Praise for *Nature's Metropolis*

"*Nature's Metropolis* is that rare historical work which treats nature and the moral force we derive from it seriously. . . . The roots of the modern environmental predicament are plainly visible in the economic dynamism that brought about the rise of Chicago in the mid-nineteenth century, which is a captivating story in its own right."

—Verlyn Klinkenborg, *The New Yorker*

"William Cronon challenges many of the conventions of both urban and western history in this pathbreaking book, and does so with unusual intelligence and elegance. More important, he helps lay the groundwork for a vital new field of scholarship: the history of the natural environment and its relationship to human society."

—Alan Brinkley, Columbia University

"No one has ever written a better book about a city. . . . No one has written about Chicago with more power, clarity and intelligence than Cronon. . . . *Nature's Metropolis* is elegant testimony to the proposition that economic, urban, environmental and business history can be as graceful, powerful and fascinating as a novel."

—Kenneth T. Jackson, *Boston Globe*

"*Nature's Metropolis* is economics, history, life, business, and national destiny, so brilliantly mingled and united that is is hard to tell what is economics and what is life, where business stops and ecology or national destiny takes over. That is, of course, the way things are; but it takes a master historian-writer to create a tableau so vividly alive, so marvelously interesting."

—Robert L. Heilbroner

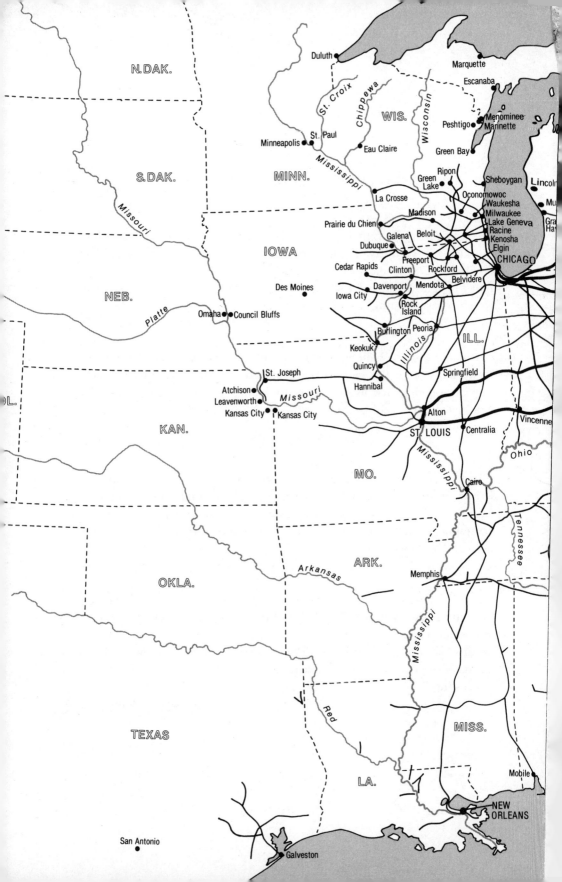

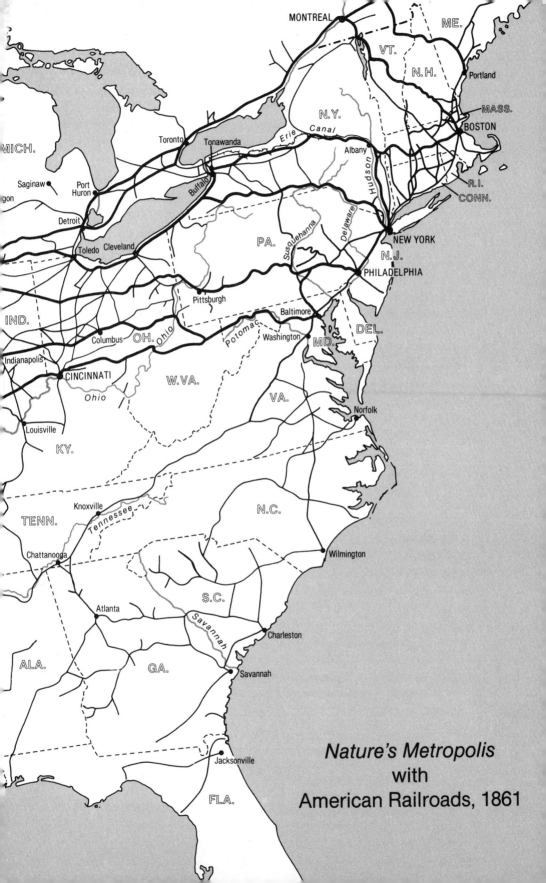

Nature's Metropolis
with
American Railroads, 1861

Also by William Cronon

CHANGES IN THE LAND:
INDIANS, COLONISTS, AND THE ECOLOGY OF NEW ENGLAND

[*coeditor*]

UNDER AN OPEN SKY:
RETHINKING AMERICA'S WESTERN PAST

NATURE'S METROPOLIS

Chicago and the Great West

WILLIAM CRONON

W·W·NORTON & COMPANY
New York London

Cover illustration: A bird's-eye view of Chicago in 1857,
from a lithograph by Charles Inger after a drawing by I. T. Palmatary.
Courtesy The Chicago Historical Society.

Printed in the United States of America.

The text of this book is composed in Baskerville,
with the display set in Radiant Bold.
Composition and manufacturing by the Haddon Craftsmen, Inc.
Book design and cartography by Jacques Chazaud.

First published as a Norton paperback 1992.

Library of Congress Cataloging in Publication Data

Cronon, William.
Nature's metropolis: Chicago and the Great West/William Cronon.
p. cm.
Includes bibliographical references and index.
1. Chicago (Ill.)—Description—To 1875. 2. Chicago, (Ill.)—
Description—1875–1950. 3. Man—Influence on nature—Illinois—
Chicago—History—19th century. 4. Chicago (Ill.)—Historical
geography. I. Title.
F548.4.C85 1991
977.3'11—dc20   90–40835

ISBN 0-393-30873-1

W. W. Norton & Company, Inc.
500 Fifth Avenue, New York, N.Y. 10110
www.wwnorton.com

W. W. Norton & Company Ltd.
Castle House, 75/76 Wells Street, London W1T 3QT

For my parents,

who took me to Green Lake and Chicago too

Contents

PART II

NATURE TO MARKET

PART III

THE GEOGRAPHY OF CAPITAL

Illustrations follow pages 168 and 328

Maps and Graphs

MAPS

GRAPHS

Preface

A s someone who believes that truth in advertising should apply no
less to books than to automobiles or toothpaste, I must warn the
reader at the outset that *Nature's Metropolis* may appear to be something that it is not. Despite what its subtitle may seem to suggest, it is a
comprehensive history neither of Chicago nor of the Great West. It is
rather a history of the relationship between those places. My contention is
that no city played a more important role in shaping the landscape and
economy of the midcontinent during the second half of the nineteenth
century than Chicago. Conversely, one cannot understand the growth of
Chicago without understanding its special relationship to the vast region
lying to its west. Although the persistent rural bias of western history has
often prevented us from acknowledging this fact, the central story of the
nineteenth-century West is that of an expanding metropolitan economy
creating ever more elaborate and intimate linkages between city and
country. To see the traditional American "frontier" from this metropolitan perspective, no place furnishes a more striking vantage point than
Chicago.

During the second half of the nineteenth century, the American landscape was transformed in ways that anticipated many of the environmental problems we face today: large-scale deforestation, threats of species
extinction, unsustainable exploitation of natural resources, widespread
destruction of habitat. It was during this period as well that much of the
world we Americans now inhabit was created: the great cities that house
so many of us, the remarkably fertile farmlands that feed us, the transpor-

tation linkages that tie our nation together, the market institutions that help define our relationships to each other and to the natural world that is our larger home. The nineteenth century saw the creation of an integrated economy in the United States, an economy that bound city and country into a powerful national and international market that forever altered human relationships to the American land. Although this book takes Chicago and the Great West as its immediate focus, its broader ambition is to explore century-old economic and ecological transformations that have continued to affect all of North America and the rest of the world besides.

Few of us, I think, fully understand or appreciate how much our modern landscape is a creation of these nineteenth-century changes. For cultural reasons that date from this same historical period, Americans have long tended to see city and country as separate places, more isolated from each other than connected. We carefully partition our national landscape into urban places, rural places, and wilderness. Although we often cross the symbolic boundaries between them—seeking escape or excitement, recreation or renewal—we rarely reflect on how tightly bound together they really are. Even professional historians often fall into this trap. Urban historians rarely look beyond the outskirts of cities to the hinterlands beyond; western and frontier and even environmental historians usually concentrate far more attention on rural and wild places than on urban ones. As a result, there are few models for a book like this one, which tries to tell the city-country story as a unified narrative. Having struggled with this book for more than a decade, I can well understand why others have shied away from such an approach. The obstacles in its way are many, and I have by no means overcome all of them in trying to make sense of my own topic. Still, throughout it all I have held fast to one central belief: city and country have a common history, so their stories are best told together.

Since my own private passion is to understand environmental change in relation to the actions of human beings, blending as best I can the insights of ecology and economics, I have organized this book around a topic that many will initially find peculiar if not off-putting: commodity flows. In the pages that follow, I have much to say about grain, lumber, meat, and other trade goods as they moved back and forth between Chicago and its hinterland during the second half of the nineteenth century. Therein has been one of my greatest challenges as a writer. Economic history is unfortunately not much read these days, even by many historians, in part because it has come to be dominated by highly mathematical approaches that are far more dedicated to theoretical rigor than to ordinary communication or understanding. Trying to combine economic and

environmental history in a way that will excite rather than squelch the
reader's curiosity has been my constant goal, especially since commodity
markets have never been a subject that has attracted much public interest
or enthusiasm. Most people find them deeply mysterious, and probably
deeply boring as well.

These two reactions—mystification and boredom—are certainly un-
derstandable, but they nonetheless seem to me unfortunate. I urge you,
reader, to resist them both, as I have resisted the urge to load my text with
statistical analyses and tables. I write of commodity markets not from
some perverse private fascination, but from the conviction that few economic institutions more powerfully affect human communities and natural ecosystems in the modern capitalist world. Even those of us who will
never trade wheat or pork bellies on the Chicago futures markets depend
on those markets for our very survival. Just as important, the commodities that feed, clothe, and shelter us are among our most basic connections to the natural world. If we wish to understand the ecological consequences of our own lives—if we wish to take political and moral
responsibility for those consequences—we must reconstruct the linkages
between the commodities of our economy and the resources of our ecosystem. This is what I have tried to do. *Nature's Metropolis* consists of a
series of stories, each tracing the path between an urban market and the
natural systems that supply it. I intend these stories as contributions to
the history of nineteenth-century Chicago and the history of the West,
but I intend them as parables for our own lives as well.

Because I spend so much time looking at commodities in this book, I
devote little or no space to subjects that many readers and scholars might
expect to find treated at some length. I have little to say about most of the
classic topics of urban history: the growth of neighborhoods within the
city, social conflicts among classes and ethnic groups, the actions of municipal authorities, even the environmental history of public services like
sewage disposal or water supply. Readers turning to this book for an
account of Chicago's architecture, its labor struggles, its political machines, its social reformers, its cultural institutions, and many other topics
are likely to turn away disappointed. Indeed, I have little to say about
individual men and women. The few who do show up in these pages are
mainly merchants, who enter my narratives less because they are significant in their own right than because they exemplify so well the broader
city-country connections I wish to trace. The book might have been better
had I given more space to any number of other important subjects; it
would certainly have been much longer. I can now understand why Bessie
Louise Pierce was never able to finish her famous history of Chicago, even
though it eventually encompassed three thick volumes. It is a big city with

a big history, and I have not even tried to do it full justice. Instead, I have kept my compass sights on the paths into and out of town, following the routes that linked the human community called Chicago to the natural world of which the city became so important a part.

I should perhaps define a few key terms that recur in this book and that may seem unfamiliar in the way that I use them. The most important are right in the book's title. By "the Great West," I mean a region that no longer exists on the mental maps of most Americans. According to nineteenth-century usage, it was the vast interior region of the nation that was neither the North (the region north of the Mason-Dixon line and east of the Appalachians or Great Lakes) nor the South (the region defined most simply as the losing side of the Civil War). The Great West began either at the Ohio River or at Lake Michigan, and extended all the way to the Pacific Ocean. By the second half of the nineteenth century, many Americans saw Chicago as the gateway to that expansive western territory.

"The Great West" is thus related to a much more controversial word, "frontier." Some western scholars have recently argued that American conceptions of frontier history are so ideologically loaded, so racist, sexist, and imperialist in their implications, that it would be better not to use the word at all. They offer instead a regional version of western history in which the West begins where it does today, at a not very well-defined line cutting across the Great Plains or the Rocky Mountains. Although I share these scholars' objections to the ideological distortions of traditional frontier historiography, I do not believe we can escape those distortions simply by changing vocabulary to redefine the historical experience that created them. In *Nature's Metropolis*, I describe one aspect of the frontier experience on a very macro scale: the expansion of a metropolitan economy into regions that had not previously been tightly bound to its markets, and the absorption of new peripheral areas into a capitalist orbit. Frontier areas lay on the periphery of the metropolitan economy, while cities like New York and London lay near its center. Chicago sat in between, on the boundary between East and West as those regions were defined in the nineteenth century. As such, its story is inextricably bound to American frontier expansion. Much as I may be uncomfortable with the shifting definitions that have plagued scholarly readings of frontier history since the days of Frederick Jackson Turner, I am convinced that regional redefinitions of the field are ultimately not much better, since I am quite confident that for much of the nineteenth century the West began in Chicago, not in Denver or San Francisco. To try to redefine the West to fit our modern vocabulary is to do violence to the way Americans in the past understood that term, since for them it was intimately tied to that other, now problematic word—"frontier." And so I have compromised by self-consciously using an anachronistic phrase to label Chicago's nineteenth-century hinterland. The very fact that we no longer speak of the Great West suggests its origins in the frontier processes that created—and then dismantled—that region.

But "frontier" and "Great West" are not the most problematic terms I use in this book; that honor is surely reserved for "nature," one of the richest, most complicated and contradictory words in the entire English language. Those who like their vocabulary precise and unambiguous will surely be frustrated by the different ways I use "nature" in this text. To them, I can only apologize: I do not believe the ambiguities can be suppressed, and I regard the word as indispensable to my purposes. The central ambiguity flows from the old dilemma about whether human beings are inside or outside of nature. At times, I use "nature" to refer to the nonhuman world, even though my deepest intellectual agenda in this book is to suggest that the boundary between human and nonhuman, natural and unnatural, is profoundly problematic. I do so because our language really has no good alternative for describing the nonhuman systems which humanity acts upon. I have tried to reduce confusion (but may only have heightened it) by resorting to the Hegelian and Marxist terms "first nature" (original, prehuman nature) and "second nature" (the artificial nature that people erect atop first nature). This distinction has its uses, but it too slips into ambiguity when we recognize that the nature we inhabit is never just first or second nature, but rather a complex mingling of the two. Moreover, the different meanings and connotations of "nature" have a rich cultural history of their own (traced most subtly in the work of Raymond Williams), and no simple definition can hope to control or capture them. Only careful, historically minded usage will do, especially when the thing one wants to convey about the human place in nature is precisely its ambiguity. My hope is that the attentive reader is already familiar with these conceptual problems of a word which is, after all, part of our everyday speech, and that my meaning in any given context will be reasonably clear.

I first conceived this book more than a dozen years ago, while working on a history of energy use in the English city of Coventry and realizing that an environmental history of a single city made little sense if written in isolation from the countryside around it. In the time since, I have incurred innumerable debts to so many people and organizations that I cannot possibly thank them all. Students and colleagues have been immensely generous with their insights and suggestions, giving me the intellectual and emotional support I needed to keep going on a project that often seemed too large and unmanageable ever to reach a satisfactory close. I hope all will recognize my gratitude for their help, but there are a few I wish to single out for special thanks.

Several institutions gave important financial assistance without which it would have been impossible for me to do this work. I continue to be grateful to the Rhodes Trust for the scholarship that took me to Oxford and resulted in the work that indirectly led to this book. *Nature's Metropolis* began as a doctoral dissertation at Yale University, where it was supported by a Danforth Fellowship and by a University Fellowship from Yale itself. The Danforth Fellowship, in particular, has remained among the most important experiences of my life, shaping my sense that scholarship should also be committed to teaching and to making a difference in the world beyond the academy. Like so many others who have benefited from the support of the Danforth Foundation, I deeply regret its decision to abandon its extraordinary program of support for American graduate education. The Newberry Library covered my living expenses while I worked in its collections. Yale's Mellon and Morse Fellowships for junior faculty members, and its generous triennial leave policy, enabled me to continue work on this and other projects. Finally, I have benefited from the financial support of the John D. and Catherine T. MacArthur Foundation. To all these organizations, which took risks on what often seemed a most unlikely enterprise, I am more grateful than I can say.

All scholarship rests on the labors of librarians and archivists, without whose work historical research would be nearly impossible. We scholars rarely thank them enough for their work on our behalf. Here at home, the collections and staffs of Yale University were my mainstays, in particular the Sterling, Mudd, Forestry, and Kline Science libraries. Karin Trainer was especially generous in helping with the illustrations I have reproduced from Yale's holdings, and I am grateful to her. In Chicago, the Newberry Library and the Chicago Historical Society were absolutely essential to my research, and both showed me great hospitality. The Newberry not only gave me my home away from home but also provided a richly stimulating intellectual environment in which to do my work; Richard Brown was particularly supportive of my work there. Archie Motley, the curator of manuscripts at the Chicago Historical Society, will always seem to me a model of curatorial generosity, giving as unstintingly of his time and advice to high school students as to senior scholars. I benefited from having access to the Northwestern University Library and the Regenstein Library at the University of Chicago, and archivists at the Chicago Tribune Company, the Chicago Board of Trade, and at Joseph T. Ryerson and Son, Inc., were also helpful. The court cases that supplied the evidence for my bankruptcy maps came from the National Archives' regional record centers in Chicago and Kansas City, whose staffs were remarkably tolerant of my requests for hundreds of documents—most of them jet black with ancient coal dust—that no one had examined for over a century. I will always be thankful to David Weber, an archivist at the Chicago record center, for serendipitously being at the right place at the right time to tell me about the existence of the bankruptcy cases among the National Archives' holdings.

In Madison, Wisconsin, I used the collections of the State Historical Society and the University of Wisconsin libraries (especially Memorial and Steenbock) as a rich source of hinterland texts and as a backup to odd gaps in Yale's collections. Elsewhere in Chicago's hinterland, I found important materials in the State Historical Society of Iowa, the Special Collections of the University of Iowa, the Nebraska State Historical Society, the Kansas State Historical Society, the Illinois State Historical Library, and the Illinois State Archives. Back in the Northeast, librarians at the Baker Library of Harvard Business School made special arrangements that allowed me to search for hundreds of bankrupt merchants in the R. G. Dun collection, and I also benefited from work in the Harvard University Archives. Finally, several institutions generously allowed me to reproduce images from their collections to illustrate this book: the Chicago Historical Society, the Iconographic Collections of the State Historical Society of Wisconsin, Sterling Memorial Library at Yale University, the Newberry Library, the Michigan Department of State's Bureau of History, the Milwaukee Public Museum, the Amon Carter Museum, the Thomas Gilcrease Institute of American History and Art, the Clay County Historical Society in Moorhead, Minnesota, the Joslyn Art Gallery, Swift-Eckrich, Inc., the Library of Congress, and the University of Wisconsin Arboretum. To all, my heartfelt thanks.

For help of a different sort, I am grateful to the Yale Computer Center and to Northwestern University's Vogelback Computer Center for providing the institutional setting and financial support that enabled me to do much of the statistical analysis that underpins (I hope not too intrusively) several sections of this book. At Yale, Richard Ferguson was especially generous in providing grants of computer time that enabled me to produce the bankruptcy maps, and Dave Bruce was a wizard at solving sticky problems in getting SAS datasets to intersect with SASGRAPH mapping routines. The Newberry Library's summer program on quantitative methods for historians introduced me to the use of statistics and computers in historical research. Richard Jensen, Daniel Scott Smith, and Nancy Fitch were masterful instructors, and later colleagues, in that program. But the person to whom I owe most of my knowledge of computers and statistical methods is Janice Reiff. Jan has been unstintingly generous in her willingness to act as a long-distance consultant for any number of computer emergencies, and spent many hours helping me work out various dataset design problems with the computer mapping routines. I am very grateful for her patience, and even more for her friendship.

At Yale, I have been lucky in the colleagues and companions who have guided and supported me during the long gestation of this book. My biggest debt is undoubtedly to Howard Lamar, who has for the past dozen years been my mentor, closest colleague, and dear friend. Howard's generosity toward his graduate students and colleagues is legendary within the community of western historians, but surely no one has ever benefited more from his largesse than myself. He has guided this book from its beginning as a dissertation, and displayed remarkable tolerance for my tendency to go off on side trips—and even another book altogether—when my curiosity headed in other directions. I hope he thinks the wait was worth it. John Morton Blum and Edmund Morgan were among the early teachers who encouraged me to take on this project. I am particularly grateful to John for having introduced me to the work of William Z. Ripley, which immensely aided my understanding of railroad economics. Other Yale colleagues and friends who have offered advice and encouragement over the years include Jean-Christophe Agnew, Diana Balmori, Troy Brennan, Elise Broach, George Chauncey, David Brion Davis, Kai Erikson, Ann Fabian, Jean Fraser, Tom Gariepy, Peter Gay, Steve Gillon, Lori Ginzberg, Jay Gitlin, John Godfrey, Michael Goldberg, Robert Gordon, Amy Green, Reeve Huston, Paul Johnson, Susan Johnson, Hugh Joswick, Jonathan Lear, Edie MacMullen, Ramsay MacMullen, George Miles, Katherine Morrissey, Kathy Morse, Jan Oscherwitz, William Parker, Jenny Price, Karen Sawislak, Gaddis Smith, Tom Smith, Jonathan Spence, Sylvia Tesh, Eustace Theodore, Florence Thomas, Conrad Totman, Alan Trachtenberg, John Wargo, Tim Weiskel, and Steven Wilf. I am grateful to all. John Demos has been especially encouraging about nontraditional literary questions that have shaped my narrative, and I have been most grateful for our conversations about the writing of history. Finally, the students and teaching assistants in my undergraduate courses on western and environmental history have been a superb audience for many of the ideas I explore in this book. From their excitement, confusion, and boredom, I have learned much about the clarity of my own thought—or lack thereof. Although I cannot name them all, they are among my most important teachers in learning how to ask the right questions and tell the right stories. It has been a privilege to work with all of them.

It is a peculiarity of academe that one's closest intellectual colleagues are often not at one's home institution, because no university has room for more than one or two people working in the same field. Several dis-

tant friends have helped shape this book in more ways than they perhaps know. Michael Conzen's remarkable work on the historical geography of metropolitan dominance furnished a powerful example for my own, and he has been generous with his time and advice since I commenced this project. Richard White has repeatedly offered profound insights from his own work, and an example of scholarly discipline and rigor that few historians can match; our conversations and friendship are among the things I treasure. Patty Limerick and I sometimes differ, at least superficially, about where we think western history is headed, but I count myself very lucky indeed to have her among my friends; even our disagreements have always been fertile, and she markedly improved the first four chapters of this book by giving them a critical scrutiny more intense than any other I received. Don Worster has likewise been a friend with whom I have sometimes disagreed, but from whom I have always learned: all of us who write environmental history follow in his footsteps, and I count him as a mentor even though he was never formally my teacher. And my dear friend David Scobey, who has discussed with me the issues underlying this book in places as diverse as Oxford, New Haven, Cambridge, and the top of Mt. Washington, remains my closest intellectual companion even though hundreds of miles now separate us; the book would have had a very different shape had it not been for his repeated interventions and unflagging willingness to challenge my assumptions with the gift for constructive criticism which is uniquely his own. Other colleagues and friends who have contributed to this book with readings, comments, and rich conversations include Tom Barron, Saul Benjamin, Sidney Bremer, Steve Brick, Vernon Carstensen, Kathleen Conzen, Ramsay Cook, Merle Curti, Owen Gregory, Scott Hancock, Peter Mathias, Arthur McEvoy, Clyde Milner, Tim Mitchell, Jim O'Brien, Donald Pisani, Steve Pyne, Martin Ridge, William Robbins, Morton Rothstein, Frank Smith, Paul Taylor, Charles Twining, and Arthur Wang. I thank all for their help.

All of us in academe recognize the degree to which our own life stories have been shaped by teachers who happened to touch us in ways that profoundly changed our lives. We are forever indebted to such people, since what they have given us becomes in the deepest sense a core part of our own being. Some of them we never meet but only read, and we record our debts to them in footnotes. In my own case, notes cannot adequately acknowledge how much I have learned from reading the likes of Raymond Williams or Aldo Leopold or David Potter or Carl Sauer or even Frederick Jackson Turner or Karl Marx. But these acknowledgments would be radically incomplete if I did not mention three people whose classroom teaching and scholarly examples set me irrevocably on the course that led to this book and to the larger intellectual project of which

it is part. One I have already named, Howard Lamar, a mentor whose kindness and wisdom are known to all who have worked with him. Another is Allan G. Bogue. During my senior year as an undergraduate at the University of Wisconsin, I happened almost by accident to take Al's course on the history of the American West. Before walking into that room, I had thought I was going to become a scholar of medieval literature: ever since, because of the world he showed me in that classroom, I have been studying and teaching the history of the American West. This book rests upon his work, and would not have been written without his example. My third great teacher was Richard N. Ringler, the man who almost succeeded in turning me into a medieval historian on the strength of his own example. I have never encountered a more brilliant teacher, or a scholar I have more wished to emulate in my own work. Although I long ago forsook the worlds of medieval Iceland and Anglo-Saxon England, the ways in which I now write about Chicago and the Great West, and about environmental change in North America generally, still follow the paths Dick Ringler showed me. I hope all three of these teachers understand how much I will always be in their debt.

I feel privileged to have been able to publish this book with W. W. Norton & Company, seemingly one of the few remaining New York houses that still hold to an ideal of publishing in which the bottom line does not overwhelmingly dictate whether a book belongs in print. Norton consistently went out of its way to make sure that the book as published would match my hopes and expectations for it. Jacques Chazaud did a fine job with the maps and graphs, and shaped its general design as well. Otto Sonntag copyedited the manuscript with a care and rigor I have never encountered before, improving it markedly in the process. And Steve Forman has been nothing less than the perfect editor: enthusiastic about the general project of the book, encouraging in times of despair, patient about my endless delays, always humane and professional in his dedication to our mutual labor. I cannot thank him enough for his good work on my behalf, or for the many kindnesses he has shown me as a friend.

Finally, I must thank my family. I hope it is apparent from the dedication and from the prologue and epilogue how much *Nature's Metropolis* has been a personal journey shaped by the examples and experiences that my parents, Dave and Jean Cronon, gave me when I was very young. I have mentioned other teachers here, but they were my first and by far my most important. From my father, who is himself a professional historian, I learned the craft of scholarship and the passion for the past that made this book possible. He taught me more about writing, and about the value of history, than any other teacher I have ever had, and was wise enough to let me find my own peculiar route into the subject. From my mother, I

learned the value of ordinary life, the little things of our day-to-day world that often fail to surface in our consciousness even though they are ultimately the most important things we do. No children ever fully repay the gifts their parents give, but I hope my parents will see this book as at least a partial payment.

During the year when *Nature's Metropolis* finally completed its overdue birth, my wife, Nan Fey, and I welcomed into our lives our first child, Hilary Fey Cronon. I could thank Nan for her patience in putting up with this book, which has been part of our lives far longer than either of us would have liked, or for her willingness to comment on draft chapters as they rolled off the word processor. But my deeper gratitude is to Nan and Hilary both, for reminding me that no history book is finally worth writing unless it manages somehow to connect itself to the present world in which past and future meet and reshape one another. The autobiographical reflections about my youthful past which open and close this book will undoubtedly seem self-indulgent to some readers, but they flow directly from the daunting and exhilarating experience of reflecting in much the same way on my daughter's future. I thank Nan and Hilary for reminding me what books like this one are finally all about.

William Cronon
New Haven
August 1990

NATURE'S METROPOLIS

Suddenly the meaning and significance of it all dawned upon Laura. The Great Grey City, brooking no rival, imposed its dominion upon a reach of country larger than many a kingdom of the Old World. For thousands of miles beyond its confines was its influence felt. Out, far out, far away in the snow and shadow of Northern Wisconsin forests, axes and saws bit the bark of century-old trees, stimulated by this city's energy. Just as far to the southward pick and drill leaped to the assault of veins of anthracite, moved by her central power. Her force turned the wheels of harvester and seeder a thousand miles distant in Iowa and Kansas. Her force spun the screws and propellers of innumerable squadrons of lake steamers crowding the Sault Sainte Marie. For her and because of her all the Central States, all the Great Northwest roared with traffic and industry; sawmills screamed; factories, their smoke blackening the sky, clashed and flamed; wheels turned, pistons leaped in their cylinders; cog gripped cog; beltings clasped the drums of mammoth wheels; and converters of forges belched into the clouded air their tempest breath of molten steel.

It was Empire, the resistless subjugation of all this central world of the lakes and the prairies. Here, mid-most in the land, beat the Heart of the Nation, whence inevitably must come its immeasurable power, its infinite, infinite, inexhaustible vitality. Here, of all her cities, throbbed the true life—the true power and spirit of America; gigantic, crude with the crudity of youth, disdaining rivalry; sane and healthy and vigorous; brutal in its ambition, arrogant in the new-found knowledge of its giant strength, prodigal of its wealth, infinite in its desires. In its capacity boundless, in its courage indomitable; subduing the wilderness in a single generation, defying calamity, and through the flame and débris of a commonwealth in ashes, rising suddenly renewed, formidable, and Titanic.

—FRANK NORRIS, *The Pit* (1903)

An ethic to supplement and guide the economic relation to land presupposes the existence of some mental image of land as a biotic mechanism. We can be ethical only in relation to something we can see, feel, understand, love, or otherwise have faith in.

—ALDO LEOPOLD, *A Sand County Almanac* (1949)

Prologue:
Cloud over Chicago

The smoke of Chicago has a peculiar and aggressive individuality, due, I imagine, to the natural clearness of the atmosphere. It does not seem, like London smoke, to permeate and blend with the air. It does not overhang the streets in a uniform canopy, but sweeps across and about them in gusts and swirls, now dropping and now lifting again its grimy curtain. You will often see the vista of a gorge-like street so choked with a seeming thundercloud that you feel sure a storm is just about to burst upon the city, until you look up at the zenith and find it smiling and serene.

—WILLIAM ARCHER, *America To-Day* (1900)[1]

My earliest memories of Chicago glide past the windows of an old green and white Ford station wagon. I was not yet in grade school. Each summer, my family drove from our home in southern New England to my grandparents' cottage on Green Lake, in central Wisconsin. Most of what remain are backseat memories: looking at comic books with my brother, checking odometer readings to measure the tunnels of the Pennsylvania Turnpike, counting different state license plates on passing cars. I remember the dramatic vistas of the Appalachians, and the descent into Ohio, but as we moved deeper into the Middle West the landscape became at once more uniform and less interesting. Little of it survives in my memory.

Until Chicago. The city announced itself to our noses before we ever saw it, and we always pressed our faces against the windows to locate the sweet pungent odor that was Gary. (Gary and Chicago blend in my child's eye view as a single place, united in a child's mythic name: The City.) The forest of smokestacks, the great plumes of white and unwhite steam, were unlike any place that I, middle-class child of a nurse and a professor, had ever lived. The place remains in my memory as a gray landscape with little vegetation, a clouded sky hovering over dark buildings, and an atmosphere that suddenly made breathing a conscious act. I remember especially one smokestack with dense rusty orange vapor rising like a solid column far into the sky before it dissipated. We always saw it there, every year, and it signaled our entrance into The City.

The orange cloud of smoke was a signpost warning us of our entry into an alien landscape. As the highway rose above city streets to give an elevated view of the South Side, I saw a world that simultaneously repelled and fascinated me. Beneath the rush and noise of traffic, lined up beside the factories, were block after block of two- and three-story houses arranged in neat rows like barracks. The landscape's natural flatness lent a sense of endless uniformity to the scene, and the buildings only added to the monotony. No matter how they were actually painted, their color in my oldest memory is always gray.

I was too young to know anything of the people who lived in those buildings, their class or the color of their skins, but I could see the shattered windows, the litter, and the dirt, and I knew this was a place in which I had no wish to linger. Not even the skyscrapers of the Loop made a favorable impression on me, and I barely remember them from those early trips. The one positive image I can conjure up (and this not until we made our way north out of the downtown) is a large white and red neon billboard advertising Budweiser beer, flashing what then seemed an astonishing variety of colors. It was my brother's and my favorite part of the trip through Chicago, not least because it was a landmark showing the way out of The City.

A few years later, my parents moved to Madison, Wisconsin, where I grew up. There, I came to know and care for a landscape that few who are not midwesterners ever call beautiful. Travelers, whether in the air or on the ground, usually see the Middle West less as a destination than as a place to pass through. Only after a long while does one appreciate that the very plainness of this countryside is its beauty: the farms with their fields of yellow corn and stench of fresh manure, the great fence-line bur oaks recalling long-vanished prairies, the dark lakes and woodlands of the . hill country to the north, the small towns with their main streets of stores and bars and bakeries. When people speak, usually with some ambivalence, of the American heartland, this is one of the places they mean. For me, it came to be home.

At the edge of this landscape, somehow in its midst without seeming to be quite part of it, was Chicago, which I eventually visited on day trips that introduced me to its museums and skyscrapers, not just its views from the highway. Never having lived in a great city, I had no idea how little I understood it, but my continuing instinct was to mistrust and dislike it. Loving the rural landscape—and later, as I discovered the West, loving still wilder lands as well—I felt quite certain that I could never call the city home. Like many who came to adult consciousness during the environmentalist awakening of the late sixties, I wished to live close to "nature." If asked to choose between city and country, I'd have felt no hesitation about my answer. More important, I'd have thought it perfectly reasonable—perfectly *natural*—to pose the choice in just these stark terms. Chicago represented all that was most *un*natural about human life. Crowded and artificial, it was a cancer on an otherwise beautiful landscape.

One of the pleasures of childhood and adolescence is that one can experience emotions of this sort without worrying too much about their possible contradictions. These feelings came easily—my love of nature and the pastoral countryside, my dislike for the city, and, beneath them, the romanticism which had schooled me in such perceptions. It took me a long time to realize that I had learned them from a venerable tradition in American and European culture, and an even longer time to suspect that they were distorting my sense of city and country alike. I can't pinpoint when it happened, but I gradually began to sense that my own life (including my affection for things natural) was not so free of the city and its institutions as I had once believed.

Reflecting on the various expeditions I made between my parents' Madison home and assorted rural retreats around Wisconsin, I became troubled by what seemed a paradox in my easy use of the word "natural." The more I learned the history of my home state, the more I realized that the human hand lay nearly as heavily on rural Wisconsin as on Chicago. By what peculiar twist of perception, I wondered, had I managed to see the plowed fields and second-growth forests of southern Wisconsin—a landscape of former prairies now long vanished—as somehow more "natural" than the streets, buildings, and parks of Chicago? All represented drastic human alterations of earlier landscapes. Why had I seen some human changes as "natural"—the farm, the woodlot, the agricultural countryside—but not the other changes that had made "nature" into "city"? How could one human community be "natural" and another not?

My puzzlement did not end there. In my eagerness to reject Chicago and embrace the rural lands around it, I had assumed that there was little chance of confusing the two. I had only to look at any midwestern map to see the same reassuringly sharp boundaries between city and country I had experienced so strongly as a child. And yet the moment I tried to trace those boundaries backward into history, they began to dissolve. City and country might be separate places, but they were hardly isolated. Chicago had become "urban," spawning belching smokestacks and crowded streets, at the same time that the lands around it became "rural," yielding not grass and red-winged blackbirds but wheat, corn, and hogs. Chicago's merchants and workers had built their warehouses and factories in the same decades that farmers had plowed up the prairie sod and lumberjacks had cut the great pine trees of the north woods. City and country shared a

common past, and had fundamentally reshaped each other. Neither was
as "natural" or "unnatural" as it appeared.

This insight disturbed me. More and more, I wondered whether it
made sense—historically or environmentally—to treat city and country as
isolated places. Might I not be fooling myself to think that I could choose
between them? I began to see that the word "city" depended for its meaning on its opposition to the word "country," and vice versa. Unpleasant as
it might be to admit, the city helped define—might even be essential
to—what I and others felt about the country. My passion for rural and
wild landscapes would have lost at least some of its focus without my
dislike for Chicago to serve as counterpoint. The city was what the country was *not:* in loving the one, I expressed a certain contempt, but also a
certain *need,* for the other. And beyond this linguistic question, city and
country also had close material ties. Would these Wisconsin farms be
here without the city in which to sell their crops? Could the city survive if
those crops failed to appear? The answer to both questions was surely no,
but then why did it make sense, in trying to understand rural nature, to
draw a boundary between it and the urban world next door? The more I
pondered that question, the more I began to doubt the "naturalness" of
the wall that seemed to stand so solidly between the country I thought I
loved and the city I thought I hated.

If that wall was more a habit of thought than a fact of nature, then
decrying the "unnaturalness" of city life in a place like Chicago was
merely one more way of doing what my own environmental ethic told me
to oppose: isolating human life from the ecosystems that sustain it. Putting the city outside nature meant sending humanity into the same exile.
And yet this is precisely what I and many other modern environmentalists
have unconsciously often done, following the lessons we learned from
nineteenth-century romantic writers like Wordsworth, Emerson, Thoreau, and Muir. The boundary between natural and unnatural shades
almost imperceptibly into the boundary between nonhuman and human,
with wilderness and the city seeming to lie at opposite poles—the one
pristine and unfallen, the other corrupt and unredeemed. Gauged by how
we feel about them, the distance we travel between city and country is
measured more in the mind than on the ground. If this is true, then the
way we cross the rural-urban boundary, the way we make the journey into
and out of Chicago, exposes a great many hidden assumptions about how
we see the larger relationship between human beings and the earth upon
which we live.

This book, then, is a series of historical journeys between city and
country in an effort to understand the city's place in nature. I choose
Chicago in part because it loomed large in my own childhood as a dark

symbol of The City, so that writing these travelers' tales about the past serves as a kind of exorcism of a way of thinking I now believe to be wrongheaded and self-defeating. But Chicago is also an appropriate focus for a less personal reason—it has been raising similar questions about the city's place in nature for well over a century now. I was certainly not the first to visit it with deeply conflicted emotions. During the nineteenth century, when Chicago was at the height of its gargantuan growth, its citizens rather prided themselves on the wonder and horror their hometown evoked in visitors. No other city in America had ever grown so large so quickly; none had so rapidly overwhelmed the countryside around it to create so urban a world. Those who sought to explain its unmatched expansion often saw it as being compelled by deep forces within nature itself, gathering the resources and energies of the Great West—the region stretching from the Appalachians and Great Lakes to the Rockies and the Pacific—and concentrating them in a single favored spot at the southwestern corner of Lake Michigan. The image is not one I would have appreciated as a child, but for these nineteenth-century observers Chicago looked for all the world like a city destined for greatness by nature's own prophecies: Nature's Metropolis. And so the journey between urban Chicago and the rural West carries a much more than autobiographical significance.

Descriptions of the cityward journey became almost a leitmotif among those who wrote about Chicago in the late nineteenth and early twentieth centuries. Hamlin Garland, Waldo Frank, Louis Sullivan, Robert Herrick—all tried to capture in words the railroad ride that first brought them to the new metropolis of the Great West.[2] However they felt about the journey, each described a passage between two worlds that could hardly have been more alien from each other. Starting in the agricultural terrain of the surrounding countryside, the railroad became a vehicle that symbolically transported its passengers as much through time as through space. At journey's end stood a city that represented the geographical antithesis of the lands around it, and the historical prophecy of what America might become as it escaped its rural past.

Travelers recognized the city long before they came to it. The air changed. "I shall never forget," wrote the novelist Hamlin Garland of his youthful first visit to Chicago in the 1880s, "the feeling of dismay with which . . . I perceived from the car window a huge smoke-cloud which embraced the whole eastern horizon, for this, I was told, was the soaring banner of the great and gloomy inland metropolis. . . ."[3] Even admitting his literary embellishments, Garland's was a prototypical Chicago journey which suggests what many rural visitors and other travelers undoubtedly felt as they approached the city. As he saw the farmhouses give way first to villages and then to Chicago's outer suburbs, Garland began to believe that the railroad's "tangled, thickening webs of steel" were carrying him into radically unfamiliar terrain.[4] From a countryside that was, if anything, oppressive in its openness and plainness—"a commonplace country, flat, unkempt and without a line of beauty"—he moved toward a city whose oppressiveness was of another sort entirely.[5] The more urban the landscape became, the more its space contracted and its time accelerated; the deeper he penetrated its interior, the more he had to fight off feelings of claustrophobia and vertigo.

At his home in Iowa, the young Garland had dreamed of the day he might finally visit Chicago for himself. Country boy that he was, he had needed a long time to summon the courage to go there, feeling "safe only when in sight of a plowed field."[6] Now, as he stepped out into the train station, he was confronted with crowds that seemed as dark and foreboding as the city itself. Writing three decades later about his feelings of fear and alienation at that moment, he sketched a frightening portrait of the hackmen who tried to grab his baggage and drive him for some outrageous fare to his hotel. Their eyes were "cynical," their hands "clutching, insolent . . . terrifying," their faces "remorseless, inhuman and mocking," their grins "like those of wolves."[7] Such were the first people he met in Chicago.

Garland's language is literary and exaggerated, but it outlines the symbolic conventions of the Dark City—in counterpoint to the Fair Country—all the more effectively because of its caricature. For Garland, the forces that had created the city and beclouded its horizon had also stolen from its citizens something of their humanity. Repulsed by the dirty atmosphere, stunned at "the mere thought of a million people," and fearful of the criminal "dragon's brood with which the dreadful city was a-swarm" in its "dens of vice and houses of greed," he and his brother spent less than a day exploring Chicago before continuing their railroad journey to the east.[8] And yet not all was negative about their experience. The tall buildings of the downtown were like none they knew back home, and at every turn they found things they had never seen: "nothing was commonplace, nothing was ugly to us." "To me," Garland concluded, Chicago "was august as well as terrible."[9] Such a double-edge description, in varying combinations of praise and revulsion, would be offered by virtually every traveler who visited the city.

A decade after his first visit, writing one of his earliest novels, Garland portrayed a Wisconsin farm girl, Rose Dutcher, making the same journey for the first time. Once again, a cloud on the horizon marked the transition from country to city:

Rose looked—far to the south-east a gigantic smoke-cloud soared above the low horizon line, in shape like an eagle, whose hovering wings extended from south to east, trailing mysterious shadows upon the earth. The sun lighted its mighty crest with crimson light, and its gloom and glow became each moment more sharply contrasted.[10]

It would be hard to imagine a more ambivalent image. The great eagle, blood red in the light of a rising sun, betokened urban growth and national pride, sent soaring skyward on jet black wings by ten thousand tons of burning coal.[11] Seen from afar, it was alive, almost magical. Whatever the claustrophobic darkness that might lie beneath it, its very presence was proof that the lands below had been remade by human industry. Chicago wore its cloud like a black halo, and few visitors failed to notice the symbolism. To transform not merely the earth but also the heavens above: this surely was a mark of great human achievement, "august" as well as "terrible." The cloud that Hamlin Garland and Rose Dutcher saw from their train windows had nothing to do with the natural atmosphere of an Illinois prairie. Only coal, human labor, and a multitude of furnaces and steam engines could produce it. Glorious and abhorrent at the same time, the polluted eagle was a wholly human creation, and carried within it all the contradictions of human progress. "See that cloud?" someone on Rose's train had asked. "That's Chicago."[12]

Chicago's murky horizon was the most immediate sign of its urban transformation, but everything about its environment, including its citizens, suggested that the place had broken from nature. As Rose Dutcher made her way out from the train station, she encountered the city beneath the cloud: "Terrors thickened. Smells assaulted her sensitive nostrils, incomprehensible and horrible odors. Everywhere men delved in dirt and murk, and all unloveliness."[13] In the face of such experiences, a new arrival in the city was bound to be reminded of its rural antithesis. Like her creator, Rose suddenly recalled the home she had left behind. An image of her father's farm rose in her mind: "At that moment the most beautiful thing in the world was the smooth pasture by the spring, where the sheep were feeding in the fading light. . . ." That pastoral scene had all the natural loveliness that the city lacked, but it was already a thing of the past, a nostalgic glance backward toward an abandoned world. Like Garland and like Chicago itself, Rose had chosen her course and could no longer turn back from her urban future. Her old country moorings were gone. "She was afloat," Garland said, "and retreat was impossible."[14]

Many other writers joined Garland in seeing their passage from country to city as an entrance into a perpetually shrouded landscape in which the darkness of the sky was proof of a moral transformation in humanity and nature alike. Such descriptions almost always suggested the city's vast power and its ability to inspire awe; but, as in Garland's cloud-eagle, power and awe flowed from deeply troubling roots. The city's beauty inverted nature and turned humanity inward upon itself. In choosing to live in such a place, one ran the risk of putting human creation above the works of God. "The manufactories," wrote Charles Dudley Warner of his visit to Chicago in 1889, "vomit dense clouds of bituminous coal smoke, which settle in a black mass . . . so that one can scarcely see across the streets in a damp day, and the huge buildings loom up in the black sky in ghostly dimness."[15] Things were no better thirty years later. "Here," wrote Waldo Frank in 1919, "is a sooty sky hanging forever lower." For Frank, the Chicago atmosphere was a nightmare out of Dante's Hell, in which the dismembered corpses of the stockyards' slaughtered animals descended to earth in a perpetual rain of ash: "The sky is a stain: the air is streaked with runnings of grease and smoke. Blanketing the prairie, this fall of filth, like black snow—a storm that does not stop. . . ."[16] As Frank's railroad swept him in "toward the storm's center," it entered an environment so entirely dominated by humanity that sun and sky both seemed to be in retreat. "Chimneys stand over the world," wrote Frank, "and belch blackness upon it. There is no sky now."[17] Whatever natural appearance the place might once have had had vanished when the sunlight died.

But however foreboding Chicago's clouds and darkness might seem, its landscape also inspired awe. One might fear the degree to which the city had declared its independence from nature, but at the same time one could hardly help feeling wonder at its audacity. The more visitors came to believe that Chicago had broken with the rural nature that surrounded it, the more fascinating it became in its own right. Only the most alienated of tourists failed to experience an unexpected attraction to the place.[18] Whether or not they thought it ugly, most Americans still believed they saw in it one of the wonders of the Republic. Exploding in two or three decades from a prairie trading post to a great metropolis, Chicago was among their proudest proofs that the United States was indeed "nature's nation."[19] Not by accident did Garland transform Chicago's smoke cloud into an image of the same bird that adorned the great seal of the nation. Especially in the years following the devastating fire of 1871, when it seemed that the city had miraculously resurrected itself from its own ashes, Chicago came to represent the triumph of human will over natural adversity. It was a reminder that America's seemingly inexhaustible natural resources destined it for greatness, and that nothing could prevent the citizens of this favored nation from remaking the land after their own image.

Seen in this light, the city became much more compelling. The Italian playwright Giuseppe Giacosa, who had initially called the place "abominable," finally admitted that its energy and industry had led him to see in it "a concept of actual life so clear, so open-minded, so large and so powerful" that it made him think better of his earlier disgust.[20] Chicago was destiny, progress, all that was carrying the nineteenth century toward its appointed future. If the city was unfamiliar, immoral, and terrifying, it was also a new life challenging its residents with dreams of worldly success, a landscape in which the human triumph over nature had declared anything to be possible. By crossing the boundary from country to city, one could escape the constraints of family and rural life to discover one's chosen adulthood for oneself. Young people and others came to it from farms and country towns for hundreds of miles around, all searching for the fortune they believed they would never find at home. In the words of the novelist Theodore Dreiser, they were "life-hungry" for the vast energy Chicago could offer to their appetites.[21]

So attractive was the city that it seemed at times to radiate an energy that could only be superhuman. Called forth by the massed resources of western nature, the city—at least in literary descriptions—became almost a force of nature itself. Mere human beings might try to manipulate or control its energy, but never to create it. This most human of places seemed to express a power that belonged less to people than to the god whose name was Nature. "It was," wrote Garland of Rose Dutcher's train journey,

> this wonderful thing again, a fresh, young and powerful soul rushing to a great city, a shining atom of steel obeying the magnet, a clear rivulet from the hills hurrying to the sea. On every train at that same hour, from every direction, others, like her, were entering on the same search to the same end.[22]

Garland's metaphors may seem a little curious as descriptions of a city, but he followed a favorite literary convention of his day. His urban metaphors are all natural: the city was the great ocean, to which all fresh streams must flow and become salt. It was the magnet, projecting invisible lines of force that determined the dance of atoms. By so massing the combined energies and destinies of hundreds of thousands of people, the city, despite its human origins, seemed to express a natural power. As Rose stood remembering her father's spring and pasture, she felt herself to be "at the gate of the city, and life with all its terrors and triumphs seemed just before her."[23] For those like Rose who heard its call, Chicago could appear to encompass a universe of living possibilities precisely because it was so thoroughly human a place.

Among those who answered the city's siren song and embraced its possibilities was the architect Louis Sullivan. Arriving as a young man in Chicago a couple of years after the Great Fire of 1871, Sullivan was instantly struck by the vision and sense of destiny of those who were rebuilding the city. In prose that sometimes seemed as windy as his chosen city, he declared that one could see in Chicago "the primal power assuming self-expression amid nature's impelling urge." For Sullivan, although Chicago's energy sprang ultimately from nature, nature expressed itself only when mortal men and women followed their own inspiration. Such people, he wrote, "had vision. What they saw was real, they saw it as destiny." In the light of Sullivan's romantic wonder, Chicago was less a place than a feeling: it was "all magnificent and wild: A crude extravaganza: An intoxicating rawness: A sense of big things to be done."[24]

For Sullivan, the wonder of Chicago was the wonder of nature transformed: the more nature had been reworked by an inspired human imagination, the more beautiful it became. It served as the vehicle and occasion for expressing *human* spirit. Nowhere was this more true than in cities, and in no city more than Chicago. Seen through Sullivan's eyes, the great buildings rising beside "the boundless prairie and the mighty lake" were the stuff less of brick and mortar than of visions and dreams. Imagination far more than nature had made their creation possible, and so their conquest of Chicago's skyline represented the triumph of "the crudest, rawest, most savagely ambitious dreamers and would-be doers in the world." Sullivan thought them and their creation wonderful, and their energy "made him tingle to be in the game."[25]

Garland and Sullivan describe the same city, but from opposite directions. By the end of the nineteenth century, those who visited Chicago had at least two general views about how "natural" or "unnatural" the city might be. For those like Garland who feared Chicago, nature became the symbol of a nonhuman creation damaged and endangered by the city's growth. For those like Sullivan who loved the city, nature became the nonhuman power which had called this place into being and enabled its heroic inhabitants to perform their extraordinary feats. Whichever perspective one held, Chicago acquired special significance, for few other American places seemed to raise so strong a question about the city's special relationship to nature.

The writer who best captured this paradoxical sense of a city within and without nature was probably Robert Herrick. "Chicago," he wrote in his 1898 novel, *The Gospel of Freedom,* "is an instance of a successful, contemptuous disregard of nature by man."[26] The city at its founding, he argued, had none of the natural advantages found in great cities elsewhere around the world: built in the midst of a great level swamp, it had no fertile valleys, no great harbors, no broad rivers. Instead, its creation depended solely on the force of human will. "Man," Herrick wrote, "must make all"—buildings, streets, even the green plants—"for left to herself nature merely hides the plain with a kind of brown scab."[27] Where nature offered such feeble support to human endeavor, the triumph of Sullivan's "dreamers and would-be doers" became all the more extraordinary.

Carrying his readers on the same railroad journey from outskirts to city center that Hamlin Garland and others had experienced so negatively, Herrick reveled in the urban growth one could see beneath the "pall of dull smoke." First came the plank walks, drainage ditches, frame houses, and electric wires that marked "the advancing lines of blocks" that were "the Chicago of the future." Here visionaries were still pursuing the metropolitan destiny which Sullivan had seen just after the fire. Then came the boulevards, the green parks, and the great houses to which the wealthy could retreat when they wished to catch their breaths in the clear air beside the lake. And when the train pulled into its station, after passing through a landscape that had become "hotter and fiercer mile by mile," the traveler stepped out into the heart of a great commercial and industrial city, where the horizon vanished altogether behind skyscrapers and darkened air.[28]

Like Garland, Herrick had carried his readers into the heart of darkness, but with a much more ironic moral at journey's end. Here nature had no place, having become at last what Emerson had once called the mere "double of the man."[29] In a remarkable passage, Herrick showed just how far a writer could go in proclaiming the city's liberation from the natural world:

> Life spins there; man there is handling existence as you knead bread in a pan. The city is made of man; that is the last word to say of it. Brazen, unequal, like all man's works, it stands a stupendous piece of blasphemy against nature. Once within its circle, the heart must forget that the earth is beautiful. "Go to," man boasts, "our fathers lived in the fear of nature; *we* will build a city where men and women in their passions shall be the beginning and end. Man is enough for man."[30]

Herrick's vision, for all its apparent exuberance, was darker than Sullivan's. He had little doubt that Chicago had in fact freed itself from nature, and he shared Sullivan's passion for the human achievement the city represented. His excitement in describing the triumph over nature was quite genuine. But his language also suggests a deeper ambivalence. Herrick felt the same disorientation that other travelers experienced as they watched the Illinois prairies give way to railroad yards and slaughterhouses. He too choked on the city's "stale air and the filth," and although he might imagine hearts that could "forget that the earth is beautiful," his own could not. His soliloquy on behalf of the unnatural city reflects his own foreboding at every turn.[31]

Moreover, Herrick's claim that Chicago was "made of man" rings hollow, for real women and real men were no more present in the city he described than real nature. Individual people and their real landscapes had dissolved into that favorite device of literary naturalism, the abstract dichotomy between man and nature.[32] In an opposition that was far more ideological than real, man was masculine, singular, active, and all-controlling, while nature was feminine, singular, passive, and ever more controlled. Their relationship was larger than life, played out upon a landscape of heroic mythology. Vast forces created and moved through the city, but they were the work of "man," not individual people. The city, no more than a flood or a storm in the wilderness, could hardly be called the creation of particular men and women—save perhaps for the bourgeois captains of industry with whom this image of "man" was most closely identified. If nature had been exorcised to create Herrick's mythic city, so had history and its human actors. For so human a place, the city had surprisingly few people, and that too characterized this genre of antinaturalistic urban description.

Herrick's Chicago is a curiously disembodied place, isolated from its natural landscape much as its inhabitants are isolated from each other. One of his characters says of Chicago, "When you are in it, you are cut off by a vacuum, as it were, from the surrounding world. You can't see outside, and you hear the voices of the others only faintly."[33] Off to the east, Lake Michigan sends out its quiet message of natural beauty at every instant, even though few bother to observe it "shifting, changing, gathering light to itself, playing out the panorama of nature close at hand for the unheeding benefit of this creature, man."[34] For some of Herrick's Chicagoans, the separation from nature and the rest of the world offers the very feeling Louis Sullivan had embraced so enthusiastically—of liberation, of freedom from the "fear of nature," of being able to realize big dreams without the constraints of natural limits or close community. Men and women could be on their own in the city and make as much or as little of their talents as they wished or were able.

But such freedom was also a kind of prison, a retreat from the sources of value that gave human life a larger meaning: closeness to neighbors, a sense of rootedness in the soil, a feeling of belonging, faith in something larger than the self or the merely human. In the city, even amid all the crowds and the human artifacts, one stood curiously alone. At the end of Herrick's novel, his central female character decides not to marry an artist who embraced this vision of urban freedom in all its sterility. "You have abandoned your own people," she tells him; "you have sneered at your own land. And what is worse than all, you have failed—to add one beautiful thing to this sore old world!"[35] She had nearly followed him in a behavior which mimicked that of the city: "You have taught me," she says, "to climb the same desolate hill where you have perched yourself. I have my freedom—I am alone now—but it would be better for me to be dead. . . ."[36] Here was a moral for the city itself. In Herrick's Chicago, by taking dominion so completely over servile nature, humanity had declared its freedom but lost its birthright: to see human passions as the beginning and end of existence was to blaspheme against creation and humanity itself. To see one's world as a self-created place opened the doorway to heroic achievement, but finally denied any other Creator, be it Nature or God.

Herrick's dark praise for Chicago's conquest of nature carries me back to my own youthful revulsion at the city. As I read him, I remember my fervent belief that the people of the city had indeed cast aside nature in favor of a wholly human creation, apparently indifferent to the ugliness they created in so doing. All these earlier visitors to Chicago had made the same journey, from a rural landscape of prairies, cornfields, and pastures to the grid of city streets, the soaring buildings of the downtown, and the dark cloud of coal smoke hanging over all like a sentry. And yet each traveler could still experience the symbolic endpoints of the journey quite differently. My own childish passage from rural beauty to urban ugliness was matched by a multitude of other possible journeys: from pastoral simplicity to cosmopolitan sophistication, from rural bondage to urban freedom, from purity to corruption, from childhood to adulthood, from past to future. Each possible journey forms a powerful narrative trajectory, a compelling token of the divided world we inhabit—and yet each also reproduces that divided world. All these rural–urban passages share one underlying assumption which is itself deeply problematic. They all assume that city and country are separate and opposing worlds, that their divisions far outweigh their connections. And so all reinforce our widely held conviction that people can somehow build a world for themselves apart from nature.

Such beliefs are deeply embedded in Western thought. We learned our city-country dichotomy from the nineteenth-century Romantics, who learned it in turn from pastoral poets stretching back to Virgil. From these traditions, we discover how to make country–city journeys of the sort I have been describing, journeys which present themselves as a passage between alien worlds.[37] On the one hand, our willingness to see country and city as separate, even opposite, is our most powerful reason

for agreeing with Herrick that civilized humanity has been able to escape
the bonds of earth. We "moderns" believe, even in a postmodern age,
that we have the power to control the earth, despite our deep ambivalence about whether we know how to exercise that power wisely. On the
other hand, our nostalgia for the more "natural" world of an earlier time
when we were not so powerful, when the human landscape did not seem
so omnipresent, encourages us to seek refuge in pastoral or wilderness
landscapes that seem as yet unscarred by human action. Convinced of our
human omnipotence, we can imagine nature retreating to small islands—
"preserves"—in the midst of a landscape which otherwise belongs to us.
And therein lies our dilemma: however we may feel about the urban
world which is the most visible symbol of our human power—whether we
celebrate the city or revile it, whether we wish to "control" nature or
"preserve" it—we unconsciously affirm our belief that we ourselves are
unnatural. Nature is the place where we are not.

The oddity of this belief becomes most evident when we try to apply it
to an actual place and time in history. At what moment, exactly, did the
city of Chicago cease to be part of nature? Even to ask the question is to
suggest its absurdity. Herrick's literary conceit—that Chicago was "made
of man," "a stupendous piece of blasphemy against nature"—becomes
meaningless as soon as one tries to look past the city's smoky horizon to
see Chicago in its proper landscape. The journey that carried so many
travelers into the city also carried them out again, and in that exchange of
things urban for things rural lies a deeper truth about the country and the
city. The two can exist only in each other's presence. Their isolation is an
illusion, for the world of civilized humanity is very nearly created in the
continuing moment of their encounter. They *need* each other, just as they
need the larger natural world which sustains them both.

The urban-rural, human-natural dichotomy blinds us to the deeper
unity beneath our own divided perceptions. If we concentrate our attention solely upon the city, seeing in it the ultimate symbol of "man's"
conquest of "nature," we miss the extent to which the city's inhabitants
continue to rely as much on the nonhuman world as they do on each
other. We lose sight of the men and women whose many lives and relationships—in city or country, in factory or field, in workshop or counting-
house—cannot express themselves in so simple an image as singular man
conquering singular nature. By forgetting those people and their history,
we also wall ourselves off from the broader ecosystems which contain our
urban homes. Deep ecology to the contrary, we cannot solve this dilemma
by seeking permanent escape from the city in a "wild" nature untouched
by human hands, for such an escape requires us to build the same artificial
mental wall between nature and un-nature. We fail to see that our own

flight from "the city" creates "the wild" as its symbolic opposite and pulls that seemingly most natural of places into our own cultural orbit. We alter it with our presence, and even with the ways we think about it. Just as our own lives continue to be embedded in a web of *natural* relationships, nothing in nature remains untouched by the web of *human* relationships that constitute our common history. And in that fact lies the measure of our moral responsibility for each other and for the world, whether urban or rural, human or natural. We are in this together.

However we draw the boundary between the abstraction called city and the abstraction called country, we must still understand that all people, rural or urban, share with each other and with all living and unliving things a single earthly home which we identify as the abstraction called nature. Recognizing nature in the city, where our language itself has taught us to believe nature no longer exists, challenges our ability to see the world clearly—but to miss the city's relation to nature and the country is in fact to miss much of what the city is. In the words of the landscape architect Anne Spirn, "The city is a granite garden, composed of many smaller gardens, set in a garden world. . . . The city is part of nature."[38] One might only add that if the urban garden is part of nature, then so are its gardeners. A city's history must also be the history of its human countryside, and of the natural world within which city and country are both located. We cannot understand the urban history of Chicago apart from the natural history of the vast North American region to which it became connected: Nature's Metropolis and the Great West are in fact different labels for a single region and the relationships that defined it. By erasing the false boundary between them, we can begin to recover their common past.

PART I

TO BE THE CENTRAL CITY

1

Dreaming
the Metropolis

Patterns on a Prairie Landscape

Before the city, there was the land. Go back just over a century and a half to the place that became Chicago, and our familiar distinction between city and country vanishes. At the mouth of the river where the city would one day stand, small human settlements came and went, but their inhabitants would no more have used the word "urban" to describe the place than the word "rural." Without those words, there could be no city here, not until people came who could dream city dreams in the midst of a cityless landscape. Chicago remained a gathering place like so many other gathering places scattered between the Great Lakes and the Rocky Mountains. What most distinguished it were the wild garlic plants that grew amid the grasses and sedges of its low-lying prairie. From them, it had gained its name: Chigagou, "the wild-garlic place."[1]

And yet if the boundary between city and country had no meaning here, that did not imply that this was a world without borders. Far from it. The city's history may have begun in the human dreams that prophesied its rise, but those dreams laid their foundations on solid earth, tracing their destiny onto the land's own patterns.

The natural feature that first defined Chicago's location was the river. In the long expanse of Lake Michigan's southern shoreline, this sluggish waterway provided one of the few sheltered spots for vessels seeking harbor. The sandbar at its mouth blocked storm surges and protected the waters behind from wind and waves. Sailors would welcome the relief it offered from the lake's angrier moods. Those traveling by canoe found in it a boundary between open and flowing waters, with their different rhythms of paddles and movement. It was also a passage into the interior. About a mile from its mouth, two prairie streams converged to form the main channel. Neither was much of a river. But less than half a dozen miles from the lake, the south fork found its source on a low wet ridge that for several months of the year flooded to become almost an open marsh. East of that ridge, water flowed down to the lake and on to the St. Lawrence River; west of the ridge, water flowed south to the Mississippi. Although barely fifteen feet higher than Lake Michigan, the ridge sat atop one of the chief natural boundaries of North America, separating the two greatest watersheds east of the Rocky Mountains. By canoeing across it—as was possible without even portaging during wet seasons of the year—one could paddle halfway across the continent, from the North Atlantic to the Gulf of Mexico.[2]

The ridge signified more than just a boundary between watersheds. Thirteen thousand years earlier, it had been part of the terminal moraine at the edge of the great Ice Age glaciers as they began their long retreat to the north. As such, it marked another, much older boundary between ice and land. Although the glaciers had long since vanished, they had altered everything in their path. Far to the north, on the ancient rocks that would become northern Minnesota, Wisconsin, and Michigan, the ice stripped the land of its soil, leaving it badly drained and not very fertile. Grinding southward, the glaciers gouged out tiny ponds and enormous lakes, finally depositing immense loads of soil and gravel wherever they paused in their advances and retreats. Illinois and Iowa, southern Wisconsin and Minnesota, and Chicago itself were all blessed with these Ice Age gifts from the north. As winds blew across the great outwash plains on the margins of the ice sheets, dust storms lifted fine-grained sediments and deposited them as rich loess soil on many of the region's hillsides. Then, as the glaciers disappeared, enormous volumes of water released from their melting ice carved new routes for the major watercourses of the region, creating or reshaping rivers as different as the Chicago, the Wisconsin, and the Mississippi.[3]

In the wake of the glaciers, the climate warmed and winter snows ceased to accumulate. Specialized communities of plants, each adapted to a different set of habitats, moved northward with the warmer weather, as did the animals that lived in their midst. Near the glacier's edge, retreating with it, were the lichens and low grasses of the arctic tundra. Behind them came spruces and other coniferous trees that ruled the landscape for thousands of years until they too moved north, to be followed by the broad-leaved oaks and hickories of the deciduous forest. And to the west, where the climate became drier and fires burned so regularly that trees could not keep a toehold, the tall grasses of the prairies moved in to make their home.[4] These postglacial migrations defined the region's vegetational geography. Three of the continent's most important biotic communities met each other in the lands north and west of Lake Michigan. Chicago stood in the borderland between the western prairies and eastern oak-hickory forests, and the lake gave it access to the white pines and other coniferous trees of the north woods. Grasslands and hardwood and softwood forests were all within reach.[5]

Before Chicago gained its version of the line separating city from country, the lands around it already carried a complex set of natural markers, each with its own meaning and story: gravel and stone, rivers and lakes, clay and loess, grasses and trees, flock and herd. The glaciers had given this landscape its flatness, its fertility, and its easiest corridors of movement. Chicago held proof of their passage in the morainal ridges, the great lake, and the wet prairie at the mouth of the river. Glaciers, bedrocks, and plant communities had together inscribed thousands of square miles with other, subtler divisions—between glaciated and unglaciated regions, between well and poorly drained watersheds, between fertile and less fertile soils, between eastward- and southward-flowing rivers, between grasslands and forests. Each of these natural legacies left patterns on the land, and each would have a part in shaping the history of Chicago and its region.

And yet none of these patterns matter to human history until we ask how the people whose lives they touched understood their significance. By using the landscape, giving names to it, and calling it home, people selected the features that mattered most to them, and drew their mental maps accordingly. Once they had labeled those maps in a particular way—identifying the muddy river flowing through the prairie grasses as a place where long-leaved plants with sweet bulbous roots might be gathered for food—natural and cultural landscapes began to shade into and reshape one another.

In that mutual reshaping, the city's history begins. As early as 1833, when the local Indians signed away their last claims to the area, the dream of Chicago's metropolitan future was cast like a net over the wide territory that nineteenth-century Americans came to know as the Great West. At its farthest extension, the region reached from the waters and forests of the Great Lakes across the treeless grasslands of Illinois and Iowa, to the lands beyond the Missouri where the Plains made their long dry rise toward the mountains, to the Rockies themselves and beyond. Glaciers and grasses alike had left these lands among the richest (and sometimes poorest) in all of North America. Chicago would eventually be the linchpin that would connect them to each other and to the rest of the world. As the city grew, it altered the way people perceived the region so as to make everything seem centered upon itself and its remarkable growth. By the second half of the nineteenth century, Chicago would stand as the greatest metropolis in the continent's interior, with all the Great West in some measure a part of its hinterland and empire.

For the city to play that role, however, the land had first to be redefined and reordered; as so often before in American history, such reordering required a conquest. Indians had been using the land along the Chicago River for centuries. Its first non-Indian occupant was a mulatto trader from Quebec, Jean Baptiste Point du Sable, who established a fur-trading post there in the 1770s.[6] The U.S. Army built Fort Dearborn near the mouth of the river in 1803; nine years later, the inhabitants of the fort were killed in a famous massacre by Potawatomi allies of the British at the start of the War of 1812.[7] The army rebuilt Fort Dearborn in 1816, whereupon it quickly became a center for a trade largely dominated on the U.S. side by the American Fur Company. Over the next decade and a half, the tiny settlement, with its military stockade and wooden cabins, outwardly appeared Euroamerican. But the lands around it were still largely Indian, with several Potawatomi communities living in the vicinity and regularly mingling with the traders.

Chicago itself was a polyglot world of Indian, French, British, and American cultures tied to a vast trading network that was no less Indian than European. Its inhabitants, like other people in the region, gained their living by a mixture of Indian and Euroamerican land practices: raising corn, stalking game, keeping livestock, gathering wild plants, and fishing the prairie streams. In all these activities, the natural patterns of the land offered clues about where and how best to earn a living. Much of what villagers ate came from nearby. They also traded at the fort and fur posts, exchanging corn, flour, skins, jewelry, pipestone, dried meat, fish, and alcohol, as they had been doing for half a century and more. But even at its height the fur trade still occurred in an elaborate social context—mediated always by gift giving, celebrations, and complex negotiations—that Indian communities controlled as much as Europeans did. Marriages between Indian families and European traders produced offspring who played key roles in these exchange relationships, and their mixed parentage symbolized the hybrid cultural universe that had emerged in the region.[8]

By 1830, signs of change loomed from several directions. Illinois had been a state for a dozen years, though most of its American settlements were still well to the south, in the farming areas upstream from St. Louis on the Illinois and Mississippi rivers. Lead mining had emerged as a major economic activity to the west, in the hill country around Galena and Dubuque. Indians and traders in such places had lost their old centrality to the economy.⁹ But in Chicago itself, the Potawatomis still controlled much of the land around the village, where they met the many peoples with whom they traded: Sacs, Foxes, French, Ottawas, English, Chippewas, Americans, and others. Although there were growing rumors that Chicago might become the terminus of a canal linking Lake Michigan to the Illinois River, life continued much as it had in the past. Villagers and their many visitors serviced the paychecks and contracts of the garrison at Fort Dearborn, brought skins to the fur post on the opposite side of the river, frequented the local taverns, and conducted their annual subsistence within the mingled rituals and celebrations of Potawatomi and French Catholic cultural life. Most of the one to two hundred village residents were French or Potawatomi or both, living in ramshackle cabins scattered along the river. People lived well and had every reason to hope that so comfortable a marketplace might continue indefinitely as a small but prosperous center for trade.¹⁰

Unfortunately for the villagers, the end of this world came quickly, and from an unexpected source that had little to do with local Potawatomis and other residents. On April 5, 1832, a group of Sac, Fox, and Kickapoo Indians under the leadership of the Sac chief Black Hawk crossed the Mississippi from Iowa in a futile effort to reclaim lands in western Illinois that they had lost to the United States under a treaty of doubtful legality signed in 1804. Black Hawk and his people had been living on their ancestral lands along the east bank of the Mississippi River for more than two decades before pressure from arriving American settlers persuaded the United States to enforce the terms of the treaty. The result was the last significant Indian uprising in Illinois.

Denying the validity of the 1804 treaty, Black Hawk declared that *"land cannot be sold."* As long as he and his people continued to use it, he said, they would retain their "right to the soil"; not even they themselves had the power to alienate it, since their lives and the land's were one. Black Hawk's people had lived by wandering across a broad landscape in their movements between cropland and hunt, a practice that fit poorly with American notions of bounded property. Like many Indians before and after him, Black Hawk defended his homeland with an argument that made no sense to American ears: "Nothing," he said, "can be sold, but such things as can be carried away."¹¹ An American government long committed to surveying and selling the lands of its "public domain" was not about to be convinced, and moved against Black Hawk accordingly. After raiding a small settlement in Illinois, Black Hawk's band of perhaps two thousand fled before an American military force over twice its size. The final defeat came on August 2, 1832, at the Battle of Bad Axe, when Illinois militiamen gunned down dozens of Indians—men, women, and children—who were trying to cross back to the western side of the Mississippi.[12]

Chicago played no part in Black Hawk's objectives and was far removed from the actual fighting. But the war nonetheless marked a sea change for the village. Soldiers who had mustered from as far away as New York, Virginia, and Louisiana sent back glowing reports about the fertility of the Illinois prairies, and spurred a wave of immigration to the region around Chicago.[13] By the spring of 1833, half a year after Black Hawk's defeat, the town's population had more than doubled. The demographic change brought a cultural and economic revolution. Newly arrived American townspeople soon outnumbered the French and Potawatomi inhabitants who had previously dominated village life, and the local economy began to revolve around the larger and wealthier immigrant group. Before long, the land in and around Chicago was owned and occupied by a predominantly Yankee community.[14]

Responding to Black Hawk's defeat and to the anxieties of new settlers, the U.S. government moved to consolidate its control of remaining Indian territory in Illinois, most of which was held by Potawatomis who had taken no part in the uprising. Vulnerable because of the war but driving the best bargains they could, the Potawatomis negotiated a series of treaties ceding the lands they held around Chicago.[15] By 1833, almost all that remained to them was a tract of about five million acres in northeastern Illinois and southeastern Wisconsin. In August of that year, the U.S. Indian agent at Chicago sent out runners announcing that this too would have to be sold.[16]

In response, most of the remaining Indians of the region began to gather at Chicago; by the middle of September, no fewer than six thousand of them had encamped on the prairies surrounding the village. When told that "their Great Father in Washington had heard that they wished to sell their land," they denied the euphemism by replying that "their Great Father in Washington must have seen a bad bird which had told him a lie, for that far from wishing to sell their land, they wished to keep it."[17] If the Potawatomis were to give up their homelands, they wanted no misunderstanding about the forced nature of the sale. For two weeks, they remained on the outskirts of the village, living off government rations, gaming on the prairie, enjoying the free-flowing alcohol, and mixing with the various birds of passage—grog sellers, grocers, Indian traders, land speculators, gamblers, thieves—who made it their business to profit from such goings-on. One visitor described the scene as "a general fair," while another remarked that "the village was in an uproar from morning to night, and from night to morning." And the curious thing, he said, was that "the whites seemed . . . more pagan than the red men."[18]

The treaties—two of them—were finally signed on September 26 and 27, 1833. Although they were long clouded with scandal because of the large sums of money they allotted to individual Indian agents and traders in the Chicago area—many of them Potawatomis of mixed French and Indian parentage—they nonetheless became the legal basis for American possession of a major part of Chicago's immediate hinterland.[19] Within two or three years, the government forced most of the Potawatomis to move from northern Illinois to new homes on the far side of the Mississippi. Even the Chicago traders who had thought to throw in their lot with the Americans found themselves exiled from their former home.

The final moments of the 1833 negotiations thus carried a heavy symbolism that was clearly visible to those who attended. Charles Latrobe, an English traveler present at the treaty signing, described the moment at sunset as the U.S. commissioners faced west and the Indians faced east, the one looking toward the lands they had just acquired, the other toward the lake and homes they would soon be abandoning. "The glorious light of the setting sun streaming in under the low roof of the Council-House," wrote Latrobe, "fell full on the countenances of the former as they faced the West—while the pale light of the East, hardly lighted up the dark and painted lineaments of the poor Indians, whose souls evidently clave to their birth-right in that quarter."[20] The hybrid cultural universe of Indians and Euroamericans that had existed in the Chicago area for decades was finally to be shattered by different conceptions of property and real estate.

Black Hawk had been wrong that land could not be sold, and the Americans immediately set out to prove his error with a vengeance. During the next three years, the village of a few hundred grew to nearly four thousand.[21] At the same time, Chicago's real estate became some of the most highly valued in the nation. The mid-1830s saw the most intense land speculation in American history, with Chicago at the center of the vortex.[22] Believing Chicago was about to become the terminus of a major canal, land agents and speculators flooded into town, buying and selling not only the empty lots along its ill-marked streets but also the surrounding grasslands which the Indians had recently abandoned. Stories abounded of men who bought land for one or two hundred dollars in the morning and sold it for several thousand before the sun set.[23] Lots that had sold for $33 in 1829 were going for $100,000 by 1836.[24] Such prices bore no relation to any current economic reality. Only wild hopes for the future could lead people to pay so much for vacant lots in a town where the most promising economic activity consisted of nothing more substantial than buying and selling real estate. Speculators dreamed of what the land might someday be, and gambled immense sums on their faith in a rising market. As the British traveler Harriet Martineau remarked, it was as if "some prevalent mania infected the whole people."[25]

When the bubble burst in 1837 and the banks called in loans that had little more than hope as their collateral, people who had counted themselves millionaires teetered on the edge of bankruptcy. The real estate market collapsed, so it became almost impossible to sell land at any price. One visitor said of Chicago's inhabitants that "they possessed at present the means of earning their subsistence, but little more," and so, "having lost all their capital, and being obliged . . . to begin the world again, they endeavoured to be content."[26] The great boom years had carried Chicago ever so speedily away from its Indian past and toward the urban future on which the speculators had based their investments; but the end of the boom left the town stranded with its promise largely unfulfilled. Business slowed to a near standstill in the general collapse of prices, and the city's growth followed suit. It was as if the town had gone into hibernation.

Although plat maps showed the grid of city streets extending four miles along the lakeshore and out into the prairie, Chicago's actual buildings in 1837 concentrated in the small business district on the south side of the river, and in the equally small well-to-do residential quarter on the north side. Rope-drawn ferries provided the principal link between the two halves of town. No block was entirely built up, and one did not have to walk more than a few minutes to be out on the prairie. Residents could still hunt wolves within earshot of city center during the 1830s.[27] A few buildings, including the finer of the town's fifteen hotels, offered elegant quarters, but most were hurried affairs thrown up at the height of the real estate speculation. The place possessed five churches, three Protestant and two Catholic, but the Unitarians could not yet afford a building and had to hold their meetings in a local tavern.[28] None of the streets was paved, and many still showed "the green turf of the prairie grass in their centre" when rain or snow had not turned everything to mud.[29] Many families continued to use pails to draw their water supply directly from the river.[30] The town served as a trade center for the growing number of local farmers and, like most frontier communities, depended heavily on selling supplies to travelers and arriving immigrants.

Little of this changed in the immediate future. After such dramatic early signs of growth, Chicagoans found it all too frustrating to watch the boom grind to a halt. And yet those who had lost their money in the collapse had little choice but to keep their land, earn a living as best they could, and hope their luck would change. They waited a long time. Another decade passed before Chicago began to fulfill the destiny speculators had dreamed for it during the mad years of the land rush.

Booster Dreams

And what was Chicago's destiny?

To answer that question is to confront much of the history of America's Great West in the nineteenth century. At Chicago's famous Columbian Exposition of 1893—an event which many interpreted as the fulfillment of the city's destiny—the historian Frederick Jackson Turner proposed for the first time his famous frontier thesis as an explanation of why the West had developed as it had. In offering what became a ruling paradigm of American history for the next half century, Turner delineated one standard version of Chicago's destiny. He argued that the different Wests of the United States had recapitulated the social evolution of human civilization as Europeans and easterners repeatedly encountered the "zone" of "free land" and "primitive savagery"—what he called "the frontier"—that was the source of American energy, individualism, and political democracy. Chicago was one end product of that evolution.

For Turner, the sequential phases of the frontier constituted a palimpsest that could be read "like a huge page in the history of society." The frontier, he wrote,

> begins with the Indian and the hunter; it goes on to tell of the disintegration of savagery by the entrance of the trader, the pathfinder of civilization; we read the annals of the pastoral stage in ranch life; the exploitation of the soil by the raising of unrotated crops of corn and wheat in sparsely settled farming communities; the intensive culture of the denser farm settlement; and finally the manufacturing organization with city and factory system.[31]

Turner never explained the mechanism whereby these stages succeeded each other, probably because they so closely matched his nineteenth-century notions of social evolution. For him and his contemporaries, it seemed quite "natural" that Indians and fur traders should prepare the way for cattle ranchers, and they for subsistence farmers, and they for complex farming communities. After all, human society had supposedly followed this same path. Only at the end of this Darwinian sequence would come an industrial city like Chicago, which as the ultimate expression of nineteenth-century progress stood as both the achievement and the antithesis of the frontier.

Whatever the merits of the Turner thesis—and both its strengths and weaknesses have profoundly shaped American historical thought—it fits poorly with the world of Chicago in the 1830s.[32] Turner would probably have interpreted the American Fur Company's trading post on the Chicago River as a "pathfinder of civilization" paving the way for "the disintegration of savagery," but it seems most unlikely that the French or Potawatomi traders would have described it that way. Neither the post nor the fur trade necessitated the treaties of 1833, which quickly destroyed them both. The forced migration of the Potawatomis was the product not of natural progress but of political choice, supported by the organized violence of an expansionist society. Moreover, the subsequent land craze posed an even greater difficulty for Turner's theory of frontier development. Chicago's population exploded after 1833 without bothering much about a pastoral stage, a settlement of pioneering subsistence farmers, or even an agricultural community at all. The town's speculators gambled on an *urban* future, staking fortunes on land they hoped would soon lie at the heart of a great city. Explaining their vision of Chicago's "destiny" means reading Turner backward, for their theory of frontier growth apparently *began* with the city instead of ending with it.

The speculators' urban dream extended to many more places than just Chicago. The land craze of the 1830s was nationwide, part of an upward swing in the business cycle and a dramatic easing of admittedly shaky credit in the wake of Andrew Jackson's victorious assault on the Second Bank of the United States. As real estate prices skyrocketed, they fueled a manic search for new places in which to invest.[33] Joseph Balestier, a Chicago attorney who had done well for himself just by processing land titles during the craze, recalled in 1840 how the speculators had remapped—and redreamed—the Old Northwest until they had nearly covered it with "a chain almost unbroken of suppositious villages and cities. The whole land seemed staked out and peopled on paper."[34] Speculators looking for big profits invested in townsites, which always sold at much higher prices than mere agricultural land. Fictive lots on fictive streets in fictive towns became the basis for thousands of transactions whose only justification was a dubious idea expressed on an overly optimistic map. With wonderful irony, Balestier described how speculators scoured the countryside for any site that might conceivably serve as the seed of a future city. If they could find a stream, no matter how muddy or shallow or small, flowing into Lake Michigan—here was the future harbor from which all else would grow:

> Then the miserable waste of sand and fens which lay unconscious of its glory on the shore of the lake, was suddenly elevated into a mighty city, with a projected harbor and light-house, railroads and canals, and in a short time the circumjacent lands were sold in lots 50 feet by 100. . . . Not the puniest brook on the shore of Lake Michigan was suffered to remain

without a city at its mouth, and whoever will travel around that lake shall find many a mighty mart staked out in spots suitable only for the habitations of wild beasts.[35]

Chicago began the 1830s as just such a site. The Chicago River may have been more than a puny brook, but it was rather less than a great waterway: short, shallow, with no current to speak of, and far better suited to canoes than to sailing ships. A visitor in 1848 called it "a sluggish, slimy stream, too lazy to clean itself."[36] It nonetheless had two great virtues. One was its harbor: bad as it might be, it was still the best available on the southern shore of Lake Michigan in the 250 miles between St. Joseph, Michigan, and Milwaukee, Wisconsin.[37] The writer Caroline Kirkland was only slightly exaggerating when she called it "the best harbor on Lake Michigan" and the "worst harbor and smallest river any great commercial city ever lived on."[38] Equally important was the river's nearness to the divide between the Great Lakes and Mississippi watersheds. If investors could arrange to dig a canal across the glacial moraine at this point, an inland ship passage between New York and New Orleans might at last be possible. As early as 1814, *Niles' Weekly Register* in Baltimore had predicted that a canal at Chicago would make Illinois "the seat of an immense commerce; and a market for the commodities of all regions." "What a route!" its editor exclaimed. "How stupendous the idea!"[39] Thirteen years later, Congress granted land to the state of Illinois to build the canal. Although nearly a decade passed before construction began, the first mapping of city lots in Chicago, in 1830, was a direct consequence of the canal surveys. So was the speculative boom that followed.[40]

No place would benefit more from a canal than Chicago, a fact that speculators were quick to grasp—and exaggerate. "Almost every person I met," reported a skeptical Scottish visitor, "regarded Chicago as the germ of an immense city. . . ."[41] One typical example was Charles Butler, a New York real estate investor who visited the area a month before the Potawatomi treaty was signed. After deciding that Chicago's prospects looked good, Butler spent $100,000 to buy 150 acres—1,000 city lots—on the north side of the river. By Chicago standards, the purchase was on the conservative side, and the paper value of Butler's lots soon rose much higher. When his brother-in-law, William B. Ogden, arrived in 1835 to look after the investment, he could scarcely believe the prices people were paying for land. Chicago speculators, he said, had become "crazy and visionary," and "he could not see where the value lay nor what it was that justified the payment of such prices."[42]

Still, Butler and those like him were not to be dissuaded, and even Ogden eventually underwent a monumental change of mind. Apparently deciding that Chicago offered good investment opportunities after all, he soon became its first mayor and a key investor in the railroad enterprises that finally assured the city's success. Such people saw Chicago in their mind's eye not as it was but as it could be: a metropolis of continental significance. "This is *the most important point* in the great west for missionary effort," Butler wrote in one of the earliest passages linking Chicago to the favorite nineteenth-century name for its hinterland. "It is a concentrating & diffusive point: it is at the head of navigation & of course a great commercial point. It has a very extensive back country extending to the Mississippi & rich beyond calculation. . . ."[43] What could be more certain than real estate investments at a site so clearly marked for greatness?

Modern readers must beware lest their knowledge of the future lead them to be too impressed by Butler's prescience. His enthusiasm for the quiet little trading post that was also—rather astonishingly—*"the most important point* in the great west" was not noticeably different from that of other investors who erected cities out of swampy air at dozens of other sites on the shores of the Great Lakes. Some of those places—Buffalo, Cleveland, Toledo—went on to become major cities; most did not. That Butler's prophecy came true should obscure neither its unlikely good luck nor its similarity to equally enthusiastic but unlucky claims for scores of other would-be "great commercial points."[44] Indeed, we should care less about Butler's accuracy than about how utterly conventional his predictions were. He and his fellow speculators all believed that cities were the keys to the Great West. And since their reasons for this belief were anything but academic, they sought to discover why some cities grew and not others, so that intelligent investors could profit accordingly.

In the speculators' dreams lay the urban promise—and the urban imperative—of frontier settlement and investment. The search for the great western cities of the future drove nearly all nineteenth-century townsite speculation, and the accompanying rhetoric always inclined toward enthusiastic exaggeration and self-interested promotion. But not all was fantasy. The "boosters," as they came to be known, expounded serious theories of economic growth that dominated nineteenth-century thinking about frontier development.[45] Although Jesup W. Scott and William Gilpin were better known than most who wrote about urban growth in the West, no one person could claim authorship of the booster theories themselves, which quickly became the common intellectual property of speculators, newspaper editors, merchants, and chambers of commerce throughout the West. Taken as a group, the boosters offered a surprisingly coherent model of urban and regional growth. Unlike Turner, they saw the engine of western development in the symbiotic relationship between cities and their surrounding countrysides. So powerful was their vision that it became a self-fulfilling prophecy. When the Potawatomis and the U.S. commissioners faced each other at Chicago in 1833, they expressed their cultural differences in the way they saw the landscape that stretched before them in the light of the setting sun. One saw the apparition of a great city upon it, while the other did not. To understand how so many nineteenth-century Americans came to share that urban vision is to discover much about their dreams for themselves and for the Great West.[46]

In the first place, the boosters felt confident that the West would produce great cities and even a future metropolis, though they argued about where such places would be. For them, the apparition that hovered over Chicago's 1833 treaty negotiations was a true prophecy, not a ghost. A writer in the 1890s captured this feeling by saying of early Chicago that "the place was pregnant with certainty."[47] Boosters sought to make their visions come true by conveying just this certainty to investors and merchants who might set up shop in the place being promoted. Almost always they identified a list of supposed "natural advantages" that would make the future metropolis a natural outgrowth of its region. Boosters believed that climate, soils, vegetation, transportation routes, and other features of the landscape all pointed toward key locations that nature had designated for urban greatness. When the newspaper editor William Bross sought in 1880 to analyze "Chicago and the Sources of Her Past and Future Growth," he began by asserting, "Nature, it is believed, or, to speak more reverently, He who is the Author of Nature, selected the site of this great city . . . and hence her future will not be subject to those causes which have paralyzed or destroyed many of the cities of past ages."[48] In the practical eyes of people seeking profitable investments, nature became the world's most reliable real estate broker.

What better guarantee of profit and prosperity could one want? If a city's growth was assured by nature or—better yet—ordained by God, then only a fool could doubt its future promise. No mere human power could alter the forces that compelled its growth.[49] Moreover, if one could identify these forces in advance, one could predict with certainty their effects—and the success of investments based on them. "I shall assume that a city is an organism," wrote Jesup W. Scott, "springing from natural laws as inevitably as any other organism, and governed, invariably, in its origin and growth, by these laws."[50] Scott, who became one of the most influential booster theorists from the 1840s to the 1880s, joined with Louis Sullivan and with other boosters in seeing the city as nature's highest creation. In stark contrast to Robert Herrick's antinatural image of a city "made of man" stood the boosters' implication that human labor was less important than nature in spurring a city's growth. As one writer put it in describing Chicago's urban promise, "nothing remained for man to do, but to gather up the gifts so profusely showered upon him."[51] Nature's Metropolis would almost build itself.

According to booster theories, the natural advantages that created cities ranged from the trivial to the cosmic but generally fell into three broad categories. The first included all the resources of the region which would center its trade on the city. The second comprised the transportation routes that would guide those resources to their natural marketplace. And the third, rather mysteriously, consisted of global climatic forces which had historically created great urban civilizations elsewhere in the world and which now, supposedly, were starting to operate in North America. These three sets of natural advantages would converge to promote a city's growth—or so the theory ran.

The boosters usually began their arguments by identifying all aspects of the region—fertile soils, forests of commercial timber, mines, coalfields, waterpower sites—that might become "resources" contributing to urban growth. The importance of such resources seemed so obvious that many boosters simply listed them and assumed that providence—nature's or God's—would send them flowing toward the future city. Jesup Scott, for instance, believed that the Great Lakes had been designed by no less an architect than God "to give them the utmost availability for purposes of trade," their waters extending from the heart of the continent and the northern limits of agriculture to the great markets of the Atlantic. The region's natural endowments were proof that God had "diversified" the land's "surface with hills, vales, and plains, and clothed them alternately with fine groves of timber, and beautiful meadows of grass and flowers." Scott's description may have been poetic, but his conclusions were wholly utilitarian. The forests would supply timber for buildings and cordwood for fuel. The meadows would become pastures and fields that would send grain, meat, and dairy products to the city. And beneath it all, "the minerals of nearly every geological era, and of every kind, which has been made tributary to man's comfort and civilization" were "properly distributed."[52] In his vision of a "properly distributed" landscape, Scott revealed just how completely he and other Americans had remapped the natural terrain of the Great West since the days when Potawatomis had gathered to collect wild garlic plants on the banks of the Chicago River.

But regional resources represented only the *potential* for economic development and urban growth. By themselves, they indicated little about which cities would benefit from exploiting those resources. And so the boosters, having satisfied themselves that nature would produce a great city somewhere, turned next to natural transportation routes to show where it would be located. Here theory turned to more practical ends. Virtually all boosters had some vested interest in promoting the growth of one particular city, so they usually became cheerleaders for the places where they resided and owned real estate. When they theorized about which transportation routes would funnel regional resource flows, they naturally chose routes that led to their own city's doorstep.

The talisman that lent authority to such arguments was almost always an actual map of North America. William Bross advised those who read his predictions about Chicago's future growth that "the latest and best map of the United States should be before the reader while perusing this paper."[53] Upon consulting such a map, readers would instantly see that the natural arrangement of waterways—rivers, harbors, and potential canal routes—suggested only a limited set of places destined to be major cities. "Let our readers look upon any well drawn map of this continent," intoned Chicago's *American Railway Times* in 1852, "and note the position of Chicago." Anyone who could read such a map should be able to see Chicago's "natural capabilities for drawing almost the entire trade" of the region between the Great Lakes and the Rocky Mountains.[54] By concentrating the region's wealth, the natural avenues of commerce would create the city.

Chicago's claim to natural transportation advantages lay principally in its harbor and canal corridor, neither of which extended very far to the west, and certainly not to the Rocky Mountains. Probably for this reason, Chicago boosters rarely stressed natural transportation advantages as much as boosters in other cities. In fact, if waterway geography were the determinant of urban growth, the major inland city would surely be St. Louis, an argument which boosters in that city never tired of making. Located at the confluence of two of the continent's greatest rivers, the Mississippi and the Missouri, St. Louis could reasonably expect to draw resources from the entire country to its north and west. Pressing their advantage, its boosters often carried the waterway argument to extreme lengths. "The laws of trade ultimately enforce obedience," wrote Logan Uriah Reavis, the most prominent of St. Louis's urban prophets. "The title of the Mississippi river to the commerce of this valley is attested with the Divine signature. The productions of the West will be borne to the tide-water through channels which the Architect of nature formed"—and so St. Louis would be the city to aid these "productions" in their journey.[55] How Chicagoans answered such arguments is the subject of the next chapter.

Boosters not content to project urban greatness on the basis of resources and transportation alone could appeal to one more group of "natural advantages." Following the writings of the German geographer

Alexander von Humboldt on world climate, several western boosters argued that great civilizations—and the great cities that went with them—were possible only within a narrow global band arranged around a mean annual isotherm of about fifty degrees Fahrenheit. Why? Because the white races who would build such civilizations retained their civilized superiority only in a temperate climate that challenged them with extremes of hot and cold. The climatic theory of urban growth rested on racist assumptions about human biology which asserted that the dark-skinned peoples of the tropics were incapable of cultural progress.[56]

The most famous booster to rely on this argument was William Gilpin, whose chief claim to fame lay in having served an abbreviated term as the first governor of Colorado.[57] Gilpin's eloquence on behalf of what he called the Isothermal Zodiac wandered off into mysticism as he referred to the "perpetual and instinctive pressure" that tended to "condense population" along an "axis of intensity" which contained all the great cities of the world.[58] By presenting maps that traced the isotherm of fifty-two degrees Fahrenheit across North America, Gilpin mustered evidence that the next world city would be located at "Centropolis," which he placed in the vicinity of modern-day Kansas City. (Other boosters of course chose isotherms that were conveniently nearer to their own cities.) So powerful were the mystical natural forces of climate and topography that any rivals would "contend in vain" to supplant Centropolis. Or so ran Gilpin's argument. But the Isothermal Zodiac encompassed such an inconveniently broad region—most of the United States fell within it—that boosters had to work overtime to make it serve the interests of any particular city. Gilpin alone rested the major part of his theory upon it.[59] Chicago's boosters seem never to have much bothered with it.

For all boosters, cities had their roots in natural phenomena but ultimately grew because, for whatever reason, people chose to migrate to them. The demographic pull of cities suggested yet another theoretical basis for predicting urban growth. Cities were like stars or planets, with gravitational fields that attracted people and trade like miniature solar systems. If this was true, then perhaps one could use the Newtonian theory of gravitation to understand their reach and influence. The strongest advocate of this "gravitational" theory of cities was an obscure figure in Cincinnati named S. H. Goodin, whose remarkable essay "Cincinnati—Its Destiny" in many ways anticipated the model of urban growth—central place theory—that has dominated twentieth-century thought about this subject.

"The law of gravitation or centralization," wrote Goodin, "or, as some designated it, the serial law, is known to be one of the laws of nature."[60] This "law" predicted that as frontier migrants displaced Indian communities in the West, new villages would emerge to serve the surrounding territory, attracting more than their share of population and trade. Such villages represented what Goodin called "the first circle in the serial law," and were followed by subsequent circles, each marking a higher stage of urban progress. People in these villages, wrote Goodin,

> desire intercourse one with another, so a road is made from village to village; but one improves faster than the others, some local advantage is the cause; then all the other villages construct their roads to it, and this makes the second circle. But among these villages of larger growth, one better situated than the rest advances with more rapidity, and the city soon stands in the centre of the third circle."[61]

Translated, Goodin's argument suggested that rural populations clustered around small villages, which clustered in turn around larger towns, which clustered in turn around still larger cities. Cities were the stars around which town and country satellites would come to orbit.[62] But the gravitational forces producing this urban solar system had not yet finished their work. For Goodin, the existing cities of the West—Cincinnati, St. Louis, Pittsburgh, Chicago, and others—were all "competing cities of the same grade of circles," and one more stage had yet to be achieved. *"The next circle beyond,"* he prophesied, *"is a central city—a city which shall have all these cities as satellites or outposts—Where shall that city stand?"*[63]

The great central metropolis: where would it be? No question more excited booster imaginations. All asked it in one form or another, and all answered with their own prophecy. For the boosters, "civilizing" the frontier—Turner's process—was scarcely more important than linking new communities to the emerging metropolis. Indeed, these seemingly separate processes were not merely parallel but identical: the growing countryside would create its central city, and vice versa. The metropolis would sit at the center of an immense circle within which would live most of the American population. Metropolitan location might ultimately depend on the geography of resources and waterways, but its more immediate cause was the spatial arrangement of human beings. As the Great West became ever more densely settled, the geographical center of the country's population would drift gradually westward, until finally it came to rest at the central city.

On this theory, boosters of a quantitative bent decided that careful study of population movements as recorded in the census, along with business and trade statistics, would reveal the location of the new western metropolis. No one made more diligent efforts at such study than Toledo's Jesup W. Scott.[64] For over three decades, starting in the 1840s,

Scott gathered a vast array of statistical evidence demonstrating the westward movement of American population, the flow of regional trade, and the more rapid growth of cities in the West as compared with those in the East. Although he never stated his argument in quite such abstract terms as S. H. Goodin, the two agreed on the importance of demographic trends for understanding urban growth. For Scott, cities grew in tandem with the increasing size and density of regional population. Geography was secondary to population increase, channeling rather than creating the underlying demographic pressures that led cities to expand. "The great city of America," he wrote, "will be in the midst of, and not far from, the centre of the great *population* of America."[65]

Unlike Gilpin, Scott was no mystic. He believed that cities grew principally for economic reasons: their main activity was to serve as marketplaces for their regions. Because people favor markets to which they have easiest access, he predicted that "the centre of trade in this country is likely to follow the centre of population."[66] Contrary to those who believed that eastern and European exports fueled western economic growth, Scott was confident that *domestic* trade was far more important. "As our internal commerce is more than ten times as great as our foreign commerce, and is increasing more rapidly," he reasoned, "it is plain that it will have the chief agency in building the future and permanent capital city of the continent."[67] As western trade and population grew, the mercantile activities of western cities would increase accordingly, and so would their manufacturing. Already they were growing more quickly than the eastern cities they would eventually surpass.

With all of his statistics, Scott sought to prove that these various phenomena were well under way in the Great West. He published article after article with long tables showing the growth rates of American cities and projecting them forward in time. Taking the 1840s as a base, he calculated that New York, Boston, and Philadelphia, all in their period of greatest expansion, needed about a dozen years to double their populations. In the West, on the other hand, Cincinnati and Toledo needed only six years to perform the same feat. St. Louis doubled in four years, and Chicago in three and a half.[68] Scott read such numbers as evidence of a shifting balance of power in the United States: "In the aggregate," he concluded, "our internal cities, depending for their growth on internal trade and home manufacture, increase three times as fast as the exterior cities. . . ."[69] He failed to note that small places can always double their size more easily than large ones for simple reasons of fractional arithmetic. But he was nonetheless right that cities in the West were expanding in trade and population much more rapidly than older cities in the East.

Scott's statistics led back to the great booster question. Just as western cities grew more quickly as a group, so too would one of them grow more quickly than the rest. Which would it be? In trying to identify that city, Scott linked his demographic arguments with booster theories of natural advantage. The great city would lie near the middle of the central valley where most Americans would ultimately dwell. It would have numerous and abundant resources in its hinterland. It would be at the location furnishing the widest access to the region as a whole, which meant that it would be on the Great Lakes, not a river. "River cities," he claimed, "gather in productions from the surrounding districts which seek an eastern market through lake harbors. . . ." Cities on the lakes could gather the products of several river valleys and so offered a wider field for trade.[70] The lake city that gave access to the most extensive group of river cities would grow most quickly. Lake, harbor, canal, and a fertile well-populated backcountry: these ingredients led to urban greatness, and Scott was quite sure that only two cities possessed them. "Chicago and Toledo," he wrote, "are believed to be the true claimants for this high destiny."[71] Not even the methodical Scott could finally resist the impulse to name his own hometown as the likely seat of future grandeur, though his analysis seemed in many ways to favor Chicago.

Metropolis and Empire

The "high destiny" of the western city: whether the boosters resorted to geographical determinism, or theorized about climatic influences on civilization, or traced imaginary circles of population on maps of North America, they always returned at last to destiny. In their eyes, nature would combine with the progress of human population to call forth a metropolis to lead the Great West. This shared vision had led Charles Butler and Jesup Scott, writing four decades apart, to the same prophecy about Chicago's future. Butler's "*most important point* in the great west" became Scott's "*ultimate* great city," but both men were convinced that the future of the West was inseparable from that of its central city. They agreed with all other boosters on this point—if not about Chicago itself—because they shared a sense of what urban greatness meant. The triumphant cities of the past, stretching back to classical antiquity, had achieved lasting fame among later generations because their destiny had been an imperial one. What Scott called "the ultimate crowning city" would achieve comparable fame by making all of North America—indeed, all the world—its empire.

Empire: its metaphors form the very core of booster rhetoric. For American patriots of the nineteenth century, the line from Bishop Berke-

ley's famous poem was less a cliché than an incantation: "Westward the
course of empire takes its way."[72] In popular conceptions of history, empire's westward course had begun in Asia with the Chinese and then
moved sequentially through "the Indian, the Persian, the Grecian, the
Roman, the Spanish, the British," and, finally, the American empire that
would emerge in the New World.[73] The sequence of empires necessarily
implied a sequence of cities, and so the boosters, in describing their own
communities, repeatedly invoked a jumbled handful of classical sites:
Babylon, Thebes, Athens, Alexandria, Carthage, Constantinople, and,
more frequently than any other, Rome. "In ancient times," wrote a Chicago newspaperman in the 1880s, "all roads led to Rome; in modern
times all roads lead to Chicago."[74]

Such references to classical sites may often have been little more than
rhetorical flourishes, but they nonetheless suggest the boosters' imperial
cast of mind. When writers spoke of Chicago as "the Rome that is to be of
the new world" or "the Rome of the railroads," they were reaching for a
metaphor that lent their city the grandeur of past urban empires.[75] One
task of such rhetoric was to suggest that Chicago had already surpassed
its midwestern rivals. For example, the cover of an 1887 Chicago guidebook presented a cartoon chariot race entitled the "Great Contest for
Supremacy." The backdrop for the race was "The World's Ampitheatre,"
a structure which distinctly recalled the Colosseum in Rome. In distant
third place, riding a chariot pulled by black horses, was a somewhat
dumpy and comic figure labeled Cincinnati; in second place, a black
charioteer pulled by four black horses carried a banner for St. Louis; and
easily in first place, a white rider, driving a chariot marked Progress and
pulled by four white horses, proudly bore Chicago's banner.[76] As Rome
had triumphed over its ancient rivals, so too would Chicago.

Classical allusions suggested other messages as well. Just as history
had progressed from empire to empire, so the emerging cities of inland
America would surpass in grandeur the older cities of Europe and the
American East. When Logan Reavis wrote that "Rome despised the barbarians, and the barbarians conquered Rome," he intended his readers to
see that the westward rise and fall of empire would be an appropriate fate
for easterners who held western aspirations in contempt. Waxing ever
more eloquent as his argument proceeded, he concluded in a passage rife
with the stock imagery of imperial decay and rebirth. "Civilization," he
said,

> like the ostrich in its flight, throws sand upon everything behind her; and
> before many cycles shall have completed their rounds sentimental pil-
> grims from the humming cities of the Pacific coast will be seen where

Boston, Philadelphia, and New York now stand, viewing in moonlight contemplation, with the melancholy owl, traces of the Athens, the Carthage, and the Babel of the Western hemisphere.[77]

We will never know what Reavis thought the condition of St. Louis would be when New York and other eastern cities lay in ruins, but San Francisco would apparently produce America's Gibbon. Passages like this one can easily seem comic, and the boosters themselves probably did not take them very seriously. But they surely did not think it silly to view American history through the epic lens of classical civilization, or to imagine that the grandeur of St. Louis or Chicago might someday, in the not too distant future, equal Rome's. To believe otherwise was to doubt the high destiny of America itself.

American boosters saw London as the current seat of world empire, heir to Rome's throne, but they also believed that New York would soon win that title for itself.[78] Many thought that the most important factor creating the next imperial metropolis would be the western trade of North America and that New York's primacy depended on such trade.[79] An Albany newspaper editor predicted, "A city sustained by that trade, can never languish. . . . [It] must be far greater than even Alexandria or Thebes."[80] New York had dug the Erie Canal to make itself the metropolis of the Great West, and had thereby earned itself the nickname Empire City. "Throw away the West," wrote one observer, "and no city on the coast could become the 'empire.' "[81]

To cast doubt on the permanence of New York's hegemony, western boosters theorized that a new "central city" would ultimately emerge as the chief agent of internal commerce. But few expected the next stage of the imperial cycle to occur in the nineteenth century. Quick as they were to compare their city to Rome, Chicago boosters usually became quite circumspect in writing about New York. Indeed, when predicting the future primacy of their own city, they generally failed to mention the eastern metropolis at all. Perhaps the classical allusions were a way of implying what might otherwise have seemed outrageous or silly: if Rome could rise and fall, so might New York, but there was no need to say so explicitly. The serial forms of empire were easiest to believe in when viewed at the safe distance of thousands of miles and thousands of years.[82]

The imperial metaphor which cropped up most frequently in booster prose, whether applied to New York or Chicago, described the "tributary" countryside that would give the metropolis its empire. In 1857, the *Chicago Magazine* reported an estimate that "700,000 square miles of Western territory" was or would be "partially tributary" to Chicago.[83] The word "tributary" conjured up the image of a great river, gathering the waters of its many branches and concentrating them at its mouth. Read in this way, it recalled the doctrine of natural advantages.[84] But the metaphor also suggested that the countryside would pay tribute to Chicago as Gaul had paid tribute to Rome. After a visit to Chicago in 1867, the journalist James Parton had written that "every acre with which it could put itself into easy communication must pay tribute to it forever."[85] Like Rome, Chicago's imperial future would arise from the wealth flowing into its coffers from the territory around it. Most who wrote about the city sooner or later resorted to such language.

One might have thought that a good republican would recoil from any metaphor that described a parasitic imperial capital imposing its rule and binding its colonies to enforced tribute, but this never seems to have troubled the boosters. If there was a contradiction between the American faith in republican democracy and the boosters' affection for imperial metaphors, few noticed it at the time. Instead, the boosters embraced the common American notion that free commerce and an enlightened democratic government would together create an expanding empire in which there were no subjects, only citizens. At least in theory, people joined the Republic by choice, and they would trade with its metropolis in much the same way. America's cities had grown by *commercial* power, not the tyrannical power of the state. Commerce was a two-way street in a manner that imperial taxes could never be, so city and country in America need not reproduce their ancient enmity. The booster vision of imperial destiny presupposed no exploitation. William Gilpin could thus wax eloquent on behalf of America's various "empires"—"the empire of our *continental* geography," "the empire of our *free* people," the empires of American politics, society, religion, and industry—and then proclaim them reconciled in "mutual concord, self-sustained: unlimited expansion: perpetual buoyancy, and perpetual life!"[86]

Gilpin went further than others in his rhetorical exuberance, but most boosters, like most nineteenth-century Americans, sought to strip empire of its dangerous connotations and leave only its epic grandeur. Because the central city of the Republic would attain its status by commerce rather than by military might, it had no need to play tyrant and so could escape the moral corruption that had been Rome's fate. The Indians might not have agreed that Americans had built their empire without violence, but boosters were not thinking about Indians when they described America's imperial promise. In 1846, Cincinnati's James Hall referred to commerce as "a mighty conqueror, more powerful than an army with banners," through whose agency "a vast region" had been "overrun and subdued." The proof of America's unique destiny, he said, was that "the conquests of the warlike Emperor have vanished . . . while a commercial people, using only pacific means, have gained an empire whose breadth and wealth might satisfy the ambition of even a Napoleon."[87] Conquest of this kind, so the theory went, expanded the national sphere of interest with mutually beneficial ties that joined all parts of the empire in free trade and liberal democracy.

Perceiving America as a commercial empire allowed boosters and others to believe that the flow of "tribute" among its various parts enriched all and impoverished none. The progress of cities and their rural areas opened markets that enabled both to prosper. Although the countryside did pay tribute that allowed a city like Chicago to grow, the exchange was anything but a zero-sum game. After all, if rural areas failed to become tributary to a metropolis, they would have no market and could only languish. Under such circumstances, commercial "conquest" yielded happy results for conqueror and conquered alike.

Chicago boosters offered a similar argument about their city's relation to potential urban rivals. Because Chicago's wealth and preeminence had been guaranteed by nature, they said, it did not need to compete with other western cities.[88] In fact, they hoped that all areas of the city's vast hinterland would enjoy the fruits of progress, since Chicago could only benefit from the general prosperity. Its leading booster, John Wright, expressed this feeling in 1869 when he announced that Chicago's motto should be "Room for them and us." The city, he said,

> is no monopolist; and instead of desiring to see other cities, either on lake or on river, dwindling like stars to leave her a glittering sun, she rejoices in the truth that we constitute no ordinary nation, but a constellation of sovereign, free and independent States, which fact of art itself tends to create many centres, while nature, in these immense vallies of thousands of miles, has ordained sites for many great cities. Because Chicago is sure of being chiefest, it is her interest and ambition that her own section should have several chief cities.[89]

William Bross offered a similar argument when he suggested that cities ranging from Milwaukee to St. Louis to Denver misunderstood their own best interests in trying to compete with Chicago. Chicago had "not a particle of jealousy in her nature," and encouraged them to improve themselves to the utmost. "Bless you, friends," he chuckled, "the more you prosper, the more you all will contribute to the wealth and the prosperity of Chicago."[90]

Boosters in other cities might gnash their teeth at such condescension, but to a considerable extent they shared Bross's assumptions about metropolitan empire. Only their assessment of which city should become "the chiefest" differed.[91] All believed that the Great West would rise as a commercial hierarchy with its foundation in the rural countryside, and its ascending levels in village, town, and city. At the apex would stand the great central metropolis which was cause, effect, and emblem of its region's continuing prosperity. A favorite booster word for that central city was "emporium," a "great marketplace" that prospered on commerce but carried at least a false etymological echo of that other mystical word, "empire."[92] By the end of the century, when Chicago was the second-largest city in the nation, with over a million and a half inhabitants, even the most die-hard champions of other places were willing to concede that it might have some special claim to being metropolis of the Great West. By then, at the place where wild garlic plants no longer grew, it almost seemed that America's urban empire had been achieved.

Reading Turner Backwards

Few people read the boosters anymore. Their unabashed optimism about progress and civilization has long since gone out of fashion, and their prose is alternately too dry and too baroque for modern tastes. But their chief historian, Charles Glaab, has rightly observed that "this kind of writing more than likely outweighs any other about the West. . . ."[93] The boosters expressed what many Americans believed—or wanted to believe—about the expansion and progress of the United States and its Great West. They offered seemingly rational arguments to reinforce the visionary faith that sustained many who lived and invested in the region. As a group, they present a strikingly consistent picture of how the western landscape would be absorbed into a commercial system revolving around a small number of urban centers. Natural advantage and the movement of human populations together determined how individual cities, towns, and villages would fit into that system. Many such places would prosper, said the boosters, but only one would emerge as the central city of the Great West. As the speculators of the 1830s dashed through the muddy streets around Fort Dearborn and paid fortunes for empty lots, some form of this vision was hovering before their eyes. Inflated prices may have reflected inflated dreams, but fifty years later a great city did in fact stand atop those lots. At least some part of the boosters' prophecy had actually come true.[94]

The West of the great emporium and its satellites bore little outward resemblance to the West of Frederick Jackson Turner's frontier. In contrast to the boosters, Turner consistently chose to see the frontier as a rural place, the very isolation of which created its special role in the history of American democracy. Toward the end of his career, he looked with some misgiving on the likelihood that there would be an "urban reinterpretation" of American history that might "minimize the frontier theme"—as if frontier history had little or nothing to do with cities.[95] For Turner and his followers, frontier development had been slow and evolutionary, with cities appearing only after a long period of rural agricultural growth. Cities marked the *end* of the frontier.[96] For the boosters, on the other hand, western cities could and did appear much more suddenly. They grew in tandem with the countryside and played crucial roles in encouraging settlement from a very early time. City and country formed a single commercial system, a single process of rural settlement and metropolitan economic growth. To speak of one without the other made little sense.

Turner, the historian, looked backward with some nostalgia from an urban-industrial world he feared was losing touch with its rural democratic roots. Men like Scott, Reavis, Gilpin, and Wright, promoters and prophets all, looked forward to an urban future they had as yet no reason to fear.[97] But different as their perspectives might be, there can be no question that Turner and the boosters were describing the same West and the same course of empire. So perhaps the frontier historian and the metropolitan prophets had more in common than appears at first glance. The boosters erected cities out of air and prophesied the appearance of great urban civilizations in the most unlikely places—towns possessing a few hundred inhabitants who had appeared the year before and who could disappear just as quickly. They wrote mainly about would-be cities, but they knew that none could survive without the rural hinterland whose "tribute" fueled urban growth. Turner wrote of frontier log cabins and sod houses as if they constituted a world unto themselves, but he also acknowledged that those who dwelt in such places needed to sell the fruits of their labors, so rural pioneers in many ways shared the boosters' hope for the future. "The pioneer," he wrote, "dreamed of continental conquests. . . . His vision saw beyond the dank swamp at the edge of the great lake to the lofty buildings and the jostling multitudes of a mighty city; beyond the rank, grass-clad prairie to the seas of golden grain. . . ."[98] When Turner spoke of the city that had arisen out of the swamp by the lake, describing the dreams of those who would dwell within its orbit, his words became indistinguishable from a booster's. He even chose the same city: Chicago, he wrote in 1901, was where "all the forces of the nation intersect."[99]

The chief difference between Turner and the boosters hinges on a seemingly minor point: Turner's Chicago rose to power only as the frontier drew to a close, whereas the boosters' Chicago had been an intimate part of frontier settlement almost from the beginning. In this, the boosters saw more clearly than the historian. When they argued that the city grew by drawing to itself the resources of an emerging region, they also implied that urban markets made rural development possible. "Chicago, the inevitable metropolis of the vigorous northwestern third of the prairie world," wrote James Parton in 1867, "has taken the lead in rendering the whole of it accessible."[100] Making a landscape "accessible" meant linking it to a market, which meant fostering regular exchange between city and country. Urban-rural commerce was the motor of frontier change, a fact which the boosters understood better than Turner.

In the twentieth century, the body of theory which analyzes urban-rural systems of the sort that both Turner and the boosters were trying to understand goes by the name of central place theory. Curiously, it traces its roots back to a contemporary of the boosters, writing in Germany at about the same time. Johann Heinrich von Thünen, an educated gentleman farmer in Mecklenburg, published the first edition of his book *The Isolated State* in 1826. In it, he tried to produce a rigorous mathematical description of the spatial relationships and economic linkages between city and country. Neither Turner nor the boosters appear to have read it, and yet it may offer a way to resolve the apparent differences between them.

Von Thünen proposed a simple thought experiment. If one imagined a completely isolated world, he said, in which a single city sat in the midst of an endless and uniformly fertile plain, certain regular patterns of agricultural activity would appear in the surrounding territory. What farmers could profitably raise at any given location would depend on two key variables: how much people in the city were willing to pay for different crops, and how much it cost to transport those crops to market. "With increasing distance from the Town," wrote von Thünen, "the land will progressively be given up to products cheap to transport in relation to their value."[101]

Von Thünen's abstract principles had strikingly concrete geographical consequences. A series of concentric agricultural zones would form around the town, each of which would support radically different farming activities. Nearest the town would be a zone producing crops so heavy, bulky, or perishable that no farmer living farther away could afford to ship them to market. Orchards, vegetable gardens, and dairies would dominate this first zone and raise the price of land—its "rent"—so high that less valuable crops would not be profitable there. Farther out, landowners in the second zone would devote themselves to intensive forestry, supplying the town with lumber and fuel. Beyond the forest, farmers would practice ever more extensive forms of agriculture, raising grain crops on lands where rents fell—along with labor and capital invest

Von Thünen's Isolated State

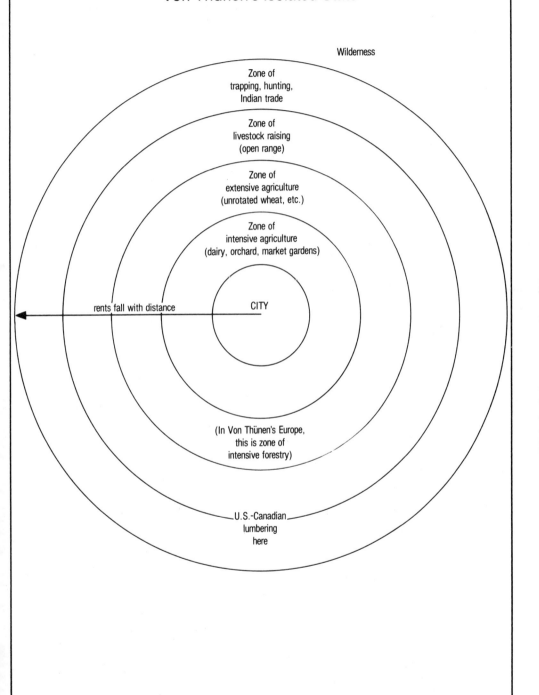

Wilderness

Zone of
trapping, hunting,
Indian trade

Zone of
livestock raising
(open range)

Zone of
extensive agriculture
(unrotated wheat, etc.)

Zone of
intensive agriculture
(dairy, orchard, market gardens)

rents fall with distance ← CITY

(In Von Thünen's Europe,
this is zone of
intensive forestry)

U.S.-Canadian
lumbering
here

ment—the farther out from town one went. This was the zone of wheat farming. Finally, distance from the city would raise transport costs so high that no grain crop could pay for its movement to market. Beyond that point, landowners would use their property for raising cattle and other livestock, thereby creating a zone of even more extensive land use, with still lower inputs of labor and capital. Land rents would steadily fall as one moved out from the urban market until they theoretically reached zero, where no one would buy land for any price, because nothing it might produce could pay the prohibitive cost of getting to market.

Von Thünen acknowledged that his abstract thought experiment departed from reality in several important ways. No city was as isolated as this one. All were surrounded by a variety of smaller towns and villages which complicated the hinterland picture. No region was as homogeneous as the hypothetical plain. The natural resources of any real landscape clustered in random patterns that inevitably distorted the abstract zones. Moreover, towns almost always appeared along rivers or canals, which drastically reduced transportation costs for lands along their banks, thereby introducing still more distortions to von Thünen's ideal geography.[102] But none of these "distortions" undermines von Thünen's underlying principles. Each in fact suggests how those principles express themselves in the more complicated geography of the real world. Von Thünen radically simplified his landscape to demonstrate what the nineteenth-century boosters knew intuitively, and what modern central place theorists have confirmed with formal mathematics.[103] Where human beings organize their economy around market exchange, trade between city and country will be among the most powerful forces influencing cultural geography and environmental change. The ways people value the products of the soil, and decide how much it costs to get those products to market, together shape the landscape we inhabit.

Von Thünen's idealized geography suggests how the boosters' urban theories might combine with Turner's rural history to produce a new way of understanding the history of colonization in the Great West and elsewhere. One has only to imagine his central city in a nineteenth-century American setting—Chicago in 1870, for instance—and then travel outward through the surrounding rural countryside, to experience an odd sense of déjà vu. Leaving the city and its factories behind, one first passes through a zone containing densely populated farm settlements practicing intensive forms of agriculture. Truck gardens, dairies, and orchards dominate the landscape, with many signs that farmers are investing their profits in outbuildings, fences, fertilizers, and other technologies for "improving" agriculture. As one travels farther west, these intensive farms gradually give way to newer and more sparsely settled communities. They practice more extensive agriculture, exploiting the prairie soil by raising unrotated crops of corn and wheat. Farther west still, these give way to the open range, where ranchers and cowboys raise animals rather than crops, on vast stretches of land with very few people and low capital investment. (This is also, in nineteenth-century North America, the zone of the forest, which was lumbered much more extensively—and wastefully—than in von Thünen's Germany, and so was located on lands of low value at greater distance from the city.)

Von Thünen's idealized landscape ended in the livestock-raising zone. But in America, to borrow Turner's admittedly problematic language, an additional zone beyond the pastoral still belonged to "the Indian and the hunter," both of whom had long since welcomed, like the Potawatomis, "the entrance of the trader, the pathfinder of civilization"—a pathfinder whom we can now recognize as an emissary from the metropolitan marketplace.[104] To read von Thünen in this way is suddenly to realize that one is reading Turner backwards, and that Turner's frontier, far from being an isolated rural society, was in fact the expanding edge of the boosters' urban empire. Seen from the midst of the city, Turner's "frontier" stages—hunters, traders, cattle raisers, extensive grain farmers, intensive truck gardeners, and urban manufacturers—look like nothing so much as the zones of von Thünen's Isolated State. Frontier and metropolis turn out to be two sides of the same coin.[105]

One can read von Thünen's map too literally and fall victim to the same sorts of distortions and simplifications for which Turner's thesis has been rightly criticized. The Great West of the nineteenth century was a much more diverse and complicated landscape than these broad zones suggest, and the sweeping abstractions of an idealized geography do little justice to the different historical experiences of the real people who lived within it.[106] Even on its own terms, this application of von Thünen's model raises technical questions about modern central place theory. Where precisely, for instance, should we locate the metropolitan core of the nineteenth-century American city system? It presumably lay somewhere off to the east—whether on the American or the European side of the Atlantic—but it clearly contained many more cities than one. What does this imply about von Thünen's zones, and where do cities like Chicago or St. Louis or San Francisco fall within those zones?

I will return to such questions in the closing chapters of this book, but for now I would offer just two observations about von Thünen's geography. First, he reminds us that city and country are inextricably connected and that market relations profoundly mediate between them. A rural landscape which omits the city and an urban landscape which omits the country are radically incomplete as portraits of their shared world. The

zoned hinterland of the Isolated State may oversimplify the diverse realities of the Great West, but it nonetheless suggests the sorts of underlying
market principles that have linked city with country to turn a natural
landscape into a spatial economy. Chicago's story remains incomprehensible without some knowledge of von Thünen's principles. But—and this
is the second point—von Thünen, like many modern central place theorists, made no effort to place his city-country system in *time*. The lone city
in the midst of the featureless plain *had no history,* and so poses real problems when one tries to apply it to the extremely dynamic processes that
reshaped city and country in the nineteenth-century West. As a historical
explanation, the Isolated State is as wanting—and as teleological—as
Turner's frontier.[107]

The concrete example nearest at hand is the best case in point: von
Thünen's zones, for all they may suggest about Chicago's later hinterland, shed little light on the city's explosive growth during the 1830s. In
just three or four years, a tiny village suddenly increased its population
twenty fold, the value of its land grew by a factor of three thousand, and
boosters began to speak of it as a future metropolis.[108] Capitalists from
the largest cities in Europe and America—London, New York, Boston,
Philadelphia, and others—raced to invest in the would-be city. To understand these events, we have to combine von Thünen's abstract geography
with the booster theories that persuaded New Yorkers like Charles Butler
and William B. Ogden to invest substantial sums to help make Chicago's
urban dream come true. Booster models of urban growth were nothing if
not dynamic, for the simple reason that they sought to prevail on wealthy
investors to turn predictions of urban greatness into self-fulfilling
prophecies. "If our National Wheel of Commerce have its Hub immova-
bly pivoted by Nature and by Art," wrote John Wright at the beginning of
a 475-page book promoting Chicago, "should not every Business Man
know it?"[109] Much as they might claim that the city's growth was "natural" and "inevitable," boosters knew that they were whistling in the dark
if they failed to attract outside capital to make their prophecies come true.

Capital held one of the most important keys to metropolitan empire,
which was why boosters wrote so many tracts making their case to potential investors. Repeatedly in the nineteenth century, western cities came
into being when eastern capital created remote colonies in landscapes
that as yet contained relatively few people. Movements of capital helped
explain why large cities developed so much more quickly in the West than
Turner's evolutionary frontier stages suggest. By linking frontier areas to
an international system of cities, these centers of capital investment
emerged as urban markets which drove the region's growth.[110] Although

no booster would have put it quite so bluntly, the center of metropolitan empire—and of Turner's frontier—was the marketplace of modern capitalism. When Turner spoke of the frontier as "the outer edge of the wave," what he unintentionally described was not some implicitly racist "meeting point between savagery and civilization" but the ongoing extension of market relations into the ways human beings used land—and each other—in the Great West.[111]

Chicago had been a marketplace long before boosters proclaimed it a metropolis. Its Potawatomi and French inhabitants made it the focus of a thriving fur trade many decades before it reached the watershed of the 1830s. The Potawatomis had been shrewd traders who bargained well for wealth and power as they understood those things, linking themselves to distant urban markets to pursue their own cultural sense of the good life. These were no "savages," noble or otherwise. They understood the market as it applied to such things as animal skins and alcohol and blankets and guns, and they had at least an equal hand with Euroamerican traders in dominating local trade before 1833. If the frontier was an expanding "wave" of market activity, they were well within its leading edge.

The Potawatomis had willingly attached themselves to the urban market for furs because it appeared to serve them as well as they served it. But what they did not understand—what they were not allowed to understand, not allowed to join, not allowed to resist—was the vision of empire behind that market, the vision that inspired those who flooded into Chicago during the 1830s hoping to make it the focus of a far more extensive metropolitan economy. The Potawatomis' own conception of the market did not extend to the lands on which they lived, at least not nearly so much as the people who supplanted them. They had little experience with how deeply land and its products could enter the marketplace, and they did not dream of how a hinterland territory could pay tribute to an imperial city.

If, then, we take 1833 as the beginning of Chicago's metropolitan story, the Indians' and boosters' different notions of land and empire marked a great cultural divide on human maps of the Great West in the 1830s. The nineteenth-century French political scientist Emile Boutmy wrote of Americans,

> Their one primary and predominant object is to cultivate and settle these prairies, forests, and vast waste lands. The striking and peculiar characteristic of American society is, that it is not so much a democracy as a huge commercial company for the discovery, cultivation, and capitalization of its enormous territory. . . . The United States are primarily a commercial society . . . and only secondarily a nation. . . .[112]

Turner bridled at so irreverent a description of American life, but he admitted the truth of Boutmy's insight insofar as "the fundamental fact in regard to this new society was its relation to land."[113] For many, if not most, Americans, "the discovery, cultivation, and capitalization" of land meant bringing it into the marketplace and attaching it to the metropolis. They might articulate their visions in terms quite different from those of the boosters' urban empire—speaking of freedom, or community, or family, or getting ahead in the world—but even these noneconomic dreams generally presupposed a growing commercial intercourse between city and country. Frontier and metropolis, and the ideas that lay behind them, would reshape the Great West together.

The Potawatomis finally sold their lands to the United States and moved west to prepare for their next encounter with American land hunger. The removal of these "dusky nuisances" fulfilled an imperial ideology that viewed the "idle and dissolute Indians" as "the first obstacle to the growth of Chicago."[114] Henceforth the Potawatomis played only the most marginal roles in the marketplace they had once dominated. The proof of their tragedy is that the history of Chicago can be written from 1833 forward as if they had never lived there. But as we watch the speculators and their frantic efforts to start Chicago down the metropolitan path of its boosters, we would do well to remember that the place had once been occupied and possessed in a way that cherished no such visions of urban empire. At precisely the moment that Charles Butler imagined the little village to be "a great commercial point," he averted his eyes and the Indians disappeared. The dream would not contain them.

Turner averted his own eyes in much the same way when he defined his frontier as "the hither edge of free land."[115] The land was not free but taken. Moreover, even if it became free in the moment that it passed from Indian control, it soon ceased to be free again as it entered the marketplace. Never again would it be without a price. Tallgrass prairies, oak openings, white pine forests, herds of bison, and the people who might choose to live amid these things: none would ever be the same again. As village became metropolis, so frontier became hinterland. The history of the Great West is a long dialogue between the place we call city and the place we call country. So perhaps the best vantage point from which to view that history is not with Turner, in the outermost of von Thünen's zones, but in the place where Turner himself said "all the forces of the nation intersect."[116] Viewed from the banks of the Chicago River, the Great West is both an urban empire and a countryside transformed.

2

Rails and Water

Market in the Mud

The boosters spoke much about "natural advantages." Resources, waterways, and climatic zones loom so large in their writings that one can almost forget that *people* have something to do with the building of cities. A river, a lake, and a fertile plain present many opportunities that intimately influence those who live nearby. And yet people make such different choices about nature's opportunities: one could hardly confuse the French-Anglo-Indian fur-trading village that was Chicago in 1830 with the speculative American boomtown that had replaced it half a decade later. Geographical arguments do not explain how the one became the other; only culture and history can do that. Whatever the advantages of a particular landscape, people seem always to reshape it according to their vision of what it should be. Just so did Americans who shared the boosters' cultural values struggle to turn the Illinois prairie into a city and its hinterland.

In manipulating Chicago's landscape, Americans did much more than simply pick and choose among its natural opportunities, for the local geography possessed features of a sort most boosters rarely chose to describe. The location with so many "advantages" turned out to have some daunting disadvantages as well. The mouth of the Chicago River, for instance, which many speculators wanted to see as a great harbor and gateway between East and West, had a sandbar seventy yards wide at its mouth. "The River," reported a visitor in 1821, passed "between this Barr and the main land below the village," so its mouth was "constantly chocked up with Sand."[1] Water at the mouth was at best about two feet deep, certainly not enough to float a vessel capable of reaching the Erie Canal. Repeatedly in the 1820s, the soldiers at Fort Dearborn tried to dig a new channel, but the sand quickly frustrated their efforts. Nature—in the form of a strong south-flowing current in Lake Michigan—evidently intended that the Chicago River make a ninety-degree bend at its mouth, obstructing navigation for all but the smallest boats. When the town began to expand in the 1830s, ships arriving from the east had to anchor a mile offshore before unloading their cargoes and passengers into small lightering boats with shallow drafts.[2]

Since river and lake apparently refused to fulfill their mutual destiny as harbor, Chicagoans decided to take fate into their own hands. In 1830, the same year that saw the first subdivision of local land into city lots, a government survey proposed a scheme of "improvements" for cutting a deep new channel and building piers that might prevent it from silting up. Three years later, shortly before the Potawatomis signed their treaties, the U.S. government appropriated $25,000 to put the plan into action. By the fall of 1835, engineers had cut a channel two hundred feet wide and three to seven feet deep across the bar, protecting it with two long piers extending hundreds of feet out into the lake. Chicago finally had a decent harbor, and much larger ships could now make their way upriver. Unfortunately, the sand continued to reappear, forming new bars as it piled up behind the north pier. Local citizens raised money to buy a dredging machine and sought additional government funds to extend the protective piers. But they won no clear victory. Nature met every new scheme with new sand, and the harbor continued to be a problem long into the future. By the late 1840s, the north pier extended nearly three-quarters of a mile out into the lake, and the government had spent almost a quarter of a million dollars on dredging and maintaining this "natural" advantage.[3]

The harbor was just one example of the many "improvements" that Chicagoans and other American settlers would bring to the landscape of the Great West. In addition to advantages and opportunities for growth, nature threw up obstacles which those who dreamed of human progress had to overcome at every turn. Each new improvement meant a shift in regional geography—a dredged harbor here, a canal or a road there—so the advantages sustaining the city came to have an ever larger human component. A kind of "second nature," designed by people and "improved" toward human ends, gradually emerged atop the original landscape that nature—"first nature"—had created as such an inconvenient jumble.[4] Despite the subtly differing logic that lay behind each, the geography of second nature was in its own way as compelling as the geography of first nature, so boosters and others often forgot the distinction between them. Both seemed quite "natural." Nowhere was this more true than in the new artificial transportation technologies that changed the ways people and commodities moved back and forth between city and country. Although early boosters had believed that rivers and lakes would carry an irresistible flow of resources to the city they favored, canals and especially railroads finally proved more important in building Chicago and other cities of the Great West. Second nature defined the corridors of commerce at least as much as first nature.

By the 1840s, before any railroad had yet reached Chicago, its merchants were doing a good business with the expanding farm communities of northern Illinois and Indiana. But the difficulty of moving agricultural produce across the landscape discouraged a wider trade and limited the city's growth. Chicago lay in the midst of a countryside that was in many ways ideal for land transport: some of the flattest, least rocky, least forested land in all of North America, with scarcely a hillock to prevent one from traveling in any direction as far as the horizon and beyond. But the same glaciers that had left Illinois flat had also left it poorly drained, with vast stretches of marshland and wet prairie threaded by meandering rivers. Even upland prairies did not remain dry all year round. Whether one moved on foot or on horseback, travel was often hard.

Too much water on land mired wagons; too little water in harbors stranded ships. Because water was critical to all kinds of travel, and because the region followed the hot-cold, wet-dry cycles of all temperate climates, transportation and trade fluctuated widely from season to season.[5] For nearly half the year, ice and storms on Lake Michigan closed shipping, with the result that Chicago merchants did no eastern business between November and May.[6] The roads that connected the city to its surrounding territory were not much more than dirt tracks, which, like the city's streets, turned into morasses during wet seasons of the year. One visitor in 1848 noted that "on the outskirts of the town . . . the highways were impassible, except in winter when frozen, or in summer when dry and pulverized into the finest and most penetrating of dust. At all other seasons they were little less than quagmires."[7] Horses had to struggle knee-deep in mud and water, so it could take a day to travel less than a dozen miles.[8] Conditions like these were a trial for even the most leisurely travelers. When Ralph Waldo Emerson visited Chicago in the winter of 1853, he began to wonder whether he should have made the trip at all. "In the prairie," he wrote, "it rains, & thaws incessantly, &, if we step off the short street, we go up to the shoulders, perhaps, in mud. . . ."[9]

All places in the region suffered these seasonal inconveniences to some degree, but mud was an especially serious problem in Chicago for reasons dating back to the Ice Age. The glacial predecessor of Lake Michigan had for thousands of years flowed south down the Illinois River to the Mississippi; only in the last four thousand years had the lake abandoned its old outlet and begun to drain toward Lake Huron. In spring, when water levels were high, the lake revisited its old southern outlet, which now went right through Chicago.[10] Such a state of affairs was hardly good for local business. At least one Chicago dry goods dealer closed his shop and went hunting on spring afternoons in the 1840s, since "people from the country, never thought of coming to Chicago during the reign of mud, except for very urgent reasons."[11] Local wags loved to tell stories about bottomless holes that had swallowed horses and riders together. Residents found the morass so annoying that they paved the streets with wooden planks to avoid at least some of the mud. "Under these planks," an 1848 visitor noted, "the water was standing on the surface over three-fourths of the city, and as the sewers from the houses were emptied under them, a frightful odour was emitted in summer, causing fevers and other diseases. . . ."[12] Nothing drained properly: sewers and water pipes were as much a nuisance as the roads, and an even greater danger to public health.[13]

Chicago's bad drainage was among the worst of its "natural disadvantages," and only heroic measures could solve the problem. Digging a new sewer system to drain away excess water was pointless, for with the water table so near the surface, there was nowhere to dig. And so Chicagoans moved in the opposite direction. If they could not lower the drainage system, they would have to raise the city. Starting in 1849, the City Council passed a series of ordinances requiring that the grade levels of streets be raised anywhere from four to fourteen feet. The process took two decades and required that large buildings weighing many thousands of tons be lifted by dozens of men turning dozens of jacks in unison so that new foundations could be built underneath. Many owners chose simply to move their buildings to new locations, and it became common to see large frame and masonry structures rolling through city traffic. Differences in building grades persisted for many years, so sidewalks rose and fell with their adjacent storefronts, but the long-term effect was to lift the city a dozen or more feet out of the mud. Like the new harbor, the new level of city streets came to seem quite natural for those who had gotten used to it, becoming yet another overlay of second nature in Chicago.[14]

All this lay in the future for merchants and farmers of the 1840s, who had to live with the seasonal transportation challenges that afflicted city and country alike. The practical difficulties of the mud season were but the flip side of the very advantages that had led speculators to identify Chicago as a prime center for water-based trade in the first place. If people wanted a town that would benefit from a natural harbor (however bad) and a natural canal corridor (however undug), they would have to live with a little water and mud. Trade and transportation therefore waxed and waned with the seasons. Just as von Thünen had predicted, the regional economy was shaped primarily by distances between city and country, expressed not in miles but in the time and expense devoted to transportation. Periods of slow trade and difficult travel became part of the cost of doing business, a kind of natural excise tax paid on virtually all movement and trade. The more time people devoted to waiting for customers or traveling to market, the less time they had for more productive activities.

Even when roads were in decent condition, the only vehicles that could use them were horse-drawn wagons, which had limited capacity and became uneconomical for moving agricultural produce over any great distance. Farmers drove such wagons to Chicago from surprisingly remote places, bringing to market their most valuable commodities—apples, ham, butter, feathers, chickens, wheat—from as far away as the Rock River in northern Illinois and the Wabash River in southern Indiana, well over a hundred miles distant.[15] But they could not make such journeys often, and that limited the entire economy. Furthermore, because farmers could carry only small loads in such vehicles, the costs of wagon, horses, and driver consumed a sizable portion of any money they earned. Wagons offered few economies of scale, and so set well-defined limits to how far one could afford to travel in them.[16] As one Chicago businessman observed, it took a nearby farmer on the Rock River five days just to bring an average-sized wagonload of thirty bushels of wheat to market, so the cost of the journey "took off nearly all the profit."[17] Along the way, rainstorms and unbridged streams often conspired to soak the wagon's contents, with the result that grain was dirty and damaged, and sometimes sprouting, by the time it reached the city. Few people got rich under these conditions, and the growth of city and country lagged in consequence.[18]

Despite the difficulties, harvest season by the middle of the 1840s saw hundreds of farmers appear in Chicago each day. The earlier depression of the late 1830s and early 1840s had finally given way to more promising times. The farmers' arrival signaled the onset of what city merchants called "business season," which contrasted in their minds with other periods—"dull seasons"—when nature's seasonal cycles slowed the town's economy almost to a standstill.[19] From September to November, the pent-up rural business that had been accumulating for a year behind ice and mud and unharvested fields finally raced into the city with winter in close pursuit. Camped in great numbers amid the tall grasses at the city's edge, the farmers' "lines of Hoosier wagons" seemed to the well-known critic Margaret Fuller in 1843 to be "the most picturesque objects to be seen from Chicago."[20] One farmer, Lester Harding, wrote home to his brother-in-law, "The last time I was in the city the number of teams loaded with wheat amounted to twelve hundred and the receipts on that day reached sixty thousand Bushels."[21] When harvest trade was at its peak, the city's central merchandising district, located on Lake and Water streets, regularly became blocked by long traffic jams as farmers crowded in to do their buying and selling. Grain and other agricultural products piled up beside the wooden buildings, while wagons, animals, mud, and manure filled the unpaved streets. For a few weeks, until ice closed the harbor, the city became a wild and lively chaos, a marketplace of the open air.[22]

The farmers chose Chicago as their destination because they received more cash for their crops there, and because they could buy more and better supplies at lower prices. River towns in the interior—Peoria, Springfield, Vincennes, even St. Louis—did not have the cheap lake transportation to the east that gave Chicago its price advantage. Wheat, for instance, often brought anywhere from ten to sixty cents more per bushel in Chicago than in downstate communities.[23] Lester Harding reported in October 1847 that Chicago prices were "70[cts] for spring and 80[cts] to 85 for winter wheat," compared with fifty cents back home in Paw Paw, Illinois. "Farmers," he said, "cannot grumble at these prices. . . . There can be no better [market] any where in the Union."[24] Harding found Chicago's prices so attractive that he made at least four separate harvest season trips to the city in 1847 alone. Each took five days, enabling him to sell just forty bushels of wheat per trip; to increase his income, he also hauled supplies back home for a local merchant.

With cash safely in hand, farmers like Harding could wander the crowded streets to visit the hundreds of retail stores which in number and variety surpassed those of all other towns in Illinois. No general store back home could compete with what this place had to offer. "The city," wrote a German woman after a visit in 1849, "seems for the most part to consist of shops. . . . And it seems as if, on all hands, people came here merely to trade, to make money, and not to live."[25] By the late 1840s, Chicago already had over three hundred stores doing more than a million dollars worth of business in dry goods and groceries alone, not to mention the more specialized firms dealing in boots, lumber, hardware, agricultural tools, and all the other items that farm families could not easily make for themselves.[26]

What the farmers found in Chicago was the western outpost of a metropolitan economy centered on the great cities of Europe and the American Northeast. Chicago, located in one of von Thünen's outer zones, was able to buy and sell so successfully because the lakes, the Erie Canal, and the Hudson River gave it better access to eastern markets—especially those of New York—than any other city in Illinois. Other lake cities had comparable advantages: Cleveland and Toledo offered their hinterlands the best markets in Ohio, and Milwaukee played a similar role in Wisconsin.[27] As in these other places, most of what farmers bought in Chicago during the early years came not from the city itself but from the Northeast. Chicago's advantage in selling such merchandise derived from its favorable price structure. Its merchants could buy goods at eastern wholesale prices in ship-sized quantities with no markup for expensive land transport. For the same reasons, they could also offer the best prices in the region for farm produce moving east. Low prices for eastern goods, and high prices for western ones: the combination was a sure recipe for success.

In Chicago, the exchange of merchandise became an exercise in regional transmutation. Whether one turned dried apples into nails, or salted hams into lumber, or bushels of wheat into bolts of printed cotton, the net effect was to link West with East, rural with urban, farm with factory. City streets became places where the products of different ecosystems, different economies, and different ways of life came together and exchanged places. "There can be no two places in the world," wrote Margaret Fuller in 1843, "more completely thoroughfares than this place and Buffalo. They are the two correspondent valves that open and shut all the time, as the life-blood rushes from east to west, and back again from west to east."[28] At Chicago's harbor, farmers and merchants moved their wares from ship to wagon and back again, so roads and waterways all converged. Second nature would lead people to regard Chicago as what one local booster called "the end of a route": the place where eastern and western journeys met each other at the boundary between lake and land.[29]

From the 1830s forward, Chicagoans distinguished themselves by the strength and extensiveness of their eastern ties. Even at the beginning of the land fever, when the city's population was only about two thousand, eastern investors and merchants already showed greater interest in its affairs than in most other western places—proof that booster arguments on its behalf were succeeding. In 1834, Chicago's first newspaper, the *Democrat,* showed a total of 865 subscriptions at the end of its first full year of publication.[30] Only a fourth of those subscriptions were sold within the city itself. Another 40 percent were mailed out to subscribers in other parts of Illinois, indicating the extent to which the city was already acting as a conduit of news for readers in the downstate region. Most strikingly, however, fully 25 percent of the *Democrat*'s subscribers lived in the East. Although the city presumably contained many readers who were not subscribers, the number of *subscriptions* from Chicago and from the East were almost identical. Of the 221 easterners who cared enough about the city's economic well-being to subscribe to its first newspaper, over half lived in New York State. The list of eastern communities whose citizens regularly read the *Democrat* was led by Detroit with 29 subscribers, Buffalo with 34, and New York City itself with 18. Together, those three cities traced the string of lakes, canals, and rivers that would channel the flow of information and resources between Chicago and the East.[31]

By using information networks like those suggested by the *Democrat*'s subscription list, Chicago merchants made business connections in New York and other eastern cities, which assured them a steady low-priced source of supply throughout the warm months of the year. Many of these merchants had eastern partners who acted as buyers whenever a store needed new stock: a typical Chicago newspaper advertisement of the 1840s offered cloth goods "at the lowest *New York jobbing prices*," promising that stock would be "constantly replenished by one of the partners permanently residing in New York."[32] Depending on how involved they wanted to be with the business, eastern partners might simply provide capital or might actively buy, sell, and warehouse goods on behalf of their western associates. Interregional partnerships of this sort typified the period, and commonly occurred in all western cities that were emerging as major wholesaling centers by 1850: Cincinnati, Toledo, Detroit, Milwaukee, St. Louis, and, much farther to the west, San Francisco, in addition to Chicago. The number and scale of such interregional trading connections critically determined a city's eventual position in the urban hierarchy. Cities with the greatest access to the East would become the new metropolises of their region; towns with less direct eastern ties would rely on western wholesaling centers for the bulk of their merchandise and develop only a local retail trade of their own.[33]

Here was the hidden foundation of the boosters' geographical determinism: natural avenues of transportation might play important roles in shaping a city's future, but the preexisting structures of the *human* economy—second nature, not first nature—determined which routes and which cities developed most quickly. Chicago enjoyed its favorable price structure because New York merchants and bankers had already consolidated for their city the role of national metropolis. By midcentury, New York had developed the most direct access to European markets, the most extensive trading hinterland, and the most powerful financial institutions of any city in North America.[34] Without New York, the natural advantages of Great Lakes shipping would have meant little. Had New Orleans, and not New York, been the chief entrepôt between Europe and North America, the evolution of western trade would surely have followed a different course.

Despite the boosters' arguments, Chicago's location at the southwestern corner of Lake Michigan carried no automatic geographical significance.[35] What gave the site its importance was the emerging commercial and industrial primacy of the American Northeast. An eastern-oriented economy "naturally" looked across the lakes to Chicago as the westernmost point of cheap water access to the agricultural heartland of the interior. Just as "naturally," easterners saw Chicago as the logical place in which to invest funds for encouraging the flow of trade in their direction. "What built Chicago?" asked the booster Everett Chamberlin in 1873. "Let us answer, a junction of Eastern means and Western opportunity."[36] From the perspective of eastern capital, it was second nature that Chicago should become gateway to the Great West.

Artificial Corridors

The muddy roads and shallow harbor gave Chicago its early hinterland, attracting farmers and other customers from a hundred or more miles away during the 1840s. But the considerable disadvantages of these early transportation routes also limited the city's business. As Judge Jesse B. Thomas complained in his report to the 1847 River and Harbor Convention, Chicago was still "merely the centre of a local retail trade of a few hundred miles of extent." Thomas's word "merely" betrayed a booster's contempt for so meager an urban hinterland, which was surely too small for a place that aspired to metropolitan stature. He joined other area residents in arguing that the poor quality of Chicago's roads and waterways would stifle its growth until people overcame the prairies' seasonal muck and completed the avenues of commerce that nature had left unfinished. Only then would transportation, breaking free from the limitations of geography, "at once, and by magic, change the conditions and prospects of our city; increase its population; introduce capital . . . enlarge every avenue of commerce, and promote the growth of manufactures. The arteries of trade will then be opened, and commerce will flow freely over them."[37] People who shared Thomas's vision would have to build artificial corridors before the city could fulfill its natural destiny and become the new metropolis of the Great West.

Boosters had initially expected that Chicago would float to greatness on the proposed canal between Lake Michigan and the Illinois River, following the old glacial channel from the days when the lake drained south toward the Mississippi.[38] Surveying the canal route had helped trigger the city's real estate boom in the 1830s, though the canal itself took much longer to get going. The first company to attempt its construction incorporated in 1825 and collapsed even before managing to sell its own stock. Responsibility for the project next passed to Illinois, which like other western states was soon embarking on an ambitious scheme of public improvements that envisioned several railroads in addition to the canal. The federal government threw its support behind the scheme by giving Illinois a large grant of land which the state could use as loan collateral or sell off to raise funds directly. In the booming speculative economy of the 1830s, the floating of state bonds to finance new transportation routes seemed an ideal way for government to provide infrastructure that would promote widespread economic growth.[39]

But the state's development schemes proved harder to finance than politicians had expected. Nearly a decade passed before ground was finally broken at the canal site in 1836. A less auspicious year to begin construction would be hard to imagine. As the national economy neared the peak of its speculative frenzy, supplies were expensive and workers hard to find; worse, the general financial panic came only a year later. Real estate values plummeted, making it impossible to raise funds by selling lots from the canal's land grant. The State Bank of Illinois, which held the canal's assets, stopped meeting its obligations in May 1837, and the fiscal condition of the government continued to deteriorate. By 1841, Illinois could easily have declared itself bankrupt had anyone wished to force the issue. No one did, but four more years had to pass before the state could convince its European creditors that new taxes and the canal's physical assets would be enough to secure additional loans. On that basis, construction proceeded, and the Illinois and Michigan Canal finally opened for traffic in April 1848.[40]

Just as its early promoters had predicted, the canal brought striking changes to the regional economy. During its first season of operation, eastern corn shipments from Chicago multiplied eightfold as farmers in the Illinois River Valley suddenly discovered an alternative to St. Louis as an outlet for their produce.[41] The explosion of corn sales furnished convincing proof of the boosters' arguments in favor of water transport. By avoiding the risks and frustrations of the muddy roads leading to Chicago, farmers could bring much more of their produce to market, and purchase greater quantities of urban manufactured goods as well. Over 90 percent of the new corn shipments came to Chicago via the canal, which was henceforth the city's chief source of corn until after the Civil War. Lumber receipts at Chicago from the forests of Michigan and Wisconsin nearly doubled in 1848, and one-fourth of this wood moved south down the canal, to be used for houses, fences, and farm buildings on the Illinois prairies.[42] By decreasing the difficulty and cost of transportation, the canal enabled larger quantities of heavier and bulkier goods to extend their geographical reach both to and from Chicago. It was as if a corridor of relatively cheap transport had suddenly appeared like a fault across the various zones of von Thünen's isolated city, displacing them and necessitating a complex series of adjustments in the region's spatial economy. The canal almost instantly expanded Chicago's hinterland southward to the Mississippi River just above St. Louis.[43]

Before people had fully adjusted to trading via the canal, however, a second artificial corridor, which would bring even more dramatic changes, augmented Chicago's access to its surrounding region. In 1836, the year canal construction began, a new company was chartered to construct a railroad between Chicago and Galena, then the chief center of the prosperous lead-mining district of northwestern Illinois and southwestern Wisconsin. Like the canal, this early railroad project foundered without laying any track in the financial debacle of the ensuing decade, but, again like the canal, it resurrected itself as prosperity returned in the mid-1840s.[44] On January 7, 1846, over three hundred delegates representing one Wisconsin and ten Illinois counties assembled at a convention in Rockford, Illinois, to pass a series of resolutions supporting the railroad. Arguing that farm property along the railroad's route would double in value as soon as it began operating, the delegates called on farmers to "come forward and subscribe to the stock of the proposed railroad to the extent of their ability."[45]

Although most residents of northern Illinois were enthusiastic about the benefits this new transportation corridor would bring, the convention was orchestrated throughout by members of the Chicago delegation, which included some of the city's most prominent businessmen. Among them were the bankers J. Young Scammon and William H. Brown, the real estate dealer Benjamin Raymond, the merchant Walter Newberry, and Chicago's first mayor and leading citizen, William B. Ogden—the onetime skeptic now wholly converted to the booster faith in Chicago. When a new board of directors for the railroad was elected the following February, all of its members—including Ogden, Scammon, Brown, and Newberry—were from Chicago. Ogden became president.[46] It was hardly surprising that the road came to be closely identified with Chicago's interests.

Even with such enthusiastic support from leading Chicagoans, however, efforts to raise eastern capital for the railroad proved unsuccessful. Investors were still wary after having lost money in the Illinois transport schemes of the 1830s, and apparently regarded the project as too speculative until local capital began construction and proved the railroad's profitability.[47] Ogden and Scammon therefore decided to raise funds from people residing along the railroad route itself. During the fall of

1847, they visited farmers and merchants throughout northern Illinois between Chicago and Galena to promote the enterprise. Many farmers—no doubt thinking of the muddy roads that caused them so much trouble in bringing crops to market—came forward to subscribe, even though, as Scammon remarked, "they had to borrow the first instalment of two dollars and fifty cents on a share, and get trusted 'till after the harvest' for the same."[48] Ogden reportedly managed to gather $20,000 worth of subscriptions in a single day from farmers who were selling their fall harvest on the streets of Chicago.[49] By the following April, over twelve hundred people had pledged to buy stock hypothetically valued at about $350,000, though they had paid only about $20,000 in actual cash. Despite the still shaky financing, construction of the first thirty-one miles of the Galena and Chicago Union Railroad started in March 1848.[50]

Chicago's earliest railroad thus began as a corporation managed by Chicago businessmen but financed in good measure by the rural and small-town communities along its line. During 1847, Chicago citizens contributed only $20,000 to the road—8 percent of the subscriptions up to that time—although this had risen to a much more respectable 35 percent by the spring of 1848, when construction actually began.[51] Men like Ogden and Scammon invested not just money but immense entrepreneurial energy as well. They expected to profit personally from their efforts, and in a variety of ways. For at least some of the Chicagoans most actively engaged in the project, the road's expected effect on real estate investments may have been as attractive as the profits it would produce in moving freight and passengers. Ogden, in particular, was accused of trying to increase the value of his land holdings on the North Side of Chicago by having the railroad locate its depot there, but he was hardly unique in this. All of the Chicago directors tried to influence the road so as to benefit their own real property.[52]

In this, they had much in common with farmers who sought to make their crops more profitable and with businessmen in other towns who wanted to promote their community's fortunes by investing in the railroad. The chief difference was that the Chicagoans on the board of directors exercised a managerial power out of proportion to the scale of their own investment. Part of their influence flowed from their early role in organizing the railroad, which was itself a consequence of their superior position in the urban hierarchy. They had better access than anyone else in the region to eastern capital, and their good financial reputation also helped reassure hinterland investors that the railroad would be managed with integrity.

But part of their influence also derived from the assumption, shared by virtually everyone in northern Illinois, that the eastern terminus of the road should naturally be Chicago. Booster arguments had convinced residents of city and hinterland alike that Chicago was where people using this particular railroad would want to end their trip. The doctrine of natural advantages which attached such significance to Chicago's canal and harbor applied to its railroads as well: first and second nature reinforced each other. The railroads centered on Chicago not because nature ordained that they *had* to do so—nature made no such pronouncements—but because investors and everyone else who acted on booster theories proclaimed that they *should* do so.

Construction of the Galena and Chicago Union during 1848 amounted to only ten miles, the railroad reaching the Des Plaines River in December. The first regular passenger service began on November 21, proving that even ten miles of rails were a big improvement over prairie roads. Within a week, Chicagoans were delighted to learn that eager farmers had delivered over thirty carloads of wheat at the line's western terminus for transportation to the city. In a ploy undoubtedly intended to increase its own passenger receipts, the railroad company was soon urging wheat buyers to conduct their business not on the streets of Chicago but on the banks of the Des Plaines River.[53] Grain dealers did not much heed this advice, but the westward extension of the railroad into Illinois's chief grain farming region meant that more and more of the city's wheat began to arrive by rail. The road's promoters had constructed it with just this purpose in mind: their first annual report gave detailed estimates of the wheat crop in eight counties surrounding Chicago and argued that the railroad would become the preferred way to bring the grain to market.[54] The initial contribution of the new line to Chicago's wheat trade is difficult to judge because much of the region's winter wheat crop failed for climatic reasons between 1848 and 1851, but the railroad's relative impact is nonetheless clear. By 1852, over half the city's wheat arrived via the Galena and Chicago Union.[55]

Underlying this remarkable growth was the line's expanding system of rails. By the beginning of 1850, the Galena was serving Elgin, forty miles west of Chicago; by 1852, the rails had reached Rockford, and a year later they were at their western terminus in Freeport, located in the northwestern corner of the state. Ironically, the Galena never reached the town for which it was named. The Illinois Central arrived in that city in 1854, and the two railroads agreed to share traffic between Freeport and Galena rather than operate competing lines that would lose money.[56] Discouraged from further westward movement by this threat of competition, managers for the Galena and Chicago Union began building several branch lines intended to increase access between Chicago and the agricultural lands northwest of it. Construction on the main line between

Galena and Chicago halted in favor of new feeders that reached out toward the profitable countryside around Aurora and Dixon, in north-central Illinois, and around Beloit and other points in southern Wisconsin.[57] These branch lines demonstrated a lesson that small-town railroad promoters like those in Galena learned repeatedly in ensuing decades: lines initially projected to benefit a particular town or rural area seemed always to point toward Chicago. Western towns might compete fiercely to bring railroads in their direction and gain stations for themselves, but the eastern terminus was never in doubt. All roads led to Chicago.

What was true of the Galena and Chicago Union was true of the railroad network as a whole. The decade of the 1850s saw some of the most rapid railroad expansion in American history, the nation's total trackage rising from 9,000 miles in 1850 to 30,000 miles in 1860. Illinois alone gained over 2,500 miles of track during the same period.[58] By 1860, eastern investors and Chicago railroad managers had succeeded in imposing a new geography on the western landscape. Almost all the new lines west of Lake Michigan focused on the city, extending from it like the spokes of a great wheel and dividing the region into a series of pie-shaped wedges, each more or less within the territory of a single Chicago-based railroad. Northwest of the city, dominating a broad arc of territory in northern Illinois and southern Wisconsin, the Chicago and Northwestern had proven so successful by 1864 that it was able to absorb the original Galena and Chicago Union into its system. Due west of the tip of Lake Michigan lay the Chicago and Rock Island, which by 1860 reached to the Mississippi and beyond, having become in 1856 the first railroad to bridge the river. To the southwest was one of the region's most extensive systems, the Chicago, Burlington and Quincy, which not only reached the Mississippi at two separate points but controlled two railroads in Iowa and Missouri as well. Still farther to the southwest, the Chicago and Alton gave Chicago access to the eastern bank of the Mississippi just above St. Louis.[59]

This tendency for railroads west of Lake Michigan to focus on Chicago was true even of the Illinois Central, which had been planned in the late 1830s as a north–south railroad running from Galena to Cairo, at opposite ends of the state. Like many of the rail and water transportation routes which Illinois had supported in its internal improvement schemes, the Central was originally to have bypassed Chicago altogether.[60] But then the federal government in 1850 gave a large grant of land to the Central as part of a north–south line that would connect the Great Lakes with the Gulf of Mexico. It was the first railroad land grant in American history, and became the model for subsequent federal support of transcontinental lines farther west—all but one of which eventually aimed to-

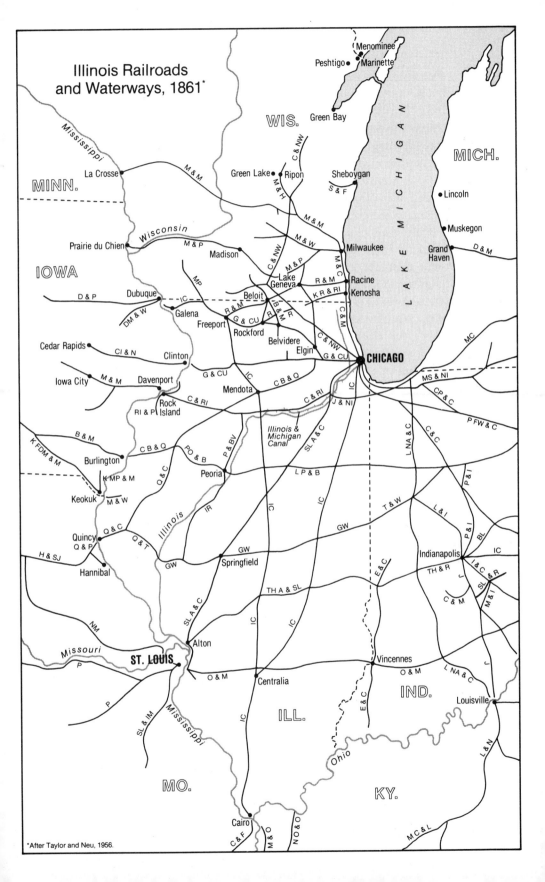

Illinois Railroads
and Waterways, 1861*

*After Taylor and Neu, 1956.

ward Chicago. As part of the land grant bill, Senator Stephen Douglas, of Illinois, inserted a clause requiring that the Central build a "branch line" from Chicago that would join the "main line" at Centralia. The addition of this route between Chicago and the Gulf drew eastern political support to the legislation and enabled it to pass: as happened so often later, powerful figures in the East saw their own interests converging with Chicago's.[61] Almost immediately, the branch became the trunk: by 1859, Chicago accounted for well over one-fourth of the Central's total freight earnings in the entire state of Illinois.[62]

By the start of the Civil War, then, the broad outline of Chicago's rail hinterland was already emerging, though it soon extended much farther to the west. An early period of unsuccessful transport improvement schemes had given way by the late 1840s to a period of rapid construction, whether of canal, railroads, or even, for a brief time, a series of plank toll roads. All of these, especially the railroads, revolutionized Chicago's access to the Great West; by 1869, the city had rail connections extending all the way to the Pacific Ocean. Until the early 1850s, these western routes linked to New York and the Northeast principally via Chicago's harbor, the trade of which grew rapidly as the city increased its connections with the interior. In 1852, however, two lines with direct rail access to New York—the Michigan Southern and the Michigan Central—finally reached Chicago, so eastward competition between lake and rail soon became a persistent feature of the city's transport economy.

The rising fortunes of the railroads meant relative decline for the Illinois and Michigan Canal, which even at midcentury was no longer what people had hoped it would be in the 1830s, the leading symbol of the city's prosperity. Less than a decade after it opened, Chicagoans would regard the canal as "an old fogy institution—one of the things that were, to be superceded by new inventions."[63] Earlier boosters had not been wrong. Waterways played crucial roles in promoting urban growth in many parts of the trans-Appalachian West, including Chicago. But their role in Chicago would be crucially mediated by the railroad. The lake, the harbor, the river, and the canal might by themselves have made Chicago the most important city in northern Illinois, but they would never have made it the interior metropolis of the continent. Water routes would help shape the railroads—by competing with them, by sharing business with them, not least by influencing where they would be built—but the last quarter of the century saw these waterways become ever more marginal to the city's economy. Only the lake continued to carry large quantities of freight; and its most important effect on Chicago's overall growth may well have been its subtle influence on railroad rate structures. As the writer Caroline Kirkland observed of Chicago in 1858, "The

'Open Sesame' in this case has been spoken through the railroad-whistle."[64]

Chicagoans had begun to realize that their city had a special relationship to the railroad even before the Galena and Chicago Union neared completion. One can gauge the shift in their attitudes by reading the annual reviews of Chicago's commerce published during the early 1850s by the city's chief newspapers, the *Daily Tribune* and the *Daily Democratic Press*. In 1850, the *Tribune*'s "Annual Review" included just two paragraphs on Chicago's only railroad, noting without much hyperbole that it had "exceeded the expectations of the most sanguine of its friends." The same article devoted nearly twice as much space to the canal and about three times as much to lake commerce.[65] The boosters' enthusiasm for the city-sustaining powers of water transport evidently remained strong.

Within a year, things had begun to change. The *Tribune*'s "Annual Review" for 1851 presented a dozen paragraphs describing more than ten new railroad projects that would ultimately benefit Chicago. More important, the paper now argued that railroads had "become essential to the prosperity of cities." Water routes were no longer enough. "It matters but little," the *Tribune* claimed, "how great may be the natural advantages with respect to a location upon navigable water, if [cities] fail to avail themselves of this new element of power, a decline is inevitable."[66] Although the paper immediately pointed out that Chicago was handsomely endowed with both sorts of advantage, water *and* rail, the changing direction of the editors' enthusiasms was clear. Without the railroad, a city could hardly expect to keep up with the pace of progress, and might well descend into oblivion.

By 1852, even the title of the *Daily Democrat*'s annual review pamphlet revealed how completely rails had triumphed over water: the publication was now called *Chicago: Her Commerce and Railroads.*[67] Nine pages—over a third of the review's total length—described various new railways and what the city would gain from them; the canal, on the other hand, received no special emphasis at all. Now, when the editors of the *Daily Democratic Press* forecast that Chicago would be "the commercial metropolis of the Mississippi Valley," they made the familiar booster suggestion that anyone wanting to confirm the prediction should consult a map of Illinois—but *not* to locate the magical point where rivers, lakes, and canals would all converge. "With the use of a map," the editors declared, "any person can see that all the [rail]roads and branches that we have noticed, aim at Chicago. From the east and west, north and south, it is the great center which they all seek. Let them come!" With railroads as the engines of growth, said the editors, "our city is capable of almost unlimited extension. . . ."[68]

As Chicagoans and other Americans groped for language to convey their excitement at the new technology, they found themselves drawn to two metaphors that would recur endlessly in booster rhetoric. On the one hand, they assimilated the railroad to the doctrine of natural advantages, merging first and second nature so that the two became almost indistinguishable. The railroad's presence was no less inevitable, no less "natural," than the lakes and rivers with which it competed. Wealth would come to Chicago because its "system of railroads branching in every possible direction throughout the length and breadth of the producing district" made it "the natural outlet and market" for its region.[69] A writer for the *Lakeside Monthly* went so far as to argue that Chicago could expect a speedy recovery from its disastrous 1871 fire because the railroads constituted a natural force compelling it back to economic health. "The routes of traffic passing through this city," he wrote,

> are as truly "natural" routes as though the great lakes were a mountain-chain, and the Mississippi, instead of flowing to the tropics, swept around the southern base of that impassable range, and emptied its volume, swollen by a score of great tributaries into the waters of New York, Delaware, or Chesapeake Bay. The routes thus established, not merely by capital, but by nature and necessity, are as truly fixed facts as are the Mississippi and the Lakes; and they are far more commanding. . . .[70]

People who wrote of the railroad in this way never paused to explain how so "natural" a route could be constructed from rails, ties, and locomotives. Instead, they seemed to see it less as an artificial invention than as a force of nature, a geographical power so irresistible that people must shape their lives according to its dictates.[71]

Wherever the rails went, they brought sudden sweeping change to the landscapes and communities through which they passed, suggesting the second metaphor that occurs repeatedly in nineteenth-century prose about them. Railroads were more than just natural; their power to transform landscapes partook of the supernatural, drawing upon a mysterious creative energy that was beyond human influence or knowledge. The steam engine on the prairie evoked genies and wands and the magic that could make dreams come true merely by wishing them so. "Railroads," wrote one Chicagoan, "are talismanic wands. They have a charming power. They do wonders—they work miracles. They are better than laws; they are essentially, politically and religiously—the pioneer, and vanguard of civilization."[72] Because the flat glaciated landscape was peculiarly suited to railroads, "adapted as it is by nature for their advantageous construction," the arrival of these "powerful iron agencies" meant that the land would "spring at once into teeming life and animation."

When the locomotive appeared on the horizon, it soon called forth "the wave of population . . . rolling a mighty tide of subjugation over the prairies," with "hamlets, towns and cities . . . springing up like magic and realizing in a day the old time history of an age."[73] One editor compared such villages to the quail that "whirls up before the whistle of the engines."[74]

Nobody probably intended such metaphors literally, so we can if we choose read them as mere rhetorical excess. There seems little question, though, that many nineteenth-century Americans did feel genuine awe in the face of the new technology.[75] The locomotive was an inanimate object that had somehow sprung to life, the mechanical herald of a new age. People who described it by appealing to nature and magic—often in the same breath—were seeking some analogue that would help them make sense of a phenomenon unlike any they had encountered before. Our own faith in technology has been so chastened by our knowledge of Faust's bargain—also magical, but finally hollow and self-destructive—that we may find it hard to take seriously the rhetoric of wonder as applied to so profane an object as a railroad locomotive.[76] We recognize such rhetoric as an exercise in mystification. Those who shrouded the railroad in the language of deep mystery, making it seem the expression of a universal life-force beyond human ken, obscured the social and economic processes that lay behind it. Despite the metaphors it evoked, the railroad was neither a direct product of nature nor the creation of a sorcerer's magic. It was a human invention at the heart of an equally human economic system. "Nature," wrote one booster who came closer than most to this perspective, "built Chicago through her artificer, Man."[77]

Still, writers who waxed poetic about the railroad were surely right to regard it as much more than just a machine. It touched all facets of American life in the second half of the nineteenth century, insinuating itself into virtually every aspect of the national landscape. As Caroline Kirkland remarked in 1858 in describing the sunset over an Illinois prairie community, "Fancy the rail gone, and we have neither telegraph, nor schoolhouse, nor anything of all this but the sunset,—and even that we could not be there to see in spring-time," because of the mud that would prevent us from reaching the place.[78] The railroad left almost nothing unchanged: that was its magic. To those whose lives it touched, it seemed at once so ordinary and so extraordinary—so second nature—that the landscape became unimaginable without it. The railroad would replace the waterways of first nature with the myriad complexities of its own geography, thereby becoming the unnatural instrument of a supposedly "natural" destiny. It would rapidly emerge as the chief link connecting Chicago with the towns and rural lands around it, so the city came finally to seem like an artificial spider suspended at the center of a great steel web. To understand Chicago and its emerging relationship to the Great West, one must first understand the railroad.[79]

Railroad Time

Compared with earlier transport systems—lakes, rivers, and canals, on the one hand, and rural roads, on the other—railroads exhibited several key innovations.[80] For one, they broke much more radically with geography. Railroad engineers certainly had to consider any environmental factors that might affect a line's operating costs—the relative steepness of topographic gradients, the bearing load of subsoil structures, the bridgeability of watercourses, and so on. Still, their chief task was to draw the straightest possible line between market centers that might contribute traffic to the road. The same principle applied to nonrail transport systems as well, but the railroads came closer to realizing it than any of their water-based competitors.

As a result, the boosters' geographical determinism affected railroads only indirectly, as a kind of cost-benefit analysis that engineers performed in selecting from among a nearly infinite set of possible routes. Railroads did follow existing rivers and valleys to reach existing harbors and towns—but not because of mysterious environmental forces. Such places usually offered the largest concentrations of prospective customers for freight and passenger traffic. Railroad engineers sought above all to route their lines through country that promised high market demand and low operating cost. Nineteenth-century rhetoric might present the railroad network as "natural," but it was actually the most artificial transportation system yet constructed on land.

The railroads' liberation from geography took many subtle forms. Aside from being able to go virtually anyplace where potential demand was great enough, they could also operate quite independently of the climatic factors that had bedeviled earlier forms of transportation. Farmers who used a railroad like the Galena and Chicago Union probably regarded its invulnerability to mud as its single greatest attraction. No longer did trade and travel have to stop during wet seasons of the year.

The railroads also alleviated many of the worst effects of winter. The period from November to April had always been the dullest season of the business year, when trade ground to a virtual halt for farmers and merchants alike. With the railroad, rural farmers could travel to urban markets whenever they had the need and funds to do so, even in the deep cold of February. Chicagoans no longer had to wait for months on end to view

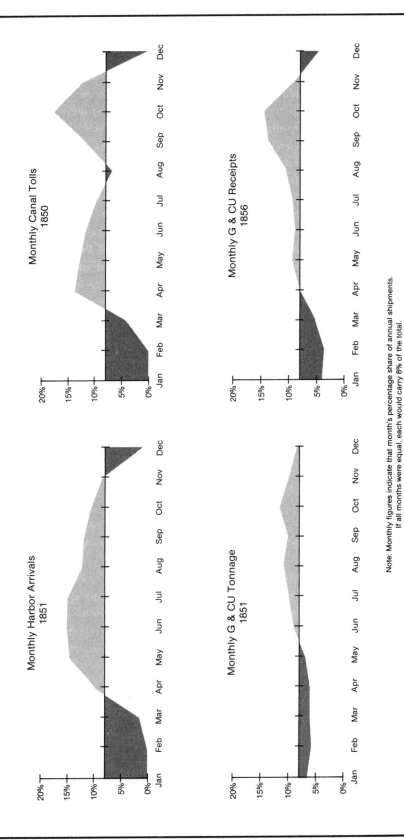

Seasonality of Chicago Shipping,
1850–1856

Monthly Canal Tolls
1850

Monthly G & CU Receipts
1856

Monthly Harbor Arrivals
1851

Monthly G & CU Tonnage
1851

Note: Monthly figures indicate that month's percentage share of annual shipments.
If all months were equal, each would carry 8% of the total.

the latest fashions from New York. As one railroad promoter wryly remarked, "It is against the policy of Americans to remain locked up by ice
one half of the year."[81] The railroads could not break the wheel of the
seasons entirely: the fall harvest, for instance, remained a particularly
active time for travel, straining all forms of transportation. But they did
reduce the seasonal economic cycles that followed the rising and falling
curves of temperature and precipitation.[82]

Just as the railroad changed the ways people experienced the seasons
of the year, so too did it begin to change their relationship to the hours of
the day. No earlier invention had so fundamentally altered people's expectations of how long it took to travel between two distant points on the
continent, for no earlier form of transportation had ever moved people so
quickly. In prerailroad days, before the Michigan Southern made its tri-
umphal entrance into Chicago on February 20, 1852, the trip from New
York took well over two weeks; shortly thereafter, it took less than two
days.[83] Even more striking was the accelerated flow of *information* after the
arrival of the telegraph in 1848: messages that had once taken weeks to
travel between Chicago and the East Coast now took minutes and seconds.[84] Railroad and telegraph systems would expand in tandem, often
following the same routes, and together they shrank the whole perceptual
universe of North America. Because people experience distance more in
hours than in miles, New York, Chicago, and the Great West quite literally grew closer as the lines of wire and rail proliferated among them.

Conversely, time accelerated and became more valuable the greater
the distance one could travel in any given period. Once farmers had access to a railroad, most no longer thought it worth their while to spend a
week or more driving a team of horses over bad roads to sell their crops in
Chicago. More than twice as much wheat came to Chicago in 1852 via the
Galena and Chicago Union than came in farmers' wagons, the latter having fallen by half in just the previous year.[85] In 1860, Chicago received
almost a hundred times more wheat by rail than by wagon; ten years later,
no one even bothered to keep statistics on the latter.[86] Beneath these
seemingly straightforward commodity movements lay a much subtler cultural change: farmers now valued their time too much to contemplate
making extended wagon journeys of the sort they had taken for granted
just ten or twenty years earlier. As one Chicagoan later remembered, the
railroad relieved "the farmers at every stopping place from their long and
tedious journeys by team, enabling them to utilize their own labor, and
the services of their teams, in improving their farms, and adding every
season to the amount of grain sown," thereby increasing the pace of
agricultural improvement throughout the hinterland landscape.[87]

As railroads decreased the cost of distance and increased the value of

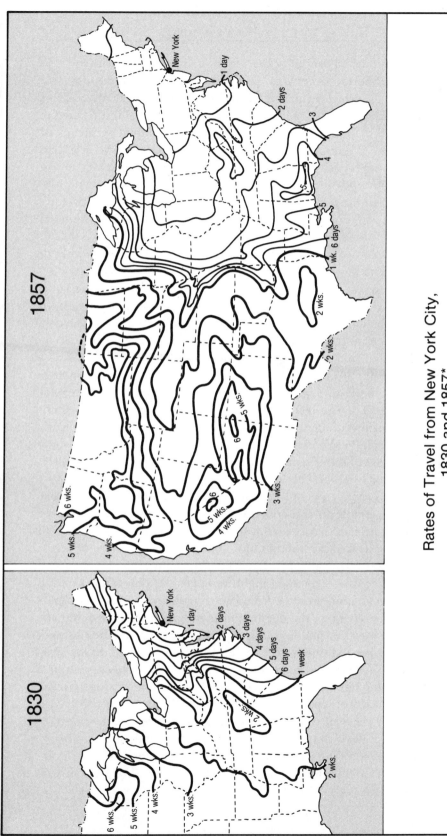

1830

1857

New York
1 day
2 days
3 days
4 days
5 days
6 days
1 week
2 wks.
2 wks.
6 wks.
5 wks.
4 wks.
3 wks.

New York
1 day
2 days
3
4
5
5
5
1 wk. 6 days
2 wks.
2 wks.
3 wks.
4 wks.
5 wks.
6
5 wks.
6
5 wks.
4 wks.
3 wks.
6 wks.
5 wks.

Rates of Travel from New York City,
1830 and 1857*

*After Paullin, 1932.

time, they also raised people's expectations about the regularity and reliability of transportation services. Earlier forms of western transport had involved single vehicles carrying small loads. The individuals or firms that ran them operated on a limited scale and had little ability to predict local demand or avert potential delays caused by weather, accidents, or other hazards. As a result, canal boats, steamships, and road vehicles had trouble keeping regular schedules. As one frustrated eastern traveler reported of his western journey in 1851, "For a boat to lie at her wharf hours after the time set for starting, and by innumerable stops to prolong her trip a day or two beyond the promised time, is an event of common occurrence." Because people had no choice but to tolerate such delays, they had to plan very loose schedules for when they might be able to conduct business, receive shipments, or complete a trip. With so erratic a transportation system, one could not place a very high value on one's own time. "Indeed," the same traveler reported, "*time* does not yet seem to enter as an element into Western thought. It answers about as well to do a thing next week as this; to wait a day or two for a boat, as to meet it at the hour appointed; and so on through all the details of life."[88]

Because railroads ran more quickly and reliably, and could carry more people and goods over greater distances, they changed this irregular sense of time. Trains too could be delayed. But whereas earlier western stage and steamship operators had measured their service by how many trips they made in the course of a *week,* railroads measured the same service in terms of the scheduled trips they made in a *day.* [89] On this scale, a train delayed by several hours was very late indeed, a fact that suggests how railroads changed people's ability to schedule and predict their use of time. The long-term consequence was to move timekeeping into the realm of the mechanical clock, away from the various natural cycles which had formerly marked the flow of time.

Distinctions that had once been crucial in dividing the days and months of the year—separating night from day, wet times from dry, hot times from cold, good weather from bad—gradually became less important to travel even if they did not disappear altogether. No longer did one have to stop traveling and find lodging for the night when the sun went down; no longer did one have to delay a journey until ice disappeared from rivers or lakes; no longer did one have to fear snowstorms as a life-threatening hazard on the open road.[90] When one boarded a train, one entered a world separated from the outside by its own peculiar environment and sense of time. Train passengers had less and less need to interact physically with the landscapes through which they were passing. They became spectators who could enjoy watching the world go by instead of working their way across it on foot or horseback. Unless an accident occurred—and railroad accidents, like those of steamboats, entailed horrors of a sort never before seen—the train promised what its passengers increasingly came to expect: the safety and clockwork regularity of an artificial universe.[91]

The most dramatic proof that this new universe had extended its influence to the outside world came in 1883, when the major railroad companies imposed on North America new, "standard" times to replace the hundreds of "local" times which had previously been used to set clocks throughout the country.[92] Before the invention of standard time, clocks were set according to the rules of astronomy: noon was the moment when the sun stood highest in the midday sky. By this strict astronomical definition every locale had a different noon, depending on the line of longitude it occupied. When clocks read noon in Chicago, it was 11:50 A.M. in St. Louis, 11:38 A.M. in St. Paul, 11:27 A.M. in Omaha, and 12:18 P.M. in Detroit, with every possible variation in between. For companies trying to operate trains between these various points, the different local times were a scheduling nightmare. Railroads around the country set their clocks by no fewer than fifty-three different standards—and thereby created a deadly risk for everyone who rode them. Two trains running on the same tracks at the same moment but with clocks showing different times could well find themselves unexpectedly occupying the same space, with disastrous consequences.[93]

And so, on November 18, 1883, the railroad companies carved up the continent into four time zones, in each of which all clocks would be set to exactly the same time. At noon, Chicago jewelers moved their clocks back by nine minutes and thirty-three seconds in order to match the local time of the ninetieth meridian.[94] The *Chicago Tribune* likened the event to Joshua's having made the sun stand still, and announced, "The railroads of this country demonstrated yesterday that the hand of time can be moved backward about as easily as Columbus demonstrated that an egg can be made to stand on end."[95] Although the U.S. government would not officially acknowledge the change until 1918, everyone else quickly abandoned local sun time and set clocks by railroad time instead. Railroad schedules thus redefined the hours of the day: sunrise over Chicago would henceforth come ten minutes sooner, and the noonday sun would hang a little lower in the sky.[96]

The railroads broke with the sun in one other respect as well. All previous forms of land transport had relied on biological sources to power their movement, in the form of food calories consumed by people, horses, or oxen to move vehicles and goods through space. All such energy ultimately derived from the sun, and its use was strictly constrained by the physiological ability of animal metabolisms to convert food into work. Speed of movement had well-defined biological limits, as did the total quantity of work that people or animals could perform in a day: a good-sized man might deliver two to three horsepower-hours in the course of a hard ten-hour day, while a horse might deliver eight to ten horsepower-hours during the same period.[97] The railroad broke this age-old restrictive relationship between biological energy and movement, much as the steamboat had done for water transport several decades earlier. Although early locomotives burned wood, they gradually shifted toward coal, and so ended their reliance on biological energy sources by replacing them with fossil fuel. Locomotives were not more efficient than horses, but they could consume vastly greater quantities of fuel much more quickly, and thus had much higher limits for work, speed, and endurance. Typical locomotives of the 1850s could deliver well over three hundred horsepower.[98] By the Civil War, they could pull enormous loads at better than twenty miles per hour for hours on end—far longer than horses or people could move a tiny fraction of that load at less than half that speed. No longer would solar energy and animal physiology set limits to human movement across the landscape.

The greater speed, distance, volume, and power of railroads enabled them to break free from the economic and environmental constraints of earlier transport systems. Compared with its predecessors, railroad geography rested on differences in degree that people experienced as differences in kind, shifting the human sense of scale in a way that itself became second nature in subtle ways. With the possible exception of great armies, no human organization had ever posed such extensive and elaborate management problems before. The railroads moved immense volumes of goods and people at high speeds on closely timed schedules over great distances, creating a far-flung network in which responsibility for the entire system fell to a small group of managers. Operating such a system required concentrations of private capital greater than ever before. By 1860, total American investment in canals, which had been the largest comparable corporate enterprises, was still less than $200 million after forty years of operation, while railroad investment, more than tripling in the preceding single decade, had already passed $1.1 *billion.*[99] Unlike their predecessors, the corporations that ran railroads generally owned the entire operation: lands, rails, locomotives, cars, and stations, not to mention the labor and fuel that kept everything moving. The companies that operated stagecoaches, ships, and canalboats generally paid only their vehicles' operating costs, not the expense of maintaining the right of way, while canal companies and toll roads maintained the right of way without owning or running vehicles themselves. Railroads did both and simultaneously incurred large fuel, labor, and equipment costs. Although such extensive ownership rights conferred great power, with them came truly daunting levels of risk and responsibility as well. Running a railroad meant trying to achieve unprecedented levels of coordination among engineering technologies, management structures, labor practices, freight rates, resource flows, and—not least—natural environments, all spread over thousands of square miles of land.

Control of this sort required techniques for gathering and interpreting information at a level much more detailed than had previously been typical of most business enterprises. The railroads faced as much of a challenge in processing data as in moving people or freight. For every station, managers had to set rates, maintain schedules, and keep records of what the firm was hauling at how much cost during which period of time, so that in the end the corporate account books would all balance. Managing this accounting problem generated vast new quantities of statistics which themselves helped revolutionize the American economy by making possible increasingly intricate analyses of trade and production.[100] Responsibility for using the new statistics fell into the hands of a new class of managers, engineers, and accountants whose emerging professional skills became essential to the system as a whole. Out of their work would come an increasingly hierarchical power structure which gradually proliferated through the entire economy.[101]

At the most abstract level, the railroads' hierarchies of corporate wealth and managerial power represented a vast new concentration of capital. Whether one understands that word to mean the accumulated surplus value extracted from rail workers, the aggregate financial investments represented by company stock, or the real resources and equipment required to operate trains, it carries one basic implication. As perceived by those who ran it, a railroad was a pool of capital designed to make more capital. Railroads spent money moving goods and passengers in order to earn a profit out of the difference between their receipts and their operating expenses. Actual practice did not always turn out so happily, but this at least was the theory of the enterprise: invested capital would grow or at least earn back costs so that the system as a whole could expand. Because investments and costs were enormous, everything that moved by railroad—and every place through which the railroad ran—became linked to the imperatives of corporate capital. The railroad thus became the chief device for introducing a new capitalist logic to the geography of the Great West.

The Logic of Capital

At no place was that logic more fully and intricately expressed than at Chicago. Already by the 1850s, Chicago boosters had begun to back away from water-based versions of the doctrine of natural advantages, having realized that their city's future depended at least as much on capital as on geography. They pointed with special pride to the fact that their municipal government, unlike many western communities, had never needed to commit municipal funds to attract railroad projects to the city.[102] As the booster William Jones observed in 1857, despite the obvious importance of railroads to its economy, Chicago had not "in her corporate capacity, *invested a single dollar in any of them.* "[103] And yet the railroads had come to the city anyway, more of them than anywhere else in the country. What better proof could one want that the interests of capital and the interests of Chicago "naturally" aligned with each other? As Chicago's leading booster, John S. Wright, argued in 1870,

> *The whole Capital of New York and New England supports Chicago.* The sagacious capitalists of the East, seeking simply their own aggrandizement, have built such roads as the East wanted, and where wanted. Of Chicago they have merely asked permission to come into the City, a boon often obtained with difficulty. Yet the East has already made her the focal point of over three-fourths of the western system.[104]

Wright concluded that Chicago's growth was nourished chiefly by its linkages to eastern areas with greater concentrations of capital. "Though weak herself," he wrote, "Chicago has found abundant strength in her unity of interest with the wealthiest region of our country."[105]

Wright was correct that Chicagoans had acquired their unique position in the nation's railroad system without actually owning the companies that sustained their city's economy. Investors from eastern cities, especially New York and Boston, came to control most of the railroad networks centering on Chicago, even when, as in the case of the Galena and Chicago Union, local investors had started the line. The Illinois Central had originally been promoted by the same New York and New England capitalists who had lobbied for the road's 1850 land grant from the federal government. Management control continued to be located in New York, though the road's equity soon moved even farther east: by 1858, some two-thirds of the Central's stockholders lived in England.[106] The Chicago, Burlington and Quincy emerged from the consolidation of several local Illinois companies by a group of Boston investors led by John Murray Forbes, and would henceforth be linked to the Forbes-controlled Michigan Central.[107] Among the larger shareholders of Burlington stock, the vast majority continued to be easterners: in 1890, for instance, 112,-968 shares were held by New Yorkers, 166,198 shares by Bostonians, and only 3,104 shares by Chicagoans.[108] And the Galena and Chicago Union was finally absorbed by the Chicago and Northwestern in 1864. Although Chicago's William Butler Ogden became the first president of the Northwestern as he had earlier been of the Galena, he and the other four Chicagoans on the new road's board of directors were immediately outnumbered by easterners. Of the seventeen directors, a controlling majority—nine—was from the Northeast, and eight of those were from New York City.[109]

The eastern ownership of Chicago railroads is hardly surprising, given the amounts of money that went into constructing them. No local source of capital could have handled such costs in the 1850s when most of the city's roads were getting started, and to that extent Chicagoans and easterners really did have a unity of interests. Furthermore, the original source of Chicago's railroad capital mattered much less than the geographical orientation of the resulting physical networks. Once corporate managers had decided to locate the terminals of more than one major railroad in Chicago, stockholders had little choice but to align themselves with the city. Their interest in Chicago's welfare depended almost not at all on where they themselves lived, for their corporation had no easy way to liquidate the capital it had spent on such fixed assets as lands or rails or station equipment. In the words of the Chicago, Burlington and Quincy's president, "Railroads are fixtures; they cannot be taken up and carried away. . . ."[110] And so investors and managers became pawns of the very geography they had helped to create. As one Chicago real estate promoter explained with some glee, "It has been said that Chicago has no capital of her own, and that her capital is from other cities; that fact admitted, can not affect her present, or her future, one tittle. That capital can never be removed."[111]

One fact above all others sustained the alliance between easterners and the railroad metropolis they had helped create on Lake Michigan. The most important feature of the new geography of capital was Chicago's location at the breaking point between eastern and western rail networks. Already by 1852, the pattern had clearly emerged that eastern railroads operating south of the Great Lakes would find their *western* terminals in Chicago, while the various western railroads fanning out from the city would locate their *eastern* terminals there. No single railroad company operated trains both east and west of Chicago. Out of this seemingly trivial fact flowed many consequences that maintained Chicago's railroad hegemony for the rest of the century.[112]

To grasp these consequences, one must first understand the uneasy relationship between railroad rates and costs.[113] As managers soon learned, the first principle of railroad rate setting was to encourage customers, whether passengers or shippers of freight, to make the longest possible journey on one's own line. Companies sought freight and passengers that traveled long distances because handling costs—incurred mainly at the beginning and end of the trip—were identical no matter how long the journey. A railroad spent just as much time and money loading and unloading a carful of wheat whether it traveled one mile or a thousand miles, making it much easier to earn back costs on long shipments. Since longer journeys cost the railroad less, its managers were much more likely to offer low rates to an Iowa farm family if it shipped wheat to Chicago instead of to a town on the Mississippi River. As one writer explained in 1873, "To the railroads, a long shipment is a large business. Short traffic, no matter how large, can be made profitable only by high rates."[114] A manager at the Chicago, Burlington and Quincy made the point even more graphically: "A Railroad is a cheap means of transportation for long distances and relatively less cheap as the distance diminishes until, when it becomes very small a wheel-barrow is the cheapest—and for still smaller distances a shovel."[115]

But managers had even better reasons for setting rates to promote long-distance travel. Much nearer the core of their capitalist geography was the relationship between a company's *variable* costs and its *fixed* costs. Variable costs changed with the volume of traffic; fixed costs did not. Because the investment needed to create a new railroad was enormous—requiring its managers to assemble all basic equipment, supplies, and workers before they had earned even a dollar of income—companies confronted very high fixed charges.[116] Taxes and interest on borrowed capital loomed large among these. Once a company had sold bonds—often at substantial discounts—to finance a road's construction and operation, it had to make regular interest payments on those bonds or risk bankruptcy. Such payments bore no relation to the road's success in attracting traffic; one paid them even when not a single train was running. Statistics on this subject are not readily available for earlier periods, but data from the last decade of the century suggest that fixed finance charges typically amounted to more than a fourth of a railroad's total annual expenses.[117]

Interest payments aside, an astonishingly high proportion of a railroad's *operating* expenses also bore no relation to the volume of goods it carried. Ties rotted, bridges collapsed, and rails rusted no matter how few trains passed over them. Workers had to clear tracks of snow so that just one train could complete its journey. Even expenditures that one might think would vary most directly with volume of operation—fuel consumption, wear and tear on engines, and workers' wages—had quite a large component of fixed costs. A locomotive consumed a tenth of its daily fuel simply heating itself to the point that it could produce steam. Another fourth of its fuel consumption went toward moving its own weight. As a result, perhaps a third to a half of all expenditure on locomotive fuel bore no relation whatsoever to how fully a train was loaded.[118] Wages followed a similar pattern. A large portion of a railroad's employees, especially its managers, clerical staff, and maintenance workers, had to stay on the job even when little freight and few passengers were riding the rails. And a train needed the same number of engineers and conductors whatever the size of its load.

These fixed charges meant that perhaps two-thirds of a railroad's total expenditures remained unaffected by how much traffic it carried.[119] Once a company had built the tracks and equipment needed to serve a given territory, it had little choice but to provide that service. Its capital investment required it to earn a minimum income, and this had a surprising consequence for the way its managers set rates. The simple but paradoxical fact was this: when railroad business was poor, a company had to attract traffic—even when that traffic did not pay the cost of its own transportation. Since the company was going to pay fixed costs no matter what, earning *something* was better than earning nothing. If one could somehow earn $90,000 of cash income on transportation that cost $100,000 to provide, one lost only $10,000; if, on the other hand, one let the railroad sit idle, one was guaranteed to lose more than $60,000 in fixed costs. Curious as it might seem to an outsider, railroad managers sometimes had to set rates they knew would lose the company money.[120]

This was the logic of capital, and it was also the logic that would make Chicago the greatest railroad center in the world. One more variable completes the equation that defined Chicago's special role: competition. The need of railroad corporations to meet fixed costs made them vulnerable to competition as no earlier transportation system had ever been. As the rail network expanded, certain large towns found themselves with more than one railroad. Although their size made such places highly attractive markets, their passengers and freight shippers also gained the ability to play railroads off against each other to drive down rates. At "competitive points," as such places came to be called, the logic of fixed costs drove railroads to cut rates to the bare minimum—below the actual cost of transportation, if necessary—in order to keep traffic from switching to other roads. An opposite logic applied to towns with only one railroad. Having no alternative, shippers and passengers at these "noncompetitive points" paid not only their full cost of transportation but often a surcharge to help make up for a road's competitive losses elsewhere.

Railroad rate schedules, no matter how many pages they filled or how intricate they might appear, thus rested on a few key principles. Short of bankruptcy—and not all roads stopped short of bankruptcy—fixed costs were inescapable. To pay them, railroad managers had to attract as much traffic as possible. Since passengers and shippers could choose between railroad companies at competitive points, those places must receive the lowest rates; at noncompetitive points, where a road had an effective monopoly over transport service, it could afford to charge much more. Within these constraints, railroad rate setters tried to maintain the highest possible ratio of traffic volume to fixed costs in order to earn the maximum amount from each station along the route. Toward that end, once passengers or freight shipments had begun their journey on a given railroad, they must be discouraged from switching to other roads so that they would travel as far as possible on the line with which they started. "The whole tendency of rail transportation," wrote one contemporary observer, "is toward the longest shipments possible without breaking bulk. . . ."[121] Railroad managers therefore gave the best rate of all, from whatever point of departure, to passengers or shipments destined for the railroad's eastern terminus. (The western end of the line mattered much less, since under frontier conditions its small population represented a much lower demand and generally had no alternative means of transportation anyway.)

Out of this complex calculus of railroad rates came the new economic imperatives promoting metropolitan growth in the Great West. By 1860, the eastern terminus for virtually every major railroad west of Lake Michigan was Chicago.[122] One reason for this was simple: as we have already seen, no western lines provided service east of the city, so any freight or passengers bound for the East Coast had to switch railroads in Chicago. But another reason amplified the effect of this east–west division in railroad corporate organization. Earlier boosters who had argued that water routes would make Chicago a great metropolis proved to be right after all, though not in quite the way they had expected. Lake Michigan, the city's single greatest "natural advantage," turned out to have surprisingly powerful effects on railroad rate structures.

Railroads were not the only carriers competing to haul western farm produce to the Northeast. Ships continued to do so as well. Despite their older technology, they were intrinsically cheaper to run than railroads, largely because the buoyancy and lower friction of water travel required less energy consumption. Sail ships had no fuel costs at all, and steamships got more mileage from the fuel they consumed than railroads did. Both types of ship enjoyed the enormous advantage of not having to maintain a right of way. The capital for harbor improvements usually came from government subsidies, and the lakes themselves were free, so the capital costs of private lake carriers were inevitably lower than those of railroads. Aside from their greater risk of water damage from leaks or shipwreck, which produced higher insurance costs, the only real disadvantage of ships was their slowness, which was the reason they soon ceased to be major passenger carriers as soon as the railroads arrived. For many kinds of freight, on the other hand, speed mattered little. To travel from Chicago to New York, a shipment of grain took fourteen to twenty days by sail, ten and a half days by steamship, and five and a half days by rail, a difference that mattered only under unusual market conditions.[123] Prior to the Civil War, before railroads were equipped to handle large shipments, more than 90 percent of Chicago's grain continued to travel east by lake. Thereafter, the lake's share of grain shipments fluctuated more widely, but rarely fell below 50 percent. The reason depended entirely on shippers' sensitivity to the price of time and distance: except at the height of harvest season, lake rates from Chicago to New York were typically 15 to 20 percent lower than comparable rail rates.[124]

Lake Michigan promoted Chicago's dominance over the regional economy in two equally important ways. First, shippers seeking to move farm produce east at the lowest possible rates chose Chicago as their initial destination in order to transfer freight to cheaper lake vessels. Only Milwaukee had a comparable harbor on the western shore of Lake Michigan, but its more northern location and weaker connections to eastern capital had left it with rail facilities far inferior to Chicago's. Given the expense of all-rail freight travel to the East Coast, shippers had a strong incentive not to use the few railroads that eventually bypassed Chicago to offer direct eastern connections at cities like St. Louis or Peoria. Instead, shippers used the railroads west of Chicago to avoid using the railroads east of it, and this could only benefit Chicago.

The lake also influenced Chicago's railroad rate structure in a second important way—by lowering the prices that eastern roads could charge outbound traffic. The eastern railroads too had to confront the need for minimum income in the face of fixed costs, and so tried to bring their rates as close as possible to those of lake shipping. The result was a curious cycling in rail rates east from Chicago. For the whole winter, while the lake was frozen, rail rates remained almost constant at a level often half again as high as the price ships would charge in the spring. As soon as the ice melted, in late March or early April, rail rates plummeted to a position just 15 to 20 percent higher than rates on the lake. For the rest of the summer, railroad rates more or less paralleled those of ships. Ship and rail rates gradually rose together until the fall harvest, when, with both systems operating near full capacity, the two were usually closer than at any other time of the year. Then, after ships completed their final trips in December, rail rates again returned to their high winter plateau.[125] A government economist described this effect in 1877 by saying,

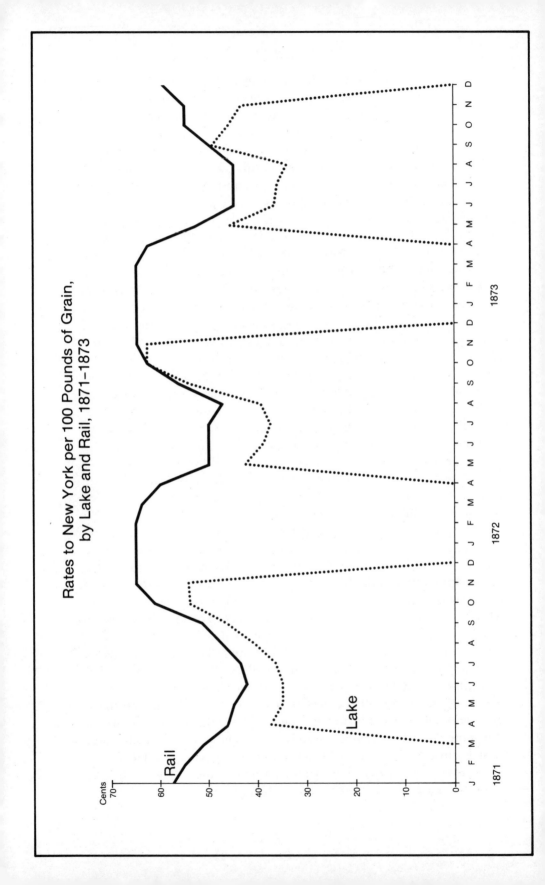

Rates to New York per 100 Pounds of Grain, by Lake and Rail, 1871–1873

"Rail-rates are very much advanced at about the time of the close of navigation, and . . . they are correspondingly lowered, at or about the time when navigation opens in the spring, thus proving the regulating power of the water-line."[126] This seasonal cycling of eastward-bound railroad rates was more pronounced at Chicago than anywhere else in the West; in many landlocked places, it did not occur at all. For half the year, in other words, lake competition gave Chicago rail rates that were even lower than the favorable ones it already enjoyed for other reasons.

But the division between eastern and western railroads that augmented Chicago's growth was only partly a consequence of the lake. In fact, the competition between lake and rail that produced the seasonal fluctuation in Chicago's freight rates was merely a special case of a more generalized eastward competition that consistently benefited the city's economy. Whether traveling by lake or rail, most traffic moving east from Chicago did not halt its journey until it reached the Atlantic Ocean; more often than not, its destination was New York City. By the Civil War, at least three major railroads and dozens of ships were servicing the Chicago–New York corridor. All competed with each other. Even when the lakes froze over, the railroads had no choice but to keep rates relatively low, lest their competitors take business away. The only thing that saved eastern lines from disastrous competition was the sheer volume of freight moving east from Chicago. (Rate-fixing was an alternative to competitive pricing, but it rarely proved successful for long.)[127] Given the strength of New York's markets, the eastern lines had little trouble encouraging freight to travel the full length of their lines, and that in turn made their low-price, high-volume operations relatively cost-effective.

An entirely different competitive logic applied to railroads operating west of Chicago. Unlike the eastern roads, they could not simply pick up enormous shipments at one city and drop them off at another. Instead, they gathered small quantities of freight along their entire route, finally assembling everything at Chicago in the much larger quantities that ships or eastern railroads would carry east. Eastern manufactured goods arriving in Chicago followed exactly the opposite process: western lines picked up large shipments in the city and delivered them in small quantities to the many stations along their route. Because western railroads had to transport so many small shipments, they faced much higher handling costs than their eastern counterparts. To make matters worse, the agricultural shipments they carried to Chicago—principally grain, livestock, and other produce—were much bulkier and filled many more cars than freight moving in the opposite direction. As a result, most trains traveling west from Chicago had to haul empty cars that earned no income at all.

For all these reasons, western railroads faced much higher costs per ton mile than eastern ones and were therefore vulnerable to disastrous competition from other roads. Fortunately for their economic well-being, the pattern of railroad construction initially worked in their favor, at least until the Civil War. Unlike routes east of Chicago, which paralleled each other because of their common endpoints, those west of the city did not run in parallel. Each of the western railroads had its own distinctive territory, which meant that each to a greater or lesser degree had a monopoly on transporting the produce of its region. Except at places where the few north–south lines crossed the much more numerous east–west ones, "competitive points" outside of Chicago itself were rare.

By 1860, then, the geography of capital had placed Chicago at a location with much subtler benefits than early booster arguments about "natural advantages" had suggested. The competition between lake and rail had given the city advantages that few communities in North America could hope to share: in railroad parlance, no other point in the Great West could be nearly so "competitive." But a deeper reason for the city's success was its location on the watershed between two quite different systems of corporate competition. East of the city, the railroads were known as "trunk" lines: low-cost, high-volume competitive routes following a tight corridor across the nine hundred miles to New York. West of the city, the visual metaphor of the railroad map changed from trunk to fan, with lines diverging like rays from a central point to spread hundreds of miles north and south before continuing their westward trend. The roads making up this metaphorical fan were high-cost, low-volume, and noncompetitive. The intersection of trunk and fan was the essential geographical fact of Chicago's location: more than anything else, it constituted the second, constructed nature that the railroads had imposed on the western landscape. In 1877, the presidents of two Chicago railroads described this phenomenon in the following way:

> The railways which radiate from Lake Michigan and run like lattice-work throughout the West, gather up business and centering at Chicago pour it by train-loads on to the through lines to the East. The latter have simply to forward it. It is this fortunate condition which gives the New York Central Railroad 16 miles of freight-cars daily. The western roads are feeders; the eastern lines are receivers. The latter are saved the expense of picking up this business by driblets. It comes to them in volumes.[128]

A Chicago railroad analyst put it even more succinctly: "western roads," he declared, "were built *from* and eastern ones *to* Chicago."[129]

Chicago thus grew to metropolitan status less from being what the boosters called *central* than from being *peripheral*. By defining the boundary between two railroad systems that operated within radically different markets—even as both sought to meet the same fundamental problems of fixed costs and minimum income—Chicago became the link that bound the different worlds of east and west into a single system. In the most literal sense, from 1848 to the end of the nineteenth century, it was where the West began. Railroad companies in both directions sought to promote the city's interests, because its unique position helped them solve the special problems which their own scale of business and capital investment had created. "The prosperity of the roads," wrote a government economist in 1881, "largely depends upon the prosperity of the city."[130]

One railroad manager, Robert Harris of the Chicago, Burlington and Quincy, called the city "that strong ally of ours," and his feelings were surely common to all managers of the Chicago roads.[131] Their decisions resulted in a myriad of daily business practices that served to benefit the city. Harris's own correspondence furnishes dozens of examples. He reprimanded one employee, a station manager in Salina, Kansas, for the inadequacy of his advertising: "It seems to me," wrote Harris, "that you do not in your circular refer to our Chicago market with that fullness that its importance would justify.—We think you would find it your strong point."[132] He told a rival railroad that the Burlington had no interest in making a pooling arrangement to share the market at Keokuk, Iowa: "Our customary way of doing our business," Harris said, "is to throw business over as much of the Road as possible. Business to & from the East into Keokuk we prefer to take via Chicago."[133] And in explaining why the CB&Q had altered rates at Hamburg, Iowa, he wrote, "A considerable effort has generally been made by the Kan. City St Joe & CB RR to foster the trade of St Joseph, and, to that end it established a very low schedule of rates St Joseph to Hamburg with a view to enable St Joseph to undersell Chicago in that town—In order to protect ourselves and the Chicago market it became necessary to reduce our rates to Hamburg."[134] Harris's actions in each of these cases reflected a coherent underlying philosophy of rate setting, which he expressed in a single sentence: "We are always desirous," he wrote, "of shaping our tariff so as to build up the prosperity of those who build up our prosperity. . . ."[135] In whatever ways they could, railroad managers like Harris sought to keep long-distance traffic flowing over their rails, and that in turn meant encouraging freight and passengers to travel whenever possible through Chicago.

By fulfilling the role that the railroads had assigned it—serving as the gateway between East and West—Chicago became the principal wholesale market for the entire midcontinent. Whether breaking up bulk shipments from the East or assembling bulk shipments from the West, it served as the entrepôt—the place in between—connecting eastern markets with vast western resource regions. In this role, it became a key participant in a series of economic revolutions that left few aspects of nineteenth-century life untouched. Henceforth, Chicago would be a metropolis—not the central city of the continent, as the boosters had hoped, but the gateway city to the Great West, with a vast reach and dominance that flowed from its control over that region's trade with the rest of the world.

Before the railroads, no such dominance had been possible. But by 1893, a New York journalist could write, "In Chicago, one-twenty-fifth of the railway mileage of the world terminates, and serves 30 millions of persons, who find Chicago the largest city easily accessible to them."[136] The changes that the railroad system initiated would proliferate from Chicago and fundamentally alter much of the American landscape. As the city began to funnel the flow of western trade, the rural West became more and more a part of its hinterland, mimicking the zones von Thünen had described even before Chicago existed as a town. The isolation that had constrained the trade and production of frontier areas would disappear in the face of what Karl Marx called "the annihilation of space by time," the tendency of capitalism's technologies and markets to drive "beyond every spatial barrier."[137] Wherever the network of rails extended, frontier became hinterland to the cities where rural products entered the marketplace. Areas with limited experience of capitalist exchange suddenly found themselves much more palpably within an economic and social hierarchy created by the geography of capital.

At its best, the new geography meant that westerners could now sell the products of nature and human labor much more readily than before, giving them new hope of fulfilling the great nineteenth-century booster dream of material progress for city and country alike. On the other hand, that same geography also left many people nervous about their growing dependency on the metropolis and the faceless institutions like railroads that seemed to serve its interests. Hinterland residents found that they now had little choice but to sell in Chicago's marketplace if they wished to participate in the economy that revolved around it. Not everyone was content with the resulting mixture of gains and losses. In comparison with the world of wagons and canalboats that preceded it, the postrailroad landscape would require much higher levels of trade, production, and resource consumption for its own sustenance, let alone its imperatives toward growth. More and more of the Great West would be drawn into that landscape, and more and more of western nature would become priced, capitalized, and mortgaged as the new capitalist geography proliferated.

The railroads had made Chicago the most important meeting place between East and West. But they also continued the process begun long before with the harbor and the canal, and before that in the trading village and the booster dreams that transformed it. In Chicago and its hinterland, first and second nature mingled to form a single world. The boosters had been indulging their rhetorical mysticism when they likened the railroads to a force of nature, but there can be no question that the railroads acted as a powerful force *upon* nature, so much so that the logic they expressed in so many intricate ways itself finally came to seem natural. In the second half of the nineteenth century, city and country, linked by "the wild scream of the locomotive," would together work profound transformations on the western landscape.[138] On the farms of Illinois and Iowa, the great tallgrass prairies would give way to cornstalks and wheat fields. The white pines of the north woods would become lumber, and the forests of the Great Lakes would turn to stumps. The vast herds of bison on which the Plains Indians had depended for much of their livelihood would die violent deaths and make room for more manageable livestock. Like von Thünen's isolated city, Chicago was remote from all of these events. And yet no place is more central to understanding why they occurred.

PART II

NATURE TO MARKET

3

Pricing the Future: Grain

Prairie into Farm

The train did not create the city by itself. Stripped of the rhetoric that made it seem a mechanical deity, the railroad was simply a go-between whose chief task was to cross the boundary between city and country. Its effects had less to do with some miraculous power in the scream of a locomotive's whistle than with opening a corridor between two worlds that would remake each other. Goods and people rode the rails to get to market, where together buyers and sellers from city and country priced the products of the earth. In this sense, Chicago was just the site of a country fair, albeit the grandest, most spectacular country fair the world had ever seen. The towns and farms that seemed to spring magically into being when railroads appeared in their vicinity were actually responding to the call of that fair. But so was Chicago itself. Its unprecedented growth in the second half of the nineteenth century was in no small measure the creation of people in its hinterland, who in sending the fruits of their labor to its markets brought great change to city and country alike. "The cities have not made the country," reflected one long-time resident of Chicago in 1893; "on the contrary, the country has compelled the cities. . . . Without the former the latter could not exist. Without farmers there could be no cities."[1] Nowhere was this more true than in Chicago.

Farmers brought a new human order to the country west of the Great Lakes, as revolutionary in its own way as the train or the city itself. Potawatomis and other Indian peoples had been raising corn on small plots of land around Lake Michigan for generations, but always on a limited scale. The new Euroamerican farmers, on the other hand, raised corn with an eye to the market, and so grew much greater quantities on much larger plots of land, especially once they could ship their harvest by rail. In addition to eating some of the grain themselves, they did things no Indians had ever done with it: turned it into whisky or fed it to hogs and other livestock, in both cases so that they could transport it more easily to market. They also began to raise crops that had never before been part of the regional landscape: old-world grains, especially wheat, as well as a wealth of fruit and vegetable species.

Like maize, which Indians had been breeding for millennia, each of these grain and vegetable crops had a long history of human use and manipulation. People had been improving them with selective breeding for countless generations, so wheat or oats or rye were themselves products of human technology—first and second nature woven together in the life of a single organism. Most varieties had become specialized enough that they could scarcely survive in a wild setting; their success thus depended on specialized habitats maintained solely by the labors of human beings. To reproduce such habitats, people resorted to a variety of tools. To prepare the heavy, dense prairie sod in order that exotic seeds could thrive in it, farmers had to turn over the grass and work the soil with plowshares and harrows made of iron and steel. To pull these heavy tools, they needed draft animals—horses and oxen—whose domestication was itself one of the great chapters in the global history of technology. Once seeds had become mature plants awaiting harvest, farmers needed still other tools—scythes, reapers, and threshers—each of which underwent important technological changes during the period of Chicago's greatest growth.[2]

The glaciers had left the region west of the Great Lakes unusually well suited to the organisms and farming techniques that American and European migrants brought with them.[3] In the valleys where braided streams had dropped their glacial silt, and on the hillsides where dusty winds had redeposited that same silt, mineral-rich soil had been accumulating for millennia. Atop it, prairie grasses had made their own contribution. The black soil they had produced measured in feet rather than inches and contained well over 150 tons of organic matter per acre in what seemed an almost inexhaustible fund of fertile earth. The parent rock beneath often contained a good deal of lime, which the prairie grasses were adept at transporting to the surface. This kept the soil from becoming acidic, making it more suitable for the crops farmers sought to raise. Considering the favorable climate as well, it would be hard to imagine a landscape better suited to agriculture.[4]

Families trying to farm such soil at first found it almost too much of a good thing, for the native vegetation so thrived upon it that traditional plows had trouble cutting through the sod. The grasses formed a mat so dense that in upland areas rainwater rarely sank more than six inches into the ground, preventing all but the hardiest of competing plants from taking root.[5] Wooden plows with cast-iron edges quickly came to grief here. What farmers needed was a steel plow that could cut the tangled roots and still hold its edge—exactly the sort of plow that John Deere and other prairie manufacturers began to produce in their shops during the 1840s.[6] Many farmers hired professional "prairie breakers" who owned oversized plows to do the initial cutting. The work had to be carefully timed, for if it was done too early the prairie grasses grew back and overwhelmed the crops; if too late, the turned-over vegetation did not rot soon enough for a successful planting in the fall. Professional prairie breaking was expensive, but well worth the cost for small landowners who could not afford to purchase special breaking equipment themselves.[7] Spared the initial plowing, and also the task of clearing the trees and stumps which consumed so much time on forested lands back east, farmers could begin at once to seed their land.

As they did so, the native grasses—big and little bluestem, side oats grama, Indian grass, and all the others—began their long retreat to the margins of cultivation. The dozens of species that together defined the prairie ecosystem quickly gave way to the handful of plants that defined the farm. The two most popular of these were corn and wheat. Unlike their Indian predecessors, who planted with hoes and human labor, American farmers could prepare large fields of corn by plowing with draft animals. They sowed corn seed, as the prairie proverb recommended, in the spring when oak leaves were the size of a squirrel's ear. To protect the young seedlings from weeds, they ran harrows and plows between the rows several times before the Fourth of July, when the plants could usually fend for themselves. Families had to harvest corn by hand, but that task could wait until October or November, or even the following spring, with little damage to the crop. Even though corn brought low prices—few Americans, and even fewer Europeans, regarded it as a prime food grain—it became a major part of prairie agriculture. People might not enjoy eating corn, but animals loved it; moreover, its crop yields were extraordinary compared with those of other grains.

Because bread was near the center of most American and European diets, wheat was the classic cash crop of western farming. Highly popular in most early frontier communities, it brought the best market prices of any grain, and was a ready source of income in a way that corn was not (unless first converted to pork or alcohol). Farmers sowed winter wheat in the fall, harrowed it to cover the seeds, and then harvested it in spring or early summer. Unfortunately, wheat farmers in Illinois and Iowa experienced a series of bad harvests in the late 1840s and early 1850s, caused by bad weather, winterkill, blight, rust, and various insect attacks. They tried many different techniques for responding to these problems, sheltering the wheat seeds to protect them from winterkill and changing the timing of crops so that they would not coincide with the life cycles of pest insects, but winter wheat continued to have difficulties. Many farmers therefore turned to spring wheat, which they planted after the thaw and harvested in late summer or fall.

Harvesting wheat was always much trickier than harvesting corn. Each ear of corn sat protected in its own husk, and so generally remained undamaged by wind, rain, or the death of its parent plant. Not so with wheat and the other small grains, which could topple from their own weight, or drop seeds to the ground when overmature, or rot if harvested wet. Timing was everything, causing considerable anxiety to farmers for whom a few days might make the difference between a profitable crop and a failed one. The hazards and hard labor of harvesting wheat were the chief reasons that prairie farmers responded quickly when Cyrus McCormick began to sell mechanical reapers from his Chicago factory in the 1840s and 1850s.

Risks such as these kept farmers from depending too heavily on any single grain. Although no farm resembled the original prairie in diversity of plant species, the typical one grew several crops, each in its own monocultural field. Wheat and corn were the most popular, wheat because it served as the classic frontier cash crop, corn because it was prolific and served well as animal feed. Farmers tried to arrange plantings of other crops so that they would not interfere with the life cycles and labor requirements of these two mainstays. Oats, rye, and barley sometimes got fields for themselves, with oats becoming more popular in the years following the Civil War as Chicago and other cities began to purchase large quantities for horse feed. For animal feed closer to home, farmers relied on hay, which they cut on remnant prairies in their vicinity. As prairies became scarcer later in the century, "tame grasses" raised in separate meadows took their place, with timothy, bluegrass, and clover the preferred crops.[8] Farm animals fed themselves on open pastures during the warm months of the year, and then subsisted on hay and corn when pastures gave out in the winter. For their part, farm families raised a variety of garden vegetables for use at home, ranging from root crops like potatoes and onions to legumes like peas and beans to cucurbits like melons and squash. Dairy cows supplied milk, cheese, and butter; poultry laid eggs; hogs produced pork; sheep yielded wool and mutton; and orchards rounded out the family diet with apples and cider. Every farm was a carefully partitioned landscape of fields, crops, and animals, each with its own unique requirements and life cycle. Farm families organized their lives around the delicate task of orchestrating these cycles, and tending the creatures that inhabited the small artificial ecosystem.

To make the farm succeed, people had to erect a variety of structures to divide the local landscape and protect its inhabitants: a farmhouse for the family, a barn and other outbuildings for the animals, sheds for tools and machinery, and fences to separate the pastures where animals grazed from the fields and meadows where plants grew. These structures were among the most visible symbols of second nature in the rural landscape, endlessly proliferating as farmers moved onto new soils.[9] But in building them, people had to confront the vice of the prairie's virtue: land that had no trees to be cleared for plowing also had no trees to be cut for lumber. The compromise solution in the beginning was to stay in the borderland between woodland and grassland. Early settlers located their farms near watercourses, which flowed like wooded ribbons through otherwise tree-less landscapes. As one emigrant handbook reported in 1838, the first prairie farms were "usually made on that part of the prairie which adjoins the timber," producing "a range of farms circumscribing the entire prairie as with a belt."[10] Farmers eventually fanned out from these woody areas but continued to rely on them for lumber and fuel. Even where no trees grew, wooden fences and buildings stood as silent reminders that those who inhabited the farm landscape survived by mingling the products of the forest with those of the prairie.

As people erected wooden structures on their land, they committed themselves to a practice that undermined the prairie ecosystem as subtly as farming itself. In addition to plowing up the sod, farmers did their best to stop the annual fires—many of them set by Indians—that had formerly kept trees from invading the grassland.[11] It made no sense to spend hundreds of hours and dollars erecting fences or building barns only to have them burn to the ground. So rural inhabitants employed various techniques—plowing firebreaks, mowing fields, reducing natural fuel sources, and fighting fires directly—to diminish the number of fires. Once fires ceased to burn back saplings, trees reappeared on whatever lands escaped the effects of plow or pasture, eventually creating a patchwork of small woodlots on land where farmers let them grow. Prairies, in other words, gave way before fields and forests alike. Still, the regrowth of oaks and other native hardwoods was too slow to supply the farmers' voracious demand for lumber and fuel. It was not long before farm families on the prairies looked to merchants in Chicago and elsewhere for alternate supplies of timber.

Fields, fences, and firebreaks were concrete embodiments of the environmental partitioning that made farming possible, but they also expressed the underlying property system that divided the land into ownership rights. Few other regions in the United States were better suited to the system which the government had used since 1785 for selling public lands, subdividing the nation into a vast grid of square-mile sections whose purpose was to turn land into real estate by the most economically expedient method. By imposing the same abstract and homogeneous grid pattern on all land, no matter how ecologically diverse, government surveyors made it marketable. As happened during Chicago's land craze of the 1830s, the grid turned the prairie into a commodity, and became the foundation for all subsequent land use.[12]

Starting in the second decade of the nineteenth century, when the government first began selling land in southern parts of Illinois, arriving settlers purchased their property in arbitrary units of sections, half sections, and 160-acre quarter sections. An apparently uniform terrain whose natural boundaries were so subtle as to seem almost invisible meant that the survey's checkerboard pattern caused few obvious problems: the grid gave shape to the pastures, meadows, and cornfields of a new agricultural order.[13] From that order would come a cornucopia of wheat and corn, livestock and poultry, all held within neatly rectilinear frames. Rectangular fields meant that farmers and horses could cut long, straight swaths whether they pulled plows, harrows, or newfangled tools like reapers. Because farm fields were large, uniform, and relatively free of rocks or other obstructions, prairie farmers enjoyed economies of scale which left them better able to adopt new agricultural machinery than many of their eastern counterparts—once they could afford to do so.

Despite the outward appearance of the grid, not all lands were equally advantageous. As the shopkeepers of Chicago learned to their sorrow, the flatness of the prairies subjected lowland areas to bad drainage and flooding. J. M. Peck's emigrant handbook warned arriving settlers in 1831 that farmers could easily get themselves into trouble by buying such land. "The emigrant," Peck wrote, "may mistake [*sic*] in the dry season, and fancy he has a rich, level, and dry farm in prospect, but the next spring will undeceive him." During wet seasons, water stood in plowed furrows and kept the soil dense and compact; during dry seasons, the land baked and cracked from drought.[14] Finding the ideal farm site entailed striking a balance between lands that had too much water and lands that had too little. Farmers tried to settle far enough from floodplains and wet prairies to avoid bad drainage, but they also needed to be near enough to a stream course to obtain supplies of wood and water.

Watercourses offered another advantage as well. Given the poor state of frontier roads, the rivers of the prairie were its highways. Farmers often sought to float their goods to market, for the land's flatness meant that prairie rivers had few rapids and were easily navigable when they held enough water. What the traveler Henry Rowe Schoolcraft said of the Illinois River in 1821 described many lesser streams as well: "the water," he wrote, "moves sluggishly, and, indeed, has more resemblance to a canal than to a stream."[15] Although one might travel slowly on such a river, one also traveled with relative ease and safety.

To go to market, farmers had either to build a raft or flatboat themselves or, as happened more often, to sell crops to a local merchant who combined them with other farmers' produce for shipment up or downstream.[16] Before 1850, typical western flatboats cost anywhere from $40 to $140 to construct, and might carry up to one hundred tons of produce.[17] On larger rivers, especially the Mississippi, one could book passage and ship goods on steamboats. Farmers still had to use wagons to reach the waterways, but one of the chief reasons they initially stayed on the margins of the prairies was to keep the trip to the river as short as possible. Just as booster theories suggested, waterways gathered produce from the countryside and swept it toward the markets—towns, cities, and would-be metropolises—that lay downstream.

For all these reasons, Euroamericans' initial agricultural occupation of the prairie country took place mainly along the spines of the chief watersheds.[18] As in Chicago, the earliest fur-trading communities had already located along the banks of important rivers and harbors. Farm settlements tended to spread out from these early market centers. When Chicago began its growth in 1833, the only sizable non-Indian populations in Illinois lived near St. Louis in the southwestern corner of the state—along the banks of the Mississippi and the lower reaches of the Illinois—and in the lead-mining district around Galena in the northwest. (Settlers occupied the Iowa side of the Mississippi at about the same time.) Two decades later, in 1850, settlements had begun to appear throughout the interior of the state, but population densities continued to be greatest along the river corridors: outside of Chicago's immediate vicinity, the Mississippi, Illinois, and Rock river valleys contained most of the state's inhabitants. The largest farm populations continued to cluster around St. Louis, which still had the best market in the region, but the construction of the Galena and Chicago Union Railroad had also begun to increase settlement west of Chicago.[19]

The settlers came from many places. Before the 1833 land rush, the major influx of population came via the Ohio and Mississippi rivers, with southern states—Kentucky, Tennessee, and Virginia as well as southern Ohio and Indiana—accounting for a disproportionate share of settlers. At the same time, a number of British families began to arrive either individ-

ually or in colonies.[20] By 1850, as the Great Lakes started to carry more
passenger traffic, increased numbers of settlers from New York, Pennsylvania, and New England were joining the stream of new arrivals. In their
midst were more and more foreign-born migrants, with Great Britain,
Ireland, and Germany contributing the greatest shares. Foreign migrants
settled disproportionately in cities: although Illinois as a whole was only
12.5 percent foreign-born in 1850, fully half of Cook County's inhabitants (most of them living in Chicago) had been born outside the United
States.[21] The relative "foreignness" of cities like Chicago, Milwaukee,
and St. Louis continued throughout the century, but rural settlements
also had their share of immigrant farm families.

A Sack's Journey

Whatever their ethnic origin, whether they spoke German or English,
increasing numbers of farmers meant increasing quantities of crops. Settlers did not solve the problem of selling those crops simply by hauling
them to the banks of the nearest river. They also had to find customers for
them, which was not always easy to do in a sparsely settled landscape with
few towns and even fewer cities. Farmers sold much of what they grew to
merchants and storekeepers in their immediate vicinity, acting out one of
the key market relationships in the emerging agricultural economy.
"There are," wrote Rebecca Burlend of her experiences as an immigrant
Englishwoman in southern Illinois during the 1830s, ". . . what are
termed store keepers, who supply the settlers with articles the most
needed, such as food, clothing, implements of husbandry, medicine, and
spirituous liquors: for which they receive in exchange the produce of their
farms, consisting of wheat, Indian corn, sugar, beef, bacon, &c."[22]
As Burlend suggests, the earliest storekeepers in rural areas wore at
least two hats: at the same time that they sold farmers retail goods, they
also served as wholesalers of farm crops because their customers had
nothing else with which to pay for merchandise.[23] Storekeepers needed
enough capital to purchase and warehouse farm produce in sufficient
quantities to justify shipping it off to more distant markets. Their financial
resources, although by no means large compared with those of urban
merchants, sometimes allowed them, as Burlend said, to "exercise a sort
of monopoly over a certain district," with the result that "their profits are
great, and they often become wealthy."[24] Compared with most farmers,
who could command little capital and credit, even the keeper of a small
village store looked well-to-do, at least in good years. But whatever the

disparity between farmers and storekeepers in relative wealth, each performed an essential function for the other. Without the farmers, storekeepers would have had neither customers to sell to nor crops to buy. And without the storekeepers' willingness to purchase produce and extend credit in advance of the harvest, many farmers could not have survived their own lack of capital in growing crops and bringing them to market.

Merchants could earn greater profits than farmers, but they also faced the prospect of considerably greater losses. Given the problems of water transport and the poor quality of information about prices in distant markets, wholesaling farm crops in pretelegraph, prerailroad days could be risky indeed. "No one can realize," wrote the merchant John Burrows of Davenport, Iowa, "the difficulties of doing a produce business in those days. We had no railroads. Everything had to be moved by water, and, of course, had to be held all winter."[25] It was all too easy to buy wheat and other crops in the fall and then find little or no market for them the following spring.

Burrows himself described a harrowing experience in the spring of 1844 involving a flatboat he had loaded with 2,500 bushels of potatoes. Although he was initially offered fifty cents a bushel for them at the mouth of the Illinois River, he refused, anticipating that he would sell them instead in New Orleans, where he had heard they were selling at $2.00 a bushel. Floating south, he discovered to his dismay that the prospect of high prices had encouraged other merchants to send potatoes toward New Orleans as well. The market was becoming glutted, so prices fell steadily as he moved downstream. By the time he reached Memphis, potatoes were bringing only twenty-five cents a bushel, and when he reached New Orleans, six weeks after he had started, there was no market for potatoes at all. He was finally forced to sell them—taking payment in coffee—to a Bermuda ship captain for eight cents a bushel, which, as Burrows lamented, "was just nothing at all," as it cost him "all of that to sprout, barrel, and deliver them."[26] One could easily go bankrupt under these circumstances, and many merchants did.

Rebecca Burlend defined the essential relationship between farmer and storekeeper when she wrote that stores "are in Illinois, nearly what markets are in England, only there is more barter in the former country."[27] Farmers bartered their produce because they were cash poor. In an economy short of cash, where credit was essential to making exchange possible, merchants served as translators between the world of rural barter and the world of urban money. Because storekeepers sold almost anything farmers needed, the general store became the outpost of a mar-

ket economy whether it was located in a town, in a village, or in the middle
of a prairie. By buying, storing, shipping, and reselling farm produce,
merchants linked farm communities to the trade of a wider world.

The gateways to that trade were almost invariably located in cities,
which acted as funnels for the increasing flood of grain and other farm
products being sent out of the countryside. Although Chicago was beginning to emerge in the 1830s and 1840s as a center for Great Lakes shipping, it lacked a water connection with inland areas until the canal opened
in 1848. For most early farm settlements on the Illinois and Iowa prairies,
the easiest markets to reach were downriver, at St. Louis or, more
remotely, New Orleans. When the English traveler William Oliver visited
St. Louis in 1842, he reported that the city had "a daily and extensive
market for all country produce," making purchases from "a large portion
of the surrounding district, within a distance of sixty or seventy miles."
The inhabitants of St. Louis consumed some of this produce themselves,
but most of it wound up in "the numerous and crowded steamers," which
Oliver said were "doubtless the cause of such a constant and large demand."[28] Goods loaded onto steamers or flatboats might be consumed
on board, sold to smaller communities along the river, or shipped to New
Orleans for resale or transfer to oceangoing vessels bound for ports on
the eastern seaboard and Europe.

Before the coming of the railroad, people traded grain at St. Louis and
Chicago in similar ways, although the physical circumstances of the two
towns differed markedly.[29] In both cities, the chief market for agricultural
produce was along the waterfront. Of the two, Chicago seemed less
suited by geography to accommodate the trade of its river. Most of the
city's grain merchants conducted their business in the vicinity of South
Water Street, immediately adjacent to the south bank of the Chicago
River.[30] Warehouses fronted directly on the water, rising three or four
stories above it and leaving little room for wagons to maneuver. Ships
were equally crowded in the narrow waterway. So hemmed in was the
river that it did not figure very prominently in people's mental image of
the city. Visitors to Chicago often mentioned the crowded bustle of its
streets and the long traffic jams that occurred when drawbridges over the
river were open, but they scarcely seemed to notice the river's wharves
and piers. Perhaps because Lake Michigan was so much more powerful as
a visual icon, the Chicago River dominated people's sense of Chicago
much less than the Mississippi shaped perceptions of St. Louis.

In St. Louis, the wharves were the heart of the town, so much so that
few visitors—most of whom arrived by boat—failed to comment on them.
The city's buildings sat well back from the riverfront to escape the Missis-

sippi's annual rise during spring floods. A broad open area known simply as the levee sloped down toward the river for the entire length of the town. The levee amounted to nothing less than a vast open-air market. As the German visitor Moritz Busch noted in 1852, "The landing square is regarded as the center of the city."[31] William Oliver said of it, "Large steamers are very frequently arriving and departing, and there is a constant bustle of lading and dislading at the levee."[32] When trading season was at its height, supplies overflowed the warehouses and piled up on the banks of the river, so the streets became "almost blockaded with boxes, barrels, bales and packages, much coming in, much also, going out."[33]

Whether on St. Louis's levee or Chicago's South Water Street, selling grain in the 1840s was a fairly straightforward business. A merchant like Burrows in Davenport would sack up the grain he had purchased from farmers in his vicinity, load it onto a flatboat or steamship, and float downstream to the docks at St. Louis. To reach Chicago during the 1840s, he would have made a similar trip by wagon. Once he arrived, he would unload his grain and try to sell it for cash to dealers who needed it to meet local demand. Much of the street and levee activity that struck visitors in Chicago and St. Louis consisted of sellers trying to find buyers and buyers trying to find sellers for the sacks of grain lying on the ground around them. One Chicago reporter said the buyers reminded him of nothing so much as "bees in a clover field."[34] As often as not, local dealers had all the grain they needed for home use, and so the would-be seller next turned to a commission merchant. Commission merchants made money not by buying grain on their own account but by arranging for its transportation to a larger city—New Orleans or New York being the two most obvious choices—where it might find a more welcoming market. The country merchant or farmer paid a commission for this service and took whatever profits or losses resulted from the final transaction.

To grasp the changes in grain marketing that occurred in Chicago during the 1850s, one must understand several key features of this early waterborne trading system. All hinged on the seemingly unremarkable fact that shippers, whether farmers or merchants, loaded their grain into sacks before sending it on its journey to the mill that finally ground it into flour. As the sack of grain moved away from the farm—whether pulled in wagons, floated on flatboats, or lofted on stevedores' backs—its contents remained intact, unmixed with grain from other farms. Nothing adulterated the characteristic weight, bulk, cleanliness, purity, and flavor that marked it as the product of a particular tract of land and a particular farmer's labor. When distant urban millers or wholesalers decided to buy the grain, they did so after examining a "representative sample" and then offering a price based on their judgment of its quality. Within any given level of market demand, price reflected how plump, clean, and pure a farm family had managed to make its grain.[35]

Intrinsic to this system of sack-based shipments was the fact that ownership rights to grain remained with its original shipper until it reached the point of final sale. The farmer or storekeeper who sold grain to a Chicago or St. Louis commission merchant continued to own it as it traveled the hundreds of miles to New Orleans or New York. This meant that the shipper bore all risks for damage that might occur during transit. If the grain became waterlogged, if it began to spoil in warm weather, if prices collapsed before it reached market, or if its ship sank, the resulting losses accrued not to the commission merchant or the transport company but to the original shipper.

Because these risks remained in the hands of farmers and merchants who were often of small means, insurance was a key service sold in large cities such as St. Louis or Chicago. Sellers of fire, marine, and commercial insurance, many of them agents of eastern companies, were among the largest businesses in Chicago by the 1840s, when at least one of them outranked city banks in financial resources.[36] Without the services of such firms, small shippers could all too easily face bankruptcy if some disaster happened before they could sell their goods. John Burrows described having been forced to delay his ill-fated potatoes on their journey to New Orleans because no one in St. Louis was initially willing to insure them: "I did not dare to send them forward without insurance," he wrote, "as my capital was all there."[37] Burrows's problem was finally solved by one of the largest St. Louis grain dealers, who supplied insurance on the condition that Burrows safeguard his potatoes by physically accompanying them on their journey downstream. Urban commission merchants often sold insurance in this way, and also advanced credit to shippers while goods were traveling to market—but both acts were implicit statements that ultimate legal responsibility remained with the shipper.

Sacks were the key to the whole water-based transportation system. Since grain originated in farms and villages that had only small quantities to sell, it had to start its journey on a modest scale, ideally suited to small groups of sacks. Once embarked on the river passage, sacks offered a convenient solution to the problem of loading the irregular holds of flatboats, keelboats, and steamboats. Moving goods by water almost always meant transferring them several times along the way, from pier to flatboat, from flatboat to levee, from levee to steamboat, from steamboat to sailing craft. Such transfers worked best if shipments were small enough that their weight and bulk did not prevent an individual worker from handling them. Moving grain on and off a ship usually meant negotiating tortuous passageways—across gangways, down stairs, through corridors, into storage bins—and the more complicated the path, the more critical the need to keep down the size of the unit being moved. Beyond these purely physical problems of water-based grain handling, the prevailing apparatus for transferring ownership rights also worked in favor of the sack system. Shippers and their customers wanted to know exactly what they were selling and buying, so it made sense not to break up individual shipments or mix them with others. In all these ways, marketing and transportation systems reflected each other. Sacks and ships seemed an ideal combination.

The water-based grain-marketing system at midcentury was thus designed to move wheat, corn, and other cereal crops without disrupting the link between grain as physical object and grain as salable commodity. At every point where grain moved from one form of transportation to another, it did so in individual bags on the backs of individual workers. Wherever it had to wait at transfer points, it did so in warehouses that kept individual lots carefully separated from each other. When shippers completed their final sales, they sold the rights to actual sacks of physical grain. A farm family sending a load of wheat from Illinois to New York could still have recovered that same wheat, packed with a bill of lading inside its original sacks, in a Manhattan warehouse several weeks later. The market had as yet devised few ways of separating grain as a priced commodity from the grain that had so recently clung to yellow stalks on the windy hillsides of former prairies.

The Golden Stream

The railroads changed all this. By giving rural shippers an alternative way to reach urban markets, they rerouted the flow of farm produce and encouraged new settlement patterns in the areas they serviced. Migrants to Illinois and Iowa had previously settled mainly in the river valleys nearest St. Louis; after 1848, they moved most quickly into the railroad corridors west of Chicago.[38] As they arrived, new settlers increased agricultural production on upland prairies which had heretofore seen little farming: the route of the Illinois Central, for instance, gave new access to the previously unsettled counties of the Grand Prairie in central Illinois.[39] Equally important were the grain shipments out of already settled areas which had formerly had no alternative to rivers for bringing crops to market.[40] By lowering land transportation costs, the railroad allowed farmers to sell more grain and heightened their expectations about the scale of their own production.

The predictable result was an explosion in Chicago's receipts of grain. As late as 1850, St. Louis was still handling over twice as much wheat and flour as Chicago, but within five years the younger city had far surpassed its older rival. The same shift occurred in the waterborne corn trade after 1848 when the Illinois and Michigan Canal began to bring corn north toward Lake Michigan.[41] As the canal and railroads increased the flow of grain into Chicago's warehouses, they simultaneously encouraged an expansion of shipping out of its harbor, contributing to a general reorientation of western trade toward the east and away from the south. Between 1850 and 1854, the net eastward movement of freight shipments via the Great Lakes finally surpassed shipments out of New Orleans.[42] No place was more important than Chicago to this redirection of agricultural trade. The city and its merchants changed forever the way prairie farmers could sell their crops. At the same time, the farmers and their crops fundamentally altered Chicago's markets.

The immense amounts of grain pouring into Chicago expanded the city's markets, but quantity alone was not the whole story. Compared with other modes of transportation, railroad cars moved grain more quickly and in standardized carloads of medium size. With whole freight cars, for instance, carrying nothing but wheat, shippers and railroad managers soon came to think of grain shipments not as individual "sacks" but as "carloads" consisting of about 325 bushels each.[43] The railroad brought grain into the city through the narrow gateways represented by tracks, sidings, and stations. As more and more trains passed more and more frequently through those gateways, adding their grain to the loads that farmers were still hauling in their wagons, freight traffic congestion became more of a problem. As the *Chicago Democratic Press* reported during the harvest season of 1854, "The piles of grain now lying uncovered in our streets, the choked and crowded thoroughfares, the overloaded teams, the bursting bags, . . . all testify to a wide-felt want of room. . . . We want more warehouses. . . . We want more cars and locomotives."[44]

Geography and the logic of capital meant that congestion *felt* different in Chicago than in St. Louis. The 2.1 million bushels of wheat that passed across the St. Louis levee in 1854 moved among hundreds of boats and ships scattered along hundreds of yards of waterfront.[45] Hundreds of individuals, many of whom possessed only small amounts of capital, shared responsibility for making sure that grain continued safely on its journey. Although the 3.0 million bushels of wheat that passed through Chicago during that same year was only moderately larger than St. Louis's shipments in total size, well over a million of those bushels entered the city via the tracks of just one railroad, the Galena and Chicago Union.[46] In Chicago, a small group of railroad managers bore the heavy financial responsibility of moving millions of bushels of grain. Given the large capital investment represented by a railroad's cars, sidings, and other equipment, managers had a strong incentive to accelerate the speed with which employees emptied grain cars and returned them to active service. Rapid turnaround was imperative if managers were to maximize their use of capital equipment and prevent congestion.

Achieving these goals meant getting grain out of its sacks, off the backs of individual workers, and into automatic machinery that would move it more rapidly and efficiently. The invention that made this possible was among the most important yet least acknowledged in the history of American agriculture: the steam-powered grain elevator.[47] First introduced in 1842 by a Buffalo warehouseman named Joseph Dart, it was soon adopted by grain dealers in Chicago as well. By the end of the 1850s, Chicagoans had refined their elevator system beyond that of any other city, leading the way toward a transformation of grain marketing worldwide.[48]

Structurally, the elevator was a multistoried warehouse divided into numbered vertical bins containing different lots of grain. But as Anthony Trollope observed of his visit to a Chicago elevator in 1861, "it was not as a storehouse that this great building was so remarkable, but as a channel or a river course for the flooding freshets of corn."[49] What distinguished an elevator from earlier warehouses was its use of machinery instead of human workers to move grain into and out of the building. Grain entered the structure on an endless steam-powered conveyor belt to which large scoops or buckets were attached. After riding the buckets to the top of the building, the grain was weighed on a set of scales—a technique that soon encouraged Chicago dealers to define their standard bushels according to weight rather than volume.[50] Grain dropped out the bottom of the scale into a rotating chute mechanism, which elevator operators could direct into any of the numbered bins inside the warehouse. Once it was inside the bins, workers could deliver grain to a waiting ship or railroad car simply by opening a chute at the bottom of the building and letting gravity do the rest of the work.[51]

Small horse-powered elevators were used in Chicago throughout the prerailroad 1840s, but it was not until 1848 that the first steam-powered grain elevator appeared. Built by Captain Robert C. Bristol, it was a four-story brick building measuring 75 feet square and having a total capacity of over 80,000 bushels.[52] Large by the standards of its day, Bristol's elevator was soon dwarfed by larger ones as the flow of grain through the city increased. Within less than a decade the largest elevators in Chicago—all either owned by or closely affiliated with major railroads—were almost ten times bigger than Bristol's.

Elevators of this size were constructed from two-inch wooden planks bolted on top of each other and bound with iron rods to form walls ten inches thick. The Chicago and Rock Island Railroad's largest warehouse in 1856, with a 700,000-bushel capacity, contained ninety bins measuring 10 feet by 22 feet and standing 41 feet high. They were served by ten conveyor belt elevators, and the entire structure weighed 2,400 tons when full of grain.[53] The multiplication of such facilities during the 1850s gave Chicago the ability to handle more grain more quickly than any other city in the world. By 1857, it had a dozen elevators whose combined capacity of over four million bushels meant that the city could *store* more wheat than St. Louis would *ship* during that entire year.[54]

Now some of the hidden costs of the river transportation system began to be more apparent. Chicago newspapers delighted in describing the way St. Louis might deal with a steamboat carrying 10,000 bushels of grain:

> It comes in sacks—which have to be taken from the boat by a crowd of lazy laborers, who wearily carry it on their shoulders, sack by sack, and pile it on the levee. There it has the privilege of laying twenty-four hours, when it has to be moved in drays, either to a warehouse, or to some part of the levee to be shipped, where the same slow process has to be repeated. Everything is done by manual labor. . . .[55]

The net result was that a 10,000-bushel shipment of grain arriving in St. Louis might involve "the labor of probably two or three hundred Irishmen, negroes and mules for a couple of days."[56] One cannot, of course, accept such descriptions at face value, given the pro-Chicago, antiblack, and anti-Irish prejudices that came easily to this booster author. The slowness of those "Irishmen, negroes and mules" had less to do with laziness than with the inherent difficulties of hauling so many burlap sacks from one vessel to another. The work was hard, the transport technology crude, and grain thus took its time passing through St. Louis.

The movement of grain on the rivers had always been labor-intensive, and remained so as long as shipments continued to travel in sacks. As a result, St. Louis enjoyed few economies of scale as the trade of its levee grew; instead, it simply increased its employment of dockworkers, many of them slaves and recent immigrants. Elevator construction was discouraged by the fact that no single carrier on the river could guarantee a steady flow of grain through such a facility comparable to the golden torrent delivered by Chicago's railroads. The ease of constructing cheap flatboats set a limit on how much capital could profitably be invested in large steamboats, which in turn discouraged the development of more expensive grain handling equipment.[57] Beyond this, the constantly changing height of the Mississippi River, which rose and fell by more than forty feet during extreme seasons, suggested to many that permanent grain elevators would never be practical on the levee: if they were constructed far enough from the river to escape the spring floods, they would be too far from the riverbank during the rest of the year.[58] (In this respect, the apparent disadvantages of the Chicago River's "sluggish, slimy steam, too lazy to clean itself," proved unexpectedly beneficial to trade.)[59] For all these reasons, antebellum St. Louis investors were unwilling to risk the hundreds of thousands of dollars needed to build elevators similar to those in Chicago.[60] St. Louis did not have a working grain elevator until after the Civil War.[61] As a result, sacks of grain passing through the river city had to pay an overhead cost of six to eight cents more per bushel for additional handling.[62] Even the sacks themselves cost two to four cents apiece.[63]

The increasing scale and efficiency of Chicago's grain-handling technology depended on one condition: moving wheat, corn, or other crops without recourse to old-fashioned sacks. Grain entering Chicago might arrive in wagons or canalboats or railroad cars, but to move up an elevator's conveyor belts, it had to be sackless. Only then could corn or wheat cease to act like solid objects and begin to behave more like liquids: golden streams that flowed like water. If farmers avoided sacks and simply loaded their grain directly into a railroad car or canalboat, an elevator chute inserted into the vehicle could lift and pour the grainy liquid into any elevator bin ready to receive it. The *Chicago Daily Press* described the process in 1857 as follows:

> Our warehouses are all erected on the river and its branches, with railroad tracks running in the rear of them, so that a train of cars loaded with grain may be standing opposite one end of a large elevating warehouse, being emptied by elevators, at the rate of from six to eight thousand bushels per hour, while at the other end the same grain may be running into a couple of propellers [ships], and be on its way to Buffalo, Oswego, Ogdensburgh or Montreal within six or seven hours. And all this is done without any noise or bustle; and with but little labor, except that of machinery.[64]

A large elevator like that of the Illinois Central could simultaneously empty twelve railroad cars and load two ships at the rate of 24,000 bushels per hour. It was, as Trollope said, "a world in itself,—and the dustiest of all the worlds."[65] When all twelve of the city's elevators were operating at full capacity, Chicago could receive and ship nearly half a million bushels of grain every ten hours. The economic benefits of such efficient handling were so great that moving a bushel of grain from railroad car to lake vessel cost only half a cent, giving Chicago a more than tenfold advantage over St. Louis.[66]

These were great benefits to derive from the simple expedient of doing away with grain sacks, but they quickly raised a serious new problem that called into question the entire legal apparatus of the earlier grain-marketing system. Formerly, the transportation network had assiduously maintained the bond of ownership between shippers and the physical grain they shipped. Farmer Smith's wheat from Iowa would never be mixed with Farmer Jones's wheat from Illinois until some final customer purchased both. Now this started to change. As the scale of Chicago's grain trade grew, elevator operators began objecting to keeping small quantities of different owners' grain in separate bins that were only partially filled—for an unfilled bin represented underutilized capital. To avoid that disagreeable condition, they sought to mix grain in common bins. Crops from dozens of different farms could then mingle, and the reduced cost of handling would earn the elevator operator higher profits. The only obstacle to achieving this greater efficiency was the small matter of a shipper's traditional legal ownership of physical grain.

The organization that eventually solved this problem—albeit after several years of frustrated efforts and false starts—was the Chicago Board of Trade. Founded as a private membership organization in March 1848, the Board initially had eighty-two members drawn from a wide range of commercial occupations.[67] In the beginning, it had no special focus on the grain trade. Its principal goals were to monitor and promote the city's commercial activity, and to resolve any disputes that might arise among its members. Like boards of trade and chambers of commerce then emerging in other western cities, it sought to represent the collective voice of business interests in the city.[68] During the Board's first few years of existence, its members passed resolutions concerning canal tolls, telegraph services, harbor improvements, and other matters affecting the city's economy. Nonetheless, its accomplishments were few, partly because its real powers were limited. Its members could issue pronouncements, lobby politicians, and exercise moral suasion on other merchants. They could also agree among themselves that all Board members must follow certain business practices, with clearly prescribed penalties up to and including loss of Board membership. This internal regulatory mechanism soon emerged as the Board's most important power, enabling its members to regulate trade in Chicago by reaching collective consensus about their own best interests.

As in all voluntary organizations, members reached consensus most easily when their common interest was clear. The Board's earliest activities in the grain trade therefore focused on improving Chicago's inspection and measurement systems, since all legitimate traders had an interest in agreeing upon uniform weights and measures as a way of suppressing fraud. Elevators, with their automatic mechanisms for handling large quantities of grain in continuously moving streams, made the old measure of grain volume—a bushel of standard size—obsolete. Starting in 1854, therefore, the Board pressed city merchants to replace the old, volume-based bushel with a new, weight-based bushel that could be used to calibrate elevator scales.[69] The need for such a standard was indisputable, but members still argued about how much a bushel should weigh. In the early 1850s, Board meetings saw considerable controversy over how much a unit of shelled corn should weigh in Chicago: some members wanted a standard bushel to weigh sixty pounds while others recommended fifty-six. In the absence of a clear consensus, both measures continued to be used for several years, with two separate sets of prices, until sixty-pound bushels emerged as the standard and did away with the confusion.[70]

The trouble members had in agreeing about even so basic a standard as this suggests the Board's ineffectiveness during its first half decade. Throughout the early 1850s, it held annual meetings in borrowed rooms, issued pronouncements, and attracted few new members. Although its officers made continual efforts to hold daily meetings at which members could trade grain and other commodities at a single central location, they had great difficulty persuading anyone to come. The membership roll for a nine-day period in July 1851, for instance, reveals that only one member showed up on four of the days; no one at all was present on four others. Even the offer of free refreshments failed to increase attendance.[71] Chicago's grain market continued to be as decentralized as ever, with traders conducting their transactions in offices, warehouses, and streets all around the city.

Not until European demand for grain expanded during the Crimean War did the fortunes of the Board begin to change. American wheat exports doubled in volume and tripled in value during 1853 and 1854, while domestic prices rose by more than 50 percent.[72] The surge of foreign buying had impressive effects in Chicago. Between 1853 and 1856, the total amount of grain shipped from Chicago more than tripled, with 21 million bushels leaving the city in 1856 alone.[73] As volume increased and traders found it more convenient to do their business centrally, attendance at daily Board meetings rose. Rather than argue over prices amid heaps of grain in streets and warehouses, traders—usually working on commission for real owners and purchasers—brought samples to the Board's meeting rooms, dickered over prices, and arranged contracts among buyers and sellers. The greater the number of traders who gathered in a single market, the more efficient and attractive that market became. By 1856, Board leaders felt confident enough of their organization's importance that they stopped serving cheese, crackers, and ale to encourage attendance. The advantages of the centralized market were soon so great that no serious grain merchant could afford not to belong, and so the Board began to issue membership cards that traders had to show to a doorkeeper before entering the meeting rooms. Daily meetings on the floor of what was beginning to be called 'Change (short for "Exchange") soon became so crowded that the Board moved to new quarters on the corner of LaSalle and South Water streets.[74]

Its membership now numbering in the hundreds, the Board finally had sufficient influence to seek a new role: increasingly, its members would take it upon themselves to regulate the city's grain trade. By promulgating rules which all traders using its market agreed to follow, the Board in effect set uniform standards for the city as a whole, and for its grain-raising hinterland as well. Its system of regulations, proposed for the first time in 1856, restructured Chicago's market in a way that would forever transform the grain trade of the world. In that year, the Board made the momentous decision to designate three categories of wheat in the city—white winter wheat, red winter wheat, and spring wheat—and to set standards of quality for each.[75]

In this seemingly trivial action lay the solution to the elevator operators' dilemma about mixing different owners' grain in single bins. As long as one treated a shipment of wheat or corn as if it possessed unique characteristics that distinguished it from all other lots of grain, mixing was impossible. But if instead a shipment represented a particular "grade" of grain, then there was no harm in mixing it with other grain of the same grade. Farmers and shippers delivered grain to a warehouse and got in return a receipt that they or anyone else could redeem at will. Anyone who gave the receipt back to the elevator got in return not the *original* lot of grain but an equal quantity of *equally graded* grain. A person who owned grain could conveniently sell it to a buyer simply by selling the elevator receipt, and as long as both agreed that they were exchanging equivalent quantities of *like* grain—rather than the physical grain that the seller had originally deposited in the elevator—both left happy at the end of the transaction. It was a momentous change: as one visitor to Chicago later remarked after a tour of one of the elevators, "It dawns on the observer's mind that one man's property is by no means kept separate from another man's."[76] The grading system allowed elevators to sever the link between ownership rights and physical grain, with a host of unanticipated consequences.[77]

The Board's grading system was initially quite informal, each elevator more or less setting its own rules for sorting grain into the new grades. Within two years, however, the Board had imposed much more formal grading regulations, for reasons that had to do with another problem that occurred when grain from different owners mixed together in single bins. Farmers had been complaining for years that prices paid in Chicago markets did not adequately reflect differences in quality among different shipments of grain.[78] One correspondent of the Chicago-based *Prairie Farmer* in 1852 told of an instance in which four farmers arrived in the city, one with sprouted wheat, one with dirty wheat, one with good wheat that had been intentionally mixed with dirt and chaff, and one with good clean wheat of prime quality. Despite such wide variations in the real value of what they had to sell, all four received from forty-seven to fifty cents per bushel—because elevator operators had no reliable way to grade and separate grains of different quality as they entered the warehouse. Under such circumstances, farmers had little incentive to keep their grain clean, and so Chicago's grain had developed a reputation among eastern buyers for being particularly dirty and bad. Indeed, as the third farmer had discovered, one could sometimes make grain more valuable by mixing it with cheaper substances—not all of them palatable—to increase its weight and hence its price. The *Prairie Farmer*'s correspondent concluded, "There is no wonder then, that our wheat should be thought so little of in Eastern markets."[79]

Dirty, mixed, and generally low-quality grain became a growing problem during the nationwide depression that began in 1857. As farmers struggled to earn adequate incomes in the wake of collapsing grain prices—spring wheat fell by more than half from the beginning of 1856 to the end of 1857—they either did not bother to clean their wheat thoroughly or mixed it with lower-priced materials like oats, rye, and chaff to increase its weight and hence its value at the elevator scales.[80] "We are credibly informed, and believe," reported a committee of the Board of Trade in 1858, "that it is a common occurrence, for farmers to send damp and dirty grain to this market, calculating that under the present system of inspection it will bring about as much as it would if it were thoroughly cleaned and in good order. . . ."[81] Grain merchants in the city found that they were having more trouble than usual selling wheat identified as coming from the Chicago market. They got better prices by claiming, falsely, that they were selling "Milwaukee Club"—the best grain from Wisconsin, which brought five to eight cents more per bushel in New York than did "Chicago Spring"—with the result, according to one newspaper report, that western merchants appeared to be selling four times more Milwaukee Club to New York than farmers had actually raised in Wisconsin.[82]

Worried that such reports would soon hurt their market, members of the Board of Trade adopted a series of reforms between 1857 and 1859 designed to improve the reputation of Chicago grain. The key step was to make formal distinctions between grains of different quality. Starting in 1857, the Board no longer recognized "spring wheat" as a single category, but instead broke it into three grades ranked from high quality to low: "Club Spring," "No. 1 spring," and "No. 2 spring."[83] Even these proved inadequate, for in 1858 a Board committee announced that "to improve the character of our grain it will be necessary hereafter to reject entirely much of the grain that has heretofore passed as standard in this market."[84] Board members therefore added a fourth category—"Rejected"—to define the bottom of the scale.

The Board adopted comparable grades for corn, oats, rye, and barley, but the greater value of wheat meant that its grading scale became more complicated than the others as traders struggled to devise a standardized system that could adequately distinguish among wheat shipments of different quality. Over the next several years, grading scales became ever more elaborate; by 1860, there were no fewer than ten different grades for wheat alone. Distinctions among grades inevitably depended to a considerable degree on subjective judgment: No. 1 white winter, for instance, required that the berry "be plump, well cleaned and free from other grains," while No. 2 white winter was "sound, but not clean enough for No. 1."[85] There was plenty of room for disagreement in these standards, but grades and the measures of quality they reflected—plumpness, purity, cleanliness, and weight—quickly became more and more clearly defined. The best grain was plumper, purer, cleaner, drier, and heavier than its competitors.

To make sure that the city's elevators applied these grades consistently in filling their bins, Board members in 1857 for the first time resolved to appoint an official "grain inspector of the city at large" who would be "competent and a good judge of the qualities of the different kinds of grain."[86] In 1860, after a brief unsuccessful period of working with inspectors employed by the elevators, the chief inspector was ordered to hire and train a committee of assistants who, for a standard fee, would examine grain shipments and certify the grade of any elevator receipt traded on the floor of 'Change.[87] To enable inspectors to do their work, the Board got the city's elevator operators to agree (not altogether enthusiastically) that they would allow inspectors to enter warehouses to make sure that the grain in individual bins was actually of the grade that the elevator claimed it to be. This last step was crucial, for only thus could the Board guarantee that people purchasing elevator receipts in its meeting rooms would receive grain of the designated quality when they went to reclaim their shipments. Inspection underpinned the integrity of the grading system, which underpinned the integrity of the elevators, which underpinned the integrity of the Board's own markets.

The Board's inspection system was not without fraud, and over the years it came under repeated attack by people who worried that inspectors might be winking at corrupt practices. But since the Board's members included just as many buyers as sellers—most members regularly operated on both sides of the market—the organization as a whole had a clear interest in honest grading. Even critics of the system acknowledged this. "That there are advantages in a well arranged and equitable grading system," observed the editors of the *Prairie Farmer* in 1861, "no one can deny—it is an incentive to send good and merchantable well cleaned grain to market. It facilitates the handling of the large amounts of grain that find their way to this market, and without which it would be difficult to do it."[88] The Board's inspectors might not always be competent, and they might not always detect the frauds that could be perpetrated in elevator bins. Everyone recognized "the great importance of placing men of character and sound judgment in these important positions."[89] Individual inspectors undoubtedly engaged in dishonest practices from time to time, but the Board of Trade as a whole had no structural reason to bias inspections in one direction or another. Quite the contrary: all honest members benefited from knowing exactly what they were buying and selling.

The Board's right to impose standardized grades and inspection rules on its members—and hence on the Chicago market as a whole—was written into Illinois law in 1859, when the state legislature granted the organization a special charter as "a body politic and corporate."[90] Under its terms, the Board gained the right to hire inspectors and measurers whose judgments about grain quality would be legally binding on Board members, who by now included among their number most grain traders in Chicago. If a dispute arose between members about whether someone had failed to fulfill a trading contract, a Board committee had the power to arbitrate between them. Remarkably, the charter declared that once the committee had rendered its decision, the ruling would have the same legal force "as if it were a judgment rendered in the Circuit Court." New members joining the organization were required to swear an oath—with the full force of binding contract behind it—that they would obey the Board's rules, regulations, and bylaws, in effect abandoning much of their right of appeal to the civil courts. The effect of the charter was that the Chicago Board of Trade—a private membership organization of grain merchants—became a quasi-judicial entity with substantial legal powers to regulate the city's trade.[91]

Futures

By 1859, then, Chicago had acquired the three key institutions that defined the future of its grain trade: the elevator warehouse, the grading system, and, linking them, the privately regulated central market governed by the Board of Trade. Together, they constituted a revolution. As Henry Crosby Emery, one of the nineteenth century's leading scholars of commodity markets, wrote in 1896, "the development of the system of grading and of elevator receipts is the most important step in the history of the grain trade."[92] The changes in Chicago's markets suddenly made it possible for people to buy and sell grain not as the physical product of human labor on a particular tract of prairie earth but as an abstract claim on the golden stream flowing through the city's elevators.

Chicagoans began to discover that a grain elevator had much in common with a bank—albeit a bank that paid no interest to its depositors. Farmers or shippers took their wheat or corn to an elevator operator as if they were taking gold or silver to a banker. After depositing the grain in a bin, the original owner accepted a receipt that could be redeemed for grain in much the same way that a check or banknote could be redeemed for precious metal. Again as with a bank, as long as people were confident that the elevator contained plenty of grain, they did not need to cash the receipt to make it useful. Because the flow of grain through the Chicago elevators was enormous, one could almost always count on them to contain enough grain to "back up" one's receipt: the volume of the city's trade in effect made receipts interchangeable. Instead of completing a sale by redeeming the receipt and turning over the physical grain to a purchaser, the original owner could simply turn over the receipt itself. The entire transaction could be completed—and repeated dozens of times—without a single kernel of wheat or corn moving so much as an inch. The elevators effectively created a new form of money, secured not by gold but by grain. Elevator receipts, as traded on the floor of 'Change, accomplished the transmutation of one of humanity's oldest foods, obscuring its physical identity and displacing it into the symbolic world of capital.[93]

The elevator helped turn grain into capital by obscuring and distancing its link with physical nature, while another new technology extended that process by weakening its link with geography. In 1848, the same year that Chicago merchants founded the Board of Trade, the first telegraph lines reached the city. The earliest messages from New York had to be relayed through Detroit and took some eighteen hours to arrive, but that seemed nearly instantaneous compared with the days or weeks such messages had taken before.[94] As the telegraph system expanded across the nation and became more efficient, hours became seconds. By the Civil War, there were 56,000 miles of telegraph wire throughout the country, annually carrying some five million messages with lightning speed.[95]

Because commodity prices were among the most important bits of information that traveled the wires, the coming of the telegraph meant that eastern and western markets began to move in tandem much more than before.[96] As a result, those with the best access to telegraph news were often in the best position to gauge future movements of prices. The *Chicago Democrat* in September 1848 related the story of a Chicagoan who had raced down to the docks after receiving word from the telegraph office that wheat prices were rising on the East Coast. "Seeking among the holders of Illinois wheat, whom he might make a meal of," he

soon came across his man, and immediately struck a bargain for a cargo at eighty cents per bushel, the seller chuckling over his trade. In less than fifteen minutes, however, the market rose to eighty-five, and the fortunate possessor of the news by the last flash pocketed the cool five hundred.[97]

Although telegraphic information created speculative opportunities of this sort, it also increased the efficiency of regional markets by giving traders throughout the country speedier access to the same news. To the extent that local price differences reflected uncertainty about conditions in other markets—uncertainty of the sort John Burrows had experienced when he launched his unlucky boatload of potatoes down the Mississippi—the telegraph brought prices in distant places closer together by reducing the chance that people would act on bad information. In the wake of the telegraph, news of western harvests brought instant shifts in New York markets, while news of European wars or grain shortages just as rapidly changed prices in Chicago. Local events—a drought, say, or an early frost—ceased to be so important in setting prices for grain or other crops. If local circumstances forced up prices at one place, the telegraph allowed knowledgeable buyers to go elsewhere, driving local prices back down. As markets became more efficient, their prices discounted local conditions and converged with regional, national, and even international price levels. The wider the telegraph's net became, the more it unified previously isolated economies. The result was a new market geography that had less to do with the soils or climate of a given locality than with the prices and information flows of the economy as a whole.[98]

As part of its new landscape of information, the telegraph helped focus attention on cities that already had large trade volumes. A farmer in

Iowa inevitably wanted to know wheat prices in Chicago, just as a banker in Chicago wanted to know interest rates in New York. Although the telegraph dispersed price information across an ever widening geographical field, it also concentrated the sources of such information in a few key markets. The dense flow of news in cities like Chicago and New York allowed their prices to reflect trade conditions not just for the local economy but for the national and even the global economy. Once such central markets had become established, people in other places looked to New York and Chicago prices before all others, enhancing the significance and geographical reach of those two cities in a kind of self-fulfilling prophecy.

The new communication technology had much to do with making the Chicago Board of Trade one of the key grain markets in the world by the late 1850s. The Board began regularly posting telegraph messages from New York in 1858, and the Chicago newspapers started carrying daily market reports from New York, Buffalo, Oswego, and Montreal shortly thereafter. When Board members moved into their new Exchange Hall in 1860, they made sure that a telegraph office occupied the western end of the trading room.[99] The same new emphasis on telegraphic information occurred in New York as well, where the New York Stock Exchange rose to prominence as the national market for securities during the same period and in much the same way.[100] News of events in these emerging central markets flashed outward along the wires and helped set prices wherever it went. One eastern traveler in 1851 remarked after seeing a telegraph line crossing the Mississippi River,

> It seemed like the nervous system of the nation, conveying, quick as thought, the least sensation from extremity to head, the least volition from head to extremity. . . . Or, like a vast arterial system, it carries the pulsations of the heart to the farthest extremity; and by these wires stretched across the Mississippi, I could hear the sharp, quick beating of the great heart of New York.[101]

But the very speed of that heartbeat's spreading rhythm created a problem: although prices might travel from New York to Chicago and back again in a matter of minutes or seconds, grain could hardly do the same. Bushels of wheat or corn still took days or weeks to complete their eastward journey. Since everything depended on buyers' being able to examine grain before they offered a price for it, at least part of the shipment had to reach its destination before parties to the sale could reach an agreement. The old grain-marketing system had solved this difficulty by sending forward a small express sample of the larger shipment, allowing eastern buyers to make their purchases before the bulk of the grain arrived. But there was no way in which even small samples could move quickly enough to lock in the prices coming over telegraph wires. By the time a sample or shipment reached its eastern destination so that buyers could make an offer after examining it, prices might already have changed drastically. Neither buyers nor sellers were happy about the risks such delayed transactions entailed.

Fortunately for both parties, there was a way around this dilemma. If buyers and sellers could complete their grain transactions by telegraph, they could escape the risk and uncertainty of a fluctuating market. However much prices might change in the future, merchants and millers could know that they would receive their grain at the price they expected. The means to this happy end were already available from the same institution that had resolved the elevators' problem of mixing grain in common bins. When the Board of Trade adopted a standard grading system, it made grain interchangeable not just between elevator bins but between cities and continents as well. Once people inside and outside Chicago began to know and trust the Board's new grades, a New York grain dealer could purchase five thousand bushels of Chicago No. 2 spring wheat solely on the basis of prices quoted over the telegraph lines. No longer was it necessary to see a sample of any particular shipment, for all grain of a given grade was for practical purposes identical. A New Yorker could simply check telegraph quotations from the floor of 'Change and wire back an order when the price seemed right, without having to examine a sample of the grain in advance.

Telegraphic orders of this sort encouraged a sharp rise in what traders called "to arrive" contracts for grain. Under these contracts, a seller promised to deliver grain to its buyer by some specified date in the future. Like the telegraph, "to arrive" contracts significantly diminished the risks of trading grain. With the advent of standard grades, it became possible to sell grain to its final customer before it actually began its journey east. A western seller could sign a contract agreeing to deliver grain to an eastern buyer at a specified price within thirty days or some other period of time. With the sale thus guaranteed, most of the *time*-related risks of grain storage or transportation disappeared: had John Burrows been able to use the telegraph to contract in advance for delivering his boatload of potatoes in New Orleans, his journey would have had a much happier ending.[102] Moreover, banks were willing to offer loans to farmers and shippers on the basis of such contracts, so commission merchants found their credit requirements significantly reduced. Customers no longer needed to borrow from commission merchants, but could get immediate cash by using their "to arrive" contracts and elevator receipts as security for bank loans.[103] Such "to arrive" contracts were an old legal form that had been in use on a small scale at Buffalo, Chicago, and other grain-trading cities since the 1840s, but the telegraph and the grading system gave them unprecedented popularity.[104]

"To arrive" contracts in combination with standardized elevator receipts made possible Chicago's greatest innovation in the grain trade: the futures market.[105] "To arrive" contracts solved a problem for grain shippers by ending their uncertainty about future price changes; at the same time, they opened up new opportunities for speculators who were willing to absorb the risk of price uncertainty themselves. If one was willing to gamble on the direction of future price movements, one could make a "to arrive" contract for grain one did not yet own, since one could always buy grain from an elevator to meet the contract just before it fell due. This is exactly what speculators did. Contracting to sell grain one didn't yet own—"selling short"—enabled one to gamble that the price of grain when the contract fell due would be lower than the contract's purchaser was legally bound to pay. By promising to deliver ten thousand bushels of wheat at seventy cents a bushel by the end of June, for instance, one could make $500 if the price of wheat was actually only sixty-five cents at that time, since the buyer had contracted to pay seventy cents whatever the market price. When June came to an end, one had only to buy the necessary number of elevator receipts at their current price on the Chicago Board of Trade, and use them to fulfill the terms of the contract. Given the enormous volume of elevator receipts in circulation, there was little reason to fear that grain would not be available when the "to arrive" contract fell due.

It is impossible to fix the earliest date at which a full-fledged futures market existed in Chicago. The city's newspapers commented on the frequency of sales for future delivery as early as the Crimean War (1853–56).[106] Such sales, however, were often "to arrive" contracts which speculators secured by borrowing elevator receipts from actual holders of grain, and so (unlike true futures contracts) were limited in scale by the number of receipts in circulation.[107] During the Civil War, the Union army's demand for oats and pork generated a huge speculative market in those commodities, which finally helped institutionalize futures trading as a standard feature of the Chicago Board of Trade. It was no accident that the Board adopted its first formal rules governing futures contracts in 1865.[108]

At whatever point we choose to locate its origins, a new sort of grain market had emerged at the Chicago Board of Trade by the second half of the 1860s. Alongside the older, more familiar market, in which traders bought and sold elevator receipts for grain actually present in the city, there was a growing market in contracts for the *future* delivery of grain that perhaps did not even exist yet. These new contracts represented a departure from the older grain market in several key ways. As defined by the Board's bylaws, they referred not to actual physical grain but to fixed quantities of standardized *grades* of grain. They called for delivery not at the moment the contract was struck but at a future date and time that was also standardized by the Board's rules. The contract, in other words, followed a rigidly predefined form, so that, as Henry Emery noted, "only the determination of the total amount and the price is left open to the contracting parties."[109] This meant that futures contracts—like the elevator receipts on which they depended—were essentially interchangeable, and could be bought and sold quite independently of the physical grain that might or might not be moving through the city.

Moreover, the seller of such a contract did not necessarily even have to deliver grain on the day it fell due. As long as the buyer was willing, the two could settle their transaction by simply exchanging the difference between the grain's contracted price and its market price when the contract expired. Imagine, for instance, that Jones sold Smith a futures contract for 10,000 bushels of No. 2 spring wheat at 70 cents a bushel, to be delivered at the end of June. If that grade was in fact selling for 68 cents a bushel on June 30, Jones could either purchase 10,000 bushels at the lower price and deliver the receipts to Smith or—more conveniently still—accept a cash payment of $200 from Smith to make up the difference between the contract price and the market price. Had the wheat cost 72 cents on June 30, on the other hand, Jones would have paid Smith the $200.[110]

In either case, Jones and Smith could complete their transaction without any grain ever changing hands. Although those who sold futures contracts were legally bound to deliver grain if requested to do so, in practice they rarely had to. As the historian Morton Rothstein has aptly put it, the futures market, when viewed in the most cynical terms, was a place where "men who don't own something are selling that something to men who don't really want it."[111] Resolving this apparent paradox reveals the extent to which the Chicago grain market had distanced itself from the agricultural world around it. The futures market was a market not in grain but in the *price* of grain. By entering into futures contracts, one bought and sold not wheat or corn or oats but the *prices* of those goods as they would exist at a future time. Speculators made and lost money by selling each other legally binding forecasts of how much grain prices would rise or fall.

As the futures market emerged in the years following the Civil War, speculative interests dominated more and more of the trading on the floor of 'Change. On either side of any given futures contract stood two figures, metaphorically known to traders and the public alike as the bull and the bear.[112] Bulls, believing that the trend of grain prices was upward, tended to *buy* futures contracts in the hope that they would be cheaper than the market price of grain by the time they fell due. Bears, on the other hand, believing that the trend of prices was downward, tended to *sell* futures contracts in the hope that they would be more expensive than the market price of grain when they expired. Except under certain special circumstances, neither bulls nor bears cared much about actually owning grain.[113] One was "long" while the other was "short," and each needed the other to make the market in future prices possible. Since both were gambling that the predictions of the other were wrong, the gains of one always matched the losses of the other. From the point of view of the traders, it mattered little whether the actual price of grain rose or fell, whether farm crops were good or bad, except insofar as these things corroborated price predictions and thereby determined which speculative animal won or lost.

Grain elevators and grading systems had helped transmute wheat and corn into monetary abstractions, but the futures contract extended the abstraction by liberating the grain trade itself from the very process which had once defined it: the exchange of physical grain. In theory, one could buy, sell, and settle up price differences without ever worrying about whether anything really existed to back up contracts which purported to be promises for future delivery of grain. One proof of this was the speed with which futures trading surpassed cash trading—the buying and selling of actual grain—at the Chicago Board of Trade. Although no one kept accurate statistics comparing the two markets, the *Chicago Tribune* estimated in 1875 that the city's cash grain business amounted to about $200 million; the trade in futures, on the other hand, was ten times greater, with a volume of $2 *billion.* [114] A decade later, the Chicago futures market had grown to the point that its volume was probably fifteen to twenty times greater than the city's trade in physical grain.[115] That the trade in not-yet-existing future grain far surpassed the number of bushels actually passing through the city's elevators was strong evidence that Chicago speculators were buying and selling not wheat or corn but pieces of paper whose symbolic relationship to wheat or corn was tenuous at best.

And yet however tenuous that relationship might have become, it could never finally disappear, for one simple reason. No futures contract ever overtly stated that it could be canceled by settling the difference between its price and the market price for grain on a given day.[116] Although the practice of "settling differences" became exceedingly common, written contracts—which after all were enforceable in a court of law—stated that grain would be delivered on the day they expired. Since

futures contracts rapidly came to have standardized expiration dates—
usually the last day of certain months—the market in future prices and the
market in real grain had to intersect each other at regular intervals. On
the day a futures contract expired, prices in the cash grain market determined its value. Because they did so, the activities of speculators working
the floor of 'Change sooner or later circled back to those of farmers
working the black prairie soil of the western countryside. Remote as the
two groups often seemed from each other, they were linked by the forces
of a single market.

Never was this clearer than when a group of speculators, working in
unison, succeeded in "cornering" one of Chicago's grain markets, an
event that became increasingly common in the decades following the
Civil War. To accomplish this feat, a group of grain traders (invariably
bulls) began quietly buying up futures contracts for a particular date,
usually just prior to a new harvest, when supplies were at their lowest.[117]
At the same time, they bought up physical ("spot" or "cash") grain as
well, in the hope that they could control most of the city's supply by the
time futures contracts fell due. Since their ultimate plan was to manipulate the market to trap unwary bear speculators who had sold grain for
future delivery, their purchases had to be as invisible as possible, lest
other traders refuse to sell. For this reason, corners often seemed mysterious events, emerging suddenly and taking traders by surprise without
anyone's being quite certain who had set the trap.

The logic of a corner lay in forcing speculators to deliver real physical
grain instead of following their usual practice of settling price differences.
If a bear speculator could not make delivery as a contract promised, because the operators of the corner owned all available grain, the seller had
no choice but to fulfill the contract by purchasing grain from the corner-
ers themselves, usually at exorbitant prices. The operators of a corner
could name virtually any price, for the futures contract had the full penalties of civil law supporting it. Those who failed to deliver on their legal
promise placed their businesses and reputations in jeopardy, and could
even face bankruptcy or jail. The sums of money that might change hands
under such circumstances were enormous, running into thousands and
finally millions of dollars. A cornered market was a painful and expensive
reminder that elevator receipts and paper contracts were ultimately
backed by real grain.

The futures market came to fruition in the years immediately following the Civil War, and so did the corner.[118] Alfred Andreas, Chicago's
leading nineteenth-century historian, remembered 1868 as "the year of
corners." "Scarcely a month" went by, he wrote, "without a corner on
'Change. Three on wheat, two on corn, one on oats, and one attempted

on rye. . . ."[119] Among the most successful was one which can serve as an example of the whole phenomenon: the corner on No. 2 spring wheat run during the month of June.[120] In late May and early June, a syndicate led by the grain traders John Lyon of Chicago and Angus Smith of Milwaukee gradually bought futures contracts for nearly a million bushels, to be delivered on June 30.[121] By June 24, as traders began to realize they were being squeezed in a corner, the *Tribune* market report declared, "The feeling has been growing for some time past that ruling prices are unnatural. . . . Wheat being held off the market by parties able to control it, the price goes up or down as they turn the screws on more tightly or relax them a little. . . ."[122] On June 30, when the cornered contracts finally fell due, No. 2 spring wheat sold for $2.20 per bushel in Chicago, twenty cents more than the same grain selling in New York. Since it cost at least forty cents a bushel to move wheat between the two cities, this meant that the corner had driven Chicago prices at least sixty cents above their normal level.[123]

As the *Tribune* reported, proof that the Lyon-Smith syndicate had successfully cornered the market came the instant June futures contracts expired:

> Five minutes before 3 o'clock yesterday afternoon wheat sold readily in Chicago at $2.20 per bushel. Five minutes after 3 o'clock it was freely offered at $1.85, but no one wanted it, and no one bought a grain. The difference of 35 cents per bushel . . . [was] a natural sequel to the "corner."[124]

For individual speculators, most of whom had sold their futures contracts at $1.80 to $1.90 per bushel, the consequences of the corner were painful indeed. They could fulfill a standard contract for 5,000 bushels at the end of the month only by purchasing grain from the corner's operators, at a loss of perhaps $1,250 per contract. In the June 1868 corner, the operators' average gain was about twenty-five cents per bushel on 875,000 bushels, producing a gross income of nearly $220,000.[125] The *Tribune*'s market report suggested that some small traders had "probably lost their all—the accumulations of long years of toil—and have received a valuable lesson almost too late to profit by it."[126] Alfred Andreas explained the lesson more explicitly: however remote the futures market might seem from the movement of real grain, "there was an actual basis of property underneath every trade; and . . . to sell what one did not possess was fraught with as much danger as to buy what one could not pay for."[127]

Who suffered from a successful corner? First and foremost, the bear speculators who had been forced to redeem futures contracts at inflated prices; in this sense, the corner was just a transfer of wealth from one group of grain traders to another. Although large speculators were by no means immune to being trapped in a corner, many of those who lost most heavily were probably smaller traders who were less in touch with day-to-day activities in the Chicago market: country grain dealers placing orders through Chicago traders, for instance, or speculators "of small means" who, "tempted by the golden offers of commission men, order them to buy or sell short, and pay a small percentage for the trouble."[128] Those who did not speculate were much less directly affected. The few farmers who still had spring wheat to sell benefited temporarily from higher prices in Chicago markets; and because the grain purchased during the corner never commanded such high prices when it finally reached New York, eastern consumers probably experienced little increase in the price of bread as a result.[129]

But the effects of the corner were not limited to the speculators who had participated in it. Its most obvious consequence was to distort the Chicago wheat market for an extended period of time both during and after the corner. By the last week in June, No. 2 spring wheat was actually selling at a higher price than the better-quality No. 1 spring wheat (which was not cornered); sales of the latter virtually halted after desperate bears bought the better wheat and had it graded down to try to meet their contracts.[130] Fewer and fewer wheat sales of any kind occurred as the end of the month approached, until June 30 itself, when nearly a quarter of a million bushels changed hands as trapped speculators closed out their contracts.

The next day, the *Tribune* reported that the wheat market had collapsed: "there were no transactions, or so few that the market was the dullest within the memory of the oldest inhabitant."[131] This too was a predictable consequence of the earlier market manipulations. The classic problem of running a corner was bringing it to a successful close. Even if one had made enormous profits when cornered futures contracts expired, one still faced the difficult task of selling off the vast stockpile of grain one had acquired to make the corner possible in the first place. Keeping the grain in store cost money, but putting it up for sale inevitably caused prices to decline, sometimes precipitously. If the bulls who had cornered the market did not have time to sell off their grain before prices fell below the level at which they had originally purchased it, they ran the serious risk of losing all their profits from the earlier transactions. The bears might get their revenge after all. In the parlance of the day, the cornered wheat was "an elephant which it is equally difficult to keep as to get rid of safely."[132] Later in the century, speculators told of how hard it was to "bury the corpse" when the corner was done.

In 1868, other traders knew that the speculators who had run the corner would have to dispose of their grain, and also feared that the Lyon-Smith syndicate might be in a position to repeat its performance in July.[133] Because uncertainty about the future direction of local wheat prices was so great, traders were "skeery," and refused either to buy or to sell until the direction of the market became clearer. "It is well known," wrote the *Tribune*'s reporter, that the corner's operators "have a large amount on hand, which may be thrown on the market at any time and swamp it. This destroys the desire to buy, while sellers are equally scarce. . . ."[134] As the stagnant market dragged on into the middle of the month, speculators who had earlier contracted to deliver wheat at the end of July started to fear that they might be caught in a corner again, and they therefore purchased grain from other cities to be able to make delivery on time. The bizarre result was that wheat began to be shipped south to Chicago from Racine, Wisconsin, "at a cost nearly equal to that required to carry it from Chicago to Buffalo," even though Chicago continued to have large quantities of wheat in store.[135] Wheat prices remained higher in Chicago than in nearby markets—Milwaukee's No. 1 spring wheat was cheaper than Chicago's No. 2—so millers and other large consumers of grain simply stopped buying from the city.[136]

This state of affairs persisted until the end of July, with only a few thousand bushels of wheat changing hands each day in a market accustomed to handling ten times that quantity. Traders lamented that "the rushing torrent of last month had become a peaceful gully, without a stream."[137] Farmers and merchants whose railroad connections to Chicago made them dependent on the Board of Trade had trouble getting any price at all for their grain. In Chicago itself, grain traders grew angry about the disruption of their ordinary business. By the end of the month, the *Tribune,* which had initially held itself aloof from commenting on the shenanigans at the Board, issued a stern indictment of the whole business:

> If anything more sick than the wheat market of the present time can be invented, we do not want to see it, and if the members of the late combination can take pleasure in viewing the demoralization they have wrought, they are exceptions to the ordinary run of human nature. The Corner was as disastrous in its influence on the wheat trade, as a long continued strike is to the business of a city. It has completely upset the order of things, kept the cereal from the city, driven operators away, and forced millers to buy elsewhere. The chances are that the exhaustion will not be recovered from in many months, though . . . the arrival of New Wheat will surely produce some current, though a small one, in this hitherto important channel of trade.[138]

Corners, in short, seemed to call into question the legitimacy of the entire futures market.

The market finally did become more active in August after traders realized that the syndicate had apparently failed (or perhaps had not even tried) to corner July wheat.[139] Just when everyone had begun to feel more comfortable, however, an equally severe corner in September corn squeezed many bear speculators so badly that some of the most prominent trading houses in the city found themselves hard pressed to honor their commitments. Even E. V. Robbins, president of the Board of Trade, became so financially embarrassed in the September corner that he felt obliged to tender his resignation to the Board's directors. They refused to accept it, on the grounds that he was an honorable man who had been caught out through no fault of his own. Instead, they castigated the corner operators themselves. On October 13, Board members passed a resolution that

> the practice of "corners," of making contracts for the purchase of a commodity, and then taking measures to render it impossible for the seller to fill his contract, for the purpose of extorting money from him, has been too long tolerated by this and other commercial bodies in the country to the injury and discredit of legitimate commerce, [and] that these transactions are essentially improper and fraudulent. . . .[140]

To put teeth in this resolution, members amended the Board's bylaws so that traders could appeal to a disinterested panel if they felt they had been cornered. The panel had the formal power to recognize the existence of a corner, and then to break it by allowing cornered bears to use nonstandard grades of grain in paying off their futures contracts. In addition, the Board could suspend the membership of anyone who tried to run a corner.[141]

If the purpose of the new rule was to put an end to corners, it failed. The Board's directors proved reluctant to enforce the anticorner regulations, and corners continued unabated to the end of the century and beyond. They became if anything more spectacular with time, the most famous being the Leiter corner of 1896, which Frank Norris immortalized in his novel *The Pit.*[142] Although members sometimes invoked Board rules to try to close out corners once they had been run, few grain traders expected corners to disappear altogether.[143] Indeed, their emotions about corners were an odd mixture of fear and admiration. A corner operator was a gambler's gambler. Whether one saw such people as heroes or as villains, one still had to admire their daring: tales of great corners and their operators became the stuff of Board legend.[144]

More important, few traders were willing to attack a phenomenon that seemed to flow from the heart of the market itself. Chicago's great innovation in the grain trade had been to simplify the natural diversity of wheat, corn, and other crops so that people could buy and sell them as homogeneous abstractions. To accomplish that task, the Board of Trade had drawn artificial boundaries to separate one abstract category of grain from another: spring wheat from winter wheat, No. 1 wheat from No. 2 wheat, and so on. Without those boundaries, neither futures nor corners would have been possible on any large scale. The futures contract depended on buyers and sellers not having to worry about evaluating the quality of the grain they were trading, especially since that grain often did not yet exist at the moment they bought and sold it. Standard grades eliminated such worries, but they also segmented the market so that grain of one grade could not legally be used to fulfill contracts for grain of another. With the market divided up in this way, speculators found it possible to buy up all rights to future grain of a particular grade. By institutionalizing the contractual boundaries which prevented traders from exchanging grains of different grades, the Board created the essential condition that made corners possible.[145] Because that condition was no less essential to the "legitimate" grain-trading apparatus of Chicago, the Board could hardly afford to attack the corner problem at its root. Corners were an almost inevitable result not just of the futures contract but of grain grading and elevators as well; all three derived from the same artificial partitioning of the economic landscape, the same second nature.

Boundary Disputes

Outsiders were much less prepared than traders to accept this newly partitioned market as natural or inevitable, and even Board members were uncomfortable with some of the changes going on around them. The late 1860s saw widespread agitation throughout Illinois for legislation to regulate what many farmers and merchants regarded as a long list of abuses in the Chicago marketplace. In that list, corners were only the most dramatic sign that railroads, elevators, standard grades, and futures contracts had imposed a new order on Chicago's grain markets. Although the complaints took many forms, most came down to the same fundamental problem: how to draw appropriate boundaries around the products of rural nature, and who should benefit from those boundaries. Despite the deep suspicion that many rural residents felt toward the Board of Trade and its mysterious market, farmers and Board members often found themselves on the same side of arguments about how to reform Chicago's grain trade. Moreover, they had a common enemy: the grain elevator operators.

The Board's new grading system, of course, touched farmers as much as traders. Each time a farmer delivered grain to an elevator and had it graded by one of the Board's inspectors, its market value depended on the particular grade it received. In 1860, the Board defined No. 1 spring wheat as weighing more than 59 pounds per bushel, while No. 2 spring wheat weighed from 56 to 59 pounds. Any spring wheat weighing less than 56 pounds was labeled Rejected; it still had a market, but brought a much lower price. Although the weight of real physical wheat varied continuously along this scale from No. 1 to No. 2 to rejected, the inspection system's boundaries defined how much farmers or merchants actually received when they finally sold their grain. Whether wheat weighed an ounce more or less than 56 pounds might make a difference of ten cents or more per bushel in its price. If a family raised 500 bushels of wheat, its income could rise or fall by more than 10 percent—$50 if the price was $1.00 per bushel—depending on which side of the grade boundary its grain happened to be placed.[146]

Because grade boundaries might mean the difference between profit or loss for a family's annual crop, arguments about inspection and grading were almost unavoidable. This was especially true when grade prices differed markedly. In the words of one country dealer, "the wider the difference between the different grades *in price,* the more particular will be the grading. . . ."[147] As graders drew sharper boundaries between grain shipments that seemed nearly identical, disputes about grading grew more frequent. Sometimes complaints reflected a farmer's or merchant's unwillingness to accept the true value of a shipment; sometimes they reflected an inspector's unfair grading; but always they reflected a dispute over how to impose artificial boundaries on the world of "natural" grain.

Disputes about grade boundaries manifested themselves as complaints about elevator fraud, which became a major political grievance of Illinois farmers and grain traders during the 1860s and 1870s. Many such complaints were well justified. Grain inspectors were sometimes dishonest, classifying a farmer's or trader's shipment into a lower grade than it actually deserved and giving someone else—usually the elevator operator—the resulting difference in value. Elevators on occasion set their scales to underweigh an entire shipment and thereby lower its grade.[148] One reason the Board hired its own team of inspectors in 1860 was to reduce the likelihood of such fraud, for Board members had as strong an interest as farmers in properly graded grain. Stories nonetheless circulated of farmers who had sent two carloads of identical grain to Chicago, one of which was then graded No. 1 and the other Rejected, with a resulting ten- to fifteen-cent difference in price per bushel.[149] The Board did not deny that such things could happen, but argued that they were much more the exception than the rule: "while general charges of a very indefinate [*sic*] character have frequently been made against [the inspectors'] decisions, by parties in interest," one Board report declared, "nothing has ever been established that would indicate they were wanting in either honesty or ability."[150] Reassuring declarations of this sort proved unpersuasive to farmers, for it did not take much anecdotal evidence to confirm rural suspicions that the entire Chicago market was corrupt. Farmers "knew" that railroads, elevators, inspectors, and "grain gamblers" were all in league to swindle the defenseless producer.[151]

But not all conflicts over grade boundaries signified obvious fraud. The grading system itself could structurally favor one group of traders over another simply by the number of grades it contained. The fewer standard grades there were, the more possible it was for buyers to benefit at the expense of sellers from variations in the true value of physical grain *within* any particular grade.[152] To take advantage of such variation, a buyer or an elevator operator had only to mix grain from different grades. If one farmer sold 1,000 bushels of No. 2 wheat weighing 59 pounds, and another sold 1,000 bushels of Rejected wheat weighing 55 pounds, an elevator could combine the two lots and instantly produce 2,000 bushels of No. 2 wheat weighing 57 pounds. If the price differential between the grades was ten cents, the simple act of mixing yielded a profit to the elevator of $100.[153]

Farmers naturally believed that this $100 had been stolen from them, but the nature of the theft was difficult to define.[154] No elevator could operate without mixing at least the grain *within* a given grade, and the opportunity for making a profit by mixing *across* grades was intrinsic to the grading system itself. "Out of this right to mix," declared the *Tribune*, "grows the whole possibility of fraud."[155] The incentive to mix across grades, like the ability to run a corner, flowed directly from the partitioning of Chicago's grain market. The Board's grading system relied on the conventional fiction that grain was uniform within grades, but physical grain remained as variable as ever. Even the Board admitted that grading could not do *"even* and *exact* justice . . . to every car load of grain," for "that would require that there should be no variation whatever in different lots of grain graded into the same class." In fact, there *had* to be such variation, for the whole point of the grading system was to simplify the minute differences among real grain shipments so that they could be more easily combined and traded. "Between a very good car of, say No. 1 or No. 2 spring wheat, and a very poor car of the same grade," observed the Board, "there may be several cents difference of actual value. . . ."[156]

Those who combined grades used the Board's necessary fiction of within-grade homogeneity to profit from the very real heterogeneity of physical grain: mixing happened on the boundary between first and second nature, and was possibly only because of the tension between them.

Whatever the logic behind it, mixing disturbed farmers and Board members alike, for it seemed to call into question the honesty and integrity of the whole grading system. What made mixing particularly objectionable was the uniquely powerful position of elevator operators, who could earn large sums of money by manipulating the physical partitions between grain bins so as to profit from the conceptual partitions between grain grades. By mixing grain to bring it as close as possible to the lower boundary of a grade, elevators could capture the hidden value of intra-grade variation for themselves, an act that seemed both dishonest and unfair.[157]

But this was by no means the only complaint that farmers and Board members had against the elevators. Equally objectionable were the legal agreements elevator operators made with the railroads to segment Chicago's grain-handling market geographically. By 1870, Chicago had seventeen elevators with a total capacity of 11.6 million bushels of grain. Each received grain from only a single railroad, and each had a contract which gave it exclusive rights to the grain delivered by that road.[158] The railroads rarely operated elevators themselves, but received a percentage of the elevators' profits as part of the agreement between them. Five private partnerships managed all the large elevators in the city. Moreover, the ten to fifteen individuals who made up these partnerships were financially so closely linked to each other, and had so successfully restricted the possibilities of competition among themselves, that they effectively acted as a single bloc. When farmers and traders complained about an "elevator monopoly" in Chicago, they knew what they were talking about.[159]

Farmers and shippers sending grain to Chicago had virtually no choice about which elevator their grain entered; this enabled elevators to set uniform rates without fear of losing business. A typical elevator charge in the 1860s was two cents per bushel, which included receiving, twenty days storage, and shipping; this amounted to about 5 percent of the total transport cost of moving grain from its point of origin to New York.[160] On that basis, the *Prairie Farmer* in 1864 calculated Chicago's total elevator income to be roughly $1 million, with about $80,000 going to an average elevator and more than double that to a large one.[161] The lack of cost data makes it difficult to estimate profit rates from these figures, but elevator operators did declare personal incomes ranging from $30,000 to $100,000 per year during the 1860s.[162]

People debated among themselves whether such incomes were legitimate. The *Prairie Farmer,* speaking to a rural audience, concluded that "no business men in Chicago are more rapidly becoming independently rich than the warehousemen. Their fortunes are being made entirely from off the farmers of the country."[163] Probably because Board members understood better than farmers the practical necessity of grain elevators in the Chicago market—some undoubtedly remembered the much higher handling costs of water-based transport before elevators existed—they were prepared to be more generous in the face of such charges. While concluding at the end of an official investigation in 1866 that the rates for storage of grain in Chicago were "quite high enough," a Board committee noted that they were no higher than rates charged by elevators in Buffalo, at the other end of the Great Lakes transportation corridor.[164] Elevators performed an important service in moving grain to market, said the Board, and those who benefited from that market—farmers and traders both—should expect to pay a reasonable charge for the service.

Board members had different fears about the elevators which farmers were less likely to share, for grain traders worried about the elevators' power to threaten the integrity of the Board's own market.[165] Whether the price of grain rose or fell on the floor of 'Change depended, at least from the supply side, on how much grain the bulls and bears thought the city's elevators contained. The elevator operators, unlike everyone else, actually *knew* such numbers to the nearest bushel, and so had an enormous advantage when speculating—usually secretly—in the market.[166] "The warehousemen," one observer reported, "had the inside track, because they knew exactly the amount of grain on hand."[167] Elevator operators could predict ordinary price movements better than most traders. They knew when a grain could probably be cornered, and when a corner could probably be broken. As one Cook County politician remarked, the elevators were not only "the largest gamblers in grain in Chicago . . . , but gamblers who play with marked cards. . . ."[168]

Gambling with marked cards involved more than just knowing how much grain Chicago's elevators contained. Both the grading system and the futures market depended on elevator receipts for their very existence, and the elevator operators controlled those receipts in a way no one else could. By issuing receipts, the elevator operators effectively printed money. The money was good as long as there was grain corresponding to each receipt. But if elevator operators illegally issued counterfeit receipts for grain that did not exist, they could mint themselves a fortune without anyone's ever knowing. Corners presented special opportunities in this respect. At the height of a corner, an elevator operator might gradually sell 10,000 bushels worth of counterfeit receipts to speculators who were desperately trying to meet the obligations of their futures contracts.

Later, after the corner was over and the price of grain had fallen, say, forty cents, the operator could buy back those 10,000 receipts and pocket $4,000 from the transaction, with no one the wiser. Elevator operators could also collude with speculators who were running a corner by refusing to admit how much grain they had in store, or by falsely declaring that the grain they did have was "heating"—spoiling—and could no longer be traded. All of these maneuvers were illegal, but they appear to have occurred with some frequency during the late 1860s. In the absence of effective means for regulating and policing the elevators, little could be done to prevent such abuses.[169]

In the years following the Civil War, then, critics of Chicago's grain market had a long list of indictments against the city's elevators: fraudulent grading, dishonest weighing, mixing grades, restricting competition, hiding storage information, and issuing false receipts.[170] Each charge began with a question about appropriate market boundaries—between one grade and another, between public and private information, between legitimate and illegitimate business practices—and ended with a question about who should have the power to set those boundaries. If people were to trade grain not as a physical good but as a categorical abstraction, then sellers and buyers were bound to fight about how to categorize it. Once grain grades existed, *someone* would benefit from intra-grade variations in real value. Farmers, elevator operators, grain traders, and millers could hardly avoid having different views about who that beneficiary should be.

Other boundaries were equally in dispute. Some believed that elevator charges were too high, and would come down only if railroads and elevators were forced to abandon their monopolies of the city's transportation markets: shippers should be able to send grain to any elevator they chose, not just the one associated with a particular railroad. Grain traders required accurate knowledge of the grain supply to set prices, and so Board members and elevator operators fought with each other over the boundaries between public and private information: elevators, critics said, should be forced to release accurate statistics about the grain they held in store. And although no one actually defended counterfeit receipts, they too marked a contested boundary, for if corrupt elevator operators insisted on issuing them, all elevator receipts—and with them the grain market as a whole—would be cast in doubt. Each of these conflicts raised serious questions about how to maintain the necessary boundaries of a partitioned market and still protect that market's integrity as perceived by all who participated in it. For just this reason, the Chicago Board of Trade and several of the city's leading newspapers— not the farmers—actually led the attack against the elevators.[171]

Efforts to reform Chicago's grain-trading institutions—to legally de-

fine their boundaries and make them more answerable to the public—
came to a head in the decade following 1865 as part of a much broader
agrarian movement, identified with the Grange, whose main targets were
the railroads.[172] In 1866, the Illinois legislature considered a bill, sponsored by Senator F. A. Eastman of Chicago's Cook County, to regulate
warehouses. The bill called for public elevator inspection, limits on mixing, mandatory publication of warehouse statistics, and open competition
among elevators. These were all reforms that individual members of the
Board of Trade had been proposing as ways to limit elevator abuses,
although the Board itself had not yet taken a stand in their support. When
members learned that the Board's directors favored a watered-down version of Eastman's bill, they called a mass meeting to repudiate the directors' action. At the meeting, members passed a resolution declaring that
they believed "that there are serious abuses exerting a very depressing
influence upon the grain trade" and therefore "that any action which may
be taken by the State Legislature towards placing the grain warehouses of
this city under wholesome legal restrictions will meet with the unqualified
approbation and cordial sympathy and support of the Board."[173] Board
members promptly raised funds to send a committee of one hundred to
Springfield to lobby in support of the Eastman bill. In the meantime,
newspapers like the *Tribune* published exposés that heightened agrarian
anger about corrupt elevator practices.

To defend themselves, elevator operators apparently bribed members
of the legislature to eliminate the most threatening provisions of the bill
and to limit its enforcement mechanisms. They also tried to get back at
the Board by having a friendly legislator add an amendment outlawing
futures as "void and gambling contracts," thereby making much of the
Board's market illegal. Irritating as this may have been to members of the
Board, no one ever seriously tried to enforce the clause, and the legislature repealed it in 1869. To the disappointment of farmers and Board
members alike, the same thing happened to the elevator regulations: because their enforcement depended on someone's bringing civil suit, and
because no one in the grain business was willing to take that risk against
such formidable adversaries, the Warehouse Act of 1867 proved ineffec-
tive from the beginning.[174]

Political agitation against both railroads and elevators continued to
grow, culminating as far as the Chicago elevators were concerned in the
Illinois constitution of 1870 and the Warehouse Act of 1871. Arguing
that the new constitution should empower the state to regulate transportation and trade within its boundaries, agrarian protesters gathered in
April 1870 in Bloomington. They were greeted upon their arrival by a
letter from Governor John Palmer promising that "freights and all that

relates to the transportation, storage, and sale of the products . . . of the country shall be relieved from the arbitrary rule of monopolies, and subjected to such regulations as may harmonize with reason and justice." There was also a letter from the president of the Chicago Board of Trade. The Board's members, he said, "feel the deepest interest in the deliberations of your body, and trust they may result in substantial good to the producing interests of the Northwest." Those in attendance "heartily applauded" both letters, pleased that such powerful allies had decided to join them: Illinois farmers and Chicago grain traders would make common cause.

The farmers' meeting at Bloomington proceeded to pass a series of resolutions urging the constitutional convention to reduce "unreasonable and oppressive" rates and to define unambiguously their "legal rights to transportation and market."[175] But they did not try to define those "legal rights" themselves. Indeed, they seemed to have a curiously abstract sense of the system that moved and marketed their crops, no doubt because the institutions of that system were so remote, impersonal, and hidden from public view. Although the farmers sought the forward-looking goal of having the government regulate railroad rates and elevator charges, several of their suggestions looked backward to older technologies and economic practices. To solve the problem of railroad "monopoly," they proposed developing new canals that might provide alternative competitive routes, not fully understanding either the fixed-cost problems of railroads or the difficulty that many waterways would soon have holding their own competitively. They and the governor speculated about making the railroads true "common carriers" like highways and canals, allowing anyone to run trains over a given set of tracks, not understanding why this made less sense for railroads than for most other forms of transportation. And they objected to "the practice of the railway companies of delivering grain to warehouses . . . without the consent and against the protest of the grain owners and shippers," apparently not fully grasping how essential elevators and their common bins had become to moving grain by rail.[176] The farmers did not address the subtleties of grading, elevator storage, or grain trading, preferring to express a generalized hostility toward the oppressive power of "monopolies." That the problems of grain marketing might be more structural, built into the very system that enabled farmers to sell their crops in the first place, does not seem to have occurred to them.

At the Illinois Constitutional Convention itself, much of the leadership that proposed concrete solutions to the elevator problem came not from hinterland farmers like those who met at Bloomington but from people in Chicago who knew the city's grain trade at first hand. Chicago-

based publications such as the *Prairie Farmer,* the *Western Rural,* and especially the *Chicago Tribune* led the way in arguing for government intervention against corrupt elevator practices. The *Tribune,* for instance, reported that among farmers in the city's hinterland, "the name of a
Chicago warehouseman has become a synonym with that of a pirate. . . . It
may be safely affirmed that no man voluntarily sends his grain to Chicago
who can send it elsewhere."[177] Negative perceptions of this sort could
only hurt the city in general, so booster editors who wished to protect
Chicago took it upon themselves to ferret out corruption and hold it up
for public condemnation. Because such newspapers were widely read
throughout the state, they helped shape public thinking about the issue.
Much of the most damaging information that farmers knew about Chicago's markets came to them via the Chicago newspapers, which had in
turn learned insider stories from grain traders at the Chicago Board of
Trade. If, as many farmers believed, Chicago was the font of corruption in
the grain trade, the city also pointed the way to its own redemption.

The constitution's proposed article for regulating grain warehouses
had in fact been drafted by none other than a committee of the Board of
Trade. This led at least one rural delegate to oppose elevator regulation
as "a grain gamblers' article, and not a farmers' article."[178] Another rural
delegate thereupon leapt to the measure's defense by declaring that although "this report came from the city of Chicago" and "had its manli-
ness and all its garments laid on there," he was still "willing to receive
anything good, that may come out of evil."[179] The *Tribune*'s reform editor, Joseph Medill, was himself a delegate and delivered what was probably the convention's most grandiloquent indictment of the elevators:

> The fifty million bushels of grain that pass into and out of the city of
> Chicago per annum, are controlled absolutely by a few warehouse men
> and the officers of railways. They form the grand ring, that wrings the
> sweat and blood out of the producers of Illinois. There is no provision in
> the fundamental law standing between the unrestricted avarice of monop-
> oly and the common rights of the people; but the great, laborious, patient
> ox, the farmer, is bitten and bled, harassed and tortured, by these rapa-
> cious, blood sucking insects.[180]

With the republican body politic so infested with vermin, Medill argued,
only the law could "step between these voracious monopolies and the
producers." The new constitution should attack the elevator plague, save
the farmer, and redeem Chicago at the same time.

Article 13 as it finally appeared in the 1870 constitution remained
largely as Board members had written it. It designated all warehouses in
Illinois to be "public," thereby asserting the state's power to regulate

their activities and confirming a grain owner's right to inspect the goods stored in such places.[181] Despite the statewide definition of public warehouses, convention delegates understood their real target and did not wish to subject rural warehouse owners to needless costs and regulations. The most important requirements of the article therefore applied only to elevators in cities with over 100,000 inhabitants—and there was only one such city in Illinois. Elevators in Chicago were to post weekly notices of how much grain of each grade they had in store. To prevent them from issuing fraudulent receipts, they were to keep a public registry of all outstanding receipts they had issued. And they were forbidden to mix different grades without permission. Furthermore, all railroads in the state were required to deliver grain to any elevator a shipper desired—and, if necessary, permit new track construction to accomplish this.[182]

The Illinois legislature supplemented Article 13 in 1871 with a series of laws assigning the task of grain inspection to a new Railroad and Warehouse Commission that would henceforth regulate all grain movement and storage in the state. Much to the chagrin of Board of Trade members, the Warehouse Act of 1871 separated the grading system from the organization that had invented it.[183] But the Board itself had abandoned internal inspection of elevators in April 1870 after a dispute with elevator operators that may also have been an effort to lobby the constitutional convention for greater inspection powers. If it was a lobbying effort, the action backfired when the Board's inspectors fell under a cloud that confirmed public perceptions that they might be nearly as corrupt as the elevators themselves. In January 1871, the Board suddenly suspended its chief grain inspector, R. McChesney, after learning that he had graded as no. 2 oats a shipment of no. 3 oats mixed with Rejected barley, apparently at the behest of one of the Board's own directors.

The *Tribune* used the occasion to attack the integrity of the entire inspection system, fanning political hostility toward the Board just as the legislature was considering the new warehouse law. As a result, the Illinois government took over all grain inspection in the state. But the Board's original system otherwise changed little. The new state control of grain inspection undoubtedly helped diminish public suspicions about Chicago grading in general. By 1874, faith in Chicago inspection had been so restored that the city's grades were accepted without dispute in New York, Philadelphia, Baltimore, Boston, Montreal, and other eastern ports. Disputes about the grading of individual shipments continued, but farmers too appear to have become more content once the state took over grain inspections.[184]

In short, Article 13 and the 1871 Warehouse Act addressed each of the boundary problems that had so concerned farmers, grain traders, and other elevator critics during the 1860s: grading, inspection, mixing, counterfeit receipts, public grain supply statistics, and the monopoly linkage between railroads and elevators. Although complaints about grain elevators persisted long into the future, the new legislation laid the essential legal foundation for regulating any abuses that might occur.[185] Elevator operators initially contested the legality of the new laws by refusing to take out licenses for themselves, thereby denying that Illinois had a right to regulate their activities. When the state prosecuted them, public outcry about the case was so strong that voters changed the composition of the Illinois supreme court to make sure that the Warehouse Act and other new "Granger laws" would be declared constitutional.

Finally, in 1877, the U.S. Supreme Court issued its famous ruling in *Munn* v. *Illinois*, establishing forever the principle that grain elevators and other such facilities were "clothed with a public interest" and could not escape state regulation.[186] The name of Ira Munn, Chicago's leading elevator operator, would henceforth be associated with the legal ruling which enabled state governments to regulate the boundary between private interest and public good in economic matters. In making their decision, the justices were clearly impressed by what they saw as the harmful public consequences of monopoly power at Chicago's grain elevators, but the case had much wider ramifications. As one early student of the subject remarked in 1928, *Munn* v. *Illinois* "was epoch making in its consequences," and "through it the Granger Movement has remained an active force in American history to the present day."[187]

Necessary Fictions

Chicago's relationship to the new "public interest" as articulated in *Munn* can only be called ambivalent. On the one hand, the city's grain elevators had significantly benefited "the public" by joining with the railroads to liberate western farmers from the constraints of water and winter, vastly increasing the amount of grain that could move to market. That farmers and merchants no longer needed to float rafts down prairie streams or haul wagons over muddy roads to sell their grain was due to the very railroads and elevators which now linked them so powerfully and troublingly to Chicago's marketplace. The *Prairie Farmer* explained, "In connection with our immense grain warehouses, but little cessation of the grain trade occurs during the close of navigation, and a market is afforded the farmer at all times."[188]

On the other hand, elevator operators had also taken advantage of "the public" by seeking to profit from virtually every ambiguous boundary in the city's partitioned markets. One delegate to the constitutional convention remarked, "I am satisfied that there is no institution in the State of Illinois that can pile up money like the elevators in Chicago."[189] The critics probably went too far in claiming that the elevators had systematically "stolen" vast sums of money from the public, but the case against them was easy enough to make. Many of Chicago's leading citizens and institutions—newspapers, politicians, grain traders, the Board of Trade itself—had made just that case, organizing downstate efforts to regulate elevator power. The willingness of these Chicagoans to criticize their own city suggests their genuine ambivalence about its markets. They attacked abuses in the interests of reform, but also to defend their own self-interest and to maintain the city's dominance. In the process, they often found themselves tarred with the same anti-Chicago brush as the elevators they attacked.

No institution reflected this ambivalence more than the Board of Trade, which led the campaign against the elevators even as it became the object of similar campaigns itself. One rural delegate used almost the same metaphors to attack the Board and its "grain gamblers" as Joseph Medill had used against the elevators: "They are leeches upon commerce and the community, that suck the life blood out of the farmers and dealers in grain, without contributing anything towards the general wealth or productions of the country. They swarm like lice upon the body politic and feed and fatten upon its substance."[190] From this perspective, those who stalked the floor of 'Change to amass fortunes by buying and selling futures, cornering markets, and trading grain without adding any value to it shared the corruption of the elevator operators. They too stole rather than earned their livelihoods. They too were parasites on the honest labor of farmers. One rural orator declared in 1866, "The Board of Trade of Chicago is one of the considerable obstructions that stand between the farmer and the ultimate market to which his grain must go. The different devices by which they shave him right and left, going through Chicago, is [*sic*] one of the greatest oppressions to which he must submit."[191]

And yet these same traders who speculated and gambled in the golden products of the fields were also the people farmers depended upon to buy and sell their crops. Despite all the cries of fraud, corruption, and monopoly directed against it, Chicago's immense grain market, with all of its speculative frenzy, served as a clearinghouse for the capital and credit that moved western crops to their final customers. It had improved the efficiency of trade and transport alike, so that many more farmers were able to sell much larger quantities of grain than ever before. The Board's grading system had created an opportunity for elevators to skim off the profits hidden within individual grades, but it also created an economic incentive for farmers to clean their grain and increase its value, while making possible the elevators' much reduced cost of grain handling generally. The daily trading on the floor of 'Change, combined with the constant supply of grain in the city's elevators, created a year-round market that had never before existed, so farmers could still sell grain in the dead of winter. Even futures trading offered real benefits by enabling buyers and sellers to contract in advance for grain deliveries, thereby shifting the risk of future price changes to speculators who were more willing or able to absorb that risk.[192] Much more than the residents of Chicago's hinterland usually acknowledged, farmers depended on the Board of Trade for their very livelihoods. Far from standing as an "obstruction" between grain and its ultimate market, the floor of 'Change was where grain *found* its final markets. As another delegate to the constitutional convention argued, "If there is nobody at Chicago or other great markets to buy grain, then the farmer does not get a reward for his labor."[193]

The ambivalence of the Board's position was structural. Although it controlled the circumstances of Chicago's trade, establishing the rules by which anyone—farmers, millers, speculators, corner runners—could buy and sell grain, it did not control the trade itself. It provided the stage on which other actors played. In serving as home to bulls and bears alike, it played host to as many losers as winners. Its members—who numbered well over twelve hundred by the 1870s—included many more small traders than elevator operators, railroad corporations, or large speculators.[194] Most members were committed to keeping their playing field level, resisting any presence that threatened either to become a monopoly or to subvert the contractual rules of the trading game. Their stance toward the grain trade was classically liberal: they defended an open market within the boundaries they had defined for that market, and did not make distinctions among those who stayed within the boundaries. Their liberal stance led them to fight elevator fraud, but also to accept corners and other peculiarities of the futures trade. This very neutrality was part of what made the Board suspect in the eyes of its critics. The Board could go so far as to write the article of the Illinois constitution governing warehouse regulation—and yet still seem a villain to delegates who, even as they voted for that article, declared their wish to "have nothing to do with the board of trade," that "monstrosity in the commercial world."[195]

Hostility toward the Board, and toward Chicago's grain trade in general, flowed from rural suspicions that there was something not quite real—something false, something dishonest—about its markets. The city was remarkable in handling the floodtide of grain that moved through its railroads, elevators, and ships, all of which seemed real enough. But it was equally remarkable for having redefined the *meaning* of grain within an intricate web of market fictions, abstracting and simplifying it to facilitate its movement not as a physical object but as a commodity. The trading of grain as a commodity was what made Chicago's market seem unreal to those who stood outside it.

Wheat and corn came to Chicago from farms that were themselves radical simplifications of the grassland ecosystem. Farm families had destroyed the habitats of dozens of native species to make room for the much smaller bundle of plants that filled the Euroamerican breadbasket. As a result, the vast productive powers of the prairie soil came to concentrate upon a handful of exotic grasses, and the resulting deluge of wheat, corn, and other grains flowed via the railroads into Chicago. And there another simplification occurred. In their raw physical forms, wheat and corn were difficult substances: bulky to store, hard to handle, difficult to value properly. Their minute and endless diversity embodied the equal diversity of the prairie landscape and of the families who toiled to turn that landscape into farms. An older grain-marketing system had preserved the fine distinctions among these natural and human diversities by maintaining the legal connection between physical grain and its owner. But as the production of western grain exploded, and as the ability to move it came to depend on capital investments in railroads and elevators, the linkage between a farm's products and its property rights came to seem worse than useless to the grain traders of Chicago. Moving and trading grain in individual lots was slow, labor-intensive, and costly. By severing physical grain from its ownership rights, one could make it abstract, homogeneous, *liquid*. If the chief symbol of the earlier marketing system was the sack whose enclosure drew boundaries around crop and property alike, then the symbol of Chicago's abandonment of those boundaries was the golden torrent of the elevator chute.

The original decision to remove grain from its sacks was undoubtedly a pragmatic one, driven by the technological possibilities of the grain elevator. Probably no one foresaw that so simple an act would have such complex consequences, imposing a new symbolic order on Chicago's marketplace and distancing it from the physical universe of fields and crops and rural nature. The shift from sack to elevator enabled grain traders to come indoors, to a market called 'Change where sheets of paper would stand as surrogates for grain bought and sold in millions upon millions of invisible bushels. The shift to standard grades meant that those sheets of paper represented not real physical grain but abstract conventions whose homogeneity was the condition that made them interchangeable. Interchangeability in turn made it possible to sell grain not only over great distances of space but over extended periods of time as well, for the futures market depended for its existence on the standard-ized fictions that enabled traders to buy and sell grain they had never seen, because it did not yet exist.[196] Those who dealt in futures extended the abstraction of Chicago's market by dealing not in grain, not even in elevator receipts, but in the prices that *future* elevator receipts would bring when they finally came into being several weeks or months later.

Chicago grain traders dealt in the physical products of an agricultural landscape by transforming them into commodities defined by the market itself. Insofar as farmers were already raising corn and wheat with the intention of selling them, these grains had been commodities long before the founding of the Chicago Board of Trade. But 'Change altered their meaning, distancing them from the rural farm and tying them ever more closely to the urban market in which they were exchanged. The very language of the market reshaped the objects traded within it. To under-stand wheat or corn in the vocabulary of bulls, bears, corners, grades, and futures meant seeing grain as a commodity, not as a living organism planted and harvested by farmers as a crop for people to mill into flour, bake into bread, and eat. As one bewildered delegate to the Illinois Con-stitutional Convention remarked after trying to read a Chicago market report, "this 'buying short' and 'buying long' and the 'last bulge' is per-fect Greek to the grain producer of the State."[197]

By imposing their own order and vocabulary on the world of first nature, the city's traders invented a world of second nature in which they could buy and sell grain as commodity almost independently from grain as crop. "In the business centre of Chicago," wrote a bemused visitor in 1880, "you see not even one 'original package' of the great cereals."[198] In Chicago, the market turned inward upon itself to trade within its own categories and boundaries. Although the futures market marked the most significant step in this direction, an equally symbolic change occurred in 1875. In that year, the Board of Trade decided that its own member-ships—roughly two thousand in number—should be offered for sale in the open market, to be bought and sold as commodities in their own right. This "policy of making these memberships merchandise" would henceforth be the way people acquired the right to trade on the floor of 'Change, offering their services to anyone on the outside who wished to buy or sell grain there.[199] By this decision, the Board began to conduct a market in the market itself: boxes within boxes within boxes, all mediat-ing between the commodified world inside and the physical world out-side.

Physical grain did not, of course, disappear from the Chicago market, obscured though it might be behind the various fictions of grain as com-modity. The success or failure of crops and the dietary needs of people around the world—however abstract these might have seemed from the floor of 'Change—remained the ultimate conditions of supply and demand underlying even the most commodified of grain markets.[200] The Board of Trade's greatest problems always occurred on the boundaries where its market fictions intersected with the real world. When speculators cornered the futures market, they succeeded because trapped traders really did have to meet expiring contracts with physical grain. Farmers believed Chicago was robbing them because standard grades really did obscure legitimate differences in the value of grain shipments, thereby creating innovative opportunities for "theft." People struggled about grading, mixing, and trading grain because Chicago's market abstractions did finally connect with the real world. Grain as crop and grain as commodity maintained an uneasy truce on the floor of 'Change, a truce that remade the agricultural landscape of the Great West.

4

The Wealth of Nature: Lumber

Where Value Comes From

The grain elevator was not the only place in Chicago where the products of rural nature entered the urban market to become commodities. Elevator receipts were an extreme case of what the market could do because grain so easily seemed to lose its physical identity while passing from hand to hand. But the process was far more general. Rural products entered Chicago in such immense quantities that their sheer concentration encouraged people to think of them as symbolic abstractions—as commodities defined by their passage through the market. When post–Civil War boosters waxed eloquent about Chicago, they declared their city to be not merely the greatest grain market in the world but also the greatest cattle market, the greatest hog market, the greatest lumber market, and so on. "Chicago," exulted the city's chief booster in 1870, "which less than thirty years since imported grain and provisions of all sorts from the East . . . is now in grain, lumber, live stock, and provisions, chief market of the world."[1]

Chicago's most striking trait in the latter decades of the nineteenth century was its extraordinary ability to trade commodities with most of the Great West, from Michigan and Ohio to Montana, Nevada, and New Mexico. All western cities served as markets for their hinterlands, but Chicago did so with greater reach and intensity than any other. By assembling shipments from fields, pastures, and forests into great accumulations of wealth, the city helped convert them into that mysterious thing called capital, what Karl Marx identified as "self-expanding value."[2] As the city's population increased, as its buildings expanded out onto the prairies, and as its factories and warehouses spewed forth a seemingly endless stream of goods, so did its capital—which served as the symbolic representation of all these things—continue its preternatural growth.

The railroad funneled commodities into the city, but it did not create their intrinsic *value*. Some portion of that value, as Marx would surely have argued, was "produced" by the human labor that had transformed prairies into wheat, forests into lumber, livestock into meat. For Marx, as for other classical economists who followed Adam Smith in embracing the labor theory of value, every economic good acquired its worth "only because abstract human labour [was] objectified or materialized in it."[3] Human hands and human sweat were the catalysts that brought the raw materials of first nature within the bounds of the human community and fashioned them into goods that people could use or exchange. As the end result of this process, capital was nothing if not the product of social relationships. Each of the city's commodities had been produced by human beings facing each other in the tumultuous relationship whose name was market: farmers and grain traders, cowboys and cattle barons, lumberjacks and lumbermen, all struggling over who would control the product of their collective work.[4] Indeed, the buying and selling of wage labor was among the most important innovations that distinguished Chicago and the lands around it from the Indian landscape that preceded it. Without such labor, the economic and ecological transformation of Chicago's hinterland would have been neither so rapid nor so profound as it was.

But the labor theory of value cannot by itself explain the astonishing accumulation of capital that accompanied Chicago's growth. Human labor may have been critical to planting, harvesting, and transporting the grain that passed through Chicago's elevators, or to logging, driving, and milling the lumber in its yards, but much of the value in such commodities came directly from first, not second, nature.[5] The fertility of the prairie soils and the abundance of the northern forests had far less to do with human labor than with autonomous ecological processes that people exploited on behalf of the human realm—a realm less of *production* than of *consumption*. In nature's economy, all organisms, including human beings, consumed high-grade forms of the sun's energy—foods—and transformed them into low-grade ones. Although plants might convert the sun's energy into usable carbohydrates, and animals might then concentrate that stored energy in their flesh, they all finally drew their sustenance from the light of the nearest star. The abundance that fueled Chicago's hinterland economy thus consisted largely of stored sunshine: this was the wealth of nature, and no human labor could create the value it contained.[6] Although people might use it, redefine it, or even build a city from it, they did not produce it.[7]

Chicago and other cities of the Great West grew within the ecological context of what the historian Frederick Jackson Turner would have called "frontier" conditions. Despite all the ambiguities and contradictions that have bedeviled Turner's frontier thesis for the past century, it still holds a key insight into what happened at Chicago in the years following 1833.[8] The "free land" that defined Turner's frontier was important not because it was "empty" or "virgin" or "free for the taking"—the Indians, at least, knew that it was none of these things—but because its abundance offered to human labor rewards incommensurate with the effort expended in achieving them. One earned great wealth from the western soil less because one expended great labor upon it than because the soil itself was already so rich. Unexploited natural abundance was the central meaning of Turner's frontier.[9] The land might have been taken from Indians, its profits might sometimes have been expropriated by absentee landlords, its small farmers might on occasion have suffocated beneath a burden of accumulating debt, but much of what made the land valuable in the first place had little to do with the exploitation of *people*. The exploitation of *nature* came first.

The United States took from the Indians an ecosystem that when viewed through the lens of the marketplace already held great treasures. The attraction of "free land" was that people could turn its natural wealth into capital with less labor than elsewhere. Settlers worked immensely hard to clear forests and plow fields, of course, but the land rewarded their labor far more generously than in older, more populous places. The settlement of the countryside, the growth of the city, and the expansion of the market that linked them, all rested on the basic premise that people could and should exploit the wealth of nature to the utmost. In the process, some people might gain more than others, certainly, but human gained over nonhuman most of all.

The social relations of production that yielded this result themselves depended on still more encompassing ecological relations of *consumption*. In any ecosystem, only the sun produces. All other beings consume in a long chain of killing and eating that stretches from the tiniest microorganism to the most aggressive carnivore. Since no organism can make energy, each must do its best to *store* it, accumulating a stockpile for use when the sun will not be so generous with its gifts. The same is true of human society: most of the labor that goes into *"producing"* grain, lumber, and meat involves *consuming* part of the natural world and setting aside some portion of the resulting wealth as "capital." To apply for a moment the language of economy to the ecology of the Great West, Chicago's explosive growth was purchased at the expense of prairies and forests that had spent centuries accumulating the wealth that now made "free land" so attractive. Much of the capital that made the city was nature's own.

From Forest to Prairie

The tallgrass prairie was one habitat that people sacrificed to human progress; the north woods was another. Although Chicago itself was at the edge of the grasslands, with prairies and scattered oak-hickory groves stretching for hundreds of miles to its west, Lake Michigan gave it easy access to the very different, densely forested country lying a hundred or more miles to the north. The lake's north–south orientation meant that it cut across—and so connected by water—radically different ecosystems. Sailing north from Chicago along the Illinois–Wisconsin shoreline, one initially passed a countryside of tall grasses and oak openings. Somewhere around Milwaukee, as the more northern climate became cooler and moister, the oaks and grasses gave way to a wetter and richer forest dominated by elms, basswoods, and sugar maples. Farther north still, near Sheboygan, the elms and basswoods became less common and gave way in turn to maples, hemlocks, and yellow birches, the classic mixed-hardwood forest of northern Michigan, Wisconsin, and Minnesota. On the hillsides, and where soils were drier, sugar maples became the dominant trees of the forest, forming dense canopies beneath which few other plants could grow. In the valleys, on north slopes, and where soils were heavier and wetter, hemlocks and yellow birches became more common.[10]

Approaching the heart of the north woods, one also began to see enormous conifers, some well over a hundred feet tall, pushing airy crowns high above their deciduous neighbors. These were white pines, and they more than any other tree were the lords of the north country. Often standing alone amid the more common hardwoods, white pines were most numerous on sandy soils where they could form thick glades whose needled floors and sparse ground cover contrasted markedly with the hardwood forests. The tree was among the most widely distributed pine species in the country, and could be found from almost the edge of the Great Plains all the way to New England. There, Thoreau could remark of it that "there is no finer tree." Visiting a grove near Concord, he said of the white pines that they were "like great harps on which the wind makes music."[11]

People visiting the Great Lakes forest at the middle of the nineteenth century rarely expressed such romantic sentiments about the tree, but they almost invariably noted it. Their descriptions make duller reading today than Thoreau's, but have the virtue of revealing an un-Thoreauvian though very common American way of looking at the landscape. "The land," wrote one traveler in 1852 of the country around Manitowoc, Wisconsin, "is heavily timbered, generally, with pine, oak, maple, and other varieties. . . ." To perceive the forest as this traveler did through the lens of that word "timber" was already to shift into the domain of resources, commodities, and second nature. The object of such language became clear as the description continued: "The lumber trade from this region is extensive, and a source of gain to the inhabitants."[12] When most nineteenth-century Americans saw a white pine, they could summarize their reaction with a single, compelling word: "lumber." No other tree was so highly prized. In a forest such as Manitowoc's, it was the only one worth sending to the sawmills.

The tree's virtues were many. Growing steadily to produce an exceptionally even-grained wood, a typical white pine in the Great Lakes region averaged fifty feet in height by the time it was half a century old and, as one forester declared, would continue "its growth in thickness with a most remarkable uniformity to a great age (200 years and more)."[13] At full growth, it could attain a height of over two hundred feet.[14] More important for those who saw in it the studs and joists of buildings, its tallness was matched by the straightness of its trunk, and its tendency to drop its lower limbs as it grew. Mature trees might rise fifty or more feet before spreading out their branches. The really large trees had trunks ranging up to six feet in diameter, which meant that their heartwood was beautifully clear and without knots. So common were these large trees, wrote one traveler, that "logs less than three feet in diameter are counted 'under size' by many lumbermen."[15] Better still, the wood was soft and light enough that one could easily work it with primitive sawmills and simple hand tools. And yet it was also very strong. "Being of a soft texture and easily worked," wrote the preeminent nineteenth-century historian of Great Lakes lumbering, and "taking paint better than almost any other variety of wood, it has been found adaptable to all the uses demanded in the building art. . . . No wood has found greater favor or entered more fully into supplying all those wants of man which could be found in the forest growths."[16]

But the white pine had another, less obvious, characteristic that mattered even more to the people who wanted to turn it into lumber: unlike the hardwoods that surrounded it, it floated. In a northern landscape that still lacked railroads, only water could move so large and heavy an object as a sawlog for any great distance. Fortunately, the same climate, glaciers, and impermeable bedrocks that had created soil conditions favorable to forest growth had also left the north woods with an intricate network of lakes, rivers, and streams. If one could only get the trunk of a pine tree to the bank of a major stream, water would do the work of carrying it to mill and market. Most of the timber-bearing rivers and streams of upper Michigan and northeastern Wisconsin flowed into Lake Michigan. With its northern end in the forest and its southern end three hundred miles away in the prairie, the lake was a natural corridor between two ecosystems. At one end were prairie people desperately short of trees; at the other, forest people who had more trees than they knew what to do with. (Farther west, the Mississippi had a similar north–south orientation between forest and prairie, and would play a similar role.)

The fertile soil of the prairie made it a wonderful landscape for farmers, but its lack of timber posed serious problems for people who relied on wood to partition their agricultural landscape. Because they realized this, early Illinois settlers had kept close to the margin between wooded stream courses and the grasslands where they meant to plant their crops. All too soon, the prairies proved to have too little timber to sustain a population of would-be farmers. Given its strength, plasticity, and ease of use, wood was second only to soil in its importance to the farm economy. Without it, houses, barns, and corncribs—not to mention churches and schools—were almost impossible to construct. Most of the tools and machinery with which farmers worked their land were made with it in whole or in part. It supplied the wagons that allowed crops to move to market, and the fences that kept livestock from straying where they were not wanted. It heated homes, cooked meals, and supplied the energy that ran steam engines. No raft, boat, or railroad could be built without it. Lacking a ready supply of wood, no town could come into being or aspire to become a metropolis. As the Chicago-based *Northwestern Lumberman* reported in 1880,

> Every new settler upon the fertile prairies means one more added to the vast army of lumber consumers, one more new house to be built, one more barn, one more 40 acres of land to be fenced, one more or perhaps a dozen corn cribs needed. But it means more; it means an extension of railroad lines with the vast consumption of lumber consequent thereupon; it means an additional incentive to other projected settlers to take farms near the first comer; it means churches, school houses and stores, sidewalks, paved streets and manufactures, and it means new channels of enterprise constantly opening which add to the yearly increasing demand for lumber.[17]

Wood was the foundation of all previous American prosperity, and of no tree was this more true than the white pine. If prairie was to become farmland, its inhabitants would have to have pine.

For all these reasons, Americans who contemplated the future of the Great West at midcentury understood that settling the western prairies meant cutting the northern forests. Most saw the need to cut white pine as a first step toward establishing farms in the north country as well, and so it was easy to imagine a reciprocal and complementary development of the two areas. Prairie farmers could raise crops more quickly than northern ones, who would need to purchase food while they were clearing their land of trees. Trade between the two would thus be the perfect way to bring prosperity to both. "The northern farmer," wrote a Green Bay correspondent of the Wisconsin State Agricultural Society in 1860, "is ex-officio a lumberman; the southern farmer, living in the 'fat of the land,' has more than he needs; and commerce thrives in bearing to and fro the fruits of the reaper and the axe, which they all are in need of."[18]

Contemplating the vast extent of the western grasslands, people began to conceive of the entire region as if it were a single productive unit. New economic relationships would bridge old ecological boundaries to the benefit of all concerned. "We cannot but imagine the valley of the Mississippi," wrote the editor of a Wisconsin lumber journal in 1873, as "a huge farm with a very small grove in the northeast corner."[19] The happy geographical conjunction of prairie and forest could not be the result of mere chance; rather, it was yet another sign that manifest destiny was showing its hand. "We are ashamed," wrote a Minnesota booster, "that we ever distrusted Providence, or suspected that our munificent Maker could have left two thousand miles of fertile prairies down the river, without an adequate supply of pine lumber at the sources of the river, to make those plains habitable." By using the waterways to float pine to its "natural" market, Americans would join two regions that had formerly been isolated from each other and, in so doing, create a landscape of mutual advantage. What might happen to that landscape if and when the white pines finally gave out was not at first a cause for much concern: after all, providence would see to that. As the same booster declared, "Centuries will hardly exhaust the pineries above us."[20]

If Lake Michigan was the corridor along which white pine lumber would flow from the forests of western Michigan and northeastern Wisconsin to the grasslands of Illinois, Iowa, and points west, it was also the funnel that would direct that flow through the city of Chicago. Once again, the city benefited from the intersecting geographies of nature and capital. On one side, Lake Michigan had given it a harbor where the northern lumber ships could unload their heavy burdens onto the waiting docks. On the other side, the spreading fan of the canal and the railroad network pointed toward the heart of the treeless country, putting the city in immediate contact with nearly every western community where tall-grass prairies were becoming farms. If the weight and bulk of lumber meant that only water and rails could move it profitably in large quantities, then no other city in the Great West was better situated to become its chief depot. When the 1848 opening of the Illinois and Michigan Canal doubled Chicago's lumber receipts in a single year, the event was a clear portent of things to come.[21] Ecology and economy had converged: the city lay not only on the border between forest and grassland but also on the happy margin between supply and demand.

At least until the end of the 1870s, the vast bulk of Chicago's lumber came floating to it via the lake.[22] Indeed, the entire journey of white pine from forest to sawmill to city yard traced a clear annual cycle whose rhythms followed the seasonal movements of water. Logging was a winter activity, roughly counterpointing the agricultural year.[23] Crews moved into the woods during November and December, just as the grain harvest drew to a close, and just as the rivers and lakes began to freeze. They labored among the trees until plowing time, in April or May when the waters had begun to flow again. In many cases, the men who worked in the camps—and they were almost all men—were the sons and husbands of farm families trying to earn cash income to supplement the produce of the farm. Most were immigrants to the region, initially from New England—whether Yankees, French Canadians, or British immigrants—but later from the wooded countries of northern Europe, with Germans, Irishmen, and Scandinavians contributing a growing share of the work force.[24]

The companies for which they worked took many forms. Some were small independent operations either managed by a single entrepreneur or run cooperatively, and these often contracted with sawmills or absentee landowners to cut trees on a particular tract of land. Larger companies with their own lands might hire crews directly, taking them on as employees for the season. A single logging crew in the 1850s was rarely larger than fifteen men. Average crew size increased dramatically during and after the Civil War as the organization of lumbering became more corporate, until camps of fifty or even a hundred were common. During the early years, the men lived in a crude log structure consisting of a single large room with an open, chimneyless fire in the middle, plank "deacon's seat" benches surrounding it, and shared bunk beds, each sleeping two or three men, stacked against the walls. Come evening, the men hung their wet clothes to dry in the smoke-filled rafters, ate their salt pork and beans, and spent the night quietly struggling with their sleeping companions over which way the group would face. All romantic images to the contrary, it was anything but a glamorous life, though conditions did become more tolerable with time.[25] Logging camps underwent steady improvement as the years passed, until by the 1880s they typically consisted of several buildings with moderately comfortable living quarters.[26]

Logging took place in the winter partly because workers were more readily available when there was less competition from farms, but even more because the huge white pine logs could be moved only during the cold months of the year.[27] Many of the poorly drained northern forests were too boggy for effective hauling when the ground was unfrozen. With only horses, ox teams, and people to supply motive power, the crews moved logs by flooding skidways with water, which froze to a glaze ice that could convey even the largest loads. After toppling the trees—axes continued until the 1870s to be more popular than saws for this purpose—teams of men stripped away their branches and cut them into manageable lengths, usually ranging from about twelve to sixteen feet.[28] Workers branded each log with a mark indicating who owned it, and then hooked it to a chain and pulled it by ox or horse team to a skidway.[29] Using block and tackle, the men proceeded to stack ten thousand or more board feet of logs onto sleds that consisted of little more than a platform resting on two pairs of runners, with chains to hold the load in place. Hauling the sleds along the icy roads was relatively easy on the flat, but trickier on the upgrade, where additional animals were often needed, and potentially catastrophic on the downgrade, where a runaway vehicle could threaten the lives of horses, oxen, and men alike. Careful icing and sanding were critical wherever the way became steep.

The journey came to a temporary halt where the skidway reached the banks of a stream. There, the men unloaded the logs from their sleds and piled them in huge stacks as close as possible to the frozen water. The task of piling was particularly dangerous, and all too many of the "top-deckers" who coordinated the work by standing astride the heap died or suffered terrible injuries from being crushed when the load shifted. Once they had finished this work, however, there was little more to do with the piled logs for the rest of the season. The logs remained stacked beside the ice and did not move again until melting snow filled the river with the frigid black waters of the spring floods.

Water again: nothing was more essential to the success of the year's work than the two or three weeks in early spring when the accumulated snow of many months recommenced its long journey to the sea. During most of the year, the vast majority of lumbering streams in the north country did not contain enough water to carry anything like their huge burden of floating logs. If too little snow fell during the winter, it was not only hard to drag logs along the bare skidways but impossible to float them on the streams. Few things more worried lumber operators than how much snow the winter would bring. Trade journals from January to April were filled with speculation about how weather would affect the year's output.[30] "From all we can hear," wrote a worried Chicago dealer to his Michigan partner in January 1858, "the winter has thus far been unfavourable for lumbering any where [?] for want of *snow.* "[31] Those who worked the upper reaches of a stream, where only a small area contributed runoff to the spring freshets, felt particularly anxious as they eyed the season's snowfall.[32] After a bad winter, most of the season's cut might wind up remaining next to the streams for over a year, with potentially devastating effects on the company that had felled it.

In good years, on the other hand, the coming of warm weather signaled the time when crews of men (many of whom had been without work for several weeks between the beginning of mud season and the arrival of the floods) headed down the streams to shepherd the logs on their journey. After shoving the piled timber into the water, the men walked and floated downstream amid the dull roar of grinding logs, doing their best with pike poles and "peaveys" to keep the mass moving.[33] It was an awesome task, fraught with great dangers and difficulties. As one contemporary observed, "If the water is high, the logs come down by thousands upon thousands, rushing, clogging up, breaking away again, piling upon each other, and requiring the constant efforts of the drivers to keep them on the go."[34] In the shifting chaos of the crowded river, death awaited any worker careless enough to fall into the water.

The worst fear of the men was that a few logs might become caught at a shallow or narrow place in the river, causing thousands of others to back up behind them in the nightmarish tangle known as a logjam. Logs might pile up for miles behind such an obstruction, overflowing the river's banks, destroying structures on shore, and wreaking havoc with the forward movement of the drive. Such occurrences were all too common, and certain locations became famous for them. The 1869 jam at Chippewa Falls, Wisconsin, for instance, backed up fifteen miles from its front, stood thirty feet high in some places, and reportedly contained something like 150 million board feet of timber. More impressive still was the 1888 pileup on the Menominee River, where over half a billion board feet of timber got stuck.[35]

Jams—and the process of breaking them up—were among the most dramatic and colorful events in all lumbering. They received great play in the newspapers when they occurred, and have gotten more than their share of attention from folklorists and historians ever since. The critical moment of a jam came when a lone daredevil, stripped to his shorts with a rope around his waist, worked his way into the growling mass to release the last few logs. As the jam lurched forward and gave way, his comrades on shore pulled on the rope with all their might to haul him ashore. With luck, he usually survived. But breaking a big jam generally involved far more than risking the life of a single hero. Large numbers of men might have to work for days or weeks on the river, dynamiting strategic locations and using horses to pull logs onto shore to weaken the obstruction. Lumber companies might have to pay thousands of dollars for wages and equipment to get the drive moving again, while often as not their mills sat idle downstream. By the late 1860s, companies were forming associations for the express purpose of breaking bad jams, and these organizations eventually became models for efforts at industrywide cooperation during the last quarter of the century.[36]

The final destination of the log drives in western Michigan and northeastern Wisconsin was Lake Michigan. There, where major rivers flowed into the lake, clusters of sawmills began to appear during the 1830s and 1840s. At a few locations, these had grown into substantial mill towns by the Civil War. The earliest lumber-milling district in Michigan grew up in the eastern part of the state, at Saginaw Bay on Lake Huron, where one of the largest river systems in the lower peninsula dropped its load of logs. Although some of the lumber produced by the Saginaw mills found its way to Chicago, most of it traveled east, toward Ohio, New York, and the Erie Canal.[37] The mill towns that fed Chicago's market were all to the west of Saginaw, and were scattered along the shores of Lake Michigan at places like Grand Haven, Whitehall, Ludington, Manistee, Traverse City, and still others whose names are today almost forgotten. Some mill towns, like Green Bay, Wisconsin, ran out of timber supplies early and had ceased to be major lumber districts by the 1870s. Others, like Muskegon, in the lower peninsula of Michigan, and Marinette-Menominee, on the Wisconsin–Michigan border, would by the 1880s become the predominant milling centers of the region.[38]

The logs that the rivers deposited at these cities' doors had to undergo a series of steps before they were ready for the next leg of their journey. Since the spring drives typically involved logs cut by many companies and destined for several different sawmills, the first problem was to sort out which logs belonged to which owners. This job was typically performed by a single organization known as a "boom company" that was collectively owned and operated by all the major mills on the river. Boom companies had evolved in Maine and Pennsylvania as a way to share the expense of building and managing the dams, booms, and holding basins that were needed while logs were being sorted. They also paid the wages of the men who did this work.[39] As boom companies expanded on major rivers like the Muskegon and the Menominee, they eventually became the most powerful economic forces of their region. Ultimately, some even regulated the flow of the river itself to aid the drive. In 1893, for instance, when the Menominee River experienced one of its driest seasons ever, only the careful release of water from boom company dams allowed the drive to take place at all.[40]

Once the boom company had delivered logs to their proper mills, the time finally came to turn them into lumber—boards of standard lengths and dimensions. The peak period for sawing, unlike logging, came after the floods, when mills received a new supply of sawlogs, lake navigation opened, and merchants could again try to satisfy the pent-up demand of prairie buyers. Early mills used gangs of muley (rip) saws mounted on light vertical frames to cut several boards at once. These were gradually replaced by circular saws, which predominated in Great Lakes milling until the last couple decades of the century, when more efficient band saws began to appear.[41] Sawing involved much waste: in the early years, until perhaps the late 1870s, only the finest "clear" parts of the log were retained after milling. The rest were either used for fuel or discarded. Muley and circular saw blades were wide, so the cut they made (the "kerf") consumed a lot of wood, often amounting to one or more inches out of every log. Before the introduction of the much thinner band saw, perhaps a third of the wood in each sawlog became waste, whether as mill scraps or sawdust. Much of it wound up back in the river and contributed to silting and shoaling, which gradually became hazardous to navigation. Once cut, the lumber was usually loaded directly onto the ships that carried it to market. It rarely had much time to dry at the mill, so it arrived in Chicago and other markets still quite green.

The Business of Lumber

No place was more important in coordinating this massive movement of water, men, and wood than Chicago. The city served as the chief lumber market on Lake Michigan, but its role went much further than just buying and selling wood. Many Chicago lumber dealers participated in every phase of regional lumber production, and Chicago capital thus often directed the movement of white pine from forest to mill to final customer. Quite a few lumber companies in northern Michigan and Wisconsin had at least one partner based in Chicago, and many of the largest regional firms managed all company operations from a head office there.

Sometimes, Chicagoans merely contributed investment capital toward establishing such businesses. This is apparently what happened in

1849 when Zebina Eastman, a prominent Chicago journalist, joined two other men in forming a partnership to saw lumber in Ulao, Wisconsin.[42] Eastman limited his involvement with the business mainly to the $1,000 he invested in it. The working relationship among the three men suggests one typical division of labor between Chicago and non-Chicago partners under such circumstances. Partners based in the lumbering districts usually took charge of acquiring wood and milling it, while Chicago partners had responsibility for purchasing supplies and marketing the mill's output. Although the company was known in the city as Z. Eastman and Company, it took the Wisconsin partner's name at the mill itself, where it was known as R. P. Derrickson and Company. Derrickson was more actively involved in the business than either of his two Chicago-based partners, operating the sawmill and devoting his "whole time and energies . . . to the prosecution of the business of the Company. . . ." Although Eastman was mainly a silent partner, the two Chicagoans were in charge of attending "to all necessary business in the City of Chicago, such as purchasing goods, effecting a sale of the company merchandize, and keeping a lumber and wood yard" if circumstances warranted.[43]

Being in charge of "all necessary business in the City of Chicago" could mean a great deal, as the experiences of another Chicago lumberman reveal. The brothers Charles and Nathan Mears, originally of North Billerica, Massachusetts, arrived in Paw Paw, Michigan, in 1836 to run a general store. Charles, a difficult, driven man whose moods swung back and forth between obsessive enterprise and depressed inertia, soon decided to branch out into other lines. He constructed his first sawmill at White Lake, Michigan, in 1837, and sent his first shipment of lumber to Chicago a year later. Although Mears initially thought his best market would be in Milwaukee, and operated a lumberyard there for a few years, by 1848 he had closed the Wisconsin yard and opened a new one at Chicago. It was henceforth the main outlet for his mills.[44] Within another three years, he had taken on two partners who would be in charge of day-to-day operations at the Chicago yard: his brother, Nathan, and the man who had previously managed affairs in Milwaukee, Eli Bates. Over the next quarter century, Mears acquired some forty thousand acres of Michigan pine land, constructed and operated no fewer than fifteen sawmills, and built five separate harbors for the fleet of boats that ferried lumber and supplies back and forth between Chicago and the Michigan shoreline.[45]

Mears was typical of Lake Michigan lumbermen in a number of ways. Although he was a citizen of Michigan and officially resided in the mill town of Lincoln—indeed, he served in the Michigan state senate during the early years of the Civil War and was instrumental in having his town's name changed to honor the Republican president—almost his entire business revolved around the Chicago market.[46] Sales at the Chicago yard determined what sort of lumber Mears cut at his Michigan mills. When he tried in 1852 to save money by sawing thinner lumber, Mears's partners in Chicago soon let him know that the market was punishing them for his error. Eli Bates warned Mears several times that the mills were cutting too much coarse wood with dimensions that were not "plump" enough to satisfy Chicago buyers. "That which has come forward," complained the yard manager, was *"not thick enough,"* and so the yard was losing sales worth tens of thousands of board feet to competitors. As Bates explained, "The only objection to it was *'it is too thin,'* " and did not meet the informal grading standards that buyers were beginning to expect when buying wood in the city.[47]

Because the Chicago markets were critical to business, Mears and other lumbermen regularly relied on the city's newspapers, especially the *Tribune* and more specialized trade publications, to learn what was going on in the markets. "Dont [*sic*] fail," Mears reminded one of his later business partners, "to send me the Tribune by every vessel. . . ."[48] Lumbermen also turned for advice to the monthly market reports issued by large Chicago brokers and commission merchants, who analyzed conditions of supply and demand with an eye to helping their customers saw and ship lumber at the greatest profit.[49] In much the same way, Mears's Chicago office occasionally forwarded to his mill on the other side of the lake special "counterfeit detector" publications to warn the firm's Michigan storekeepers about dubious banknotes that might be circulating in their area.[50] No single location had more information than Chicago about the regional lumber trade, and so dealers and manufacturers from Michigan all the way west to the High Plains looked to the city as they tried to gauge what strategies their businesses should pursue.

Despite his official residence on the eastern shore of the lake, Mears often found himself working as much in Chicago as in Michigan. He employed a resident manager at each of his various mills and thus was able to spend much of every year either in Chicago or on the road. To take just one year as an example, New Year's Day in 1856 found Mears at his mill in Lincoln, Michigan, where he remained for six idle weeks. He did not make his first trip to Chicago until the middle of February.[51] Upon arrival in the city, he made a quick social excursion to Cincinnati and then returned to Chicago, where he stayed until the middle of March. While there, he gathered information about possible pineland acquisitions in Michigan, something which, ironically enough, he could do more easily in the city than he could back home in Michigan. He also bought the government warrants that he would use to purchase the pine lands he had just identified; ordered mill supplies; and lobbied to get a post office located in one of his towns. All these tasks pertained to his firm's Michigan mills rather than its Chicago yards, but Chicago was still the best place to take care of them.

On March 18, Mears returned to Michigan—not bothering to stop at any of his mills—to visit the state capital and buy the lands he had previously located. Once he had them, he mailed the deeds not to Lincoln but to Chicago. Continuing on from Lansing, he was in Cleveland by the end of March to examine the propeller-driven steamship he had commissioned from an Ohio manufacturer. He devoted the first half of April to traveling around Ohio in search of various pieces of machinery—saws, boilers, and engine parts—for his mills. By April 16, however, he was back in Chicago, where he remained for an entire month to purchase supplies and hire workers. Late May and June found him in Cleveland again, supervising the completion of his new ship and accompanying it to his mill at Duck Lake, where it arrived in early July. Two days after reaching Duck Lake, Mears was back in Chicago, and there he remained for the entire second half of the year. Although 1856 was perhaps unusual in seeing Mears away from his mills for such extended periods, the account of the year still conveys an accurate sense of his activities. Mears and many others who called themselves "Michigan" lumbermen often managed to do much if not most of their Michigan work from the distant southwestern corner of the lake.[52] After Mears finally married in 1874, at the age of sixty, it came as no surprise when he announced to one of his managers that he and his wife would probably "never return to reside" in Michigan. Henceforth, they would consider Chicago their true home.[53]

Michigan lumbermen had many reasons to spend so much time in Chicago. The city's concentration of commodity markets made it ideal for the purchase of every resource other than land (and some heavy machinery) needed to manufacture lumber. The agricultural produce that flooded into Chicago from western farms included many of the basic staples that a logging camp or a mill town needed during its peak months of operation. Among the individual purchases that Mears made in the city during the fall months of 1856 were 75 barrels of salt, 77 kegs of butter, 4 tons of cornmeal, 2,500 bushels of corn, 100 barrels of flour, 13 barrels of beef, 83 barrels of salt pork, 4 tons of fresh pork, 100 bags of oats, and over 50 tons of hay.[54] As Mears's shopping list suggests, Chicago served as pantry, butcher shop, and barn for the entire Lake Michigan lumber district. The city's wholesale markets made it easy to purchase provisions in large quantities, and to do so at prices better than those anywhere else in the region. The flow of supplies from city to mill complemented the flow of lumber from mill to city: ships that might otherwise have returned to Michigan empty could partially fill their holds with whatever items mill town stores needed for their customers.

Chicago was also the ideal place to purchase one other key commodity for lumber production: wage labor. Mears went to Chicago, and sometimes to Milwaukee, to hire many of the workers for his mills. In addition, he scoured the city docks to locate sailors and ship captains to crew the lake vessels he owned. He and other lumbermen counted on Lake Michigan's urban markets to serve as gathering stations for potential employees and to supply reserve labor whenever it was needed. Being able to turn quickly to the cities for workers became especially important to lumbermen at certain key times: when demand for lumber was suddenly greater than expected and mills had to run round the clock, when workers suddenly left or were fired for disciplinary reasons, or when strikes occurred. A strike by twenty of his workers in 1867 prompted Mears to write the Chicago office, "We need good men to fill their places very much." Having heard that workers were "plenty in Chicago," Mears directed, "All our Captains should endeavor to bring over as many good hands as they can. . . ."[55] In just this way, Mears could frustrate his workers' efforts to organize, and thereby keep their wages in line with those of others in the region. The floating populations of laborers concentrated in cities hundreds of miles from the lumber districts gave millowners a crucial measure of control over their local work forces.

Unlike the more seasonal labor arrangements that characterized logging camps, Mears's contracts for mill workers during the late 1850s typically lasted for one year, during which the employee agreed to work at Mears's discretion either in Chicago or at one of the Michigan mills. The typical workday was from sunrise to sunset except when the hours of daylight were under twelve hours; at no time was an individual to work less than eleven hours in a day. Men signing Mears's contracts agreed to bring their own axes, to pay their own passage across the lake, and to abstain from intoxicating liquors. They spent their days hauling logs to the mill, pushing them past the dangerous saw blades, stacking green lumber for drying and shipping, and generally maintaining the whole operation in good repair. In return, they received room, board, laundry, and a wage that, depending on the general economy, ranged from $100 to $200 per year.[56]

Occasionally, a man's wife and children were included in the labor contract he signed. One father, for instance, agreed to have his wife and daughter "work in the house" while he himself did "outside work."[57] In such cases, Mears wrote just one contract to cover the entire family, with no wage for anyone but the father. He made these arrangements only if he could get workers' wives to do the mill's cooking and laundry, at an unstated wage far below their husbands'. When he instructed his partners to hire workers for him in Chicago, he advised them to choose "good men and good Families without Children" to guarantee that women would not waste the firm's time in child-rearing. Mears could sometimes hire a man with a childless wife for the same wage given to a man with no wife at all, and he regarded this as the best possible arrangement, for "family men" were the steadiest and most reliable workers and brought underpaid female labor as a bonus.[58] Whether or not a woman had children, Mears was adamant that she contribute to the work of the mill. "I am sure," he told one of his managers, "my Business will not warrant the payment of wages sufficient for any one to keep his wife as a Laidy [*sic*]."[59]

Like the prices of all other commodities, the wages workers were getting on the streets of Chicago and other lake cities drew Mears's close attention. Because his contracts obligated him to keep workers for an entire year, he became anxious whenever the prevailing price of labor dropped below what he was paying. This was particularly true during the panic of 1857. Having hired his men with contracts guaranteeing them $180 or more for a year's work, Mears grew nervous as he watched wage rates in Chicago drop below $10 per month—a third less than what he was paying. He therefore urged his managers to pay off any men who were willing to leave early, so that he could hire new ones at the lower Chicago rates. "I can now," he wrote one manager, "hire a plenty of good hands at from 8 to $10 per month by the year and would be glad to pay off all who are willing to give up their contracts & leave & hire others at the going wages. . . ."[60] Mears kept track of wages in several cities, but his standard comparison was almost always with Chicago. The city served as his leading indicator of the cost of labor and, as such, helped set regional wage rates for Mears and others like him throughout the lumber districts.[61]

Cash flow was a perennial problem for Mears and most other lumbermen. When economic conditions turned bad, how and when to pay wages became the biggest single source of conflict between a firm and its workers. Although men and their families often earned board and laundry as part of their contract with Mears—so some of their wages came as continuous payments in kind—they were much less certain about when they would receive their cash wages. Money, a firm's most liquid form of capital, became its most critical resource when lumber was hard to sell. Whenever the market turned against him, as it often did during the winter and always during financial panics, Mears tried to avoid paying actual cash to his workers until the last possible moment. During the 1857 panic, when the firm had few liquid assets, Mears offered store credit to workers who were willing to take it—but no money. Their angry reaction was hardly surprising. As Christmas approached, one mill manager reported, "There has been great dissatisfaction about my not giving them cash. . . ." To let Mears know how angry men were becoming, the manager reported that he feared for his own safety: "I have been told . . . ," he said, "how I should be served" if wages did not appear by Christmas. The holiday ball was coming up soon, he told Mears, adding, "I hope you will be here to supply them with the money."[62]

It proved a vain hope. Those not satisfied with Mears's offer of store credit during the panic had only one recourse: quitting and demanding back wages. Unfortunately for them, Mears had no money and was not prepared even then to make good on their contracts. Instead, he offered them not the liquid capital of cash but the nonliquid capital of nature itself: the raw materials that in better times constituted his chief source of profits. The best he could do while hard times continued, he told one manager, was to offer departing workers payment in kind: "Those who leave I think might as well take most of their pay in good[s] & supplies which would be quite as good for them as money, & go in to some Business for themselves for the winter, as they will without doubt find it most impossible to get work elsewhere." The irony of an entrepreneur's giving up his capital at just the moment it no longer promised him any profits could hardly have been lost on his workers. One can imagine their reaction to Mears's closing gesture of magnanimity: "You may give them," he wrote, "the priviledge [*sic*] of chopping wood on my land below the Middle House & have the wood. . . . I am willing they shall have all they can make till Spring. . . ."[63] How they would sell such wood when Mears himself was unable to do so was a question he did not try to answer.

Harsh as Mears's actions may seem, he had good reason for them: under the depressed economic conditions of 1857, his own business was no longer profitable. Markets in Chicago and elsewhere had collapsed, and the backward flow of money that ordinarily paid for shipments of lumber had dwindled to nothing. "We are now," he wrote, "having the hardest times with the most *Gloomy* prospects for Business in Future that this Country has ever seen."[64] In such circumstances, it hardly mattered to Mears that he had signed contracts requiring him to pay workers no matter what the price of lumber. Even if he had possessed funds enough to meet his obligations, he would have been unwilling to spend good money on labor that had no prospect of earning back its own cost. "They certainly cannot expect me," he observed about his workers' requests for money, "to pay them more wages than can be realized from their labour." To Mears, it seemed that the men should be grateful just to have jobs, even if they did not receive cash for their work. "I supposed considering the condition of affairs in the Country," he fumed, "that all hands would be obliged to me for giving them imploy at such wages as I could afford to pay & be willing to take part of their wages in trade at that."[65] If the men could not see that their true interest was to have any job at all under such circumstances, so much the worse for them.

Mears's occasional inability to meet his payroll points to a deeper problem that he shared with other Great Lakes lumbermen in the era immediately surrounding the Civil War. Like many frontier entrepreneurs, most lumbermen were undercapitalized.[66] Despite the high book value of a typical lumber company's *fixed* capital—the lands, mills, and machinery that easily ran to hundreds of thousands of dollars for even a medium-sized firm—many companies often lacked the *liquid* capital needed to turn trees into lumber and lumber into cash. Even if a lumberman owned ten thousand acres of prime timber and a state-of-the-art sawmill, neither was any good without the money to hire workers or buy supplies. Lack of capital was undoubtedly the industry's single most persistent and prolific source of sleepless nights and ulcers.

Shortages of liquid capital made the many financial risks confronting lumber operators all the more severe. Some of these risks lay in the very wood that composed their fixed capital. Sawmills were notoriously vulnerable to fires that could destroy them in a single night. In 1858, for instance, Charles Mears's manager at Duck Lake sent him the laconic message "Last night we retired to bed at 9 o'clock, at 10 o'clock we was all aroused—the Mills are entirely ruined."[67] In this and other cases, the conflagration had been set by an aggrieved worker who found in fire a ready weapon against his employer.[68] Whether a fire occurred by accident or by intent, the same thing could easily happen to the stacked wood in lumberyards, and even to whole forests. The annual fire reports of Chicago's chief lumber journal always ran to dozens of entries.[69]

Water too posed risks. Ships on Lake Michigan had an unnerving tendency to sink or run aground during storms, a danger that grew as lumbermen tried to get in a last shipment before the cold of winter finally sealed the harbors.[70] Once winter had set in, too much or too little snow could mean trouble for loggers in the woods, just as springtime floods or droughts could wreak havoc with the river drives. Perennial as these risks may have been, given the very nature of the lumber trade, they always served as grim reminders of just how close to the edge a firm was operating. Although lumbermen might try to insure against them, even a single such disaster could mean bankruptcy for a company whose capital was too meager to absorb the blow.

But the greatest risks of the lumber trade flowed less from its occasional disasters than from the ordinary cycling of its natural year, which created long periods when a company had to pay out far more money than it earned. Throughout the fall and winter months, firms had to spend thousands of dollars on food, supplies, and wages, even though they could ship no lumber to market as long as Lake Michigan and the port cities were locked in ice. Because they depended in opposite ways on the freezing and thawing of water, the natural rhythms of supply and demand seldom moved in harmony: the most expensive time of the year came exactly when it was least possible to earn income. Success in the lumber industry required enough capital to meet costs during the long winters when shipping and sales fell to a minimum. Some operators found themselves short of money every winter, while others, like Mears, generally had enough funds to do all right except during financial panics. Sooner or later, however, almost everyone faced cash shortages that threatened business.[71]

When this happened, lumbermen could resort to several tactics that might mean the difference between bankruptcy and survival. One was to follow Mears's example during the 1857 panic: pay out as little cash as possible. This could be accomplished by such cost-cutting measures as not buying supplies, reducing production, refusing to pay old debts, making payments in kind, or firing workers. When the Holt Lumber Company faced hard times in 1877, its Chicago office directed its mill in Oconto, Wisconsin, to adopt almost all of these measures. "In regard to paying the men," directed the Chicago partner,

> I agree with you that it is better to pay what we can from the store, if we can do it to any advantage, but I have no idea of putting in a large stock of goods there and getting in debt for them and trusting them out. . . . I want every man discharged that can possibly be spared [a]bout the Mill[,] Store & everywhere else. Our expenses [no]w are eating us up, and must be curtailed.[72]

All such measures were ways of tightening the account books to cut away as many financial obligations as possible. At the same time that lumbermen were reducing costs in these ways, some scrounged to find any alternative source of income they could. Mears, for instance, went so far as to urge his mill managers to gather and sell blueberries, blackberries, peaches, and furs.[73]

An equally important survival tactic was to concentrate a firm's cash reserves wherever they were most needed. In practice, this meant regularly shifting money among a firm's logging operations, lakeshore mills, and Chicago yards—assuming its business included all these activities. Mears, who was more conservative about credit than many, regularly dealt with cash-flow problems by ordering his managers, "Send us every dollar you can spare. . . ."[74] The Chicago partner of the Holt Company responded to its capital crisis in 1877 by writing his Wisconsin mill, "I will send you what money I can," but telling his partners, "You will have to pay out money as sparingly as possible. We have a large amt of paper falling due the 1st of the month and we are getting in almost nothing to meet it."[75] Such movements of capital occurred during calmer times as well. For example, Mears's brother, Nathan, informed him in October 1852 that the Chicago yard had "plenty fund on hand if you want to the amount of six to ten thousand dollars."[76] In this way, sales at Chicago yards helped keep Michigan and Wisconsin mills operating when money was short, while store income from the mills helped on a smaller scale to pay for supplies in Chicago. Any lumber company that ran logging operations, a Lake Michigan mill, and a Chicago yard was by definition an interstate business with resources widely distributed across the region.[77] It thereby gained the ability to transfer its funds from mill to yard and back again—from forest to city to prairie, and from cornfield back to pinery—to meet the needs of trade. Just as lumber and supplies shuttled between Chicago and the lumber towns, so did money and capital.

But something else moved in this way as well: credit. When firms found themselves, as they regularly did each winter, having to spend money they did not possess, the most attractive solution was to spend money belonging to someone else. If one could acquire goods without paying for them, or get workers to cut trees and saw lumber without giving them cash, one could survive the seasonal downturn until sales of lumber brought in the funds to pay off accumulated debts. If a firm had too little cash to conduct business entirely with its own capital, it could purchase supplies on credit. It thereby transferred the burden of its own capitalization to a third party, more often than not a merchant or banker located in a major city like Chicago. By relying on Chicago wholesalers to advance them funds, small or undercapitalized Michigan and Wisconsin firms could survive the winter months when demand was at its worst. Come spring, they could then hope that the flow of natural capital from the forests would meet the demand of the farmers, turning lumber into cash and enabling companies to pay off their debts.

As the experiences of Charles Mears show, the dangers of the seasonal cycle were compounded by the business cycle. The same shortage of liquid capital that led lumbermen to fear the winter months threatened catastrophe when the economy jolted into a financial panic. In years like 1857, 1873, and their lesser cousins, many lumber companies found themselves caught in a trap of their own making. Not only had they incurred debts with their suppliers, but more often than not they had also extended credit to their own customers, who were now unable to pay. Under such circumstances, the long chain of debts and credits broke at its

Tallgrass prairie. Courtesy University of Wisconsin—Madison, Arboretum.

Henry Rowe Schoolcraft's view of Chicago in 1820. The sandbar at the mouth of the river is in the foreground, and Fort Dearborn is on the left bank. The site of the building on the right had been a fur-trading center since the 1770s. Reproduced from *Chicago Magazine* (1857), author's collection.

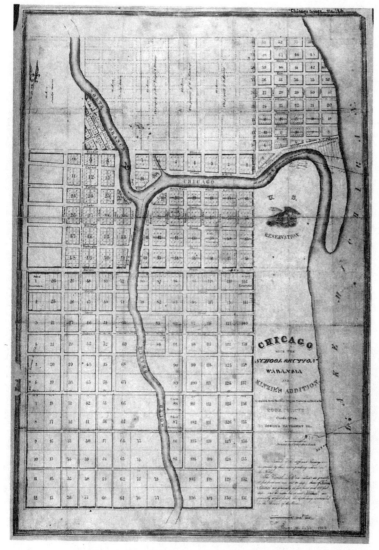

Joshua Hathaway's plat map of Chicago in 1834. Despite the urban appearance of this map, most of this land was as yet unoccupied. Note the two branches of the Chicago River, the site of Fort Dearborn, and the sandbar that still blocked the river's mouth. Courtesy Chicago Historical Society.

James Palmatary's bird's-eye view of Chicago in 1857. This detail from the famous bird's-eye shows the tracks of the Illinois Central Railroad, in the left foreground, leading to two large grain elevators at the mouth of the Chicago River. Ships line the main branch of the river, loading and unloading in the warehouse and business district, which is clearly visible as the line of larger buildings on the south bank. Courtesy Chicago Historical Society.

A one-family Dakota wheat farm in the 1880s. A farmer is at work on a reaping machine at the edge of the uncut grain, and carefully gathered piles of wheat sit drying in the field. Grazing animals in the pasture to the right are prevented from eating the cash crop by a wooden post-and-rail fence. Note the train on the right horizon—a familiar icon of the transportation revolution that had helped call this scene into being. Reproduced from William M. Thayer, *Marvels of the New West* (1887), author's collection.

The St. Louis levee in the heyday of water transportation. Dozens of steamboats line the riverbank, and the shore is abustle with activity as laborers and merchants move goods from one place to another. Note the sacks of grain that have been taken from the flatboat at the left and are about to be loaded—all by hand—onto the steamboat behind. Reproduced from *Harper's Weekly,* October 14, 1871, courtesy Yale University Library.

"The World's Railroad Scene." When the Illinois Central Railroad sought to convey a sense of its own importance with this 1882 lithograph, it superimposed its routes on a globe-scale map of the United States. In the foreground, wondering observers watch as a train leaves the station. Note the telegraph lines, steamship, and grain elevator at left, and the inset images of old-fashioned road and water transportation in the upper right and lower right. Courtesy Library of Congress.

The Great West as Chicago's corncob. In 1891, the Chicago, Burlington and Quincy Railroad distributed a deck of playing cards to favored customers, backed with this image—which speaks for itself! Reproduced from author's collection.

Wheat arriving at a Moorhead, Minnesota, elevator in 1879. Farmers brought their crops to country elevators like this one in wagons filled with burlap sacks. For grain to move through the elevator and into waiting railroad cars, its owners had to pour it from the sacks and mix it in common bins, an act that had far-reaching implications for the agricultural economy. Note the large heap of fuelwood in the left foreground to power the elevator's steam engine. Courtesy Clay County Historical Society, Moorhead, Minnesota.

Cutaway diagram of Chicago's Armour Elevator A and B in 1891. Grain was transported to the top of the elevator in buckets attached to an endless belt. There it was weighed in a pair of hoppers before falling down one of several chutes into a bin specially designated for its grade. It was finally carried by gravity to the holds of lake vessels waiting on the Chicago River. Reproduced from *Scientific American*, October 24, 1891, courtesy Yale University Library.

Detail of the chute sorting mechanism atop Armour Elevator A and B. Each bin in the elevator corresponded to a particular grade of grain. The rotating chute from the weighing hopper allowed workers to send grain into the appropriate bin. Shippers got receipts that entitled them to withdraw from the elevator an equal quantity of the same grade of grain they had put in—but they could not get back their own grain. Reproduced from *Scientific American*, October 24, 1891, courtesy Yale University Lib ary.

Buying and selling grain in the streets of Chicago. Before the advent of the elevator, dealers spilled samples of the grain they wished to sell right out onto the street in a great open-air market. The trading pits of the Chicago Board of Trade eventually replaced this institution. Reproduced from *Harper's Weekly*, October 31, 1868, courtesy Yale University Library.

The great hall of the Board of Trade. 'Change consisted of a series of octagonal platforms, each with several wooden steps leading down to a central pit. Traders faced each other in a crowd encircling the pit, using shouts and elaborate hand signals to indicate what they wished to buy or sell. Although the system has since been computerized, these pits are still the heart of the Board's market. Courtesy Chicago Historical Society.

FACING PAGE: *A flurry in wheat.* This famous image suggests the frenzied excitement of trading on the floor of 'Change when speculators were trying to run a corner. Reproduced from *Harper's New Monthly Magazine,* October 1880, courtesy Yale University Library.

Logging crew in northern Wisconsin, 1890s. These woodsmen display the chief tools of their trade for the camera: an ax, a crosscut saw, a yoke of oxen. Coming from a wide variety of ethnic and occupational backgrounds, laborers such as these often spent only the winter months cutting lumber, working elsewhere when the weather was warm. Courtesy State Historical Society of Wisconsin.

Sawyers working on a pine tree. In the early days of Great Lakes lumbering, even large trees were cut with axes. But by the 1880s, it had become more common to notch one side of the tree and then cut through the opposite side with a crosscut saw. The technique not only was easier for workers but allowed more precise control over where the tree fell. Courtesy State Historical Society of Wisconsin.

Logs moving along a skidway in northern Wisconsin, 1890s. Logging was mainly a winter activity because only then was it possible for huge loads of wood to move along iced skidways. A dozen or more logs could travel on a sled which consisted of a simple pair of wooden runners pulled by a team of four or more horses or oxen. Courtesy State Historical Society of Wisconsin.

Logs piled on a riverbank near Antigo, Wisconsin, 1886. Almost always, the end of the skidway was a frozen river. Workers arranged the logs into careful piles lining the riverbanks, and then awaited the spring thaw. Courtesy State Historical Society of Wisconsin.

Workers handling logs on the Muskegon River in Michigan. When the ice finally broke up at winter's end, woodsmen rode the floodwaters with their harvest of logs down to the mills on Lake Michigan. They guided the logs with tools called peavies, long wooden poles with a metal point and hook on the ends. It was hard, cold, dangerous work. Courtesy Michigan Bureau of History.

Chippewa River logjam, 1869. A logger's worst nightmare happened when logs suddenly got stuck in the river and blocked everything behind them. Logs could back up for hundreds of yards, and the immense pressure could lift them thirty or more feet in the air. A jam like this one emitted an eery dull roar as the logs scraped and creaked against each other. Courtesy State Historical Society of Wisconsin.

Breaking a jam. A logjam could be broken by using teams of horses to pull logs onto the shore, or even by dynamiting strategic logs in the hope of loosening the rest. But in the end, workers often had to go out onto the face and hack away by hand at the roaring mass. It was not a job for the faint of heart. Courtesy State Historical Society of Wisconsin.

Logging railroad near Cadillac, Michigan. As forests began to retreat from riverbanks that were increasingly devoid of trees, railroads allowed lumbermen to continue cutting the remaining pines. More and more of the cut moved by rail, eventually undermining the system of lake transport that had been so central to Chicago's lumber market. Courtesy Michigan Bureau of History.

Chicago's cargo market. At this location, Chicago lumber merchants met the ships from Lake Michigan milltowns, examined their contents, and bought wood by the shipload. This was the greatest lumber market in the world in the decades following 1850. Buyers purchased lumber here at the forks of the Chicago River, and then sent it on to lumberyards lining the South Branch (toward the viewer in this photograph). Courtesy Chicago Historical Society.

Chicago's lumber district. In this immense city within a city, lumber sat on the banks of the South Branch waiting to be shipped by rail out to customers in the grasslands. The stacks of wood dwarfed the lumber merchants' offices, and an aroma of pine mingled with the smell of sewage from the river. Note the masts of ships and the grain elevator on the horizon. Reproduced from *Harper's Weekly,* October 20, 1883, courtesy Yale University Library.

The Cutover. The lands around Deward, Michigan, had one of the last remaining white pine forests in the Lower Peninsula at the beginning of the twentieth century. Within a decade, they too had become part of the Cutover, that abandoned ghost landscape which Chicago played such an important role in creating. Courtesy Michigan Bureau of History.

White pine forest. Courtesy State Historical Society of Wisconsin.

weakest links, and firms had to scramble to avoid becoming one more victim in the ensuing series of defaults. Declaring in October 1859 that "these are the hardest times for the lumber trade I have ever seen," Mears wrote one of his managers, "I . . . have hardly been able to attend to any thing but money matters and have hardly been able to collect enough to pay expenses." After repeating his ritual injunction "I hope you will not fail to send me all the money you can spare," Mears added, "Many of the lumber Dealers will be obliged to fail if these times last a month longer."[78] Such were the perils of juggling debts in the troughs of the business cycle.

Risky as the dependence on credit could be, there was almost no way to escape it. Buyers and sellers were both short of cash, which meant that both had to offer customers their best natural alternative—lumber, grain, meat, and other provisions—in return for a promise to pay cash in the future. During ordinary years when the economy was healthy, one could do a reasonable business in this way; during panics, one had to hope that creditors would be patient while one waited for one's own customers to pay for goods they had bought on time. Although the obvious way to escape such risks was to avoid selling (or buying) on credit—Mears repeatedly reminded his managers, "I do not wish to extend a dollars credit to any man"—this was much more easily said than done.[79] As one lumber merchant explained in a letter to the *Northwestern Lumberman,*

> You can not do it! Why? Because credit is not an extraneous substance which exists on the outside of the business; it is not a wash upon the surface; it is a part of the innermost. If it is a disease, it lies next to the most vital parts. To suddenly remove it would be to endanger life.[80]

The greatest threats to a lumber firm's economic well-being were thus, ironically, also the fount of its prosperity. The mills whose cheap wooden construction made them affordable also made them susceptible to fire. The late-season shipments of lumber that reached Chicago in time to take advantage of the city's winter market also faced the threat of shipwreck in December storms. And the credit that allowed companies to do a larger business than their capital justified also laid them open to financial disaster in a panic. The risks of the lumber trade were indeed a disease lying "next to the most vital parts." A lumberman's greatest challenge was to prevent that chronic condition from becoming fatal.

Cargo Market

It was for this very reason that Chicago emerged during the 1850s as the single greatest lumber market in the world. The solutions to seasonal and business cycles alike came to center on the city in such a way that Lake Michigan lumbermen had little choice but to turn to Chicago as their safest port in good economic weather and bad. The natural capital they held in their trees, logs, and lumber became valuable for trade only if they could turn it into the liquid capital of cash and credit. To work that transformation, they needed a dependable market—and no western market was more dependable than Chicago. In the city's marketplace, the commodities of the forest underwent their crucial conversion into money, and so provided the basis for another cycle of production: lumber became cash, and cash became the wages and provisions that would sustain the next round of logging and milling. In this cycle of cash and capital lay the source of Chicago's influence over the supply side of the market.

The conversion of wood into money could happen in at least two ways. Mill operators like Mears who owned Chicago yards could simply have their ships pick up lumber in Michigan or Wisconsin and deliver it directly to their docks in the city, taking upon themselves the different roles of manufacturer, shipper, wholesaler, and sometimes even retailer. Many sawmill operators, however, did not possess the resources to handle all these roles at once, and thus could not afford to maintain their own Chicago yard. Unlike Mears and other large operators, they had to adopt a second strategy. After loading their output into the hold of a Lake Michigan ship that they might or might not own themselves, they then consigned it to Chicago in the hope that some purchaser—usually a commission merchant or an independent wholesale dealer—would buy the lumber after it arrived in the city. This was a riskier way to do business, but if one lacked the capital to handle sales directly, there were few alternatives.

From the 1850s forward, independent lumber ships arriving in Chicago generally made their way up the Chicago River to the foot of Franklin Street, just before the river split into its north and south branches. There, on a few hundred feet of wharves collectively known as the wholesale docks, the buyers and sellers of Chicago lumber met in the "cargo market"—probably the only place in the United States where traders conducted a wholesale market in unsold shiploads of lumber throughout the warm months of the year. Not even such major lumber centers as New York, Albany, Boston, or Philadelphia had a comparable institution.[81] "Chicago," wrote the *Northwestern Lumberman* in 1878, "is about the only point in the country where there is a 'market' for lumber, as between manufacturers and wholesale dealers."[82] Each morning, starting sometime after sunrise and continuing until about noon, the city's commission merchants and wholesale dealers "went on the market" by boarding the ships to inspect whatever wood they could see below deck. On the basis of the volume and quality of the cargo, they offered a price for the entire shipload of lumber. Once buyer and seller had completed their transaction, the ship was towed to the purchaser's yard in the lumber district proper, along the banks of the South Branch. There, its new owner unloaded it and prepared it for wholesale or retail sale.[83]

Several features of the Chicago cargo market made it unique on Lake Michigan, if not in the entire country. These features almost guaranteed the city's dominance in the lumber trade once large numbers of independent ships began to use the wholesale docks in the 1850s. One was simply its reliability. So great was the demand concentrated in Chicago by the city's railroad lines that its lumberyards had an almost insatiable appetite for whatever the ships could bring them. "No lumber market but this," remarked a Chicago correspondent of the Milwaukee-based *Wisconsin Lumberman* in 1874, "could dispose of an average of three million feet per day . . . for the space of nearly seven months each year."[84] Lumbermen could be confident that Chicago would always have someone ready to buy their wood, no matter how large the shipment. The fierce competition at the docks kept prices lower than they might be elsewhere, but that mattered less than knowing one could always make a sale. Much like railroad managers, lumbermen had to worry about buying supplies, paying debts, and meeting fixed capital costs, and so they often cared more about earning a reliable income quickly than about getting the highest possible price for their product.

To see why Lake Michigan mill operators chose to send the bulk of their output to Chicago, one has only to consider their alternatives. The city's nearest competitor on the western shore of the lake was Milwaukee, but its much smaller railroad network gave it an equally small wholesale hinterland for lumber. Even in the 1870s, it maintained stocks of lumber that were less than a seventh of Chicago's total.[85] Most wood went to Milwaukee only if a dealer had already purchased it in advance. Lumbermen knew from hard experience that buyers were "not particularly numerous" in Milwaukee, making it difficult to sell lumber at the city's docks. "Sometimes," wrote one observer, "after fruitless lingering on the meager market, a lumber vessel is forced to pull out for Chicago, the caresses of sharp-clawed friends being preferable to a supreme cold shoulder."[86] The bottom line was simple: Chicago was the only place on Lake Michigan where one never had to wait long to sell lumber. Its prices might be low, but at least its merchants were always willing to strike some sort of deal.

Two other features of the cargo market made it even more attractive to Lake Michigan lumbermen: Chicago dealers bought lumber by the shipload *and* they paid hard cash for it. Nowhere else was this true. As the

Wisconsin Lumberman reported to its readers in 1874, "Chicago is not only the largest lumber market in the world, but it has always had an eminent reputation as a market upon which almost any amount of lumber could be placed at any time and sold for cash."[87] For lumber vessels whose owners and captains were eager to return to the mills as soon as possible for another shipment, there were enormous advantages in being able to sell large quantities quickly. A rapid sale meant reducing the amount of time a ship sat idle (and paying dock charges) in port. It lowered the transaction costs that came with each additional buyer. It avoided the need to unload lumber onto the docks so that potential purchasers could inspect it piece-meal. And it eliminated the very real possibility that at the end of several sales low-quality lumber might remain that no one would buy at any price. Being able in one transaction to sell everything a ship contained allowed lumbermen from Chicago's hinterland to shift these costs and risks onto the shoulders of the city's merchants. Even more important, though, buy-ers at Chicago's cargo market always paid cash. For mill operators peren-nially short of money, the prospect of converting lumber instantly from natural capital into liquid capital justified adding many extra miles to its journey. "Lumber," explained one Chicago dealer, "comes here because it can be sold for cash."[88]

As soon as the ice broke up in the spring, lumberman around the lake sent off shipments to raise the cash with which to repay their winter debts. As they did so, they made a simple calculation about where to send their output. If they shipped lumber to lake towns other than Chicago, they would in all likelihood have to sell to customers who had to buy on credit—which was of no help in meeting their own financial obligations. No such problem existed in Chicago. Furthermore, Chicago's other wholesale markets sold food and provisions in bulk at some of the lowest prices in the region, so lumber ships could bring back supplies rather than return to their home ports empty. All arguments pointed to Chicago as the best destination for most lumber shipments. As a result, lumber vessels accounted for most of the ships that visited Chicago's harbor: of the nearly thirteen thousand arrivals there in 1872, over nine thousand carried lumber.[89] One visitor to Chicago recorded that on a single day in 1867, "a favorable wind blew into port two hundred and eighteen vessels loaded with timber."[90] The *Northwestern Lumberman* was not exaggerating in 1879 when it remarked, "It may almost be said that the few hundred feet of dock at the head of Franklin street is the center around which the vast industry represented in the handling of lumber revolves." [91]

Lumber arriving at the cargo market came from all around the shores of Lake Michigan; some even came from as far away as the Canadian and Michigan ports on Lake Huron. In 1859, Chicago's two most important trading partners were Muskegon, Michigan, and Green Bay, Wisconsin, both at the mouths of river systems that drained extensive areas in the interior of their respective states. Important as they were, Muskegon accounted for only 18 percent of Chicago's total lumber supply and Green Bay for 14 percent.[92] Only one other port—Oconto, Wisconsin, north of Green Bay—contributed more than 10 percent of Chicago's supply, a fact that suggests the extent and diversity of the city's lumber hinterland. The rest of Chicago's wood came from dozens of small sawmill towns scattered up and down the lakeshore. Although Lake Michigan lumber operators depended heavily on Chicago wholesalers to buy their wood, the converse was not nearly so true of the wholesalers. Chicagoans were in the happy position of being able to buy from as many sellers as they wanted. Competition to sell was fierce, which meant that wholesalers could accumulate large stocks at very favorable prices. They could afford to have sharp claws.

But Chicago's central role in the lumber trade had still other sources that were at least as important as the cargo market's ability to attract many sellers from a wide area. The attractiveness of the Franklin Street docks as a cash market was attributable to the wealth and organization that allowed the city's wholesale yards to sustain an open market in lumber. For the three decades following 1850, Chicago wholesalers were the largest and most important lumber operators between the Appalachians and the Sierra Nevada. It was their capital, made available either as cash purchases or credit advances, that permitted so many small sawmills and logging operations to do business with what would otherwise have been insufficient financing. By 1880, the city's lumber merchants jointly controlled an estimated capital of over $80 million, a sum several times larger than the aggregate capital held by all the city's banks.[93]

The wholesalers amassed this enormous fortune by acting as intermediaries between the original suppliers of lumber in the Lake Michigan forests and the ultimate consumers of it in the small towns and farming areas of the prairies. As go-betweens, they performed several crucial functions for manufacturers and retail customers alike. The most important was simply to smooth out the seasonal oscillations of supply and demand by holding vast quantities of lumber. One could order even the largest shipment of lumber from Chicago no matter what the time of year. The stock in the city's yards far surpassed that in any other western city, so much so that at the beginning of 1879, for instance, Chicago yards were holding over 400 million board feet of lumber. By the best contemporary estimates, this amounted to over one-fifth of the milled lumber waiting to be sold at urban yards in the entire region streching from Cleveland to Minneapolis.[94] So concentrated a supply meant that, just

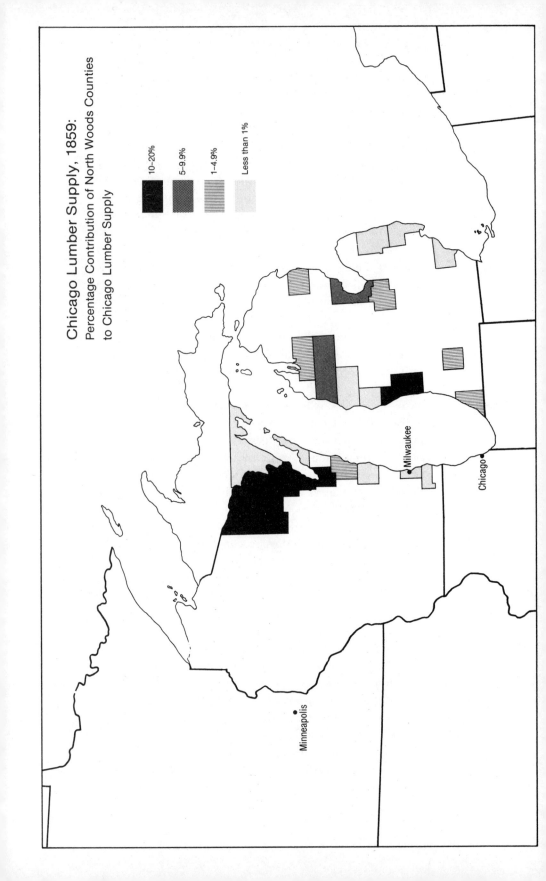

Chicago Lumber Supply, 1859:
Percentage Contribution of North Woods Counties
to Chicago Lumber Supply

10–20%

5–9.9%

1–4.9%

Less than 1%

Minneapolis

Milwaukee

Chicago

as millowners could always find someone in the Chicago cargo market who would buy their lumber, so could retail dealers and customers always find someone in the Chicago lumber district who would sell it to them. Because the wholesale market was highly competitive, its prices were attractively low, and that often enabled Chicago firms to outsell lumber dealers located hundreds of miles away.

For anyone who visited it in the years following the Civil War, the lumber district was an astonishing place, almost a city within a city. As one passed the Franklin Street wholesale docks and rounded the bend to float onto the South Branch of the Chicago River, one entered a world that appeared to consist almost entirely of stacked wood. As a stunned British visitor remarked, "The timber yards are a considerable part of the city's surface, there appearing to be enough boards and planks piled up to supply a half-dozen States."[95] Especially on the west bank of the river, whole city blocks might contain nothing but docks and seemingly endless heaps of pine lumber ten or more feet high. All told, the district contained twelve miles of dockage devoted solely to handling lumber ships.[96] The smell of sap and sawdust hung in the air, mingled with the less pleasant odors of sewage from the river. Here and there above the square woodpiles, one could glimpse the masts of docked ships as they unloaded the lumber in their holds, as well as the looming shapes and smoking stacks of nearby grain elevators. Otherwise, though, the vista stretching off into the gray middle distance was raw lumber and nothing else. The woodpiles dwarfed the offices of individual lumber merchants, which were barely distinguishable from their surroundings. After dark, it was a lonely and abandoned landscape, the gloom broken only by the wandering lanterns of night watchmen making their rounds to guard against fire and theft.[97]

The heart of the district lay along the mile of riverfront south of Twenty-second Street and west of Halsted. There, more than a dozen short canals, each over a quarter mile long, fingered north from the river. Along these canals were hundreds of standard lots measuring 244 by 100 feet. Each one had 100 feet of canal frontage, and at the back of each was a railroad siding connecting the yard via the Chicago, Burlington and Quincy with every railroad line in the city. Once a wholesale dealer had purchased a shipload of lumber at the cargo market the entire vessel floated down the river to a dock at one of these yards. A crew of "lumber-shovers" then unloaded and stacked the lumber onto the dealer's lot. There, the boards sat until some retail dealer purchased them for shipment to another city, whereupon they had only to be moved no more than a couple of hundred feet to the railroad car that carried them to their final destination.[98]

More went on in these yards than the simple receiving, stacking, and shipping of wood. Because of the sawmill operators' urgent financial need to sell their lumber as quickly as possible, most of it arrived in Chicago still green with moisture and sap. The wholesale yards therefore contributed to the final stage of lumber manufacture by drying wood that was still too damp for safe use. In effect, this was yet another capital cost they absorbed for the sawmills, since money invested in lumber did not earn any income while wood sat drying in the yard.[99] One reason wholesalers kept so many woodpiles in the lumber district was to give themselves enough of an overstock that they could fill any orders that came in while newly arrived shipments were still drying. But just how seriously they took this part of their job is open to question. Given the high demand even for green lumber in Chicago's hinterland markets, and given that wholesalers viewed stacked wood as capital that was not earning its keep, they had strong incentives to declare lumber ready for sale even when it still felt damp to the touch. Chicago dealers shipped wood that was much greener than many of their country customers liked, with consequences that have been evident in the warped walls and floors of many a farmhouse ever since.[100]

Chicago wholesalers may not have taken very seriously the task of drying wood, but they were much more serious about another of their chief activities: sorting wood. Because the sawmills hurried their product to market by the shipload, they made little effort to separate good wood from bad. Instead, they sent literally everything that was remotely marketable. A typical shipment might contain pieces of lumber that differed widely in dimension, dryness, knottiness, sappiness, degree of finish, and overall quality. This meant that when wholesalers at the cargo market bought everything in a ship's hold, they inevitably purchased different pieces of lumber that would bring widely varying prices from retail customers. To obtain full value from their purchase, therefore, they had to sort the wood into categories that customers would recognize.

After unloading wood at the yards, lumber workers graded it according to informal rules that superficially resembled those used for grain at the Chicago Board of Trade. How many knots did the wood have, and how large were they? How wide and long was it? Did it have sap stains? Was it warped? And so on. Once graded and inspected according to these rules, lumber was sorted into the appropriate part of the yard, so the physical layout of the lot came to reflect the yard's grading scheme. With the completion of this step, the timber that had arrived at the cargo market as a raw, homogeneous mass was carefully differentiated into the conventional categories of the marketplace. What had begun as a natural pine tree had been progressively transformed from log to board to artificially standardized commodity. The Chicago wholesale yards were thus a long way—in thought as much as in space—from the forests that had been cut down to supply them.

When customers, most of whom were dealers located in hinterland towns, placed an order with one of the Chicago yards, the prices they paid depended on the grade of wood they selected. Lumber, shingles, and lath each had separate standards that identified them as "clear," "first common," "second common," and so on. The broadest distinction in grades was between "clear" stock, which tended to be sold at higher prices for use in finishing, and "common" stock, which was cheaper and of lower quality. The best clear lumber—broad boards entirely free of knots or sap stains—often went to merchants in towns and cities where wealthier residents were willing to spend good money to give their homes a fine appearance. "Common" lumber sold more widely, since it was used by everyone to frame buildings and was also popular with poorer customers, many of them in rural areas, who could not afford to worry about the finish of their houses.[101]

In effect, the enormous concentration of supply in Chicago's lumberyards encouraged its dealers to attempt the same abstraction of a natural resource that had occurred in the city's grain market. As in the grain trade, in the lumber trade buying by rail often meant that hinterland customers had to wire their orders to Chicago without seeing in advance the products they were buying. Doing this was possible only with some sort of grading scheme. Chicago wholesalers reached a rough agreement about how the city's lumber should be graded, and because they so dominated the western market, their grading system, like that of the Board of Trade, proliferated across the region to become the basis for sales in hinterland towns.[102] Competing lumber districts adopted it as well: sawmills on the Chippewa River in northwestern Wisconsin hired Chicago lumber inspectors to make sure that their output conformed to Chicago grades.[103] Remembering the feverish speculative market that emerged after the Board of Trade standardized grain grades, a few Chicago merchants even hoped that the city's lumber market might develop along similar lines. Where standard grades existed, could futures contracts be far behind? If so, surely the profits from a full-scale futures market in lumber would make the city's existing trade look like small kindling.

But the story of Chicago's lumber trade would have a much different ending: no speculative market in wood ever really developed there during the nineteenth century.[104] The city's lumber grades never became so standardized as its grain grades, probably because buyers of wood continued to insist on differentiating its qualities much more carefully than those of grain. Once one built something from wood, one had to live with

it for a long time. For those who marketed it, lumber was bulky, expensive
to store, and easy to damage. It had none of the liquid qualities that had
allowed grain elevators to transform the handling of wheat and corn.
These characteristics all made if difficult to treat lumber quite so abstractly as grain, and thus made it less suited to the speculative needs of a
futures market.[105] Moreover, the Lumberman's Exchange of Chicago, the
city's chief organization of lumber wholesalers and manufacturers after
its founding in 1869, never attained anything like the power or prominence of the Chicago Board of Trade.[106] Although Chicago lumbermen
during the 1870s and 1880s regularly sought to promote national lum-
ber-grading standards that resembled their system, none of their efforts
succeeded.[107] Regional grading schemes with effective enforcement did
not appear in the lumber industry until the 1890s, and they were based on
Mississippi Valley standards, not Chicago ones.[108]

Although Chicago's grades for lumber quality did not become wholly
standardized across the region, the sizes in which city dealers sold their
wood did set informal but widely recognized standards. The customers
who purchased the bulk of Chicago's lumber sought it in certain regular
dimensions, among which the humble two-by-four was just one of several
popular choices. The huge and growing market for such essential
wooden objects as fence posts and railroad ties demanded that logs be cut
according to rigidly consistent scales. The same was true of the wooden
structures that rural farmers and townspeople were building for themselves. Obtaining the designs of their houses, farms, and commercial
buildings from popular pattern books and builders' manuals, people
were eager to buy wood that came as close as possible to the specifications
in those books. A good sawmill could supply pieces of wood with almost
identical width and depth measurements, so carpenters had only to cut
them to proper length—thus significantly reducing the labor involved in
construction. For all these reasons, lumber of standard dimensions became more and more popular with American builders during the course
of the nineteenth century.

Here again they followed Chicago's example. In 1833, just as the city
was experiencing its first major real estate boom in the wake of the canal
fever, the builder Augustine D. Taylor devised a new architectural framing system while constructing St. Mary's Catholic Church.[109] In designing
the building, Taylor rejected the strong but laborious timber-frame construction—with heavy beams held together by hand-carved mortise-and-
tenon joints—that had typified wooden architecture since the European
Middle Ages. Instead, he turned to the new, lighter, mass-produced
pieces of lumber that were beginning to be available in the city, and
combined them with an even more unpretentious product of America's

machine age: the nail. Taylor used these simple materials to erect a structural skeleton consisting of sills, floor joists, studs, and roof rafters, all nailed together and covered with a wooden sheathing of clapboards and shingles. Because his design supported the load of the building with a cage-like framework consisting of many lightweight studs and joists rather than a few massive wooden columns and girders, it came to be known as the balloon frame.

As a popular farmer's manual defined it in the 1880s, what distinguished the balloon frame from its more stolid predecessor was that it consisted of "a strong frame made with few mortises and tenons, spikes and nails holding all firmly together."[110] Mundane as this simple description may sound, it proclaimed an architectural revolution. Because the balloon frame consisted of light, milled wood, a small number of workers could erect it quickly; because it was held together with nails instead of intricate carved joints, it required less skill than earlier buildings; and because its components were easy to modify and repeat, it was wonderfully adaptable to buildings of different shapes and forms. Perhaps its only real drawback was that the tall two-by-four studs supporting both the second-floor joists and the roof rafters formed continuous air spaces that ran from basement to roof. Because builders did not at first grasp the implications of these air spaces, early balloon-frame structures had few or no fire-stops in their walls.[111] In the event that any part of the structure started to burn, the walls quickly began to act as flues, and the building became an inferno. Chicagoans would learn this lesson all too well during the Great Fire, which devastated their city in October 1871.[112]

Despite this one invisible danger of the balloon frame, Chicagoans and other nineteenth-century Americans had every reason to embrace it as the quintessential building form of the age. In a world where wood was cheap and readily available, Taylor's design was ideally suited to the task of occupying a frontier landscape as quickly and with as little labor as possible. "Everything new," wrote a traveler to Chicago in 1880, "is of wood. . . ."[113] The balloon frame was no less well adapted to the needs of humble farm outbuildings than to the elaborate architectural fantasies it soon helped inspire in the domestic residences of the well-to-do. Even inexperienced carpenters could use it with reasonable success, and builders' manuals promoted it accordingly. By the second half of the nineteenth century, the vast majority of America's wooden buildings were using it.

Appropriately enough, the decades following 1850, during which the balloon frame triumphed in American architecture, also constituted the period when Chicago emerged as the greatest lumber market in the world. The fences, railroad ties, and buildings that fueled the prodigious

American demand for wood were in common use throughout the country, but nowhere was the demand for them more concentrated than at Chicago. In no other city on the planet was there a neighborhood to compare with the vast, strange landscape of stacked wood that dominated the South Branch of the Chicago River. In no other city did so large a lumber fleet gather to deliver so immense an output from so many different sawmills. And in no other city did so many customers from so extensive an area gather to buy so much wood.

Buying by Rail

If the lumbermen of Lake Michigan had good reasons for selling their product in Chicago, the settlers and retail lumber dealers of the western grasslands had equally good reasons for buying it there. The most obvious was the familiar ecological one: for the first time in the history of North American frontier settlement, would-be farmers and town builders had moved out of the forest and into a grassland ecosystem where they had to rely on sources of wood lying far outside their immediate locales. "The prairies," wrote one traveler, "to which Nature has been so variously bountiful, do lack this first necessity of the settler, and it is Chicago that sends up the lake for it and supplies it to the prairies."[114] The same attractions that had pulled sellers to the Chicago marketplace drew buyers there as well: the sheer volume of wood its dealers could handle, the variety of assortments they stocked, and their readiness to offer cash to sellers and credit to buyers. In Chicago, lumber supply met lumber demand on an unprecedented scale.

But the mere conjunction of forest and prairie could not by itself have produced Chicago's extraordinary wholesale market in lumber. The geography of capital was no less crucial than the geography of nature in bringing so many sellers and buyers together, for both depended finally on the iron and steel rails that were Chicago's gateway to the western prairies. Because the city by 1860 was already the central rail depot of the upper Mississippi Valley, Chicago's wholesale lumberyards became the chief suppliers to inhabitants in a broad fan-shaped swath of land reaching to the Great Plains and beyond. Farmers and townspeople in Illinois, Iowa, and southern Wisconsin were among the chief customers of Chicago's lumber dealers, but the city's reach extended much father west, to wherever the rails ran. For many grassland customers, the rail network made Chicago the best option for obtaining lumber. The superintendant of the Chicago, Burlington and Quincy could thus write in 1868 of the lumber dealers at St. Joseph and Kansas City, "They get from Chicago their lumber because they cannot ge[t] it any other way."[115] By the end of the 1860s, Nebraskans and Kansans were buying much of their lumber from Chicago, and the city's wood was framing buildings as far away as Colorado and Wyoming.

Sometimes entire buildings rode the rails west from the city. One Chicago firm, as an 1867 visitor described it, went so far as "to despatch timber in the form of ready-made houses" to customers throughout the Great West, its proprietors being "happy to furnish cottages, villas, school-houses, stores, taverns, churches, court-houses, or towns, whole-sale and retail, and to forward them, securely packed, to any part of the country."[116] Chicago firms that manufactured building components—doors, sashes, and blinds—shipped goods even greater distances, and not just to the West. By 1880, an eastern tourist could report that he saw railroad cars at one Chicago factory that were destined "not only for Denver, Leadville, Santa Fe, and Salt Lake City, but—tell it not in New England—for Connecticut as well."[117] Wherever the city's lumber went, and in whatever form, it reached its destination by rail.

Just as they did with grain, the railroads had powerful reasons of their own for making Chicago central to the lumber trade. One was simply the sheer volume of business it generated for them. By 1860, the city's yards were annually shipping over 220 million board feet of lumber.[118] Nearly 80 percent of it rode the rails. By 1870, the city's lumber shipments had risen to over 580 million board feet, and by 1880, to over a *billion* board feet—of which the railroads' share had grown to 95 percent. For individual lines passing through treeless country, these aggregate numbers meant big business. In 1870, for instance, the Illinois Central, the Chicago, Burlington and Quincy, and the Chicago and Alton each carried over 120 million board feet of lumber. Only the city's grain shipments could compare in total volume.[119]

For the railroads, the direction of these shipments was at least as important as their size. The vast bulk of Chicago's lumber exports moved west, toward the prairies.[120] By so doing, they helped counterbalance the opposing movement of grain from western farms, the vast bulk of which moved east. Many of the trains that carried wheat and corn east would have gone back empty—at a loss—had there been no lumber to help pay for the return journey. Because railroad companies had to meet their fixed costs no matter what, and because railroad cars had to return to the western granaries whether or not they had anything to carry, railroad managers had good reason to be generous in setting their westbound lumber rates. Lumber therefore moved cheaply relative to many other goods—and from nowhere more cheaply than from Chicago. Since most western railroad companies had their farthest eastern terminals in Chicago and since they sought to encourage the longest possible haul over their own lines, they competed with each other more intensely there than anywhere else. The best way to maximize the return on invested railroad capital was to keep the average cost per ton-mile for lumber lower from Chicago than from anywhere else.

By the 1870s, the whole railroad rate structure for Great Lakes lumber was revolving around Chicago, in ways that made the city's preeminence a self-fulfilling prophecy. Shippers at other locations found that westward-bound railroads charged them for carrying lumber by setting a "differential" between their own rate and Chicago's rate to the same point. To establish the rate from Burlington, Iowa, to Omaha, Nebraska, for instance, a railroad company determined what it would charge for carrying the same quantity of lumber from *Chicago* to Omaha, and then subtracted a fixed number of cents to set the Burlington rate.[121] As long as these differentials remained fixed on a railroad's books, its rates could fluctuate from month to month without ever upsetting the balance of power among Chicago and its competitors.

This system was formalized for the entire rail network in 1884 when George M. Bogue, a railroad arbitrator, announced an official schedule of differentials—differences in cents per hundredweight between Chicago's lumber rates and those of other cities—that would henceforth set rates on all participating railroads for every major shipping center east of the Rockies.[122] With the Bogue award in place, railroads could set identical rates (and hence avoid competing with each other) simply by maintaining the Chicago-based differentials that the arbitrator had established. By so doing, they reinforced the advantages Chicago already enjoyed as a lumber center, and revealed just how much people had come to regard those advantages as a natural condition of trade. Bogue himself felt little hesitation in attributing Chicago's favored status to the logic of a railroad geography that he apparently saw as "natural." In explaining how the city could afford to ship lumber more cheaply even than towns located in the heart of the north woods, he wrote,

> It is no doubt true that the roads reaching Chicago—which is the largest primary grain and stock receiving point in the world—can in their return make rates on lumber without loss, which would net a loss if applied to the roads reaching the pineries direct; and it is doubtless true, also, that the actual cost of the haul from Chicago does not greatly exceed the shorter haul from the Mississippi river; and so long as this is the case, it is natural to expect that the Chicago roads will support the Chicago market.[123]

Support it they did, though for reasons having less to do with nature than with the railroads' own need to employ capital as fully as possible to meet fixed costs and remain profitable. Whatever their reasons, the railroads made Chicago, a city located in one of the nation's most treeless landscapes, the greatest lumber center in the world. In consequence, customers could often buy wood from Chicago more cheaply than from towns whose "natural" advantages—nearness to the pine forests or nearness to prairie customers—seemed superior to Chicago's. Merchants in other lumber towns sometimes complained about the unfairness of not being able to compete against a lumber metropolis located so far from the forests, but they were a distinct minority.[124] Most people saw nothing odd about Chicago's favored position. The geography of capital had once again insinuated itself so successfully into the geography of nature that the primacy of the city's wholesale lumberyards came to seem inevitable—in Bogue's word, "natural."

It must have seemed equally natural for George Hotchkiss, the most important nineteenth-century chronicler of Chicago's lumber industry, to write in 1884, "The history of the lumber trade is the history of the city."[125] Had he sought to show proof for those words, he need only have gestured toward the South Fork of the river, where over half a billion board feet of lumber sat drying in seemingly endless woodpiles whose appearance from afar was like nothing so much as a great gray forest lopped off and squared by some gigantic ax. More than a quarter million trees had died to build those woodpiles, trees that had been growing for more than a century in forests located well over a hundred miles north of the city.[126] If the history of the lumber trade—or rather, the history of those trees—was in fact "the history of the city," one suspects that few Chicagoans recognized it as such. Few had ever seen those forests, and fewer still had seen what those forests were becoming as the ax wielders continued their relentless work on behalf of Chicago's merchants and customers. Although the city, its railroads, and one of its most important industries had all required the sacrifice of those trees, few acknowledged their deaths. They had died so far away, and the years in which they had grown were so much out of mind, that it was easy to forget the roots from which the city had sprung. And where a quarter million white pines had fallen in a single year, surely another quarter million would always stand ready to take their place.

Lost Hinterlands

Or perhaps not.

Just three or four years after Hotchkiss wrote, many Chicagoans began to realize that the city's wholesale lumber industry had entered a new era. During the three decades preceding 1882, the city's lumber dealers had enjoyed an average annual growth in their incoming shipments of nearly 15 percent; during the golden years that preceded the 1857 panic, the city's receipts had bounded upward at average rates of over 35 percent per year. The early 1870s, on the other hand, had seen the market stagnate for more than half a decade before it finally turned upward again. Then, in 1882, Chicago's lumber industry entered an era of upheaval and decline. From then until the end of the century, its receipts actually fell by an average of just under 1 percent per annum, and fluctuated wildly from year to year, seriously destabilizing lumber company profits.[127]

The 1880s marked a sea change for an industry addicted to exuberant growth. Never again would Chicago lumber merchants be able to take for granted the "naturalness" of their city's special relationship to the northern forests. As they moved into the final decade of the century, they found themselves in the unaccustomed position of taking "a rather dreary view of the prospect," knowing that their city had permanently lost its role as lumber wholesaler to the West.[128] Many lumber dealers began to cast about for other lines of business. Some reoriented and reduced the size of their operations; some left the trade; some moved elsewhere; some went bankrupt. In the last few years before his death in 1895, Charles Mears was reduced to promoting an unsuccessful harbor-development scheme in Michigan and to writing bitter, plaintive letters to bankers no longer interested in financing the visions of a lumberman whose time had passed.[129] As his generation began to retire and die, so did Chicago's wholesale trade in white pine lumber.

What had happened?

Ironically, the same forces that had made Chicago the world's leading lumber center gradually began to work against it in the years following the Civil War. As the railroad network spread more deeply into Chicago's hinterland, its competitive logic began to undermine rather than promote the city's interests. New forested regions that lay well outside Chicago's tributary rail system began to compete with the city in selling wood. At the same time, the white pine forests that had supplied Chicago with lumber began to vanish, consumed by the same voracious appetite that had given the city its market. The very success of Chicago in dominating the regional lumber trade was among the most important factors contributing to its decline. Starting in the 1870s, groups that had once seen their interests converge in Chicago's cargo market began to drift apart: Chicago wholesalers, Lake Michigan lumbermen, hinterland lumber dealers, and prairie customers no longer seemed so closely tied to the city's trade. Those who had relied on Chicago's market increasingly resented the power it held over them. As they sought to improve their circumstances, one of their strongest wishes was to find alternative markets that would reduce their dependence on Chicago.

Competitive conditions at Chicago affected even the retail lumber dealers of Kansas and Nebraska, and it was there, out in the retail hinterland, that Chicago's lumber wholesalers saw the first storm clouds beginning to gather. In the face of declining prices, Chicago dealers sought to shore up their profits by sending "drummers"—traveling salesmen—out into the hinterland to persuade farmers and builders to buy lumber direct from their yards.[130] Drummers were men of little means, sometimes failed lumber dealers themselves, who worked on commission to obtain orders on behalf of Chicago lumber wholesalers. At times, they took orders from retail dealers in small towns; at other times, they sold direct to retail customers. By contracting for one of these "direct sales," retail customers who paid cash for large quantities of wood could get wholesale prices for their shipments. Because drummers worked on commission, they had a strong incentive to make as many such sales as possible.

Not surprisingly, lumber dealers in hinterland towns did not take kindly to the drummers' activities. Country yards earned money by purchasing large amounts of lumber at wholesale and reselling them in smaller quantities at higher retail prices. The retail markup generated the income that allowed dealers to pay yard workers' wages, offer credit to customers, stock a wide assortment of lumber, and earn income from invested capital. Country dealers incurred the cost and risk of purchasing and storing lumber so that it would always be available when their customers needed it.[131] From their perspective, the difference between wholesale prices in Chicago and retail prices at the country yard was their legitimate reward for anticipating and meeting the needs of their local customers.

During the 1870s, drummers threatened to snatch the best part of this reward and carry it off to Chicago. Country yards depended for their profits on a mix of sales: their customers included those who needed to buy only a few pieces of lumber, which brought the yard little money, and others who bought lumber for an entire building, which brought much more income to the yard. But it was exactly these latter customers whom the drummers most successfully pursued. By offering wholesale rates to the largest and most profitable buyers, drummers undercut country dealers at their most vulnerable point. Worse, drummers from different Chicago firms competed fiercely for business, driving prices down still further. "Chicago salesmen," wrote a reporter in Iowa in 1876, "are too numerous to mention, and the cutting of price lists is fearful to behold."[132] By contributing to the downward pressure on prices in an already depressed market, drummers made it ever harder for retail yards to sell their stocks at a profit.[133]

In this, the drummers were aided by a group of local entrepreneurs known as scalpers. Rather than incur the high costs of maintaining a lumberyard, scalpers sought to identify retail customers who had to make large purchases, and then offered to place an order for them in Chicago at lower prices than the local yard could afford. Since the lumber came direct to its final customer, scalpers had no yard costs and so needed smaller markups to earn a profit. According to irate retail dealers, the scalpers' stock-in-trade was merely their ability to ferret out potential customers, "which information they usually obtain by loafing around lumber offices, or in some other underhanded way."[134] Moreover, they could sometimes take advantage of their customers' inexperience by ordering inferior grades of lumber and pricing them as if they were top quality. Reputable dealers who wanted a long-term relationship with their customers could not afford to resort to such tactics.

To country dealers, drummers and scalpers represented just one thing: unfair competition, much of it emanating from the city of Chicago. The root of the problem was not the drummers and scalpers themselves but the wholesalers who called them into being. By offering to sell lumber to farmers at the same prices that dealers got, wholesalers were competing with their own customers. One angry Illinois dealer argued, "This ought not to be; it is an injustice that every country dealer ought to denounce. . . . It is taking trade from us that we worked hard to obtain, and which we cannot well get along without, as we depend upon the patronage of our immediate vicinity to enable us to keep a stock on hand for the accommodation of the public."[135] The irony of the situation was that retail dealers continued to be among the largest purchasers of Chicago lumber, so wholesalers potentially undermined their own sales. "Manufacturers," wrote the *Wisconsin Lumberman* in an attack on direct sales, "depend more or less on the capital of retail dealers to assist in the disposal of their manufactured stock. That capital is worth at least a fair interest compensation."[136] For country dealers whose profits were disappearing in the face of the new competition, it felt as if wholesalers had violated the most fundamental covenant of the wholesale-retail relationship, and were threatening to dismantle the entire lumber distribution system.

The notion that retail distribution might disappear altogether did not seem farfetched in the 1870s. The direct-sales controversy in the lumber trade was linked to the same post–Civil War agrarian protest movements that had attacked the Chicago grain elevator system. By the 1870s, these protests had become identified with various branches of the Patrons of Husbandry, otherwise known as the Grange. One of the Grangers' chief economic complaints was having to pay exorbitant prices to "middlemen" who stood between manufacturers and customers in order to siphon off illegitimate profits for themselves. From the point of view of the Grangers, retail lumber dealers were no better than any other middlemen.[137] To escape their clutches, state Grange organizations sought to create cooperative buying agencies that would make wholesale purchases and resell goods to their members with only an "equitable" markup. Although most of these buying cooperatives ultimately lost money and collapsed, their efforts to organize farm customers struck, at least in theory, at the very heart of the country lumber business. When attacking the practices of wholesalers, therefore, retail dealers directed their greatest indignation at sales to members of the Grange. The *Wisconsin Lumberman* argued in 1874, for instance, that "it is the manifest duty of lumber manufacturers to refuse grange representatives the same rates at which legitimate retail dealers are now purchasing. . . . The grange element is assuming the dictatorial tone of monopoly in its worst form."[138]

With their customers seemingly organizing to drive them out of business, and with Chicago wholesalers apparently standing ready to help, retail dealers decided that it was time to organize in their own defense. In August 1877, an Illinois retailer wrote a letter to the *Northwestern Lumberman* suggesting that he "would not buy a foot of lumber" from a dealer who would sell to one of his customers.[139] In its next issue, the *Lumberman* editorialized that such a boycott would be a powerful way to pressure wholesalers into changing their practices, but only if dealers acted collectively. "One thing is certain: individually nothing can be accomplished, but let the dealers throughout Illinois . . . unite in an organization for the protection of their trade, and they would wield a power which would make itself felt beyond all question."[140] The *Lumberman's* editor, W. B. Judson, said that he would throw the full support of his publication behind such an organization, and began in subsequent issues to promote it with great energy. If anything proved the centrality of Chicago's role in the western lumber trade, this was it: a Chicago-based journal seeking to unite dealers in Chicago's hinterland to resist the power of Chicago wholesalers in Chicago's market.[141]

Judson's efforts soon bore fruit. On November 7, 1877, thirty-two retail dealers, mostly from downstate Illinois, gathered in Chicago to form the Northwestern Retail Lumber Dealers' Association.[142] (The name would soon change—reflecting the organization's ambitions more than its actual scope—to the National Association of Lumber Dealers, or NALD.)[143] The preamble to its constitution stated the group's chief goal:

"We believe that the practice of selling lumber to consumers by manufacturers and wholesale dealers at the same prices given to retail dealers, is
unjust and injurious to our trade. . . ."[144] To solve this problem, the
group proposed a simple enforcement mechanism. If one of its members
complained to the association's secretary that a firm had sold direct to a
retail customer at wholesale prices, the secretary would write the wholesaler and ask that it pay a fine to the association.[145] If it agreed to do so,
the secretary would distribute the money to association members living in
the area, giving them the retail profit that the direct sale had denied them.
If the wholesaler refused to pay the fine, the secretary would post an
announcement calling on all members to boycott that firm. In this way,
the dealers sought to enforce the principle that wholesale and retail markets be clearly partitioned from each other. To defend their interests,
they elected a slate of officers to organize the boycott, among whom the
most important was undoubtedly the enforcing secretary. The first holder
of the post, predictably enough, was the *Northwestern Lumberman*'s own
W.B. Judson, based in Chicago.[146]

Retail dealers immediately greeted the NALD with great enthusiasm.
Within half a year of its founding, over five hundred dealers from eight
different states had joined.[147] Despite the group's hope of achieving national status, it drew its membership from the territory where Chicago
wholesalers clearly dominated the lumber trade. A map showing the locations of country dealers who had joined the NALD by the end of 1879
looks like nothing so much as a map of Chicago's lumber hinterland:
aside from the handful of NALD members in Indiana and Ohio, the vast
majority did business in the region bounded by Illinois and southern
Wisconsin on one side and western Kansas and Nebraska on the other.[148]

With so many people joined in defense of the retailers' interests, the
NALD quickly began to affect the way Chicago wholesalers did business.
Although the Chicago Lumbermen's Exchange passed a resolution in
February 1878 stating that "the lumber dealers of Chicago will not in the
future consider any [NALD] demands made upon them," individual
wholesalers did start to pay penalties when they were caught making
direct sales.[149] By the end of its first year, the NALD had collected some
$2,000 in fines—not a huge sum but a symbolically important one.[150]
Wholesalers began to signal their acquiescence in the organization's demands by printing the phrase "We sell to dealers only" on their price
lists. By 1880, the NALD had been so successful that Secretary Judson
could report to the membership that "the practice of selling to consumers
has practically stopped."[151] The problem of direct sales had diminished
so much by then that some members began to lose interest in the organization. Income from fines dropped precipitously, membership rolls de-

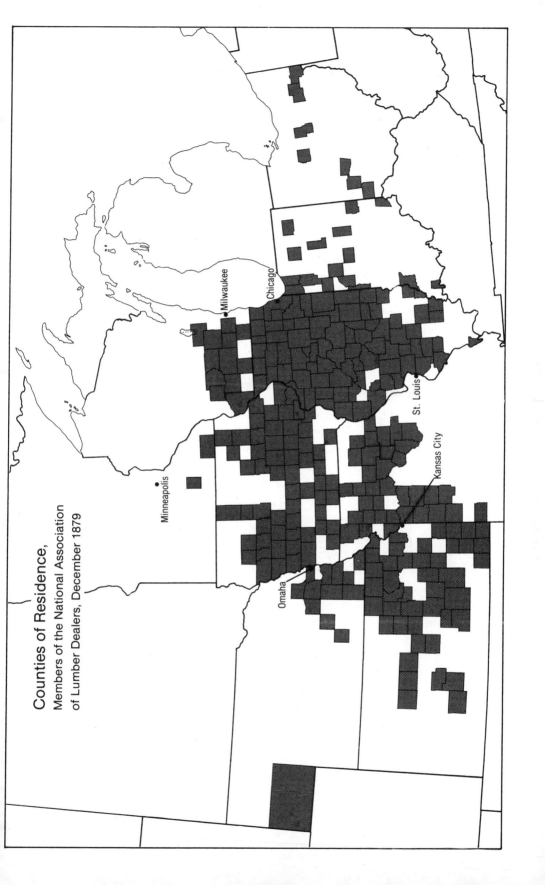

Counties of Residence,
Members of the National Association
of Lumber Dealers, December 1879

Minneapolis

Milwaukee
Chicago

St. Louis

Kansas City

Omaha

clined, and the NALD budget went into the red. By the mid-1880s, the association had abandoned fining wholesalers altogether and was a shadow of its former self.[152]

But the decline of the NALD was testimony to its success: by the mid-1880s, most Chicago wholesalers and hinterland retailers had agreed to protect dealers' markups. The movement to shield retailers from direct-sale competition came just as Chicago's influence over western lumber markets reached its peak. The retailers' efforts to organize on their own behalf contributed to the changing fortunes of Chicago wholesalers, but other, more powerful forces were also at work. These involved direct sales as well, but at the opposite end of the marketplace. If the NALD signified that Chicago merchants were losing control of the demand side of their business, comparable actions by lumber manufacturers were having a similar effect on the supply side. Together, the two would bring irresistible pressure on Chicago's lumber trade.

Lake Michigan sawmill operators had long been struggling against competitive conditions that encouraged overproduction. In the short term, overproduction meant that they suffered from chronically low prices; in the long term, it meant that they consumed their forest resources and thus undermined their own enterprise. Because most operators were small and undercapitalized, they had no choice but to undercut each other's prices when bringing their product to market. Like the railroads, lumber manufacturers had fixed costs—wages, debts, and taxes—that had to be met no matter what, so they sometimes had to sell at little profit, or even at a loss, to meet costs. "By the time the lumber is ready to ship it often becomes less a question of profit than of cash with the mill owner . . . ," wrote the *Northwestern Lumberman* in 1879. "But what can he do? With rapidly maturing notes to meet, and with his credit already strained to its utmost limit of endurance, there is no course left open to him but to send his stock as fast as it can be loaded and shipped to this market, and get what he can for it."[153]

Millowners rarely got as much as they wanted. Once shipments arrived in Chicago, the sale was handled by a commission merchant who had more interest in selling lumber quickly than in getting the highest price for it.[154] The commission merchants' eagerness for a fast sale, combined with the need to clear the Franklin Street docks within twelve hours to avoid demurrage charges, encouraged rushed auction sales that only diminished prices further.[155] Worse, wind conditions on the lake often caused lumber vessels to arrive simultaneously, exacerbating the already fierce competition among them. "Being subject to the wind and weather," lamented the *Lumberman*, "it universally happens that the stock arrives here in fleets, and the larger the fleet the greater the slaughter."[156]

The mill operators' own financial urgency allowed Chicago to become a buyer's market that yielded some of the lowest prices in the region. The manufacturers' acute seasonal need for short-term credit drove them to the one market where they knew they could get quick cash, even if it meant that they were forever selling lumber at lower prices than they liked. Under such circumstances, the only way they could keep up with costs was to cut more trees, contributing still further to the overproduction and saturated markets that had created low prices in the first place. Chicago thus became the focal point of a vicious circle: undercapitalization caused overproduction, which in turn kept prices low and accelerated the destruction of the northern forest.[157] The *Lumberman* summed up the problem by attributing it to "so many men . . . striving to carry on a larger business than their capital will warrant" and, as a result, having to turn natural capital into liquid capital merely to survive. "The only reasonable explanation of this paradoxical state of affairs . . . ," the *Lumberman*'s editors wrote, "is that the mill men . . . are using up their capital, as it exists in the form of stumpage, for no other end than to simply keep themselves in business."[158]

For all these reasons, Michigan and Wisconsin sawmill operators had long begrudged their dependence on the Chicago cargo market. Although many of them desperately needed it for the cash and credit that kept them in business, they disliked having to accept its low prices, having to trust its commission merchants, and being at the mercy of its wholesalers. The extent of their dependency reveals itself in maps of Chicago's supply hinterland at the peak of the city's dominance, in 1879.[159] A comparison with the earlier, 1859 map (see page 174) shows that Chicago's supply area had gradually shifted to the north; less visible but no less real was its movement into the interior of Wisconsin and Michigan as timber began to disappear from the lower reaches of the logging rivers. Green Bay had ceased to be a significant source of lumber for the city, having been replaced by the new twin lumber towns of Marinette and Menominee, which received their logs from the Menominee River, on the Wisconsin-Michigan border. The mills in those two communities now accounted for roughly 14 percent of Chicago's total lumber supply. Only Muskegon, on the eastern shore of the lake, continued to surpass them. It now accounted for almost 30 percent of Chicago's total receipts—more than half again as much as any other city in 1859. This suggests the extent to which Chicago was beginning to depend on fewer sources of supply. But the individual mill towns of its hinterland were still far more depen-

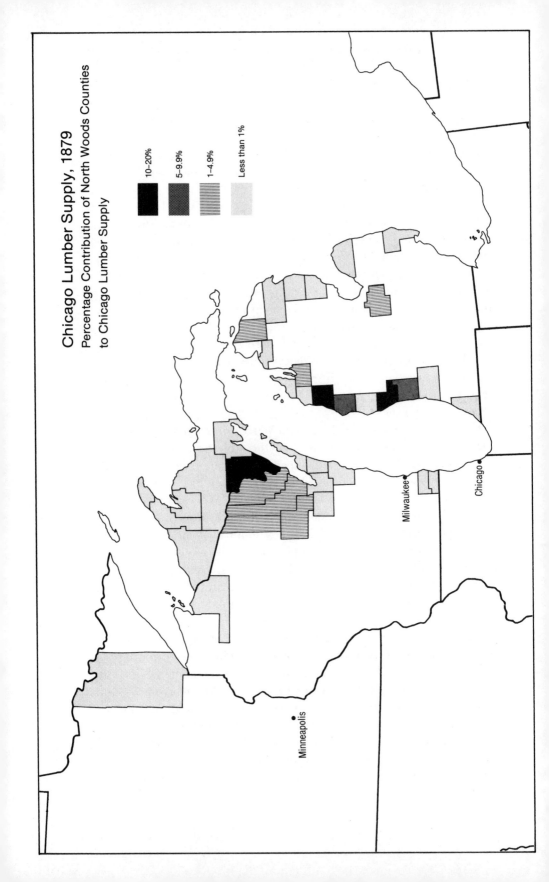

Chicago Lumber Supply, 1879
Percentage Contribution of North Woods Counties
to Chicago Lumber Supply

10–20%

5–9.9%

1–4.9%

Less than 1%

Minneapolis

Milwaukee

Chicago

dent on it than it was on them. All three of these towns sold 85 percent or more of their output to Chicago in 1879.[160]

Given the extent of their dependency on Chicago's markets, it is hardly surprising that millowners began to seek customers in places where people would pay better prices.[161] Many of them saw Chicago's wholesalers in much the same way that Grange members saw retailers: as middlemen who siphoned off a lion's share of the profits from lumber sales.[162] Beginning in the early 1870s, millowners started speculating about how much they might benefit if only they could sell wood to retailers direct from the sawmill instead of sending it through Chicago. In 1873, for instance, the *Michigan Lumberman* offered the prescient observation that "if we handled, piled, seasoned, assorted, and sold our own product, we would save to ourselves the amount which makes the middle men rich."[163] Making direct sales from mill to retailer required Lake Michigan lumbermen to take over all the tasks that the yards in Chicago had been handling for them since the 1840s. This consolidation entailed new infusions of capital and greater annual expenses, but it held out the promise of liberating the mill towns from the hold of Chicago's market.

Fortunately for the millowners, the means of liberation were just at hand. The railroad network had continued to expand in the years following the Civil War, and by the 1870s various roads for the first time began to make their way directly into the lumber districts. Muskegon acquired its first rail connection to what became part of the Lake Shore Railroad in 1869; and Marinette-Menominee became a station on the Chicago and Northwestern in 1871.[164] Although railroad rates were initially high enough that lake shipments to Chicago continued to be more profitable, that would soon change. Roads passing through the relatively unpopulated north country had to carry freight if they were to earn any money at all, and freight in the pine forests meant lumber. Railroad companies therefore began to modify their rate structures to try to attract shipments away from Lake Michigan, which in turn meant diverting lumber from Chicago's market.

The late 1870s also saw the railroads change their rate policies at Chicago itself in a way that delivered a body blow to the city's lumber trade. Until 1876, the railroads had charged for lumber either by the carload or by how many thousands of board feet a car contained. Wholesalers benefited from this policy because it did not differentiate loads of lumber by how much they weighed. Everyone assumed that a carload weighed somewhere between 20,000 and 24,000 pounds, the official maximum load for most freight cars, and few bothered to check this assumption against reality.[165] But because much of the wood leaving Chicago was still green, the railroads were in fact carrying a lot of excess weight in damp lumber—and not charging for it. Railroad managers began to discover that many lumber shipments weighed an undeclared 40,000 pounds or more, potentially damaging car and roadbed alike while paying nothing for the extra burden.[166] Toward the end of 1876, therefore, the principal roads operating out of Chicago began to charge for lumber on the basis of weight rather than volume.[167] This initially put Chicago at a disadvantage in competing against towns where railroads still measured shipments by volume, but by 1880 a regionwide cartel involving all the major railroads had adopted weight as the only permissible way of measuring lumber shipments.[168]

"By requiring the transportation of lumber to be paid for by the pound, instead of the thousand feet," wrote the *Northwestern Lumberman* in 1877, the railroads' new policy had "practically cut off the trade in green lumber while it has proportionately increased the demand for dry."[169] Innocuous as this change might seem on the surface, it was a disaster for the Chicago wholesalers. Previously, retail yards and other hinterland customers had ordered their lumber by the carload, in the knowledge that transportation costs made this by far the most economical way to buy wood. With every additional piece of lumber now increasing the freight charge for a shipment, retailers became much pickier about the amounts and kinds of lumber they bought. "Now that every hundred pounds costs so many cents . . . ," declared the *Lumberman,* "it is much better to buy from the yards the dry stock in just such quantities as may be most wanted."[170] The new freight rates enabled dealers to place many more small orders for lumber, and still compete effectively with those who bought large shipments.

Chicago's chief advantage as a lumber market had always been its ability to move wood in large volume, which was partly attributable to the hidden discount its merchants earned by not paying full freight rates. With rates reassessed and retailers more selective in their orders, part of that advantage disappeared. In response, the Chicago wholesalers became warier themselves about buying green lumber. Knowing that it would sit in their yards—on expensive urban real estate—until it dried, Chicagoans began to urge the Lake Michigan manufacturers to hold their cut at the mill until it had lost weight. In so doing, the wholesalers cut their own throats. With dry lumber suddenly at a premium, and with railroad service becoming available direct from the mill towns, lumber manufacturers finally saw the opportunity to change their earlier policy of shipping lumber to Chicago as soon as they milled it. By the 1880s, the largest sawmills at places like Muskegon and Marinette-Menominee had become financially secure enough that they no longer depended so heavily on the cash they could obtain from the Chicago cargo market.[171] Instead, they set aside land at their mills and began to stack lumber to dry before shipping it to market.

But once it was dry, there was no longer as much incentive to send it to Chicago. Rather than sell it at auction in the notoriously competitive and low-priced cargo market, why not ship it direct to the retail dealers who were willing to pay premium prices for the driest and best wood? By sending only inferior wood to Chicago, sawmill operators could keep for themselves the most profitable lumber that most easily paid for its own rail transportation. They could finally cut themselves loose from the market whose dominance had irritated them for so long. "The manufacturer who piles his lumber," wrote the *Northwestern Lumberman* in 1881, "occupies a comparatively independent position toward those who buy. He does not stand in mortal fear of a break in prices, or run the chance of sending a heavy consignment to the cargo market at the wrong time, and having to stand the consequent loss. . . . He has his stock where it will keep, and he is prepared with the facilities for holding it. . . ."[172]

By the mid-1880s, the Chicago yards were finding themselves in the unaccustomed position of not being able to maintain full assortments of lumber, especially not in the higher grades. The cargoes that came to the Franklin Street docks for sale at auction were less and less satisfactory as a source of supply. Instead, wholesalers who wanted to keep up the quality of their stock increasingly had to journey up the lake to buy direct from the mills.[173] There, they had no more of an advantage than any other buyers, and found themselves having to compete for wood—sometimes against their own retail customers—much harder than before.[174]

Early signs of how bad things were getting for the wholesalers came in 1883, when the big Menominee mills, which had long maintained yards in Chicago, began to discuss closing their operations in the city.[175] In 1885, one of the largest of them, the Kirby-Carpenter Company, actually did so, while others substantially cut back their operations. In explaining their actions, Kirby-Carpenter officials identified what they regarded as the growing disadvantages of the Chicago market: "big dock rents, heavy switching charges, outside prices for labor, the cost of keeping a large fleet of barges in commission, and all the other expenses of maintaining a yard here." Given these problems, they concluded that the most profitable course would be to sell lumber "as near the saw as possible."[176] Few statements more succinctly captured the declining influence of the Chicago marketplace. Some of the city's most prominent lumbermen were in charge of the Menominee mills, and that only drove home the lesson more powerfully.

The decision of the Menominee millowners to abandon Chicago paralleled another broad change in the industry: the migration of lumbering into new regions that lay outside the city's "natural" tributary territory. Since at least the Civil War, Chicago had been competing with the lumbermen of the Mississippi Valley. Trees cut on the northern reaches of such rivers as the Wisconsin, the Black, and especially the Chippewa floated downstream to the Mississippi and thence to major mill towns in Iowa: Clinton, Davenport, Muscatine, and others.[177] Although Chicago's privileged railroad rates had earlier allowed the city to ship lumber even into Iowa—the immediate hinterland of these mills—the changing railroad economics of the 1880s made that harder to do. Moreover, the lumber interests of the upper Mississippi had by then come under the control of Frederick Weyerhaeuser's Mississippi River Logging Company.[178] Weyerhaeuser had begun as a mill operator in Rock Island, Illinois, but had gradually built a coalition of millowners and logging companies along the Mississippi and the Chippewa River in Wisconsin. The Weyerhaeuser syndicate was still in its early stages and had not yet gained the full corporate organization that characterized it in the twentieth century. Still, it represented a regionwide coordination of lumber production and marketing that had no analogue in Chicago's highly competitive market. By the 1880s, Mississippi Valley lumber firms were competing ever more effectively against Chicago's wholesalers.

Worse still was the arrival of competition from a different sector entirely: the South. In the years following the Civil War, lumbermen who found their supplies diminishing in the Northeast and Great Lakes regions began to buy up timber acreage—most of it in yellow pine—in Arkansas, Louisiana, and other southern states.[179] As railroads extended their lines into the southern forests, manufacturers began to sell yellow pine lumber direct from their mills. Some of that lumber headed north into the heart of white pine territory. The first of it arrived in Chicago in 1877, where the *Northwestern Lumberman* observed that it took "a much handsomer finish" than white pine and declared that it would "not be long before yellow pine flooring will be extensively used in this section."[180]

The prophecy proved correct, and conservative. Yellow pine could be used for most of the same purposes as its northern cousin, and it had even greater strength.[181] By 1884, it was arriving in ever larger quantities even for use in Chicago itself.[182] Kansas City soon emerged as a major rail center for the western distribution of Arkansas yellow pine, but, in keeping with the other innovations of the decade, most southern pine sold direct from the mills.[183] As if to prove that great urban wholesale centers were no longer so important to the lumber trade, by the end of the 1880s yellow pine had succeeded in claiming most of the trans-Missouri region for itself. In consequence, Chicago could no longer sell much lumber in Kansas or Nebraska and lost much of Iowa and Missouri as well.

As the Great Plains ceased to be an effective outlet for white pine, competition in the upper Mississippi Valley became more severe. At the same time that Chicago wholesalers were losing their western markets, sawmills in the Mississippi Valley and interior mills at places like Marinette-Menominee and Wausau, Wisconsin, were losing theirs. All had to look for possible sales to the same customers in the same reduced area, which consisted almost entirely of Chicago's old hinterland. "Chicago," announced the *Northwestern Lumberman* in 1886, "can no longer claim any portion of the prairie northwest as exclusively its own."[184]

Much to their horror, the city's wholesalers for the first time found that they were having trouble competing in southern Wisconsin and even in Illinois. By 1890, the *Lumberman* was reporting that the city's trade in "piece stuff"—lumber for the studs and joists of balloon-frame buildings, the most basic mainstay of the Chicago market—had been reduced to "a scramble, with a hard pushing competition in this state and a few counties in Indiana." "The western trade in such lumber," it added, "has been given up, probably for all time."[185] Unbelievable as it must have seemed to old-time lumbermen, the editors suggested that the only way Chicago dealers could continue to compete would be to purchase and pile wood *at the sawmills* and then ship direct from there without ever bringing it to the city. Operations in Chicago would be reduced merely to taking orders for customers. The Chicago dealers' only other hope was to try to "confine themselves to territory in which they know that they can sell lumber in competition with anybody"—even though "very little of such territory, if any," was left.[186]

Railroad expansion was undoubtedly the single most important cause of these changes. Increasing quantities of the region's lumber were cut at mill towns that used rails, not rivers or lakes, to carry their output to market. People nicknamed them rail mills because of their location away from the waterways that had once been mandatory to lumber manufacture. Loggers had been so thorough in their work that few remaining forests were anywhere near the banks of rivers large enough to carry a log drive. To continue cutting, lumbermen had to make expensive investments in narrow-gauge railroads, raising capital costs to such a degree that small logging operations had little hope of competing. The coming of the logging railroads in northern Michigan and Wisconsin (already evident in interior regions of the Upper Peninsula on the 1879 map of

Chicago's supply areas) meant that logging was less bound to the flooding streams and the wheel of the seasons.[187] Woodsmen could cut and
transport trees year-round, effectively breaking the old reign of the winter ice. In much the same way, loggers could finally cut and market species other than white pine. Trees that had never before been marketable,
because they did not readily float—ash, oak, hickory, maple, and other
hardwoods—sold at a profit now that they could ride the rails.[188]

Perhaps the most revealing proof of how much Chicago's market
changed during the 1880s and 1890s was the way the city itself acquired
lumber. Until 1880, over 90 percent of Chicago's lumber arrived via Lake
Michigan.[189] In that year, the railroads for the first time accounted for
more than 10 percent of the city's supply, and their share soon increased
dramatically. By 1890, they were supplying nearly 30 percent of Chicago's lumber; by the end of the century, well over 60 percent. The days
of lake transportation were rapidly drawing to a close. Chicago's unique
role in the lumber trade had been possible only at the intersection of lake
and rail, where the products of the forest met the needs of the prairie.
Now that lumber was leaving the lake, the reasons for Chicago's dominance were disappearing as well.

The glory years were over. Although they continued to handle enormous quantities of lumber, the Chicago merchants who had once grown
rich by selling wood as far west as the Rocky Mountains now had to work
hard to sell it in their own backyards. The same railroad that had given
the city its dominance now took it away, driving "beyond every spatial
barrier" to achieve "the annihilation of space by time"—to repeat Marx's
phrase.[190] The editors of the *Northwestern Lumberman* would hardly have
agreed with Marx's politics, but they shared his analysis in lamenting what
had happened to the old "natural" boundaries of the lumber trade. "The
integrity of sectional fences," they wrote, "has been utterly destroyed.
The distributers of lumber are seeking a market anywhere and everywhere, without reference to old lines of territory, with the result that
nobody's trade is safe or profitable, as it should be."[191] But they failed to
note how artificial those original "sectional fences" had been, dependent
as they were on the brief moment when Chicago's rail network had been
the sawmills' only effective passage to the Great West. By "seeking a
market anywhere and everywhere," the merchants of the new rail mills
were only doing what Chicagoans had done a generation before. In the
perennial instability of the marketplace, the geography of capital had
shifted yet again, replacing one version of second nature with another.

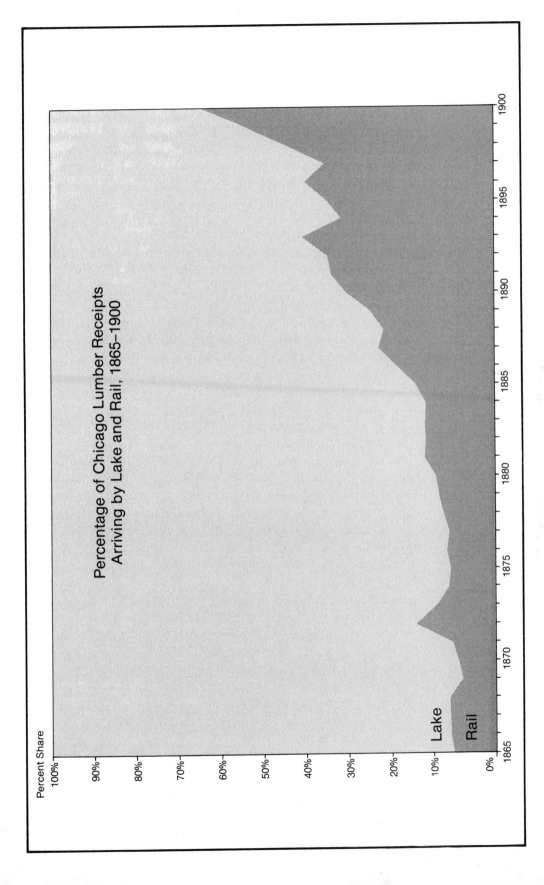

Percent Share

Percentage of Chicago Lumber Receipts
Arriving by Lake and Rail, 1865–1900

Lake

Rail

100%
90%
80%
70%
60%
50%
40%
30%
20%
10%
0%

1865   1870   1875   1880   1885   1890   1895   1900

The Cutover

Beneath the geography of capital, underpinning it and sustaining it even as the two transformed each other, there was still the geography of first nature. To explain why Chicago lost its wholesale lumber trade, one must ultimately turn to that older geography. Behind the retailers' resentment of the Chicago drummers, behind the millowners' efforts to escape the influence of the cargo market, behind the competition of other regions and the coming of yellow pine, behind even the proliferation of the railroads, there remained the forest itself. Without it, none of the others would have mattered. Chicago lost its lumber trade because the forest was finally exhausted by the effort to bring it to market.

Even as late as the early 1870s, few had believed this possible. *"Will our pine timber soon be exhausted?"* asked a journalist in a popular Chicago magazine in 1870. "We say no. None of our generation will see our pine forests decimated."[192] Efforts by early conservationists to suggest that the forests of Michigan, Wisconsin, and Minnesota were finite and should be used more carefully were greeted with scorn by the lumber press.[193] A case in point was the reaction to James S. Little, a wealthy Canadian lumberman unusually concerned about preserving forest resources, who wrote a long article in 1876 on the timber supply of the United States and Canada. In it, he suggested that Great Lakes loggers were "not only burning the candle at both ends . . . but cutting it in two, and setting the match to the four ends to enable them to double the process of exhaustion."[194] In the face of Little's estimates, the editors of the *Northwestern Lumberman* simply argued that his statistics were inadequate and his economic assumptions naive. They showed no real concern about whether he might be right in the long run about the potential destruction of the forest. They were equally hostile to the special report on the nation's forests published in the 1880 census, and devoted many columns to refuting its pessimistic estimates of the remaining timber supply.[195]

During the 1880s, however, as Chicago lumbermen reeled from one bad piece of news after another, there were more signs that the white pines might in fact be giving out. For instance, sawlog prices, along with the prices of forested real estate, were steadily rising. Michigan sawlogs in 1879 were selling for $14 per thousand feet, when just four years earlier even fully milled coarse lumber had not cost as much.[196] Just as worrisome was the general decline in the quality of trees that loggers were

cutting. In 1870, the typical sawlog reaching a Michigan mill town measured sixteen to eighteen inches in diameter, and no one considered a
tree worth cutting if it was not at least a foot wide. Ten years later, the
minimum size had fallen to six to eight inches, so the average log contained far less lumber than before.[197] The costs of logging rose accordingly. By 1883, loggers in the Muskegon district were cutting trees higher
into the branches than they ever had before; they cut almost the entire
tree into logs.[198] To make matters worse, trees still worth cutting were
located farther and farther from the lumber streams. In 1879, for instance, the *Lumberman* reported, "There is not to-day a navigable creek in
the state of Michigan or Wisconsin and we may, with little risk, add Minnesota, upon whose banks, to the head waters, the better grade of timber
is still standing within a distance of two to three miles."[199]

Many of the technological and economic changes sweeping the western lumber trade were responses to these fundamental shifts in the nature
of the forest. With suitable trees no longer in easy reach of the watercourses, logging railroads became an ever more necessary, if expensive,
investment. The rising sale of hardwood lumber from Michigan and elsewhere occurred partly because railroads could now carry such wood, but
also because there was so little white pine lumber left to compete with it.
The rapid disappearance of uncut pine land led lumbermen to realize
they were running out of timber, and many of them therefore began
looking to the uncut forests of the South and the Pacific Northwest. Frederick Weyerhaeuser's decision to move his chief field of activity to Idaho
and Washington was only the most celebrated of these movements, for
the rise of the southern yellow pine industry also followed the search of
Great Lakes capital for new timber investments.

The ability of yellow pine to compete at all in the heart of white pine
country was among the most telling signs that the best of the white pine
was already gone. When Chicago wholesalers started having trouble obtaining the higher grades of white pine, it was not just because manufacturers were holding back those grades to sell directly from the mill but
also because higher grades no longer existed.[200] In 1890, sawmill operators in the Mississippi Valley met to suggest that regional grading scales
be shifted downward so that lower-quality wood could be graded higher
than before. In the very act of trying to obscure the truth, they acknowledged that their forests were disappearing.[201] By the 1880s, that realiza-
tion was dawning on even the most skeptical. As early as 1881, the *Northwestern Lumberman* was admitting that "the old prophets must be
accredited with a remarkably correct appreciation of the timber supply."[202] By 1887, its editors had joined the prophets of doom to declare

that "the end of the, at one time supposed inexhaustible, supply of white and norway pine timber is altogether too near."[203]

Lumber production in the Great Lakes peaked in the early 1890s, and began to decline precipitously thereafter. The Michigan white pines gave out first, followed by those in Wisconsin and finally by those in Minnesota.[204] As the loggers finished their work in the forests they had consumed, they left behind a literal wasteland. Great piles of slash—small timber, branches, and other debris that had little economic value—remained on the ground where they fell, sometimes in piles ten to fifteen feet high. They accumulated over a vast area, turned brown in the summer heat, and waited for the dry season, when a spark might set them alight.

Fires had long been common in the Great Lakes forests. Indeed, fires were an important reason why the white pine was so abundant in the region, for the tree was adapted to reproduce most effectively in newly burned-over lands. The most extensive stands of white pines were often on the sites of old forest fires. But the fires that followed in the wake of the loggers were not like earlier ones. As the loggers cleared the forest, farmers—believing the old theory that the plow followed the ax—moved onto the newly cleared land to plant their crops. To remove the loggers' debris and to ready their fields for plowing, they typically followed the pioneer practice of setting fire to the ground in the fall. In so doing, aided by an occasional spark from the logging railroads, they ignited the immense tracts of clear-out land to produce some of the worst forest fires in American history. The 1871 fire at Peshtigo, Wisconsin, killed perhaps fifteen hundred people, far more than died in Chicago during the fire that burned down the city at almost the same time. Comparable holocausts occurred in Michigan in 1881, at Hinckley, Minnesota, in 1894, and—the last of the great slash fires—at Cloquet, Minnesota, in 1918.[205]

But human deaths and the destruction of would-be farming communities were not the only consequences of the great fires. They killed much of the remaining white pine forest as well. The tree's ability to flourish in the wake of natural fires depended on the seeds its cones released after undergoing the intense heat of burning. After a fire, tall parent trees ordinarily released their seeds to the newly cleared, now sunny ground beneath them, where young trees thrived and achieved maximum growth. In logged areas, few parent trees remained to reseed after a burn. As a result, other species, especially the deciduous aspens and birches with their ability to reproduce from stumps and suckers, began to invade the pine's old territory. They were aided in this at the end of the nineteenth century when people accidentally introduced to North America a European plant disease, the white pine blister rust. Fatal to a majority of white pines in moist areas like the north woods, the rust had reached the Great Lakes forest by the second decade of the twentieth century, and it diminished still further the chances that the white pine forest would ever fully reproduce itself. Aspen and birch, in alternation with balsam fir, appear to have permanently replaced the pines in areas where the forest has been left to its own devices. In many places, however, people in the twentieth century have systematically replanted pines and other desirable tree species, so stands of pines do still exist in many areas of the north woods.[206]

The dream that the "Cutover" district would become a fertile agricultural landscape proved within two or three decades to be an illusion. Clear-cutting and the fires that followed it reduced what little natural fertility the soil already had, and contributed to problems of erosion and flooding. More important, the poorly drained, heavily glaciated soils typical of the northern forests were inherently inhospitable to agriculture, as was the climate. Farmers who tried to earn a livelihood amid the stumps of the old pines quickly discovered that doing so was very hard indeed. Potatoes might survive in the poor soil, but few other crops did well there. Already by the late 1890s, a government report could foresee "no prospect that our denuded lands will be put to agricultural uses."[207] Old pinelands, whether abandoned by lumbermen or farmers or both, became an increasing burden on county and state tax rolls as their owners went into arrears and let the government claim the lands. The problem of what to do with the resulting depopulated landscape continued to haunt Great Lakes states well into the twentieth century.[208] As time went on, the north woods found new economic possibilities in the rise of the paper industry, which made good use of fast-growing species like birch and aspen; and the regrowing forests also became prime recreational country for Chicagoans and other inhabitants of the Great Lakes region. All of that lay in the future. In 1900, the Cutover was just that: cut over, and abandoned.

The newly treeless countrysides of northern Michigan and Wisconsin were far from the minds of most Chicagoans by the 1890s. Even though the city's wholesalers were abandoning their old western haunts to new competitors, they never lost their home market. Ever since the Civil War, people in Chicago itself had consumed a gradually rising share of the lumber that entered its yards. This home consumption eventually became the mainstay of the lumber trade, with regional wholesalers shifting toward a local retail business. No one feared that Chicago itself would run out of wood, for the city was now attracting lumber from across the entire nation. The demise of the white pine forest thus posed no permanent problem for the Chicago lumber trade.

The internal growth of the city had replaced the settlement of the

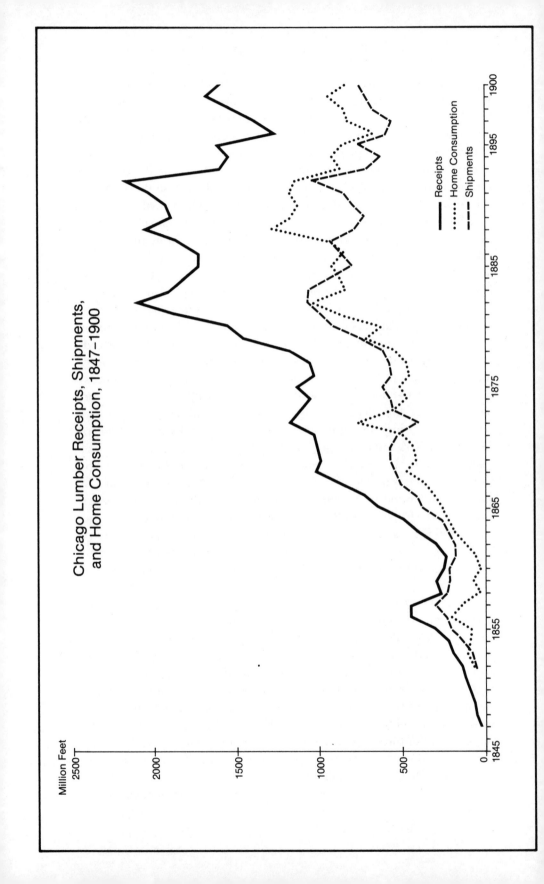

Chicago Lumber Receipts, Shipments, and Home Consumption, 1847–1900

prairies as the driving force behind lumber sales. Some even saw in the wholesalers' adversity the signs of future opportunity: by losing the trade of western farmers, hadn't the lumbermen acquired the much more profitable trade of the new metropolis? "The time is rapidly approaching," wrote the *Northwestern Lumberman* in 1889, "when the city demand will be much more important than that in the rural districts."[209] Cities, and especially Chicago, had become the centers for great concentrations of wealth, and the wealthy were likely to spend huge sums on mansions and other expensive structures for which white pine was hardly needed. How fortunate, then, that just as the northern forests were disappearing, "hardwoods have come in and pine has been in a great measure ruled out"—a wood unworthy of the new urban elite.[210] Demand for cheaper lumber would continue to come from people building the growing numbers of working-class houses in the city, as well as the prosperous farmers living in the immediate vicinity of Chicago, so lumber dealers could look forward to ongoing business from those markets as well.[211]

And what of the ravaged pinelands to the north? What was their relationship to this new vision of urban harmony and grandeur? Presumably those Chicagoans who thought about it, like most other Americans, saw the vanished forests as a worthy sacrifice to the cause of civilization. The fate of those forests had been prophesied as early as 1868, when a visitor to upper Michigan could declare in a remarkable passage, "The waste of timber is inevitable." He went on,

> The pioneer is insensible to arguments touching the future supply; to him the forest is only fit to be exterminated, as it hinders his plough and obstructs his sunlight. When Northern Michigan becomes, like Southern Illinois, a great rolling prairie of grass and grain, whose horizon is unbroken as the horizon of the ocean, the want of foresight that permitted the destruction of these magnificent forests will be bitterly lamented. But the lament will come from the next generation: the people of this will only boast the swift change of the wood and the wilderness to the fertile field, and exult in the lines of towns and cities which spring up along its watercourses and overlook its lakes.[212]

What made this vision so remarkable was its partial truth. The deaths of the forest trees had indeed built farms on great rolling prairies, and towns and cities had indeed sprung up as a result of the white pines' sacrifice— but not on the forest soil itself. The wealth that the northern pines had stored as natural capital had been successfully transformed into a more human form of wealth, but the vast bulk of it had been moved to another soil, another landscape, another ecosystem. The forest had been consumed in pursuit of a vision that would triumph in the grasslands and,

even more, in the city of Chicago—but not in the Cutover. The old black-
ened stumps would continue to serve as reminders, like the gray stones in
an abandoned churchyard, that the city and its hinterland had originally
been the products of a kind of theft that few now wished to remember. A
sizable share of the new city's wealth was the wealth of nature stolen,
consumed, and converted to human ends. The task of forgetting that fact
was easier the farther one traveled from the north country, and easiest of
all when one stood in the shadows of the tall stone buildings of Chicago's
Loop.

A few remembered nonetheless. Toward the end of his life, Isaac
Stephenson, one of the most successful of the Marinette-Menominee
lumbermen, would write in his autobiography,

> The habitual weakness of the American people is to assume that they have
> made themselves great, whereas their greatness has been in large measure
> thrust upon them by a bountiful providence which has given them forests,
> mines, fertile soil, and a variety of climate to enable them to sustain them-
> selves in plenty. . . .[213]

From the wealth of nature, Americans had wrung a human plenty, and
from that plenty they had built the city of Chicago. Chicago's relationship
to the white pines had been exceedingly intricate, emerging from ecological and economic forces that for a brief time had come together into a
single market, a single geography. The tensions in that market and that
geography finally destroyed the distant ecosystem which had helped create them—but by then it no longer mattered. Perhaps the greatest irony
was that by surviving the forests that had nurtured its growth, Chicago
could all too easily come to seem a wholly human creation.

5

Annihilating Space:
Meat

The Great Bovine City of the World

A lthough in retrospect the significance of Chicago's nineteenth-century grain elevators and lumberyards seems undeniable, visitors to the city in the years following the Civil War often failed to recognize their import. The scale of these structures might be outsized, but their essential function still appeared familiar and ordinary. The elevators concealed most of their machinery and far-reaching effects behind tall, windowless façades that did not invite closer scrutiny. One could marvel at them without much understanding what they did, and without sensing their relationship to the daily pandemonium at the Board of Trade. The fragrant piles of drying pine, for all their vast extent, bore enough resemblance to lumberyards elsewhere that they rarely became part of a tourist's itinerary. In each case, one could easily miss their implications for city and country alike.

The same could hardly be said of that other great institution where western nature met the Chicago market: the stockyards. Tourists might hesitate to subject themselves to the stench and gore of the place, but all knew that something special, something never before seen in the history of the world, was taking place on the south side of the city. Opinion differed about whether it should be an essential stop on a visitor's itinerary. Many saw in it the pinnacle of Chicago's social and economic achievement, the site, above all others, that made the city an icon of nineteenth-century progress. "Great as this wonderful city is in everything," wrote a British traveler, "it seems that the first place among its strong points must be given to the celerity and comprehensiveness of the Chicago style of killing hogs."[1] A New Zealand tourist told of having shown an American visitor one of his nation's great natural wonders, the geysers at Rotorua, only to have the American, unimpressed, remark, "Well, I guess, stranger, you would reckon it a grander sight to see a man standing to his waist in blood sticking pigs. We do that in my country." Although the New Zealander had been taken aback by this remark, which appeared "at the time a leap from the sublime to the ridiculous," he decided after finally visiting the Chicago stockyards for himself that the American "was quite right. It was a wonderful sight, and almost true to the letter."[2]

Others might be no less impressed, but also feel appalled that the taking of animal life could have become so indifferent, so efficient, so calculating and cold-blooded. The stockyards might be "of vast importance and of astounding dimensions," one such visitor admitted, but "the whole business [is] a most unpleasant one, destitute of all semblance of picturesqueness, and tainted with cruelty and brutality."[3] A person could visit the grain elevators and lumberyards without pondering their meaning, but such equanimity seemed somehow less appropriate at the stockyards. Rudyard Kipling was appalled at what he found there, and even more appalled by the apparent indifference of some of the visitors. He described one young woman who looked on quite cooly, standing "in a patch of sunlight, the red blood under her shoes, the vivid carcasses tacked round her, a bullock bleeding its life away not six feet away from her, and the death factory roaring all round her. She looked curiously, with hard, bold eyes, and was not ashamed."[4] Her indifference seemed to Kipling the most frightening thing he saw at the stockyards, and made him worry about the effect of so mechanical a killing house on the human soul. As Upton Sinclair would remark in the most famous passage ever written about the place, "One could not stand and watch very long without becoming philosophical, without beginning to deal in symbols and similes, and to hear the hog-squeal of the universe."[5] Kipling's young woman to the contrary, few who heard that squeal, or who saw the vast industrial landscape devoted to its exploitation, could avoid wondering what it might signify about animals, death, and the proper human relationship to both.

Chicago merchants had been dealing in hog squeals for decades before the Union Stock Yard opened for business on Christmas Day in 1865.[6] The wagons and cars full of grain that jammed Chicago-bound roads and railroads were not the only means by which hinterland farmers could send their crops to market. Corn in particular became more profitable in its travels by undergoing an alchemist's transmutation into denser, more valuable substances: kegs filled with whisky or animals that could carry themselves to market. "The hog," wrote a British journalist, "is regarded as the most compact form in which the Indian corn crop of the States can be transported to market. Hence the corn is fed to the hog on the farm, and he is sent to Chicago as a package provided by nature for its utilization."[7]

For years, shippers had driven their animals through crowded streets to reach one of several small stockyards scattered in various districts in the southern parts of the city. As early as 1837, Willard F. Myrick had built a fenced area next to his South-Side boardinghouse where hogs and cattle could eat prairie hay before being butchered. The key attraction of these early yards was the hotel where drovers lodged and entertained themselves while completing their transactions. As with many other Chicago businesses, customers came to the city as much to participate in its broader cultural marketplace as to buy and sell produce and merchandise. Myrick's yard, Bull's Head, Sherman Yards, and other stockyards of the 1840s and 1850s each possessed hotels and saloons where more than just animals and money changed hands. Restaurant food, whisky, and prostitution were among the many services they provided.[8]

The coming of the railroads reoriented these yards, so by the mid-1850s all but the smallest had rail connections allowing shippers to send packed meat and live animals east. Like the grain elevators, individual yards had connections with only one or two railroads, and their scattered locations made it difficult for drovers to move among them. "Lying in different parts of the city" wrote one early observer,

> on different and diverging streets, in several instances two or three miles apart, these yards were found inconvenient for the transaction of business. A drover bringing a herd of cattle or hogs into the market, was obliged to drive them through the crowded streets of the city, to yard after yard, thereby suffering the greatest inconvenience, and in many instances loss, occasioned by the difficulty of driving, and rough pavements, which lacerated and tore the hoofs of the animals, producing disease and many other evils.[9]

The problems of handling livestock in Chicago only became worse with time. Although most stockyards were initially located on prairie land just outside the built-up area of the city, they were soon surrounded by houses and factories that limited their expansion and cut off their original supply of hay and grazing land. The congestion of city streets inconvenienced drovers, endangered pedestrians, and injured animals; worse, it also broke up the Chicago market, making it difficult for buyers and sellers to compare the prices being offered in different yards. Financial reporters for the city's newspapers had trouble gathering information about price movements, and the inaccuracy of the resulting reports compounded the difficulties of those in the trade. The problem grew steadily during the 1850s and reached crisis proportions in the early years of the Civil War, when the Union army's demand for provisions led Chicago to surpass Cincinnati as the largest meat-packer in the world. By the mid-1860s, as an early Chicago historian described it, "centralization was urgently demanded, as a means of competition, from both buyers and sellers."[10]

The railroads would provide the means to escape these problems and transform Chicago's role in the meat trade. The solution—a single unified stockyard that would concentrate the city's livestock business at one location—was proposed in the fall of 1864, when Chicago's nine largest railroads, in conjunction with members of the Chicago Pork Packers' Association, issued a prospectus for what they called the Union Stock Yard and Transit Company. Capitalized at nearly a million dollars, the new company purchased a half square mile of land in the town of Lake, just south of the Chicago city limits in the open prairie lying west of Halsted Street. Four miles from city center, it seemed far enough away to avoid being overtaken by urban growth at least for the immediate future. The chief engineer of the Chicago and Alton Railroad drew up plans for the site, and construction began on June 1, 1865.[11]

It was in all ways an extraordinary project, gargantuan in proportions. Chicago guidebook authors were soon regaling their readers with its most impressive statistics. The greatest initial problem its builders faced was the wet prairie itself, which lay two feet below the level of the Chicago River and regularly flooded with standing water in spring and after severe rainstorms.[12] The marshy ground required over thirty miles of drainage and discharge pipes before it could support the proposed structures of the stockyard. The drainage system emptied into two great sewers that carried away water and offal to the South Branch of the Chicago River, which soon grew polluted past all recognition, with a stench that visitors did not soon forget. From the same river, upstream of the sewer outlet, came the fresh water that filled three miles of water troughs at a rate of 500,000 gallons per day. Paralleling the water troughs were an amazing ten miles of feed troughs that held the corn and the one hundred tons of hay animals would consume during each day of the stockyard's peak season.[13] The animals were kept in some 500 pens covering sixty acres of ground; within another three years, these numbers would grow to 2,300 pens on a hundred acres, capable of handling 21,000 head of cattle, 75,000 hogs, 22,000 sheep, and 200 horses, all at the same time. The pens were grouped into four great shipping and receiving yards, each of which was assigned to one or more railroad companies. Surrounding everything was a broad loop of rail line that made it easy for shippers to load and unload from every corner of the facility.[14] Simple in basic plan, the stockyard was a triumph of the engineer's craft.

Pigs and steers were not the only creatures the Union Stockyard could accommodate. Hough House, the hotel, stood six stories high and contained 260 sleeping rooms for livestock dealers and their guests. Its long dining hall measured 38 by 100 feet, and it also had a parlor, barbershop, and billiard room. From the cupola on its roof, one could gaze out across acres of wooden fences and thousands of bellowing animals to try to place the stockyard in its surrounding landscape. To the south, stretching all the way to the flat horizon, were mile upon mile of farms and open prairies, still more or less untouched by signs of urban growth. To the east lay Lake Michigan, close enough that one could see both shores on opposite sides of a broad expanse of water. And to the north—the structures of an expanding city, rising up out of a familiar haze: "the city," wrote one guidebook author about the Hough House view, "lies seemingly at your feet, wrapped in a thick cloud of smoke, as if you were standing above the clouds."[15] For its part, the stockyard was soon contributing "the smoke of scores of chimneys" to that cloud and to the progress it represented.[16] On a cold winter day, the pens steamed with the breath and sweat of restless animals, and the pungent odor of urine and manure filled the air.

A visitor standing atop Hough House and taking in the sights of what Chicagoans were fond of calling "THE GREAT BOVINE CITY OF THE WORLD" could hardly fail to be impressed that this vast network of rails and fences had only one purpose: to assemble the animal products of the Great West, transmute them into their most marketable form, and speed them on their way to dinner tables around the world. The economic miracle of the stockyard had much in common with that of the grain elevator. It concentrated an abundant but scattered natural resource to create a new kind of commodity. For cattle, this meant traveling east by rail in heretofore unheard-of numbers while still alive, since beef packing was not at first a major activity at the Chicago stockyards. For pigs, it meant passing through the "disassembly line"—pioneered in Cincinnati but perfected in Chicago—that divided animals into their most minute constituent parts so that the greatest possible profit from their sale could be gained. In each case, the fundamental process remained the same: moving animals ever further in their passage from pulsing flesh to dead commodity.

At the stockyards, this economic alchemy was accomplished in a yellow limestone structure located next to the hotel. Known as the Exchange Building, it contained a bank that during the 1860s regularly handled up to half a million dollars worth of transactions each day, as well as telegraph facilities that gathered meat prices and livestock news from every corner of the globe. Its most important feature, though, was the great hall where dealers conducted their daily business in much the same way as the grain traders at the Board of Trade. As one New Yorker described it, "In this elegant Exchange room two classes of cattle men meet,—those who collect the cattle from the prairie States,—Texas, Missouri, Kansas, Illinois, Iowa, Wisconsin, Minnesota,—and those who distribute the cattle among the Eastern cities."[17]

Here, then, was the whole point of the stockyard, the ultimate meeting place of country and city, West and East, producer and consumer—of animals and their killers. Its polished wood surfaces and plush upholstery offered an odd contrast to the wet muck and noisy, fecund air in the pens just outside its doors. The Exchange Building seemed somehow at a distance from the animals in whose flesh it dealt, as if to deny the bloody consequences of the transactions that went on within it. For some, this was a sign of civilization, whereby "a repulsive and barbarizing business is lifted out of the mire, and rendered clean, easy, respectable, and pleasant." Those who handled the animals in their pens had little to do with those who bought and sold them, and vice versa. "The controlling minds"—the large traders and meat-packers—were thereby "left free to work at the arithmetic and book-keeping of the business," undisturbed by manure or blood or the screams of dying animals.[18]

By following out the logic of their arithmetic, those controlling minds would work an economic transformation in American life. Like those behind the grain elevators, they would remake international meat markets with new technologies for selling and distributing cattle and hogs. Like their counterparts in the lumberyards, they would produce enormous ecological changes in American landscapes that at first glance could not have seemed more remote from the heady air of the Chicago stockyards. But the Chicago livestock dealers and meat-packers went further still. They established intricate new connections among grain farmers, stock raisers, and butchers, thereby creating a new corporate network that gradually seized responsibility for moving and processing animal flesh in all parts of North America. One long-term result of this new network was a basic change in the American diet, and in that of people in many other parts of the world as well. Another was a growing interpenetration of city and country. With it, seemingly, came an increasing corporate control over landscape, space, and the natural world, so much so that by the end of the century the new meat-packing companies had nearly freed themselves from dependence on any single location—including Chicago. The growing distance between the meat market and the animals in whose flesh it dealt may have seemed civilizing to those who visited the Exchange Building in the 1860s, but it also betokened a much deeper and subtler separation—the word "alienation" is not too strong—from the act of killing and from nature itself.

Slaughtering the Bison

Chicago and the lands lying several hundred miles to its west had originally been covered by plants of the tallgrass prairie: wild rye, slough grass, switch grass, the bluestems, and others. Growing in the lush abundance of a well-watered land, grasses like the big bluestem could rise to over six feet in height—so high, the artist George Catlin reported, that he and his companions were "obliged to stand erect in our stirrups, in order to look over its waving tops," as they rode through it.[19] Such grasses had been maintained in part by the wildfires, some set by lightning and some by Indians, that regularly swept across them. The fires destroyed the woody stems of trees (mainly oaks and hickories) that might otherwise have dominated the terrain, and gave the abundant root growth of the grasses an injection of nutrients that accelerated their recovery. Settlers destroyed the prairies by plowing them up for crops, by fencing them for pasture, and by taking steps to prevent the annual fires.[20] Once the farmers had finished their work, the tallgrass prairie was doomed to a cornered-up existence in fugitive spots where conditions allowed a few of its species to survive. They managed to hang on only in occasional fence rows, at the corners of carelessly mowed fields, and, ironically, along the margins of railroad lines where sparks from coal-fired engines kept prairie fires alive on a much diminished scale.[21]

A different fate would befall the drier grasslands farther west. As one traveled out of Illinois and Iowa into the country beyond the Missouri River, annual precipitation diminished steadily in quantity and regularity, so taller grasses like the big bluestem became ever scarcer until finally they disappeared altogether. They were succeeded first by the midheight grasses of the mixed prairie, among which the two- to three-foot-high little bluestem was most common. Still farther west, in the foothills of the Rockies, these gave way in turn to the dominant plants of the shortgrass prairie, especially blue grama and buffalo grass, growing as a turf or in clumps three to six inches high. Here the climate was so dry that plants used all available moisture before their growing season had finished: seasonal rainfall rather than temperature determined their annual growth. As the subsoil became parched, the grasses went dormant in the hot summer sun, producing the yellowed hillsides characteristic of the High Plains. Only their root systems, extending much deeper into the ground than their leaves rose above it, enabled such grasses to survive until fall rains or spring meltwater permitted them to commence another growth cycle.[22]

The tallgrass prairie of the upper Mississippi Valley would vanish during the years of Chicago's greatest growth, to be replaced by some of the most fertile farmlands in the world. The rise of agricultural markets in Chicago and elsewhere meant that wheat and especially corn would become the new artificial dominants of the old prairie ecosystem. As the railroads fingered their way beyond the eastern margins of the Great Plains, agricultural settlement of the grasslands increased its pace, almost exploding with the completion of the first transcontinentals in the late 1860s and early 1870s. In their exuberance to repeat the success of settlers in Illinois, Wisconsin, Minnesota, and Iowa, would-be farmers swept out into Kansas, Nebraska, and Dakota Territory without realizing that they were entering new landscapes and climates that would render their own ventures much more precarious. Families migrated by the thousands during years when rainfall was abundant. The fields they plowed soon began to yield great quantities of grain, but only so long as the rain persisted—which inevitably, in some years, it did not. The rains failed far more regularly in the mixed and shorter grasslands of the plains than they had in the tallgrass prairies farther east. Drought became an ever more frequent phenomenon the farther west one went. By the 1880s, it was clear that only irrigation or special dry-farming techniques would allow farmers to produce crops reliably in such country.[23]

The precariousness of grain crops on the arid lands of the High Plains meant that many settlers turned to agricultural regimes better suited to a dry climate. If they could not profitably grow wheat or corn, they could usually raise livestock successfully. The mixed and shortgrass prairies would prove to be wonderful rangeland for domesticated grazing animals, a fact already evident from the vast herds of wild grazers that had long made homes there. An English visitor in the 1860s offered an accurate prophecy when he wrote, "Nothing short of violence or special legislation can prevent the plains from continuing to be forever that which under nature's farming they have ever been—the feeding ground for mighty flocks, the cattle pasture of the world."[24] But if livestock was to become the new foundation for agriculture on the High Plains, would-be settlers and ranchers had to alter the earlier landscape of the region. In particular, they had to confine or eliminate its original human and animal inhabitants.

Among the latter, none was more astounding in its abundance than the American bison. At the beginning of the nineteenth century, the plains had been home to a bison population numbering upward of twenty, thirty, or even forty million animals.[25] So numerous were they that they significantly modified their habitat, shifting the species composition of grasslands toward shorter and more resilient species (especially the well-named buffalo grass) that could best withstand heavy grazing.[26] The bison lived in scattered herds of fifty to two hundred individuals that, in a desultory and almost random way, migrated north and south with the seasons, and hither and yon between burned and unburned prairie, in search of fresh grass for forage. During the late summer, these small herds congregated for what was called the "running season," when bulls challenged each other for territorial mating rights. When assembled in this way, the great mass of animals became an awe-inspiring sight for all who witnessed it, indisputable proof that the grasslands were an extraordinarily productive environment for grazers.[27]

No one could visit the plains in the years before 1875 without reporting astonishment at the number of bison they saw there. George Catlin, writing about his experiences in the 1830s, spoke of the bison congregating "into such masses in some places, as literally to blacken the prairies for miles together." One could easily see "several thousands in a mass, eddying and wheeling about under a cloud of dust," with "the whole mass . . . in constant motion; and all bellowing (or 'roaring') in deep and hollow sounds; which, mingled together, appear, at the distance of a mile or two, like the sound of distant thunder."[28] Such herds could easily be several miles wide.

So numerous were the enormous shaggy beasts that travelers found themselves groping for verbal images to describe them adequately. They were like fish in the sea, an army in battle, a biblical plague of locusts, a robe that clothed the prairies in all directions to the horizon. Perhaps the most common observation, made by many before and after Catlin, was that the animals literally changed the color of the landscape, "blackening the whole surface of the country."[29] They seemed, as the Reverend Robert Rundle said in the borrowed words of Milton, "in numbers—numberless."[30] When William J. Hays sought to record the vast scale of a stampeding herd in a painting he made while visiting the plains in 1860, eastern critics attacked him for his exaggeration and want of accuracy. Yet those who had seen the great herds for themselves could testify that Hays had gotten his image exactly right.[31]

Hays produced his painting at almost the last possible moment he could have made it from life. The bison were already doomed. Their numbers, like those of the beaver and other North American fur-bearing mammals, began to dwindle as soon as the market economy placed a price on their skins. In the early years, that price was measured in liquor, firearms, and other trade goods sought most actively by Plains Indian tribes. As early as the 1830s, Catlin heard tell of a party of six hundred

Sioux warriors in the Dakota country who had exchanged fourteen hundred fresh buffalo tongues for "a few gallons of whiskey"; somewhere nearby, fourteen hundred carcasses presumably lay unused and rotting in the summer sun.[32] During the first half of the nineteenth century, Plains tribes began to consider the bison an object of trade as much as of subsistence. A market in robes sprang up in the East to encourage such ventures. At the same time, fur traders and U.S. Army posts grew to rely on the animals for food. The great herds came under increasing pressure, and their numbers began to decline.

But the real collapse of the bison population did not come until after the Civil War. With the arrival of the Union Pacific in Nebraska and Wyoming during the 1860s, followed a few years later by the Kansas Pacific farther south, the railroads drove a knife into the heart of buffalo country. As everywhere else, trains introduced easier, faster travel into territory that had formerly been much less accessible. They made market demand more effective as the cost of transportation fell, extending von Thünen's urban-rural zones rapidly westward. Suddenly it became possible for market and sport hunters alike to reach the herds with little effort, shipping back robes and tongues and occasionally trophy heads as the only valuable parts of the animals they killed. Sport hunters in particular enjoyed the practice of firing into the animals without ever leaving their trains. As they neared a herd, passengers flung open the windows of their cars, pointed their breechloaders, and fired at random into the frightened beasts. Dozens might die in a few minutes, and rot where they fell after the train disappeared without stopping.[33]

Then, disastrously, in 1870 Philadelphia tanners perfected techniques for turning bison hides into a supple and attractive leather.[34] The next year, all hell broke loose. Commercial hunting outfits—"pot-hunters"—descended on the plains in greater numbers than ever before, shipping back hundreds of thousands of skins to eastern manufacturers. So great was their enthusiasm and so little their skill that three to five animals died for every robe that eventually made the rail journey back east. "Every man," wrote Richard Dodge, an army officer who witnessed the height of the slaughter, "wanted to shoot; no man wanted to do the other work. Buffalo were slaughtered without sense or discretion, and oftentimes left to rot with the hides on."[35] Now that the dead animals were a more reliable source of cash, such waste made less economic sense, and so merchants soon organized more professional hunting parties. A typical outfit came to consist of four men: a shooter, two skinners, and a cook who was also responsible for stretching hides and taking care of camp. They were supported by a growing network of depots and smokehouses that served as gathering stations where merchants assembled their stock for shipment to Omaha, St. Louis, Chicago, and finally the great leather manufacturers in Philadelphia and especially New York.

The bison had once had few predators. As a herding animal, it instinctively responded to attack either by standing its ground or stampeding. Both behaviors proved lethal in the face of market hunters carrying guns. Professional marksmen could generally take down an animal with a single bullet. If shot from a great enough distance, a bison could drop to the ground without arousing more than the curiosity of its companions, who became in turn the next potential victims. Dodge reported having counted no fewer than 112 carcasses within a radius of two hundred yards from the spot where a single hunter had successfully brought them down in less than forty-five minutes.[36] Such shooting was hardly hunting at all; it was almost literally like working in a slaughterhouse, and the plains soon gained the appearance of a vast, nightmarish abattoir. "Where there were myriads of buffalo the year before," Dodge wrote, "there were now myriads of carcasses. The air was foul with sickening stench, and the vast plain, which only a short twelvemonth before teemed with animal life, was a dead, solitary, putrid desert."[37]

The result was just what George Catlin had prophesied forty years earlier: "the ranks must be thinned, and the race exterminated, of this noble animal, and the Indians of the great plains left without the means of supporting life. . . ."[38] Dodge's image was more poetic but no less accurate. "The buffalo," he wrote, "melted away like snow before a summer's sun."[39] Within four years of the appearance of the railroads and a market in tannable hides, well over four million bison died on the southern plains alone. In Kansas, the slaughter reached its peak between 1870 and 1873, and then collapsed.

Rather than draw the obvious lesson from that event, the hunters simply moved elsewhere. Texas became the center of the attack between 1874 and 1878, by which time nothing remained of the southern herd. The bison of Dakota, Montana, and the Canadian prairies hung on for only a few years longer. Perhaps the bitterest and most poignant moment came in 1883. Montana hunters, eager to repeat their successes of the year before, bought their usual annual supplies and headed out for the kill. But apart from a few lone stragglers, they found nothing. The great herds had vanished from the face of the plains. By midsummer, most of the hunters were bankrupt.[40]

The hunters were not alone in their disaster. As the bison disappeared, the Great Plains Indian tribes found their subsistence more and more threatened. Custer's defeat at the Little Bighorn may have been the climactic event in Plains Indian resistance to the American invasion, but it was the last stand of a people whose ecological homeland had nearly vanished. The Indian wars of the 1870s took place in the shadow of hunger and starvation occasioned by the loss of the animals on which Indian economies and cultures had been relying for generations. Sitting Bull and his followers may have won their great battle, but they lost the war to defend their earlier way of life: Henceforth, they would have to find new lives for themselves without the great herds to sustain them.

Open Range and Feed Lot

The disappearance of the bison was but a prelude to complicated changes in Great Plains ecology and economy. Although Chicago had not played as significant a role as the eastern manufacturing cities in the skin trade that destroyed the herds, it nonetheless benefited more than any other city from the long-term effects of the animals' annihilation. The bison had met their end because their ecosystem had become attached to an urban marketplace in a new way. The very market forces that had led hunters nearly to exterminate the species now encouraged other people to find a suitable replacement so that the rich fertility of the western grasslands should not go to waste. Even before the bison had entirely gone, their heirs apparent—horses, sheep, and especially the longhorn cattle working their way north from Texas—were already beginning to make buffalo country their own. Called into being by the same urban markets that had sent the hunters scurrying across the plains in the first place, the new herds would be tied to the cities by the same iron rails that had turned the plains into a slaughterhouse.

The new livestock economy linking Chicago and the Great Plains emerged at the very moment that the destruction of the bison neared its climax. The Civil War had cut off the ranchers of south Texas from their ordinary markets in the Caribbean islands and the slave states of the southern Mississippi Valley, allowing the cattle population of the region to grow dramatically during the war years. By the time the South surrendered, millions of Texas longhorns were wandering freely in the region east and south of San Antonio. Would-be entrepreneurs who wanted a herd could simply capture some animals, brand them, and call them their own. Worth only a few dollars on the Texas range, they would sell for ten times that much in the East—if only entrepreneurs could get them to market. Drovers had once taken Texas cattle to places as far away as New Orleans, but the war had left that city and other southern markets in a state of collapse. Demand was greater in the North, where cattle brought much higher prices. If only one could somehow get one's animals to the new Union Stockyard in Chicago without paying too much for transportation and (what amounted to the same thing) without diminishing their weight too much along the way, one could make a fortune.

Like that of many other places, the old market geography of the grasslands was transformed by the railroad. At the end of the war, construction crews for the Kansas Pacific began to work their way out into the buffalo country of the southern plains, surveying a line west from St. Louis and Kansas City into the heart of the mixed-grass prairie. As the hunters set about their bloody work with the bison, other entrepreneurs began to speculate about how best to solve the transportation problem of the Texas longhorns. Somewhere along the route of the new line it ought to be possible, as one such entrepreneur explained, "to establish a market whereat the Southern drover and Northern buyer would meet upon an equal footing."[41]

Just such a place came into being at Abilene, Kansas. Starting its existence as "a very small, dead place, consisting of about one dozen log huts," Abilene began its brief time of glory in 1867 when an Illinois livestock dealer named Joseph G. McCoy purchased 250 acres and established a stockyard near the rail depot there.[42] Texas cattlemen had already learned of the railroad's westward extension but had been uncertain about where best to meet it. McCoy gave them their answer. He developed and promoted an old trading route, the Chisholm Trail, as the best corridor for bringing livestock north. It ended in Abilene. Cattle began to arrive there by August, and the first twenty-car shipment of animals left the city on September 5. Their destination, predictably enough, was Chicago.[43]

The great cattle drives of the 1860s, 1870s, and 1880s are among the best known and most romantic of American frontier icons. The classic image is that of cowboys on horseback working to round up scattered cattle, assembling great herds of hundreds or even a thousand or more animals before urging the bellowing mass forward.[44] The lonely life of the trail has entered American mythology by way of folk songs, dime novels, and western films as a series of familiar moments: the long march across windswept prairies, the potential disaster of river crossings and thunderstorms, the ever present threat of stampedes, the smell of beans and salt pork cooking over open campfires, the uneasy quiet of the night watch.[45] The cowboy rapidly emerged as the new nomad of the Great Plains, driving and trailing his herds along the same paths that bison and Indians had followed just a few years before. But wherever he did his work, however remote the landscapes he called home, his essential task remained the same: bringing the fatted herd to market.[46] The cowboy was the agent who tied von Thünen's livestock-raising zone to its metropolitan market. Far from being a loner or rugged individualist, he was a wageworker whose task was to ship meat to the cities—above all, to Chicago.

Starting in 1867, hundreds of thousands of animals made the journey north from Texas each year, to widely varying destinations. Initially, most went to Abilene and the boisterous cattle towns that succeeded it: Ellsworth, Wichita, Caldwell, Dodge City. None of these lasted more than a few years as a railhead for the drovers. Each eventually lost its cattle trade as the country around it filled in with farms whose owners soon lobbied against the damage and disease the Texas cattle caused.[47] As conflict between Texas cowboys and Kansas farmers grew more intense, the center of beef production shifted elsewhere. Within a decade, ranchers had driven cattle as far north as Colorado, Wyoming, and Montana, where they began raising herds right up to the foothills of the Rockies.[48] By 1883, when the last northern bison herd finally disappeared, there were over half a million cattle in eastern Montana alone.[49]

Everywhere, from Texas to Saskatchewan, the old buffalo range became ranchland. Bison gave way to livestock. In part, cattle (and with them sheep) produced many of the same grazing effects as bison. Intensive grazing had helped maintain the old shortgrass prairies of the High Plains, since tall and medium-height grasses like the bluestems died back when trampled or eaten too close to the ground. Cattle helped ensure that the short grasses would continue their dominance of the western plains, and were consequently in some ways a force for stability and continuity in the landscape.

But the livestock brought subtle changes as well. Unlike the buffalo herds, they moved within the property boundaries their owners set for them, even where the open range continued to exist. Large ranchers sought to eliminate their competitors' access to grazing land by buying up the areas around springs and streams, gaining control of surrounding territory that depended on these sources of water and hay.[50] Intensive grazing thus tended to concentrate along the very watercourses where taller grasses had once been most abundant. Worse, cattle seemed to find taller species like the big and little bluestem especially palatable, and grazed them so thoroughly that they gradually disappeared.

In their place came species that were either less tasty to livestock or better able to survive grazing. Inedible forbs like the native ironweed and stiff goldenrod, or the invading Canadian thistle, expanded their range in intensively grazed areas, as did certain grasses. Some of the latter were natives like side oats grama, while others were exotics—none more successful than Kentucky bluegrass—that followed the herds wherever they went. As taller grasses disappeared, more sunlight became available for short grasses and annual weeds. These colonized the bare spots created by trampling hoofs and by piles of dung that smothered the plants on which they fell. The shift from bison to cattle thus brought with it parallel shifts in regional vegetation that, while initially almost imperceptible, became ever more widespread with time.[51]

The extent of such effects depended on the density of livestock populations, which rapidly increased once the bison herds had vanished. As competition for grazing land became more severe, conflicts between farmers and ranchers, or between cattlemen and sheepherders, brought an end to the open range in many areas. Owners of animals sought to keep their herds separate from each other, and farmers were no less eager to keep cattle and sheep away from their crops. Like the farm families that raised livestock and corn together on the tallgrass prairies of Illinois and Iowa, ranchers needed a way to partition the plains landscape with physical barriers to animal movement.[52]

The technology for accomplishing this task was the fence, that key symbol of European agriculture that distinguished it from its Indian predecessors.[53] But the traditional wooden fences of earlier American frontiers were simply not feasible in a landscape whose most distinctive feature was its lack of trees. Ranchers could of course get any amount of wood they needed from lumber merchants in Chicago and the Mississippi Valley—if they could afford it. Earlier fencing styles were so wood intensive, however, that they were simply too costly for wide use in the open spaces of the High Plains. Large-scale fencing there became possible only in the 1870s, after Joseph Glidden's invention of barbed wire in 1873 dramatically reduced the amount of wood that went into a typical fence.[54] The railroads that allowed ranchers to ship their animals to Chicago's market brought in return the fence posts and barbed wire with which to partition the grasslands.

Fences hastened the transition from prairie to pasture by further concentrating grazing in certain areas and by reducing the frequency of fires. Close-cropped grasses meant less fuel to burn, and that in turn helped reduce the temperature and destructiveness of fires when they did occur. Moreover, the capital investment represented by a fence gave ranchers a strong incentive to stop prairie fires wherever they got started.[55] Although fire suppression techniques were not fully effective on the plains until the twentieth century, ranchers were already actively fighting fires by the 1880s. Just as in the tallgrass prairie farther east, livestock, fences, and suppressed fires all accelerated the demise of the older grassland ecology that Indians and bison had constructed on the plains.

But the environmental consequences of the new livestock economy extended well beyond the Great Plains, for they were part of an integrated system of meat production that reached from the Rockies across the tallgrass prairies of Iowa and Illinois all the way to Chicago and beyond. At the same time that cattle were replacing bison in the short-grass regions of Wyoming and Montana, they were coming to play a new role in the Mississippi Valley as well. As late as 1860, Illinois had been the leading livestock producing state in the nation, with cattle and hogs ranging freely on the state's still abundant prairie grasses. But as the state became more settled and as its linkages to the Chicago market increased, land values rose. Under these circumstances, the usual logic of von Thünen's urban-rural zones encouraged a shift from extensive to intensive agriculture. For Illinois farmers, this meant a steady conversion of grasslands to cornfields so that animals could eat domesticated rather than wild grain. A mixed crop-livestock system emerged, with the bulk of the region's immense corn production going to feed not people but animals.[56]

Most Illinois and Iowa farmers initially operated on relatively small tracts of land. They kept only a few animals for meat and dairy products, depending on grain more than on meat for their cash income. Some individuals, however, had since the 1820s devoted much more extensive acreage to grazing, raising hundreds of animals at a time and becoming true "cattle kings." By grazing pasturelands that were sometimes many square miles in extent, their operations anticipated the ranches that appeared several decades later on the plains.[57] But the immense size of their landholdings and their emphasis on cattle production exposed Illinois grazers to market pressures different from those faced by their neighbors who were not so dependent on livestock. The advent of rail shipments from Kansas and elsewhere put them in direct competition with cheaper western range-fed cattle; at the same time, rising real estate values, and especially the taxes that went with them, made it less profitable to "waste" land by feeding Illinois cattle on grass.[58]

The solution was to feed them corn. Some livestock raisers grew corn themselves, but the larger their operation, the greater their need to purchase feed from neighboring grain farmers or from the Chicago elevators. This increased costs still further, and led producers to look for other ways to make their operations more efficient. The general strategy to which they gradually turned was to eliminate the time-consuming task of breeding young animals, concentrating instead on fattening animals that were already nearly grown. By purchasing two-year-old steers—"stockers"—from ranchers on the Great Plains, midwestern livestock raisers could make sure that the corn their "feeders" consumed would go into meat and fat rather than into inedible bone and other less marketable body parts.

Under the resulting feedlot system, steers lived in fenced outdoor enclosures and each day enjoyed a feast of shocked corn spread on the ground before them or placed in feeding troughs. Hogs wandered in their midst and happily scavenged whatever food the cattle found inedible, even consuming undigested food from the dung of the larger animals. The system thus maximized the efficiency of meat production by yielding beef and pork at the same time, and was generally more profitable than selling corn directly.[59] Speaking of the fifteen hundred bushels of corn he had raised the preceding year, one farmer in Jacksonville, Illinois, wrote home in 1838 that he would "not sell a bushel, but feed it all to the stock." Although he planned to keep raising corn himself, he added, "Whether we raise much or little, we shall give it all to hogs & cattle, as we think it more profitable than to sell the corn."[60] Some farmers did keep female cows either for milk or to breed new varieties of stock that put on weight more quickly, produced more milk, or had other desirable qualities. For these specialized breeders, profit came from manipulating the genetic characteristics of their animals so that other farmers would wish to purchase them.[61] But many farmers abandoned breeding altogether and kept only steers that would bring the best price in Chicago markets. By the end of the century, feedlots were the predominant form of meat production in Illinois and Iowa.[62]

The livestock industry that emerged in the Great West between 1860 and 1890 was another manifestation of second nature, noteworthy for its economic complexity and geographical extent. Although the product of thousands of people each making innumerable independent decisions about their own livelihoods, it had a coherent collective shape consistently structured by the logic of the market. As grassland gave way to pasture, and pasture to feedlot, the general tendency was for people to replace natural systems with systems regulated principally by the human economy. The old migratory patterns of the Great Plains, in which Indians had organized their subsistence around the wanderings of the bison herds, now gave way to a more unidirectional movement in which cowboys drove livestock northward out of Texas and eastward out of the High Plains.[63] Driving cattle was expensive, not just because cowboys received wages but because fast-moving animals lost weight as they traveled. And so cowboys sought to minimize weight loss by moving slowly, pasturing cattle along the way, and delivering animals to railroads that reduced their muscular expenditure of stored body fat by shifting the energy cost of transportation to locomotives burning wood or coal. Whereas the bison had moved north and south following the seasons of the year, cattle moved from pasture to slaughterhouse according to the dictates of the market. Both grew fat on prairie grasses, but the bison lost their fat each winter as they consumed the energy they had stored the previous summer. For the cattlemen, such weight loss was unprofitable, and so animals were hurried to market in the fall or sojourned for a time in Illinois and Iowa, where they could continue to gain weight all winter on feedlot corn.

Long drives in Texas, ranches in Wyoming, cattle towns in Kansas, feedlots in Illinois: all became linked in a new animal landscape that was governed as much by economics as by ecology. Considered abstractly, it was a landscape in which the logic of capital had remade first nature and bound together far-flung places to produce a profound new integration of biological space and market time. By century's end, the old shortgrass prairies of the High Plains had become pastures for range-fed cattle. Some of those animals rode the rails directly to market. Others, especially young males, headed to the old tallgrass prairies, which farmers had dismantled and partitioned into feedlots and cornfields. Animals' lives had been redistributed across regional space, for they were born in one place, fattened in another, and killed in still a third.

Because young steers grew more quickly than old ones, their owners arranged that they should lead shorter lives. Improvements in breeding eventually meant that animals could be slaughtered profitably by the end of their second year, thereby saving the costs of many months of feed.[64] Time itself gained new meaning under these circumstances, for in the most literal sense it had become money. During an animal's foreshortened life span, the old seasonal alternation of fat summers and lean winters gave way to a system of continuous growth, in which food supply—whether in the form of hay or shocked corn—was grown and stored so that there need be no interruption to the steady accumulation of future cash in well-muscled flesh. Farmers and ranchers thus truncated the cyclical time of natural reproduction to make agricultural production as rapid and linear as possible. Once an animal had completed its work of converting grass and corn to meat, its owners sought to protect its value by keeping it from losing weight on the journey to market. If time was money, so was distance, and stock owners could economize on both by increasing the speed at which living creatures moved across the landscape. And so meat on the hoof became meat in a railroad car, as steam locomotives consumed the energy of wood and coal to preserve the energy in living flesh. Once the animals were aboard the final cattle car, their only remaining journey was to the butcher. Just so did market logic create a new region in the shadow of the Union Stockyards; just so did Chicago extend its reach a thousand and more miles to the west.

Porkopolis

For cattle that had grown fat on the grasses of the High Plains and the corn of the Iowa feedlots, Chicago was the end of the line. It was the place, more than any other, where animals went to die. In the grimy brick buildings that sprang up beside the great stockyard, death itself took a new form.

The actual task of killing was not the biggest problem Chicagoans had to solve as they faced the thousands of animals that poured into the stock-yard. Killing was a relatively simple matter—a blow to the head, a knife to the throat—complicated only by how much one cared about the pain or terror animals felt in dying. The real problem was what to do with animals once they were dead, for unless people intervened at once they soon went the way of all flesh. Decay was the great enemy of the meat-packer, wasting an investment in fatted hogs and steers far more quickly than the animals lost weight on a long drive. Unless consumed or preserved immediately, beef and pork went through a series of mutations that rendered them first unpalatable, then inedible, and finally dangerously toxic. At each step in their decay, their value at market declined, destroying the long months of work, management, and natural growth that had gone into producing them. Preventing such waste was the chief task of the packer.

The meat-packing industry of Chicago and the Great West had begun not with cattle but with hogs. There were several good reasons for this. Up until the 1870s, the best available means for halting natural decay—salt and smoke—were much more effective with pork than with beef.[65] Although England had made small purchases of pickled beef from the United States since the 1840s, most Americans preferred their steaks fresh.[66] Pork, on the other hand, had been salted and smoked since colonial times, so that many of its most eagerly sought forms were packed rather than fresh: bacon, ham, sausage, lard, and various sorts of pickled pork.[67] Domestic demand for packed pork was enormous.

Aside from the differences between beef and pork as meats, the animals from which they came—being quite unlike each other in size, shape, and temperament—lent themselves to different kinds of marketing. Cattle, with their long legs, large size, and easygoing nature, did not generally object to being driven. If well handled, they could walk hundreds of miles without losing so much weight that they became unprofitable to sell. Hogs, on the other hand, were smaller, closer to the ground, and more ill-willed toward their keepers. Their bad humor made them so hard to drive to market that drovers sometimes stitched shut the eyelids of particularly obstreperous animals. Once blinded in this way, they could still keep to the road by following their companions, but were less inclined to make havoc.[68] Hogs lost weight quickly while on the road, and this too made it unprofitable to drive them very far.

For these reasons, American beef and pork markets developed differently during the first half of the nineteenth century. Farmers raising cattle in the trans-Appalachian West might drive them all the way to New York or Philadelphia before selling them. That way, local butchers could slaughter the animals just before their final customers ate them.[69] The Texas longhorns made their journey to the Kansas cattle towns for much the same reason: they boarded the railroads and traveled as close as they could get to the dinner table before dying. The story with hogs was quite different. Although hog drives did occur on a larger scale than one might suppose, over surprisingly large distances, there were strong economic incentives to slaughter and pack pigs near the place where farmers raised them. Pork packing was thus one of the earliest and most important of frontier industries, springing up wherever people established new agricultural settlements.[70]

Frontier farmers raised hogs as their great residual crop. Unlike cattle, pigs were perfectly willing to fend for themselves even in the earliest days of settlement, whether in prairie or in woodland. Often allowed to run wild, they grazed, ate acorns, foraged in cornfields, and consumed any household garbage not being put to other uses. From the perspective of a farm family struggling to establish itself in a new location, they were wonderfully productive animals, converting grain to meat with two or three times the efficiency of cattle or sheep. A hog contained considerably more usable meat and fat as a proportion of its body weight than a steer. Moreover, a sow could start reproducing when only a year old, whereas a cow did not become fertile until sometime in its third year. A sow dropped her litter of several piglets after only four months gestation, whereas cows took nine months to produce only a single calf (or occasionally two). As a result, pigs multiplied at a much greater rate.[71] Their prodigious meat-making powers meant that once farmers had harvested their corn crop, pigs (along with whisky) were generally the most compact and valuable way of bringing it to market. Farmers tried hard to gauge the ratio of pork prices to corn prices, and fed corn to their pigs whenever it seemed the most profitable course to follow.[72] As one nineteenth-century commentator put it, "The hog eats the corn, and Europe eats the Hog. Corn thus becomes incarnate; for what is a hog, but fifteen or twenty bushels of corn on four legs?"[73]

The new farming areas of the tallgrass prairie had a large crop of pigs whose owners were eager to sell them for cash. Unwilling to waste their investment by driving the animals far, farmers instead chose to sell them to seasonal pork packers in the nearest town. Before railroads arrived, pork-packing operations existed in many western communities, usually run by general merchants who hired casual workers to slaughter and dress pigs in unused warehouses.[74] Typical of many such pork packers was John Burrows of Davenport, Iowa, who was luckier handling hogs than handling potatoes. A merchant who bought and sold virtually any produce local farmers were willing to trade, Burrows used the lower floor of an old mill he owned to cut up carcasses which he purchased, already dressed and frozen, from local farmers. During one winter in the early 1850s when he had no competitors in the trade, pigs came in four times more quickly than Burrows's workers could cut them up. Soon, he reported, "every warehouse and cellar in town [was] filled with frozen hogs." To keep up, he had to work "two sets of hands, night and day," and packed a total of nineteen thousand animals that winter alone.[75]

Burrow's operation was impressive for an early agricultural settlement, but still small by later standards. Like most such packing, it required moderate capital, few specialized tools, and only a few weeks worth of labor. Merchants like Burrows could pack pork on the margin, as a way to use capital at a time of little trade. The needs of the business were simple: nearby farms to supply pigs, the cash or credit with which to buy them, a source of barrels, salt and saltpeter as preservatives, inexpensive transportation, and, not least, cold weather.[76] Like everything else in the prerailroad economy, packing depended on the seasons. Hogs, especially those that had spent their lives foraging, were at their fattest after gorging themselves on the seeds and fruits of autumn. Early winter was an advantageous time in the labor market as well, since farmworkers were more willing to take on other jobs once the fall harvest was complete. Most important, subfreezing temperatures were critical if a packer hoped to chill a carcass quickly. For all these reasons, early winter was prime packing time.

Winter also marked the close of navigation on the rivers, which meant that a merchant had little choice but to hang on to most barrels of pork until warm weather returned, even though doing so tied up scarce capital for several months. That was why Burrows had to fill so many of Davenport's basements with his bacon and pickled pigs. There might be a small local demand for meat, but only with the coming of spring would the rivers thaw and downstream markets reopen. The reluctance of farmers to drive their pigs any great distance thus combined with the dependence of merchants on a river-based transportation system to keep western pork-packing operations widely diffused across the agricultural land-scape. In this, they were much like the eastern slaughterhouses that had preceded them: local, unconcentrated, numerous, and small. They en-joyed few economies of scale.

One western city, however, was an exception to most of these rules: Cincinnati. Its site at the confluence of several major rivers drew to it the produce of a wide farming region in Ohio, Indiana, and Kentucky. Its merchants had initially served as intermediaries for the flatboat trade to New Orleans, but during the early decades of the nineteenth century they took up pork packing as well. By concentrating the supply of the city's large hinterland, its packers handled tens and then hundreds of thou-sands of animals each year. By the 1830s, Cincinnati was the largest pork-packing center in North America, and had proudly claimed for itself the nickname Porkopolis. The thousands of pigs moving through its streets, the color of blood staining its streams, the fetid odor filling its air: all testified to a scale of operation well beyond that of other western towns. "I am sure I should have liked Cincinnati much better," wrote Frances Trollope in the late 1820s, "if the people had not dealt so very largely in hogs."[77] When Frederick Law Olmsted described the country around Cincinnati in the winter of 1853–54, he commented that his party saw "as many hogs as trees."[78]

Just as Buffalo had invented the grain elevator that would revolution-ize Chicago's grain trade, Cincinnati pioneered the manufacturing tech-niques that would transform Chicago meat-packing. The enormous num-ber of pigs that filled Cincinnati's streets each fall, and the urgent need to stop the clock of their decay, led the city's packers to develop new ways of organizing the traditional process of butchering. The earliest step toward mechanization was a large horizontal wheel from which dead pigs hung. As it rotated, workers at the eight points of its compass cleaned and gutted the animals in eight separate steps before sending them off to a storage room for cooling. Once cold, they were taken to tables where master butchers systematically cut them into pieces to be packed and marketed. Cincinnati packers later supplemented the wheel with an over-head rail which carried pigs through each step of the butchering process, and with multistoried packing plants in which animals and carcasses moved by the force of gravity from station to station.[79] The most power-ful description remains that of Olmsted:

> We entered an immense low-ceiled room and followed a vista of dead swine, upon their backs, their paws stretching mutely toward heaven. Walking down to the vanishing point, we found there a sort of human chopping-machine where the hogs were converted into commercial pork.

A plank table, two men to lift and turn, two to wield the cleavers, were its component parts. No iron cog-wheels could work with more regular motion. Plump falls the hog upon the table, chop, chop; chop, chop; chop, chop, fall the cleavers. All is over. But, before you can say so, plump, chop, chop; chop, chop; chop, chop, sounds again. . . . Amazed beyond all expectation at the celerity, we took out our watches and counted thirty-five seconds, from the moment when one hog touched the table until the next occupied its place.[80]

The whole system came to be called the disassembly line and was among the most important forerunners of the mass production techniques that swept American industry in the century to come. In relation to what would soon happen at Chicago, several key facts stand out about Cincinnati. One was that the disassembly line's chief innovation depended much more on the minute division of human labor than on new mechanical technologies. Chicago would go much further with mechanization, but ultimately the organic irregularities that made each animal unique also made human eyes and human hands indispensable for most of the packing process. The division of labor allowed packers to accelerate the rate at which workers handled hogs, and led to specialized ways of dealing with each constituent body part. The enormous volume of animals meant that even body parts that had formerly been wasted now became commercial products: lard, glue, brushes, candles, soaps. Because of such economies, Cincinnati packers in the 1840s could pay seven to ten cents more per hog than packers in other places.[81] But the very rivers that had brought Cincinnati its flood of pork also tied it to the same seasonality that governed the activities of John Burrows and other lesser packers. Even Porkopolis did most of its work in the winter, leaving its immense capital plant idle for the rest of the year. The natural cold that could slow death's decay still held ultimate sway over production.

Chicago merchants had conducted a substantial meat trade even before the coming of the railroad, but they did not come close to the Ohio city in total volume. At the start of the 1850s, Chicago packed 20,000 hogs, compared with Cincinnati's 334,000.[82] Chicago pork packing was still largely the domain of the general merchant, who did business much like John Burrows in Davenport. Then, as the railroads extended their network west, they worked their transforming magic. Chicago's western hinterland grew, bringing ever greater quantities of live hogs and chilled carcasses to the city's merchants. Interior communities could now ship their animals eastward via Chicago rather than southward via the river towns. Cincinnati's rivers had brought it more pork than any other American city, but the trade had reached its natural limits by midcentury; Chicago, on the other hand, was just beginning to grow.

The Civil War clinched Chicago's dominance of American pork pack-ing and enabled it to seize the much-sought title of Porkopolis. One and a half million men enlisted in the Union army during the war; while in the field, they consumed over half a billion pounds of packed meat.[83] At the same time, the Union blockade of the lower Mississippi closed off from western farmers their ordinary markets for produce in New Orleans and the southern cotton country. With unsalable corn on their hands, they had little choice but to feed it to their pigs. Chicago benefited from in-creases in both supply and demand. Its pork packing exploded during the war, while Cincinnati's grew by less than half.[84] Between 1859–60 and 1862–63, Chicago's pork output grew more than sixfold.[85] It surpassed the older city's during the winter of 1861–62, and from that moment on became the greatest pork-packing center in the United States. By the early 1870s, it was processing well over a million hogs per year.[86]

Storing the Winter

By creating a vast pork hinterland that extended all the way across the corn region of Illinois and Iowa, the railroads gave Chicago economies of scale that even Cincinnati could not match. Borrowing a lesson from the river town, Chicago packers abandoned the simple warehouses that had sufficed in earlier days. They constructed elaborate factories designed to slaughter animals and move them past a long chain of workers, each of whom helped disassemble a small part of the carcass into its constituent parts. During the Civil War decade, Chicago firms invested immense sums in specialized buildings, steam engines, and other equipment that enabled them to handle an ever larger number of animals. In 1860, the average capital invested in an Illinois pork-packing plant had been just over $50,000; a decade later, Chicago's pork packers had an average capitalization four times that amount, and the largest had invested over half a million dollars in buildings and equipment.[87]

Capital investment on such a scale underscored the seasonal prob-lems of pork packing as an industry. During the first decade of rail-based packing in Chicago, the vast majority of the city's pork receipts occurred during November, December, and January. Although a trickle of live hogs continued to arrive during the rest of the year, they were slaughtered mainly for fresh consumption within Chicago itself. Few if any animals were packed, for warm temperatures made that impractical. Inefficient use of capital was the seemingly unavoidable result. Half a million dollars in buildings and equipment might pay handsomely for themselves during the early months of winter when they processed the immense stream of carcasses and live hogs that flooded into Chicago from western farmlands. But for the rest of the year, capital plant sat idle, earning little or no return for its owners. This was the trade-off between the simple warehouse facilities that hinterland merchants like Burrows used for their packing and the more specialized factories of Chicago pork packers. Specialization yielded greater meat output from each pig and each human worker, but only by employing equipment that was useless for other purposes during warm seasons, when the meat trade fell off. Seasonal fluctuation meant using capital inefficiently.

Faced with this problem, Chicago pork packers took the obvious step: they began to consider ways of manipulating the seasons of the year. If only winter temperatures could somehow be stored for use during the hot Illinois summers, expensive capital plant need not sit idle. The railroads provided the means for performing even this improbable feat. Merchants in the East had for half a century been cutting ice from ponds near cities like Boston and New York to supply the urban demand for refrigeration. Stored in insulated warehouses and delivered by wagon to commercial and residential customers, ice was traded locally by land and over great distances by sea, so Boston ice merchants could supply the West Indies and American South as well as their own city.[88] But ice was a large-bulk, low-value commodity and had to await the coming of the railroad before it could travel far by land. Chicago was again in the right place at the right time: rail-shipped ice became available at just the moment that rail-shipped hogs began to pose problems.

Local traders started to cut ice from the Chicago River during the 1840s, and had called nearby ponds into service by the end of the 1850s.[89] This ice was consumed primarily within the city itself; breweries in particular were among the heaviest users. But the increasing capital intensity of pork packing created new demand, and in 1858 Chicago firms for the first time used stored winter ice to pack pork during the summer.[90] Thereafter, ice moved in ever larger quantities by rail, coming to Chicago primarily from the shallow glacial lakes that ringed the city in Illinois and Indiana. Summer packing generally went to foreign markets—American consumers still preferred winter pork—but it accounted for a growing share of the total annual output.[91] One measure of its effect was the increase in Chicago's July hog receipts, which had never before been packed, compared with receipts in December, the annual peak of packing. In the years immediately before the Civil War, July receipts were only a tenth of December ones. By the late 1860s, they were about a third, and by the early 1880s they were regularly more than half.[92] July's rising share of Chicago's annual pork output directly reflected the growing ice trade.

The effect of this shift in receipts was exactly what the packers hoped.

It reduced seasonal variation in pork packing, and so permitted factories to use capital plant more efficiently. Packing could now go on year-round, employing equipment, buildings, and workers more steadily. Chicago received pork in two forms: as live animals and as dressed carcasses that hinterland packers had slaughtered and cut into pieces. In 1859, city receipts of the two types of pork followed nearly identical annual curves, with large quantities arriving during the peak period from October to February, and not much arriving at any other time. By 1879, the effect of the ice trade on Chicago pork packers was evident in their very different month-to-month hog purchases compared with those of hinterland packers. Dressed hogs, slaughtered outside Chicago, still came to the city almost entirely during the winter. Live hogs that would be slaughtered in Chicago, on the other hand, peaked only slightly during the winter and arrived steadily throughout the rest of the year.

Farmers could now count on finding a year-round market in Chicago for their corn-fattened pigs—because the city's packing plants never closed. Access to the Chicago market changed the agricultural calendar, spreading pork production across the entire year.[93] Ice and rails together enabled Chicago to pack an ever larger share of the western hog supply; by 1882, its peak year, the city processed nearly half the Midwest's total urban output.[94] The railroads, by carrying hogs to the city even when older modes of transportation proved impassable, had helped Chicago break the wheel of the seasons. The packers had learned to store the winter.

Although the ice trade undoubtedly increased the volume of pork packing in Chicago, its effect on the city's beef market was revolutionary. Because American consumers preferred their steaks fresh, the cattle that railroads brought to Chicago from as far away as Texas, New Mexico, and Montana did not generally end their journey in the city. Initially, most steers at the Union Stockyard, aside from the fraction destined for dinner tables in Chicago itself, were transferred to eastbound railroads and sent to butchers in New York and other cities. As late as 1871, less than 4 percent of the cattle that arrived in Chicago were packed there, those few being shipped mainly to England and imperial outposts like India.[95] Packing as an industry relied almost entirely on pigs, not cattle.

Pork packers used ice to do artificially in summer what cold air had done naturally in winter: cure carcasses before actually preserving them with salt. But Americans' preference for unsalted beef suggested to a few packers an alternative way to use ice. If one could butcher cattle in Chicago and then ship them in refrigerated form to eastern markets, beef packing might become a more profitable activity. Chilling beef in Chicago was easy enough, given the infrastructure already devoted to the ice trade for pork packing. The problem was how to keep meat cold once it began its eastbound journey. The earliest solution was that of George H. Hammond, a Detroit packer who in about 1868 used a special refrigerated railroad car—an icebox on wheels originally designed for fruit shipments—to send sixteen thousand pounds of beef to Boston. The new invention had problems but was enough of a success that Hammond decided to commit himself more fully to the trade. Toward that end, he decided to move nearer to the main source of supply for cattle, and so shifted his operations to Chicago. Given his great need for ice, Hammond chose to build his plant on the banks of the Calumet River next door to an already existing ice-harvesting operation. There, in what would become Hammond, Indiana, he began to introduce the nation to this new form of beef. By 1873, he was doing a million dollars worth of business annually.[96]

Hammond and several other packers expanded the business during the 1870s, but the man most responsible for solving the marketing problems of dressed beef was Gustavus F. Swift.[97] Swift was a New England farm boy who had gotten his start in the meat business by purchasing steers at Boston's Brighton market, cutting them up himself and selling them door-to-door on Cape Cod. He had gradually established several butcher shops that sent out daily wagons to sell direct to their customers. In the early 1870s, he became the partner of a large Boston meat dealer and, like Hammond, decided to pursue his market closer to the original source of supply. This carried him first to Albany and then to Buffalo, but left him thinking that a location even farther west would have still greater benefits. As his son explained, "the cattle on their way from the farms and the ranches and the plains made Chicago their first stop. Then why was not Chicago the place where, inevitably, cattle could be purchased to the best advantage? At Chicago must be the greatest selection, with the minimum of commissions and handling charges accrued against the animals."[98] And so Swift moved to Chicago, where he arrived in 1875. He came to the city with no plans of becoming a packer, intending mainly to act as a livestock dealer who would supply his firm's New England butcher shops. But the losses he experienced in shipping live animals led him in 1877 to try the experiment of shipping two carloads of dressed beef back home. He had no refrigerator cars, so instead he arranged to ship at midwinter, using stripped-down express railroad cars with their doors left open to keep cold air moving across the meat.

The success of the experiement convinced Swift that he should explore refrigerator cars in earnest. Any number of inventors had been working on them to solve several key problems. For one, they sought to prevent meat from touching the ice and freezing, which discolored it and

encouraged spoilage. This could be solved as Swift had done in his earliest shipment, by hanging sides of beef from an overhead rail in the center
of the car. Unfortunately, the suspended carcasses swayed in unison as
the train rounded curves, causing wear on equipment and even train
wrecks. Tighter and more careful packing helped reduce the risk of shifting loads, but often meant that not all parts of the car stayed equally cold.
The solution that Swift's engineer finally used to assure uniform cooling
was to put boxes filled with ice and brine at both ends of the car, venting
them so that a current of chilled air constantly flowed past the meat.[99]
First introduced by Swift in the late 1870s, this improved refrigerator car
was soon in use by all major firms in the dressed beef trade. In addition to
Swift, these included Hammond, Nelson Morris, and Swift's most important competitor, Philip Armour.[100]

The refrigerated railroad car, like the grain elevator, was a simple
piece of technology with extraordinarily far-reaching implications. The
most obvious was the steep growth in Chicago beef packing that began in
the mid-1870s. In 1883–84, the number of cattle slaughtered in Chicago
surpassed the number shipped east for the first time; henceforth, "meat-
packing" would replace "pork packing" as the name of the industry.[101]
The packers themselves attributed their success to the new technology.
"The refrigerator car," announced Swift and Company in a later brochure, "is one of the vehicles on which the packing industry has ridden to
greatness."[102]

Before the refrigerator car could reveal its full implications, however,
the packers first had to link it, again like the grain elevator, to a complex
new infrastructure. Predictably enough, one element of the new system
had to do with ice. As their demand for refrigeration increased, Chicagoans had to look ever farther afield for natural sources of supply. Ice cut
from the Chicago River was terribly polluted, releasing offensive odors
when it melted and endangering the very food it was supposed to preserve. Looking for alternatives, the packers turned first to Lake Calumet
on the Indiana border, as Hammond had done, but it soon proved inadequate in volume: by the 1880s, Swift alone was using 450,000 tons of ice
per year.[103] And so he and his Chicago competitors moved outward toward the city's colder and less polluted hinterland. Lakes in Wisconsin
with good rail connections were particularly attractive candidates for ice-
harvesting operations. Not only were they cleaner, but the northern climate produced a more extended crop of thick, clear ice that was easy to
pack and ship.

The peak years of the Wisconsin ice industry came during the 1880s
and 1890s, when Chicago firms conducted operations from the Illinois–
Wisconsin border all the way north to Green Bay. At Pewaukee, for in-

stance, the Armour Company erected an immense structure 1,200 feet long and 200 feet deep, capable of holding 175,000 tons of ice. Surrounding it were ramps, rail lines, boiler rooms, storage sheds, and boardinghouses to accommodate the hundreds of workers who assembled each winter to cut and handle ice. Swift had a comparable facility on Brown's Lake, in Racine County, and independent Chicago firms worked the lakes in Madison and elsewhere.[104] Harvesting the winter was a major activity of Chicago's Wisconsin hinterland for more than two decades. Only the expansion of artificial refrigeration at the turn of the century made this cheap yet sometimes unreliable source of natural cold obsolete.[105]

But the problem of ice supply was more complicated even than this. Chicago firms had to cool not just their meat-packing plants and the refrigerated railcars that left the city; they also had to resupply those cars several times in their journey as the initial load of ice melted. Swift was the first to grapple with this difficulty, and he solved it by opening a chain of icing stations along the route his beef would follow. Each station required its own icehouse and ice-harvesting operation, quickly giving Swift "an ice-consuming capacity . . . greater than any other ice user's in the country."[106] By 1883, he had developed five such stations—at Battle Creek, Michigan; Sarnia, Ontario; East Buffalo, New York; Waverly, New York; and Port Jervis, New York. Each car of refrigerated beef required an average of a thousand pounds of ice per station on a typical four-day journey east. Swift estimated that it took "as many tons of ice as you expect to ship tons of dressed beef," plus seven hundred pounds of salt, to complete a shipment.[107]

Triumph of the Packers

Refrigeration may have been the key technological problem that packers faced in expanding Chicago's dressed beef trade, but they also had to solve equally complex problems in marketing their product.[108] For one, they needed to overcome consumer resistance to the very thought of purchasing beef that had been butchered a thousand miles away. Spoiled meat represented a serious health threat, from which people had heretofore protected themselves by buying only freshly slaughtered beef from nearby butchers. "The idea of eating meat a week or more after it had been killed," wrote Swift's son, "met with a nasty-nice horror."[109] But the Chicago packers had a great ally in overcoming this horror: price. Dressed beef was typically one-half to one cent cheaper per pound than fresh beef.[110] Since the base price of beef was about ten cents per pound retail, the differential represented a 5 to 10 percent advantage.[111]

One explanation for the lower cost of dressed beef lay in von Thünen's zones: cattle raised in the West cost less than those raised in the East because of the lower cost of western rangeland and corn. For just this reason, growing numbers of the cattle that eastern butchers slaughtered came from the West. But the Chicago packers had an even stronger advantage. Beef dressed in Chicago and shipped east was inherently cheaper than beef shipped live from Chicago and dressed in the East. Assuming reliable refrigeration, dressed beef presented few of the problems that afflicted shippers of live animals. It suffered no injury from the horns of jostling neighbors. It experienced no stress or overheating in closed railroad cars. It lost no weight by refusing to eat. It did not die in transit.

But the biggest advantage of dressed beef was more basic still. The usable meat in a typical steer was only about 55 percent of its total body weight.[112] The rest—bones, joints, entrails, gristle—was largely waste or, if salable, did not justify shipment one thousand miles to its final market. This meant that shippers effectively threw away 45 percent of the money they paid to railroads. Meat paid a surcharge for traveling in a living package that contained a large share of nonmeat. Shippers of dressed animals, on the other hand, avoided this surcharge by filling their refrigerated cars with nothing but beef. Their more efficient use of expensive railroad space translated into lower prices for their ultimate customers.

In this way, the refrigerated car bore another important resemblance to the grain elevator. Both partitioned a natural material—a steer or a bushel of wheat—into a multitude of standardized commodities, each with a different price, each with a different market. No. 1 spring wheat found customers different from no. 2's. The same was true of different animals raised at different locations, and even of the different parts of a single animal. Chicago's No. 1 cattle were the corn-fed animals raised in Illinois, Iowa, Kentucky, and Indiana. They produced the fattest and most desirable meats and went to "first-class customers," swank urban hotels, and the discriminating English buyers in Liverpool. No. 2 cattle were from Colorado and Montana and were the heaviest and best tasting of the western range animals. No. 3 cattle were the common Texas longhorns and went mainly to domestic markets that were not so selective in their tastes.[113] Different supply areas in the West became linked to customers of different classes in different regions, even in different countries.

Beef and pork did not develop formal grading systems in the same way that grain did at the Chicago Board of Trade (though a futures market in pork did emerge). Live animals varied too much in weight and quality to be traded as completely abstract commodities at the stockyard. Unlike buyers of grain, livestock purchasers continued to examine individual animals before offering prices for them. Standardization happened later, after a sale was complete and animals had entered the packing plant. Then, their transmutation into commodities went even further, since a single living creature could be divided into literally hundreds of different products. Whereas the local butcher in a city or small town had little choice but to sell the parts of an animal to nearby customers for whatever they were willing to pay, the Chicago packers could amass body parts and ship them wherever they would bring the best price. Profits from one body part could help subsidize the sales of other parts, giving the Chicago firms an enormous competitive advantage. When a carload of dressed beef arrived in an area, it could contain only the cuts of meat most likely to sell there, with none of the other material local butchers had to try to sell.

The real genius of the refrigerator car had more to do with marketing than with technology. The proof of this came when customers examined the cuts of meat Swift offered for sale. Traditional butchers, especially wholesale ones, kept few if any samples of their final products on display for customers. The bulk of their meats hung as carcasses in a cooler and were cut to order. Swift's insight was to realize that customers (including retail butchers) would buy more meat, doing so essentially on impulse, if a variety of different products met their eyes when they walked into a shop. The most important of those products from Swift's point of view were cuts like the plate and chuck and round, which were not ordinarily as desirable as ribs or loins. If one could sell parts such as these at favorable prices, one would get maximum profits from the animal as a whole. The best way to accomplish this goal was to cut meat cosmetically into the most attractive possible pieces and display them to best advantage, an idea Swift had first tried in his Massachusetts butcher shops. Now he applied it to dressed beef, urging his agents to "cut it up and scatter the pieces," for "the more you cut, the more you sell."[114] The strategy showed real insight into consumer psychology, and Swift's competitors soon adopted it as well.

Shrewd marketing and low prices had precisely their intended effect. Once customers overcame their initial reluctance, they sought Chicago dressed beef whenever they could get their hands on it. And yet this at first was harder to do than one might think, for both they and the packers faced formidable adversaries. Dressed beef profoundly disrupted the traditional American beef trade. The opportunity it represented for Chicago packers seriously threatened others in the trade: livestock shippers, eastern packers, wholesale butchers, and, not least, the railroads themselves. Its effects paralleled changes already going on in Chicago's grain and lumber markets. Dressed beef vastly extended the geographical reach of Chicago's market, enabling one city to transform the economic landscape of a broad region, rearranging its environment according to the dictates of capital. Dressed beef went beyond grain and lumber in proliferating the logic of the market, for people in the East felt some of its greatest effects as much as people in the West. Dressed beef brought the entire nation—and Great Britain as well—into Chicago's hinterland.

Perhaps the most serious hurdle that Swift and the other dressed beef firms faced came from the very institution that had made their success possible in the first place: the railroads.[115] The transport companies did not welcome refrigerated beef with open arms. They had long tried to move livestock as far as possible by rail, and had invested a great deal of capital toward that end. They had built immense stockyards not just in Chicago but throughout the country, especially in the northeastern cities where butchers ordered large shipments of western cattle for local slaughter. Those stockyards would become worthless if the dressed beef companies managed to shift most slaughtering to Chicago. Livestock shippers were among the railroads' biggest and most favored customers, served by a vast fleet of cattle cars in which the roads had invested hundreds of thousands of dollars. Such cars were more flexible than the new refrigerator cars, since they could easily carry eastern manufactured goods on their return journey and avoid the cost of traveling empty. This was one reason why the roads refused to furnish the Chicago packers with refrigerated cars, calling them "speculative." Swift and the others had to build and operate their own cars on the model of the express companies, which had been running fast freight cars on contract with the railroads since the Civil War.[116]

From the railroads' perspective, livestock was a bulkier, heavier load than dressed beef. All other things being equal, live animals intrinsically generated more freight charges than meat—which was, after all, why dressed beef had a competitive advantage over them. Faced with protecting their investment, and with their classic problem of fixed capital costs in a competitive economic environment, the roads tried to support livestock shippers who could guarantee them a large and reliable volume of freight traffic. Probably the best example of this was the "evener system," which the railroads east of Chicago—the New York Central, the Erie, and the Pennsylvania—used as a pooling device during the late 1870s.[117] Originally intended to reduce competition among these roads, the system designated a small group of Chicago livestock shippers as "eveners" who would guarantee to each road a predetermined share of the total trade east of the city. In return for this service, the eveners received a rebate of $15 for every carload of cattle they shipped east. This gave them a great advantage over other shippers, especially those in cities other than Chicago, for it allowed them to offer better prices than anyone else in the West. Its effect was to increase still further the already strong tendency of western cattle to travel through Chicago before moving east, and it also helped reduce the number of buyers in Chicago's market and elsewhere. Many livestock shippers blamed the evener system for the decline of St. Louis's cattle market relative to Chicago's.[118] As one angry commission merchant later described the system, "It lasted until it ruined every Western shipper from shipping East. . . . It changed the cattle trade entirely."[119]

Ironically, the railroads' efforts to concentrate the livestock trade at Chicago also created conditions that encouraged the development of the dressed beef industry there. The city's prices, facilities, and handling charges had all made it the obvious location when Hammond, Swift, and Armour had been deciding where to set up operations. (Nelson Morris, more ironically still, had himself been one of the eveners.) But this did not prevent the railroads from responding to dressed beef with a kind of passive resistance. They refused to provide capital equipment in the form of refrigerator cars and icing stations. They were reluctant to guarantee a steady volume of traffic or the rapid handling that was essential to iced shipments. They set rates that put dressed beef at a disadvantage against live shipments, charging it at the traditional rate for barreled beef, which was about three times higher than that for livestock.[120] Although they could not forbid dressed beef shipments entirely, they did what they could to make them inconvenient and unprofitable.

Fortunately for Swift, there was one eastern railroad with no significant interest in live animal shipments: the Grand Trunk. Saddled with the longest and most northern of cross-country routes, the Grand Trunk skirted the Canadian shores of Lakes Erie and Ontario before connecting with American railroads near Montreal to reach the Boston and New York markets. Because its line was so much more circuitous than those of its competitors, and because cattle required constant feeding and watering while they traveled, the Grand Trunk had never succeeded as a livestock carrier. Locked out of the highly profitable American meat trade, its managers were delighted when Swift approached them about carrying dressed beef.[121] Travel distance mattered little for chilled meat so long as ice was available along the way—and on that score the Grand Trunk's colder northern route was a positive advantage. The railroad quickly became the leading carrier of Chicago dressed beef. By 1885, the Grand Trunk was hauling 292 million pounds of the commodity, over 60 percent of the city's output.[122]

Long before that time, the other eastern railroads realized they could not keep dressed beef off the market indefinitely. Unless they wished to cede the business entirely to the Grand Trunk, they would have to change their obstructionist tactics toward the Chicago packers. Moreover, the evener system had collapsed in 1879 and been replaced by Albert Fink's Eastern Trunk Line Association as a pool for enforcing uniform rates and stable market shares on the competing railroads. When the roads sought a new policy for dressed beef in 1883, Fink's group faced the delicate task of determining an appropriate rate.[123] They gathered minute statistics about the relative costs of shipping livestock as opposed to dressed beef, and heard arguments from both sides about how each was at a disadvantage because of current railroad policy. Livestock shippers, unaware or unconvinced of the technological advantages of dressed beef, were certain that the only possible reason they were having trouble competing with it was unfair treatment by the railroads. Packers, on the other hand, knowing the denser and more valuable load their cars were carrying, argued that the railroads were preventing them from enjoying the full advantage of their more efficient handling.

For both sides, it was an explosive issue. Cattle shippers, having recently seen dressed beef surpass live shipments to New England, and noting that dressed beef shipments to New York were also growing rapidly, feared for their very survival. They told Fink that "unless modifications are made in the present relative rates of Live Stock and Dressed Beef, they would have to give up the Live Stock business entirely and go into Dressed Beef."[124] The packers, though not so worried about absolute survival, argued that their product sold for half a penny more per pound in New York than beef slaughtered fresh by the city's butchers. Given what they knew about the relative costs of production for the two, this seemed a clear sign of railroad discrimination, which they saw as "retarding and demoralizing to business."[125]

Faced with such arguments, Fink and the railroads tried to assume what they saw as a neutral stance. Asserting that shippers of the two commodities should be placed "upon an equal footing," Fink said rates should be set "to make the cost per pound for the transportation of Dressed Beef, when slaughtered in Chicago, the same as the cost of transportation of Dressed Beef when the same is obtained from the steer transported alive from Chicago to New York or Boston, and slaughtered there."[126] In 1884, this principle was adopted after formal arbitration as the famous Cooley award, in which the rate for cattle from Chicago to New York was set at forty cents per hundredweight and for dressed beef at seventy cents.[127] It was no accident that the ratio between these two numbers was 57 percent—almost exactly the percentage of meat contained in a living steer. The new rate at least in theory eliminated the advantage the packers gained from sending meat east without the accompanying bones and offal. "Neutrality" in this instance apparently meant erasing the benefits of a new technology to protect those who continued to use traditional methods. The new rates primarily benefited the railroads' easternmost terminus, New York City, which soon became the only significant packing center on the East Coast.

"Neutrality" was necessarily a fiction, albeit a suggestive one. The railroads were trying to have their meat and eat it too. They did not wish to undermine their profitable trade hauling livestock, but could protect that trade only by agreeing to maintain a stable differential between live and dressed shipments. The latter were potentially so remunerative, however, that each individual railroad—and none more than the Grand Trunk—had a strong incentive to secretly cut rates to attract the packers' dressed beef. This produced great instability, and rate wars followed. Matters worsened for the railroads with the creation of the Interstate Commerce Commission in 1887, which outlawed pools like the Eastern Trunk Line Association without placing any similar constraints on shippers. Faced with the growing oligopoly of Chicago's packing companies—now nicknamed the Big Four—the railroads lost much of their ability to defend shippers of live animals. The packers had become too powerful to resist, since they controlled such a large share of each railroad's carrying trade. The unavoidable result was a dramatic rearrangement of the geography of the American meat trade.

The collapse of the older system affected no one more than wholesale butchers in eastern states from Ohio to New England. Their ordinary habit had been to buy livestock from local farmers or from Chicago itself, slaughtering the animals and selling cuts of meat to retail butchers and their final customers. Shrewd marketer that he was, Swift realized that it would be better to have the wholesale butchers as allies than as enemies, so in many towns he approached the leading butcher—usually a person of considerable means—about becoming a partner in the dressed beef business. Those who agreed took a one-third interest in the local trade, while Swift and his brother took the remaining two-thirds. In this way, he and the other Chicago firms linked their business to an already existing trade network and source of local capital, and encouraged wholesale butchers of live animals to become wholesale distributors of dressed beef.

In many communities, butchers refused to handle Chicago dressed beef, claiming that the product was unsanitary and that no customer should buy meat that had been killed a week or more before. One butcher, when approached by an agent of Nelson Morris about introducing dressed beef to the Pittsburgh area, replied, "I sell no beef unless I see it killed."[128] The wholesale butchers believed that only live animals

could be safely inspected for disease, and feared the loss of their traditional role slaughtering all meat sold in a particular community. Most
lacked the icehouse facilities to store large quantities of chilled beef, and
were unwilling or unable to invest the capital needed to acquire refrigeration technology for themselves.

When a Chicago packer appeared in a new town offering to sell
dressed beef, local butchers often formed an organization to fight the
incursion. Members agreed not to deal with the packers and put signs in
their windows saying, "No Chicago dressed meat sold here."[129] By 1887,
opposition had become widespread enough that butchers met in a nationwide convention to create the Butchers' National Protective Association,
with the express purpose of defending themselves against Chicago
dressed beef. Stating that their only object was the public good, they
declared their intention to "secure the highest sanitary condition" for
food by fighting "diseased, tainted, or otherwise unwholesome meat." In
a pattern that became typical of meat industry controversies from this
time on, public health was a convenient way of putting the best face on a
deeper and more self-interested economic issue. Much as they might regard tainted meat as a bad thing, the butchers were even more worried
about "monopolies and combinations which ultimately injure and op-
press the people by controlling and manipulating the market in a staple
and indispensable article of human food." Whether or not "the people"
were actually injured by the "combinations" of the Chicago packers, the
butchers certainly were. So, taking a somewhat contradictory stand on
principle, they organized a combination to fight a combination. In the
butchers' eyes, dressed beef represented disease, monopoly, and tyranny.[130]

But it was a losing battle. When the packers encountered such resistance, they quickly moved to break open the local market. A company
agent might appear at the local railroad depot with a carload of beef—
nicknamed a peddler car—and sell it at cut-rate prices directly off the
tracks. The more permanent approach was to build a refrigerated warehouse in town, called a branch house. From it, the packers sold meat to all
comers at whatever price it took to gain a foothold in the market.[131] A
butcher in Akron, Ohio, ruefully described how Armour and Company
had used two local branch houses to bring the city's meat dealers to their
knees:

> Upon opening these markets they were supplied in enormous quantities
> with the best the country produced in everything that was made out of
> meats and in all the finest appliances of the markets of our largest cities.
> These markets were advertised thoroughly throughout the city to sell at

never-before-heard-of prices. Dodgers were scattered, like leaves of the forest, stating the time of the first opening to be at 6 a.m. on Saturday. Long before that hour people were waiting for the doors to open. After they commenced business the crowd seemed to grow with the passing hours until the markets would not contain the people, and the waiting crowd upon the sidewalks almost, if not entirely, obstructed travel. So great was the crowd that it was necessary several times to call policemen to preserve order and permit travel.

With such proof of their customers' enthusiasm for the new product, it took less than a week of "sitting around doing nothing" for Akron's sixty butchers to realize they were licked. They signed an agreement with Armour whereby local agents purchased the city's branch houses, and dressed beef became a permanent feature of the Akron market.[132]

The Chicago packers were ruthless competitors, and had little compunction about selling dressed beef at whatever price would bring customers. They had good reasons for this. Their product was perishable and had to be sold quickly before it spoiled. If potential customers were prejudiced against dressed beef, the only way to convince them otherwise was to use bargain prices to get them to try it for themselves. Since chilled beef required expensive capital equipment for refrigeration, the unwillingness of local jobbers to handle it meant that the packing firm had to set up its own branch house to sell the product at all.[133] Swift's motto was "If you're going to lose money, lose it. But don't let 'em nose you out."[134] Market share was the paramount concern, and the packers were willing to do almost anything to gain it. They sold meat below its cost of production to break the resistance of local butchers, raising their prices once they had succeeded in entering the market. In this, they gained considerable price flexibility from the disassembly line itself, since they could recover losses on some cuts and body parts with the profits from others. The same was true geographically: with the proceeds from a successful struggle in one town, they could move on to the next. The sheer scale of their production, the reach of their marketing activities, and their accumulated capital made it impossible for any local butcher to withstand them. A Pennsylvania butcher described the experience of those who tried by declaring, "We are working for glory now. We do not work for any profit. I can give you that straight."[135]

The packers' efforts led to a radical change in the structure of American meat markets in little more than a decade. One by one, local butchers in most cities touched by the Chicago market closed their slaughterhouses. A New York wholesale butcher in 1888 declared that up and down the eastern seaboard, except in New York City itself, "the slaughtering of cattle by butchers is a thing of the past."[136] Local meat merchants found it cheaper to become retailers of Chicago beef, for they could no longer afford to purchase, slaughter, and butcher livestock themselves and still earn a profit if forced to sell at dressed beef prices.[137] To be sure of this, the packers made it their practice to monitor the purchases of any butcher who tried to buy livestock directly, to make such transactions unprofitable by undercutting prices.[138] Even as far away as New Mexico, stock raisers found that eastern buyers were unwilling to purchase cattle directly, for fear of what the Chicago packers might do to them. One New Mexico cattleman went all the way to Hartford, Connecticut, to ask meat dealers there why they would not buy his stock. They replied "that they were afraid to do so; that the Chicago combination . . . would run them out of the business if they attempted to come into our markets and buy."[139]

The strategy worked. By the late 1880s, Chicago packers dominated much of the American meat supply.[140] The most dramatic proof of this fact was in northeastern areas that had previously been part of New York City's meat hinterland. By 1889, the wholesale butchers of New York were finding it difficult to compete with Chicago even at so near a location as the eastern end of Long Island. When a U.S. senator expressed astonishment that a Long Island butcher would buy from faraway Chicago instead of nearby New York, the New York wholesaler who was testifying before him quickly explained. "I beg pardon," the wholesaler replied, "the Chicago dressed beef he got next door to his house. They had a refrigerator right there."[141] For retail butchers in small towns, the long trip to a metropolitan meat market was a significant cost of doing business. Unable to buy frequently enough and in large enough volume to get special discounts, they found it cheaper and more convenient to buy from the refrigerated branch warehouses the Chicago packers opened in their communities. Although New York slaughterhouses and wholesale markets could survive such competition—because of the sheer size of metropolitan demand and the special kosher requirements for fresh slaughter—even the nation's largest city found its hinterland contracting. Everywhere else, the triumph of the Chicago packers over wholesale butchers was nothing less than a rout.

As dressed beef drove local slaughterhouses and butchers out of business, the packers gained greater freedom to price their products as they saw fit. By 1889, four companies controlled over 90 percent of the beef slaughtered in Chicago.[142] Their oligopoly and nationwide influence led them to seek new ways of diminishing competition among themselves.[143] The packers had made massive investments in capital infrastructure— Chicago factories, refrigerator cars, icing facilities, dozens of branch warehouses—and thus faced all the problems of fixed costs that had created competitive nightmares for the railroads. Just as the railroads had imposed a new capitalist geography on the western landscape in response to their fixed costs, so would the dressed beef companies.

The packers could afford to service their capital costs only by keeping the volume of their output as steady and high as possible; this was why they had worked so hard to smooth out fluctuations in Chicago's meat-packing seasons. They sought to stabilize market shares among them-selves to reduce the chance that they would undercut each other's prices in locations where more than one was operating a branch store. Like the railroads, they resorted to pooling mechanisms "to equalize the busi-ness," working toward ever greater regional integration of the nation's meat markets.[144] When successful, a pool might temporarily produce uni-form prices on particular cuts of meat across as many as seven or more states, a condition that would have been impossible to imagine even just a decade before. Such arrangements were always unstable and usually worked only for brief periods of time. But they did not have to work long to drive wholesale butchers out of the slaughtering business. In so doing, they helped expand still farther the reach of the packers' markets, and made it all the more difficult for small competitors to stand up against the onslaught.

Such market changes were not limited to packing alone. When local butchers stopped slaughtering cattle, farmers in their immediate vicinity had to look farther afield for markets. Either they could start selling all their livestock in Chicago (or in the western cities that continued to have significant slaughtering operations), or they could stop raising cattle alto-gether. An alternative solution was to switch to dairy cattle if that was an option, but even a dairy farmer occasionally wished to sell animals for slaughter and so faced the same dilemma. Among the first to experience this change were farmers in the immediate vicinity of Chicago itself. A dairy farmer near Elgin, Illinois, about forty miles from Chicago, re-ported in 1889 the great change that had happened to Elgin's cattle mar-ket in the previous two years. Formerly, he said, "we had a home market. Our butchers bought without much trouble all we had to sell, but now we have scarcely any market at all at home for our beef cattle. . . . Chicago is the only market now."[145] The same thing happened at greater distances from the city. Farmers throughout Illinois and Iowa found their local markets contracting, and so had to ship to Chicago. A farmer in eastern Iowa reported, "A few years ago nearly all of our cows and heifers, what is called butcher stuff, were bought by butchers in Davenport, Rock Island, and the cities about us. Now Armour furnishes the meat in those places, which throws us off that trade. . . . Our market has changed alto-gether."[146]

For Corn Belt farmers, the obvious response to the disappearance of local slaughterhouses was to ship cattle to Chicago. And yet this made them feel even more vulnerable to the vagaries of a distant market than they had before. Iowa stock raisers began to resent what seemed to them the price manipulations of the Chicago packers. Informed by wire of favorable prices in the city, farmers rushed to send their stock on the next possible train; but when the animals arrived, prices had fallen again and the sale had become less profitable.[147] Whether the cycling of prices was caused by concerted manipulation or by the periodic glutting of supply in response to outdated price information, the economic and emotional effect was the same. The Union Stockyards charged fixed rates to house and feed the animals who stayed there: $1 per hundredweight for wild prairie hay, $1.50 per hundredweight for domesticated hay, $1 per bushel for corn, and twenty-five cents for yardage.[148] These rates were high enough that cattle literally ate up their profits within a short time. Farmers or shippers had little choice but to sell as quickly as possible; this forced them to give up their animals at lower prices than they had hoped.

They therefore joined the wholesale butchers—in much the same way as the grain farmers and retailer lumber dealers had done—in blaming the lakeside city and its markets for these troubles. "Some of our stock drovers," observed an Iowa farmer, "complain bitterly of Chicago."[149] The *Western Rural* described the nature of their complaints: "Next to the railroad extortions there is no greater outrage perpetrated on the country than is practiced three hundred and sixty-five days in the year at the Union Stock Yards in this city. . . ."[150] The general impression was that the city's firms were using unfair and dishonest means to achieve their success. Recognizing their political vulnerability, the packers sought to disguise what they were doing by keeping all pooling transactions under "fictitious names, so that a party going through the ledger would never discover it unless he was familiar with the business of the firm."[151] Hiding a pool was tantamount to admitting its illegitimacy. When the bottom dropped out of the cattle market toward the end of the 1880s, the Senate Select Committee on the Transportation and Sale of Meat Products—the "Vest Committee"—conducted the first of several major government investigations of the packers and their activities. Its conclusion was that the farmers and drovers trying to sell animals in Chicago found "no competition among buyers." "We have no hesitation," the senators declared, "in stating . . . that a combination exists at Chicago between the principal dressed-beef and packing houses which controls the market and fixes the price of beef cattle in their own interest." For the Vest Committee, this, rather than the speculative overproduction that had swept the livestock industry during the 1880s, was the chief reason for low prices. Cattlemen and butchers alike were suffering from "the artificial and abnormal centralization of markets, and the absolute control by a few operators thereby made possible."[152]

What seemed "artificial and abnormal" at the end of the nineteenth century would look conventional in the twentieth, for the economic concentration of the meat-packing industry, and the new technologies that went with it, never returned to earlier conditions. Whether that development was good or bad is less important for the purposes of this discussion than the committee's most fundamental conclusion about Chicago itself: "for all practical purposes the market at that city dominates absolutely the price of beef cattle in the whole country." Although other cities continued to buy and sell cattle, their prices were "regulated and fixed by the great market on the Lake."[153] An economic earthquake had taken place, and there could be little doubt about the location of its epicenter. In the first rumblings of that quake, Chicago's role had perhaps seemed distant and benign enough, for without its markets the farmers and cattlemen would not have profited so easily from the animals they produced. But the longer-term consequences were more unsettling. By giving Chicago their business, stock raisers had reinforced the city's growth as the greatest and most integrated meat market the world had ever seen. With that growth had come power, and with power a new set of institutions that would forever change the structure of American meat-packing. Whatever those institutions may have meant to the farmers, butchers, and meat eaters of America, their deepest and subtlest meaning pertained to nature itself.

Unremembered Deaths

Most visible of all were the altered landscapes from which Chicago obtained its great tide of animal flesh. By 1890, the ten million or more bison that had still grazed the Great Plains at the end of the Civil War were gone. In their place were nearly as many cattle, eating the same buffalo grass but living within a newly partitioned ecosystem that was now managed toward new human ends.[154] The shortgrasses of the High Plains, although augmented by exotic species, were surviving their new use better than the tall grasses farther east, for the plow was as much a part of the livestock economy as the fence and the open range. Although prairie hay might still be purchased at the Union Stockyards, "tame" hay, cultivated by Illinois farmers, was taking its place. More important still was the emergence of the midwestern feedlot system, in which farmers raised corn and hay together to fatten western cattle and midwestern hogs before their final journey to the Chicago slaughterhouses. Without the sweeping environmental manipulations these developments represented, none of the other changes at Chicago would have been possible.

The packers could claim more direct responsibility for severing the natural relationship between death and decay. Their most basic technical innovation had been to devise new means for protecting meat, especially beef, from its own perishability. To separate an animal's death from the decay that ordinarily followed hard upon it, they had harvested the winter's cold and suspended the wheel of the seasons. In the chilled factories by the stockyards, livestock died but did not rot. Their flesh could stay for days or weeks, long after the time it would otherwise have become inedible, in the well-iced branch stores that packers built throughout the nation.

The ability to preserve animal flesh would in itself have been impressive, but the more important effect of the packers' new technology was on the market. No longer did the natural seasonality of a steer's life mean alternating gluts and famines in the beef supply. No longer did farmers have to concentrate their selling during the few months after the harvest. No longer did valuable meat-packing capital have to sit idle in the heat of summer. By creating a market in ice (and later a market in mechanical refrigeration), the packers smoothed the cycling of the natural year and committed themselves to a comparable smoothing of the market. Having achieved this end for meat, they soon expanded into other areas where their chilled warehouses gave them special advantages. One of these was fruit, the crop for which the refrigerator car had originally been invented. By the 1890s, Philip Armour had invested heavily in the California fruit industry, and he soon dominated the eastern marketing of oranges.[155]

The scale of the packers' markets and investments gave them immense advantages over potential rivals. Competitors who were tied to local areas, whether western livestock raisers or eastern butchers, had little hope of stopping packers from entering new markets. Not even the railroads could hold out against them for long. The packers' efforts at coordinating their oligopoly to hold down animal prices and raise those of meat were not always so successful as populist critics imagined, for they did constantly have to worry about competing at least with each other. Even so, they represented a gigantic concentration of economic power.

Philip Armour, in particular, straddled the city's economy to become not just its largest pork and beef packer but one of its largest grain dealers as well. By 1891, he owned half a dozen grain elevators with a total capacity of over nine million bushels, 30 percent of Chicago's total—and more than any other single person on the planet.[156] He speculated at the Board of Trade on both the bull and the bear sides of the market, and was a key player in the famous Leiter corner, the largest in Chicago history. When European crop failures in 1896 allowed Joseph Leiter to corner and drive up the price of September and December wheat past $1.00 per bushel, Armour used his extensive elevator capacity and railroad connections to flood the city with wheat and eventually break the corner. The story of how he made good on his shorted futures contracts by ordering a fleet of ships out into the threat of winter storms to bring extra December wheat from Duluth would became one of the legends of the Chicago Board of Trade.[157]

Armour, as one admirer described him, was "something more than the richest man in Chicago"; he was "perhaps the greatest trader in the world."[158] But his ability to hold sway over such far-flung markets in beef, pork, wheat, oranges, and other commodities was unusual only in its primacy. He was otherwise characteristic of the Chicago packers. All of them based their businesses on much more than just meat. Indeed, if any single factor was more important than refrigeration in accounting for their success, it was their tireless efforts to use every single part of the animals they dismembered. Chicagoans made the boast so frequently that it became a cliché: the packers used everything in the hog except the squeal.[159]

Like the progressive reformers who followed them, the packers worshiped at the altar of efficiency, seeking to conserve economic resources by making a war on waste.[160] This was their most important break with the past. Chicago pork packers in the 1850s had relatively limited options in utilizing the nonmeat portions of the animals they killed. They could boil them down into tallow and lard, which a number of firms used for making candles, soap, and other products.[161] They could feed packing wastes to scavenger pigs, practicing an early form of recycling in which pig flesh people were unwilling to eat was reconverted into pig flesh they were willing to eat. But whatever was left sooner or later made its way as refuse into the Chicago River. The stench that hung over the South Branch and the filthy ice harvested from it were clear signs of its pollution. Decaying organic matter, whether in the form of packing wastes, manure, or raw human sewage, was the chief water supply problem the city faced by midcentury. Seeing it as a threat to health and comfort alike, Chicagoans were trying to do something about it as early as the 1850s.

One solution was to try to send the filthy water elsewhere, out of sight, out of smell, out of mind. By 1871, city engineers had accomplished the extraordinary feat of reversing the Chicago River, sending its ordinary flow via the Illinois and Michigan Canal southwest into the Illinois River rather than east into Lake Michigan. The city could thereby count on fresher drinking water from the two-mile tunnel it had built under the lake bottom just after the Civil War. Only during storms, spring runoffs, and other periods of heavy flow did meat-packing debris from the South Branch continue to threaten the urban water supply.[162] Reversing the river did not, of course, mean that its pollution had vanished. It may have appeared less frequently in Chicago's tap water, but downstate residents had a clear idea of where it had gone. "Ever since the water from the Chicago River was let down into the Illinois River," wrote one furious resident of Morris, Illinois, "the stench has been almost unendurable. What right has Chicago to pour its filth down into what was before a sweet and clean river, pollute its waters, and materially reduce the value of property on both sides of the river and canal, and bring sickness and death to the citizens?"[163]

Since industrial wastes produced pollution wherever one threw them away, a better solution might be to avoid throwing them out in the first place. If the packers could devise ways of using meat-packing refuse for productive purposes, it would cease to be waste at all. The refuse would pollute the river less, and—better still—turn a tidy profit for its owner. "There was a time," remembered Philip Armour at the end of the century, "when many parts of cattle were wasted, and the health of the city injured by the refuse. Now, by adopting the best known methods, nothing is wasted, and buttons, fertilizer, glue, and other things are made cheaper and better for the world in general, out of material that was before a waste and a menace."[164]

As the packers pushed the disassembly line toward its fullest possible development, they turned what had been a single creature—a hog or a steer—into dozens and then hundreds of commodities. In the new chemical research laboratories that the packers installed during the 1880s and 1890s, older by-products like lard and tallow were joined by more exotic items like oleomargarine, bouillon, brushes, combs, gut strings, stearin, pepsin, and even canned pork and beans.[165] One visitor described the output of the plants as follows:

Everything—without particularizing too closely—every single thing that appertains to a slaughtered beef is sold and put to use. The horns become the horn of commerce; the straight lengths of leg bone go to the cutlery-makers and others; the entrails become sausage-casings; their contents make fertilizing material; the livers, hearts, tongues, and tails, and the stomachs, that become tripe, all are sold over the butchers' counters of the nation; the knuckle-bones are ground up into bone-meal for various uses; the blood is dried and sold as a powder for commercial purposes; the bladders are dried and sold to druggists, tobacconists, and others; the fat goes into oleomargarine, and from the hoofs and feet and other parts come glue and oil and fertilizing ingredients.[166]

The portion of any single animal that might go into one of these by-products was very small. More than half of a steer's bodyweight became dressed beef, but less than 1 percent of it became glue or dried blood or neat's-foot oil.[167] No ordinary butcher could afford the capital investment needed to deal in such small quantities, and so waste was inevitable when traditional methods were used.[168] Not so for the packers. Because they dealt in enormous numbers of animals and because they could search out customers anywhere in the world, they were able to find specialized markets for even the most minute of body parts. By-products became an ever more important source of packers' profits. Armour estimated that a 1,260-pound steer purchased in Chicago for $40.95 would produce 710 pounds of dressed beef. When sold in New York at an average price of 5 and ⅜ cents per pound, this beef would earn only $38.17—a clear loss even without deducting production and transport costs. Only by selling by-products could the packers turn this losing transaction into a profitable one. Indeed, the income from such sales was crucial in enabling the packers to lower dressed beef prices far below those of ordinary butchers. As Swift and Armour saw it, they earned their profits on the margin largely from things that butchers threw away.

Armour's Estimates of Dressed Beef By-product Costs and Profits[169]

Steer, 1,260 lbs @ $3.25 per cwt* (becomes 710 lbs dressed beef)	$	40.95
Cost of killing, processing, salt, icing, etc	$	1.75
Freight on 710 pounds @ $0.45 per cwt	$	3.20
New York selling charges @ $0.35 per cwt	$	2.48
Costs of purchase, processing, and transport		−$48.38
Sale in NYC of 710 lbs dressed beef @ 5⅜ ¢ per lb.	$	38.17
(Net loss on dressed beef in NYC)		−$10.21
Sale of hide, 70 lbs @ $.09 per lb	$	6.30
Sale of by-products	$	4.50
Yield from all by-product sales		10.80
Net profit from all transactions	$	0.59

*hundred-weight

The rise of the by-products industry had several other implications. For one, it undoubtedly changed the rate and character of pollution entering the Chicago River from the packing plants. Packingtown remained one of the smelliest and most environmentally degraded neighborhoods in all of Chicago, and the water that flowed from its sewers was extraordinarily foul. Upton Sinclair could still describe Bubbly Creek in 1906 as "a great open sewer a hundred or two feet wide" in which grease and chemicals underwent "all sorts of strange transformations," so it was "constantly in motion, as if huge fish were feeding in it, or great leviathans were disporting themselves in its depths."[170] Visitors and residents assaulted by the smell of the place could hardly have believed that it represented any kind of improvement over the past, but in a sense it did. Compared with those of an ordinary butcher's slaughterhouse, the packers' wastes constituted a smaller share of the animals they killed. They might be more concentrated and no less dangerous, but their total volume had grown less quickly than the total production of the plants.[171]

Rather more sinister was the packers' increasing ability to sell products which customers would never have purchased, let alone eaten, in their original form. By shrewdly manipulating bone and offal and even spoiled meat in myriad ways, Chicago companies could convert them not just into salable commodities but into substances which had all the appearance of human food. It seems unlikely that anyone objected to the idea that waste hair be turned into brushes, dried blood into fertilizer, bones into buttons, cartilage into glue. But people were more suspicious about the packers' sometime practice of marketing mixed, altered, or adulterated products as pure food. One butcher complained about having to sell his own kettle-rendered lard in competition with a lower-priced packinghouse product that was "as solid as a rock; it looks white; but is a compound of cotton-seed oil, stearine, etc."[172] Although vegetable shortening and oleomargarine were "unnatural" products, they would gain steady ground in the American market and diet, however much traditionalists like this butcher might oppose them. Dairy farmers in Wisconsin tried to discourage oleomargarine consumption in that state well past the middle of the twentieth century, even as most Americans quite happily traded butter for its cheaper alternative.

But other manufactured foods seemed less benign even to people who ate oleo without a second thought. Most drew the line when packers took otherwise inedible materials—or spoiled, diseased, or tainted meats—and altered them so that they would appear to be ordinary, healthy food. Dressed beef was always open to the suspicion that it had been cut from diseased cattle, and processed meats were most suspect of all. Bologna sausage became the great waste disposal product because it could hide such a multitude of sins. Once ground up and combined with spices and potato flour, all manner of body parts could go into it: inferior meats that drew lower prices on the open market, meat from diseased cattle, meat that had spoiled and begun to smell, sweepings from other production processes, even sawdust and dirt.[173] Meat inspectors were supposed to catch such adulterations, but in fact did not. Although the butchers had used public health as a battle cry since the start of their war with the packers, their obvious self-interest (and the fact that the same brush could easily tar them as well) muted the effectiveness of their criticisms. Public fears about the health hazards of dressed beef and its by-products did not finally explode until 1906, when Upton Sinclair published his muckraking novel *The Jungle* and Congress passed the Meat Inspection and Pure Food and Drug Acts, which subsequently imposed much stricter inspection standards on the packers and their products.[174]

Waste, then, was one of the symbolic paradoxes of meat-packing in Chicago. For those like Upton Sinclair who saw in the city all that was most evil in capitalism, Packingtown represented the decline of corporate morality and the end of an earlier, more familiar and trustworthy way of life. The stench in the Chicago River and the insidiously invisible substances that might make their way into a package of bologna appeared to be the product of companies so intent on their own profits that they were indifferent to the harm they did the public. Obsessed with turning waste into profit whatever the noneconomic cost, they sold what they should have thrown away—and yet did little to prevent pollution from the wastes that finally washed down their sewers. "Under the system of rigid economy which the packers enforced," wrote Sinclair, "there were some jobs that it only paid to do once in a long time, and among these was the cleaning out of the waste barrels. Every spring they did it; and in the barrels would be dirt and rust and old nails and stale water—and cart load after cart load of it would be taken up and dumped into the hoppers with fresh meat, and sent out to the public's breakfast."[175] Public health was not alone in being jeopardized by such perfidy. The packers drove honest butchers out of business with their deceitful products, so that in the end there would be nothing left but the Big Four and their foul meats. The Chicago packers had wasted honesty and community alike in their single-minded drive to extract every last penny from the wretched animals that walked through their doors. The tyranny of monopoly, and the public revolt against it, would be their final legacy.[176]

And yet such a description was surely not the whole truth, if it was truth at all. Armour was right: his profits, like those of the other packers, came because he managed to save what others threw away. He had built his empire on waste. This seemed akin to making something out of noth-

ing, which was surely not such a bad thing to do. Writing a decade and a
half after the Vest Committee, another government investigation was
more willing to acknowledge the public benefits that had accompanied
what the earlier committee had seen as the "artificial and abnormal centralization" of Chicago's markets. "The margins between prices of stock
and prices of meats," the later committee wrote,

> have been kept during recent years, by reason of the thorough utilization
> of by-products, at a point lower than would have been possible under the
> methods of slaughtering and packing which prevailed thirty or more years
> ago. By virtue of the economies secured in the handling of former wastes,
> and in other ways, the development of huge packing establishments has
> beyond question been beneficial to cattle raisers and meat consumers.[177]

Because of the Chicago packers, ranchers in Wyoming and feedlot farmers in Iowa regularly found a reliable market for their animals, and on
average received better prices for the animals they sold there. At the same
time and for the same reason, Americans of all classes found a greater
variety of more and better meats on their tables, purchased on average at
lower prices than ever before. Seen in this light, the packers' "rigid system of economy" seemed a very good thing indeed.

It was no mean achievement. Taking advantage of Chicago's ability to
concentrate the market, Swift, Armour, and the others had succeeded in
distributing the immense tide of beef that had appeared in less than two
decades upon the old buffalo grazing grounds of the plains. They had
opened new markets for beef and its by-products and made meat in general more salable across the seasons of the year. They had reduced its cost
of transportation and constructed a far-reaching network of branch stores
for delivering their chilled product to the consumer long after it would
otherwise have decayed and gone to waste. In so doing, they had made
many meats available at lower prices. If they had sometimes cut corners
and gone beyond the limits of merely "preserving" meat, their basic ac-
complishment was nonetheless much as Armour had testified before the
Vest Committee. The packers, he said, "are making beef more palatable,
attractive, and wholesome, by a proper and advanced system of refrigeration, than it was when the small slaughterer butchered a steer during the
night and hung the still warm carcass in the market next morning, and are
distributing this beef throughout the country at the lowest possible
charge for the service rendered."[178]

They had achieved these things by creating immense, vertically integrated corporations capable of exercising managerial control over the
food of many nations on a scale never before seen in the history of the

world. Nothing in Chicago at the end of the nineteenth century better symbolized the city's profoundly transformed relationship to the natural world than its gigantic meat-packing corporations. Although they joined the Board of Trade and the lumberyards in guidebooks that sought to impress visitors with the ways in which Chicago stood first among cities, the packers in fact represented the city's greatest break with nature and the past. At the Board of Trade, hundreds of grain traders vied with each other to profit from the sale of wheat and corn drawn from Chicago's broad western hinterland, but none of them could control the market for long. A handful of meat-packers, on the other hand, could do just that. By managing supply and demand, they effectively rearranged the meat trade of the entire world.[179] Ranchers on the plains, feedlot farmers on the prairies, butchers in the cities, and meat eaters the world over increasingly inhabited a system in which the packers called most of the important shots. "A few enterprising men at Chicago," wrote the Vest Committee, "engaged in the packing and dressed beef business, are able through their enormous capital to centralize and control the beef business at that point."[180]

However impressive individuals like Swift or Armour might be, their real achievement was to create immense impersonal organizations, hierarchically structured and operated by an army of managers and workers, that would long outlive their founders. No one person was essential to such enterprises. The very scale on which they operated made them increasingly susceptible to the same abstract logic which the railroads had first discovered in their balance sheets. Fixed costs meant an inescapable need to service debt. Unused capital—whether in the form of equipment, employees, or raw materials—meant waste. Waste meant inefficiency, and inefficiency in a competitive economic environment could all too easily mean death. It must be eliminated with every strategy and device that managerial ingenuity could muster against it. Summer must be made to seem like winter so that the great factories could continue their work all year. Death's hand must be stayed to extend by hundreds and thousands of miles the distance between the place where an animal died and the place where people finally ate it. Prices must be standardized so that markets in distant places would fluctuate together if they fluctuated at all. An industry that had formerly done its work in thousands of small butcher shops around the country must be rationalized to bring it under the control of a few expert managers using the most modern and scientific techniques. The world must become Chicago's hinterland.

The combined effect of these many managerial strategies was to make meat seem less a product of first nature and more a product of human artifice. With the concentration of packing at Chicago, meat came increasingly to seem an urban product. Cows and cowboys might be symbols of a rugged natural life on the western range, but beef and pork were commodities of the city. Formerly, a person could not easily have forgotten that pork and beef were the creation of an intricate, symbiotic partnership between animals and human beings. One was not likely to forget that pigs and cattle had died so that people might eat, for one saw them grazing in familiar pastures, and regularly visited the barnyards and butcher shops where they gave up their lives in the service of one's daily meal. In a world of farms and small towns, the ties between field, pasture, butcher shop, and dinner table were everywhere apparent, constant reminders of the relationships that sustained one's own life. In a world of ranches, packing plants, and refrigerator cars, most such connections vanished from easy view.

The packing plants distanced their customers most of all from the act of killing. Those who visited the great slaughterhouses came away with vivid memories of death. Rudyard Kipling described being impressed much more by the "slaying" he saw in Chicago than by the "dissecting." "They were so excessively alive, these pigs," he wrote. "And then they were so excessively dead, and the man in the dripping, clammy, hot passage did not seem to care, and ere the blood of such an one had ceased to foam on the floor, such another, and four friends with him, had shrieked and died."[181] The more people became accustomed to the attractively cut, carefully wrapped, cunningly displayed packages that Swift had introduced to the trade, the more easily they could fail to remember that their purchase had once pulsed and breathed with a life much like their own. As time went on, fewer of those who ate meat could say that they had ever seen the living creature whose flesh they were chewing; fewer still could say they had actually killed the animal themselves. In the packers' world, it was easy not to remember that eating was a moral act inextricably bound to killing. Such was the second nature that a corporate order had imposed on the American landscape. Forgetfulness was among the least noticed and most important of its by-products.

The packers' triumph was to further the commodification of meat, to alienate still more its ties to the lives and ecosystems that had ultimately created it. Transmuted by the packing plants into countless shape-shifting forms, an animal's body might fill human stomachs, protect human feet, fasten human clothes, fertilize human gardens, wash human hands, play human music—do so many amazing things. The sheer variety of these new standardized uses testified to the packers' ingenuity in their war on waste, but in them the animal also died a second death. Severed from the form in which it had lived, severed from the act that had killed it, it vanished from human memory as one of nature's creatures. Its ties to the earth receded, and in forgetting the animal's life one also forgot the grasses and the prairie skies and the departed bison herds of a landscape that seemed more and more remote in space and time. The grasslands were so distant from the lives of those who bought what the packers sold that one hardly thought of the prairie or the plains while making one's purchase, any more than one thought about Packingtown, with its Bubbly Creek and its stinking air. Meat was a neatly wrapped package one bought at the market. Nature did not have much to do with it.

There was a final irony in this for Chicago itself. The new corporate order, by linking and integrating the products of so many ecosystems and communities, obscured the very connections it helped create. Its tendency was to break free from space altogether, managing its activities with organizational charts that stressed function rather than geography.[182] The traditional butcher shop had belonged very much to its particular place, bound to customers in the immediate neighborhood and farmers in the surrounding countryside. The packing companies had none of these ties, not even to the place that had nurtured their own birth. By the 1880s, their managers could already see that Chicago's advantages—its transportation facilities, its concentrated market, its closeness to western supplies of cattle—were by no means unique. Conditions at the Union Stockyards were crowded, there was little room for expansion, and the city was not as close to the chief grazing regions of the country as were certain other cities that lay still farther to the west. The sensible thing to do was not to invest more capital in Chicago but to set up new plants that could take advantage of more favorable conditions elsewhere.

All the major Chicago packers saw the logic of this analysis; it was, after all, the logic of capital. Swift's behavior was typical of the group. In 1888, he built an entirely new packing plant, replicating his operations at Chicago, in Kansas City, Missouri. Because it was well suited to handle the livestock output of the southern plains but did not have good rail connections with areas farther north, he built another new plant at Omaha just two years later. East St. Louis received a Swift factory in 1892 and St. Joseph in 1896.[183] Swift and the other Chicago packers invested increasing amounts of capital in these new operations, and so the major cities of the Great Plains began to rival Chicago for primacy in the cattle trade.[184] By the end of the century, Omaha was butchering nearly a third as many steers as Chicago was, while Kansas City was packing more than half of the lakeside city's total volume.[185]

It was the beginning of the end. Chicago retained its primacy, but had lost the quality that had made its nineteenth-century experience so remarkable. Its growth had stopped. Its production of pork and beef flattened out from the 1880s forward, while other cities surged to accommo-

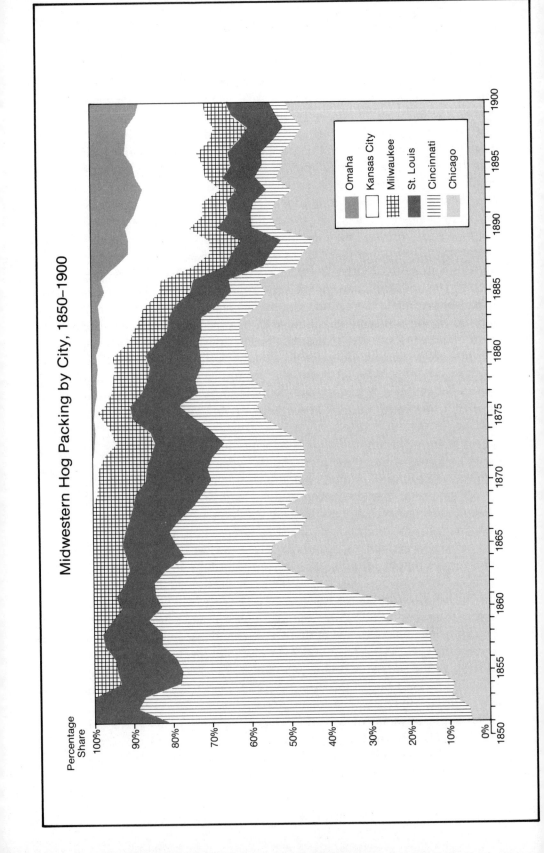

Midwestern Hog Packing by City, 1850–1900

Percentage Share

Legend:
- Omaha
- Kansas City
- Milwaukee
- St. Louis
- Cincinnati
- Chicago

date new packing facilities and output. Chicago continued for the next half century to handle an immense number of animals, never fewer than thirteen million per year, but its relative share declined as the industry continued its steady westward movement onto the plains. The rise of the diesel truck eventually undermined the technological tendency toward centralization that the railroads had promoted, until finally Chicago lost its earlier advantages altogether.[186] By the 1930s, the output of the stockyards was in steady decline; by 1960, all the major packers had shut down their Chicago factories.[187] Ten years later, the stockyards finally closed altogether. The familiar odor of manure vanished, and the strange silence of abandonment fell over the old animal pens. Grass began to grow again amid the ruins.[188]

The whole point of corporate meat-packing had been to systematize the market in animal flesh—to liberate it from nature and geography. Chicago had been the place to accomplish that feat, but the industry the city fostered ultimately exercised its independence even from the great Union Stockyard itself. Corporate headquarters might remain for a time in Chicago, directing vast networks for the production and distribution of food and other commodities, but they ultimately had only the most marginal reasons for preferring one location to another.[189] Once within the corporate system, places lost their particularity and became functional abstractions on organizational charts. Geography no longer mattered very much except as a problem in management: time had conspired with capital to annihilate space. The cattle might still graze amid forgotten buffalo wallows in central Montana, and the hogs might still devour their feedlot corn in Iowa, but from the corporate point of view they could just as well have been anywhere else. Abstract, standardized, and fungible, their lives were governed as much by the nature of capital as by the nature that gave them life. It was perhaps nothing more than simple justice that the city which had remade them in this way should be subject to the same alchemy. In losing control of its corporate meat-packing hinterland, Chicago's stockyard fulfilled the logic of its own birth.

PART III

THE GEOGRAPHY
OF CAPITAL

6

Gateway City

Mapping Capital

By the end of the nineteenth century, Chicago was filled with temples of commerce that were also, less obviously, mausoleums of landscapes vanishing from the city's hinterland. The grain elevators and Board of Trade celebrated the new speculative furor of the futures markets while simultaneously commemorating the tallgrass prairies being plowed and fenced into oblivion. The acres of sweet-smelling lumber stacked along the South Branch of the Chicago River testified to the fencing of the prairie and the growth of the city itself, but were also graveyards for the white pine forests rapidly disappearing from Michigan, Wisconsin, and Minnesota. Chicago's refrigerator cars and packing plants betokened a revolution in the way its citizens killed and sold animals, but were also monuments to the slaughtered bison herds. Behind each urban structure were the ghost landscapes that had given it birth. In sinking roots into the western soil, the city was remaking the countryside after its own image.

Though hardly as elegant as the department stores on State Street or the millionaires' mansions on Prairie Avenue, Chicago's elevators, lumberyards, and stockyards were the most basic symbols of the city's wealth and power. Never top tourist attractions, they nonetheless earned a place in every guidebook. For those who bothered to visit them, they seemed to commemorate more the city that housed them than the countryside that poured its wealth through their gates. Their bustling energy and sheer scale obscured the web of ecological and economic relationships in which they were enmeshed. It was easy to wonder at the pandemonium on the floor of 'Change or at the torrents of grain and flesh that flowed through the city's elevators and stockyards. It was much harder to make sense of them. An 1891 guidebook urged tourists to visit the public gallery at the Board of Trade, but offered no explanation of what people would see there. "From this gallery a perfect view may be had of the operations on the floor," it reported, "operations which it would be impossible to describe, and impossible for the average visitor to understand."[1] The view might be perfect, but it captured only the city's frenetic surfaces, not its deeper meanings.

This failure of understanding was twofold. First there was the forgetfulness that split asunder the rural and the urban, separating the field from its grain, the forest from its lumber, the rangeland from its meat. As natural ecosystems became more intimately linked to the urban marketplace, they came to seem more remote from the busy places that so impressed tourists who visited Chicago. This was the alchemy of the elevator receipt, converting wheat into a graded abstraction, and of the refrigerator car, separating the killing of an animal from the eating of its flesh. The easier it became to obscure the connections between Chicago's trade and its earthly roots, the more readily one could forget that the city drew its life from the natural world around it. "The city is made of man," Robert Herrick had written in 1898; "that is the last word to say of it."[2] Like other urban places before and since, Chicago seemed to break free from the soil and soar skyward as a wholly artificial creation. In appearing to be a triumph of human labor and will, it concealed its long-standing debts to the natural systems that made it possible.

But the city's dependence on this first, original nature was not all that Chicago's monuments obscured. They also hid much of the human economy, that second, constructed nature of which the city itself was the most visible expression. This second nature was what the 1891 guidebook author found impossible to describe when looking down from the visitors' gallery at the Board of Trade. The commodities that flowed across the grasslands and forests of the Great West to reach Chicago did so within an elaborate human network that was at least as important as nature in shaping the region. The emergence of the city required that a new human order be superimposed on nature until the two became completely entangled. The result was a hybrid system, at least as artificial as it was natural, that became second nature to those who lived within it.

At the heart of this new system was the twin birth of city and hinterland. Neither was possible without the other. Before Chicago became a metropolis, one could have described the processes of ecological change in the landscape west of the Great Lakes without making any reference to that particular place. One could have captured the dynamics of local ecosystems by speaking of the seasonal cycling of climate and vegetation, the weathering processes of bedrocks and soils, the migrations of animals, the activities of Indian communities, the perennial return of the prairie fires. But the coming of the city added a crucial new variable to the equation. As its influence extended farther and farther to the west, it drew every local ecosystem into the web of its markets, so the environmental dynamics of western places eventually had as much to do with their hinterland status as with their ecology. The catastrophic changes that forever altered the prairies and north woods had little to do with the ecological processes that had created them. To explain those changes, one must look instead toward the city by the lake, and to the market it represented.

Chicago was not alone in restructuring the environment of the midcontinent during the nineteenth century. Hundreds of lesser places were arrayed beneath it, a handful of cities tried hard to equal it, and a few—New York chief among them—bore the same relation to Chicago that Chicago did to the Great West. Changing ecosystems and economies were much more the product of the urban-rural system as a whole than of any single place, including Chicago. Had Chicago not been so successful in extending its reach toward the Rockies, some other city or cities would surely have done so, for the task of binding together city and country was the preoccupation of the age. And yet the universality of the process makes Chicago's explosive growth all the more exemplary. Other cities soon had railroads and elevators and refrigerator cars as well, but it was Chicago that first revealed the importance of such things for the West. Moreover, as Chicago grew to metropolitan stature, hundreds of other towns and cities grew with it, becoming part of its hinterland while simultaneously developing hinterlands of their own. City, town, and country might come into conflict in any number of ways, but they also worked together as a system, joining to become the single most powerful environmental force reshaping the American landscape since the glaciers began their long retreat to the north. One cannot understand the environmental or economic history of the Great West—one cannot understand the merged worlds of first and second nature in the midcontinent—without exploring Chicago's nineteenth-century hinterland and the urban-rural relationships that defined it.

Viewed abstractly, what distinguished the new regime from its predecessor—what separated first from second nature—were the broad outlines of von Thünen's Isolated State, with its lone city exerting far-reaching market influences on the territory around it. The flat glacial plains of Illinois may not have been entirely featureless, and the city by the lake may not have been entirely isolated—quite the contrary—but the economic geography of Chicago's markets mimicked uncannily the pattern von Thünen had first predicted in 1826. Beyond the central city lay the zone of intensive agriculture, filled with orchards, market gardens, dairy farms, and feedlots; beyond it the zone of extensive agriculture, with its farms raising mainly wheat and corn; beyond it the zone of livestock and lumber production; and beyond it the zone of the hunters, where fast-disappearing game species were opening new niches for cattle, to say nothing of farmers, miners, and lumbermen. Each element of this new market geography had its roots in the original ecosystems that had assigned pine trees to the north woods and bison to the Great Plains. But each was no less affected by its distance from the city and its ability to pay the transport costs of getting there.

Bison and pine trees had once been members of ecosystems defined mainly by flows of energy and nutrients and by relations among neighboring organisms. Rearrayed within the second nature of the market, they became commodities: things priced, bought, and sold within a system of human exchange. From that change flowed many others. Sudden new imperatives revalued the organisms that lived upon the land. Some, like the bison, bluestem, and pine tree, were priced so low that people consumed them in the most profligate ways and they disappeared as significant elements of the regional landscape. Others, like wheat, corn, cattle, and pigs, became the new dominant species of their carefully tended ecosystems. Increasingly, the abundance of a species depended on its utility to the human economy: species thrived more by price than by direct ecological adaptation.[3] New systems of value, radically different from their Indian predecessors, determined the fate of entire ecosystems.

Differential pricing of species produced dramatic shifts in far-flung regional landscapes. The ecology of first nature had been more local than not: climate aside, species succeeded and failed mainly because of circumstances they encountered in their immediate habitats.[4] Quite the opposite was true of second nature. Chicago, and the economic demand it represented, put new pressures on species hundreds of miles away. Its markets allowed people to look farther and farther afield for the goods they consumed, vastly extending the distance between points of ecological production and points of economic consumption. Now food and other resources made ever longer journeys to reach the places where people consumed them. The cattle that grazed on a Wyoming hillside, the corn that grew in an Iowa field, and the white pine that flourished in a Wisconsin forest would never ordinarily have shared the same landscape. All nonetheless came together in Chicago. There they were valued according to the demands and desires of people who for the most part had never even seen the landscapes from which they came. In an urban market, one could buy goods from hinterlands halfway round the world without understanding much if anything about how the goods had come to be there. Those who bought plants and animals from so far away had little way of knowing the ecological consequences of such purchases, so the separation of production and consumption had moral as well as material implications.

Von Thünen's zoned landscape meant increasing specialization among different ecosystems, the production of each becoming concentrated on a few economically profitable species. The more Iowa moved into Chicago's orbit, the more its ecosystem was dominated by corn, hogs, and feedlot cattle. What had once been a diverse prairie landscape produced fewer and fewer species. Although the local ecological conditions of first nature continued to influence which species grew where, the economic imperatives of second nature—distance from the city, cost of transportation, supply and demand, price—played an ever more important role in determining the shape of the landscape. As the human inhabitants of Chicago's hinterland responded to the siren song of its markets, they simplified local ecosystems in the direction of monocultures.

The merging of first and second nature was thus a shift from local ecosystem to regional hinterland and global economy. Any late-nineteenth-century map of the country west of Chicago outlines the new hinterland patterns that had emerged there. The substrate of such a map was first nature itself: the soils, plants, animals, and habitats on which even the most artificial human system continued to depend. Despite the importance of these things, a typical map generally recorded their presence with nothing more than blank paper. Only the watercourses got much attention, chiefly because they remained important corridors of human travel. Most maps emphasized the demography of human settlement more than anything else, the hierarchy of metropolis, town, and country. That hierarchy revealed itself on paper with place markers and typefaces of different sizes, and with lines representing railroads and highways. Rural areas rarely earned even a name on the map, remaining as blank as the ecological substrate itself. Villages, of which there were many, were marked with small dots and had one or two roads linking them to the surrounding countryside. Towns earned larger letters for their names and had one or two rail connections in addition to a few roads. Large cities, of which there were only a few, usually had access to water transport, several railroads, and many roads. And the great city—the metropolis, Chicago—in addition to its million or more inhabitants had railroads, highways, and watercourses that seemed to reach everywhere.

The map of these places—large and small, accessible and inaccessible—was also, at least in outline, a map of second nature. It recorded the location and size of human settlements, but also, implicitly, the subtler web of connections among them—what geographers call the system of cities. These connections in turn traced flows of economic power. Some places were not only larger than others; they were also easier to get to and had more influence over the city system as a whole. The paths of least resistance, whether for people and commodities or for less tangible things like information and capital, seemed always to lead toward the cities. What gave a large city its influence—what made Chicago a metropolis—was that many small places could communicate more easily with it than with anywhere else. In so doing, they tied the fates of their local ecosystems—their farms, their forests, their rangelands—to the movements of urban markets and the fate of the city system as a whole. Although other cities and towns participated just as fully in the regional networks of market exchange, none in the West was so central or powerful as Chicago. By the time of the Civil War, its metropolitan status was itself second nature to those who lived in its shadow.

Second nature, no less than nature itself, is necessarily an abstraction. If it exists in the world at all, it does so only as a multitude of real things and their even more multitudinous relationships to each other. Size and accessibility may have been the abstract features of second nature that placed Chicago atop the regional hierarchy of the Great West. But they found their concrete embodiment in things like steel rails, telegraph wires, flour mills, log drives, icing stations, and the like—to say nothing of factories, department stores, millionaires' mansions, and workers' cottages. To grasp Chicago's relationship to Iowa farmers, it makes less sense to speak of "second nature" than of things like prairie soils, steel plows, grain elevators, feedlots, cattle cars, and railroad rates. Just as an ecosystem consists of the creatures that live within it, so does an economy consist of the day-to-day actions of real people working to make their way in the world, turning the soil and reshaping its products to construct a life for themselves.

But abstractions have a certain reality too. The near infinity of real objects that human beings had assembled on the landscape of the Great West by the end of the nineteenth century was a vast collective construction. Taken as a whole, these objects gave new shape to the land. They represented the accumulated labor of several generations, and the accumulated wealth of ecosystems that had been at least partly dismantled in their creation. To understand their meaning, a certain degree of abstraction is unavoidable. To read the landscape west of Chicago without trying to see these larger patterns would be to join the tourists in the public gallery at the Board of Trade, fascinated by the apparent chaos but understanding nothing. Outward chaos hid a deeper order, the architecture of which was no less real than the bricks and mortar of which more tangible structures were composed. By peering into that underlying order, one can begin to see the blueprint that made city and country into a single region, economy and ecology into a single system. In the vocabulary of the human landscape, second nature has another name, and it is under that alias that one must sooner or later grapple with its meaning. Drawing a map of second nature means coming to terms finally with capital itself.

Credit Flows

But where is one to find such a map, and how is one to read it?

Trying to trace the flow of capital in Chicago's hinterland is a task fraught with difficulty. Although nineteenth-century Americans were no less concerned than their modern counterparts with keeping track of what they bought and sold, who owed money to whom, and how much wealth a person had accumulated, they were just as secretive about such information as we are today. There were usually plenty of good reasons not to let one's competitors and creditors know how well one's business was doing, and even better reasons for not letting such information fall into the hands of the tax collector. Neither the government nor the banks gathered much information about regional flows of capital. The result is a paucity of historical data that would let us trace the flow of money through Chicago and other cities.

Under these circumstances, it might seem that a map of second nature—of capital—would be an impossible undertaking. As with most such historical dilemmas, however, one can find ways around this apparent lack of evidence if one is willing to play detective. There are two possible moments in an individual's life when personal assets and debts come into full public view: death and bankruptcy. This was as true in the nineteenth century as it is today. Then as now, when a person died or became insolvent, the courts seized control of the remaining estate in order to divide it among creditors and heirs who had some claim on the wealth it contained. Suddenly, the usual impulses toward financial secrecy disappeared, since those who hoped to gain from carving up the economic corpse had every reason to assert their legal right to a place at the accounting table. This means that the archives of probate and bankruptcy courts contain long lists of economic assets, and even longer lists of people trying to claim them. These lists can serve as vital clues for mapping the geography of capital in the hinterland of nineteenth-century Chicago.

In trying to use probate or bankruptcy court records to trace past movements of debt and capital, one must always ask how representative such records are. Death takes a disproportionate toll of the sick, the young, and the elderly, people whose economic circumstances are often far different from those of individuals in the prime of their adult lives. Probate court records strongly reflect the wealth that has accumulated at the *end* of a life, and are more helpful in defining their owner's final socioeconomic status than in revealing his or her role in the commerce between city and country. They tell little about capital flows and commercial indebtedness.

Bankruptcy records are in this respect a more promising source. When an individual or firm becomes legally insolvent, the task of the bankruptcy court is to identify all outstanding debts and the assets that can be used to pay them. The court proceedings become a kind of economic snapshot of the debtor's business affairs, focusing especially on the capital he or she owned and owed at the moment of bankruptcy. For every bankrupt debtor, the court compiles a list of creditors, where they live, and how much each of them is owed. With such data, one can explore whether debtors in Chicago were systematically different from debtors in St. Louis or Peoria or rural farming areas in downstate Illinois. By examining how debtors and creditors arrange themselves in space, one can construct maps of how capital flowed between city and country.

But here too there are problems. Like death, bankruptcy is hardly a random event: by definition, it takes a disproportionate toll of those who are already in economic trouble. There is no small irony in using bankruptcies as a measure of capital flows, since an insolvent debtor's chief problem is that capital is *not* flowing—there is too little money to keep business going. Under ordinary circumstances, the relations between bankrupt debtors and their creditors are probably atypical of the population as a whole. This flaw in the data is to some extent irreducible, but there is a possible way to mitigate its effects. If one looks at bankruptcies when large numbers of people are finding themselves unexpectedly insolvent because of broader changes in the economy as a whole—during, say, a financial panic or depression—one might reasonably expect their circumstances to be more typical than at other times. If one applies this logic to the nearly four hundred people who went bankrupt in Chicago and its hinterland during the first nine months of the panic of 1873—and to the nearly twenty thousand creditors to whom they owed money—one can learn a great deal about capital flows in the region.[5]

Take, for instance, the case of the Garden City Manufacturing and Supply Company of Chicago, a large sawmill which at the beginning of 1872 had an estimated capital of over a quarter million dollars.[6] At that time, it was reported to be of "high" creditworthiness by the nation's most respected credit rating firm, the Mercantile Agency of R. G. Dun in

New York. Although it enjoyed favorable business conditions in the immediate aftermath of the great Chicago fire of 1871, the company had
fallen on hard times by the summer of 1873 as the economy turned downward and credit became tighter. By July, the Bradstreet credit agency of
New York was reporting to its subscribers that Garden City Manufacturing was failing to pay its debts on time; by December, the firm had filed
for bankruptcy.

As the court sifted through the claims held by hundreds of Garden
City Manufacturing's creditors, it constructed a picture of the company's
business that mimicked that of Chicago's lumber industry as a whole.
Among the firm's creditors were well over a hundred of its workers, often
identified in the records with no known address and with single nick-
names like Big Mule, Little Cuss, or Tom. Few were due more than $50 in
back wages, which they were entitled to receive before any other creditor.
Although large in number, these employees held only a tiny share of the
firm's debts, their total being less than a tenth of what the firm owed to a
single Connecticut insurance company. Looming much larger among
Garden City Manufacturing's debts were the sums it owed to other Chicago firms: sometimes dozens, sometimes hundreds, sometimes thousands of dollars to the companies that had sold it wood, machinery, and
other supplies on credit. Roughly 65 percent of nearly $300,000 in debts
was owed to firms located in the immediate Chicago area. The rest was
scattered across the countryside, with the largest remaining share predictably being held by the Michigan and Wisconsin companies that had
sold the mill unfinished lumber. To round out the picture, Garden City
Manufacturing owed over $2,000 to the Chicago, Burlington and Quincy
and the Chicago and Northwestern railroads. Workers, wholesalers, and
transport companies: these three types of creditors figured in the account
books of almost every nineteenth-century firm, bankrupt or not.

Balanced against these debts were several dozen unpaid bills from the
firm's customers for the doors, windows, and other finished wood products that had been shipped just before the bankruptcy occurred. Nearly
$50,000 was still outstanding from these customers, all of whom lived in
Chicago's lumber hinterland: Illinois, Iowa, Missouri, Nebraska, and
Kansas. In effect, the bankruptcy of Garden City Manufacturing revealed
in microcosm the movements of lumber through the entire region.
From the lists of individuals and firms that appeared in its court proceedings, one can trace a familiar map of interlocking ecosystems and economies: rough pine lumber from the northern shores of Lake Michigan
making its way to Chicago, where it was finished in the city's mills and
lumberyards before being shipped by railroad out to ranches and farms in
the treeless grasslands of the prairies and Great Plains. Far from being an

anomaly because of its bankruptcy, Garden City Manufacturing and its court records confirm just how typical it was. In the final account books of a long-defunct company, one can thus rediscover the outlines of a ghost landscape, the shape-shifting boundaries of second nature itself.

Bankruptcy records are particularly useful in showing relations between city and country because so much of the debt they track is commercial in nature. Although one might think that a bankrupt's debts would consist principally of the direct loans one obtains from a bank today—to finance a mortgage, say, or a business expansion—the more common form of debt in the nineteenth century consisted of what one might call commercial paper. The most familiar modern analogue is probably a checking account or credit card. When a hinterland storekeeper ordered goods from a wholesaler in Chicago, he or she paid for the shipment with some sort of IOU or promise to pay, as happens today in a credit card transaction. As long as the goods were in transit and the IOU remained unpaid, the storekeeper was a debtor and the wholesaler a creditor. If the storekeeper then went bankrupt, the wholesaler who had shipped the goods suddenly became a party to the bankruptcy proceeding, and had to compete with other creditors for a share of the debtor's remaining assets. To the extent that commercial debts of this sort constituted most of a bankrupt's estate, the court's list of creditors reflects the flow of capital that underwrote the entire mercantile economy.

Each individual bankrupt had his or her own way of doing business, and each set of court records tells a particular story of struggle and failure. For example, Ferdinand C. Lighte moved to Chicago to open a piano business after the death of his father, who had manufactured musical instruments in New York. Although he started out expecting to receive $10,000 from his father's estate, and worked diligently to succeed at his new business, legal problems with the will and the general economic downturn eventually drove the young man to drink. Like many small business people before and since, Lighte discovered that he lacked the capital to get off to a sound start. He was in bankruptcy court by January 1874.[7]

Bankruptcy could also happen to people with far more capital than this would-be piano dealer. Freeland B. Gardner was among Chicago's most prominent lumber dealers in 1871, with extensive timber property in Wisconsin, a hotel in the city, and over half a million dollars in capital. Although he had once been financially embarrassed in the panic of 1857, fifteen years later R. G. Dun and Company considered him a superb credit risk: "Strong, wealthy, and v[er]y good in every way."[8] But Gardner believed that the most effective way to make money was to expand business on borrowed capital, a strategy that worked only so long as the general economy was healthy. When times turned bad, he was caught in the same credit crunch that had trapped him in 1857. His business collapsed in August 1873, leaving over $700,000 in bad debts to the Chicago and Wisconsin firms that had been his suppliers. His son, who had managed the Chicago hotel, soon followed him into bankruptcy, so father and child shared in the general disaster of the family.[9]

The Gardners suffered their fate because they gambled on living beyond their means. Others came to the same end because bad luck or inadequate resources kept them perennially undercapitalized. This was the case with the unfortunate furniture firm of McCabe, Wilkins, and Spaulding, whose total assets never amounted to more than a few tens of thousands of dollars. After losing their inventory—most of it uninsured— in the great Chicago fire of 1871, the partners decided that the only honorable course was to pay their creditors in full even for goods that had been destroyed. It was the honest and ethical thing to do—not everyone chose to respond to the fire with such high-mindedness—but it ate up their remaining capital. They struggled diligently for the next couple of years to recover from the blow, limping along with late payments to friendly suppliers who were still willing to sell to them on credit. Then the economy collapsed, and with it all hope that the firm would recover. A Cincinnati wholesaler finally grew restless about an unpaid bill, and on April 16, 1874, a U.S. marshal appeared at their door and threw them into bankruptcy.[10]

Each of these stories is a small tragedy, and there are hundreds like them in the records of bankruptcy courts and credit-rating agencies even for the brief, arbitrary period of nine months following the 1873 panic. Sad as such narratives may be, however, their pathos is of less interest here than what they reveal about the geography of capital, the daily transactions not of business failure but of ordinary life. Abstracted from the details of his or her personal tragedy, each bankrupt reflected a more general way of doing business that characterized a particular industry and the economy as a whole. Individual businesses had special needs, so a piano dealer, a lumberman, and a furniture merchant look quite different when seen in the context of their daily transactions.

Ferdinand Lighte's most important creditors outside the city of Chicago, for instance, were several musical instrument manufacturers in New York, and he owed most of his debts within the city to other music dealers. Although some of his debts were common to any line of business—an unpaid bill to a painter for the sign that hung above his shop, a fee for insurance to cover his equipment—most were unique to his fellow piano dealers. In these special patterns, one can begin to discover the broader geography of trade, and of capital itself. Freeland Gardner and his son revealed their affection for unsecured loans by the number of round-numbered debts from firms all around the Chicago area that appear in their bankruptcy proceedings. But the Gardners also left debts recording the purchases from sawmills in Wisconsin that were typical of all lumbermen, and the purchases from local grocers, linen merchants, and furniture dealers that characterized all hotels. McCabe, Wilkins, and Spaulding, furniture dealers themselves, bought most of their wares from chair, bed, and sofa manufacturers in Michigan, Indiana, and Ohio. It was no accident that the firm finally sending them into bankruptcy was located in Cincinnati.

One begins to understand the significance of these patterns if one combines the lists of creditors for all Chicago bankrupts who shared a particular line of work and examines where they lived geographically. The result is a map of the hinterlands that supplied each major commodity bought and sold in the city. Take, for instance, the creditor map of the three Chicago lumber merchants and manufacturers who went bankrupt between August 1873 and April 1874. In a pattern common to all such maps, Chicago lumbermen owed more money to other Chicagoans than to creditors in any other location, suggesting how heavily local merchants relied on each other for credit to finance the flow of trade. But the rest of their creditors, like those of Freeland Gardner, clustered around the shores of Lake Michigan, in the Wisconsin and Michigan counties from which they bought most of their raw pine. Although hinterland lumbermen usually played debtor to Chicago firms, dealers like Gardner often ordered wood direct from mill operators, who in the case of a bankruptcy suddenly found themselves unlikely creditors to large urban manufacturers and wholesalers. The bankruptcy maps thus confirm and deepen our sense of Chicago's broad regional trade relationships as revealed in other lumber industry sources.

Contrast this lumber map with the one for Chicago's five bankrupt boot and shoe dealers. Aside from their heavy trade with other merchants in Chicago, which by the 1870s housed a substantial local leather industry, almost all of these merchants' creditors were in the Northeast, in cities like New York, Philadelphia, Boston, and especially Lynn, Massachusetts, the best-known shoe manufacturing center in the nation.[11] This pattern of debt paralleled yet differed from that of the city's two bankrupt hardware dealers. Although they too traded with a favored group of northeastern wholesalers, especially in New York City, they also bought heavily from the stove and hardware manufacturers of western New York, Pennsylvania, and Ohio. Each different industry had its own patterns of trade, its own characteristic geography of debt, credit, and capital.

These maps of the creditors to whom Chicago's bankrupt merchants

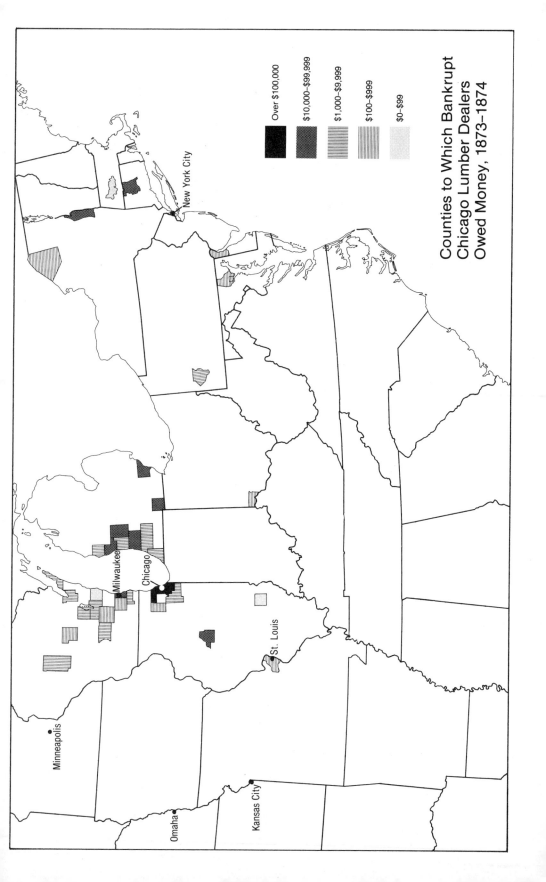

Counties to Which Bankrupt
Chicago Lumber Dealers
Owed Money, 1873–1874

Over $100,000

$10,000–$99,999

$1,000–$9,999

$100–$999

$0–$99

New York City

Minneapolis

Milwaukee

Chicago

St. Louis

Omaha

Kansas City

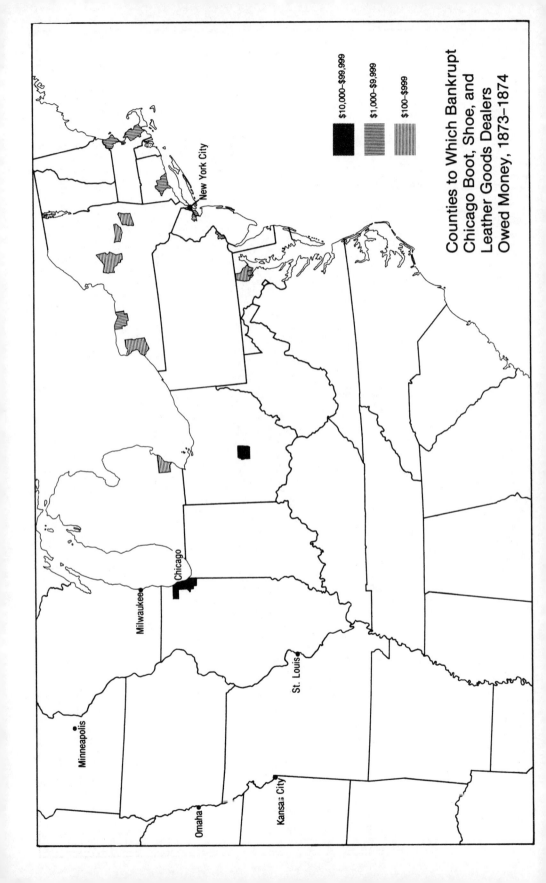

Counties to Which Bankrupt
Chicago Boot, Shoe, and
Leather Goods Dealers
Owed Money, 1873–1874

$10,000–$99,999

$1,000–$9,999

$100–$999

New York City

Chicago

Milwaukee

Minneapolis

St. Louis

Omaha

Kansas City

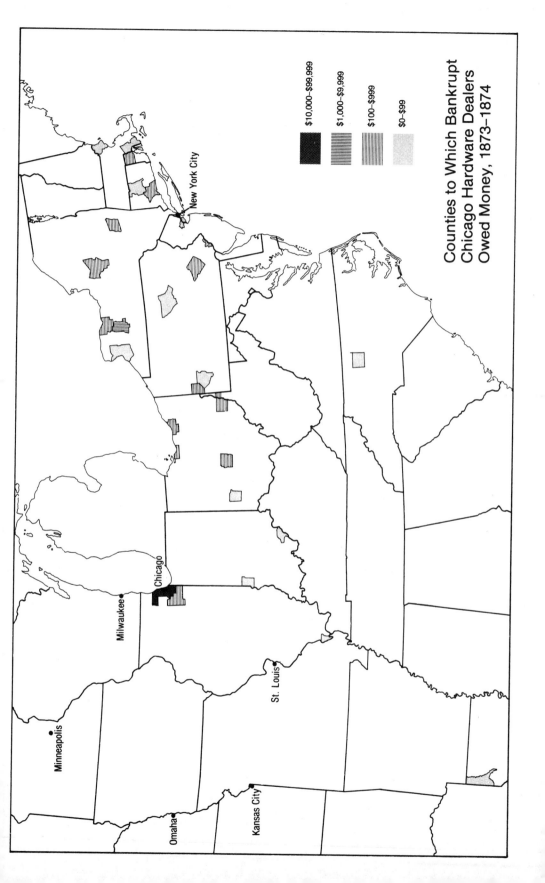

Counties to Which Bankrupt
Chicago Hardware Dealers
Owed Money, 1873–1874

$10,000–$99,999

$1,000–$9,999

$100–$999

$0–$99

New York City

Chicago

Milwaukee

Minneapolis

Omaha

St. Louis

Kansas City

owed money make an important point about the city's "hinterland": it had no single identity. Rather than being one easily traced region dominated by one Chicago market, the city's hinterland was actually thousands of overlapping regions, each connected in myriad ways to the thousands of markets and thousands of commodities that constituted Chicago's economic life. Each different commodity had unique sources of supply and demand—and hence a unique set of environmental linkages to the natural world. "The trade of the city," wrote Joseph Nimmo, a government economist who was one of the shrewdest trade analysts of his day, "in almost every commodity, has different geographical limits."[12]

This was no less true of the city's manufactured goods than of the agricultural commodities that had made Chicago famous. There were sound ecological reasons why Chicago's lumber supply hinterland lay around the shores of Lake Michigan, and why its lumber demand hinterland reached far across the prairies and plains to the Rocky Mountains. There were equally sound reasons why its grain commodities moved in exactly the opposite direction, with supply hinterlands in the west and demand hinterlands in the north and east. Subtly differing hinterlands of demand and supply existed for everything bought and sold in the city. Its supply hinterland for leather goods included New York City and Lynn, Massachusetts, but also reached into Chicago's own packinghouses, with their vast output of hides and skins that had arrived in the city on the backs of living animals. The boots and shoes manufactured in Chicago were of coarser quality than those of eastern cities, but this made them eminently salable in southern and western regions where cost and stoutness counted for more than fashion. The market hinterland in which Chicago wholesalers competed effectively in selling boots and shoes stretched all the way to eastern Tennessee and Georgia in the South, and to Utah in the West—only in Reno, Nevada, did San Francisco merchants begin to compete effectively with Chicagoans. "The Chicago trade in boots and shoes," declared the secretary of the city's Board of Trade in 1879, "probably extends over a larger area of territory than any other."[13]

In economic and environmental terms, we should think of a city and its hinterland not as two clearly defined and easily recognizable places but as a multitude of overlapping market and resource regions. This suggests in turn that we should revise von Thünen's suggestive but simplistic map of concentric agricultural zones surrounding an isolated metropolis. His core insight remains sound: goods do travel to market according to their value, weight, bulk, and ability to pay their cost of transportation. But von Thünen's model becomes much more complicated as soon as we recognize that no real city exists in such grand theoretical isolation. Precisely because a city's markets create so many different regions of supply and demand, neighboring cities and towns inevitably share hinterlands. "Thus each commercial city," wrote a nineteenth-century economist, becomes "very sharply the rival of every other commercial city."[14] Merchants in different places compete with each other to sell goods in surrounding areas wherever they can offer attractive prices. Economic geographers have struggled in the century and a half since von Thünen to understand the spatial implications of this competition among urban merchants, and the result has been the arcane body of mathematical models known as central place theory. It is time now to revisit that theory to learn what it can reveal about the geography of capital in these maps of bankrupts and their creditors.

The Urban Hierarchy

Central place theorists seek to explain the geographic phenomenon I noted at the start of this chapter: the tendency of human settlements to organize themselves into hierarchies.[15] All cities in the modern capitalist world—not just Chicago during the nineteenth century—exist within *systems of cities*. A few large metropolises link with a larger number of big cities, and each of those links in turn with a still larger number of small towns.[16] Urban populations arrange themselves into rank order by size: population increases exponentially with rank, so the higher a city's rank, the more people it contains. By 1890, the year when Chicago finally surpassed Philadelphia to become the second-largest metropolis in the United States, there were only 3 cities in the nation with populations greater than 1,000,000. Beneath them were 25 large cities with populations less than 1,000,000 but more than 100,000. Still smaller were the 326 cities with populations less than 100,000 but more than 10,000. Beneath them were the more than 994 towns with fewer than 10,000 inhabitants, and the 6,490 villages and rural areas with fewer than 2,500 inhabitants. The number of towns and rural areas with low populations was exponentially larger, by three orders of magnitude, than the number of great metropolises.[17]

The difference between a high-order metropolis like Chicago and a lower-order town like Peoria or Burlington was not merely Chicago's much larger population. Chicago's high rank meant that its market attracted customers for many more goods and services from a much wider region. No less important, it attracted demand for much more specialized goods and services. Just as one can rank human settlements according to the number of people who live in them, so can one rank all economic goods according to the number of people and concentrations of wealth needed to create a market for them. The hierarchy of urban settlements is also a hierarchy of markets.

Some goods are so common, and the demand for them so widespread, that even a small number of people create a market for their consumption. This is true in western societies, for instance, of everyday food-stuffs—bread, eggs, milk, meat—and of the most basic items of shelter and clothing: frame houses, say, or simple dresses, shirts, and trousers. Assuming people exchange such things at all—as opposed to making them at home—their markets are extremely diffuse. No matter how small a nineteenth-century central place might be, even if it consisted only of a general store at a rural crossroads, it provided at least some of these basic retail items. Low-ranking towns sustained markets in low-ranking, unspe-cialized goods. Their trade hinterlands extended no more than a couple of dozen miles beyond their own boundaries, approximately the distance customers could travel on horseback and still return home in a single day.[18] The buildings that lined the main streets of such places contained general stores, grocers, hardware dealers, dry goods merchants, and tav-erns, all selling their wares entirely to retail customers. The small town was quintessentially a *retail* place, and counted for its customers on the rural residents who lived in its immediate vicinity.

But not all retail goods and services are of such low rank. Some are high enough in price, and are purchased rarely enough, that they require greater potential demand before it makes sense for a merchant to try to sell them. A classic example is jewelry; books are another. One would not have expected to find a jeweler or a bookstore in a small western village during the nineteenth century, but would have had to travel instead to a town or even a medium-sized city that could support such businesses. Comparable goods and services would have included dealers in stoves, large agricultural machinery, fashionable clothing, legal and medical ser-vices, photographs, and other specialized retail items. It was characteris-tic of medium-ranked urban places in the nineteenth century that they could sustain specialized retail shops: not just general stores but stores concentrating on only one article of clothing, such as shoes or millinery; not just hardware dealers but dealers in stoves or agricultural imple-ments. Specialist retailers could carry a narrower line of products because a medium-ranked city—by virtue of its better transportation connec-tions—could draw wealthier customers from a wider area that included smaller towns as well as farms. The more diverse and numerous its cus-tomers, the more concentrated and varied its market—and hence the more specialized its shops could become.

There are goods and services that are even higher in rank, so high that only a few urban places can offer them. One example is government: in each American state there is today only one capital city that houses a legislature, a governor, and the highest court. Those wishing to lobby a politician or seek legal redress for any number of problems within a state's jurisdiction must go to that city and that city alone. At a higher level still, if one wants to deal with the federal government, only one city in the country will finally do: Washington, D.C. Such cities typically develop markets in government-related services—specialist lawyers, lobbyists, printers, stationers, newspapers—that can be found nowhere else.

Economically, one can go higher still. The special role of the highest-ranking urban places in America has often had less to do with their formal political position than with the very high-ranking economic goods and services only they supply.[19] Some of the most important of these products are financial. In the nineteenth century as now, only great cities could sustain the largest commercial banks, law firms, corporate headquarters, brokerage houses, and unique economic institutions like the New York Stock Exchange or the Chicago Board of Trade. Organizations like these that depended on concentrated flows of information and capital for their success almost always located themselves in metropolitan centers. No smaller city could hope to compete for their business, and so places like New York and Chicago emerged as regional and national centers for the control of financial exchange. The same was true of most institutions of high culture: professional orchestras, theaters, libraries, art galleries, publishing houses, and the like. The number and quality of such institutions that a community could sustain related directly to its rank in the urban hierarchy.[20]

But the demand of a great city's market even for more ordinary goods and services differed from that of smaller cities, because the metropolis could handle such goods in greater volumes, with higher discounts, at lower prices. A city like Chicago was first and foremost a center of *wholesale* trade.[21] Merchants in small towns and medium-sized cities sold principally to the retail customers in their immediate hinterlands. To do so, they bought their own supplies from wholesale merchants in Chicago, New York, and other metropolitan markets. Chicago earned its high rank partly by being a retailer itself, offering its customers a greater variety and number of retail establishments than any other city in the Great West. These ranged from large department stores selling every conceivable product to small firms specializing in exceptionally narrow lines. But the city's metropolitan status derived above all from the ability of its wholesalers—many of them just as specialized as its retailers—to supply discounted goods to virtually any retailer in the country.[22] The city was a shopkeeper for shopkeepers, a market for other markets. By the end of the century, only New York came close to matching the reach and influence of Chicago's wholesalers, who had succeeded in turning the entire midcontinent into their city's hinterland. From the Appalachians to the Sierra Nevada, the Great West was Chicago's domain.

A metropolis like Chicago contained within its hinterland hundreds and even thousands of smaller places. Hinterland villages and towns sold food and clothing to their immediate retail customers, and medium-sized cities sold more specialized retail products to the towns and farms that surrounded them. But all bought their supplies from the wholesale markets of Chicago, just as local farmers, ranchers, and lumbermen sold their output to the city's grain elevators, packing plants, and lumberyards. The map of towns and settlements reflected this hidden network of markets within markets, low-ranked places within the fields of high-ranked ones. Modern central place theorists have offered elaborate formal geometries to describe these nested urban hinterlands, with intricate layers of large and small hexagons describing like so many honeycombs the markets for high- and low-ranked goods in high- and low-ranked places.

Central place theory has an elegant mathematical simplicity as it confronts the complex hierarchies of human settlement and trade, but it shares with von Thünen's agricultural zones one great flaw: it is profoundly static and ahistorical. Reading the treatises of the German theorists who originally developed it, one is struck by the abstract neatness of this geography. Its nested hexagons have none of the messiness one expects of real historical places and landscapes. In its original, most undiluted form, central place theory offers a purely formal explanation of how market hierarchies evolve. In the fantasy of a flat, featureless plain which the central place theorists share with von Thünen, population grows until small village centers begin to appear with the expansion of local market demand; they in turn eventually create a market for medium-sized towns; they in turn create larger cities; they in turn create a great metropolis.[23] Like the economic logic of capitalism itself, the entire process easily comes to seem second nature, as organic and evolutionary as Darwin's model of biological change.

But the growing city system in the region west of nineteenth-century Chicago followed a more precipitous course. Far from being a gradual, bottom-up process in which villages called forth towns, towns called forth cities, and cities at last called forth the metropolis of Chicago, nearly the opposite was true. The highest-ranking regional metropolis consolidated its role at a very early date, and promoted the communities in its hinterland as much as they promoted it.[24] The region underwent its greatest growth during a period when urban-industrial capitalism had already established itself on the eastern seaboard, tying the American economy to an international trade system that stretched across the Atlantic to European ports and markets. Because Chicago enjoyed unique transportation advantages by virtue of its position on the divide between the Great Lakes and Mississippi watersheds, and because the profound centralizing tendencies of the railroads amplified those advantages, the city emerged as a metropolis strongly linked to eastern markets long before the villages and towns of its expanding hinterland had filled out their eventual hierarchy of settlements. In so doing, Chicago disrupted the trade patterns that had already been developing in the region to its west.[25] By the terms of central place theory, Chicago grew too large, too high-ranked, too quickly.[26] This in turn suggests that something other than gradual market evolution was responsible for its metropolitan status.

The hierarchy of city, town, and country that appeared so quickly in the Great West during the second half of the nineteenth century represented a new phase of American frontier expansion, far more rapid than anything Frederick Jackson Turner described.[27] Its accelerated pace was driven by the new rail technologies, but the growth of Chicago's metropolitan hinterland was an extension of the urban hierarchy that had already emerged in the East, particularly in relation to New York City. Chicago's high-ranking urban functions as a wholesaler and financial metropolis flowed directly from its special relationship to the city on the Hudson. By choosing Chicago to be the greatest concentration of railroad capital on the continent, and by giving Chicago merchants special access to the credit and discounts that made wholesaling possible, New Yorkers and other eastern capitalists placed it atop the western city system at the very moment that settlement in the region began its most explosive growth. John M. Binckley, a Chicago booster of the 1870s, struck a familiar imperial note in describing this process:

> Chicago is the war of Eastern business carried into the Africa of the West. Montreal, Boston, New York, Philadelphia—and now very soon Baltimore—all have their outpost in Chicago. Through her, those cities have spun their webs about St. Louis; they have tapped her Pacific railroad; they have seduced Kansas City and St. Joseph; they have annexed to their commercial kingdom all Iowa, Nebraska, and North Missouri, and the southeast section of that State; they have preoccupied Texas against New Orleans; and all the Rocky Mountain region, British America, and the mouth of the Oregon, against the world; and Chicago is their instrument. Chicago is not Eastern; Chicago is not Western. Chicago is altogether *sui generis*. . . .[28]

The Canadian geographer A. F. Burghardt has used less grandiloquent language to describe this same process. In his phrase, Chicago became a "gateway city" by serving as the chief intermediary between newly occupied farms and towns in the West and the maturing capitalist economy of the Northeast and Europe.[29] Although the city's gateway status lasted only a few decades, while the capitalist economy completed its colonization of the Great West, that was long enough to make Chicago second only to New York in the reach and power of its markets.

When one adds to the abstract models of central place theory this more historical perspective on capitalist expansion and colonization, one can read the bankruptcy court records in a new way. If one combines all the creditors of everyone who went bankrupt in midwestern federal courts between August 1873 and April 1874, and then draws a map of the total debt held by creditors in each of the region's counties, the individual patterns of each bankrupt's business disappear and a new picture emerges.[30] Rather than see the different trading hinterlands that distinguished a piano dealer from a furniture merchant, we suddenly glimpse the western urban hierarchy as it had developed by the 1870s. At the top of that hierarchy, holding more debt than any other cities in the region, were Chicago and St. Louis, each with well over a million dollars in creditor debt.[31] Immediately beneath them were other places that were already emerging as the major cities of the region: Milwaukee, Minneapolis, and Kansas City, each with creditor debts in the hundreds of thousands of dollars. Beneath them were more numerous smaller places, with creditor debts measured in tens of thousands of dollars: Peoria, Burlington, Oshkosh, Omaha, and others.

Although hardly following the neat hexagonal geometry of central place theory, these cities did display some of the regular market distributions and ranked urban functions that the theory would have predicted. In particular, each had a clearly defined debt hinterland, a region in which people were most likely to owe money to creditors in that city. One sees this most easily if one examines a series of maps showing where bankrupts lived who owed money to the creditors of a particular town. Debtors who owed money to people in Peoria, for instance, clustered tightly in the rural counties immediately surrounding that city; almost none lived outside Illinois. Debtors who owed money to Milwaukeeans were more widespread, but still concentrated primarily in southern Wisconsin and in the counties along the upper Mississippi River. A similar pattern applied to the Twin Cities of Minneapolis–St. Paul: bankrupt debtors who owed money to creditors there were almost all located in the upper Mississippi Valley, mainly in the Minnesota counties immediately south and west of the two cities. Although the Twin Cities soon emerged as a major regional metropolis for the northern tier of states reaching nearly to Seattle, the bankruptcy map accurately suggests that their hinterland in 1873 was largely confined to Minnesota and Dakota Territory.[32]

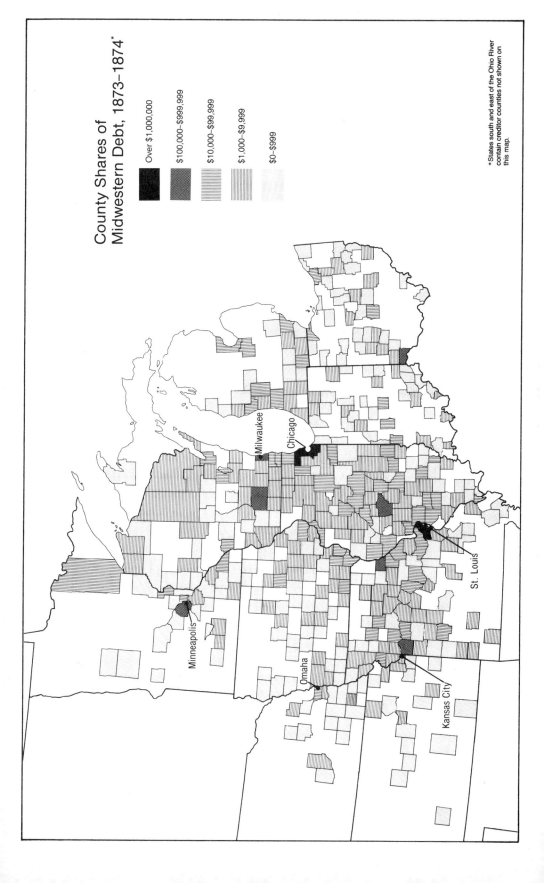

County Shares of
Midwestern Debt, 1873–1874*

Over $1,000,000

$100,000–$999,999

$10,000–$99,999

$1,000–$9,999

$0–$999

*States south and east of the Ohio River contain creditor counties not shown on this map.

Milwaukee

Chicago

Minneapolis

Omaha

St. Louis

Kansas City

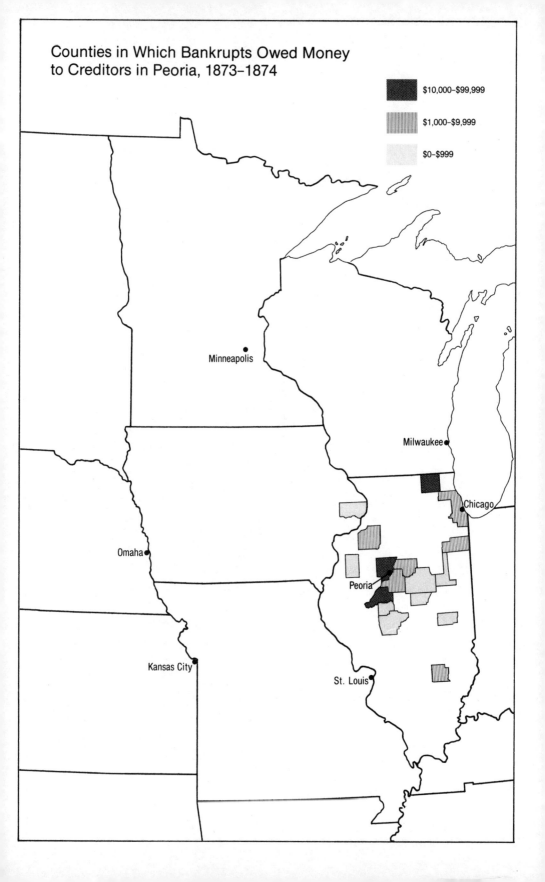

Counties in Which Bankrupts Owed Money
to Creditors in Peoria, 1873–1874

$10,000–$99,999

$1,000–$9,999

$0–$999

Minneapolis

Milwaukee

Chicago

Omaha

Peoria

Kansas City

St. Louis

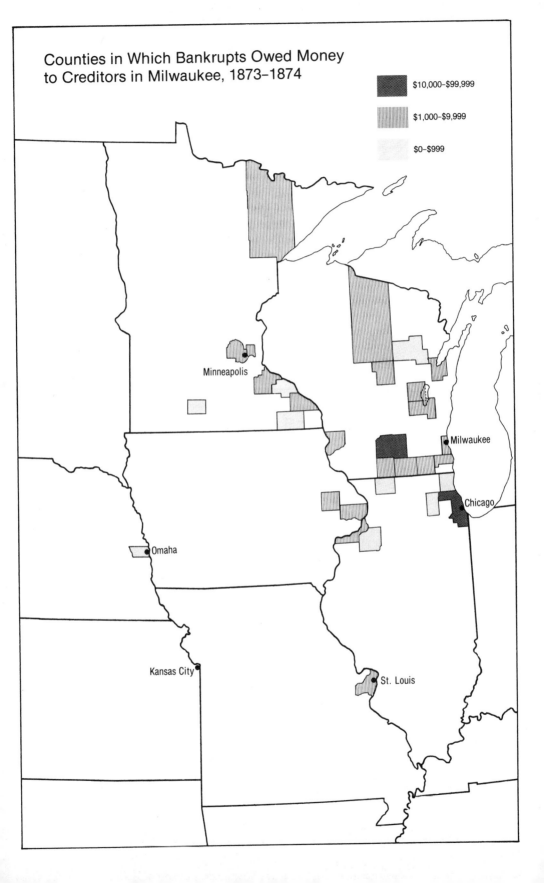

Counties in Which Bankrupts Owed Money
to Creditors in Milwaukee, 1873–1874

$10,000–$99,999

$1,000–$9,999

$0–$999

Minneapolis

Milwaukee

Chicago

Omaha

Kansas City

St. Louis

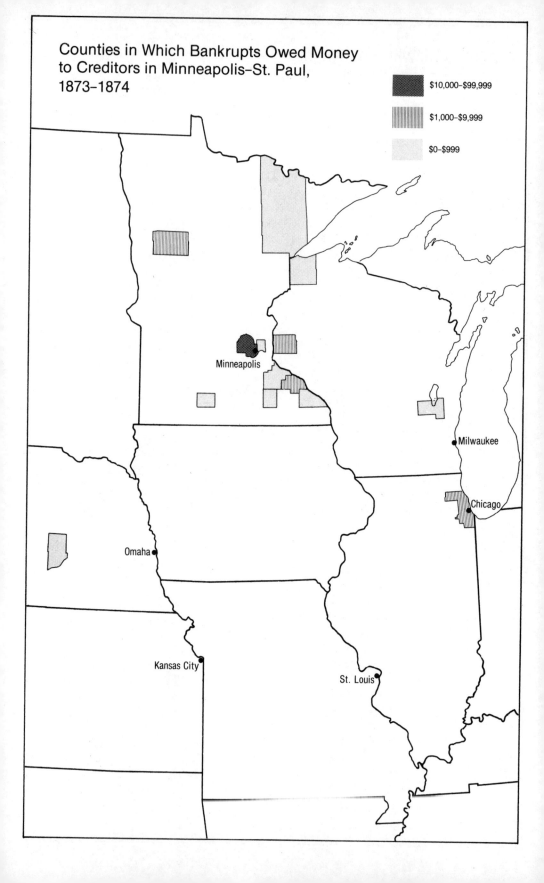

Counties in Which Bankrupts Owed Money
to Creditors in Minneapolis–St. Paul,
1873–1874

$10,000–$99,999

$1,000–$9,999

$0–$999

Minneapolis

Milwaukee

Chicago

Omaha

Kansas City

St. Louis

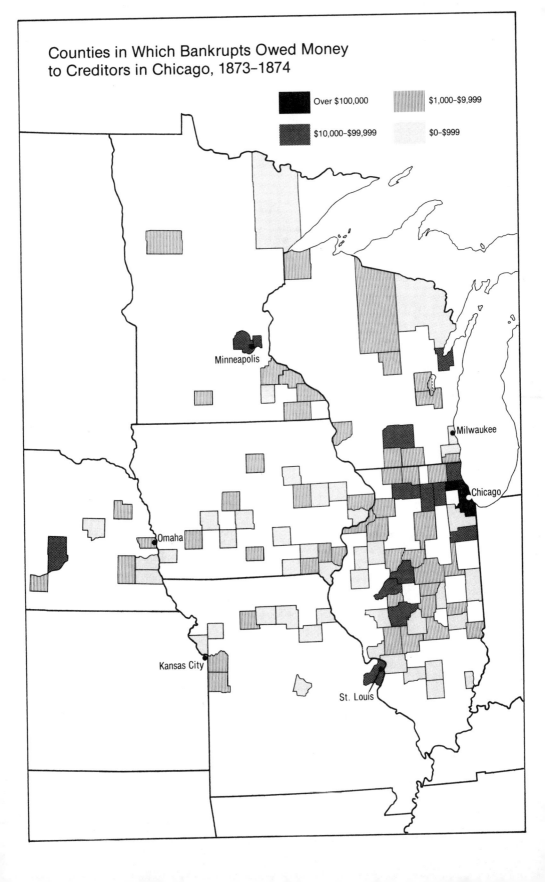

Counties in Which Bankrupts Owed Money
to Creditors in Chicago, 1873–1874

Over $100,000 $1,000–$9,999

$10,000–$99,999 $0–$999

Minneapolis

Milwaukee

Chicago

Omaha

Kansas City

St. Louis

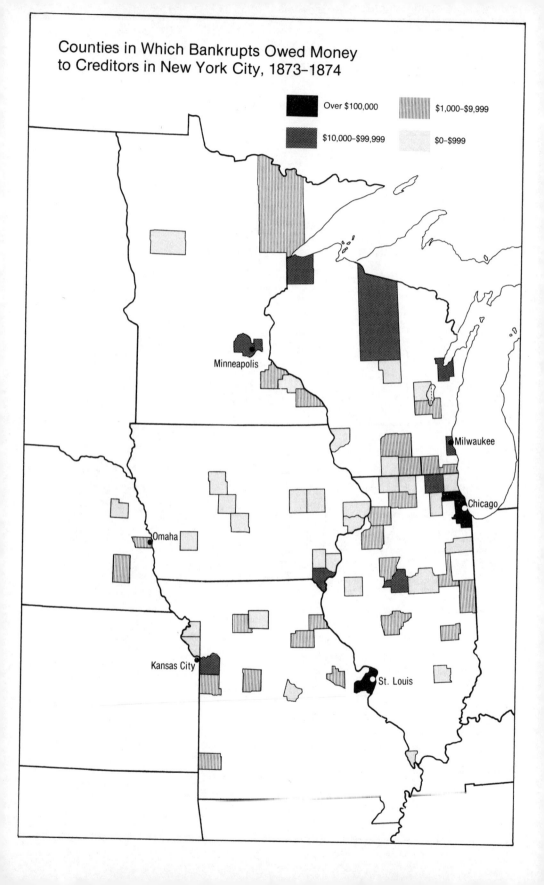

Counties in Which Bankrupts Owed Money
to Creditors in New York City, 1873–1874

Over $100,000 $1,000–$9,999

$10,000–$99,999 $0–$999

Minneapolis

Milwaukee

Chicago

Omaha

Kansas City

St. Louis

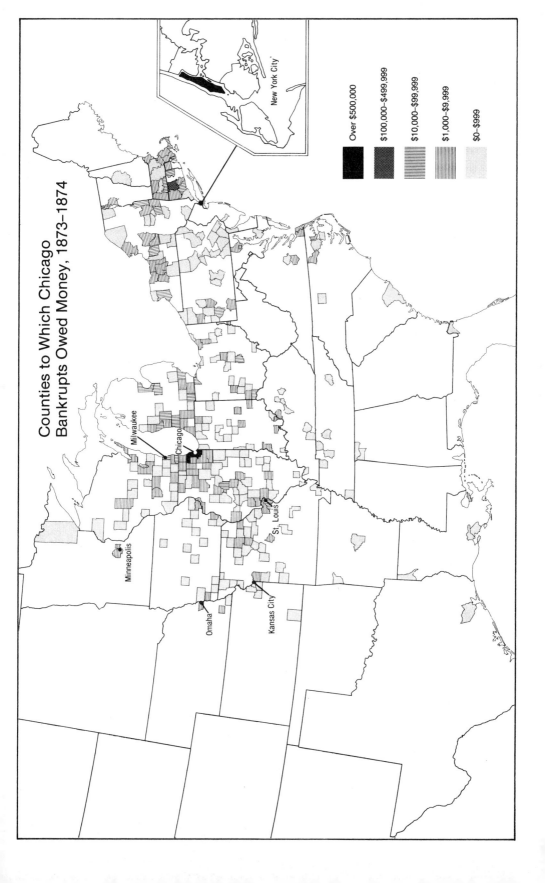

Counties to Which Chicago Bankrupts Owed Money, 1873–1874

New York City

Over $500,000

$100,000–$499,999

$10,000–$99,999

$1,000–$9,999

$0–$999

Milwaukee

Chicago

Minneapolis

St. Louis

Omaha

Kansas City

Contrast these places with Chicago. Significantly, Chicagoans appeared among the bankrupts who owed money to creditors in all three of these other cities, something that was true of no other place in the region. More important, Chicago's debt hinterland was more extensive, reaching farther to the west, than that of any other city. Although the densest concentration of bankrupt debt owed to Chicago creditors was in the region immediately adjacent to the city—in Chicago itself, as well as in northern Illinois, southern Wisconsin, and eastern Iowa—it reached all the way west to Nebraska and presumably well beyond.[33] Only one other city came close to Chicago as a creditor to midwestern bankrupts: New York. The striking overlap between the debt hinterlands of New York and Chicago suggests the extent to which the two cities acted in tandem as metropolitan centers for the region as a whole.[34]

Chicago's prolific connections to northeastern sources of capital reveal themselves most dramatically when one examines the city's debtor-creditor relationships from the opposite direction. If one maps the counties in the eastern United States in which creditors lived to whom Chicago's bankrupts owed money, one instantly sees that the city's most important extraregional trading partners were in New York, Massachusetts, and Pennsylvania, the most concentrated centers of wealth and power in the entire nation. By skillfully manipulating these special relationships, Chicago's merchants successfully placed themselves atop the urban hierarchy of their region.

Chicago's railroads and its unusual access to eastern capital were the foundations on which its citizens built its metropolitan status, but these advantages were accompanied by a host of subtler ones. Merchants doing business in Chicago benefited immensely from the mere fact of being located there. Because the city concentrated the demand of customers living in such a wide hinterland, one never had to look far to find a buyer or seller, no matter what merchandise one wished to handle. The same economic concentration that had allowed the city to develop daily cash markets in grain and lumber—markets that were unique in the nation—assured its merchants a steady and reliable demand for almost any product they might try to sell.

The hundreds of thousands of people who lived within the city created a huge retail demand quite apart from customers in the hinterland. A businessman said of Chicago, "Its own immense population, and the varied enterprises and industries within its own limits, create demand and supply for an inconceivable variety and quantity of wares and work."[35] Even the most ordinary clothing and foodstuffs found ready customers among the city's immigrants and factory workers, and there were also millionaires more than willing to pay steep prices for the rarest and most luxurious of specialty products. With high- and low-ranked goods equally easy to sell, no single product or activity dominated the local economy. Unlike lesser places that depended on a few staples for their livelihoods, the metropolis was comparatively immune to cyclical downturns in any one of its industries. "A city merchant, with an established business," explained a credit agent, "has fewer risks and interruptions to contend with, than where one industry is depended on for the support of the community where he is located."[36] Only the most general economic depression could seriously affect the overall trade of a city like Chicago.

With such diverse and concentrated markets came economic infrastructures that were entirely absent lower down the urban hierarchy. Almost any business could benefit from up-to-date information about its markets, and the more firms concentrated in a single location, the greater the demand for news and communication services. Merchants were willing to pay dearly for good intelligence about their customers or suppliers, and their combined expenditures produced economies of scale for those who made it their business to collect market news. As a result, the flux of commercial information at Chicago was better than almost anywhere else in the country. By 1891, the city had two dozen daily newspapers and well over three hundred other periodical publications. Many were specialized trade journals devoted to tracking market news for a single industry or wholesale sector. Magazines such as the *American Commercial Traveler,* the *Chicago Dry Goods Reporter,* the *Farm Implement News, Railway Age,* the *National Livestock Journal,* and the *Northwestern Lumberman* supplied commercial information to retailers and wholesalers throughout the city's hinterland. Chicago annually sent twenty million pounds of periodical literature through the mails, more than Boston, Cincinnati, New Orleans, Buffalo, and Baltimore combined.[37]

The geographic reach of the city's trade journals reflected the extent of its markets. Chicago wholesalers developed a habit of viewing the entire nation as their proper domain for doing business. "It is one of the peculiarities of Chicago," wrote a New York journalist in 1893,

> that one finds not only the capitalists but the storekeepers discussing the whole country with a familiarity as strange to a man from the Atlantic coast as Nebraska is strange to most Philadelphians or New-Yorkers. But the well-informed and "hustling" Chicagoan is familiar with the differing districts of the entire West, North, and South, with their crops, industries, wants, financial status, and means of intercommunication. As in London we find men whose business field is the world, so in Chicago we find the business men talking not of one section or of Europe, as is largely the case in New York, but discussing the affairs of the entire country. The figures which garnish their conversation are bewildering, but if they are analyzed,

or even comprehended, they will reveal to the listener how vast and how wealthy a region acknowledges Chicago as its market and its financial and trading centre.[38]

If one wanted to know where to buy or sell something—anything—one could find the answer more easily in Chicago than anywhere else in the Great West.

Chicago matched its concentration of commercial information with a comparable concentration of goods. No matter what the merchandise or commodities might be, Chicagoans traded them in immense quantities. In so doing, they achieved the same economies of scale that had allowed the elevator to revolutionize grain handling. Volume discounts on large purchases, favorable railroad rates, reduced handling expenses, the ability to warehouse large stocks in anticipation of customer's orders: these were all routine benefits of the city's wholesale trade.

The large number of wholesalers made it easy for local retail merchants to keep their shelves filled without having to warehouse a large overstock themselves. This in turn reduced their need for capital. "A retailer in Chicago," explained one businessman, ". . . can do a large business on a comparatively small capital. He is not required to carry stock beyond his daily or weekly wants. He can buy and sell, from 'hand to mouth,' and draw his supplies from the jobber, who practically answers the purpose of a warehouse."[39] This contrasted sharply with the owner of a general store at a remote rural location, who might only be able to reorder supplies every few months. Not knowing what customers would buy in the meantime, he or she would have to stock larger quantities of each item in a wide line of goods, tying up much more capital for an extended period. The same quantity of business in the more remote location might thus require two or three times the capital, and be that much less profitable as a result.[40]

In short, a Chicagoan could often do a greater volume of business with the same amount of money than a person in the same line of trade lower down the urban hierarchy. True, competition was fiercer in Chicago, certain costs (such as rents) were higher, and it was harder to gain an initial foothold in the market. But competition also helped keep prices down and made the city all the more attractive to customers, fueling its greater volume of trade. One could make up for lower prices and profit margins by turning over one's money more quickly. As long as one had the capital to hold one's own in the market, one could do quite well.

Here too Chicagoans benefited from the metropolitan infrastructure of their city's financial markets, which gave them easier access to credit, at better interest rates, than their hinterland counterparts. Not just banks but local merchants and wholesale suppliers were willing to extend credit to make a sale, which made it easier to leverage small amounts of capital for all they were worth. In places lower down the urban hierarchy, local sources of capital were often inadequate to finance business, so it was not unheard of for bankrupts to owe 80 or 90 percent of their debts outside the limits of their home county. The large share of debts that Chicago's bankrupts owed to other Chicagoans—58 percent, as opposed to only 34 percent for the region as a whole—suggests just how much the city's businesses were able to finance each other.

Moreover, compared with merchants in other locations, Chicagoans found it easier to gain access to eastern sources of credit as well. In counties throughout the Mississippi Valley, bankrupts owed an average of 27 percent of their debts to creditors living outside the region; for Chicagoans, on the other hand, extraregional debt amounted to 34 percent of their total. Much more impressively, 83 percent of Chicago's out-of-county debts were owed to creditors living entirely outside the region; the same figure averaged for counties in the Midwest as a whole was only 40 percent. This suggests that although Chicagoans could rely much more heavily than people elsewhere on local financing for their businesses, they were also more involved in interregional trade and finance. Among the city's bankrupts, even people of limited means managed to carry on regular business with customers and suppliers located hundreds of miles away.[41]

Gateway Rivalry: Chicago and St. Louis

The many advantages that merchants enjoyed by doing business in Chicago reflected its position atop the western hierarchy of cities. Once the city had developed the high-order wholesale trade and specialized economic functions that made it a regional metropolis, those functions reinforced each other and helped maintain its relative position. The more stable and self-sustaining the urban hierarchy became, the more inevitable it looked to people living within it—and to historians looking back on it. But it would be a mistake to believe that Chicago had *always* offered these advantages, or that there was anything "natural" about them. The hierarchy of cities revealed in bankruptcy maps from the early 1870s had only recently come into being, having replaced an earlier set of trade relationships that had existed long before the Civil War. Contrary to what central place theory might suggest, towns and cities did not occupy fixed positions in the rank ordering of regional markets but could shift dramatically as their circumstances changed. Even great regional centers could decline in rank, as happened to Cincinnati during the Civil War when Chicago surpassed it as a center of the pork-packing industry, and as happened again when Kansas City and Omaha emerged as regional meat-packing centers still farther to the west. The ranks and functions of any community could change, for the city system reflected the shifting geography of capital more than the underlying geography of nature.

No place better demonstrates this instability of the regional hierarchy than St. Louis.[42] Located at the confluence of the Missouri and Mississippi rivers, the city had been a major trade center for nearly three-quarters of a century before Chicago even became an incorporated town.[43] From the beginning, St. Louis established itself as the chief upriver trading partner of New Orleans, and by the 1820s had become a wholesaling center serving the growing frontier populations of Missouri, southern Illinois, and eastern Iowa. Its great fur-trading families organized a far-flung network of forts and rendezvous sites, stretching deep into the Rocky Mountains, primarily stocked and maintained by St. Louis merchants. In an era when all commodities moved by water, the city's broad levee served as a break-in-bulk point for goods traveling up and down the river, whether merchandise from the south and east or furs and agricultural commodities from the north and west. The Mississippi's shallow channel north of the city and its deeper one to the south meant that large steamboats coming upstream from New Orleans had to stop in St. Louis to transfer their contents into smaller boats that could continue upriver.[44] By the early 1840s, nearly the entire extraregional trade of the Missouri, Illinois, and upper Mississippi rivers passed through St. Louis.[45] Few in the city doubted that it was and would remain the chief metropolis of the midcontinent.

Then came the railroads, and Chicago's sudden rise: the story could hardly be more familiar, and is a case study in the ways capital can rearrange geography. First to reach the Mississippi was the Chicago, Alton, and St. Louis in 1852–53, which extended as far as Alton, on the eastern bank of the Mississippi about twenty miles upstream from St. Louis. It put Chicago and St. Louis in competition by rail without actually connecting them, encouraging the rivalry that had already become apparent with the opening of the Illinois and Michigan Canal in 1848. Alton was perfectly located to capture downstream traffic from the river and shunt it toward Lake Michigan before it could reach St. Louis—one reason why the road's owners were in no hurry to complete a connection to the river city.

The more important event was the arrival of the Chicago and Rock Island at the Mississippi in 1854, soon to be followed by several other roads in the next two years.[46] River travel upstream from St. Louis had always been troubled by two major rapids, one 200 miles above the city near Keokuk, Iowa, and the other 150 miles farther upstream at Rock Island. Between the two, the channel was filled with submerged rocks where ridges of hard limestone crossed beneath the river, making passage tricky for much of the way. Even shallow-draught steamboats had trouble navigating this stretch of river safely, and often had to unload their cargo onto flatboats to get it through. The result was much higher transport costs. To travel the 200 miles from St. Louis to the lower rapids, freight cost 10 to 15 cents per hundred pounds. For the next 150 miles between the two rapids, on the other hand, the charge was five times higher, from 50 to 75 cents per hundred pounds, and could even go as high as $1.50. These high steamboat rates added to the cost of any goods bought or sold along the river in Iowa and northern Illinois, putting the entire area at a serious competitive disadvantage.[47]

Small wonder, then, that upriver residents regarded the coming of the Chicago and Rock Island as a solution to their most serious transportation problem. Rather than face the risks and uncertainties of buying and selling via St. Louis and the river, they reoriented regional trade east, toward Chicago. The railroad spared them the danger of losing cargoes in the rapids, and avoided all the charges that accrued from loading and unloading goods on different vessels along the way. Much as the St. Louis levees were no match for Chicago's grain elevators, so did the usual advantages of rail over water transport—greater speed, more predictable schedules, and year-round movement even when rivers and lakes were frozen—pull other commodities in Chicago's direction as well.

The lake city's *Daily Democratic Press* described the festivities celebrating the Chicago and Rock Island's arrival at the Mississippi by noting,

> The faces of the men of business of the valley of the Upper Mississippi, who have heretofore looked Southward and downward, will now look upward and Eastward, and their affections are already turning from the mother city, St. Louis, to her glorious rival, Chicago. They will turn away from the former with many regrets. . . . But how can they resist it?[48]

How indeed? As railroads began to cross Iowa, and as farmers started shipping crops east, it made less and less sense to trade downriver. George Frazee, a customs agent at Burlington, put the point succinctly: "but little grain, once upon the cars, stops at the river. It goes direct to Chicago or farther east."[49] For St. Louis merchants accustomed to having the river sweep trade to their doors, this was hardly a happy change.

But transport technology alone does not fully explain the shifting importance of the two towns; the city system itself also played a key role. St. Louis had traditionally looked to New Orleans as its chief trading partner in the southward movement of agricultural produce, and (in addition to its trade with New York) had relied heavily on Philadelphia wholesalers for the merchandise it purchased from the East. Both these older cities were in relative decline by midcentury, and their competitive weakness did not help St. Louis in its rivalry with Chicago.

New Orleans was far from the centers of manufacturing and European trade that supplied the West with merchandise. The opening of a lake and rail route east from the upper Mississippi put it at a serious disadvantage, for the rail distance from Rock Island to New York was only a little more than the river distance to New Orleans. Any goods shipped from the East Coast via the mouth of the Mississippi had to make a sea journey of seventeen hundred miles before even beginning their trip up the river. Although shipping goods via this long water route was still considerably cheaper than sending them the shorter distance by rail, the much higher risks and low speed of travel more than made up the difference for merchandise of any value. Partly because of these problems, New Orleans remained much more heavily committed to export than to import, with a growing emphasis on cotton as its mainstay. The city was capital poor, its markets were undependable, and it had poor facilities for warehousing goods that passed through it. Produce and merchandise sat out on the levees for days at a time with no protection from weather or theft. As a wholesale center, New Orleans simply could not compete with cities in the Northeast. As long as there was no other outlet for the trade of the Mississippi, New Orleans (and with it St. Louis) could hardly fail to thrive; but when another route to a stronger market became available, the "natural" advantages that had once sustained the river cities would rapidly disappear.[50]

St. Louis's other major trading partner, Philadelphia, had declined relative to New York as a wholesaling center after 1820, in part because its economy shifted more toward manufacturing with the rise of the anthracite coalfields to its west.[51] Its earlier trade with the Mississippi Valley had involved shipping goods 240 miles overland to Pittsburgh, where they were loaded onto flatboats to float down the Ohio River, eventually reaching St. Louis via the Mississippi. The journey was slow, and the risk of damage along the way was high, but it was still the easiest route west until the opening of the Erie Canal. Philadelphia's harbor was much inferior to New York's, and its canal and railroad connections with the West could not compete with its northern neighbor's. Imports, and the wholesale demand they represented, concentrated more and more at the mouth of the Hudson, so St. Louis's old trading relationship with the City of Brotherly Love came to be less valuable than Chicago's new relationship with New York. As in the case of New Orleans, the fact that St. Louis's

chief supplier could not offer the best prices in the country did not matter
so long as no other city had access to trade with a more competitive
market. But the growth of Chicago's rail network provided just that competition, giving westerners sudden new access to the most attractive market in the East. Although St. Louis merchants could and did shift their
wholesale trade to New York, rail networks and rate structures put them
at a disadvantage relative to Chicago in trying to communicate with the
eastern metropolis.[52]

The river city's merchants were slow to recognize the threat these
various changes meant to their business. Long after the railroads started
shearing away its upriver hinterland, local boosters were still proclaiming
that the water-based "laws of trade" would guarantee the city's future. As
late as 1869, Logan Uriah Reavis was still intoning, "At least 10,000 miles
of navigable rivers bear their commerce in the interest of St. Louis. . . . No
inland place on the continent holds so favored a position. It is the great
point of radiation."[53] Focused as they were on the Mississippi River, defenders of St. Louis would lobby hard for the millions of federal dollars
that went into improving its channel during the nineteenth century.[54]

They also fought a rearguard action to prevent construction of new
obstacles to river navigation, among which, unsurprisingly, railroad
bridges were the most hated. In 1856, the Chicago and Rock Island became the first railroad to bridge the Mississippi. Although a steamboat
soon crashed against the supports and the owners sued the bridge company for damages, the courts refused to declare the bridge a hazard to
navigation.[55] Thereafter, the St. Louis Chamber of Commerce declared
war on any additional bridges over the river:

> If we are beaten in this suit, or abandon it, two years will not pass over our
> heads before we shall see the Mississippi bridged in at least three addi-
> tional places, and perhaps more. A half a dozen bridges in the rapid cur-
> rent and changing channel of this river, would render navigation ex-
> tremely hazardous, if not impracticable; and the commercial position of
> St. Louis, which is now the pride and boast of her citizens, would be
> counted among the things that were. The city always has been and must
> necessarily remain dependent upon her rivers for the bulk of her trade,
> and it well becomes her to watch with a jealous eye all attempts to en-
> croach thereon.[56]

The city's jealous eye proved inadequate to its task. Other Chicago-based
railroads soon joined the Rock Island in bridging the river—at Clinton in
1865 and at Burlington and Quincy in 1868—thereby drawing away more
commerce from west of the river.[57]

Finally, St. Louis sought to construct railroads of its own. Although its citizens lavished their most energetic efforts to promote a "Pacific Railroad" from St. Louis to San Francisco, the sectional deadlock in Congress during the 1850s prevented the line from obtaining the federal support it needed to succeed. St. Louisans projected several less ambitious railroads west from their city during the 1850s, but all ran into problems with weak financing and bad management. Presumably because eastern capitalists were concentrating their efforts farther north, they proved unwilling to invest the funds necessary to make St. Louis a major rail center. As a result, the great fan of railroads that drew so much western produce to Chicago never materialized at the river city.

The only really successful road constructed in Missouri during the 1850s was an exception to prove the bitter rule. The Hannibal and St. Joseph, completed in 1859, crossed the northern part of the state, its two terminal cities being located on the Mississippi and Missouri rivers. Its St. Louis supporters expected the road to draw agricultural produce from along the route and deliver it to the Mississippi, where it would then float downstream to St. Louis. Instead, the line soon came to be controlled by John Murray Forbes and his famous group of Boston and New York investors, who incorporated it into their system with the Michigan Central and the Chicago, Burlington and Quincy. Far from delivering produce to the St. Louis steamboats, it effectively sheared off the northern third of Missouri and added it to Chicago's hinterland. Worse, it gave Chicago its first rail link to the Missouri River, seriously hurting passenger steamboat traffic between St. Louis and St. Joseph. When the Hannibal and St. Joseph finally gained a bridge across the Mississippi at Quincy in 1868 (and access to Kansas City, with its Missouri River bridge, in 1869), the road's defection to Chicago was complete.[58]

On the other side of the Mississippi, the efforts of St. Louis boosters to establish eastern railroad connections for their city proved not much happier.[59] The first road to approach it from the east, the Chicago, Alton, and St. Louis, was so clearly directed toward Chicago that it dropped St. Louis from its name altogether in 1861 and became yet another of the lines that drew trade away from the river.[60] The Terre Haute and Alton, which might have supplied an eastern connection that did *not* pass through Chicago, had no line between Alton and St. Louis—and so it too pulled trade from the river. More promising was the Ohio and Mississippi Railroad, which was intended to connect St. Louis with Cincinnati. But between its end points, it passed through countryside distinguished mainly by its lack of commercial and urban development, so its traffic was initially too low for the road to turn a profit. It was finished with much fanfare in 1857, linking St. Louis with the eastern port city of Baltimore, but the timing of its completion could hardly have been worse. Caught in the panic of 1857, it went into receivership within the next year and was not successfully reorganized until 1859. Although it eventually became St. Louis's most important eastern rail connection, and crossed the Mississippi in 1874, it could not halt St. Louis's decline relative to Chicago.[61]

The clinching blow to the metropolitan dreams of St. Louis's citizens came with the Civil War and the blockade of New Orleans by Union forces in 1862. Just as Cincinnati's pork trade suffered during the war, so did all commerce between St. Louis and its usual outlet at the mouth of the Mississippi. "We in the North," wrote a visitor five years later, "can but faintly realize the desolation and misery of the war in Missouri and St. Louis. The blockade of the river reduced the whole business of the city to about one third its former amount. . . ."[62] With downstream demand drastically curtailed and the risk to waterborne commerce multiplied severalfold by military action, inhabitants of the upper river looked entirely toward Chicago for trade. Whether to meet the enormous demand of the Union army or to purchase goods from booming eastern wholesale centers, the commerce of the region turned ever more thoroughly away from its old channels. The war also broke the sectional deadlock in Congress, so federal funds finally went to a transcontinental railroad project, with Omaha its eastern terminus and Chicago—not St. Louis—its foremost beneficiary. One Iowan recalled that "the war, with its instant and complete diversion of trade," gave Chicago's commerce with the West "a wonderful impetus, and sustained it throughout. At the close of the war the direction of trade had become fixed, and Chicago had become the chief mart of the West, a position it is likely to sustain."[63]

By 1870, the river had reopened and St. Louis had regained much of its earlier trade. The city's boosters proclaimed as loudly as ever its natural superiority over Chicago, and continued to extract congressional appropriations for river improvements even as they finally gave in and constructed the great Eads Bridge across the Mississippi. In their hopeful eyes, none of the wartime changes seemed permanent or absolute. Indeed, a modern reader of the 1870 federal census might easily think that Chicago and St. Louis were still neck and neck in their race for metropolitan status: St. Louis County in that year reported a population of 351,189, while Chicago's Cook County trailed slightly with 349,966.[64] But these census figures obscure more than they reveal. It turns out that the citizens of St. Louis were so concerned about their city's reputation as a metropolis that they were not above tampering with evidence to the contrary. As one journalist later reported, "By a curious mistake in the census of 1870, or the act of enumerators driven to unscrupulous lengths by morbid ambition in the race with rivals, about 100,000 names too many were added to the [St. Louis] list."[65] Given the tainted census, we can never know for certain, but the Civil War decade saw Chicago much more than double its population, while St. Louis grew by perhaps only a third.

Both, of course, remained large, prosperous, and growing cities. St. Louis retained a substantial western hinterland, and could generally out-compete Chicago in the region to its southwest: southern and central Missouri, Arkansas, and much of Texas. (Ironically, its trade with this territory had nothing to do with rivers, depending instead almost entirely on rail transport.) The city's wholesale trade with the East grew during the 1870s because of its new rail connections until it finally became an active competitor with its old partner, New Orleans.[66] But its boosters' hope that it would become the great central metropolis was gone. In the upriver regions it had once easily dominated—the Mississippi north of Hannibal, the Missouri north of St. Joseph, and much of the broad swath of country north and west of Iowa to the Rocky Mountains—Chicagoans more or less controlled trade. Even in Kansas, Oklahoma, and the northern part of Texas, Chicago merchants could meet St. Louis prices on at least equal terms. Proof of this change came in the subtlest ways. Perhaps the most suggestive anecdote was that of a post–Civil War observer in Omaha. The Nebraska town had once been entirely dependent on St. Louis steamboat trade but was now on the direct rail line from Chicago to San Francisco. "The ancient store boxes in the cellar," this visitor wrote, "have 'St. Louis' stenciled on them; those on the pavement, 'Chicago.' " Without budging an inch, Omaha had shifted hinterlands. "Omaha eats Chicago groceries, wears Chicago dry goods, builds with Chicago lumber, and reads Chicago newspapers."[67]

Nineteenth-century Americans who sought to understand the relative decline of St. Louis had two favorite explanations, both of which have been repeatedly echoed by later historians. The most popular was that the city's leaders had been so complacent about their "natural advantages" that they failed to respond with sufficient energy to the danger represented by Chicago's railroads. Had they only possessed greater vision and entrepreneurial initiative, history might have turned out differently. Chicagoans had a special fondness for this argument, and so did St. Louisans who thought that jeremiads might rouse their fellow citizens to action before it was too late. A St. Louis newspaper in 1855 could lament,

> We in St. Louis are looking quietly on—relying on our past glory, as Virginians on illustrious ancestry—while new cities sustained by a new country, whose trade we ought to share threaten our preeminence. Last spring we spent a month in the Northwest. We found all through Wisconsin, Minnesota, and Iowa, the drummers and traders of Chicago. We can call to mind having met but one business man of St. Louis. We wait for the

apples to fall. Chicago picks all she can reach, and then shakes the tree for the balance.[68]

The other explanation was more generous to St. Louis egos, but offered even less solace about the future: the decline of St. Louis was inevitable. The same "natural advantages" that had once apparently destined the city for greatness now seemed just as bent on assuring its relative decline. "The men of St. Louis," wrote George Frazee in 1879, "may dream that the wealth of the Northwest will eventually pour into their city . . . but they are deceived. The laws of trade are against them."[69] Nature itself had proclaimed that lakes and rails were superior to rivers, and no mere human effort could resist the destiny they had proclaimed for Chicago.

In fact, neither of these explanations does justice to the complex changes occurring in the economies of the two cities. Whatever games St. Louisans might try to play with the 1870 census, the deeper reasons for their city's slowing growth and weakening trade are suggested in the regional bankruptcy maps of 1873–74. If one compares the map of Chicago's creditors with the same map for St. Louis, one instantly gets a clear sense of why the river city was failing to gain population as quickly as its rival on Lake Michigan. (For creditor counties of Chicago, see page 291.) The regional credit hinterland in which St. Louis's bankrupts did most of their business consisted principally of southern Illinois and central Missouri. Chicago's trade region, on the other hand, included these two areas in addition to the rest of Illinois, Wisconsin, Minnesota, Iowa, and the settled areas of the Great Plains, to say nothing of the widely scattered communities still farther west. As for the two cities' extraregional trading partners, both dealt heavily with New York City and New England, but Chicago's connections to the Northeast were much more extensive. St. Louis did more trade with the South, but that was hardly a promising foundation for urban growth in the post–Civil War world.

In aggregate terms, although Chicago's *population* in 1870 was at most a third larger than St. Louis's, its *credit,* as measured by the debts of its bankrupts in 1873–74, was more than two times greater. This general pattern is confirmed by statistics from the same period for Chicago's banks. In 1872, there were nineteen national banks in Chicago, compared with only eight in St. Louis. Although the Chicago banks' total capital was only a third greater than that of the St. Louis banks, the value of individual deposits in Chicago was $19,469,985—six and a half times larger than the deposits in St. Louis. Deposits by hinterland banks that relied on Chicago to handle their metropolitan financial services were three and a half times greater, $8,071,967. As a result, banking in Chicago was "done

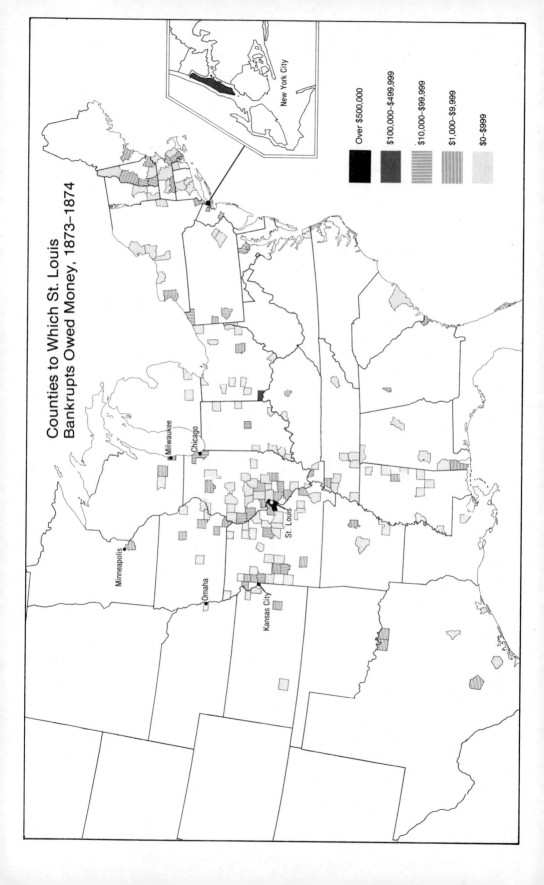

Counties to Which St. Louis
Bankrupts Owed Money, 1873–1874

New York City

Over $500,000

$100,000–$499,999

$10,000–$99,999

$1,000–$9,999

$0–$999

Minneapolis

Milwaukee

Chicago

Omaha

St. Louis

Kansas City

more largely on the capital of depositors than in other cities, except New York." Its ratio of deposits to capital—258 percent—was higher than for any other city in the country, again excepting only New York.[70] Whatever the city's population, or transport linkages, or natural advantages, the bottom line was that Chicago controlled and had access to more capital. That more than anything else placed it atop the regional system of cities.

What was already evident in the bankruptcies of 1873–74 became even more so as time went on. The most striking proof of Chicago's growing financial hinterland comes from the work of the geographer Michael Conzen, who has mapped regional banking linkages in the late nineteenth and early twentieth centuries.[71] No matter where in the country they were located, banks low in the nineteenth-century urban hierarchy had to establish "correspondent" relations with larger metropolitan banks in order to redeem banknotes, process out-of-town checks, gain access to credit, and perform any number of other financial functions. By the last quarter of the century, New York City was the undisputed banking center of the nation: in 1876, the first year for which records are available, 96 percent of the banks in major cities around the country kept deposits with correspondent banks in New York. But Chicago was quickly rising into an equally undisputed second place as a national financial center for other banks, even though banks in Boston and Philadelphia held much greater total assets. By 1881, nearly half the banks in the country's major cities were relying on Chicago banks for at least some of their correspondent work.[72] The First National Bank alone held the deposits of eighty national banks from fifteen states, and its larger competitor—the Union National, the records of which have not survived—probably had even more extensive regional dealings.[73] In 1884, a Chicago guidebook author could report, "Our banks are now depended on to a great extent to furnish Eastern exchange for other cities, and Chicago has become the recognized financial center of the West—bearing indeed the same relation to the West that New York does to the entire country."[74]

If one moves further down the urban hierarchy, the implications of these banking linkages for Chicago's regional hinterland become clearer still.[75] By looking at medium-sized cities that used Chicago banks for their principal correspondent relations, one discovers that Chicago's financial hinterland in 1881 extended from Cleveland in the east to Denver in the west. Three decades later, in 1910, it extended all the way west to Seattle, San Francisco, and Los Angeles. In contrast, St. Louis had a much humbler banking hinterland by the 1880s. The most important medium-sized city that depended on correspondent banks in St. Louis was St. Joseph, within the boundaries of the same state, and the rest of St. Louis's regional banking was with cities in Arkansas and east Texas.[76] The city that

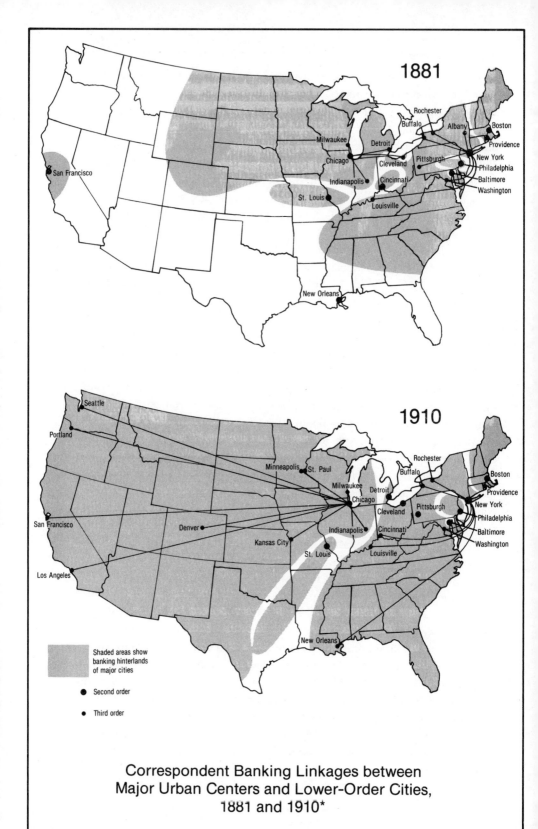

1881

Rochester
Buffalo
Milwaukee
Detroit
Albany
Boston
Chicago
Cleveland
Pittsburgh
Providence
San Francisco
Indianapolis
Cincinnati
New York
Philadelphia
St. Louis
Baltimore
Louisville
Washington

New Orleans

1910

Seattle
Portland
Minneapolis
St. Paul
Rochester
Buffalo
Boston
Milwaukee
Detroit
Chicago
Cleveland
Providence
San Francisco
Denver
Pittsburgh
New York
Indianapolis
Cincinnati
Philadelphia
Kansas City
Baltimore
St. Louis
Louisville
Washington
Los Angeles

New Orleans

Shaded areas show
banking hinterlands
of major cities

● Second order

• Third order

Correspondent Banking Linkages between
Major Urban Centers and Lower-Order Cities,
1881 and 1910*

*After Conzen, "Maturing Urban System in the United States," 1977.

had once looked upriver and toward the West for the sources of its metro-politan greatness had conceded the financing of both the upper Missis-sippi Valley and the Great West to its northern rival. In banking terms, all that remained of its once proud empire was the narrow band of three states running southwest toward the Rio Grande.[77]

In short, Chicago had taken over St. Louis's earlier role as gateway city to the West. From its founding in 1763 through its launching of the Lewis and Clark expedition and its monopolizing of the Missouri River fur trade, St. Louis had been the city that controlled all communication with the thinly populated river country to its north and west. Anyone and anything heading up the Mississippi or out across the northern plains had almost inevitably stopped at the city's levee on its journey. Now that role was gone, because the fastest and easiest route between east and west was no longer by water but by rail. The new gateway sat not at the confluence of rivers on the route to New Orleans but at the Lake Michigan railhead on the route to New York.

Gateway cities were a peculiar feature of North American frontier settlement. To return to the argument of the Canadian geographer A. F. Burghardt, they were not central places, and did not conform to the ex-pectations of central place theory that a metropolis should sit like von Thünen's isolated city at the center of a symmetrical network of medium- and low-ranked cities, towns, and farms.[78] Instead, the gateway served as the entrance and exit linking some large region with the rest of the world, and it therefore stood at one end—usually the eastern end—of a large tributary hinterland that had no other means of communication with the outside.[79] Often, as in the case of St. Louis and then Chicago, the gateway city's hinterland was extremely elongated, stretching hundreds and even thousands of miles to the west but a much shorter distance to the east. It was undoubtedly a metropolis, but there was nothing *central* about it.

Compared with that of a typical central place sharing its high rank, the gateway city's economy was much more committed to long-distance transportation and wholesaling, and for a simple reason: it was the princi-pal colonizing agent of the western landscape. The gateway city served as the go-between linking the settlements and natural resources of the Great West with the cities, factories, and commercial networks of the Northeast. On one side, westerners used it as the most effective way to gain access to the eastern markets that could transmute their land and labor into cash. On the other, eastern capitalists used it to design a system of transport and commerce that would concentrate western supply and demand—and profit—at their doorsteps. The two groups met at the gateway to do busi-ness, and so joined east and west in a single market system. The gateway metropolis represented a revolution in political economy, a complex transformation of culture, and an ecological watershed all at the same time.

As early as 1847—before the first iron rail had even been laid in Chicago—the booster Jesse Thomas had argued that eastern capital had a special interest in promoting Chicago's metropolitan status. "Inasmuch as Boston and New York," he wrote, "have a vital interest in directing business on to the lakes, to prevent it from taking a more Southerly direction to their rival cities Baltimore and Philadelphia, they cannot do otherwise than aid Chicago to the full extent of their ability, in stretching its iron arms in every direction, particularly to the South. . . ."[80] For just this reason, it had been the Bostonian John Murray Forbes who had gained control of the Hannibal and St. Joseph Railroad, thereby swinging northern Missouri into the orbit of Chicago and New York rather than St. Louis and Baltimore. St. Louis's troubles in trying to raise capital for its railroads were symptomatic of the weaker position of its eastern partners. Although the Baltimore and Ohio ultimately gave the city its access to the East (and Jay Gould later cobbled together a system linking it to New York as well), these roads were no match for those that linked Chicago to New York. A frontier gateway rose and fell on its relationship to the commercial centers that underwrote its growth, and by 1870 St. Louis was coming to the end of its frontier moment. Henceforth, it was one of the major interior cities of North America, a great central place in its own right, but it was never again a gateway in any but symbolic terms. The monumental arch that would eventually stand by the Mississippi to commemorate the city's historical relationship to the West expressed the nostalgic memory of a long-vanished era.

As for Chicago, by the 1870s it was approaching the climax of its own frontier moment as gateway to the West. After a careful investigation of the nation's internal commerce, the government economist Joseph Nimmo concluded about Chicago's hinterland that

> in the sense of being a primary market for the purchase and sale of agricultural products of the western and northwestern States and Territories, and for supplying general merchandise throughout this region, the range of the trade of Chicago embraces Illinois, Wisconsin, Northern Michigan, Iowa, Northern Missouri, Kansas, Nebraska, Colorado, the Territory of Dakota, the Indian Territory [Oklahoma], New Mexico, and the other Territories as far west as the eastern borders of the States of California and Oregon, an area constituting more than one-half of the territorial limits of the United States exclusive of Alaska.[81]

Chicago in no way had this territory to itself. Merchants from St. Louis, Milwaukee, Minneapolis, Kansas City, San Francisco, and the eastern port cities all contested it for the trade of western customers. But only New York competed so effectively over so wide an area. No other western city before or since has embraced such a large region as its gateway hinterland.

As the urban hierarchy west of Lake Michigan gradually filled out the system of central places, it in effect did so beneath Chicago. The city system of the Great West grew up in Chicago's shadow, with consequences too numerous to trace. When Kansas City and Omaha emerged as regional meat-packing centers competing with Chicago in purchasing and slaughtering western livestock, they did so under the corporate control of Chicago firms. Chicago companies would organize shipments of fruit from California to New York. Chicago banks would finance and oversee investments throughout the West.[82] But perhaps the most telling evidence of Chicago's western shadow was nearer to home: the state of Iowa never developed a regional metropolis of its own. A resident of Clinton, Iowa, could report in 1876 that the state had "no market-town for her surplus products," so that "the great bulk" went "to Chicago and to points farther east."[83] Chicago remains the chief metropolis of Iowa to this day. Just so did Chicago's gateway and city system leave a permanent imprint on the western landscape.

And yet the reshaping of that landscape was subtler still. The distribution of high- and low-ranked urban places was only one expression of the new market system that Chicago helped impose on the region to its west. Cities and towns were the empty vessels within which farmers, workers, merchants, and manufacturers did their business, whether in grain elevators, packing plants, or retail stores. The geography of capital expressed itself not just as these physical structures but as the ways people lived, worked, and traded within them. It *mattered* that residents of Omaha had relegated their old St. Louis crates to basements, and that so many of the barrels and boxes heaped on the city's sidewalks now had "Chicago" stenciled on their sides. To people in Omaha, those boxes were as much a part of the changing landscape as the system of cities that identified their town's position on the map. Beyond the maps of rank-ordered central places, after all, beyond the abstractions of capital and credit, were the ordinary markets of daily life, in which people went to town to buy the many things that merchants unpacked from many boxes piled up on many sidewalks. Those boxes were part of second nature too, and we would do well to have a closer look at their contents.

7

The Busy Hive

Reaping the Factory's Harvest

To understand the market, open the boxes: see the objects inside, then ask where they came from, who brought them here, who will buy them, and where they will go next. Follow the seller, follow the buyer.

Country folk sent grain, lumber, and livestock to Chicago, and received in return a nearly endless variety of merchandise. The exotic materials and manufactured goods they purchased with the produce of their land and labor came from all over the world, assembled by Chicago wholesalers for distribution to rural and small-town customers throughout the city's hinterland. This westward flow of merchandise complemented the stream of natural resources moving in the opposite direction. The Iowa farm family who raised corn for cattle purchased from Wyoming and who lived in a farmhouse made of Wisconsin pine clothed themselves with Mississippi cotton that Massachusetts factory workers had woven into fabric, worked their fields with a plow manufactured in Illinois from steel produced in Pennsylvania, and ended their Sunday meal by drinking Venezuelan coffee after enjoying an apple pie made on an Ohio stove from the fruit of a backyard orchard mixed with sugar from Cuba and cinnamon from Ceylon. These were all store-bought goods mingling ever more deeply with a homemade world, the endless small treasures with which the market rewarded those who labored in its service. In bringing these goods to rural communities throughout the Great West, merchants supplied the other side of the exchange relationship that drew so much western produce to Chicago, sustaining and motivating rural and urban production alike. The elaborate hierarchy of central places, from the largest metropolis down to the smallest town and most remote rural farm, existed largely to sustain this movement of goods and produce shuttling between city and country.

Chicago contributed to the flow of manufactured goods from a growing number of its own factories. In the beginning, Chicagoans simply processed hinterland resources, so the earliest industries included lumber milling, meat-packing, tanning, soapmaking, flour milling, and others.[1] Primary processing of this sort made good economic sense in the city because raw materials were abundant there, because such industries did not require complicated capital equipment, and because the large local labor pool made it easy to accommodate high turnover of unskilled workers. The demand for manufactured goods grew in tandem with local population and the extension of the city's hinterland, so factory workers became an ever larger share of Chicago's population. In 1860, they still constituted only 5 percent of the city's residents. A decade later, after the intense economic growth of the Civil War, their numbers had increased nearly sixfold and their share of the population had doubled, to 10 percent. By 1880, 15 percent of all people in Chicago labored in its factories. Many of the new industrial workers were themselves part of an extended rural–urban migration, having come to the city from countrysides as near as Illinois and as far away as Germany, Ireland, England, and Scandinavia.[2]

The period between 1860 and 1880 saw in Chicago, as in the rest of the Great Lakes region, the rise of a diversified secondary-manufacturing sector that did much more than just process natural resources. Factories in the region found it hard to compete with northeastern firms that had a head start in manufacturing high-value goods like textiles, but they could compete successfully if no eastern firms yet dominated the national market for a product. The population of the Ohio and Mississippi river valleys was now large enough to sustain a significant regional market in machine tools, hardware, furniture, agricultural implements, and other such products.[3] In the absence of serious eastern competition, midwestern firms got started successfully before entry into the national market for these goods became too difficult. Not all such firms were based in major cities, since factories often had less need for high-order urban services than did other businesses. But by 1880 Chicago had the largest industrial work force—over 75,000 people—west of the Appalachians.[4] In that year, its factories and shops produced nearly a quarter of a billion dollars worth of goods, including $85 million in meat-packing products, $19 million in clothing, $10 million in iron and steel, $9 million in foundry and machine shop products, $8 million in beer and liquor, $6 million in furniture, $6 million in printed matter, and $3 million in agricultural implements, to say nothing of many smaller product lines.[5]

The railroads supported Chicago's growth as a manufacturing center in much the same way that they supported every other aspect of the city's economy, giving factories the broad regional market that allowed them to expand and diversify. But Chicago manufacturers (like Chicago lumber merchants) derived at least one special benefit from a perennial problem that railroad managers faced in the city. Most agricultural produce moved from west to east. This meant that thousands of grain cars entered Chicago filled with wheat and corn, but had to go back empty—earning no return on invested capital—unless the railroads could find something else to fill them. Like lumber, factory products met that need nicely, and so Chicago firms often got such favorable rates that they could outcompete manufacturers elsewhere. "The *local* manufacturer," explained one non-Chicagoan, ". . . must have some very great advantages in location and materials peculiar to the local place to enable him to compete successfully against the allied advantages of cheap transportation and combined competition."[6]

One sure sign of Chicago's expanding industrial output was its growing demand for iron and steel. Railroad cars and rails, agricultural equipment, machine tools, wagons, hardware: all required iron, which people began to mine in the Upper Peninsula of Michigan during the 1840s and 1850s. The bulk of this Michigan ore initially traveled from the port towns of Marquette, on Lake Superior, and Escanaba, on Lake Michigan, to smelters in Cleveland, Ohio. But the distance from Escanaba to Cleveland was eight hundred miles; Chicago was five hundred miles closer. For the same reason that railroads offered favorable rates on shipments filling cars that might otherwise have traveled west empty, so did ships on Lake Michigan. Because ships moving west had more trouble filling their holds than ships moving east, ore going from Michigan to Chicago got better rates than ore headed in the opposite direction. Once Chicagoans recognized their advantage in obtaining ore via the lake, they began to consider building smelters of their own as an alternative to purchasing pig iron from Ohio and Pennsylvania. The only other thing they needed to start smelting was a cheap source of coal, which by the 1860s was becoming available by rail in large quantities from mines in southern Illinois. And so, in 1868, the Chicago Iron Ore Company began manufacturing the city's first pig iron.[7] By 1880, ten other firms had joined it, employing nearly three thousand workers to produce over $10 million worth of iron and steel.[8] Chicago thereby gained yet another set of supply hinterlands, receiving Illinois coal and Michigan iron ore at smelters that in turn sold pig iron to factories throughout the city.

Among those factories, probably the most famous was the McCormick reaper works, which can serve as a case study in the growth of Chicago industry and the sale of manufactured goods to hinterland customers. Cyrus McCormick invented his first reaper to mechanize grain harvesting in his home state of Virginia in 1831.[9] He realized by the mid-1840s, however, that the best market for his invention lay beyond the Appalachians, among the prairie farmers who were producing a growing share of the nation's wheat output. He therefore decided to move his manufacturing operations west, where he would be nearer to his potential customers, and so built a factory in Chicago in 1847.[10] Why he chose Chicago remains something of a mystery—other western cities in Pennsylvania and Ohio had much better manufacturing facilities—but whether by luck or shrewd booster logic, his timing could not have been better. The next year saw the city acquire its first canal, railroad, telegraph, stockyard, and grain elevator, and its Board of Trade.[11] McCormick successfully manufactured 450 reapers in his first year of production; within two years, that number had tripled. He found enthusiastic customers among the farmers in Chicago's immediate hinterland, where the flatness of the local terrain and the size of its checkerboard fields made the machine more attractive to farmers than it had been in the East. Prairie farmers also saw it as a solution to the high labor costs they regularly faced during harvest season.[12]

Still, farmers' adoption of the reaper was hardly automatic, for McCormick's early designs had serious flaws.[13] Grain too easily jammed the cutting blades until a divider was added to separate stalks as they entered the machine. The cutting bar had to undergo several changes before it became truly efficient and could be used for mowing as well as reaping. The wheat cut by McCormick's earliest reapers fell onto a platform, and a laborer walking beside had to rake it off by hand. Adding a chair for this person (and one for the driver as well) increased productivity, and helped persuade more farmers to buy the machine. Not until all these changes were perfected in the mid-1850s did acceptance of McCormick's reaper become more widespread. Future improvements—self-rakers, automatic twine binders, and eventually wire binders—would enlarge the market still further.

Technical improvements were only part of the story, however, for McCormick faced the same marketing problems as any other Chicagoan trying to sell urban goods to hinterland customers. Although he operated a factory, he was at least as much a merchant as a manufacturer.[14] Farmers had no experience with mechanical harvesting, and so had little idea that they even needed a reaper, let alone how they should use it. This machine that no one had ever heard of cost well over $100, placing it among the most expensive items other than land or buildings that a farm family could buy. Reapers were so costly that ordinary dealers in agricultural implements had trouble keeping even one of them in stock, so McCormick could not count on existing wholesale-retail channels to distribute his product. He would have to market it himself. At the same time, he had to grapple with the problem that faced all wholesalers and manufacturers who sold large, expensive products to customers of modest means: how to get people to spend more money than they ordinarily possessed. McCormick's responses to these many challenges suggest the directions in which Chicago merchandising evolved over the next half century, anticipating challenges that the city's meat-packers, lumber wholesalers, and other merchants would confront in the future.

He solved his educational problem with advertising.[15] He ran long ads in the nation's leading agricultural periodicals, filled with testimonials from happy customers whose lives had been changed by the new machine. He usually illustrated the text with a carefully labeled woodcut so that farmers could get an idea of how the new invention worked. He arranged for his reapers to appear at county and state fairs, often in competitive field trials with products of other manufacturers to add some excitement for onlookers who might not realize they were viewing a salesman's demonstration. "To sell," McCormick declared, "I must advertise," and his advertising campaigns became a tool for educating members of a broad rural public about the wondrous new technology spewing forth from the firm's Chicago factory.[16]

McCormick next faced the task of obtaining orders for these machines in rural communities. Toward that end, he began in the 1840s and 1850s to commission agents who would handle reaper sales in small towns throughout the region. Their names figured prominently in the company's advertisements so that potential customers would know whom to contact about purchasing a reaper in their area. Early each year, McCormick sent his agents a sample reaper from the new line, which they could move to different communities and display at county fairs or in courthouse squares, often next to the products of competing manufacturers. (Agents eventually operated "machinery halls"—showrooms—where farmers could examine equipment before placing their orders.) In return for handling retail distribution, agents received several benefits: exclusive sales rights to a well-defined area, discounts ranging from 10 to 15 percent of the retail price, and small advance payments to defray advertising costs.[17] Agents learned how to assemble and repair any equipment they received. They dealt in spare parts, taught farmers how to use the machines, handled orders, arranged credit, and were responsible for all collections. They were in effect the front guard of a carefully planned campaign to introduce mechanization to American farming.[18]

To solve the perennial problem of how to sell expensive equipment to cash-poor retail customers, McCormick arranged for agents to make sales on credit to farmers who placed an order. In 1849, for instance, he offered a reaper for $115 to anyone who could pay cash, or for $120 to those who put $30 down and paid 6 percent interest.[19] Payment was due on December 1, just after the peak of the harvest, when farmers had more cash on hand than at any other time of year. As in all lines of western commerce, a willingness to extend credit to his customers was essential to McCormick's success in the new reaper trade.

There was one final problem. The reaper was a large, heavy piece of equipment. Even when shipped in pieces, it was still expensive to move. Shipping it any considerable distance by wagon was prohibitively expensive, so the availability of cheap transportation was essential to developing a large regional and national market for the reaper. When McCormick opened his factory, there were still no railroads anywhere near Chicago, and even in 1850 the city's sole line reached only a few dozen miles into the Illinois countryside. McCormick's earliest sales network therefore had to rely on water. If one examines a map of the firm's sales in 1850, one sees that the heaviest concentrations of reaper purchases were around Chicago, and in the more densely settled agricultural areas of St. Louis's upriver hinterland, in counties lining the Illinois and Mississippi rivers.[20] McCormick shipped his reapers out on the Illinois and Michigan Canal, and agents arranged for delivery from canal and river towns to customers' farms.

As one might expect, the upsurge in the company's business came after 1854, when the railroads west of Chicago reached and then crossed the Mississippi River. The technical and marketing apparatus McCormick had organized—the improvements on his basic invention, the advertising campaigns, the agency contracts, the arrangements for sale on credit—suddenly bore fruit with the extension of Chicago's rail hinterland. The McCormick factory's sales rose to over two thousand for the first time in 1855, and to nearly four thousand just one year later.[21] By 1860, sales showed a striking geographical reorientation.[22] No longer were the counties with heaviest reaper purchases located along the canal or the river. Instead, they followed the routes of Chicago's railroads so precisely that one can almost trace rail lines by connecting counties with maximum purchases. Demand in these areas of rapid settlement was so intense that the company's sales enjoyed nearly uninterrupted growth in the decade following 1851. Even the serious economic depression after 1857

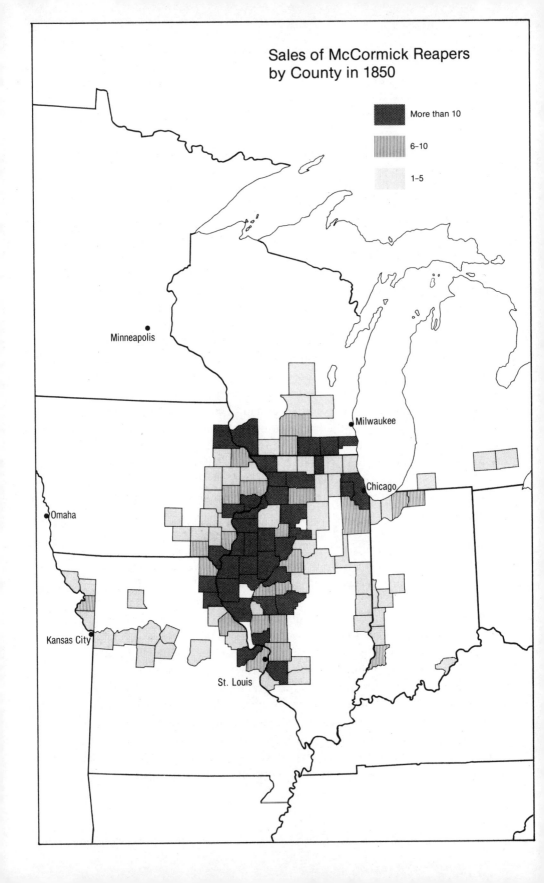

Sales of McCormick Reapers
by County in 1850

More than 10

6–10

1–5

Minneapolis

Milwaukee

Chicago

Omaha

Kansas City

St. Louis

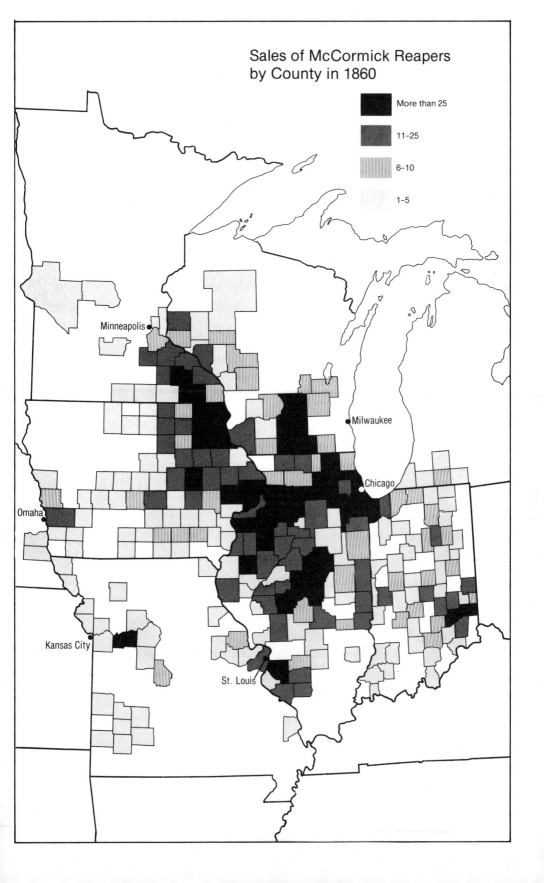

Sales of McCormick Reapers
by County in 1860

More than 25

11–25

6–10

1–5

Minneapolis

Milwaukee

Chicago

Omaha

Kansas City

St. Louis

brought only one year in which sales fell, and then only by 2 percent—
minuscule when compared with the catastrophic declines that hit other
businesses. By 1860, farmers had apparently decided that the machine
from McCormick's urban factory had become almost a necessity of rural
life.[23]

The Merchant's World: Prerailroad

McCormick's success in persuading his customers that modern farming depended on his invention was typical of the era. The marketing
institutions he developed during the 1850s were widely adopted by merchants and manufacturers in many lines of business, so a new culture of
buying and selling emerged simultaneously with the growth of Chicago
and its hinterland. The city system that arrayed towns and farms in rank
order beneath the young western metropolis came to be matched by an
equally hierarchical set of arrangements for wholesaling and retailing the
products that moved back and forth between city and country. Of all the
many revolutions that marked nineteenth-century life, none was more
pervasive than this. By using speed to lower the cost of space, the new
technology of rail transportation made it possible for urban markets to
extend their reach not just geographically and economically but culturally
as well. Just so did McCormick cast his net of agents across the western
landscape and flood the western mails with advertisements educating
rural citizens about the new laborsaving devices that would make life on
the farm every bit as "modern" as life in a city like Chicago. The lessons
of the urban market were about *newness*. The merchandise one could buy
was new, the way one bought it was new, the life one could live with it was
new. Buying from the city meant participating in the progress of the age.
It meant becoming modern.

To see how much life had changed, reflect back on what it was like to
be a merchant in, say, Iowa, before Chicago extended its hinterland as far
as the Mississippi River. Consider, for instance, John McDowell Burrows
of Davenport, who has already turned up several times in these pages.
Burrows came to Iowa from Cincinnati in 1838 to set up shop as a grocer.
His memoirs, written half a century later, supply a vivid portrait of a
frontier merchant's activities, and offer a baseline against which to measure the changes emanating from Chicago and other urban markets with
the extension of the railroads.[24] Living in a thinly settled district that was
linked to larger urban markets—principally St. Louis and New Orleans—
mainly by water, he faced all the usual problems of a prerail economy. His
rural customers usually had little or no money. When they came to his

store to buy merchandise, they rarely had cash to offer. Instead, they brought with them the produce of their farms—sacks of wheat or corn, frozen hog carcasses, potatoes, onions, eggs, butter, anything that might be of value—and expected to purchase groceries, dry goods, and hardware in return. If Burrows wanted their trade, he had to be willing to take what they offered, even if he wasn't sure "what . . . to do with the produce." Some merchants tried to avoid dealing in such things, but Burrows believed that they came with the territory. "I felt," he wrote, "that this country had to be settled up, and to accomplish this, some one must buy the farmers' surplus, or it would remain a wilderness."[25]

Because his customers were so cash poor, Burrows found himself playing two roles that in the modern economy are generally quite distinct. On the one hand, he regularly purchased a full line of merchandise from wholesalers in St. Louis, Philadelphia, and elsewhere, to be marked up and sold at retail to his customers. On the other hand, he also became a produce merchant, buying a wide range of farm commodities and shipping them downriver to urban markets.[26] Burrows handled one group of products as a seller and another as a buyer. In this way, he acquired the cash and credit he needed to purchase more merchandise and begin the cycle again. The concrete consequence of living at the bottom of a poorly developed central place hierarchy, in other words, was that frontier merchants could rarely afford to specialize. Instead, they had to be generalists, often operating on both sides of the market.

Their reward for so doing was to attract heavy trade from a wide rural clientele, so that a store frequently had to stay open very late to handle all its customers. Burrows described how farmers from several surrounding counties traveled nearly a full day to be able to buy and sell at Davenport. "Our store," he reported,

> was well patronized, and we hardly ever closed it until midnight. In the forenoons, the farmers in our county, from the Groves and points within a circuit of ten or fifteen miles, would come in with their grain, etc., and by the time they had unloaded and done their trading, another section would begin to arrive from Clinton and Cedar Counties and the territory still farther distant—a big day's travel—and would not all get in until near bedtime. They wanted to unload and do their trading, so as to start home early next morning, that they might reach home the same day. This made our business very laborious.[27]

Farmers sold their crops to Burrows because they lacked the time, inclination, and money to market produce themselves. Steamboat service was infrequent and expensive, and shipping goods by flatboat often meant building the boat oneself—not cheap either, and a lot of work.

Always there was the threat that shipments might be lost in a wreck, bringing financial ruin to anyone unprepared to absorb such a catastrophe. Although farmers might have valuable crops to sell, getting them to market was so difficult and expensive that it was often hard to find a buyer. And so the residents of Davenport's hinterland turned to Burrows, who made it his special business to find buyers. He and other frontier merchants had literally to *create* markets where otherwise there would have been none. Doing so was a tricky proposition that required a lot of capital and not a little luck, but there was money to be made by those who could stomach the risks.

Looking back on his ventures of the 1840s, Burrows emphasized how much of his time he had devoted solely to finding a market for the goods he needed to sell. "My great trouble," he wrote, "was to know where to place the products. There was no Chicago then, not much of a market in St. Louis, and I had to make frequent trips to every landing north of Davenport as far as Fort Snelling," where the army post at what is now St. Paul—three hundred miles north—was one of the few reliable purchasers of farm produce.[28] Burrows's earliest customers were primarily soldiers, fur traders, and steamboat captains, scattered up and down the length of the Mississippi between St. Louis and St. Paul. Each was in some way the emissary of a distant urban market. Whether produce was purchased with the salaries and food budgets of the War Department, with the expense accounts of large corporations like the American Fur Company, or with the tickets of immigrants and travelers spending their savings on river journeys, each represented an influx of money from remote cities like Washington or New York. Capital flowed from the urban hierarchy. Income from such sources was crucial in sustaining a merchant's business, and in enabling farm families to participate in a cash economy beyond the limits of their own subsistence production.

One of a merchant's biggest problems was getting good information about supply and demand along the river. Market news moved only as quickly as a steamboat or a person on horseback, so word of someone's need for produce might take days or weeks to reach a potential seller. "We have a great demand here for Eggs," wrote a storekeeper in Illinois to a merchant in Iowa, "and hear that there are plenty of them in your place, and request you, to send us 5 or 6 Barrels of them immediately. . . ." (Remembering the risk in such a shipment, he also thought to add, "But you must pack them in plenty of oats, for which you may charge us.")[29] There was good money in such a letter, but only if one could get the eggs to their would-be buyer before anyone else. All too often, a merchant went to great expense to send goods in the direction of a recent rumor, only to find the market glutted by the time they arrived. Burrows's ill-fated shipment of potatoes to New Orleans—which brought only eight cents a bushel instead of the $2.00 he had expected—was hardly a unique occurrence.[30] In 1842, a would-be competitor arrived in Davenport and announced on the basis of recent market news that he would pay double Burrows's price to any farmer who would sell him onions. The result was an enormous heap of the pungent vegetables, so glutting the market that they eventually had to be abandoned, and were eaten by cows. The investment was completely wasted—and it spoiled Davenport's milk besides![31]

But the biggest challenge of being a frontier merchant was undoubtedly the winter. The seasonal cycle that froze rivers and closed down the regional transportation system for almost half the year affected nearly every aspect of a storekeeper's business. The problem with winter was not just that customers had difficulty coming to town, or that merchants could not reach distant wholesalers to restock goods when they sold out.[32] Much more troublesome was the freezing up of the cash economy. The only way a frontier area acquired money—whether in the form of gold, silver, or banknotes—was to send something to the outside world for which the outside world was willing to pay. Winter prevented this from happening. Worse, the greatest surge of agricultural products came to market just as the rivers were becoming dangerous to travel, which meant that a merchant who bought them would almost certainly have to store them through the winter. At the very moment when trade was about to slow nearly to a standstill and prospects for sales were at their worst, merchants had to pay out a large share of their capital to purchase the harvest from farmers in their neighborhood. Then, for the rest of the winter, they sold merchandise on credit to those same farmers, who had spent all their cash on fall supplies and mortgage payments. Burrows's situation as the weather began to warm in 1841 was familiar to all his fellow merchants. "I found my means," he wrote, "all locked up in produce—corn, flour, pork, bacon, etc.,—and that it would be necessary for me to realize on a good portion of my stock early, in order to replenish my store."[33] Burrows's phrase captures the problem perfectly: winter *locked up* capital.

The seasonal cycling of the economy, along with the slowness of travel, meant that frontier merchants had to be prepared to handle large surges of income and expenses. Boom and bust were their normal mode of operation. Since they made money mainly by turning over their capital as produce, cash, and merchandise, they needed a large enough means to absorb the heavy risks of such transactions. The cost of travel in time and money, and the big expense involved in laying up a stock of merchandise, meant that they could afford to make only one or two large buying trips

each year. Frontier merchants journeyed for well over a month to Philadelphia and New York, guessing all the while about what their customers
might be willing to buy in the next year, and then spent as much as they
could afford on supplies. Because they purchased so much merchandise
at once, and because they had to hold such large quantities of farm produce during the winter, they also had to devote a lot of capital just to
warehousing their stock. Storage facilities were among their most significant costs of doing business. During a big harvest, a merchant could easily
overflow his warehouse capacity. As we have seen, Burrows was known to
commandeer basements and sheds all over Davenport just to hold his
purchases until the river thawed.[34]

Finally, there was the cost of money. Because merchants were the
people who linked frontier areas with the larger cash economy, they
needed access to some form of money in the outside world. This could
take many forms. Best of all was cash itself—real gold and silver—but that
was extremely hard to find in most western communities outside the mining districts. Next best were banknotes—checks drawn on a bank that
promised payment in gold or silver to anyone who submitted them. Since
nineteenth-century America had no national currency guaranteed by the
federal government, these were the best available form of paper money.
Not all banknotes were of equal value, though, since many banks, especially in the West, issued far more of them than they could ever redeem.[35]
Worse still were the all-too-common counterfeit notes. Most banknotes
circulated at a discount from their face value, so a merchant taking them
as payment had to know the proper discount before accepting them. (One
learned such information from regular bulletins called "counterfeit de-
tectors," which published discount rates for all the common notes in
circulation.) Unsurprisingly, the most trustworthy banknotes came from
major metropolitan banks of unimpeachable soundness, but these were
often almost as rare as cash in western locales.[36] Merchants had to make a
special effort to acquire metropolitan notes, paying out heavily discounted western bills to acquire money that distant suppliers would be
willing to accept. "New York Exchange" was the phrase merchants used
for notes that could circulate anywhere; by the 1860s, they held "Chicago
Exchange" in equally high regard.[37]

But there was a simpler way to solve the problem of frontier money
shortages: credit. If one could form an alliance with a merchant in some
nonfrontier location, preferably a metropolitan center, it became possible to draw a check on that merchant's bank account without having to
use regular banknotes at all. One could buy and sell entirely on account.
Burrows's whole operation got its start and was sustained in just this way.
When he first moved to Davenport, his capital consisted of a large stock of

groceries and dry goods that he had on loan from his cousin John, one of Cincinnati's largest wholesale grocers.[38] Burrows eventually went on to establish a regular working relationship with the wholesale firm of Henning and Woodruff in St. Louis. It in turn was linked to John O. Woodruff and Company in New Orleans and to James E. Woodruff and Company of New York. Family networks of this kind were endemic to early American wholesaling, because the success of long-distance trade depended so heavily on being able to trust one's partners and associates even when they were far away. Merchants could often trust their own kin more readily than anyone else, but long-standing business relationships also became a basis for trust, enabling a hinterland merchant like Burrows to draw on large stores of urban capital from the Woodruffs whenever he needed to buy or sell goods in metropolitan markets. In return, Burrows agreed to trade primarily with the wholesalers who underwrote his business. On at least one occasion, the only thing standing between him and bankruptcy was the willingness of the Woodruffs to extend liberal credit when all other sources of income had failed him.[39]

Without credit, frontier economies would quickly have collapsed. Communities typically had so little cash that even local banks could run out of money, as happened when Davenport's banker told Burrows that the merchant's heavy produce buying had nearly broken the bank. "We are cleaned out," he announced. "We could not pay for your checks another day to save our lives." Burrows's solution was to start issuing notes on his own behalf, with a promise to redeem them for currency the next April or for merchandise in the store whenever the customer pleased.[40] Such was the heavily leveraged world of frontier exchange. Everyone owed money to everyone else, and for much of the year the only way to sell anything at all was to do so "on time." It was little wonder that frontier interest rates were so high. Urban banks and wholesalers lent their credit to small-town merchants, and they in turn lent merchandise to their rural customers. The farmers, Burrows reported, "used all the money they could get hold of, to break, fence, and stock their farms, spending as little as they could with the merchant, and what trading they did was generally on a year's credit."[41]

It was a risky world, with bankruptcy or foreclosure lurking around every corner. The letter that a worried farmer sent another Iowa merchant during the hard times of 1858 captures the underlying anxiety of the economy perfectly:

Dear sir
i suppose that you are in grate need of your money i have been trying my
very best to get it for you i have some eight five dollars due me now i have

been trying all day to day and did not get one five center i have my wheat on hands yet, i am going to set for something as soon as posable and pay up if I can dont put me to any cost you shant loos any thing by me i will pay all as fast as I can times are very hard but you know that. . . .[42]

Letters in the opposite direction—from creditors trying to extract payment from tardy debtors—were rarely so sympathetic, but the problems they described were no less real or serious. "We dislike to crowd you very much," wrote a St. Joseph wholesaler to a hardware dealer in Lincoln, Nebraska, "but our obligations the next week are particularly heavy and we shall need every available cent. We shall have to ask you to help us out to the amount of 300.00."[43]

This, then, was the world of money, credit, and merchandise—of capital—that existed in the upriver hinterland of St. Louis during the 1830s, 1840s, and 1850s. In it, one sees concretely what it was like to live and trade within the nascent urban hierarchy of the prerailroad Mississippi Valley. In a landscape of scattered settlements, markets were few and far between. They sprang up wherever a merchant succeeded in linking a producer of farm crops with a seller of manufactured goods—and disappeared just as quickly. They were completely unreliable. Buyer and seller often failed to find each other. One never knew how prices might change from day to day, because there was no quick way of knowing the condition of markets in other parts of the country. Cash was always in short supply, especially during the winter months when everything—river, farms, stores, trade—froze beneath the blanket of cold. Those who could survive under these circumstances—farmers and merchants alike—needed lots of credit from anyone willing to lend it to them. Merchants had to buy their stock months in advance, hoping that they could anticipate their customers' needs because eastern visits to suppliers happened so rarely. Once purchased, goods had to be held in warehouses for months at a time, locking up capital and preventing it from earning any interest during the long winter wait. For their part, farmers paid heavily for the inefficiency of the system that brought their goods to market, and lived on credit from harvest to harvest as they tried to scrape together the funds to pay off a mortgage. It was not an easy place for anyone to earn a living.

The Merchant's World: Postrailroad

Such was frontier Iowa—and at one time or another every other part of the Great West—as it existed in 1854 when the Chicago and Rock

Island Railroad finally pushed its way to the Illinois side of the Mississippi opposite Davenport. The immediate implications of the rails pointing back toward the eastern horizon should by now be so familiar that they barely need repeating. The railroad meant speed. It meant regular, predictable schedules. It meant year-round movement, even in winter. It meant escaping the river. It meant the East, and not the South. It meant Chicago, and not St. Louis. It meant the future.

Most people welcomed the new technology almost as a savior, but for some it was an ill wind. Not just the merchants of St. Louis worried about what it might do to their business. Even Chicago retailers had initially been nervous that "the Railroad would ruin Chicago, because it would destroy all the team and retail trade of the city and transfer it to the country." Some storekeepers had even circulated a petition calling for limits on railroad expansion.[44] Laughable as this idea might seem in retrospect, it was not without foundation. Chicago's retail trade *did* suffer in the immediate wake of the railroads as area farmers stopped having to make the same long trips that Burrows's customers made to reach Davenport.[45] The railroad *did* eventually destroy the horse team trade. Indeed, the coming of the Chicago and Rock Island was not good news for John Burrows, for it meant the end of the way of doing business on which he had built his life and fortune. To understand what finally happened to Burrows, one must look at the railroad yet again, this time through the eyes of those who had lived in the frontier world that preceded its coming.

By lowering the cost of travel—reducing the time spent moving through space—the railroad brought country and city closer together. It elaborated the urban hierarchy by proliferating towns and villages beneath the emerging metropolis of Chicago, but also brought the layers of that hierarchy closer together. It had once taken Burrows several days to make the round-trip between Davenport and St. Louis. Now he could reach Chicago in a little over eight hours.[46] Moreover, he could find in that city most of the same goods that had once required a journey of many weeks for a Mississippi River merchant to purchase on the East Coast. No longer did buying trips have to be an annual affair. No longer did one have to purchase all one's stock in a single expedition that tied up most of one's capital for the rest of the year. Merchants did not have to buy such large quantities when they could travel frequently to the wholesaling center that supplied them. On the railroad, they could travel to the city once or twice a month, refilling their store shelves whenever goods sold out. This afforded the great advantage of cycling capital more quickly: instead of tying up $10,000 in merchandise for six months or a year, one could turn over $1,000 ten times in the same period and perhaps earn just as much profit. One could carry smaller quantities of a larger variety of goods, knowing that one could replenish any popular item simply by placing an order to Chicago.[47]

The same was true on the other side of the business for produce merchants who purchased crops from farmers. The availability of rail transport, and the existence of a reliable cash market in Chicago, meant that merchants did not have to invest nearly so much money in the warehouse facilities they had formerly needed to hold the harvest until spring. Railroad cars could serve as warehouses of a sort, and the enormous grain elevators and packing plants in Chicago also removed some storage burdens from smaller towns. Crucially, this allowed people of much more limited means to contemplate becoming merchants. Advantages that had once accrued mainly to retailers in metropolitan wholesaling centers like Chicago now became available lower down the urban hierarchy. As one Iowan reported, Chicago gave the frontier merchant "a market that can be relied upon, easily reached, and from which rapid returns are made to the seller, thus enabling him to do a large amount of business on a small capital."[48]

With the railroad—and the access it gave to Chicago—one needed neither as much wealth nor as much credit to be as successful as Burrows had been in frontier Davenport. For Burrows, this was a disaster. Long accustomed to dominating the Davenport market, he suddenly found himself confronted with intense new competition from small dealers with much less money. The warehouse facilities that a few years before had enabled him to handle large quantities of agricultural produce now became a serious disadvantage, tying up his money while competitors without such investments could devote all their capital to buying and selling goods. "The opening of the Chicago & Rock Island Railroad," Burrows recalled, "rather bewildered me." With its arrival, produce merchants suddenly became "as thick as potato-bugs." Dealers with only a few hundred dollars to their names—without a shop, office, or warehouse—could do business right at the railroad station, filling a car with wheat, barley, or oats in the morning and shipping it off by midafternoon. In pork season, there was no longer any need to hire butchers or chilled warehouse space. Instead, a dealer could "place a scale on the sidewalk in some convenient place, weigh his hogs as he bought them, pile them up on the sidewalk, and, in the afternoon, load them up and ship them."[49]

The result was a striking reduction in the capital costs of doing business, for dealers under the new system "were at no expense of rent or labor."[50] Burrows tried to respond in a variety of ways. He invested in new flour mills. He opened a sawmill. He tried to start a reaper factory. Perhaps most suggestively, he decided that "it would be necessary, in order to retain our trade, to follow the railroad," and so opened branch stores in other Iowa towns as a way of trying to become a wholesaler himself. Nothing worked. The new structural conditions created by the railroad and by Chicago's metropolitan market were simply too alien to his familiar way of doing business. The panic of 1857 put his investments under increasing pressure, and when his local bank finally went under in 1859, so did Burrows. After two of his mills burned down, he had no money left to rebuild them and was forced to abandon business altogether. The man who had once been among the most powerful and influential merchants in Davenport found himself a victim of the new economic regime. Looking back on the last quarter century of his life from the vantage point of a lonely and bitter old age, he concluded by saying, "And so I turned my attention to farming and gardening, which I found a hard way to earn a living; but I persevered until a year ago, when my health broke down, and since then I have been shelved."[51]

Burrows's personal tragedy, like the misfortunes of other bankrupt merchants, should not obscure the larger, more impersonal changes that were reshaping the regional economy as a whole. The hierarchy of towns and villages that was emerging in Chicago's hinterland was matched by an increasingly elaborate trading network that tied wholesalers in the metropolis with small-scale retail dealers of the sort that had helped drive Burrows out of business.[52] As Chicago became the chief wholesaling center of the midcontinent, its merchants placed themselves between eastern cities and western customers. As early as 1845, some Chicago firms were offering to act as intermediaries who could supply eastern goods to western merchants wishing to avoid an annual buying trip to New York.[53] By the 1850s, Chicagoans were pointing out that country merchants could avoid many of the risks associated with eastern buying trips by traveling only so far as their city, using the railroad to visit frequently, examine goods in person, and order only what customers were buying.[54] By making small, frequent purchases in Chicago instead of large, infrequent purchases in the East, retailers could increase their profits. In 1877, the secretary of the Chicago Board of Trade could report, "About ten years ago western merchants from all important towns and cities at the West, visited the East at least semi-annually, for the purpose of replenishing their stocks. Now such visits are rare, as full stocks and as favorable terms are presented here, and the business of the merchants at the smaller towns at the West has been gradually transferred from the eastern cities to Chicago."[55]

These changes produced a geographical reorientation so subtle that a casual observer might easily have missed it, for it was recorded mainly in the goods that sat on shopkeepers' shelves, and in the destinations between which merchants traveled as they went about their business. To discover it today, one has to examine the few account books that have survived from merchants in Chicago's nineteenth-century hinterland. Though hardly the most enthralling of documents, they trace in their own dry way the large changes taking place in western commerce and retailing.

Charles Brewster, for instance, was a dry goods merchant and banker in Fort Madison, Iowa, who began his career in much the same way as John Burrows, running a general store and bartering for farm produce. As late as 1859, most of the invoices in his files came from wholesalers in St. Louis, New Orleans, Pittsburgh, Boston, New York City, and especially Philadelphia.[56] During the Civil War, Brewster began to make many small transactions with wholesalers in Chicago, even though he continued to rely on Philadelphia for a large share of his supplies. Then, in the years following the war, he dramatically reduced his reliance on eastern wholesalers. Only a few orders to Philadelphia show up in his records between 1865 and 1871, and none at all to New York. In their place are numerous orders to large Chicago firms like John V. Farwell and Company; Field, Leiter and Company; and others. Brewster also began to rely on Chicago for most of his out-of-town banking.[57] His correspondence reveals that he adapted himself more effectively than Burrows to the opportunities offered by the railroads. He made numerous buying trips, placed frequent small orders responding to shifts in customer demand, and showed an intimate knowledge of how to use urban markets to best advantage.[58] Buying trips carried him and his associates mainly to Chicago and St. Louis, where they kept track of the goods they could buy most advantageously in each city. After one such trip in 1864, his buyer reported of St. Louis, "I have scoured this market pretty well & am satisfied that my Chicago purchases were prudent & advantageous, except on soap I could have bought here 1/2 lower. . . ."[59]

Chicago wholesalers tried to encourage retailers like Brewster by making it as easy as possible to place orders. Potter Palmer, who became one of the city's greatest merchants, began in the late 1850s to place large, foot-long advertisements in Chicago newspapers with out-of-town readerships, describing the elegant fashions that his buyers had purchased in New York and other eastern cities. He promised customer satisfaction by offering a money-back guarantee to anyone unhappy with a shipment. This eliminated much of the risk associated with buying goods at a distance. But Palmer and other Chicago wholesalers went further still, offering goods "on approval" to retailers who wished to examine samples without having to visit Chicago at all. By paying only a modest

High Plains buffalo country. Detail of Karl Bodmer's *Buffalo and Elk on the Upper Missouri,* 1833, courtesy Joslyn Art Museum.

William J. Hays's The Herd on the Move, *1862.* When Hays first exhibited this painting in the East, critics complained that he had wildly exaggerated the size of the plains bison herds. Those who had visited the region for themselves leaped to Hays's defense and declared the image quite authentic. Courtesy Thomas Gilcrease Institute of American History and Art.

Slaughter of bison along the Kansas Pacific Railroad. The coming of the railroad meant death for the great herds. Travelers fired rifles from train windows and left the animals to rot where they fell, but the railroad's role in opening the plains to eastern markets was far more important in motivating the slaughter. Reproduced from Richard Irving Dodge, *The Plains of the Great West* (1877), courtesy Yale University Library.

Rath and Wright's buffalo hide yard, Dodge City, Kansas, ca. 1874. Hunters stripped off bison hides, stretched and dried them as robes, and then shipped them east by the hundreds of thousands. Later, after the herds had vanished, settlers gathered tons of bleached bones and sold them to eastern fertilizer factories. Courtesy Amon Carter Museum.

Cattle seeking water on the Great Plains. With the bison gone, their ecological niche could be filled by new herds of domesticated grazing animals. Longhorn cattle from Texas were driven as far north as Wyoming, Montana, and Saskatchewan to turn buffalo country into cattle range. Reproduced from William M. Thayer, *Marvels of the New West* (1887), author's collection.

Cattle arriving at a Kansas stockyard. Cattle began their journey to the slaughter-house with the famed long drives. Whether cowboys drove them from Texas to Kansas or simply from eastern Wyoming to Cheyenne, the goal was to get animals from their home range to a railroad with as little weight loss as possible. Reproduced from *Scribner's Magazine,* June 1892, courtesy Yale University Library.

G. S. Chadwick's feedlot farm in Fremont Co., Iowa. Farmers in the tallgrass prairie contributed to the livestock economy by fattening young steers that had been purchased from breeders on the High Plains. Cattle lived in fenced enclosures and were fed prairie hay and corn to increase their weight before they finally boarded the railroad for Chicago. Pigs wandered among them eating whatever the cattle left behind. Reproduced from A. T. Andreas, *Atlas of Iowa* (1875), author's collection.

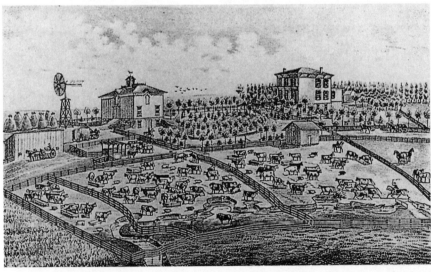

Driving hogs to the Chicago market. Cowboys and cattle drives have exercised such a powerful sway over the American imagination that we often forget that pigs were an equally important part of the livestock economy. Before the Civil War, farmers drove hogs to Chicago from well over a hundred miles away—but note the railroad, symbol of future change, on the horizon. Reproduced from *Harper's Weekly,* October 31, 1868, courtesy Yale University Library.

Workers in a Chicago packing plant gutting pigs. The disassembly line was pioneered in Cincinnati but perfected in Chicago. In the city's packing plants, pigs found themselves lifted by their hind legs onto an overhead rail, whereupon their throats were cut and they bled to death. The carcass then moved past an army of workers who cut it into dozens of different parts, each destined to be processed into different products bound for different markets. Reproduced from *Scientific American,* November 7, 1891, courtesy Yale University Library.

Clouds over Packingtown. The black clouds of smoke that belched from the smoke-stacks of Chicago's factories became a powerful and ambivalent symbol for travelers who visited the city in the late nineteenth century. The packing plants in particular evoked much comment about the pungent odor that greeted visitors long before they reached the actual stockyards. An incongruous field of cabbages is in the foreground. Courtesy Chicago Historical Society.

Market room in a Chicago packinghouse, 1892. Once living cattle had been converted into dressed beef, the butchered carcasses sat in immense cooling rooms before being shipped by rail to the retail butchers who sold them in turn to local customers. Such places were chilled with ice that had been cut from frozen ponds the previous winter. Courtesy Chicago Historical Society.

Cutting ice near Milwaukee. The ice that cooled Chicago's breweries and packing plants, and that allowed dressed beef to travel in refrigerated railroad cars, came to the city from ever greater distances. Here ice is being cut on a Wisconsin lake and moved into an immense insulated warehouse for use over the course of the next year. Courtesy Milwaukee Public Museum.

Interior view of a loaded refrigerator car. During the 1870s and 1880s, Chicago packers perfected the refrigerated railroad car as a way of transporting meat hundreds of miles without it spoiling. In the process, they drove local wholesale butchers out of business and revolutionized the American diet and food distribution system. Courtesy Swift-Eckrich, Inc.

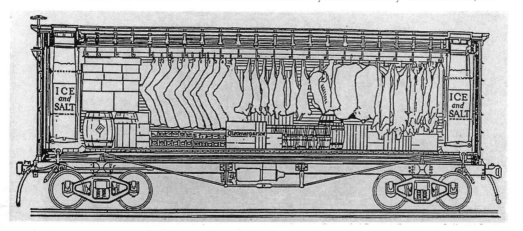

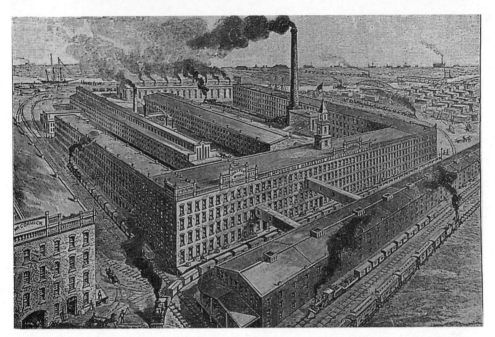

McCormick Harvesting Machine Co. factory in the 1880s. Cyrus McCormick moved to Chicago in 1848 to manufacture his reaper and sell it to farmers on the tallgrass prairies. His factory eventually became one of the largest in the city. Reproduced from Andreas, *History of Chicago,* author's collection.

McCormick reaper in action. McCormick's success depended ultimately on the prosperity of his customers and their willingness to adopt the new agricultural machinery he sold. This picturesque rural scene was endlessly repeated in Chicago's hinterland, and at first glance could hardly seem more remote from the industrial cityscape above. And yet neither could have existed without the other. Courtesy State Historical Society of Wisconsin.

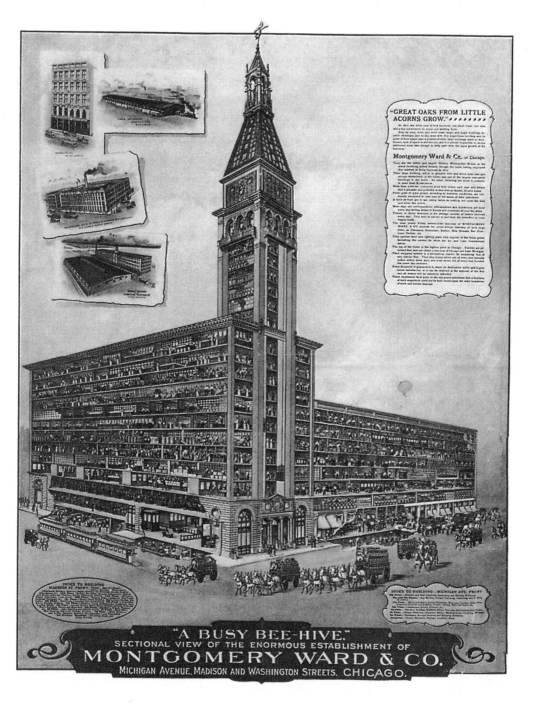

"A Busy Bee-Hive." This famous cover of Montgomery Ward & Co.'s 1900 catalog peeled away the walls of Ward's Michigan Avenue warehouse to reveal the hierarchical corporate order within. Like McCormick's factory, it seemed a powerful symbol of Chicago's urban civilization—and yet it too was a marketplace where city and country mingled and did business. Courtesy Chicago Historical Society.

The Jackson Park Lagoon, July 1891. This was the swampy site of the World's Columbian Exposition before the fair's planners began reshaping its landscape to fit their vision of urban utopia. Reproduced from Rossiter Johnson, ed., *A History of the World's Columbian Exposition* (1897), courtesy Yale University Library.

On the Roof of the Manufactures Building. This was what the lagoon looked like less than two years later. The fairy-tale city that sprang up in Jackson Park was never intended to last—the buildings were sheathed in plaster that could never survive Chicago's winter climate—but the vision it expressed helped redefine public space in American cities for the next generation and beyond. Reproduced from J. W. Buel, *The Magic City* (1894), courtesy Yale University Library.

Chicago Day on the Plaza. October 9, 1893, was designated as Chicago Day at the fair, in commemoration of the city's rebirth from the Great Fire that had obliterated the downtown just twenty-two years before. More than half the city's population turned up to celebrate, and three-quarters of a million people crowded onto the grounds. Reproduced from Rossiter Johnson, ed., *A History of the World's Columbian Exposition* (1897), courtesy Yale University Library.

The Wisconsin State Building. Not all architecture at the fair was neoclassical Beaux Arts; individual states built structures intended to display their own cultural achievements. Some Wisconsin visitors complained that the state hadn't taken the fair seriously enough, and lamented that this comfortable but unassuming building did not do justice to their state's special qualities. Reproduced from Julian Ralph, *Harper's Chicago and the World's Fair* (1893), courtesy Yale University Library.

The phoenix reborn. In the wake of Chicago's Great Fire of 1871, no metaphor came more quickly to people's minds than that of the phoenix, the mythical bird that rose from the ashes of its own funeral pyre. Chicago's growth had been remarkable even before the fire; afterwards, it seemed to most visitors quite astonishing, even frightening. Reproduced from *Scribner's Monthly,* September 1875, courtesy Yale University Library.

Dearborn Street, north across Madison Street, 1892. This was Chicago's downtown shopping district as it appeared the year before the World's Columbian Exposition. Bustling with pedestrians, horses, wagons, and streetcars, it was the liveliest shopping center west of New York. Courtesy Chicago Historical Society.

Scene in Jefferson Park. At the same time that Chicago's downtown was soaring with the new postfire skyscrapers, the city's well-to-do citizens were trying to escape into pastoral suburbs and parks. This scene is typical of the picturesque ideal they embraced: a bucolic image of rural retreat framed wholly in leisure-class terms, a landscape of reverie rather than work. Reproduced from *Scribner's Monthly,* September 1875, courtesy Yale University Library.

An "adventuress" snaring her victim. Rural people who visited Chicago may have admired its wealth and splendor, but they also feared its vices even as they were tempted to try a sample for themselves. Here a guidebook to the city's "Blooded District" warns interested male readers that the pleasures of alcohol, gambling, and sex can sometimes have unexpectedly dangerous consequences. Reproduced from [Harold Vynne,] *Chicago by Day and Night* (1892), courtesy Chicago Historical Society.

The Enchanted Summer-Land. As railroad companies began to realize that passenger traffic could be increased by catering to the summer tourist market, the lakes of Wisconsin became ever more attractive destinations for well-to-do Chicagoans. Here, a Chicago and North-Western Railway brochure promotes Wisconsin as an ideal rural retreat for middle-class families eager to escape the troubles of the city. Courtesy Yale University Library.

1879.

GREEN LAKE RESORT

— FOR —

SUMMER IDLING.

SHERWOOD FOREST.

THIS charming Lodge, to be opened on the **20TH OF MAY**, is embowered by a hundred acres of grand old oaks, lying with gentle grade along the north shore of Green Lake. It is within two miles of Green Lake Station, on the Sheboygan & Fond du Lac Railroad. It is reached from Chicago via the Chicago & North-Western Railway and Chicago, Milwaukee & St. Paul Railway, without the least delay. Omnibuses and carriages always awaiting the arrival of trains.

RAND, McNALLY & CO., PRINTERS, CHICAGO.

Sherwood Forest Lodge brochure. By 1879, Green Lake, Wisconsin, was typical of many rural resorts in Chicago's tourist hinterland. It boasted a number of elegant hotels, each sporting a suitably pastoral name, which offered all the comforts and amenities of urban life in a beautiful rural setting. They explicitly marketed themselves to wealthy city dwellers, carefully detailing the railroad routes that Chicagoans could take to reach them. Courtesy State Historical Society of Wisconsin.

GREEN LAKE, WIS.—VIEW FROM OAKWOOD.

The View from Oakwood, Green Lake, Wisconsin. Reproduced from "The Enchanted Summer-Land" tourist brochure, Chicago and North-Western Railway (n.d.), courtesy Yale University Library.

one-way express charge, Palmer said, storekeepers gained "an OPPOR-TUNITY, AT A TRIFLING EXPENSE, Of seeing a choice selection from the largest stock of Goods west of New York."[60] These new marketing arrangements encouraged small-town retailers to develop a personal relationship with the firm, relying on it for regular purchases.[61] George Kepner, a storekeeper in Davenport, Iowa, clearly felt flattered when Marshall Field, one of Potter Palmer's partners, came courting his business. Kepner reported to his partners that Field had promised him that "anything we want by order shall come right."[62] Personal contacts of this sort went a long way toward motivating hinterland merchants to look to Chicago for their needs instead of New York or Philadelphia.[62]

Like Chicago lumber dealers, Chicago wholesale merchants became famous—some said notorious—for their use of "drummers," or traveling salesmen.[63] Drummers scoured the western landscape, using every conceivable hard-sell technique in their efforts to gain orders for themselves and their firms. One could recognize them instantly in any railroad station: "the number of shrewd, business like men," wrote one observer, "to be seen with grip sack or sample cases in hand, evidently belonging to the genus 'travelling salesman,' is almost incredible. . . . They penetrate the country in every direction, from seaboard to seaboard, and from the lakes to the gulf." Chicago firms relied heavily on drummers to compete for business throughout the city's hinterland, hoping "to secure business to themselves and to the city by bonds which may be soft as silk, yet powerful as steel."[64] So successful were Chicago's wholesalers in dominating western markets, said one early historian, that "eastern drummers gradually found their occupation going, and at last withdrew from the field, satisfied that they could not hope to compete with the enterprising spirit of Chicago men."[65]

Drummers were effective in attracting trade, but aroused strong criticisms from many directions. Hinterland merchants often complained that drummers undercut their trade by selling goods too cheaply to competitors or—far worse—directly to retail customers. Even wholesalers felt nervous that drummers, whose commissions depended more on the number of orders they placed than on the price they received, could compete so fiercely and drive prices so low that profits might disappear altogether. Compelled to use drummers by their competition with each other, wholesalers nonetheless grumbled that "the system of competing through traveling salesmen has been carried to a ruinous point." The *Milwaukee Journal of Commerce* voiced a feeling common among Chicagoans and non-Chicagoans alike that "the best kind of drummer" might be an advertisement in a newspaper or magazine because:

It travels in all directions at once.

It visits your customers every week. . . .

It doesn't get drunk.

It doesn't play faro.

It doesn't lie—very much.

It doesn't bring in any supplementary fancy bill of "expenses."

It requires no "commissions."

It doesn't swell around on the credit and name of your house. . . .

It doesn't add so much to your store expenses as to reduce to zero the margin you would like to offer good customers.

It doesn't cost you many thousands of dollars a year—at the most, only a very few hundreds.[66]

Chicago wholesalers and manufacturers spent enormous sums on such advertising—the hundreds of newspapers and magazines pouring out from the city depended on their doing so—but they continued to be among the nation's largest employers of traveling salesmen as well.

Whatever the marketing strategy that captured their attention, retailers typically came to rely on a few wholesalers for the bulk of their purchases, going elsewhere only when goods were unavailable or when prices from another firm were irresistibly lower. For instance, Francis E. Newton, a hardware dealer in Lincoln, Nebraska, relied on the Chicago firm of Rathbone, Sard and Company for the bulk of his stove purchases in the late 1870s. Although he ordered supplies from firms all over the country, from New York to Pittsburgh to Kansas City, this single Chicago firm was clearly his dominant trading partner.[67] In the mid-1880s, the Hayden Hardware Store in Sun Prairie, Wisconsin, bought approximately two-thirds of its supplies from just two firms, one in Chicago and one in Milwaukee, placing orders with them on an almost weekly basis.[68] Even when retailers did not depend so much on one or two firms, they still tended to concentrate on a single wholesale market. Darwin Clark, who owned a furniture store in Madison, Wisconsin, bought nearly a fourth of his stock in 1870 from two Chicago suppliers. When he visited these firms in the city, he found it easy to shop other wholesalers as well, and so wound up placing fully half his orders in Chicago. The city's wholesale firms in effect reinforced each other even as they competed, since a customer's ability to peruse many stores for the best goods and prices made the market in general that much more attractive.[69]

As one would expect from the bankruptcy maps of regional debt and credit flows, each individual product had its own unique wholesaling geography. Retail hardware dealers, for instance, handled a particularly heavy line of products. Because they had to worry about high transporta-

tion costs, they were more likely than other storekeepers to purchase a
large share of their goods from a wholesaler in their immediate vicinity. A
Wisconsin hardware store might buy the bulk of its line from Chicago or
Milwaukee, while a Kansas store placed orders with a wholesaler in Kansas City or another nearby town.[70] Dry goods dealers, on the other hand,
whose stocks of fabric and clothing were light relative to their value,
could afford to buy from much farther afield because transportation costs
were much lower.

This in turn meant that wholesalers of cheap, heavy goods, and also
perishable ones, appeared sooner in growing frontier cities—nearer to
their retail customers—than did wholesalers of more expensive, lightweight products. It also meant that a wholesaler in Chicago could expect
hinterland customers to place their orders differently, depending on their
distance from the city and the availability of alternative wholesalers in
their immediate locale. Charles B. Sawyer, a wholesale boot and shoe
dealer in Chicago just before the Great Fire of 1871, sold to retailers from
Lake Superior all the way west to Kansas. His biggest customers, unsurprisingly, were storekeepers in the counties of northern Illinois immediately west of Chicago. Because they lived so close to the city, and could
visit Sawyer's warehouse often, these retailers placed many small orders
at frequent intervals. Retailers who lived farther away, on the other hand,
could not travel to Chicago as often, and so placed larger orders at less
frequent intervals.[71]

One can best see the results of this wholesaling geography in the
behavior of retailers like grocers who kept a wide variety of goods in their
stores, many of them perishable. No single wholesaler—whether nearby
or far away—could meet all their needs. The example of Henry Veith,
who ran a grocery in Lincoln, Nebraska, starting in the 1870s, suggests
how complicated a retailer's trading relationships could be. To supply his
store, Veith bought from dozens of different firms. He relied on other
Lincoln merchants for meats which could easily spoil, as well as for lumber and hardware items which were particularly bulky and heavy. Flour
came from a couple of nearby gristmills. Two local wholesalers were his
most important trading partners, supplying him on a weekly or monthly
basis with goods which they in turn ordered from Chicago and more
eastern cities. Veith himself dealt directly with Chicago merchants whenever he needed to buy products that were not readily available in Lincoln.
He bought certain special kinds of meats from firms in the city, especially
fish and oysters. Coffee, tea, and spices came from Chicago firms that
specialized in those products, as did nuts, sugar, yeast, and tobacco. The
general pattern of these orders was clear: staples and local agricultural
produce came from nearby, while specialty goods came from Chicago.[72]

But the more important phenomenon these wholesalers and retailers illustrate is that in the postrailroad world one could buy in a small hinterland town many of the products offered in the regional metropolis of Chicago. Chicago remained a high-order market, with a wealth of goods and services that no other city west of the Appalachians could match, but the growth of its rail-based distribution network made urban goods and services more readily available to people lower down the central place hierarchy. Henry Veith's ability regularly to place orders with dozens of firms hundreds of miles away—and to stock fish and oysters in his Nebraska grocery—suggests how different his world had become from that of John Burrows in Iowa two decades before.

City and country were growing closer together. The diminishing distance separating them was measured not just in the similar products one could buy in their stores but in the information that passed between them. Crucial to the success of all the new linkages among factories, wholesalers, retailers, and final customers was the ability of each to communicate with the others. At the same time that railroads were revolutionizing transportation in the West, other new technologies and institutions were revolutionizing communication. The same telegraph that facilitated grain futures trading at the Chicago Board of Trade also enabled western storekeepers to communicate almost instantly with their suppliers. If they were willing to pay for the service, they could walk to the railroad station and send a telegram via Western Union, restocking their shelves almost as soon as an item sold out.[73] Most of the information that sped along telegraph wires was commercial in nature: orders, instructions about payments, schedules for meetings, reports of shipments, and news about price changes.[74] The ability to convey price information by telegraph allowed wholesalers in different parts of the country to respond to each other's competition almost instantly. "You seem to think it queer," wrote one Iowa storekeeper to a colleague in Philadelphia, "that goods should come down in Chicago as soon as they do in New York. They get the news by Telegraph in there [sic] large house 2 or 3 times a day as to the markets and of course go up & down with the market. . . . New Y[ork] & Chicago are very closely connected in the dry good trade."[75]

Hinterland merchants gained most of their knowledge about Chicago's markets by more traditional means, like the buying trips they all took at frequent intervals. Except when their need to telegraph was urgent, retailers placed orders with Chicago wholesalers either in person or through the regular mail. Mail service accelerated in the years following the Civil War as the post office learned how to take better advantage of railroad technology. In the late 1860s, the Chicago postmaster tried an experiment in which postal employees sorted letters while still in transit on railroad cars, reducing delays once they reached their destination. The system was so much more efficient than its predecessor that metropolitan post offices in other parts of the country adopted it as well.[76] Rail-based mail shipments were critical in delivering Chicago newspapers to the surrounding countryside, and in making the *Tribune* and later the *Daily News* the leading regional newspapers west of the city. Their articles kept hinterland readers informed about national and regional news, while their advertisements kept merchants posted about the state of metropolitan markets.[77]

Just how important metropolitan newspapers and mails had become to hinterland residents was suggested in 1884, when the post office contracted with the Chicago, Burlington and Quincy to establish a new fast mail service between Chicago and Council Bluffs, Iowa, on the Missouri River. Under the terms of its contract, the Burlington agreed to run a special train, the "Fast Mail," six days a week at an average speed of 31.5 miles per hour. Trains pulled out of Chicago at 3:00 A.M.—in time to catch the earliest print runs of the morning newspapers—and reached Council Bluffs fifteen hours and fifty minutes later.[78] Among the most important benefits of this service was that readers could receive their Chicago papers a full workday earlier than before. Responses along the line were euphoric. A correspondent in Monmouth, Illinois, 180 miles from Chicago, reported that the *Tribune* had arrived at 7:00 A.M. "Heretofore the Chicago dailies were not received until 7 p.m. Now we can see them almost as soon as the citizens of Chicago."[79] From Des Moines came the word that the *Tribune* had arrived eighteen hours earlier than before. "It is almost an annihilation of distance," wrote an enthusiastic reader. "There is already a strong demand among the business public to have it delivered to their counting-rooms. This has not heretofore been the practice, but it is a result certain to follow." Newsdealers in every station reported that papers sold out within an hour of their arrival, and many doubled or quadrupled their orders for the next morning. The fast mail was so obvious a success that the Milwaukee and St. Paul Railroad hurried to add a similar service the next day. And so the reach of Chicago's informational hinterland expanded as the time taken to deliver newspapers and mail contracted.[80]

Catalogs on Kitchen Tables

Railroads, urban manufacturing, wholesaling, improved postal service, advertising, and the many other new linkages between city and country all came together in 1872. In that year, Aaron Montgomery Ward founded a new marketing institution that in many ways represented the logical culmination of the merchandising techniques that Chicagoans like Cyrus McCormick and Potter Palmer had been exploring since the middle of the century. Having begun his adult life as a day laborer in a barrel-stave factory and a brickyard, Ward took a job in a Michigan general store at the age of nineteen. Discovering that he had a knack for marketing, he moved to Chicago three years later, in 1865, and became an employee of the city's greatest dry goods establishment, Field, Palmer and Leiter. He stayed with them for two years, and then went to work as a traveling salesman for a dry goods wholesaler in St. Louis. His time on the road introduced him to rural customers throughout the Mississippi Valley, and convinced him that it ought to be possible to extend the advantages of metropolitan markets—high volume, wide selections of goods, efficient handling, and low prices—directly to retail customers in rural areas. The logical place to attempt such an experiment was Chicago, to which Ward returned in 1870. He was nearly ready to go into business in 1871 when most of his savings were destroyed in the Great Fire. Ward was undaunted. In the spring of 1872, he and his brother-in-law George R. Thorne launched what would become the first general mail order company in American history.[81]

Montgomery Ward and Company came into being at a time when residents of rural areas were organizing against the many new institutions they saw dominating their lives. Believing that railroad companies, grain elevator operators, and corrupt merchants were stealing the profits from their hard-earned harvests, farmers organized themselves into the first large-scale agrarian protest movement of the post–Civil War era, the Patrons of Husbandry (otherwise known as the Grange). In addition to seeking new state laws to regulate the charges of railroads and grain elevators, they attacked the entire wholesale-retail distribution system. Among their most hated villains was "the middle man," most visibly embodied in the produce merchant who seemed to pay farmers the lowest possible prices for grain, and the storekeeper who seemed to charge them the highest possible prices for goods they bought at retail. A typical protest song nicely captures their mood:

> It is an ancient farmerman, And he is one of three,
> He said unto the middleman, "We have no need of thee."
> This man here makes his cloth so strong, And sells it unto me;
> He buys my wheat and thus we save The slice that went to thee.
>
> Your eyes too dim are growing, sir, "Get spectacles," said he,
> "That you may see some higher grade Of wheat than number three."

The cunning middleman laughed out, Ha, ha, you think 'twill be?
Upon your back I'll stand and fill My pockets from the tree.

Then turned that ancient farmerman The middleman about,
And with some words of kind advice, He gently kicked him out.
And he was right; and so we say To such in ev'ry three,
To ev'ry meddling middleman We have no need of thee.[82]

Embracing the physiocratic notion that all value in the economy sprang from workers of the soil, and believing that transportation companies and store owners added no value to the products they carried and sold, the Grangers sought to form cooperatives that would sell at wholesale direct to the final customer, thus avoiding the "middle man's profit."

Although not himself a Granger, Aaron Ward knew an opportunity when he saw one. His own idea for direct-mail marketing was close to what the Patrons hoped to accomplish with their buying cooperatives. Offering to sell to Grange members (and anyone else) at the same prices retail storekeepers paid for their wares, he quickly received the official seal of approval from Grange organizations around the country. For the next several years, he advertised his firm as "THE ORIGINAL WHOLE-SALE GRANGE SUPPLY HOUSE," declaring that it sold to "Patrons of Husbandry, Farmers and Mechanics at Wholesale Prices."[83] His initial device for reaching these customers was deceptively simple: a single eight-by-twelve-inch sheet of paper listing a variety of products at prices far below what most rural inhabitants were accustomed to paying in their local stores. So astonishing were Ward's prices that the *Chicago Tribune* ran an article warning its readers about what seemed an obvious fraud. "Don't Patronize 'Montgomery Ward & Co.,' " it cautioned. "They are Dead-Beats. Another attempt at swindling has come to light." No firm that advertised such low prices, that offered its goods only by mail, and that did not even maintain a storefront address could possibly be legitimate. Ward's prices, said the *Tribune,* were "Utopian," and the only people who might be taken in by them were "credulous fools, who place boundless faith in anything which is set up in type and printed." More intelligent customers would know a fraud when they saw one.[84]

But Ward was no swindler, and a month later the *Tribune* took the unusual step of retracting its earlier story, saying that it had been "grossly unjust, and not warranted by the real facts. The firm of Montgomery, Ward & Co. is a bona fide firm, composed of respectable persons, and doing a perfectly legitimate business in a perfectly legitimate manner."[85] How did Ward manage to offer such low prices? The *Tribune* explained to its readers that Ward purchased all his merchandise with cash, and sold to his customers on the same basis, so none of his prices had to be inflated to cover interest on borrowed money. Like other wholesalers, he bought in large volume, getting the lowest possible prices for his purchases. By selling direct to the final customer, he could offer prices that included no retailer's markup. He avoided the costs of operating a store and had no sales force, thereby avoiding a retailer's rents and salaries. And the real proof that Ward was running a legitimate business, said the *Tribune*, was his guarantee. Customers who received their orders at the express office were entitled to open the package and examine its contents before paying their bill. If they were dissatisfied for any reason, they could simply refuse payment. "It is difficult," said the *Tribune*, "to see how any person can be swindled or imposed upon by business thus transacted."[86] Although very different from the old personal and familial trading networks on which John Burrows had relied, Ward's money-back guarantee was a new institutionalized basis for long-distance transactions, in which cash payments and direct inspection took the place of personal acquaintances and credit.

The success of Ward's scheme can best be traced in the pages of his catalogs.[87] The early single-page price lists contained only 163 items, and were sent out to forty Grange members as a trial balloon. The response was so enthusiastic that at the beginning of 1874 Ward issued an 8-page booklet measuring three by five inches. By year's end, it had grown to 72 pages and had begun to include woodcut illustrations of select products like the famous Grange Hat. Henceforth, the firm's growth was nothing short of phenomenal. By the end of the 1880s, Ward's catalog measured eight by eleven inches, contained 540 pages, and offered over 24,000 items to its readers. They responded by doing more than a million dollars worth of business with it, requiring a work force of nearly three hundred clerks to respond to the 750,000 letters that arrived in the mail that year alone. Business continued to grow throughout the 1890s, despite the emergence of Sears, Roebuck and Company—another Chicago firm—as an aggressive competitor in Ward's mail order territory. By the dawn of the new century, the Montgomery Ward catalog contained 1,200 pages and 17,000 illustrations, offering no fewer than 70,000 separate items for sale. Two thousand clerks now handled the orders of two million customers. The firm's yearly postal money order business was greater than that of entire cities like Cincinnati, New Orleans, or San Francisco. The incoming mail each day brought between 15,000 and 35,000 letters, while a daily average of 13,000 packages moved in the opposite direction. There had never been anything like it before. By 1900, Montgomery Ward and Sears, Roebuck were the two greatest merchandising organizations in the world.

In 1898, Montgomery Ward and Company moved its operations into an immense new building on Michigan Avenue, crowned by what was then the highest tower in the city. Two years later, customers found in their mail a Ward's catalog that used a picture of this building for its cover illustration. It is one of the most striking images in Chicago's history. Company artists had peeled away the outer façade of the structure to reveal its inner anatomy and suggest its extraordinary complexity. Each of the building's twenty stories handled a different economic function, much like the pages of the catalog itself. Most were little more than warehouses. The nineteenth floor was devoted to sewing machines and musical instruments, the ninth to ready-made clothing, the fourth to hardware and stoves, the third to guns and athletic goods. The eighth floor probably captured the firm's ambitions best, housing what company copywriters modestly called "Dry Goods, a complete line of everything."[88]

Down below, the first and second floors were the nerve center of the business. There, an army of clerks, mostly women, did nothing but open letters and direct them to the appropriate department elsewhere in the building. The cashier's department handled the firm's immense flow of money, the correspondence department answered the flood of letters, while shipping and receiving took charge of moving merchandise in and out of the building. Tucked away in the basement were the dynamos that sent electricity to the 200 arc lamps and 7,500 incandescent bulbs that lit these many floors and offices. All the key managerial divisions were within a floor or two of the ground, with only one telling exception: advertising. The employees who designed the company's catalogs and planned its advertising campaigns had their office on the highest working floor of the tower. There, they could look out their windows to the curving shore of Lake Michigan, to the gridiron streets stretching out toward the western horizon, and glimpse the hither edge of the empire that their words and images had built.

The title that the advertising department chose for this particular catalog cover was richly suggestive: "A Busy Bee-Hive." Surely there were few more powerful symbols of modern urban life than this vast buzzing tower of human enterprise, like nothing so much as a swarm of anonymous insects performing their intricate labors according to the dictates of a mysterious collective intelligence. Carrying nearly every consumer product manufactured in the United States, Ward and Sears seemed the ultimate expressions of an advanced civilization. Organized to employ the most minute division of labor, the most elaborate managerial hierarchies, the most advanced manufacturing technologies, and the most efficient distribution systems, they bespoke in every particular the progress of the age. One might possibly look at a grain elevator or a lumberyard or a meat-packing plant and think of the farms, forests, and pastures upon which their prosperity rested. But one looked at the Montgomery Ward building and thought *people*. The busy hive was a perfect emblem of the city itself, a creation so complicated, so artificial, so remarkable that one could only marvel at the human ingenuity that had built it.

And yet the deeper meaning of Chicago's great mail order establishments did not reside in their huge warehouses or office buildings, which were after all but larger versions of the wholesale firms that had been operating in the city since the middle of the century. If one wants to understand the busy hive, one has to follow the bees to their honey. The real monuments to Montgomery Ward and Sears, Roebuck were the catalogs they sent by the hundreds of thousands to eager rural customers across the United States. The pages of those much-thumbed volumes contained an encyclopedic description of modern life in the products and inventions whose purchase would carry their owners onto a higher plane of material well-being and social progress. Chicago Honey Cured Hams. Ladies Fine Shirt Waists. American Chatelaine Watches. Giant Acme Gasoline Stoves. Princess Tonic Hair Restorers. Yukon Gents' Bicycles. Beckwith Thermo Ozone Batteries. Highest Grade Columbus Carriages. Acme Grocers' Refrigerators. New Model Stereoscopic Cameras. And so on and on and on.

The list seemed endless, and as such conveyed an important message to the farm families who devoted long hours of leisure to learning the lessons of these textbooks. Mail order catalogs brought city and country together by affording their readers at least a fantasy glimpse of what civilized life was like. No matter how remote the community in which one lived, no matter how limited the retail stores in one's neighboring village, one could open the catalog and take a stroll down State Street, the richest, most glamorous retail market anywhere west of Broadway. "The Montgomery Ward catalog," wrote a Nebraska farmwoman, ". . . was a real link between us and civilization."[89] Henceforth, it needn't really matter whether one lived in city or country, for the good life could be purchased by mail wherever one made one's home. The advent of the post office's rural free delivery in 1896 was an immediate consequence of the public demand that Ward and Sears had helped create, and it pointed the way to the roads, telephones, electrical networks, and chain stores that would transform the rural landscape of America in the twentieth century.

But if the mail order catalog brought State Street to Iowa, and urban cultural values to rural landscapes and communities across the interior of the continent, it was also the conduit for transmitting rural wealth, dreams, and desires back to the metropolis. Just as the grain elevator used railroad cars to gather wheat, the busy hive used catalogs to gather cash and transmute it into whatever money could buy. The significance of

Montgomery Ward and Sears, Roebuck, like that of the grain elevator, did not reside in physical buildings but in the relationships that linked those buildings to a larger world. This was the ultimate message hidden beneath a thousand different disguises in the emerging central place hierarchy of the Great West, in the financial hinterlands recorded by Chicago's bankruptcy courts, in the decline of St. Louis relative to Chicago, in the shipments of reapers from Cyrus McCormick's factory, in the new wholesale-retail relationships that had driven John Burrows out of business and that allowed Montgomery Ward to reach out from his great Chicago tower to sell wares to customers everywhere. This was the meaning of those boxes and barrels standing on the sidewalks of Omaha. All were about buying and selling, about city and country confronting one another to discover their common ground in the marketplace. All were about capital, which was itself not a thing but a relationship. The geography of capital was about connecting people to make new markets and remake old landscapes.

The mail order catalog was only the purest expression of this much broader cultural tendency. Even more than an ordinary piece of cartography, it offered its readers a map of capital, of second nature. In its pages, these relationships all came together, so one can read in its advertisements the ties between metropolis and hinterland, the flow of debt and credit, the assembly of labor and natural resources into manufactured goods, the movement of commodities and information, and the structure of the distribution system as a whole. And yet the most remarkable thing about the catalog, like capital itself, is how thoroughly it *obscures* these relationships. On its pages, each product stands alone, just one more item among the tens of thousands that a customer might wish to consider. There was no need to wonder where such things came from—how they had been created, by whom, from what materials, with what consequences for the place in which they had been made—for the answer to that question stopped at the busy hive. All these many products came from Ward, or Sears, just as McCormick's reapers came from his factory.

Iowa farmers perusing the grocery section of the Sears catalog might not forget that Aunt Jemima's Pancake Flour or Queen Mary Scotch Oatmeal had originally come from farms like their own, but customers in Chicago may not have remembered so easily. The workers in Philip Armour's Chicago packinghouse might know all too well what kind of labor and what sorts of materials went into preserved meats, but the customers who bought Sears, Roebuck Summer Sausage had a foggier idea. Once a product had been processed, packaged, advertised, sold, and shipped within the long chain of wholesale-retail relationships, its identity became more and more a creature of the market. The natural roots from which it had sprung and the human history that had created it faded as it passed from hand to hand. Wherever one bought it, that was where it came from. Just as one could eat an Armour ham without remembering the act of killing that brought it to one's table, one could buy from a Montgomery Ward catalog without reflecting upon the web of economic and ecological connections that stretched out in all directions from oneself and the busy hive.

The paradox of nineteenth-century Chicago was that the same market that brought city and country ever closer together, giving them a common culture and fostering ever more intimate communication between them, also concealed the very linkages it was creating. The geography of capital produced a landscape of obscured connections. The more concentrated the city's markets became, and the more extensive its hinterland, the easier it was to forget the ultimate origins of the things it bought and sold. The ecological place of production grew ever more remote from the economic point of consumption, making it harder and harder to keep track of the true costs and consequences of any particular product. Even as Chicago's markets reshaped the landscape of the Great West, one did not "naturally" place the city in that larger context. One thought instead of the busy hive, the huge building selling commodities to an entire nation from the heart of the city's downtown. Visualizing Chicago's markets from the opposite direction was much harder because the images were so much more diffuse: millions of families around the country with dog-eared Ward and Sears catalogs sitting at their kitchen tables, innumerable dinner table conversations about possible purchases, countless gadgets in kitchens and farmyards and bathrooms and barns for making life a little easier in so many different ways. Hive and catalog were different sides of the same coin, and yet it was second nature not to see them upon their common landscape, as links in a long chain stretching from metropolis to hinterland and finally to nature itself.

8

White City
Pilgrimage

The Great Fair

The wonder that was Chicago reached its climax in the final decade of the nineteenth century. In 1893, the city played host to the most famous fair ever held on American soil, the World's Columbian Exposition. Having gained that honor from Congress in an open competition with New York, Washington, and St. Louis, Chicagoans proceeded to organize a national celebration of the four hundredth anniversary of Columbus's journey to America. Knowing that the eyes of the world would be upon them, they sought to create a fair worthy of that event. In it, they would demonstrate the progress of American civilization and the special role Chicago had played therein. In effect, they would suggest that their own city was itself the fulfillment of a destiny that Columbus had long ago set in motion.[1]

Like everything else about the city, Chicago's World's Fair was to be bigger and grander than any before it. Its planners indulged the local affection for hyperbole even before they had completed a single building, promoting it with their usual statistical enthusiasm. The grounds of the exposition, not far short of two square miles in area, would be more than three times larger than the most recent such fair, in Paris four years earlier.[2] Paris's Eiffel Tower would be rivaled by Chicago's newly invented Ferris Wheel. The Manufactures building would be the largest such structure on earth, covering twice the area of the Great Pyramid. The buildings would be lit with 7,000 arc and 120,000 incandescent lamps, which would be among the most striking technologies on display, demonstrating the newfangled wonders of electricity.[3] Like the city itself, the Exposition would be a place of superlatives.[4]

But the Chicago fair was special for more than just grand scale and impressive statistics. Nicknamed the White City, it became almost overnight a much praised vision of urban life at its noblest and most civilized. An army of artists, builders, and laborers under the direction of the Chicago architect Daniel Burnham drained the swampy soil of Jackson Park on the city's South Side, and created a lagoon (designed by none other than Frederick Law Olmsted) that gave formal aesthetic unity to the main exhibition buildings. Sheathing their steel skeletons with an easily sculpted but short-lived mixture of plaster and jute fiber, the fair's designers used classical motifs to create a Beaux Arts architectural fantasy of domes, arches, fountains, and colonnades. They divided each building according to an encyclopedic plan that encompassed all human knowledge as they understood it: Agriculture, Machinery, Transportation, Liberal Arts, Electricity, and so on. Into these temples of intelligence and industry, they poured representative inventions and treasures from around the world. Thirty-six nations and forty-six American states and territories built exhibits to display their contributions to civilization in what one guidebook, quoting Tennyson, called "the Parliament of Man, the Federation of the World."[5] At a time when the national economy was wracked by depression, when farmers were organizing mass protest movements, and workers were marching in the streets, the Columbian Exposition stood as a remarkably self-assured reminder that the nineteenth century was, after all, the greatest era of civilized progress the world had ever seen.

Contemporary visitors recognized this lesson at once, and for the most part appreciated it. William James, who never attended the fair, was being ironic when he reported, "Everyone says one ought to sell all one has and mortgage one's soul to go there, it is esteemed such a revelation of beauty. People cast away all sin and baseness, burst into tears and grow religious, etc. under its influence!"[6] But actual visitors described feelings that were only a little less rapturous than James's parody. James Fullarton Muirhead, the Scot who for many years edited the standard Baedeker guidebook to the United States, said of the fair's main Court of Honour that it was "perhaps the most flawless and fairy-like creation, on a large scale, of man's invention," superior aesthetically to any of the European cities on which it was modeled.[7] One visitor who traveled all the way from New Zealand just to see the exposition left "feeling assured that if I lived to the age of some of the most ancient patriarchs I could never again have a chance of beholding its superior or even its equal."[8] The socialist Eugene V. Debs praised the healthy effect it would have on the American character as a symbol of labor's high achievements, and the novelist William Dean Howells even had his traveler from the fictional utopia Altruria say that it reminded him of home.[9] Almost everyone agreed that it was one of the wonders of the world.

The majority of the exposition's visitors were not foreigners or eastern intellectuals but more ordinary folk. Attendance at the exposition started so slowly—an average of 33,687 people per day in May—that it looked as if the event might prove a financial disaster.[10] Then, as the summer went on and word got out that this was no ordinary fair, attendance swelled, so the daily average grew to over 150,000 by September and October, when the fairgrounds contained a daytime population bigger than that of all but the largest western cities. In the end, more than twelve million people managed to come, many for more than one visit.[11] The largest share undoubtedly came from Chicago itself. The fair's all-time attendance record was set in October on "Chicago Day," when schools, businesses, and factories all closed, and three-quarters of a million people spent the day celebrating at the exposition. Something like half the population of Chicago so jammed the White City that visitors in some buildings were unable to move until guards prevented additional people from entering.[12]

The next-largest group of visitors came from Chicago's hinterland. Most were rural farmers and residents of small towns in the Mississippi Valley, and they too had their special celebrations. Iowa Day drew 60,000 people from that state, including the governor and the state band in full dress uniform, to celebrate the forty-seventh anniversary of Iowa statehood.[13] Wisconsin Day was somewhat less successful, but still brought in 25,000 state citizens.[14] Out-of-town residents who came to the fair made a special point of looking in on their own state's exhibition building. They far outnumbered everyone else who toured the state exhibits, so—like Chicago's markets—each part of the fair in effect drew on a different hinterland of visitors.[15] Those who stopped by their home state's building often cast a critical eye to see how it compared with others at the exposition. One young woman said of Wisconsin's building that she thought "it was a mistake" not to put on more of a display. "A state like Wisconsin," she wrote, "could have made so fine a show—woods building stone—manufactures—ores—fine scenery—commercial interests stock raising—fisheries—I was daily pained that all this was not shown— visitors in general judged the states by state buildings. . . ."[16] The fair reminded people of something not always so obvious back home: the place in which they lived was a hinterland, whose cultural worth would be measured by the metropolitan vision that the White City so clearly exemplified.

Although visitors took real pride that America and the Great West could mount such a show, most who joined the throngs were more than a little overwhelmed by what they saw. A reporter for the *Chicago Daily Inter Ocean* commented, "Two-thirds of the people who visit the Exposition do not know what they are looking at nor why they should look."[17] Some dashed from exhibit to exhibit, barely stopping to look at anything, so that they could at least say they had been inside every building.[18] Many sought help from guidebooks to sort through the seemingly endless displays, and some even purchased diaries with preprinted chapter headings suggesting quintessential fair experiences they ought to record: "My first day in the 'White City' "; "How I went to the Fair"; "My hotel and how I liked it"; "Queer happenings"; "New inventions"; "That day it rained, O!"; and "Going home," among others.[19] Many thought they glimpsed a mystery in this place—a mystery about art and progress and civilization itself—that deserved careful study and attention. One writer described a fictional farmer's experience by saying that "his mind perceived so much that was strange and new that he became as that one who saw men as trees walking. His eyes were opened to a new world."[20]

What did the fair *mean?* Everyone who attended asked this question in one form or another, but it was left for Henry Adams, that most perceptive but detached of contemporary observers, to say it best. Adams was so fascinated by the exposition that he traveled to Chicago a second time to wander through its exhibits for half a month. He was struck in part by the incoherence that lay just beneath the surface of its apparent unity. This singular monument to civilization was in fact a great jumble. "Since Noah's ark," he wrote, "no such Babel of loose and ill-joined, such vague and ill-defined and unrelated thoughts and half-thoughts and experimental outcries as the Exposition, had ever ruffled the surface of the lakes."[21] Had he thumbed the pages of a Montgomery Ward catalog, he might have recognized that the chaotic collections of the fair were but a more concentrated version of the jumble that was Chicago itself. An English visitor and reformer, William T. Stead, noted as much when he said that the fair resembled "the contents of a great dry goods store mixed up with the contents of museums."[22] But to recognize the familial resemblance between a world's fair and a mail order catalog only underscores the problem that intrigued Adams and other visitors. "Chicago," he wrote, "asked in 1893 for the first time the question whether the American people knew where they were driving." If one wanted to understand the nation and its civilization, one must answer the riddle of the White City. "Chicago," Adams said, "was the first expression of American thought as a unity; one must start there."[23]

Miracle of the Phoenix

Adams was not alone in this perception. Everything about the fair suggested its ties to the larger miracle that was Chicago. Guidebook authors made a point of reminding visitors that they should venture beyond the exposition grounds in planning their itineraries, for the fair's city was "in itself the foremost wonder of the World."[24] People—not just Chicagoans—repeated claims of this sort endlessly in 1893, and they had something more specific in mind than the usual booster rhetoric. Among the things that made the White City seem so remarkable was its occurrence only a little more than two decades after that other key mythic event in Chicago's history—the Great Fire of October 8–9, 1871. On that terrible night, the blaze that began in the barn behind Patrick O'Leary's cottage at 137 De Koven Street spread in the dry prairie winds of a drought-stricken autumn until it finally devastated a swath of land four miles long and two-thirds of a mile wide. Terrified inhabitants fled amid scenes of gothic horror: parents searching for lost children, looters picking through abandoned buildings, mobs crowding collapsing bridges, whole city blocks engulfed in flames. None who lived through the experience ever forgot it. Almost three hundred people lost their lives, a hundred thousand were left homeless, and nearly $200 million in property was destroyed. The entire downtown—the great department stores, wholesale warehouses, Board of Trade, hotels, the very heart of the city—was laid waste in a single night.[25]

But the mythic lesson that linked the Great Fire to the White City had less to do with destruction than with resurrection. Even as the embers lay smoking amid the ruins, all the old booster arguments about the predestined inevitability of Chicago's metropolitan growth reemerged. They soon coalesced in a metaphorical image that appeared repeatedly for the next quarter century: the city as phoenix, that magical bird that could find rebirth even in the ashes of its own funeral pyre.[26] The fire may have destroyed the downtown, but it left Chicago's essential infrastructure intact: most of the grain elevators still stood, and the lumber district, stockyards, and factories were well outside the burn. Most important, the vast network of rails pointing toward Lake Michigan—the crucial geography that capital had imposed on the landscape of the Great West—could hardly be touched by so local an event. The city still had its hinterland. Relief poured in to aid the homeless and rebuild the residential neighborhoods of the city, but the main flow of capital that sustained Chicago's economy had precisely the same sources as before the fire. William Bross, a onetime lieutenant governor of Illinois, understood this perfectly when he declared five days afterward that "the capitalists, the mercantile and business interests of this country and of Europe cannot afford to withhold the means to rebuild Chicago."[27]

It was not long before Chicagoans were claiming that the destruction of the downtown had done more good than harm. By clearing away the old wooden building stock, the catastrophe enabled businesses to erect new structures using the latest techniques for fire prevention; these safety measures were enforced by the passage of new ordinances imposing strict new building codes and fire limits.[28] More important, the burn produced a construction boom that drove up the price of downtown real estate. On the first anniversary of the fire, the city's *Lakeside Monthly* could report that land values had risen well above their prefire levels, so what had seemed "horrible" had actually proved "wonderful": "Was not the Great Fire a blessing in disguise?"[29] Rising land values encouraged architects to design ever taller structures to extract more rent from the expensive property on which they stood, demonstrating that von Thünen's market in space operated as much within the city as without. Iron and steel skeletons clad in masonry were more secure against fire and could rise much higher than their wooden predecessors. The result was the invention of the "skyscraper." By the time of the World's Fair, Chicago had become famous for the height of its downtown office buildings. Men like William Le Baron Jenney, John Root, Dankmar Adler, Louis Sullivan, and Daniel Burnham were soon recognized as leading exponents of the "Chicago School of Architecture."[30]

The fire accelerated an ongoing rearrangement of Chicago's internal geography that paralleled changes in the city's regional hinterland. "The great fire," wrote a guidebook author in 1884, "modernized the city, leveling the ground and rendering possible the uniform elegance of the business portion."[31] By the time people arrived to view the fair, almost every part of the city, not just the burned-over district, had been significantly rebuilt. The same rise in land values that sent downtown buildings soaring skyward also made them too expensive for residential use. The new fire limits outlawed wooden buildings and fire-prone industries from the central business district, which meant in turn that working-class neighborhoods moved out as well. Especially on the West and South Sides, Chicago's landscape became a sprawling gridiron of small wooden cottages surrounding the factories and warehouses where their residents worked. Fire laws encouraged the already existing tendency for related economic activities to cluster in well-defined areas: lumber districts, manufacturing districts, meat-packing districts. To take only the most familiar example, the partitioning of regional nature that had turned shortgrass prairies into rangelands and tallgrass prairies into feedlots was matched by a partitioned urban environment in which packing plants and working-class houses clustered around the Union Stockyards, and a steady stream of immigrants from the European countryside defined a new labor hinterland of workers and residents alike. Every industry had its own special geography linking particular urban neighborhoods with particular rural hinterlands, but the general patterns were common to all. Those who suffered the worst social and environmental hardships associated with the new city-country linkages—cheap construction, occupational disease, polluted air, and bad water—were invariably the working families whose limited resources kept them inside factories by day, and downwind and downstream of them by night.[32]

Those who owned, managed, and financed the industrial and warehouse districts did much of their work in the downtown office buildings, but they too moved their homes away from city center during this same postfire period. The higher the downtown became, the greater the horizontal spread of the residential neighborhoods that housed its daytime inhabitants: skyscraper and suburb created each other. The process was aided by the same transportation technology that had given the city its hinterland. Middle- and upper-class Chicagoans who could afford to do so turned to the railroad as an ideal way of removing their residences from the crowds, noise, and pollution of the downtown and factory areas. The result was Chicago's extraordinary suburban growth in the decades following the fire. "Chicago, for its size," declared the *Chicago Times* with the usual local jingoism in 1873, "is more given to suburbs than any other city in the world. In fact, it is doubtful if any city, of any size, can boast of an equal number of suburban appendages."[33]

At the very moment that Chicago's markets and railroad networks were bringing a metropolitan economy to the Great West, wealthy Chicagoans were seeking to recover (or, more accurately, create) an ideal landscape that combined urban comforts with a carefully selected subset of rural amenities. Although the wealthiest of the Chicago suburbs stretched out along the northern shore of Lake Michigan—Evanston, Winnetka, Wilmette, Highland Park, and others, all far upwind from factory smokestacks—one of the most influential was Riverside, designed by Frederick Law Olmsted in 1868 but not really a thriving community until after the fire.[34] "The essential qualification of a suburb," wrote Olmsted in his plan for the town, "is domesticity. . . ."[35] A suburb was a place of trees, lawns, winding lanes, and comfortable houses. Children could safely play there and middle-class families could escape from urban squalor and danger. Neither the work of the farm nor the work of the city

was supposed to happen in it, save for the work women did in caring for
their children, and the work domestic servants did in keeping the house-
holds and tending the grounds of this park-like landscape.

Unlike the rural countrysides of Chicago's hinterland, the suburb had
paved streets, gaslights, water mains, sewage lines, and eventually electricity; unlike downtown Chicago, it had clean air, quiet domestic seclu-
sion, and little chance that rich and poor would rub up against each other
in a threatening way. As the promoters of Riverside declared in their
prospectus, the suburb was "the country with the discomforts eliminated;
the country *plus* city conveniences." It was "the golden mean between the
two kinds of life."[36] That it was also a parasitical landscape that required
both the crowded city and the uncomfortable country to sustain its consumer retreat, that its "nature" was profoundly artificial and fundamentally urban, bothered few of those who praised it as an ideal solution to
the problems of modern life. In this, it had much in common with the fair
itself.

When people came to the World's Columbian Exposition in 1893,
they experienced all these things together as "Chicago": tall office buildings and suburban retreats, crowded slum neighborhoods and smoke-
belching factories. All symbolized the reborn phoenix. When the Board
of Trade moved into its new skyscraper in 1885, a local minister offered a
prayer of thanks that expressed what had become almost a myth of origin
for the modern city: "We went through fire and water, but Thou brought-
est us out into a wealthy place."[37] For those trying to make sense of the
fair, the symbolic pairing of White City and Great Fire was irresistible. It
was no accident that the exposition's Chicago Day was scheduled for
October 9. Unconsciously echoing the 1870s boosters, a visitor in the
1890s could draw the same lesson as they from the fire: "at this moment
no one doubts that it was a great blessing. It was the death of old Chicago
and the birth of a new and better Chicago, better fitted in a thousand ways
to fulfil destiny."[38] Just so could the city's residents celebrate their worst
disaster as the most potent symbol of their modern progress.

If the fire began this epic, the fair pointed to its end. Nothing better
symbolized Chicago's resurrection and transfiguration than the White
City, which glorified Chicago's past by seeming to offer a blueprint for its
future.[39] The fair, after all, was no less an idealized city than the suburbs
were an idealized countryside. Both seemed at far poles from the downtown and factory districts, holding up a vision of what urban life could be
if only the crowded and ugly parts of the city could be remade according
to these genteel visions. James Muirhead compared the city's downtown
with its suburbs while attending the fair and declared Chicago the "City
of Contrasts." "In the one—height, narrowness, noise, monotony, dirt,

sordid squalor, pretentiousness; in the other—light, space, moderation, homelikeness."[40] When William Dean Howells had his Altrurian traveler describe the exposition as America's "earliest achievement of a real civic life," he was praising all that downtown Chicago was not. In the fair's electric vehicles and lack of horse manure, its carefully cleaned streets and landscaped grounds, its architectural beauty and leisurely crowds, visitors saw an urban equivalent of the suburban ideal.

To be sure, both fair and suburb achieved this effect by obscuring their essential connections to the rest of Chicago, much as the city's markets obscured their connections to the countryside around them. Both succeeded by eliminating from their precincts the one essential foundation of city and country alike: productive labor. Neither was a working landscape. Both were fantasies that achieved "perfection" by segregating urban and rural utopias from the economy and environment that sustained them. What the architecture critic Montgomery Schuyler shrewdly said of the White City was no less true of Chicago's elite suburbs:

> It is essential to the illusion of a fairy city that it should not be an American city of the nineteenth century. It is a seaport on the coast of Bohemia, it is the capital of No Man's Land. It is what you will, so long as you will not take it for an American city of the nineteenth century. . . . To fall into this confusion was to lose a great part of its charm, that part which consisted in the illusion that the White City was ten thousand miles and a thousand years away from the City of Chicago, and in oblivion of the reality that the two were contiguous and contemporaneous.[41]

Schuyler pointed to the chief paradox of the fair: it hid most of what the fire had supposedly created. The exposition secluded itself from the very city it celebrated, for fear that Chicago's realities might call its vision into question at nearly every turn. Its proffered "real civic life" was achieved by creating a fantasy city with no real citizens, a fantasy landscape with no real connection to the land.

In the tension between the fairy city and the real lay the heart of the question that Henry Adams and many others asked while visiting the exposition. For many, the trip to the fair marked a first direct encounter with Chicago. Touring the one meant touring the other, and trying to sort out the relation between them. "Chicago," wrote a reporter for *Harper's Weekly,* "will be the main exhibit at the Columbian Exposition of 1893."[42] Over and over again, those who commented on the fair compared its visionary buildings and exhibits to the brash young metropolis that had created them.[43] "This vast civilization," said the French writer Paul Bourget, "with its contrasts of extreme refinement and primitive crudity, is unmistakably symbolized by its central city—miracle of native will; summary of calculating, panting energy and inexhaustible impulse." And then he echoed Adams's question: "But to what end does this impulse tend, toward what goal marches this new world . . .?"[44] The fair seemed a consummate achievement of human idealism and beauty; the city—apart from its suburbs—an irresistible expression of materialism and uncouth power. How the one could have given birth to the other seemed a troubling paradox, and would haunt Chicagoans for the next generation as they tried to build cultural institutions that would recapture the civilized refinement of the fair.[45]

Metropolitan Vice

Intellectuals like Adams and Bourget expressed their thoughts about the fair and the city in the abstract language of high culture, but other tourists were no less struck by the contrasts they discovered during their visit. Mable Treseder, an eighteen-year-old girl from the small town of Viola, Wisconsin, used precisely the same metaphor as Adams to describe Chicago. "I hardly know what to say of the city," she wrote. "It was worse than the confusion of tongues at the Tower of Babel. Humdrum noise and confusion existed al[l] day and all night long."[46] Not all was noise, of course. For Treseder, some sections of Chicago's partitioned landscape were as appealing as the fair. The department stores that occupied entire city blocks offered extraordinary shopping no matter what the line of goods one wanted—far different from her father's hardware store back home. The mansion of the millionaire retailer Potter Palmer seemed nearly the perfect home, if only one could afford it. The views from the downtown skyscrapers were breathtaking, as was the elevator ride to reach their tops; some rural visitors were so taken by elevators that they half expected to pay for the ride.[47]

Treseder was impressed above all by the suburbs. Just as their promoters hoped, they struck her as an ideal combination of city and country, far better maintained than anything she remembered in Wisconsin. On an excursion to Evanston, she said, "We saw the most beautiful stretch of country which was as fresh and green as sun and rain could make it. Farms were ideal with everything present necessary to make them so, the houses being complete with all conveniences and barns and sheds well built and painted." The fences in particular struck her as a sign of Evanston's superiority, for they "were up and running straight, a contrast indeed to the Kickapoo farms where the houses are mere sheds in some places and barns sometimes not worthy of the name, and fences, where are they? We usually have for a few rods a fence that might once have been called board but now hard to tell what it was meant for."[48] The farms of Treseder's childhood suddenly looked humble and unkempt as she compared them with the comfortable estates of Evanston. Measured by the standards of its suburban ideal, Chicago seemed far more civilized and desirable than rural Wisconsin.

But the city also had a darker side, which repelled Treseder as much as these other things attracted her. On the same trip that took her to Potter Palmer's mansion, she wrote, "Our eyes witnessed some of the contrasting sights of the great city where want, misery, and crime hold sway and where poverty deals out a full measure to all. It would fairly make one's heart sick to see the distress manifested on some of those wretched alleys and lanes." Here the contrast with Wisconsin reminded her of the things she most valued about her home. "We who live in the pure fresh country air can gain no idea of the wretchedness of these back alleys until we can see them in reality as they are."[49] Rural Wisconsin had no wealth to match Potter Palmer's, but it also had no poverty to match the slum neighborhoods that encircled Chicago. The journey to the Columbian Exposition gave one a glimpse of those neighborhoods, and the juxtaposition of the two made one wonder about the city's contrasts all the more.

Treseder was hardly alone in her reactions. Hinterland residents who attended the fair approached Chicago with a great deal of apprehension, less because of its poverty than because of its crime and vice. Early newspaper reports about the exposition warned that thieves, pickpockets, and confidence men were swarming the grounds, so tourists would be lucky to hold on to their wallets or purses during their stay. "What has kept hundreds and thousands of people away" from the fair, reported a railroad passenger agent in Michigan, "is simply fear of what would befall them if they came to Chicago." Many would-be travelers had heard that the exposition charged exorbitant rates, that hotels and restaurants were outrageously overpriced, and that coach drivers were not much better than racketeers. Common criminals would happily take any remaining money one might still have after the "honest" tradespeople of the city were done with one. "There are thousands and thousands of people throughout the country," said the same agent, "who believe that every man, woman and child in Chicago is lying in wait to rob them if they come to the fair."[50]

The text that best captures these rural fears of the urban fair was one of the exposition's best-selling publications, *The Adventures of Uncle Jeremiah and Family at the Great Fair,* written by Charles M. Stevens under the pseudonym Quondam.[51] Brought out amid the flood of titles catering to the exposition market, it eventually sold 300,000 copies, a remarkable achievement for any nineteenth-century volume.[52] Describing the trials and tribulations of Jeremiah Jones, a fictional farmer from "Villaville," it

conveys an exceedingly ambivalent portrait of country and city alike. On
the one hand, Uncle Jeremiah is clearly a country bumpkin, profoundly
unwise to the ways of the urban world and nearly overwhelmed at every
turn by what the city has in store for him. On the other hand, although the
exposition has genuine wonders, Chicago is indeed a dangerous place,
with villains waiting everywhere to ensnare the family. Even before they
have disembarked from their train, a confidence man has tried to use a
money-changing trick to "flim-flam" ten dollars from Uncle Jeremiah.
Only the intervention of an honest newsboy—who becomes the family's
streetwise guardian angel—saves the old man his money.[53]

From this beginning follows a long sequence of sometimes comic,
sometimes frightening encounters between rural visitors and urban landscape. When they arrive at the exposition, the Joneses find that nothing in
their past experience has prepared them for it. Uncle Jeremiah "had been
for a good many years taking in a daily landscape of stubble-field, orchard
and straight country roads. His experience had taught him that a red
two-story hay press was a big building. . . . Then he was rushed into
Chicago."[54] Jeremiah reacts to the fair as if "oppressed by a great sorrow," while his niece Fanny and nephew Johnny fume at the "fakery" of
the buildings and exhibits. They are embarrassed when they try to strike
up conversations with wax figures on display.[55] Giant models of hop lice
and potato bugs terrify them, to the great amusement of Chicagoans
standing nearby.[56] They even observe a tourist who has gone mad from
the shock of seeing the exposition's electric lights at night.[57] The sophisticated displays of the fair seem to the Joneses like so many falsehoods.

But the Joneses' sense of Chicago's duplicity is not just a product of
their unsophisticated perception. The city *is* a dangerous place. Johnny is
attacked by a street gang, and loses his knife and apple before being saved
by the same newsboy he met on the train.[58] Uncle Jeremiah again encounters, but does not recognize, the confidence man who had earlier tried to
rob him, this time pretending to be a long-lost rural boy from "Barn-
ville," a community near the family's town. Claiming that he wants very
much to go home, he says he needs only for Uncle to cash his $200 check
so that he can make the journey. The good-hearted Jeremiah is about to
do so when Johnny recognizes the man and calls the police. They inevitably misunderstand the situation and promptly arrest Uncle. When the
family finally manages to retrieve him from jail, his only comment is "Ah,
children, this is Chicago!"[59]

And that is by no means the worst of it. Early in the family's visit,
Fanny is befriended at the exposition by a man named Mr. Blair, who
shows her a detective star and says he can introduce her to "the best
society of Chicago." When she confides in him her wish to go shopping in

the big stores downtown and her fear that she won't know how to do so, he offers to introduce her to his mother and sisters, who will be happy to show her around. Mr. Blair has gotten Fanny to the very doorstep of his "mother's" house when Johnny and the newsboy, in the proverbial lucky coincidence, happen by. The newsboy, knowing Chicago as he does, instantly recognizes that Fanny is about to be trapped in the white slave trade: Mr. Blair is taking her to a brothel, "one of the vilest and most dangerous places in the city." The newsboy warns Johnny, "I tell you if he gits your sis into one of them houses, she'll never come out alive fer she'll kill herself." The two boys try to enlist a policeman to save Fanny, but he proves to be not much better than Mr. Blair, pooh-poohing their fears with the cynical remark "The gal knows her biz." And so the boys have to rescue her themselves, barely getting Fanny out in time. On learning the fate she just escaped, she "shuddered and she whispered a fervent prayer of thankfulness."[60]

The Adventures of Uncle Jeremiah and Family is of course fiction. Its success as a best-seller depended on its ability to position its readers in the borderland between city and country, simultaneously chuckling at the family's foolishness and sharing their outrage at the city's vices. Uncle Jeremiah was such an extreme example of rural ignorance that even country readers could feel sophisticated in recognizing his blunders, which probably accounts for part of the book's popularity. Its exaggerated portrayal of urban-rural differences united its readers into what seemed to be a single cultural community, much as the Montgomery Ward catalog was already doing. But Jeremiah's fictional experiences reflected a real rural perception of Chicago's urban dangers. When asked whether he intended to visit the exposition, one man from western Michigan retorted, "Not I. I am not going. . . . Do you think I am going to be fleeced, not only by the people that are running the fair, but by everybody whom I run against? That world's fair is nothing but a great big fake, got up for the sole purpose of enabling Chicago people to rob innocent people from the outside who may go to visit it."[61] Uncle Jeremiah could not have said it better himself.

Chicagoans did what they could to allay such fears. The exposition maintained a semimilitary corps of 1,700 policemen, as well as a secret service of 250 undercover officers specially trained in detecting "the thieves and sharpers of all descriptions that might be expected to gravitate to Chicago during the progress of the Exhibition."[62] Guidebooks tried to educate visitors about how to avoid the city's dangers. "Don't trust your checks with unauthorized individuals," recommended Rand McNally's guidebook to the fair. If confronted by a solicitor on the street, visitors were advised to just "Say 'No,' and walk quickly along until you are out of their reach. Don't let them take hold of your hand-baggage, and do not be persuaded to do anything by their eloquence." Guidebook authors had to walk a delicate line here, for they wanted above all not to alarm skittish travelers by confirming their fears. And so Rand McNally closed its brief warning about potential threats with the reassuring message that Chicago's street people were "harmless but persistent individuals, and if they perceive you know your business and pay no attention to them will soon let you alone. . . ." If by chance something worse did happen, one could always be confident that "the inevitable policeman looms up on the slightest suspicion of serious trouble. . . ."[63] Chicago would take good care of its visitors.

Hinterland tourists who worried about what might befall them in Chicago were expressing a long-standing rural anxiety about the dangers and corruptions of urban life. Uncle Jeremiah's encounters with the confidence man, and Fanny's close call with a fate worse than death, hardly happened to every rural traveler—but such things did occur. No place where extremes of wealth and poverty mingled so closely could fail to have its share of crime. In the partitioned landscape of postfire Chicago, the vice district was just one more urban neighborhood, with its own rural hinterland like every other part of the city. The two main illegal businesses that went on there, gambling and prostitution, were fed in no small measure by the desire of some hinterland travelers—not the Joneses, but others more knowing about Chicago's offerings—for pleasures best purchased in the anonymity of a great city.

Some even viewed the vice district as a necessary adjunct of the wholesale trade. William T. Stead, a visiting English clergyman who wrote an exposé of Chicago's underworld after attending the fair, reported, "Entertainers are attached to the large wholesale houses, and when the country customer comes in to make his purchases the entertainer personally conducts him round the sights of the town." At least a few wholesalers believed that their customers demanded this service and would go elsewhere for business if it was not provided. "They say that the first night a country customer comes to town he is taken to the theater; next he is taken round to the questionable resorts; and on the third night he insists upon going to the gambling hells," which led at long last to the brothels.[64] Travelers who wished to visit such places more discreetly could purchase a guidebook catering specifically to parts of the city that somehow never showed up in more polite publications. The *Sporting and Club House Directory* offered tips on how to identify only the "safe," "first-class" houses—"the quiet, respectable and legitimate establishments"—among Chicago's nine hundred or more brothels. These distinguished themselves from "dives" by the reduced likelihood that patrons would face robbery or blackmail while doing business there.[65]

One indication of the size of Chicago's vice trade was the mere fact that such guidebooks could be published at all. Harold Vynne's *Chicago by Day and Night* appeared in 1892, just in time to catch the more adventurous World's Fair visitors.[66] Calling Chicago "the Paris of America," Vynne declared that no other city on the continent could offer such a wide variety of amusements: "All tastes may be promptly satisfied, all preferences catered to."[67] Calling himself "a man-of-the-world" who recognized "the desire of the average man to be amused when the cares of business are done," Vynne offered his readers a curiously genteel view of the city's underworld.[68] His book described many entertainments that were perfectly respectable—it even included a chapter on the city's churches—and it never went so far as to list brothels or describe places where one might actually engage in illegal acts. But its double entendres and knowing winks to the male reader gave all the necessary hints for those willing to read between the lines.

Vynne listed the hotels that were the center of what he called "THE BLOODED DISTRICT," which " 'high-rolling' young men of the city have made . . . a sort of headquarters or rendezvous."[69] He described "opera houses" where the performers' costumes "could not possibly convey a more liberal view of 'the female form divine.' "[70] He introduced the reader to massage parlors and Turkish baths where "other entertainment will not be difficult to procure."[71] He even recommended that the tourist might like to visit one of the city's numerous carrousels, since "wherever a carrousel is located a large *clientele* of girls of tender age seems to follow in its wake." Such girls, Vynne said, "do not seem to be burdened with a great supply of innocence. . . ."[72] He left it to the reader's sense of propriety to figure out what to do with such information.

Viewed one way, these "entertainments" constituted a market in vice and corruption; viewed another way, they traded in a furtive sort of moral freedom, at least for the men who used Vynne's book as a guide for their nights in the city. Far from the watchful eyes back home, one could indulge oneself amid the crowds of the metropolis in ways that were unthinkable, or much more hidden, in rural farming communities. In a large urban marketplace like Chicago, sex was a commodity like any other. As the Reverend Stead suggested in describing one of the city's leading madams, "She regards the question from the economic standpoint. Morals no more enter into her business than they do into the business of bulls and bears on the Stock Exchange." Girls unable to support themselves as clerks or stenographers could sometimes do better, at least for a while, in less respectable occupations. "If they have youth, health and good looks they can realize these assets at a higher price down Clark Street, or on Fourth Avenue than at any other place in the city."[73]

Some girls did enter the trade by being trapped into it in the way Fanny Jones had narrowly escaped. Stead told of corrupt cabmen in Chicago who "if they find a pretty girl who has not enough money to pay her fare" could "usually raise the money by delivering her at a sporting house."[74] Other reform tracts spoke of procuresses who befriended young country girls traveling alone on trains, or of the regular importation of French girls from Quebec to supply Chicago brothels.[75] Horrifying as such stories might be to some, however, rural prostitution and other vices were markets like any others. Vice was yet another example of city and country being linked to each other by an invisible network of supply and demand. As Vynne's guidebook suggested, a fair share of the money that sustained Chicago's "Blooded District" came from outside. Like every other neighborhood in the city, the vice district had its own regional hinterland. Its customers were often male travelers seeking to purchase more than just supplies in the metropolis; its retailers were often female migrants who had made their way to the brothels out of homes far away from Chicago.[76]

That the buyers and sellers of vice might both come from the same countryside only made the corrupting influence of Chicago seem all the worse. The rural residents who feared what might happen if they came to the White City and were ensnared by Chicago's darker side knew only too well that the metropolis was a place where morality came cheap. They knew that its brewers and saloonkeepers had consistently frustrated the efforts of downstate legislators to prohibit the sale of alcohol, that font of so many other vices.[77] They read in their newspapers about the corruption of machine politics in the city.[78] They had experienced at first hand the hard-selling dishonesty and fraudulent dealings of Chicago's traveling salesmen.[79] They loathed the cynical and immoral grain speculators on the Chicago Board of Trade, who seemed to prosper by gambling with the foodstuffs on which farmers' and workers' lives depended.[80] "A full hand must win," one farmer said of the Board, "though it be held by Satan himself."[81] Having heard so many terrible things about the city, rural residents were more than ready to believe the *Western Rural* when it labeled Chicago "The Grand College of Vice." After all, the city produced "a vast host of vagabonds and criminals to overrun the State of Illinois and the Northwest," whether in the form of drummers, speculators, confidence men, prostitutes, or tramps. "From the barrooms and dens of vice in this city," said the *Rural*, "is pouring a cloud of immorality and pauperism" threatening the entire region.[82]

The Moral Economy of City and Country

Vice: in all its hydra-headed forms, this was where the contrast between city and country seemed greatest and most menacing. The urban market concentrated hinterland trade, even the supply and demand for sin. "Criminals," wrote the *Western Rural,* "do not huddle together in the rural districts, for there is nothing for them to prey upon." The market wasn't large enough. "In the cities, however, they are found in all degrees of degradation and in all degrees of combination."[83] What really worried rural and small-town residents of Chicago's hinterland was their perception that the city acted as a *magnet* for sin. Criminals and vice merchants flocked to its underworld. On its face, this might have seemed a good thing, sparing the countryside their presence. But in the city these servants of Satan became a concentrated source of moral infection, seducing others who might not otherwise have chosen a life of sin. Young people drawn to the city by its energy and excitement could all too easily give in to pleasures and temptations that would finally jeopardize their souls. Farmers, in short, worried that Chicago and other great cities might steal their children.

Agricultural publications regularly addressed this issue in articles that ran under titles like "Stay in the Country" or "How to Keep Boys on the Farm."[84] A poem printed in the Wisconsin State Grange *Bulletin* in 1878 summarizes the genre nicely:

> *Don't Leave the Farm*
> Come, boys, I have something to tell you;
>   Come near, I would whisper it low;
> You are thinking of leaving the homestead,
>   Don't be in a hurry to go.
> The city has many attractions,
>   But think of the vices and sins!
> When once in the vortex of fashion,
>   How soon the course downward begins. . . .[85]

Such pieces lamented the tendency of farm children, especially young men, to abandon the family homestead to seek better lives in the city. Almost always, they made a sentimental appeal to the virtues of rural life, and itemized the moral dangers to which impressionable young people exposed themselves in the city. "All will admit that the country is the natural abode of man," wrote one Missouri correspondent to a Chicago-based farm periodical, for "there the youth is in constant communion with nature. . . ." Things were far different in the great urban centers. "The object of the city is trade,—trade that so often ruins the character— trade that leads men into all the intricacy of vice. . . . The city seems to be the natural home of vice. . . ."[86] The plain, simple life of the soil, with its honest hard work and moral uprightness, was "all forgotten in the extravagant and senseless worship of the hollow glitter . . . of the metropolis."[87]

And yet it was just this "hollow glitter" that so attracted young men and women tired of the drudgery of the farm. Few things more troubled rural parents than the adolescent flight from the countryside, and farm periodicals regularly offered advice about how to counteract it. Parents should remind their children that the cities were crowded, dangerous, wracked with unemployment, and full of moral snares for the unwary.[88] Although a young man might dream about the great success stories of country boys who had made their fortunes in the city—including some of Chicago's richest millionaires—they should know that the majority got trapped in dull, repetitive jobs with no hope of advancement. A thousand failed for every genius who succeeded.[89] A young person of "average" talents was far more likely to prosper on the farm than elsewhere.[90] "Always remember," one article remonstrated, "that the odds are fearfully against success in the city, and that they are largely against failure in the country."[91] Children should ponder the poorhouse, the brothel, the prison, the scaffold, and the drunkard's grave as the most likely endings of an urban dream turned nightmare. Most of all, they should know that metropolitan sophistication was false, a deceit against honest men and women drawn to the city's shining surface without reflecting upon its hollowness. Even if wayward farm children managed to escape an urban life of vice and crime, they would still lose the purity that was their moral birthright.

In urging this last point, defenders of farm children mobilized every available rhetorical tool to express their passion. Only an extended passage can do justice to their anti-urban argument:

> The apparent indolence and dazzling exterior of fashionable life in the city, the luxurious sparkle of professional and mercantile pursuits in these great centers, have a peculiar charm to the youth of the country, who soon begin to see nothing but dull monotony and uninteresting drudgery on the farm and in the village. But once in the city and the novelty worn off, they awaken from their sweet dreams, step from their castles in the air, and find that city life is terribly in earnest, alarmingly treacherous, and indescribably irksome and unremunerative. If they escape the allurements of vice, they find themselves surrounded by such unbounded selfishness, and trickery, and insincerity, that the loveliest of their nature is poisoned

and withered, the divinity of their manhood and womanhood is shockingly marred, and that which came from the country a beautiful gem, reflecting the soft light of generous love, and tinging its surroundings with the hue of heaven's purity and sweetness, becomes a shriveled, graceless, and loveless crudity, vexatious to itself and a thorn to its fellows. If we wallow in the mud it will be miraculous if we escape the soiling of our garments; if we live amidst contageon [sic] it is folly to wonder why we become contaminated, and if we walk among vice, and mingle with impurity, and listen to the teachings of corruption and selfish treachery, it is certainly not remarkable that we should become bankrupt in principle, in honor, and in virtue.

Such a sermon had only one possible ending: "Young men, remain in the country."[92] The country was the natural wellspring of a good and moral life. Most of all, it was *home,* where a child could remain in the bosom of the family and in joyous contemplation of a life lived close to nature.

The trouble with these arguments was that their moral lamentations and scare tactics failed to get to the bottom of why rural children were leaving home in the first place. Reading them, one would think that Chicago was the home of Satan, and that only the devil's own temptations could explain the attractions of the place. But these idealized portraits of country life represented the conventions of sentimental literature more than the actual world of the farm. One bemused correspondent wrote to the *Western Rural* after reading its "pieces of advise [sic] . . . interlined with scraps of poetry, giving glowing accounts of life on the farm," to declare that it just wasn't so. Farmhands had to be up with the sun and be all day at chores, even long into the night, for a grudging monthly wage of $20 plus board and washing. In the city, on the other hand, the hours of work were from seven to noon and from one to six, with plenty of time left over for reading, entertainment, and time with friends. An intelligent young person in the city could become a clerk, bookkeeper, or telegraph operator, doing jobs that were considerably more pleasant than the hard manual labor of a farmhand. Best of all, the monthly wage for such work was about $50 a month. Was it any wonder that young people opted for the city? Morality and vice had nothing to do with it: "they are going where they can get the most pay."[93]

From the perspective of rural parents, saying that children were leaving the farm because they could earn more money in the city did not help much. Why, after all, was the city able to pay higher wages? Because it extracted from the country profits that rightfully belonged to farmers. Farmers got poor prices for their crops, so the story ran, because railroads, grain elevators, speculators, and merchants—"monopolies"—all extracted unearned profit as goods passed from one buyer to the next.

Agrarian protesters ranging from the Grangers to the Populists embraced the physiocratic doctrine that attributed all economic value to tillers of the soil, the rest of society being entirely sustained by the farmers' labors. Since, as one early protester argued, "the process of transferring an article from hand to hand produces no value," it stood to reason that wholesalers, retailers, and perhaps even the railroads contributed nothing of real value to society. "It is evident that not only the cost of their support, with that of their families, clerks and other employes, but also the whole of their wasteful expenditure in handsome stores, gilt signs, and every costly device of advertising and solicitation . . . has to be subtracted from the productive labors of those who create value."[94] Urban culture rested on the backs of rural farmers.

Viewed in this way, most of the income that city people "earned" was an illegitimate tax on the countryside. When the city of Chicago succeeded in rebuilding itself so quickly after the Great Fire, at least a few farmers wondered suspiciously where all the money had come from to pay the bill. "They sometimes visit the great metropolis," wrote one rural protester, "and see for themselves the palaces, the chariots and the liveried coachmen. . . ." Puzzled at "the means by which multitudes live and fare sumptuously who have no visible means of support," such farmers "have come to the conclusion after all that it is the producer who foots the bill."[95] Urban wealth was nothing more than stolen booty from a confidence game played by urban merchants at the expense of rural farmers. Here was a deeper reason for rural anxiety about farm children departing for the city, and even for suspicion about Chicago's hosting the World's Fair. The city's merchants were little better than thieves; they too were representatives of urban vice and dishonesty. If farm children went to work in the city, they would join those who profited at their parents' expense. A report of the Wisconsin State Grange captured this view succinctly with a single telling quotation: "Trade pays the whole bill; the city is the *fleece;* officials, professions and tradesmen the *shearers;* farmers the *sheep,* and in these times . . . the *hide goes with the fleece.* . . ."[96]

How should farmers combat this process? In addition to demanding new laws to regulate railroads and agricultural markets, both the Grangers and the Populists made several recurrent suggestions.[97] One was to improve agriculture with science and to revamp education for farmers and farm children.[98] New machines and new techniques would make farming more efficient and profitable. State schools of agriculture would put the findings of modern science at the disposal of farmers. Then they too could enjoy the increased leisure that made urban life so attractive; their children could work less and be more likely to stay at home. Rural areas would become as cultured and civilized as their urban counterparts.

In pursuing this line of argument, farmers were likely to admit that rural life was not such a sentimental idyll after all. Farm work was hard and unrelenting; one could scarcely blame children for trying to flee it. "Go into the country," said Dudley Adams, master of the Iowa State Grange, in 1872, "and you will find numberless cases of men with poor health, crushed energies, ruined constitutions, and stunted souls, and women the slaves of habits of excessive labor, more fatal than the pernicious and much-condemned customs of fashionable society. You will find children prematurely old, with the bright light of happy childhood extinguished, and everywhere a lack of that life and cheerfulness which gives to life its greatest charms." The city was not to blame for these problems. No, said Adams, "Most of these evils can be traced directly to overwork."[99] The rural countryside was not adequately participating in the progress of the age, for reasons that could be solved only from within. Those who wanted to save themselves and their children had best look to the *virtues* of the city and strive to give their rural homes the cultured benefits of urban life.

The farmers' biggest problem, argued many, was that they saw their calling as brawn work rather than brain work. The modern age rewarded intelligence above all other virtues, so farmers who wanted to improve their lot must *think* more about the efficient operation of their farms. Agriculture should be placed on a business footing, with the same attention given to costs and profits that enabled urban merchants to succeed. The loneliness of farm life, and the barrenness of too many rural homes, should be fought at every opportunity by enhancing the life of the mind. A farmer should keep a library of books and "give a liberal share of his time to thought, study, and recreation."[100] The farmhouse should be surrounded by a lawn and lovely gardens. Work should be kept within reasonable limits so that children would understand the genuine pleasures of rural life. The family should gather in the parlor regularly to read poetry and tell stories, and join in Grange celebrations to fight the isolation that kept them from knowing their neighbors. If farmers wanted to keep their children in the country, the best remedy was not to rail against the city but to *"make home attractive."*[101]

In sum, intelligent farmers would follow a threefold strategy: they would associate in organizations like the Grange, educate themselves about new ways of farming, and then work together economically and politically to give agriculture the same status and advantage in society enjoyed by other professions. The Grange's motto was "Cooperation, Association, Education," with the first of these being its most direct economic response to the forces its members saw hurting them.[102] No matter where farmers traded, their urban antagonists—railroads, grain elevators, wholesalers, retailers, manufacturers—were working to suppress competition by forming alliances and creating "monopolies." With all other branches of the economy—transportation, distribution, and manufacturing—having united for their own advantage, agriculture would suffer until it did likewise. "The present," declared E. E. Bryant before the Wisconsin State Agricultural Convention in 1873, "is an age of co-operation." Merchants, corporations, and even political rings were all trying to extract maximum gains by combining and cooperating, so it was foolish for farmers not to do likewise. "With this tendency to unite for mutual strength and protection so rife among the other occupations . . . ," Bryant said, the farmer's hand "is altogether to [sic] poor to play it alone. In his present condition, he is a mere bushwhacker, confronting organized and well-equipped armies."[103]

For farmers, "cooperation" became an almost mystical symbol of modern civilized life, allowing people in large cities and corporate institutions to join forces in the service of their collective interests. Agrarian protesters felt ambivalent about some possible consequences of cooperation—particularly the tendency of large organizations like railroads to work for their own gain rather than the public good—but cooperation itself seemed wholly positive, a pathway to improved rural life, to local control, and to a stronger sense of rural community. If only farmers, the last economic individualists in an increasingly collective world, could form associations and work to support their common interests as every other sector of society seemed to be doing, they too would participate in the progressive changes that had heretofore been concentrated in cities.

To many, it seemed that the concrete way to achieve these ends was to form buying and selling cooperatives, which would replicate and modify urban mercantile institutions to serve rural ends. State Granges would hire agents to handle the collective marketing of farm produce, and make arrangements with manufacturers for mass purchases that would avoid the "middle-man" profits of urban wholesalers and retailers. If agrarian theory was correct, the result would be much lower prices. Farmers could escape the metropolitan "tax" that seemed such a heavy burden on their economic well-being. Freed from having to support the nonproductive classes that filled the great cities, they would gain the benefits of the urban marketplace without having to pay the unnecessary costs associated with it.

But the rewards of cooperation proved much more elusive than farmers had expected. To be effective, selling cooperatives had to hold farm produce off the market to escape the low prices that always came with harvest season, and this required a larger capital investment than farm organizations could muster. With railroads resisting cooperative selling as well, it did not become a reality until much later, in the 1920s and 1930s.[104] Cooperative buying met with some success when a few urban wholesalers—Montgomery Ward among them—saw it as an opportunity to reach a wider rural clientele. Much to their surprise, however, the Grange cooperatives soon found themselves in the same boat as the retailers they were trying to circumvent. Montgomery Ward and some other metropolitan wholesalers were more than happy to sell to the Grange at lower prices than local retailers could afford—but they were just as willing to offer low prices to anyone else, including the Grange's own members. In 1879, the agent for the Wisconsin State Grange complained, "Many of the merchants offer, and do sell goods as cheap to our members as they cost to get them through the Agency."[105] Grange prices in many cases turned out to be no better than those of other retailers. Some loyal members continued to buy from the organization, but all too often there were few economic reasons to do so.

The deeper explanation for the failure of Grange cooperatives lay in the farmers' critique of the existing distribution system, for they rarely recognized why manufacturers, wholesalers, and retailers relied on each other to do business. In effect, Grangers ignored—or didn't believe in— the central place hierarchy and the distribution networks that went with it. Many manufacturers refused outright to deal with Grange agents, and members usually took this as proof of their monopolistic corruption. But as merchants throughout Chicago's hinterland had recognized for years, wholesaling and retailing were tricky, difficult businesses, with high risks.[106] Manufacturers relied on wholesalers to distribute their products, and they in turn depended on retailers to absorb the large costs of carrying stock and making numerous small sales to customers of limited means in hundreds of towns and rural communities. None of the three was eager to disrupt the complex trading relationships they had developed with each other, and retailers in particular felt themselves sorely threatened by wholesalers and manufacturers who sold direct to final customers.

Each element of this distribution network had associated costs and risks—advance payments, interest charges, unsold stock, nonpaying customers, transportation and storage charges—which the Grange cooperatives soon found cropping up on their own balance sheets as well. Far from avoiding the "middle-man's profit," they began to experience the middleman's *loss.* [107] Some part of the metropolitan "tax" was apparently intrinsic to distribution, and was a more legitimate part of the cost of doing business than agrarian theory had suggested. John G. Otis, the Kansas State Grange agent, reported in 1875 that he now understood why so many manufacturers had refused to sell to him. "It was not altogether a whim, on their part . . . ," he said. "The truth is, we did not show them a thoroughly united, and well digested system, to take the place of the one they are already using."[108] To make Grange cooperatives successful meant reproducing the existing wholesale-retail network, with all its attendant costs.

The effort usually failed, and in the places where it did succeed it came to look more like the usual wholesale-retail system than not. Moreover, competition among regular wholesalers and retailers eventually produced many of the same benefits Grangers had expected from their cooperatives.[109] To take just the two most obvious examples, Montgomery Ward and Sears, Roebuck succeeded in lowering prices and reducing the "middle-man's profit" by applying the farmers' rural cooperative logic in an urban corporate setting. How one interpreted this oddly mixed failure and success of the cooperatives depended on one's ideology. Perhaps the merchants in places like Chicago were simply too powerful to beat. Or perhaps they and other urban institutions were not so intrinsically corrupt as the rhetoric of protest suggested: perhaps they performed a genuine service to rural areas after all.[110]

City and Country as a Unity

All these things—urban vice, the flight of farm children, the squalor of the countryside, the difficulties of agrarian cooperation, the need for rural education and "improvement"—called into question the simple moral dichotomies between city and country that were so close to American hearts in the nineteenth century, and that remain as cultural residues to this day. By the 1890s, half a century of metropolitan growth and thirty years of sporadic agrarian resentment toward "the city" had left Chicago and its hinterland with an exceedingly ambivalent relationship. Country and city met each other—at the World's Fair and elsewhere—at the intersection of two symbolic axes, with a continuum of complex moral imagery arrayed between them. At the two extremes of the urban axis were the White City and the Dark: the city as pinnacle of civilization versus the city as abyss of moral despair. At opposite poles of the rural axis were similar images: the country as pastoral utopia versus the country as stultifying backwater. No real place could ever fall so neatly into these categories, but the rhetorical oppositions were ready at hand whenever one needed to use them. Depending on what one wanted to attack or defend, the contrast between city and country was always good for an argument.

The census of 1890, for instance, revealed that a large number of rural townships throughout the Mississippi Valley had lost population in the preceding decade, a sure sign, some thought, of their cultural deterioration. In Illinois, only 579 townships had grown; 800 had lost residents. Most of Iowa's townships (893) were still expanding, but over 40 percent (691) had shrunk.[111] Social commentators worried that falling populations meant dwindling trade, industry, wealth, and public spirit. These were all "signs of decay," as was the weakening of small towns relative to large ones in the competition among levels of the urban hierarchy. Rural decline was compounded by the flight of young people to the city, and "the benumbing effect it has upon those who remain behind."[112] More than just Grangers and Populists feared that rural areas were lagging behind the rest of American civilization. The sociologist Walter Wyckoff, wandering around the Iowa countryside disguised as an itinerant worker, noted in some areas "a cheerlessness in farm-life the gloom of which would be difficult to heighten." Some farmers spoke of "the tyranny of 'the money power,'" and thought they were "fast sinking to a condition of 'vassalage.'" In their eyes, images of rural backwardness and material decline were proof of exploitation, of the continuing influence of a corrupt and corrupting urban economy.[113]

But there were others, apparently more prosperous or with longer memories, who reported that "the hardships were all gone from farming. . . . An accessible market, admirable labor-saving machines, ready intercourse with neighbors and with the outside world, had changed the original struggle under every disadvantage to a life of ease in contrast."[114] By this reading, country life was fast improving, so differences between the urban and the rural diminished each year. With new agricultural technology, improved roads, regular rural mail service, and new transportation systems, who could doubt that progress was helping the farm as much as the city? As the secretary of agriculture predicted in 1893, "when the country home is equal in comfort and culture to that of the city, no argument will be needed to prove its superiority to the latter."[115]

Whether the countryside was progressing or declining depended on where one stood and with whom one was arguing. Even agrarian protesters could become confused about which image of rural life to invoke. A classic instance was the editorial page of an 1883 antimonopoly newspaper in Nebraska, the *Pawnee Banner*. In adjacent columns, it ran two articles. One attacked the railroads and the "rings" for preventing farmers from getting ahead, forcing them to live "from hand to mouth." The other sought to encourage migration to the prosperous and fast-growing agricultural districts of Nebraska, declaring that the state's increase in population and wealth had "far exceeded the expectation of the most sanguine." A farmer who came to this favored land could rest assured that "the fruits of his labor" would not be "snatched from him to gratify the appetite of tenacious corporations."[116] Apparently one could have one's rhetorical cake and eat it too, embracing competing rural images even when they pointed in opposite directions.

So too with the metropolis. Ignatius Donnelly, a leading Populist politician, described in his anti-utopian novel, *Caesar's Column,* a future urban world so dehumanized that society set up voluntary suicide centers for those who could take it no longer. "The truth is, that, in this vast, overcrowded city, man is a drug,—a superfluity,—and I think many men and women end their lives out of an overwhelming sense of their own insignificance."[117] Things might not yet have gone so far in Chicago, but by the 1890s at least a few intellectuals were writing of the anomie that the city encouraged in its inhabitants, a rootlessness akin to the lurid images that agricultural papers used when describing what happened to rural children in such a place. Henry Blake Fuller in his 1893 novel, *The Cliff-dwellers,* described a Chicago in which "nobody really knows who he is, or who his people are, or where he is from . . . a town full to overflowing with single young men . . . from everywhere."[118] Under such conditions, a person could feel emotions rather like the ones Donnelly described, so one of Fuller's characters "had no sense of any right relation to the community in which he lived."[119] This might not lead to overt vice of the kind rural parents feared, but it surely corrupted the spirit.

Fuller began his book with an extended description of life in Chicago's skyscrapers, epitomized in the fictional building he called the Clifton. His opening conceit is that Chicago's downtown is a wilderness directly analogous to the mountains and canyon lands of the Great West, so as an "explorer" wanders through its savage landscape "the rugged and erratic plateau of the Bad Lands lies before him in all its hideousness and impracticability. It is a wild tract full of sudden falls, unexpected rises, precipitous dislocations. The high and low are met together."[120] Fuller's Chicago landscape is as moral as it is physical. His city expresses a sublime, unforgiving nature, and its inhabitants perceive it as such. Only a few know all its perilous trails, for most who reside in this wilderness prefer to stay within their own small domains. The four thousand people who work in the Clifton range from bankers, lawyers, and brokers to their clerical staffs, building engineers, and janitors. They are served by a lunch counter, a tobacconist, and a newsstand, and the mechanisms of the building handle their other creature comforts: light, shelter, warmth, water. They can work in this place without having much to do with the city outside, let alone the greater countryside beyond. As Fuller says, "the Clifton aims to be complete within itself."[121] The building's autonomy and self-sufficiency were akin to the image of Montgomery Ward's "Busy Hive," but also mirrored for Fuller the familiar urban emotions of loneliness and disconnection that residents experienced in the midst of a crowded metropolis.

For many middle-class critics, the very scale of Chicago prevented its inhabitants from belonging to anything like a real community within its borders. A place like the Clifton isolated its occupants from their neighbors in a way that would have been unthinkable in the country, so even those who worked in adjacent offices could remain strangers. And if neighborliness did not exist within a single building, how could it survive the spatial separation of neighborhood from neighborhood, class from class, person from person? When William T. Stead wrote his attack on the city in 1894, he reserved special praise for the settlement workers at Jane Addams's Hull House, telling in a chapter called "Who Is My Neighbor?" of their efforts to reform precisely this aspect of urban life. To describe what they were trying to achieve, Stead turned quickly to rural metaphors. "The healthy natural community," he wrote, "is that of a small country town or village in which every one knows his neighbor, and where all the necessary ingredients for a happy, intelligent and public-spirited municipal life exist in due proportion."[122] The partitioning of Chicago's landscape had destroyed its residents' sense of *belonging* to a place and community. If the city was to locate its civic heart, it would first have to recover its rural roots.

And yet: Donnelly, Fuller, and Stead all wrote their books lamenting the dislocations of Chicago's urban world within two years of the World's Columbian Exposition, that "earliest achievement of a real civic life."[123] Stead himself had visited the fair the day before it closed, and declared, "nothing that I have ever seen in Paris, in London, in St. Petersburg, or in Rome, could equal the effect produced by the illumination of these great white palaces that autumn night." Only one memory from his childhood—his first visit to Edinburgh—could match the thrill of this "ivory city, beautiful as a poet's dream, silent as a city of the dead." It left "an impression of perfect beauty."[124] When Stead published his attack on Chicago's vices two years later, he ended it with a prophetic chapter depicting a reformed Chicago of the twentieth century. In describing that place, he remembered not a rural village but this landscape. The Chicago of the future would itself become the White City.[125]

Whatever Chicago's faults, few who visited it in 1893 were left unmoved by what they found. Especially when they remembered how quickly it had grown, and how completely its downtown had been destroyed just twenty-two years before, they could hardly doubt they were seeing one of the great cities of the world, a wonder of the modern age. Perhaps it was, as one journalist remarked, "somewhat too careless of appearances, with dirty streets and smoke-filled atmosphere; a trifle bumptious, vaunting itself in an unseemly way; paying less heed to culture than to profits, unmindful, at times, of good form . . . yet big-hearted, open-handed, self-reliant, and moving forward with the strides of a giant to great destiny."[126] Such metaphors were typical, and occurred so frequently in descriptions of the period that they quickly became clichés. The city's accomplishments were those of an infant prodigy, its faults those of an energetic and inexperienced youth. For an adolescent to have achieved such extraordinary things in so short a time held great promise for its future adulthood.

If Chicago was indeed the main exhibit of the fair, visitors found much there that expressed the ideals of the White City. Country folk like Mable Treseder saw in Chicago's suburbs partial embodiments of the way of life that agrarian reformers were trying to bring to rural farmsteads. Its less idyllic working-class neighborhoods, with their cramped but freestanding cottages, were still far better than tenements, and attracted country people from halfway around the world: the farming folk who lived in them came not just from Iowa but from communities all over Europe. The city's art galleries, libraries, and museums were the finest west of the Hudson. Its park system was "truly her crown" and "as free from harm and eyesore as any in the land."[127] Its skyscrapers defined America's urban future, just as the Beaux Arts architecture of the fair would shape the downtowns of cities across the nation—Washington, D.C., not least among them—for the next generation. Even Uncle Jeremiah, in the midst of all his trials, said of what he saw, "I believe I have felt more of the Lord in my soul in the last few days than I ever did before in so many years."[128]

However much city and country might oppose each other in the rhetoric of moral economy, however much reformers and protesters might try to use the one as a tool for criticizing the other, neither had a monopoly on ideals or moralizing visions. That their descriptions often appeared in counterpoint, to underscore what each needed of the other's world, suggests as much about their unity as about their differences. Grange cooperatives and rural improvements sought to bring the advantages of metropolitan living to the heart of the countryside, just as urban parks and suburban bungalows sought to bring the virtues of rural openness to the heart of the city. Those who visited the great fair saw in its exhibits a promise of future progress for city and country alike. Despite the ease with which rhetoric could set the two against each other as warring visions of the good life, the habit of seeing them in opposition was a big part of the moral dilemma they seemed to pose. Regarding them as distinct and separable obscured their indispensable connections. Each had created the other, so their mutual transformations in fact expressed a single system and a single history.

Hard as it might be to remember this mutuality, it was surely a part of what Henry Adams felt when he said of the White City that it expressed "American thought as a unity." Given the way Americans' urban and rural visions often seemed to bifurcate and head in opposite directions, Adams and others might rightly wonder "whether the American people knew where they were driving."[129] But city and country had emerged from the same past, and would grow toward the same future. Back in 1849, just when Chicago and its hinterland had begun to discover each other, the *Prairie Farmer* had prophesied the history they would share:

> The country produces that without which the city could not live; and did the city not exist, the produce of the country for all but family consumption would be valueless. Its outlet, its market is the town. There is thus a mutual interest between them, one sustaining the other, ministering and being ministered to. There is no better index of the thrift of a country, than the thrift of its towns. They are the heart through which pours the tide of its life for the sustenance and health of the whole.[130]

The insight was easy to forget, and certainly did not keep the people of city and country from repeated skirmishes that were as material as they were rhetorical. Metropolis and hinterland themselves divided into neighborhoods and subregions whose conflicts seemed often to outweigh their connections. But one can understand neither Chicago nor the Great West if one neglects to tell their stories together. What often seem separate narratives finally converge in a larger tale of people reshaping the land to match their collective vision of its destiny. In that vision—of a White City and its thriving countryside—the people of metropolis and hinterland stood far more united than not.

Epilogue:
Where We Were Driving

All ethics so far evolved rest upon a single premise: that the individual is a member of a community of interdependent parts. . . . That man is, in fact, only a member of a biotic team is shown by an ecological interpretation of history. Many historical events, hitherto explained solely in terms of human enterprise, were actually biotic interactions between people and land. . . . Is history taught in this spirit? It will be, once the concept of land as a community really penetrates our intellectual life.

—Aldo Leopold, *A Sand County Almanac* (1949)[1]

Growing up in Wisconsin in the 1960s, I found it easy not to think much about Chicago, except as a place that had little to do with my own life and that I didn't much care to visit. (Like many midwestern children, I made an exception for the wonderful exhibits of the Museum of Science and Industry—those last remaining echoes of the World's Fair—and later for the Art Institute as well, but the rest of the city offered few attractions.) Although my mother's parents owned a hardware store in a small Wisconsin town and bought most of their supplies from Chicago wholesalers like Ace Hardware, I gave no thought to how much my family history was tied to that place. I could not have told you how many of the things I consumed in my daily life had passed through the city, or how much I depended on its markets to sustain my existence. Unconscious of my material ties with Chicago, I understood it in symbolic terms not very different from those of nineteenth-century farmers. Budding environmentalist that I was, I saw it as an unnatural, dangerous place with much dirt, little beauty, and few humane qualities. I pitied those who had to live in it, and I had no desire to join them.

I was of course quite different from those farmers, many of whom shared my dislike for the city without any illusions about how much their lives depended on it. I was a suburban child, used to thinking of supermarkets as the place where my family got its food, and department stores as the place where we got its clothing. That Chicago might have been an intermediary between myself and the farms and factories from which our food and clothing actually came did not occur to me until I was much older. I was a baby boomer, and mine was a "consumer" generation, very conscious of looking after our own needs in the market, but not nearly so aware of how the things we purchased were actually produced. Only now do I realize how much my own youthful perspective was shaped by the connections and disconnections between city and country, consumer and producer, humanity and nature, that occurred at Chicago—and many other places as well—during the late nineteenth and early twentieth centuries.

That I was unconscious of living in Chicago's hinterland is one important ending to the long story I have been telling in this book. The irony of the World's Columbian Exposition is that it marked the climax—and the beginning of the end—of Chicago's role as gateway to the Great West. By the time of the fair, the city that had so successfully dominated markets from the Great Lakes to the Sierra Nevada was already meeting serious competition from other urban centers to its west. In this, it was very much a victim of its own success. By combining with the railroads to open so large a market for so vast a region, it had encouraged the human migrations, environmental changes, and economic developments that produced other great cities—Minneapolis, Omaha, Kansas City, Denver—which could in turn supply urban services to their own emerging regions. The nearness of these cities to western markets gave them the same sorts of advantages that had allowed Chicago wholesalers to compete so effectively with eastern merchants not much more than a generation before.

To make matters worse, growth had hidden costs that also diminished Chicago's competitiveness. Diseconomies of scale began to hamper enterprise in Chicago, so the very market concentration which had earlier been the city's proudest boast became its greatest problem. Chicago had once immensely benefited from being the meeting place of eastern and western railroads. With the two sets of lines arriving in the city in different stations on opposite sides of town, passengers moving between east and west had no choice but to get off one train, travel crosstown to a different station, and get onto another train to continue their journey. "It is one of the peculiarities of Chicago," wrote a visitor in the 1890s, "that she arrests a great proportion of the travelling public that seeks destinations beyond her limits in either direction."[2] All spent time—and money—in Chicago before departing. In the early days, this enforced crosstown movement through the business district significantly benefited Chicago's commerce. But by the late 1860s it was starting to create traffic problems. Railroads centering in Chicago started having to defend themselves against non-Chicago competitors who claimed in advertisements that passengers traveling through the city could not escape *"long and tedious omnibus rides"* even if they had booked through tickets.[3] As time went on, the filling-in of the nation's rail network offered ways to avoid the delays and inconvenience of traveling through Chicago, and the city's earlier advantages began to erode.

By the 1870s, the high cost of renting railroad cars and elevator storage in Chicago was encouraging shippers to consider alternative routes for their grain and other products. Indeed, it was not just farmers who supported the new "Granger laws" regulating transport and warehousing interests. As we have already seen, Chicago merchants, newspapers, and Board of Trade members saw the business of their city being harmed by the high costs of shipping goods through it, and played important roles in lobbying for new regulations.[4] In such cases, it was easy to blame the elevators for their "monopolistic" behavior, but the deeper problems of Chicago's congestion were structural. The city's main railroads had all been built in the 1840s and 1850s, when Chicago was still a small town. Since then, the grid of city streets had steadily engulfed the tracks. High-volume freight and passenger traffic moved through urban neighborhoods with no separation between them.

The railroad companies had done nothing to raise or lower their tracks, so all crossed the city's streets at grade level. As Chicago grew, trains had to cross more streets to reach their stations. Large freight trains posed especially awkward problems, blocking streets for such extended periods that the city passed ordinances and posted policemen to limit how long trains could remain in one place. To reduce the risk of collisions and injury to pedestrians, railroads by the late 1860s were having to take a number of new precautions. Since electrical gates and warning systems were technologies of the future, the companies had to station flagmen at busy intersections, incurring new wage costs for each such crossing. They had to slow trains to six miles per hour, so it took the better part of an hour just to reach city limits. And on very busy intersections, companies started building overpasses in order that trains and street traffic could cross each other on different grades with no risk of interference. All these new rules and restrictions added capital costs to the expense of handling traffic in Chicago as opposed to other cities.[5]

Worse, the new measures failed to solve the biggest problem. Injuries at railroad grade crossings became a daily fact of life in the city; by the time of the World's Fair, approximately six hundred people each year— almost two a day—were being killed by trains. This remarkable statistic includes none of those who were merely injured, the people William Stead described as "those legless, armless men and women" who were "merely the mangled remnant of the massacre . . . constantly going on year in and year out."[6] Julian Ralph, a New York journalist who had much praise for Chicago and its fair, resorted to unaccustomed sarcasm in describing the railroad officials who argued "that they invented and developed Chicago, and that her people are ungrateful to protest against a little thing like a slaughter which would depopulate the average village in a year."[7] One obvious response to grade killings was to slow trains still more, but as Ralph acknowledged, this would further inconvenience the cross-country travelers and suburban commuters who were already being delayed by Chicago's congested rail system. The ultimate solution would separate rails and roads much more completely, but that was an immensely expensive proposition that would seriously increase the capital costs of transportation in the city.

Had I read of comparable problems in the Chicago of my youth, I would have seen them as one more proof of the city's nastiness, but I would not have thought them particularly connected to my own life. Not so the residents of Chicago's hinterland in the 1890s. They naturally saw the grade-crossing deaths as horrible, and added them to the list of unpleasant things to hold against the city. But any solution such as elevating railroad tracks to raise them above grade throughout Chicago, and spending as much as $200 million to do so—that was another matter. Some rural residents recognized immediately that their own transportation rates would ultimately bear the cost of this urban improvement: yet another metropolitan tax on the hinterland. In Iowa, the editor of the *Clinton Age* felt moved to argue, "Iowa has a large interest in such a scheme." The state might be willing to help solve Chicago's grade-crossing problem if this could be done in a cost-effective way, but the schemes being put forward by the city's newspapers and reformers were far too expensive, raising all the old rural resentments against the metropolis. "Iowa," he said, "has paid an immense cash tribute every year to Chicago, for a score or more of years, and no doubt always will continue to do so. The state has been bled almost to depletion by Chicago."[8] The cost of raising the city's railroad grades should not be added to Iowa's burdens. Such feelings of exploitation were a classic reflection of city-hinterland relations at the end of the nineteenth century.

It would be hard to imagine a comparable editorial fifty years later, which suggests the first ending to this story. Congestion—with its attendant costs in time, money, and human life—was an inevitable price of Chicago's success as a railroad metropolis.[9] No transport technology in history has been more centralizing than the railroad, a fact that accounts in no small measure for Chicago's unique role in the development of the Great West. But congestion set a limit to railroad centralization, and Chicago had already reached that threshold by the 1880s and 1890s. In 1905, the novelist Robert Herrick wrote in his *Memoirs of an American Citizen* about a fictional Chicagoan who increased his personal fortune by bringing western commodities to market without shipping them through Chicago. "Already," this character observed at one point, "the wheat and corn and meat of this Western land had begun to turn southward, avoiding the gate of Chicago with its heavy tolls, to flow by the path of least resistance out through the ports of the Gulf to Europe and Asia," and through alternative northern routes as well.[10] There was nothing fictional about this observation or its consequences. Henceforth, a host of investment decisions by the same people and institutions that had financed Chicago's growth would begin to work against it. Capital—even Chicago's own capital—flowed increasingly to new locations, in ways we have already encountered.

The rise of meat-packing in Omaha and Kansas City was a striking example of Chicago corporations deciding that Chicago was no longer an optimal location to invest in new business expansion. And so the city's meat-packing reached a plateau while that of its western rivals traced the same exponential curves of growth that Chicago had followed two or three decades earlier. Later, new technologies diffused the industry still further. Electrical refrigeration freed the packers from having to collect ice, and combined with diesel trucks and paved rural highways to make smaller plants more efficient. By the middle of the twentieth century, the immense packing operations of nineteenth-century Chicago no longer made economic sense. If the railroad was a force for centralization, the diesel truck and the automobile would be forces for *de*centralization, which was why my hometown of Madison had an Oscar Mayer packing plant that managed quite well on a modest scale under the new economic conditions of the twentieth century. And some things did not change: my professional-class academic family lived on the west side of town, upwind from the city's only significant factory, and the hams we ate were still stamped with the names of Swift and Armour.

Similar processes characterized the lumber industry, though here the new limits to metropolitan growth had to do less with congestion than with exhaustion. Chicago lost its early supply hinterland with the passing of the white pine, and the Mississippi River loggers who had been the city's chief competitors remained in the industry for only a decade or two longer. For reasons peculiar to lumber as a commodity, Chicago did not become a corporate center of the lumber industry as it did of meat-packing. Instead, the new corporate organization of lumbering evolved from the innovations of Frederick Weyerhaeuser and his allies in the upper Mississippi Valley. As Chicago's sources of supply gave out, the city's lumber firms became less competitive with Weyerhaeuser west of the Mississippi, and the city's own growth soon made it a net importer of lumber.[11] Weyerhaeuser himself headed west as the meat-packing companies had done, establishing vast new operations in the Pacific Northwest that soon started shipping Douglas fir back to Chicago. Other lumber operations, including some originally based in the city, headed south to the yellow pine districts, so that yellow pine flooring became increasingly common in Chicago homes during the 1890s. The balloon-frame house where my mother was born in Princeton, Wisconsin, was made of white pine from the northern part of the state; my parents' ranch-style house in Madison, on the other hand, is framed with Douglas fir from the Pacific Northwest. My mother and I grew up in similar landscapes but different hinterlands.

Perhaps the most interesting story was that of grain. The areas to Chicago's west that had initially supplied it with wheat—Illinois, Iowa, and Wisconsin—shifted toward corn, feedlots, and dairy herds after the 1860s. As the centers of wheat production moved north and west, toward Minnesota and Dakota Territory, Minneapolis became the gateway to a new wheat-raising hinterland.[12] Two key innovations transformed that city's economy and, with it, Chicago's. One had to do with the kind of wheat Minneapolis handled, and the other with how it milled that wheat into flour. Farmers on the northern plains faced shorter, colder growing seasons than their counterparts to the south and east, and they had trouble raising the soft winter wheat that traditional gristmills could process most effectively. They turned instead to hard spring wheat, which fared better in northern climates but had the disadvantage of a hard outer kernel—the bran—which tended to clog and burn in ordinary millstones. How to turn such wheat into flour posed new technological problems.

Minneapolis had the locational advantage of a large waterfall on the Mississippi, the Falls of St. Anthony, and entrepreneurs were eager to make use of the site for flour milling. To do so, they imported a new technology from eastern Europe, in which pairs of rollers with progressively shorter gaps between them cracked and crushed the wheat kernel in a series of steps. Multistaged milling had the effect of separating bran and germ from the rest of the wheat kernel during the initial cracking stage. Since these darkened the flour, and the oil of the wheat germ quickly turned rancid, the millers removed them with a device called a "middlings purifier," which sent a blast of air through the wheat as it moved between rollers. Bran and germ were blown away and separated. The resulting "new process" flour had a beautiful pure white color, unlike most whole grain flours then available in the United States.

Because people had long associated white flour with diets of the wealthy, it had a higher status than other flours did. Minneapolis millers could now mass-produce such flour, and it quickly swept the American marketplace. The millers built a railroad to Duluth at the western end of

Lake Superior to create a non-Chicago water route to the East, thereby giving themselves competitive rate advantages similar to the ones Chicago enjoyed. They also formed a buying cartel to control the price they paid to farmers in the city's hinterland. As a result, Minneapolis quickly emerged as the largest flour-manufacturing center in the world, with firms like Pillsbury and General Mills eventually playing the same dominant corporate role in the flour industry that Chicago firms played in meat-packing. Chicago had lost another part of its hinterland. Along the way, Americans stopped including whole grain flours in their diet, so I grew up eating white bread. Only in later years have I come to appreciate the nutritional advantages I lost by so doing.

For each of these commodities in turn—grain, lumber, and meat, along with all the other merchandise the city's wholesalers handled— Chicago had begun its career as the gateway metropolis for an immense hinterland extending far to its west. As such, it played the classic frontier role one sees repeatedly in such gateways during the history of North American colonization. As a gateway, Chicago linked its hinterland with the markets of much wealthier communities farther to the east. Because no other place in the Great West could match its markets or services, it drew trade to itself as no other city could do, becoming a metropolis second only to New York through its privileged relationship to the West. And yet the story of each gateway city in American frontier history has always ended in similar ways as each encountered self-induced limits to growth.[13] The market which the gateway provided for its hinterland reproduced itself in the hierarchy of central places that emerged beneath it. As other cities grew to dominate subregions within the original territory of the gateway, these cities captured more and more of its hinterland. In the end, the gateway became a central place like all the others.[14] Gateway status was temporary, bound to the forces of market expansion, environmental degradation, and self-induced competition that first created and then destroyed the gateway's utility to the urban-rural system as a whole.

Over and over again, other gateway cities had lived through this ending to their boosters' original vision. St. Louis lost its gateway status in the competition between water and rail transportation. Cincinnati invented the technologies that then allowed Chicago to seize for itself the title of Porkopolis. Bangor, Maine, had once been the gateway to the northeastern lumber trade, followed by Albany and Tonawanda, New York, before their forests gave out much as Chicago's did a generation or two later. Buffalo and Albany had been the leading grain centers of the West as a result of their location on the Erie Canal, but by 1877 Albany's western trade was "nearly abandoned, [and] that at Buffalo reduced to insignificant proportions."[15] Gateway cities did not last, for their eccentric frontier hinterlands eroded to make them central places serving a much more symmetrical region in their immediate vicinity. They survived as great cities, to be sure, but henceforth played very different historical roles as regional markets.

Chicago's fall from gateway dominance was not so great as these other cities', largely because the railroads and their capitalist geography gave it a reach in space and time unique to its historical moment. Not until a new set of transport technologies produced another great metropolis on the West Coast—Los Angeles—would Chicago fall from its number two position as an American population center. At least a few of its gateway legacies have remained to this day.[16] Probably the most striking is the Chicago Board of Trade, which through its commodity markets continues to help set grain prices for the entire world, even though Chicago long ago ceased to be a major handler of grain as a physical commodity.[17] The Board's futures markets are now used as much by farmers and millers as by speculators. "Hedging"—the ability of those who grow grain and manufacture flour to protect themselves from price changes by buying and selling in the futures market at the same time—has become the Board's best defense against the old agrarian critique of speculative gamblers. Grain elevators are no longer much a part of the Chicago landscape, but the power of the market and the institutional structures of capital have long outlived the tall windowless buildings that helped create them. The Board is a place about which I knew nothing as a child, and I am still not at all sure that I fully grasp the many ways it affects my life. But I am quite certain that I encounter a fragment of Chicago's hinterland each time I sit down to eat a meal.

One ending to this story, then, is about the rise and fall of the greatest gateway city of the Great West. Viewed from Chicago, the process which the historian Frederick Jackson Turner described as the reenactment of social evolution in isolated frontier places has a very different meaning. From the heart of the city, the frontier history of the Great West looks to be a story of metropolitan expansion, of the growing incursions of a market economy into ever more distant landscapes and communities. Nothing was left unchanged by this process. It brought massive Euroamerican migrations and the ensuing military conquests of Indian peoples. It profoundly altered existing ecosystems, remaking prairie and forest landscapes into farms, ranches, and Cutover districts. Perhaps most important, it imposed on the land a new geography of second nature in which the market relations of capital reproduced themselves in an elaborate urban-rural hierarchy that would henceforth frame all human life in the region.

The temporary nature of Chicago's gateway status in no way diminishes the significance of this history, for its legacy is everywhere around us. The integrated city-country system in which all of us now live is so widely diffused across the landscape that we no longer identify it with any single place. It would not occur to us to think of any city as Nature's Metropolis. In much the same way, we no longer speak in this country of the "Great West." The immense region between the Appalachians and the Pacific has in the twentieth century been partitioned into the subregional hinterlands of the many cities and physiographic provinces of the continent's interior. When we speak of "the West" today, we mean at least the Great Plains, if not the Rocky Mountains or beyond; the area served by Chicago's central place is today clearly labeled on our mental maps as "the Middle West"—not a very western place at all.[18] As the expanding market economy sheared hinterlands away from the gateway city that had helped create them, Nature's Metropolis and the Great West both passed into oblivion, joining the ghost landscapes of tallgrass prairie, white pine forest, and shortgrass bison range as past places no longer a part of living memory. But before these things disappeared, they created a good share of the world we inhabit today.

That is one ending to this story. There is another that is more personal.

During my family's cross-country drives to Wisconsin, when I first saw Chicago through the eyes of a young child, our destination was a small cottage my grandparents owned at the western end of Green Lake, a beautiful, low-key resort area in the central part of the state. It was about seven miles from the town where my mother had grown up behind the family hardware store, and she spent her childhood vacations at "the Lake" much as I did. Lined with cottages and filled with pleasure boats, Green Lake had nothing very wild about it, but it was a lovely place to be a child. We swam and canoed. We played croquet and softball. We got to know the farm family that lived about half a mile from us, and looked forward each summer to the sweet corn harvest, when shucking corn on the front stoop was the delightful prelude to a meal of steaming golden ears that had been picked just an hour or two before—we made sure of that. We rambled through the woods behind the cottage, collecting butterflies and leaves. Many nights, we walked the mile down the lakeshore to the Terrace Grocery, where we bought ice cream cones before heading home to watch the rising moon create rivers of light across the surface of the lake. The cottage was a modest structure which my grandparents had built with their own hands—hardware store owners in those days had to be jacks-of-all-trades—but it would be hard to imagine a luckier, happier place in which to grow up.

Looking back on those days and trying to see them through the disin-

terested eyes we historians are supposed to possess, I now understand
that my family was reenacting a retreat from the city into pastoral nature
that has deep roots in nineteenth-century Romanticism and in European
culture stretching back to classical Rome.[19] That easy mixture of the
"human" and the "natural" which Frederick Law Olmsted and others had
tried to achieve in places like Central Park, the Hudson River Valley, and
Chicago's own suburbs found one of its most important incarnations in
resort areas like this one. The pastoral retreat in its mythic form is a story
in which someone becomes oppressed by the dehumanized ugliness of
urban life and so seeks escape in a middle landscape that is halfway between the wild and the urban. Contemplating the beauty of that place,
relaxing in its nurturing comfort, one experiences a simpler life closer to
nature, recovering one's natural bearings and sense of self. Restored in
this way, one can finally return to the urban world which, for all of its
problems, is still one's home.

Olmsted's description of urban parks captures this pastoral landscape
well. "The park should, as far as possible," he wrote, "complement the
town. . . . The beauty of the park should be . . . the beauty of the fields, the
meadow, the prairie, of the green pastures, and the still waters. What we
want to gain is tranquillity and rest to the mind."[20] The pastoral countryside was a physical place, but it was defined by its relationship to another
physical place—the city—and by the quality of mind that went with it. It
was a way of living most of all, albeit an elite way of living that remained
the special province of a bourgeois leisure class at least until the automobile made it more widely available in the twentieth century. A healthy life
moved back and forth between the urban and the pastoral, so the week-
end visit to a city park and the summer vacation in a rural resort were
necessary parts of humane middle-class living. For those who could afford it, the daily retreat from downtown to suburb, combined with longer
holiday excursions to more wild or rural places, was the best practice of
all. As a child of the suburbs who knew the joys of a place like Green Lake,
I would surely have accepted this way of living as plain common sense
even if I did not then understand its historical roots.

Wealthy Chicagoans had embraced the vision of pastoral retreat quite
early, first in their suburbs and then in their vacations. As they cast about
for rural landscapes suitable for summer holidays, they "naturally"—
given their cultural expectations about rural beauty—looked northward
to the glaciated landscape of Wisconsin, with its thousands of lakes and
streams. Rural Illinois had nothing to match those lakes. As the Chicago
and Northwestern and the Chicago, Milwaukee and St. Paul pushed their
tracks farther north, they opened up the possibility of comfortable travel
to leisurely resorts. The result was a new recreational hinterland for the

city, in which the quality linking the rural countryside to the metropolitan economy was the simple fact that it matched urban expectations of what a nonurban landscape should look like. Certain rural Wisconsin lakes began to receive large numbers of tourists from Chicago in the summer, at about the same time that other Wisconsin lakes began to send ice to Chicago in the winter.

The first lake districts in Wisconsin that became tied to Chicago in this way were located in the southern part of the state. Oconomowoc, west of Milwaukee, emerged as a particularly favored site for estates like Montgomery Ward's La Belle Knoll mansion, where the mail order tycoon bred fine racehorses for himself.[21] The optimistic town of Waukesha, in the same general area, distributed advertisements describing itself as "the Saratoga of the West," and said of Wisconsin that it was "the summer paradise of the fashionable world, the angler's Mecca of inexhaustible resources, the huntsman's bonanza, the invalid's acme of sanitary perfection, in short, the complete Utopia for the tourist and pleasure-seeker."[22] But the most popular of the Wisconsin resort communities was Lake Geneva, just across the Illinois–Wisconsin border. "At Lake Geneva," said a promotional brochure for the Chicago, Milwaukee and St. Paul Railroad in 1902, "Nature did her best; man came and successfully did the rest." One could come to Lake Geneva confident of leaving none of Chicago's comforts behind. "It is surrounded by hotels, club houses, and villas. Here are the finest of summer residences. Millions have been spent, and the tour of the lake shows a constant panorama of beautiful structures and grounds." Yachting, tennis, and golf were readily available. The resort could even boast of "several curious, but pleasing, structures, relics of the Columbian Exposition of 1893," which had been transported there so that visitors could take a stroll by the lake and enjoy fond memories of the White City.[23] What better evidence could there be that urban and rural ideals converged in a single vision of civilized life?[24]

Because one could reach Lake Geneva from Chicago in less than three hours, it quickly developed the population cycles one associates with Wisconsin resort areas to this day. Dense populations of well-to-do tourists spent large amounts of urban money there during the summer, and sparse local populations did their best to get by on summertime savings during the winter. Many people who worked at the lakes—as cooks, waitresses, janitors, and staff—were themselves urban migrants who returned to the city (or to college campuses) for the winter. The economy of such places, and the urban-rural amenities they offered, rested on their hinterland status. The Wisconsin lake country was an outpost of the metropolitan market, and remained so long after Chicago had lost the western hinterlands of its gateway days. Although the state's own residents are heavy users of its recreational resources, and although visitors come from many other parts of the country, Wisconsin tourism depends in good measure on Chicago to this day.

Few places in central or northern Wisconsin enjoyed the posh facilities and great wealth of Lake Geneva, but they too became a part of the tourist hinterland. In the far north of Wisconsin and upper Michigan, the bankrupt economy of the old cutover district was redeemed by urban travelers who sought a place to hunt and fish. "Now that a railway has penetrated the woods," reported one sportsman, "a night's ride in a sleeping car from Chicago to Tomah, and part of a day's journey up the Wisconsin Valley Division will transport the happy man who can get away from the city to the very centre of the lake district."[25] This was wilder country, of course, but that was just what men like Ernest Hemingway, who had grown up in the tame suburbs of Chicago, were seeking as a more extreme version of the pastoral retreat.[26] I too would make that journey, as I discovered with others of my generation the more dramatic landscapes of northern forests and western mountains and began to prefer them to Green Lake for my summertime recreations.

As for Green Lake itself: in 1866, David Greenway, who owned a small variety store in Ripon, Wisconsin, decided to build a summer resort at the eastern end of the lake. He purchased thirty-five acres with 2,000 feet of lake frontage and proceeded to erect a large hotel—"Oakwood"—capable of accommodating 75 guests. It had no railroad service at first, so tourists disembarked at Ripon and rode by horse carriage the remaining six miles to the lake. It was an instant success, drawing southern travelers from as far away as New Orleans and Memphis who hoped to escape the devastating yellow fever epidemics that plagued those cities in the summer. But before long it attracted guests from closer markets—Milwaukee and Chicago—and expanded in scale as its popularity increased. Greenway added buildings, dining rooms, cottages, servants' quarters, a pavilion, an amusement hall, and a barn for horses, until finally the place could serve 480 guests at a time. The hotel operated a telegraph service for those who needed to stay in touch with their business affairs, installed gas lighting in all buildings, operated a small fleet of steamboats for cruising the lake, and offered a wide variety of recreational activities, ranging from swimming to boating to croquet.[27] Although never so grand as the resorts at Lake Geneva, it developed its own loyal clientele.

Encouraged by Greenway's success, the Sheboygan and Fond du Lac Railroad (later incorporated into the Chicago and Northwestern system) built the first depot at Green Lake in 1871.[28] As the attractions of the lake became more widely known, other hotels appeared in the years between 1873 and 1891, each with a good pastoral name: the Sherwood Forest, the Pleasant Point, the Forest Home, the Spring Grove, the Maplewood, and others. All were rambling wooden structures with wide verandas that offered comfortable shade and lovely views of the water on languid afternoons. Guests paid by the week, and many came for stays that lasted for a month or even an entire summer. This hotel style of vacationing—which depended heavily on the railroad and its centralizing impulse—changed in the twentieth century as automobiles made it easier for visitors to come and go as they pleased. More people began to buy tracts of land for themselves and build private dwellings around the lakeshore. The wealthiest bought large estates and constructed mansions with extensive lakefront views, while the more middling classes bought small lots and erected single-family cottages. My grandparents were among the first to build at the western end of the lake, far away from where the big hotels had been. By the time I began visiting in the 1950s, perhaps half the lakeshore was lined with vacation homes, which have become nearly omnipresent in succeeding decades. Most of the shore is now built up, and the lake has responded to its large part-time human population by growing ever greater quantities of algae and weeds, which thrive on the effluent fertilizer that leaches from thousands of septic tanks draining thousands of washing machines, toilets, and dishwashers.

I knew none of this history as a child, and certainly had little sense that my family's summer retreat had anything to do with Chicago's recreational hinterland. But I did know that the people who lived in the cottage next to ours came from Chicago, as did the owners of many other dwellings along the shore, from the big mansions down to the humblest cottages. Probably because my mother was a local girl from a nearby town—a farming center with no pretensions to recreational pastoralism—we knew very few of the Chicagoans, and unconsciously assumed we had little in common with them. My memories of those nameless, faceless folk are few, but I think we believed they had more money than we—many seemed to own big powerboats—and that they were somehow "outsiders" in a way we were not. I saw no connection between my childhood experiences at the cottage and the pastoral recreations that Chicagoans had been seeking at Green Lake—and all across Wisconsin—for the past century. And in that fact lies a second ending for my story.

Throughout this book, I have written of Chicago in two different ways. Much of the time, I have described the very particular history of an extraordinary city during a remarkable time in its history. Viewed in this context, Chicago really does deserve that overused word "unique," and really did play a pioneering role in shaping the markets and landscapes of North America as we know them today. But at other times I have allowed Chicago to stand as a representative for cities and markets more generally, so that much of what I have said about it would also hold true for other places. Similar things could be said even more dramatically about New York City. Many of Chicago's characteristics apply just as easily to the other gateway cities I have described, and one could write similar books for each of them as well. And the most general question of all—how a city's life and markets connect to the countryside around it—can be asked of every urban place that has ever existed, no matter how large or small. I embarked on this book because I was and am troubled that we so rarely ask just that question. And so this book about Chicago has also been a book about The City, in its largest, most mythic sense as a place somehow separate from that other key human landscape, The Country.

If I am honest about the childhood emotions that have defined my adult passions and given a sense of direction to my life, I have to admit that I am still—like many if not most Americans who care about "the environment"—a captive of the pastoral myth. I still prefer the country to the city. But I have been certain for a long time now that there is a moral schizophrenia in that preference. Like most who prefer the country to the city, I live in the city, and am entirely dependent on the intricate systems with which it sustains my life. What now most strikes me about my urban home is how easily it obscures from me the very systems that enable me to survive. Much as I say I love "nature," that word usually remains an abstraction in my daily life—a non-urban quality of aesthetic or sacred beauty to be looked at and "appreciated," not the gritty web of material connections that feed, clothe, shelter, and cleanse me and my community. Living in the city means consuming goods and services in a marketplace with ties to people and places in every corner of the planet, people and places that remain invisible, unknown, and unimagined as we consume the products of their lives. The market fosters exchange relationships of almost unimaginable complexity, and then hides them from us at the very instant they are created, in that last moment when cash and commodity exchange hands and we finally consume the thing we have purchased.

This ability of the market to construct and obscure relationships has been expanding for a long time now. The market existed long before there was a Chicago, and although it attained new complexity in that city, it has since gone on to become a fact of life in most places, no matter how urban or rural. We are consumers all, whether we live in the city or the country. This is to say that the urban and the rural landscapes I have been describing are not two places but one. They created each other, they transformed each other's environments and economies, and they now depend on each other for their very survival. To see them separately is to misunderstand where they came from and where they might go in the future. Worse, to ignore the nearly infinite ways they affect one another is to miss our moral responsibility for the ways they shape each other's landscapes and alter the lives of people and organisms within their bounds. The city-country relations I have described in this book now involve the entire planet, in part because of what happened to Chicago and the Great West during the nineteenth century. We all live in the city. We all live in the country. Both are second nature to us.

I began this book with my most vivid childhood memory of The City, an orange column of vapor rising from a smokestack in Chicago's steel-milling suburb of Gary. It was and is an evil memory, a symbol of an urban world doing harm both to nature and to the people and other creatures who lived downwind of that cloud. As a child, I was always happy when we reached the end of our journey, the cottage on Green Lake that seemed about as far from that smokestack as I could imagine. Now I am not nearly so sure. It turns out that the green lake and the orange cloud had more in common than I thought. The things I experienced in each sprang from a common history, as did my very ability to make the journey between them. Even the ease with which I saw them as separate and disconnected, a pair of alternatives with an obvious choice between them—that too was part of their common past.

So when I now imagine a group of Chicagoans sitting on the veranda of David Greenway's Oakwood Hotel in the 1890s, on the far side of the lake that would be my first childhood experience of The Country, I also think about the cloud of dark smoke that so many nineteenth-century travelers saw hanging over the Chicago skyline. I imagine the coal from southern Illinois fueling locomotives bound for San Francisco, lifting Kansas wheat to the tops of grain elevators, sawing pine lumber from Wisconsin, butchering steers from Colorado, building reapers destined for the Dakotas, powering lights and elevators in skyscrapers, heating the homes of wealthy suburbanites and poor immigrants, carrying travelers north to the lake country. Like my orange smoke, that nineteenth-century cloud raised serious questions about the city's alienation from nature. But those questions were not to be answered by a flight to the country, for the country had helped make that cloud, and vice versa. Green Lake was and is no alternative to Chicago. To do right by nature and people in the country, one has to do right by them in the city as well, for the two seem always to find in each other their own image. In that sense, every city is nature's metropolis, and every piece of countryside its rural hinterland. We fool ourselves if we think we can choose between them, for the green lake and the orange cloud are creatures of the same landscape. Each is our responsibility. We can only take them together and, in making the journey between them, find a way of life that does justice to them both.

Appendix:
Methodological Note
on the Bankruptcy Maps

The bankruptcy maps in chapter 6 are undoubtedly the hardest-won documents in this book, representing many hundreds of hours in archives and at computer terminals. In the text, I have suppressed the statistical manipulations that went into creating them, and have tried not to trouble readers with the many technical issues and problems they represent. But since historians and geographers have not previously used bankruptcy records to track regional credit relationships in this way, I should offer a few observations about the underlying data and how I manipulated them to create the maps.

Bankruptcy was a much contested terrain in nineteenth-century politics and law, with debtors and creditors struggling with each other about how easily one should be able to declare or be forced into bankruptcy, and with what sorts of penalties. The most useful survey remains that of Charles Warren, *Bankruptcy in United States History* (Cambridge: Harvard University Press, 1935), though this should be supplemented by Peter J. Coleman, *Debtors and Creditors in America: Insolvency, Imprisonment for Debt, and Bankruptcy, 1607–1900* (Madison: State Historical Society of Wisconsin, 1974). Because my regional analysis required me to compare bankrupts across state boundaries, and because the state court records were a more daunting prospect than I was willing to face, I chose to examine only those individuals who went bankrupt under the uniform standards of federal law. Congress passed three bankruptcy laws in the nineteenth century: one in 1841, which quickly proved unworkable; another in 1867, which lasted until widespread protest forced its repeal in 1878; and a final law in 1898, which remains the foundation for bankruptcy as we know it today. Those who wish to understand the legal and political controversies surrounding these laws should consult Warren, but the history of bankruptcy as a *cultural* phenomenon cries out for further examination by scholars.

Given the time frame of this book, only the 1867 law (39th Cong., 2d sess., chap. 176, "An Act to establish a uniform System of Bankruptcy throughout the United States," March 2, 1867) provided cases from the appropriate period. As I have already explained in the text, I reasoned that bankrupts would be most representative of the population as a whole during a period of general economic depression, when more individuals from a wider variety of backgrounds than usual would find themselves in straitened circumstances. I therefore chose to examine every person who went bankrupt under the 1867 law between August 1, 1873, and April 30, 1874, during the height of the panic of 1873. I drew them from the most populous states of Chicago's western hinterland: Illinois, Iowa, Minnesota, Missouri, Nebraska, and Wisconsin. The less populated territories farther west generated too few cases to be statistically meaningful; even Kansas and Nebraska produced sparse records, and I was forced to omit Kansas altogether because the courts there for some reason chose not to include summary lists of creditors in their records. The following federal district courts are represented in the dataset: Chicago and Springfield in Illinois, and Madison and Milwaukee in Wisconsin, all housed in the National Archives Regional Record Center in Chicago; and Keokuk, Council Bluffs, Des Moines, and Dubuque in Iowa; the Minnesota U.S. District Court; Omaha in Nebraska; and Jefferson City and St. Louis in Missouri, all housed in the National Archives Regional Record Center in Kansas City. I assumed that the uniform conditions of the federal law would make the bankrupts in these different districts and states roughly comparable with each other. Readers should nonetheless note that these states had their own bankruptcy laws, so differences in leniency between state and federal rules may have encouraged different choices about whether a bankrupt entered the state or the federal court system. For a sense of how contemporaries understood these differences, see "Assignment and Exemption Laws," *Northwestern Lumberman,* October 19, 1878, 5.

Since I was less interested in bankruptcy per se than in the geographical relationships among debtors and creditors, a particular bankruptcy proceeding was of use to me only if it contained three key sets of data: a list of creditors, the places where each lived, and the total debts owed to each. Under the 1867 law, people could enter bankruptcy either voluntarily or involuntarily. If voluntarily, they were required to produce a schedule of creditors of the sort I needed; if involuntarily, such a schedule might or might not appear in the court proceedings, so I could include only a portion of involuntary bankrupts in the dataset. In many cases, court cases that lacked schedules probably represent instances in which the debtor escaped bankruptcy, so their exclusion from the dataset is altogether appropriate; there is in any event no way in which they could have been included, given their lack of relevant data. Of the 299 individuals for whom records appear in the Chicago Court District, for instance, 44 percent were involuntary cases that lacked a schedule of creditors; 39 percent were involuntary bankrupts who did leave a schedule of creditors; and 17 percent were voluntary bankrupts for whom a schedule was required by the court. The bankruptcy dataset contains the records of 401 bankrupts, 290 of them involuntary and 110 of them voluntary, with one missing value. Their distribution by state is as follows: 199 from Illinois (116 of these from Chicago and Cook County); 38 from Iowa; 29 from Minnesota; 95 from Missouri (44 of these from St. Louis); 12 from Nebraska; and 28 from Wisconsin.

In coding each bankrupt for computer processing by the Statistical Analysis System, SAS, I created variables for first and last name, court district and case number, filing status (voluntary or involuntary), date of filing, the bankrupt's place of residence, and the place of residence of the creditor who brought the proceeding if the bankruptcy was involuntary. Since the computer mapping program I used required that this information be aggregated at the county level, I determined the bankrupt's county of residence and entered that information as well. Because the geography of debt varies so widely depending on a person's line of work, I also needed to enter each bankrupt's occupation, but here I encountered a curious problem. Nineteenth-century Americans understood bankruptcy as a process that happened to people who had failed in their occupation: the court proceeding represented a formal recognition that the bankrupt no longer had an economic identity, so the court made no provision for recording the bankrupt's prior occupation in its records. I therefore faced the task of locating 401 individuals in more than 175 towns in six states, to determine what they had done for a living before finding themselves insolvent in 1873–74.

In a few cases, I could reasonably infer the bankrupt's prior occupation from debts that appeared in the creditor lists: a bankrupt whose debts were all for shoe purchases, for instance, was almost certainly a boot and shoe dealer. But most cases were much more ambiguous than this, so I chose to make as few inferences as possible from the internal evidence of the court proceeding itself. Instead, I turned to other sources. First among these were various state and city business directories, which eventually yielded occupations for about one-fourth of the bankrupts. The directories on which I relied were as follows: *Sixteenth Annual Directory of Chicago* (Chicago: Richard Edwards, 1873); *Wisconsin Business Directory* (Milwaukee: M. T. Platt, 1873); *Gould's St. Louis City Directory* (St. Louis: David B. Gould, [c. 1873]); *St. Paul Census Report and Statistical Review, Embracing a Complete Directory of the City* (St. Paul: Richard Edwards, 1873); *Root's Burlington City Directory* (Burlington, Iowa: O. E. Root, 1866); *Holland's Keokuk City Directory for 1873–74* (Chicago: Western Publishing, [1873]); *Omaha City Directory, 1872–73* (Briggs & Lowry, [c. 1873]); *Corbett, Lowe & Co. 's III Annual City Directory for 1873 of . . . Kansas City* (Kansas City: Corbett, Lowe, 1873); and

Davenport City Directory (Davenport: Griggs, Watson & Day, 1873). I examined a number of others, but none yielded information about bankrupts in the dataset.

Most nineteenth-century business directories covered large towns and cities, so they missed most of the widely scattered individuals in the bankruptcy dataset, many of whom lived in small towns or rural areas. The directories were also surprisingly bad even at identifying people in places such as Chicago and St. Louis. I therefore turned to a second source: the credit rating reports of *R. G. Dun & Company's Reference Book* (New York: R. G. Dun, January 1872); and of *Bradstreet's Commercial Reports* (New York: J. M. Bradstreet & Son, July 1873). R. G. Dun and J. M. Bradstreet began as separate businesses but eventually merged, and historians have been blessed by Dun and Bradstreet's decision to deposit the nineteenth-century records of R. G. Dun and Company at the Baker Library of Harvard Business School. Credit-rating agencies were an innovation of mid-nineteenth-century commerce, themselves a fascinating example of the metropolitan economic institutions I discuss in this book. Their job was to track the financial reliability of individuals across the nation, so bankers and merchants in distant cities could know whom to trust in making loans or offering credit on business transactions. On their history, see James D. Norris, *R. G. Dun & Co., 1841–1900: The Development of Credit Reporting in the Nineteenth Century* (Westport, Conn.: Greenwood Press, 1978); on their utility to historians, see James H. Madison, "The Credit Reports of R. G. Dun & Co. as Historical Sources," *Historical Methods Newsletter* 8 (1975): 128–31; and on the cultural assumptions behind credit reports, see the fascinating text P. R. Earling, *Whom to Trust: A Practical Treatise on Mercantile Credits* (Chicago: Rand, McNally, 1890).

I looked up each bankrupt in the published reports of Bradstreet and Dun, and then if necessary in the original Dun manuscript records at Harvard. To my surprise, I fared much better there than in the business directories. Of the 401 bankrupts, 239 showed up in Bradstreet, 143 in Dun (for which my published report was a year earlier than it should have been), and an additional 35 in the R. G. Dun manuscript collection at the Baker Library. When I combined what I had learned from the directories with the credit agency reports, I was able to attach definite occupations to all but 80 of the 401 bankrupts, an astonishing 80 percent rate of record linkage that says a great deal about the national coverage of the New York credit agencies by the 1870s. With the internal evidence of the court cases themselves, I felt confident in assigning occupations to 340 of the bankrupts in the dataset. Where available, I also included credit ratings and the credit agency's assessment of the size of each bankrupt's business. Although I did not use this information in the text of this book, it offers an opportunity to test the effectiveness of nineteenth-century credit ratings as predictors of financial stability under panic conditions.

With the dataset of bankrupts complete, I turned to the 19,973 creditors to whom they owed money. Much less information was available about these people, so their computer dataset contained fewer variables: their town of residence, how much money they were owed, and the nature of the debt (mainly whether it was secured or unsecured). Each creditor also received an ID variable linking him or her to the appropriate bankruptcy proceeding. The creditors lived in more than fifteen hundred towns, and in order to map these on a computer, I had to determine the county in which they were located and add that to the dataset as well, using a geographical code that SASGRAPH could use in constructing its cartographic output. With the addition of this geographical information, the creditor dataset was complete.

By merging the datasets for bankrupts and their creditors, I produced a master file in which each case represents a single debtor-creditor pair. From this master, I aggregated debt information to the county level. The working datasets which produced the maps in the text contain information about the total debt for individual counties, and how much of each county's debt was owed to each of the counties in which its creditors lived. By subsetting these working datasets, I produced maps and statistical analyses showing the geographical distribution of debt-credit relationships by place, by occupational groups, by how wealthy bankrupts were, and by other such variables. SASGRAPH overlaid this information onto a map of *modern* American counties, the boundaries of which have in some cases shifted since the 1870s. To make sure that the maps in this book correspond to the actual county boundaries of the period, a professional cartographer, Jacques Chazaud, transferred my original computer maps onto a new base map showing county boundaries as they existed at the time of the 1870 census. This base map is from Thomas D. Rabenhorst and Carville V. Earle, eds., *Historical U.S. County Outline Map Collection, 1840–1980* (Baltimore: University of Maryland Department of Geography, 1984), a superb working collection that should be in the library of every historian and geographer who uses census data and other historical statistics at the county level. I am grateful to Carville Earle and his colleagues for producing the county boundary base maps that appear in the text, and to Jacques Chazaud for his work in reproducing my computer maps in more elegant form. In this context, I should also acknowledge the helpful assistance of the staff of the Yale Computer Center, and the unstinting advice and support I received from my good friend Jan Reiff, who taught me most of what I know about doing statistics on a mainframe computer.

The bankruptcy dataset and its associated maps represent a unique resource for examining regional capital and credit flows in the nineteenth century, but they have many problems, some of which I have discussed in the notes to chapter 6. For instance, one can certainly question the representativeness of bankrupts as an economic group, though I would argue that the bankruptcy maps so clearly fit independent theoretical expectations about the urban hierarchy that they do seem representative at this very high level of aggregation. The various controversies associated with state and federal bankruptcy laws in the nineteenth century undoubtedly produced behaviors among debtors and creditors that varied from state to state, undermining the accuracy of cross-state comparisons. An additional source of trouble was the fact that some of the smaller bankrupts in the dataset were mainly carrying very old debts that dated back to the 1860s or even the 1857 panic, making them not very comparable with bankrupts who became insolvent in the midst of an active business; but since there was no clear principle for eliminating such "old debts," I chose to include them and live with any slight distortions they might introduce. Perhaps most important from a statistical point of view, the data are frustratingly scattered, with too few bankrupts being located in most places to make trustworthy generalizations about those places. I was lucky that Chicagoans had recourse to the federal bankruptcy law more than the citizens of any other place in the region—but it is of course no accident that they did so, given the size of their city and its role in the urban hierarchy. The 111 Chicagoans who went bankrupt under the 1867 law represented more than a fourth of my entire dataset, compared with 44 bankrupts from St. Louis; 19 from Minneapolis–St. Paul; 10 from Kansas City, Missouri; and far fewer from most other places in the region. The small number of bankrupts from any but the largest cities makes it dangerous to draw conclusions except about very broad patterns in regional debt relationships. I have limited my discussion in the text to broad patterns of just this sort, and feel confident that the urban hierarchy they reveal is a genuine reflection of the city system as it existed at that time.

Notes

ABBREVIATIONS

Annals Assoc. Am. Geog.	*Annals of the Association of American Geographers*
Ag. Hist.	*Agricultural History*
AHR	*American Historical Review*
Bull. Mo. Hist. Soc.	*Bulletin of the Missouri Historical Society*
Bus. Hist. Rev.	*Business History Review*
CB&Q Archives	Chicago, Burlington and Quincy Archives, Newberry Library
CBT	Chicago Board of Trade
CHS	Chicago Historical Society
FTC	Federal Trade Commission
Hunt's Merch. Mag.	*Hunt's Merchants' Magazine and Commercial Review*
ICPSR	Inter-University Consortium for Political and Social Research
Ill. Const. Debates	*Debates and Proceedings of the Constitutional Convention of the State of Illinois* (Springfield: State of Illinois, 1870)
JAH	*Journal of American History*
JEH	*Journal of Economic History*
J. Ill. State Hist. Soc.	*Journal of the Illinois State Historical Society*
J. Pol. Econ.	*Journal of Political Economy*
J. Urban Hist.	*Journal of Urban History*
Minn. Hist.	*Minnesota History*
Mich. Hist.	*Michigan History Magazine*
Mo. Hist. Rev.	*Missouri Historical Review*
MVHR	*Mississippi Valley Historical Review*
No. Am. Rev.	*North American Review*
Nimmo, *Rept. Int. Commerce*	Joseph Nimmo, Jr., *Report on the Internal Commerce of the United States,* 1877, 1879, 1881
NWL	*Northwestern Lumberman*
SHSI	State Historical Society of Iowa
SHSW	State Historical Society of Wisconsin
UISC	University of Iowa Special Collections
USDA	United States Department of Agriculture
Vest Rept.	U.S. Senate, *Testimony Taken by the Select Committee on the Transportation and Sale of Meat Products,* 51st Cong., 1st sess., 1889–90, Sen. Rept. 829 (Serial 2705)
WHQ	*Western Historical Quarterly*
Wis. Mag. Hist.	*Wisconsin Magazine of History*

PROLOGUE

1. William Archer, *America To-Day: Observations and Reflections* (1900), 91.
2. See Carl S. Smith, *Chicago and the American Literary Imagination, 1880–1920* (1984), 101–20.
3. Hamlin Garland, *A Son of the Middle Border* (1917), 268.
4. Ibid., 269.
5. The quotation describes the countryside surrounding James Whitcomb Riley's Greenfield, Ind., in Hamlin Garland, *A Daughter of the Middle Border* (1921; reprint, 1929), 12.
6. Garland, *Son of Middle Border*, 261.
7. Ibid., 269.
8. Ibid., 268–69.
9. Ibid., 271, 268.
10. Hamlin Garland, *Rose of Dutcher's Cooley* (1895), 181.
11. CBT, *Annual Report for 1889*, 182–83. I have converted the city's 1889 coal consumption of 4.7 million tons to its mean daily equivalent.
12. Garland, *Rose of Dutcher's Cooley*, 181.
13. Ibid., 182. I should note in passing the class character of these perceptions. Raymond Williams has pointed to the tendency in English literature for pastoral nature to stand as a landscape whose beauty exists without the intervention of human labor; the city becomes ugly precisely because the bourgeois observer can less easily forget the workers whose presence makes the city possible. This tendency is less evident and more problematic in the United States, where the nineteenth-century landscape could be seen as "natural" without having to erase its working class (only the Indians had to be forgotten, usually by being assimilated to a vanishing version of nature itself). Nonetheless, the images of fallen urban humanity one finds in Garland and other writers tend to be working class. A quotation from Emerson encapsulates the problem nicely: in speaking of "what discord is between man and nature," he remarked that "you cannot freely admire a noble landscape, if laborers are digging in the field hard by. The poet finds something ridiculous in his delight, until he is out of the sight of men." Although the second sentence tries to cover the earlier reference to laborers by generalizing to the apparently more collective "men," the bias of the first sentence remains: wild nature was less an *unpeopled* landscape than an *unworked* one, and the "poet's" relationship to it was intrinsically that of a leisured class. Ralph Waldo Emerson, *Nature* in *Essays and Lectures* (1983), 42; Raymond Williams, *The Country and the City* (1973).
14. Garland, *Rose of Dutcher's Cooley*, 183.
15. Charles Dudley Warner, *Studies in the South and West with Comments on Canada* (1889), 185.
16. Waldo Frank, *Our America* (1919), 117. Later, on p. 120, Frank wrote of the Chicago stockyards that "Dante would have recognized this world. A sunken city of blood."
17. Ibid., 118. Other classic descriptions of Chicago in which smoke or odor plays a key role include Upton Sinclair, *The Jungle* (1906; reprint, 1960), 29–30; and Robert Herrick, *Memoirs of an American Citizen* (1905), ed. Daniel Aaron (1963), 266.
18. Rudyard Kipling, undoubtedly among the most alienated, was proof against the city's charms. "Having seen it," he said of the city, "I urgently desire never to see it again. It is inhabited by savages. Its water is the water of the Hugli, and its air is dirt." Rudyard Kipling, *From Sea to Sea: Letters of Travel* (1899), 139. The Hugli is the principal river of Calcutta.
19. Perry Miller, "The Romantic Dilemma in American Nationalism and the Concept of Nature" (1955), in Miller, *Nature's Nation* (1967), 197–207.
20. Giuseppe Giacosa, "Chicago and Her Italian Colony" (1893), in Bessie Louise Pierce, *As Others See Chicago: Impressions of Visitors, 1673–1933* (1933), 276, 283.
21. Theodore Dreiser, *Dawn: A History of Myself* (1931), 159; see also Theodore Dreiser, *The "Genius"* (1915, 1923; reprint, 1954), 30, 39, 59.
22. Garland, *Rose of Dutcher's Cooley*, 181. At the novel's end, Garland makes clear his belief that Rose's choice of city over country to be with the man she loves, despite her own preference for the countryside, is the necessary decision of adulthood. Her lover tells

her, speaking of Chicago, "Down there life is. Infinite novelty, ceaseless change. As you love the country, so I love the city." That said, she decides to go with him. "It was well, it was inevitable, and it was glorious to set her face toward wifehood and fame with such a man as companion, friend and lover" (p. 402). As country had been to the girl, so must city be to the woman.

23. Ibid., 183. For one of the most powerful descriptions of the city as a force of nature, see Paul Bourget, *Outre-Mer: Impressions of America* (1895), 117: "Men! The word is hardly correct applied to this perplexing city. When you study it in more detail, its aspect reveals so little of the personal will, so little caprice and individuality, in its streets and buildings, that it seems like the work of some impersonal power, irresistible, unconscious, like a force of nature, in whose service man was merely a passive instrument. This power is nothing less than that business fever which here throbs at will, with an unbridled violence like that of an uncontrollable element. It rushes along these streets, as once before the devouring flame of fire; it quivers; it makes itself visible with an intensity which lends something tragical to this city, and makes it seem like a poem to me."

24. Louis H. Sullivan, *The Autobiography of an Idea* (1924; reprint, 1956), 200–201.

25. Ibid., 201–2.

26. Robert Herrick, *The Gospel of Freedom* (1898), 101.

27. Ibid., 102.

28. Ibid., 102–3.

29. Emerson, *Nature*, in *Essays and Lectures*, 28. Although I have been assiduous in my own text about avoiding the collective noun "man" to refer to *people*—men and women— one should notice that virtually all these writers followed the practice—still common in our own time—which Emerson uses here: "man" is male and "nature" is female. A growing body of scholarship suggests that these gender identifications are fundamental to the oppositions I have been describing in this chapter, whether between humanity and nature or between city and country. For a sampling that suggests the range of this literature, see Sherry Ortner's essay "Is Female to Male as Nature Is to Culture?" in Michelle Zimbalist Rosaldo and Louise Lamphere, eds., *Women, Culture, and Society* (1974), 67–87; Annette Kolodny, *The Lay of the Land: Metaphor as Experience and History in American Life and Letters* (1975); Susan Griffin, *Woman and Nature: The Roaring inside Her* (1978); Carolyn Merchant, *The Death of Nature: Women, Ecology, and the Scientific Revolution* (1980); Carol P. MacCormack and Marilyn Strathern, *Nature, Culture and Gender* (1980); Sherry B. Ortner and Harriet Whitehead, *Sexual Meanings: The Cultural Construction of Gender and Sexuality* (1981); Annette Kolodny, *The Land before Her: Fantasy and Experience of the American Frontiers, 1630–1860* (1984); Susan Armitage and Elizabeth Jameson, eds., *The Women's West* (1987); Vera Norwood and Janice Monk, eds., *The Desert Is No Lady: Southwestern Landscapes in Women's Writing and Art* (1987); Lillian Schlissel, Vicki L. Ruiz, and Janice Monk, eds., *Western Women: Their Land, Their Lives* (1988); and Glenda Riley, *The Female Frontier: A Comparative View of Women on the Prairie and the Plains* (1988).

30. Herrick, *Gospel of Freedom*, 103–4.

31. Ibid., 104.

32. Sidney H. Bremer suggests that this tendency was shared by most of the male authors who wrote about Chicago. The city's female writers were less homogenizing in their impulses, less inclined to emphasize individuals over community, and less likely to set the city in opposition to "nature" in their fiction. See her "Lost Continuities: Alternative Urban Visions in Chicago Novels, 1890–1915," *Soundings* 64 (1981): 29–51.

33. Herrick, *Gospel of Freedom*, 113.

34. Ibid., 104.

35. Ibid., 282.

36. Ibid., 283.

37. The great work on this subject is Williams, *The Country and the City*.

38. Anne Whiston Spirn, *The Granite Garden: Urban Nature and Human Design* (1984), 4.

1: Dreaming the Metropolis

1. Gurdon Saltonstall Hubbard, *The Autobiography of Gurdon Saltonstall Hubbard, Pa-pa-ma-ta-be, "The Swift Walker"* (1911), 40–41; George R. Stewart, *American Place-Names*

(1970), 92. Hubbard reported, "The wild onion grew in great quantities along the banks of the river, and in the woods adjoining, the leek abounded, and doubtless Chicago derived its name from the onion and not, as some suppose, from the (animal) skunk. The Indian name for this animal is chi-kack, for the vegetable chi-goug; both words were used to indicate strong odors." Milo M. Quaife, *Checagou: From Indian Wigwam to Modern City, 1673–1835* (1933), 17–20, works hard on behalf of his city to argue that the broader etymological meaning of the Indian place-name was "anything great or powerful," but admits that the earliest French authority, Joutel in 1687, attributed the name to "the quantity of garlic growing in this district, in the woods."

2. Irving Cutler, *Chicago: Metropolis of the Mid-Continent*, 2d ed. (1976), 5–13; Harold M. Mayer, "The Launching of Chicago: The Situation and the Site," *Chicago History* 9, no. 2 (Summer 1980): 68–79; and Douglas C. Ridgley, *The Geography of Illinois* (1921), 37–65.

3. Glenda Daniel and Jerry Sullivan, *A Sierra Club Naturalist's Guide to the North Woods of Michigan, Wisconsin, Minnesota and Southern Ontario* (1981); Lawrence Martin, *The Physical Geography of Wisconsin*, 3d ed. (1965); Ridgley, *Geography of Illinois*, 25–36; J. Harlen Bretz, *Geology of the Chicago Region*, Illinois State Geological Survey, Bulletin no. 65 (1939); P. K. Sims and G. B. Morey, eds., *Geology of Minnesota* (1972); and Jack L. Hough, *The Geology of the Great Lakes* (1958). For a time, the predecessor of Lake Michigan drained south toward the Mississippi River through an outlet in the vicinity of Chicago. Only in the past two millennia or so has the lake found its modern drainage into Lake Huron, and only then did the Chicago River begin to flow *into* Lake Michigan instead of *out* of it. See Jack L. Hough, "The Prehistoric Great Lakes of North America," *American Scientist* 51 (1963): 84–109.

4. For a general treatment of these complex changes, see Betty Flanders Thomson, *The Shaping of America's Heartland: The Landscape of the Middle West* (1977). More technical are H. E. Wright and David G. Frey, eds., *The Quaternary of the United States* (1965); Margaret B. Davis, "Palynology and Environmental History during the Quaternary Period," *American Scientist* 57 (1969): 317–32; H. E. Wright, Jr., "Late Quaternary Vegetational History of North America," in Karl K. Turekian, ed., *Late Cenozoic Glacial Ages* (1971), 425–64; and Thompson Webb III, "The Past 11,000 Years of Vegetational Change in Eastern North America," *Bioscience* 31 (1981): 501–6.

5. John T. Curtis, *The Vegetation of Wisconsin: An Ordination of Plant Communities* (1971).

6. On the early history of the site, see Bessie Louise Pierce, *A History of Chicago*, vol. 1, *The Beginning of the City, 1673–1848* (1937), 3–42; and Robert P. Howard, *Illinois: A History of the Prairie State* (1972), 49–172.

7. Arthur H. Frazier, "The Military Frontier: Fort Dearborn," *Chicago History* 9, no. 2 (Summer 1980): 80–85.

8. Bruce G. Trigger, ed., *Northeast*, vol. 15 of *Handbook of North American Indians*, ed. William C. Sturtevant (1978); George Irving Quimby, *Indian Life in the Upper Great Lakes: 11,000 B.C. to A.D. 1800* (1960); James A. Clifton, *The Prairie People: Continuity and Change in Potawatomi Indian Culture, 1665–1965* (1977), esp. 179–278; R. David Edmunds, *The Potawatomis: Keepers of the Fire* (1978), esp. 215–275. Richard White's forthcoming *Empires, Indians, and Republics: The Middle Ground of the Pays d'en Haut, 1600–1850* gives an excellent picture of this hybrid cultural universe.

9. For a rich portrait of agricultural life in southern Illinois during this period, see John Mack Faragher, *Sugar Creek: Life on the Illinois Prairie* (1986).

10. Jacqueline Peterson, " 'Wild' Chicago: The Formation and Destruction of a Multiracial Community on the Midwestern Frontier, 1816–1837," in Melvin G. Holli and Peter d'A. Jones, eds., *The Ethnic Frontier: Essays in the History of Group Survival in Chicago and the Midwest* (1977), 25–71; Jacqueline Peterson, "Goodbye, Madore Beaubien: The Americanization of Early Chicago Society," *Chicago History* 9, no. 2 (Summer 1980): 98–111; E. Colbert, *Chicago: Historical and Statistical Sketch of the Garden City* (1868), 16. The fullest early description of Chicago during this period is Mrs. John H. Kinzie, *Wau-Bun: The "Early Day" in the North-West* (1856), ed. Louise Phelps Kellogg (1948).

11. Black Hawk, *An Autobiography* (1833), ed. Donald Jackson (1955), 101. I discussed the relationship between Indian conceptions of property and land-use practices in an earlier book about New England during colonial times. Black Hawk's people followed a comparable regime. See William Cronon, *Changes in the Land: Indians, Colonists, and the Ecology of New England* (1983).

12. For the history of the conflict, in addition to Black Hawk's autobiography, see Anthony
    F. C. Wallace, "Prelude to Disaster: The Course of Indian-White Relations Which Led
    to the Black Hawk War of 1832," *Collections of the Illinois State Historical Library* 35
    (1970): 1–51; P. Richard Metcalf, "Who Should Rule at Home? Native American Poli-
    tics and Indian-White Relations," *JAH* 61 (1974): 651–65; Roger L. Nichols, "The
    Black Hawk War in Retrospect," *Wis. Mag. Hist.* 65 (1982): 238–46; William T. Hagan,
    The Sac and Fox Indians (1958), 141–204; and, for a compilation of the relevant docu-
    ments, Ellen M. Whitney, ed., *The Black Hawk War, 1831–1832, Collections of the Illinois
    State Historical Library* 35 (1970).
13. Black Hawk, *Autobiography,* 17–20; Alfred T. Andreas, *History of Chicago from the Earliest
    Period to the Present Time,* vol. 1 (1884), 121–22; *Report of Jesse B. Thomas as a Member of the
    Executive Committee Appointed by the Chicago Harbor and River Convention, of the Statistics
    concerning the City of Chicago* (1847), 9.
14. Peterson, "Goodbye, Madore Beaubien," 98–111. On the growth of the post–fur trade
    community, see Charles Cleaver, *History of Chicago from 1833 to 1892* (1892), 46–89.
15. Edmunds, *Potawatomis,* 241–45; Clifton, *Prairie People,* 228–38.
16. Colbee C. Benton, *A Visitor to Chicago in Indian Days: "Journal to the 'Far-Off West' "*
    (1957), 70.
17. Charles Joseph Latrobe, *The Rambler in North America, 1832–1833* (1835), 2:151.
18. Patrick Shirreff, *A Tour through North America* (1835), 228; Latrobe, *Rambler,* 2:153.
19. "Treaty between the United States of America and the United Nation of the Chip-
    pewa, Ottowa, and Potawatamie Indians. Concluded September 26, 1833—Ratified
    February 21, 1835."; Anselm J. Gerwing, "The Chicago Indian Treaty of 1833," *J. Ill.
    State Hist. Soc.* 57 (1964): 117–42; James A. Clifton, "Chicago, September 14, 1833:
    The Last Great Indian Treaty in the Old Northwest," *Chicago History* 9, no. 2 (Summer
    1980): 86–97; Clifton, *Prairie People,* 238–45; Edmunds, *Potawatomis,* 247–50; Milo
    Milton Quaife, *Chicago and the Old Northwest, 1673–1835: A Study of the Evolution of the
    Northwestern Frontier, Together with a History of Fort Dearborn* (1913), 348–70; Quaife,
    "The Chicago Treaty of 1833," *Wis. Mag. Hist.* 1 (1918): 287–303.
20. Latrobe, *Rambler,* 2:158.
21. Colbert, *Chicago,* 16. For the general historical context of these changes, see Malcolm
    J. Rohrbough, *The Trans-Appalachian Frontier* (1978).
22. Andreas, *History of Chicago,* 1:133–38. Important secondary works on the 1830s specu-
    lation include Homer Hoyt, *One Hundred Years of Land Values in Chicago: The Relationship
    of the Growth of Chicago to the Rise in Its Land Values, 1830–1933* (1933), 3–44; Pierce,
    History of Chicago, 1:43–74; Arthur H. Cole, "Cyclical and Sectional Variations in the
    Sale of Public Lands, 1816–1860," *Review of Economics and Statistics* 9 (1927): 41–53;
    Paul Wallace Gates, *History of Public Land Law Development* (1968), 145–76; Patrick E.
    McLear, "Speculation, Promotion, and the Panic of 1837 in Chicago," *J. Ill. State Hist.
    Soc.* 42 (1969): 135–46; Donald R. Adams, Jr., "The Role of Banks in the Economic
    Development of the Old Northwest," in David C. Klingaman and Richard K. Vedder,
    eds., *Essays in Nineteenth Century Economic History: The Old Northwest* (1975), 208–45; and
    Michael J. Doucet, "Urban Land Development in Nineteenth-Century North Amer-
    ica," *J. Urban Hist.* 8 (1982): 299–342. See also the brief survey in Everett Chamberlin,
    Chicago and Its Suburbs (1873), 28–48.
23. Harriet Martineau, *Society in America* (1837), 1:181.
24. Andreas, *History of Chicago,* 1:137.
25. Martineau, *Society in America,* 1:180.
26. J. S. Buckingham, *The Eastern and Western States of America* (n.d.), 267.
27. Charles Fenno Hoffman, *A Winter in the West: Letters Descriptive of Chicago and Vicinity in
    1833–4* (1835), Fergus Historical Series, no. 20 (1882), 24–29.
28. Robert Fergus, *Fergus' Directory of the City of Chicago, 1839* (1876), 37.
29. Buckingham, *Eastern and Western States,* 262.
30. Cleaver, *History of Chicago,* 84.
31. Frederick Jackson Turner, *The Frontier in American History* (1920; reprint, 1962), 11.
32. Turner emphasized the supposedly progressive evolutionary stages of isolated fron-
    tier development in his most famous essays, but his monographic writings pay more
    attention to the role of cities, commerce, and speculators in the West. See especially
    chap. 5 of his *Rise of the New West, 1819–1829* (1906). I assess Turner's legacy more
    fully (and rather more favorably) in "Revisiting the Vanishing Frontier: The Legacy of

Frederick Jackson Turner," *WHQ* 18 (1987): 157–76; and in "Turner's First Stand: The Significance of Significance in American History," in Richard Etulain, ed., *Writing Western History: Essays on Classic Western Historians* (1991).

33. On the history of this episode, see Bray Hammond, *Banks and Politics in America from the Revolution to the Civil War* (1957); and Robert V. Remini, *Andrew Jackson and the Bank War: A Study in the Growth of Presidential Power* (1967).

34. Joseph N. Balestier, *The Annals of Chicago: A Lecture Delivered before the Chicago Lyceum, January 21, 1840* (1840), Fergus Historical Series, no. 1 (1876), 29.

35. Ibid. For an amusing satire of speculators in action, see James Fenimore Cooper, *Home as Found* (1838; reprint, 1961), chap. 7. For a comparison of townsite speculation in a later period, see John C. Hudson, *Plains Country Towns* (1985).

36. John Lewis Peyton, *Over the Alleghanies and across the Prairies* (1848), 2d ed. (1870), 325.

37. "Chicago in 1856," *Putnam's Monthly* 7 (1856): 608.

38. [Caroline Kirkland,] "Illinois in Spring-time: With a Look at Chicago," *Atlantic Monthly* 2 (1858): 487.

39. *Niles' Weekly Register,* Aug. 6, 1814.

40. James William Putnam, *The Illinois and Michigan Canal: A Study in Economic History* (1918), 17–18; "James Thompson's Plat of Chicago: A 150-Year Perspective," *Chicago History* 9, no. 2 (Summer 1980): 66–67.

41. Shirreff, *Tour through North America,* 226.

42. Charles Butler, in Pierce, *As Others See Chicago,* 52; Butler's 1881 letter describing the land speculation is reprinted in its entirety in A. T. Andreas, *History of Cook County, Illinois from the Earliest Period to the Present Time* (1884), 128–31.

43. Extract from Charles Butler's diary, Aug. 4, 1833, as reprinted in Pierce, *As Others See Chicago,* 48. For Butler's general investment activities in Chicago, see John Denis Haeger, *The Investment Frontier: New York Businessmen and the Economic Development of the Old Northwest* (1981).

44. The literature on land speculation is enormous, although much of it deals with rural areas. For a good brief survey, see John W. Reps, *The Making of Urban America: A History of City Planning in the United States* (1965), 349–81.

45. The most important work on the boosters is that of Charles N. Glaab, to which my own discussion is indebted. See Glaab, "Visions of Metropolis: William Gilpin and Theories of City Growth in the American West," *Wis. Mag. Hist.* 45 (1961): 21–31; Glaab, "Jesup W. Scott and a West of Cities," *Ohio History* 73 (1964): 3–12, 56; Glaab, *Kansas City and the Railroads: Community Policy in the Growth of a Regional Metropolis* (1962); Glaab, "Historical Perspective on Urban Development Schemes," in Leo F. Schnore and Henry Fagin, eds., *Urban Research and Policy Planning* (1967), 197–219; and Glaab and A. Theodore Brown, *A History of Urban America,* 3d ed. (1983), 67–73. Other general works worth consulting include Daniel J. Boorstin, *The Americans: The National Experience* (1965), 124–34; and the useful survey by J. Christopher Schnell and Katherine B. Clinton, "The New West: Themes in Nineteenth Century Urban Promotion, 1815–1880," *Bull. Mo. Hist. Soc.* 30 (1974): 75–88. Monographs which focus on local booster controversies include Wyatt Winton Belcher, *The Economic Rivalry between St. Louis and Chicago, 1850–1880* (1947), which should now be read in conjunction with J. Christopher Schnell's not entirely generous critique, "Chicago versus St. Louis: A Reassessment of the Great Rivalry," *Mo. Hist. Rev.* 71 (1977): 245–65; James W. Livingood, *The Philadelphia-Baltimore Trade Rivalry, 1780–1860* (1947); R. Richard Wohl and A. Theodore Brown, "The Usable Past: A Study of Historical Traditions in Kansas City," *Huntington Library Quarterly* 23 (1960): 237–59; Harry N. Scheiber, "Urban Rivalry and Internal Improvements in the Old Northwest, 1820–1860," *Ohio History* 71 (1962): 227–39, 289–92; Robert R. Dykstra, *The Cattle Towns* (1968); Carl Abbott, "Civic Pride in Chicago, 1844–1860," *J. Ill. State Hist. Soc.* 63 (1970): 399–421; Don Harrison Doyle, *The Social Order of a Frontier Community: Jacksonville, Illinois, 1825–1870* (1978); Doug Owram, *Promise of Eden: The Canadian Expansion Movement and the Idea of the West, 1856–1900* (1980); Carl Abbott, *Boosters and Businessmen: Popular Economic Thought and Urban Growth in the Antebellum Middle West* (1981); Alan F. J. Artibise, "Boosterism and the Development of Prairie Cities, 1871–1913," in Artibise, ed., *Town and City: Aspects of Western Canadian Urban Development* (1981), 209–35. Booster writings that emphasize railroads appear in the notes to the next chapter. An important new book by David Hamer, *New Towns in the New World: Images and Perceptions of the Nineteenth-Century Urban*

Frontier (1990), appeared just as my own manuscript went to press. Hamer surveys booster rhetoric and beliefs in the United States, Australia, Canada, and New Zealand and thus offers a much more comparative perspective on boosterism than my own single-city focus can accommodate. Our arguments nonetheless converge at many points, suggesting their general applicability well beyond Chicago and even the United States.

46. In the discussion that follows, I draw on texts written during the half century between 1840 and 1890 without trying to distinguish chronological differences among them. Although booster arguments in later, post–Civil War works tend to be fuller and more systematic and their imperial themes become more overt, their core ideas are all present in the work of authors writing in the 1840s. For my purposes, their similarities are far more important than their differences.

47. Melville E. Stone, "Chicago before the Fire, after the Fire, and To-day," *Scribner's Magazine* 17 (1895): 664.

48. William Bross, *Chicago and the Sources of Her Past and Future Growth* (1880), 3.

49. Cf. John S. Wright, *Chicago: Past, Present, Future Relations to the Great Interior, and to the Continent* (1870), 17: "No earthly power—not even the dissolution of the Union—can divert from Chicago the business and traffic of the great Northwest."

50. J. W. Scott, *A Presentation of Causes Tending to Fix the Position of the Future Great City of the World in the Central Plain of North America: Showing That the Centre of the World's Commerce, Now Represented by the City of London, Is Moving Westward to the City of New York, and Thence, within One Hundred Years, to the Best Position on the Great Lakes,* 2d ed. (1876), 6. Rarely does a book's title summarize its central argument so well!

51. "Chicago," *The Land We Love* 6 (1868): 469.

52. [Jesup W. Scott,] "Internal Trade of the United States," *Hunt's Merch. Mag.* 8 (1843): 447–48.

53. Bross, *Chicago and Her Growth,* 3.

54. *American Railway Times,* as quoted by the *Chicago Tribune,* Dec. 20, 1850. Cf. "Chicago in 1856," *Putnam's Monthly* 7 (1856): 608.

55. L[ogan] U[riah] Reavis, *A Change of National Empire; or, Arguments in Favor of the Removal of the National Capital from Washington City to the Mississippi Valley* (1869), 36. Chicagoans countered by saying that, when it came to transportation, the Architect of nature was less important than the architects of the railroads—but then, there was little that was natural about the railroads. On Reavis, see Patrick E. McLear, "Logan U. Reavis: Nineteenth Century Urban Promoter," *Mo. Hist. Rev.* 66 (1972): 567–88.

56. Humboldt, following Buffon, called these "excessive" climates.

57. On Gilpin, see Glaab, "Visions of Metropolis"; Bernard Devoto, "Geopolitics with the Dew on It," *Harper's Magazine* 188 (March 1944): 313–23; Henry Nash Smith, *Virgin Land: The American West as Symbol and Myth* (1950), 35–43; and Thomas L. Karnes, *William Gilpin: Western Nationalist* (1970).

58. William Gilpin, *Mission of the North American People, Geographical, Social, and Political,* 2d ed. (1874), 112; see also Gilpin, *The Cosmopolitan Railway: Compacting and Fusing Together All the World's Continents* (1890), 125.

59. Cf. Scott, *Future Great City,* 9–15. Logan Reavis adopted the approach more enthusiastically. Climatic interpretations of civilization enjoyed a renaissance among the geographical determinists of the twentieth century, most notably Ellsworth Huntington.

60. S. H. Goodin, "Cincinnati—Its Destiny," in Charles Cist, ed., *Sketches and Statistics of Cincinnati in 1851* (1851), 306.

61. Ibid., 310.

62. A Chicago example of this gravitational language comes from the journalist D. C. Brooks in 1872: "In commerce, as in nature there are centres and centres. . . . Every city is, in some sort, the centre of a tributary system, great or small; and all these in every country—their confines overlapping one another—are auxiliary at last to the metropolis." D. C. Brooks, "Chicago and Its Railways," *Lakeside Monthly* 8 (1872): 264.

63. Goodin, "Cincinnati," 312.

64. On Scott, who is probably the most interesting of the boosters, see Glaab, "Jesup Scott"; and Smith, *Virgin Land,* 155–64. Scott's earliest essays contain most of the themes that appear later in his writings, and so are a good way to become acquainted with his work: Scott, "The Internal Commerce of the United States" (in three parts), *Hunt's Merch. Mag.* 8 (1843): 321–30, 447–58; 9 (1843): 31–47.

65. [Jesup W. Scott,] "The Progress of the West," *Hunt's Merch. Mag.* 14 (1846): 163.
66. Ibid.
67. [Jesup W. Scott,] "Westward the Star of Empire," *De Bow's Review* 27 (1859): 131.
68. [Jesup W. Scott,] "The Growth of Towns in the United States," *Hunt's Merch. Mag.* 25 (1851): 562. One reason western growth rates were higher than eastern ones is that the former began from a much smaller base; the denominator of the fraction was lower. Scott did not bother to mention this simple fact of arithmetic.
69. [Jesup W. Scott,] "Commercial Cities and Towns of the United States," *Hunt's Merch. Mag.* 19 (1848): 385.
70. Scott, "Westward the Star of Empire," 129. Note the implicitly hierarchical model Scott constructs in this sentence, echoing Goodin. See also [Scott,] "Our American Lake Cities," *Hunt's Merch. Mag.* 31 (1854): 410–11; and "Internal Trade," pt. 3, 38. Logan Reavis, not too surprisingly, emphatically rejected what he called "the Lake theory," and proposed a St. Louis–favoring "River theory" instead, in which cities at the junctions of major rivers had advantages over all others. See Reavis, *Change of National Empire,* 125–26. Scott's predictions that the lake cities would grow as a result of their privileged access to eastern trade was not entirely consistent with his claim that interior cities would grow primarily through the growth of internal as opposed to external commerce. The lake harbor argument has much in common with modern export-base theories of urban and regional development, whereas the internal-commerce argument resembles the internal-demand model of economic growth that Diane Lindstrom has offered in her *Economic Development in the Philadelphia Region, 1810–1850* (1978). Scott presumably could have rescued himself from this seeming contradiction by proposing some sort of staged model in which an early export sector fuels the growth of internal commerce that eventually becomes more important; had he done so, he would actually have placed himself squarely in the export-base camp. These remain vexed questions even in modern economic growth theory.
71. Scott, *Future Great City,* 32. The Chicago booster Jesse Thomas quoted this prophecy of Scott's approvingly and then commented that any "disinterested" person would have little hesitation in choosing between Toledo and Chicago; see Thomas, *Report,* iv.
72. George Berkeley, "Verses on the Prospect of Planting Arts and Learning in America," in *The Works of George Berkeley,* ed. Alexander Campbell Fraser (1901), 4:366. See too the classic discussion of American conceptions of empire and national destiny in Henry Nash Smith's *Virgin Land;* and Richard Slotkin's more recent exploration of these themes in *Regeneration through Violence: The Mythology of the American Frontier, 1600–1860* (1973) and *The Fatal Environment: The Myth of the Frontier in the Age of Industrialization, 1800–1890* (1985).
73. Gilpin's Isothermal Zodiac, that fruitful breeding ground for great cities, was also birthplace to the empires which made such cities possible. Over the course of human history, the theory went, cities and their empires had risen and fallen along the Zodiac in a regular pattern, with each new imperial center emerging to the west of the one which had preceded it. Gilpin, *Mission,* 112; Gilpin, *Cosmopolitan Railway,* 125–29.
74. D. J. Kenny, *Historical, Statistical, and Descriptive: Chicago: Identifying Those Firms Who Have Contributed Most to Its Prosperity and Grandeur* (1886), 3.
75. Ibid., 4; *Chicago's First Half Century* (1883), 65. Such phrases became increasingly popular in the 1880s and 1890s, when European nations, particularly England, were emphasizing classical analogues for their own empires. On European uses of the Roman imperial experience, see Raymond F. Betts, "The Allusion to Rome in British Imperialist Thought of the Late Nineteenth and Early Twentieth Centuries," *Victorian Studies* 15 (1971): 149–59; and William L. Vance, *America's Rome,* vol. 1, *Classical Rome* (1989).
76. *A Business Tour of Chicago* (1887), cover. The racial implications of these riders' and horses' colors were surely not accidental.
77. Reavis, *Change of National Empire,* vii. For an early Chicago example of this kind of rhetoric, see Henry Brown, *The Present and Future Prospects of Chicago: An Address Delivered before the Chicago Lyceum, January 20, 1846,* Fergus Historical Series, no. 9 (1876), 10–11; also Kenny, *Chicago,* 6, which used almost the same Gibbonesque language as Reavis.
78. Cf. Scott, *Future Great City,* 32.
79. This emphasis on the trade of the "great interior" was a marked change from earlier concerns about locating a "passage to India" which would link Asian and European

commerce in the heart of North America. Although interest in a route to the Orient persisted among the urban boosters, especially Gilpin, it gradually lost importance as they came to see the Great West itself as the justification for imperial urban growth. For an example of how Chicago boosters thought the opening of a transcontinental railroad might affect the city's role in the China trade, see "Chicago to China," *Chicago Evening Journal,* Nov. 25, 1868, reprinted in C. Exera Brown, *Brown's Gazeteer of the Chicago and Northwestern Railway, and Branches, and of the Union Pacific Railroad: A Guide and Business Directory* (1869), 37–39.

80. *Albany Argus,* n.d., quoted in Scott, "Progress of the West," 163.
81. John A. Wright, "Effects of Internal Improvements on Commercial Cities: With Reference to the Pennsylvania Central Railroad," *Hunt's Merch. Mag.* 16 (1847): 264.
82. Given the no-holds-barred way that Chicagoans promoted their own city, their relative silence about New York may seem a little surprising. It undoubtedly flowed from the two cities' special relationship to each other and to the railroads. Chicago's much resented status as "second city" has been an important part of the city's identity almost from the start; see the next chapter for further development of this argument. And despite the general hesitancy among Chicago boosters about challenging the eastern metropolis, a few threw caution to the winds. See, for instance, Chicago Building & Loan Association, *Statistical and Historical Review of Chicago* (1869), 45, which asserted that Chicago would "surpass the city of New York in population, wealth and trade," compared the two cities to their classical analogues, and then used past growth rates to predict that New York's population in 1890 would be 3,043,931 as against Chicago's 10,926,540! John S. Wright was more realistic, remarking, "New York has been and still is the emporium of the continent, for all sections have more dealings with her than with any other city. Philadelphia, Baltimore, and Boston, heavy centres of business as they are, are her tributaries. Not for several years can Chicago stand in that relation to the chief cities of the West, because New York will still be their emporium. For that reason, and that only, the whole West cannot be now claimed as Chicago's territory. The time must come, as we shall see, when the West will have far more traffic with itself than with the seaboard; and then, unless this argument be fallacious, Chicago will be its emporium." Wright, *Chicago,* 115.
83. *Chicago Magazine* 1 (1857): 94.
84. For St. Louis, the image could be quite literal: Logan Reavis intended no hyperbole when he spoke of the "imperial Mississippi" which would "yet assert its commercial sovereignty." Reavis, *Change of National Empire,* 36.
85. [James Parton,] "Chicago," *Atlantic Monthly* 19 (1867): 330.
86. Gilpin, *Mission of the American People,* 104.
87. James Hall, "The Commercial Growth and Greatness of the West: As Illustrating the Dignity and Usefulness of Commerce," *Hunt's Merch. Mag.* 17 (1847): 502.
88. It need hardly be added that this perspective did not prevent Chicagoans from being among the most competitive and jingoistic self-promoters in the West.
89. Wright, *Chicago,* xvii. On Wright's life, see Lloyd Lewis, *John S. Wright: Prophet of the Prairies* (1941); and Patrick E. McLear, "John Stephen Wright and Urban and Regional Promotion in the Nineteenth Century," *J. Ill. State Hist. Soc.* 68 (1975): 407–20.
90. Bross, *Chicago and Her Growth,* 18. Cf. John Dean Caton, "An Address Delivered at the Reception to the Settlers of Chicago prior to 1840, by the Calumet Club of Chicago, May 27, 1879," in Mabel McIlvaine, ed., *Reminiscences of Early Chicago* (1912), 165.
91. At least in the early years of Chicago's existence, boosters in rival cities gave as good as they got. In 1853, the *Detroit Free Press* lampooned Chicago's pretensions, Davy Crockett–style, by reporting that Chicago's City Council had voted "to extend the limits of that city, so as to take in all east of the Rocky Mountains; all south of fifty-four degrees of latitude; and all north of Patagonia." *Detroit Free Press,* n.d., as quoted by the *Chicago Tribune,* Jan. 6, 1853. The *Tribune* answered these gibes by saying that Detroit had better be on its best behavior if it hoped to become one of Chicago's suburbs.
92. "Emporium" derives from the Greek word *emporion,* from *emporos,* "traveler" or "trader," whereas "empire" derives from Latin *imperium,* from *imperare,* "to command."
93. Glaab, "Jesup Scott," 3.
94. Readers should again remember that the portrait of booster thought that I offer in this chapter brings together texts from a fifty-year period, most written after the 1830s.

Not all the boosters' later arguments were part of Chicago's land craze; some were absent for reasons (having to do with the railroads) that will only become apparent in the next chapter. Nonetheless, the general idea of a city growing to wealth and power by dominating its hinterland's development was undoubtedly much on people's minds during the speculation of the 1830s.

95. Frederick Jackson Turner to Arthur M. Schlesinger, May 5, 1925, reprinted in Wilbur R. Jacobs, ed., *The Historical World of Frederick Jackson Turner with Selections from His Correspondence* (1968), 163–65; see also Arthur M. Schlesinger, "The City in American History," *MVHR* 27 (1940–41): 43.

96. Again, I speak here of the early Turner, whose "The Significance of the Frontier in American History" attempted to "explain" American history in terms of the frontier experience. The later Turner, in emphasizing American sectionalism, was more closely allied to the boosters as I portray them here.

97. On Turner's nostalgia, see Lee Benson, *Turner and Beard: American Historical Writing Reconsidered* (1960); and Richard Hofstadter, *The Progressive Historians: Turner, Beard, Parrington* (1968).

98. Turner, *Frontier in American History,* 153.

99. Ibid., 150.

100. Parton, "Chicago," 327.

101. Johann Heinrich von Thünen, *Von Thünen's Isolated State* (1826, 1842), trans. Carla M. Wartenberg, ed. Peter Hall (1966), 8.

102. Ibid., 171–74.

103. Central place theory has evolved into an arcane field with a huge literature. See the notes to chapter 6 for a survey of major works.

104. Turner, *Frontier in American History,* 11.

105. Articles that apply von Thünen's model to the expansion of agriculture in the nineteenth century include John T. Schlebecker, "The World Metropolis and the History of American Agriculture," *JEH* 20 (1960): 187–208; J. Richard Peet, "The Spatial Expansion of Commercial Agriculture in the Nineteenth Century: A Von Thünen Interpretation," *Economic Geography* 45 (1969): 283–301; and Peet, "Von Thünen Theory and the Dynamics of Agricultural Expansion," *Explorations in Economic History* 8 (1970–71): 181–201.

106. For a powerful corrective to the many dangers of such overgeneralization, see Patricia Nelson Limerick, *The Legacy of Conquest: The Unbroken Past of the American West* (1987).

107. See the fuller discussion of these issues in chapter 6.

108. Even Joseph Balestier, whose skepticism about the 1830s land craze was as deep as anyone's, was quite certain that Chicago was no ordinary speculator city. Balestier noted that "The Illinois and Michigan Canal, when completed, will render Chicago a place of vast importance. . . . Chicago [will be] the grand avenue for the transportation of merchandise bound westward. . . . An immense traffic will grow out of the interchange of commodities, and no limit can be assigned to the prosperity of the place." Balestier, *Annals of Chicago,* 38–39.

109. Wright, *Chicago,* frontispiece.

110. A metropolitan perspective has traditionally come more easily to historians in Canada than to those in the United States. Despite the roughly similar settlement histories of the two countries, historians of the American West, with a few notable exceptions, have continued to follow Turner's emphasis on the region's rural aspects; even where they have focused on cities, they have rarely emphasized the city-country relationship. Canadian historians, on the other hand, have more or less rejected the Turnerian frontier and have pursued what has come to be called the metropolitan thesis. Those familiar with the nineteenth-century boosters will instantly recognize its main features. As J. M. S. Careless, a leading Canadian historian, describes it, metropolitanism "implies the emergence of a city of outstanding size to dominate not only its surrounding countryside but other cities and their countrysides, the whole area being organized by the metropolis, through control of communications, trade, and finance, into one economic and social unit that is focused on the metropolitan 'centre of dominance' and through it trades with the world." In Canada, this city was Montreal; in the United States, it was New York. Beneath the central metropolis were smaller cities playing similar but less extensive roles, since "the metropolitan relationship is a chain, almost a feudal chain of vassalage, wherein one city may stand tributary to a bigger centre and

yet be the metropolis of a sizable region of its own." The examples here were Toronto in Canada, and Chicago in the United States. J. M. S. Careless, "Frontierism, Metropolitanism, and Canadian History," *Canadian Historical Review* 35 (1954): 17.

The classic work on the role of the metropolis in Canadian economic history is by Harold Innis; see especially his *Problems of Staple Production in Canada* (1933); and his "Significant Factors in Canadian Economic Development," *Canadian Historical Review* 18 (1937): 374–84. The most recent synthesis of subsequent historiography is J. M. S. Careless, *Frontier and Metropolis: Regions, Cities, and Identities in Canada before 1914* (1989). See also D. C. Masters, *The Rise of Toronto, 1850–1890* (1947); W. L. Morton, "The Significance of Site in the Settlement of the American and Canadian Wests," *Ag. Hist.* 25 (1951): 97–104; Melville H. Watkins, "A Staple Theory of Economic Growth," *Canadian Journal of Economics and Political Science* 29 (1963): 141–58; Ramsay Cook, "Frontier and Metropolis: The Canadian Experience," in Cook, *The Maple Leaf Forever: Essays on Nationalism and Politics in Canada* (1971), 166–75; Alan F. J. Artibise, *Winnipeg: A Social History of Urban Growth, 1874–1914* (1975); Alan F. J. Artibise, ed., *Town and City: Aspects of Western Canadian Urban Development* (1981). On the place of this theme in Canadian historiography generally, see Carl Berger, *The Writing of Canadian History: Aspects of English-Canadian Historical Writing, 1900 to 1970* (1976). American exponents of the metropolitan thesis have tended to be geographers, sociologists, and economists rather than historians. The most important American contemporary of Innis is N. S. B. Gras, whose *An Introduction to Economic History* (1922) is entirely organized around the theme of metropolitan development; see also his "The Significance of the Twin Cities in Minnesota History," *Minn. Hist.* 7 (1926): 3–17, which derives in part from Mildred Lucile Hartsough, *The Twin Cities as a Metropolitan Market: A Regional Study of the Economic Development of Minneapolis and St. Paul* (1925); Howard W. Odum, *American Regionalism: A Cultural-Historical Approach to National Integration* (1938); and N. S. B. Gras and Henrietta M. Larson, eds., *Casebook in American Business History* (1939), esp. 385–402. Among sociologists, R. D. McKenzie, *The Metropolitan Community* (1933), is the most systematic attempt to look at the metropolis in its regional context. The many works of Lewis Mumford are also relevant; see in particular *The Culture of Cities* (1938); and *The City in History: Its Origins, Its Transformations, and Its Prospects* (1961).

For the United States, the classic work on early western cities remains Richard C. Wade, *The Urban Frontier: The Rise of Western Cities, 1790–1830* (1959), which does not, however, deal much with issues of metropolitan dominance; it is overloaded with detail, and its themes can be gotten quickly from Wade's earlier article "Urban Life in Western America, 1790–1830," *AHR* 44 (1958): 14–30. For a later period, Lewis Atherton, *Main Street on the Middle Border* (1954), remains an excellent study of small-town life but, like Wade, is less concerned with city-country linkages. The late Charles Gates adopted the metropolitan theme in his interpretation of western cities but unfortunately never published his work in this area. Suggestions of its directions can be found in his "The Role of Cities in the Westward Movement," *MVHR* 37 (1950–51): 277–78; and "The Concept of the Metropolis in the American Western Movement," *MVHR* 49 (1962–63): 299–300. Earl Pomeroy has ably focused on the importance of major cities of the Far West in his *The Pacific Slope: A History of California, Oregon, Washington, Idaho, Utah, and Nevada* (1966), esp. 120–64, as well as in his essay "The Urban Frontier of the Far West," in John G. Clark, ed., *The Frontier Challenge: Responses to the Trans-Mississippi West* (1971), 7–29. Other studies of western urbanism have tended to emphasize small-town life. For bibliographical surveys, see J. Christopher Schnell and Patrick E. McLear, "Why the Cities Grew: A Historiographical Essay on Western Urban Growth, 1850–1880," *Bull. Mo. Hist. Soc.* 28 (1972): 162–77; Bradford Luckingham, "The City in the Westward Movement: A Bibliographical Note," *WHQ* 5 (1974): 295–306; Oliver Knight, "Toward an Understanding of the Western Town," *WHQ* 4 (1973): 27–42; and Lawrence H. Larsen and Robert L. Branyon, "The Development of an Urban Civilization on the Frontier of the American West," *Societas* 1 (1971): 33–50.

111. Turner, *Frontier in American History*, 3.
112. Emile Boutmy, *Studies in Constitutional Law: France—England—United States* (1891), 127–28.
113. Turner, *Frontier in American History*, 211.
114. Parton, "Chicago," 328. The work of Reginald Horsman is suggestive about the relationships between manifest destiny and U.S. Indian policy; see Horsman, *Race and*

Manifest Destiny: The Origins of American Racial Anglo-Saxonism (1981). A student at Illinois College in 1841 captured this same sense of the "vanishing Indian" as an icon of frontier progress, while simultaneously striking a more melancholy note, when he wrote his sister in Portland, Maine, "Stop awhile 'schooling, scholding & training' and come with me. It is early morning. You have no need of that cloak, put a handkerchief round your neck, and take my hand and let us go. fear not the 'fever and ague,' it is not the admirer of Nature she seeks, but rather he who contrary to the laws of *God* & man shuts Nature out and confines his gaze with brick and mortar[.] let us take this little path so beautifully straight. 'tis an Indian trail and as we walk along, we may look back the short space of fifty years and see the untamed savage treading the same little path fearless & undisturbed and then the melancholy question will arise 'where are they now?' what has become of that mighty race that once covered this fair land. ah! it *is* a melancholy question. would that they had been some other than Columbia's sons that had erased their very name from off the Earth. But look and see the sun as he rises so gloriously above his prairie land, see the dew-drops glisten, and the wild-flowers nod their heads for joy, as we can almost read the sweet words of Nature's sweetest poet." John Barnwell Shaw to Miss E. A. C. Shaw, Nov. 22, 1841, Shaw Family Papers, Newberry Library. See also *Illinois in 1837 & 8* (1838), 135, for a similar contemporary passage directly tying Chicago's growth to Indian removal; and Traffic Department, Chicago and North-Western Railway Co., *The Indian, the Northwest, 1600 . . . 1900: the Red Man, the War Man, the White Man, and the North-Western Line* (1901), for a text that suggests later uses of the vanishing-Indian myth.

115. Turner, *Frontier in American History*, 3. In the same paragraph where Turner defines the frontier as "free land," he also calls it "the meeting place between savagery and civilization." Although he followed a long American tradition in equating the two, they were not at all the same. Historians for at least the past quarter century have criticized Turner—and rightly so—for the racism and ethnocentrism of defining "free land" in terms of "savagery." But in the heat of the attack, Turner's critics have often overlooked the effects that abundant and cheap natural resources—"free land" in a different sense—had on the market economies and the cultures that absorbed them. Although we must never forget the acts of conquest that seized those resources, neither should we lose track of the broader political economic consequences of resource abundance, which are to a considerable degree analytically separable from the original invasion. Turner's modern critics usually fail to recognize that this narrower definition of "free land" continues to offer important insights into the history of the United States. See Cronon, "Revisiting the Vanishing Frontier" and "Significance of Significance in American History."

116. Turner, *Frontier in American History*, 150.

2: RAILS AND WATER

1. John Tipton, "Surveying Line between Indiana and Illinois, 1821," as reprinted in Pierce, *As Others See Chicago*, 28.
2. Pierce, *History of Chicago*, 1:90–91.
3. For later details about the harbor, see Andreas, *History of Chicago*, 2:70–72; and Harold M. Mayer, *The Port of Chicago and the St. Lawrence Seaway*, University of Chicago Department of Geography Research Paper no. 49 (1957). On the challenges of financing harbor and other lakeshore improvements, see Robin L. Einhorn, "A Taxing Dilemma: Early Lake Shore Protection," *Chicago History* 18, no. 3 (Fall 1989): 34–51.
4. On the Hegelian concept of "second nature" as the cultural transformation of "first nature," see Alfred Schmidt, *The Concept of Nature in Marx* (1971), 42–43; for a critique and elaboration of the concept, see Neil Smith, *Uneven Development: Nature, Capital and the Production of Space* (1984), 19–20.
5. The best study of seasonal cycling in frontier trade and transportation of the trans-Appalachian West remains Louis C. Hunter, "Studies in the Economic History of the Ohio Valley: Seasonal Aspects of Industry and Commerce before the Age of Big Business," *Smith College Studies in History* 19, nos. 1–2 (Oct. 1933–Jan. 1934): 1–49.
6. Thomas Butler Carter, "Some facts and incidents in the early life of THOMAS BUTLER CARTER from boyhood and on until 1889, but especially during the last fifty years from the date of his arrival in Chicago Sept. 15th., 1838," manuscript autobiog-

raphy, Sept. 15, 1888, CHS, 41. Aside from the inherent dangers to ships of winter storms on the lakes, the critical locations where ice closed the shipping lanes were the Erie Canal and the Straits of Mackinac. Cf. Chicago Building & Loan Association, *Statistical and Historical Review of Chicago*, 37.

7. Peyton, *Over the Alleghanies*, 327.

8. Cleaver, *History of Chicago*, 80.

9. *The Letters of Ralph Waldo Emerson*, ed. Ralph L. Rusk (1939), 4:342.

10. Hough, "Prehistoric Great Lakes," 84-109; and Hough, *Geology of the Great Lakes*.

11. Carter, "Facts and Incidents," 40. For other descriptions of the problems Chicagoans experienced with mud, see Charles Cleaver, *Early-Chicago Reminiscences*, Fergus Historical Series, no. 19 (1882), 28-31. Business reports in the Chicago papers regularly noted the slowness of trade during the wet months. One example from among many is the following market report from the *Chicago Tribune* of April 23, 1849: "Nothing doing in the streets, even in the Family Provision trade."

12. Peyton, *Over the Alleghanies*, 326.

13. Pierce, *History of Chicago*, 1:204-5. Cf. Daniel Lyman Chandler to Henry P. Chandler, July 22, 1855, Newberry Library.

14. Pierce, *A History of Chicago*, vol. 2, *From Town to City, 1848-1871* (1940), 316-19; Harold M. Mayer and Richard C. Wade, *Chicago: Growth of a Metropolis* (1969), 94-99.

15. John Dean Caton, " ' 'Tis Sixty Years Since' in Chicago," *Atlantic Monthly* 71 (May 1893): 590-91.

16. That farmers traveled as far as they did to sell goods in the city testifies to the inelasticity of their demand for the goods they purchased in Chicago.

17. Cleaver, *History of Chicago*, 111.

18. Ruby Yetter, "Some Aspects of the Commercial Growth of Chicago, 1835-1850" (M.A. thesis, Univ. of Chicago, 1937), 33, 57.

19. Thomas Butler Carter to Aaron Carter, Feb. 24, 1865, in Carter Collection, CHS.

20. S. M. Fuller, *Summer on the Lakes in 1843* (1844), 80. Fuller visited Chicago in late spring, which was another time when the city's business tended to peak.

21. Lester Harding of Paw Paw, Ill., to Jerimiah Hall of Abington, Penn., Oct. 24, 1847, CHS, Xerox of original which is property of the Lackawanna Historical Society, Scranton, Penn.

22. William Bross, *History of Chicago* (1876), 36.

23. Yetter, "Chicago Commercial Growth," 32; Pierce, *History of Chicago*, 1:127.

24. Harding to Hall, Oct. 24, 1847, CHS.

25. Fredrika Bremer, *The Homes of the New World; Impressions of America* (1853; reprint, 1968), 605. Bremer's general impression of Chicago was not favorable; she thought it "one of the most miserable and ugly cities" she had yet seen in America, resembling "rather a huckstress than a queen."

26. Thomas, *Report*, 14-17.

27. *U.S. Census of Population*, 1840, 1850; Lawrence H. Larson, "Chicago's Midwest Rivals: Cincinnati, St. Louis, and Milwaukee," *Chicago History* 5 (1976): 141-51; Bayrd Still, *Milwaukee: The History of a City* (1948), 570. Chicago's ultimate triumph over Milwaukee resulted directly from its privileged relationship with the railroads. On Chicago's competition with other port cities on Lake Michigan, see Patrick E. McLear, "Rivalry between Chicago and Wisconsin Lake Ports for Control of the Grain Trade," *Inland Seas* 24 (1968): 225-33.

28. Fuller, *Summer on the Lakes*, 30.

29. Thomas, *Report*, 25.

30. John Calhoun Papers, CHS, Subscription book for the *Chicago Democrat*, dated Dec. 3, 1834. The statistics in this paragraph are based on my own rough tabulations of the names and addresses listed in this volume. The account book arranged subscribers by mailing address and divided them into two groups, "western" mail and "eastern" mail. The "western mail" included Missouri (5), Iowa (13), Wisconsin (36), Louisiana (1), and Mississippi (2), with 7 missing locations; the "eastern mail" included New York (117), Michigan (47), the District of Columbia (9), Tennessee (1), Massachusetts (6), Pennsylvania (7), Ohio (10), Upper Canada (4), Connecticut (3), Vermont (2), New Jersey (3), Virginia (3), and New Hampshire (1), with 11 missing locations. (For reasons that are not clear—perhaps having to do either with shipping routes or with simple clerical errors—1 Wisconsin and 13 Iowa subscribers were listed under the

"eastern mail" and 1 Virginia subscriber under the "western"; I have shifted each to its more logical location in the above list.) There were 342 Illinois subscriptions outside of Chicago, and 226 Chicago names on what was called the "village list." I have not included newspaper exchanges (free subscriptions exchanged between newspapers in different localities) in my tabulations, although they generally reflect the same patterns as the individual subscriptions. A number of names on the list were crossed out, presumably because the subscriber had not paid or renewed, but in the interest of capturing the fullest possible geographic coverage, I have included all such crossed-out names in my calculations. The paper's agent for a given community was usually listed first, and I have included that person's name in the list of subscribers. Finally, I have *not* made a thorough effort to eliminate duplicate names on the list, but these do not appear to have been numerous. On the history of the *Democrat*, see Andreas, *History of Chicago*, 1:360–412.

31. Subscription book for the *Chicago Democrat*, Dec. 3, 1834, CHS.

32. "New and Cheap Goods, Phillips & Co.," *Chicago Tribune*, April 23, 1849; emphasis in original. On Chicago advertising practices during this period, see Erne Rene Frueh, "Retail Merchandising in Chicago, 1833–1848," *J. Ill. State Hist. Soc.* 32 (1939): 149–72.

33. For a full discussion of these issues, see Lewis E. Atherton, *The Frontier Merchant in Mid-America* (1939; reprint, 1971), 59–162. On the importance of wholesaling to urban hierarchies in general, see the discussion in chapter 7 below, and also James E. Vance, Jr., *The Merchant's World: The Geography of Wholesaling* (1970).

34. See Robert Greenhalgh Albion, *The Rise of New York Port, 1815–1860* (1939); and David Maldwyn Ellis, "New York and the Western Trade, 1850–1910," *New York History* 33 (1952): 379–96. New York's dominance was of course not absolute. Other eastern cities continued to compete for western trade, with entrepreneurs in Boston, Philadelphia, and Baltimore playing especially important roles. For discussions of eastern port competition in different periods, see David T. Gilchrist, ed., *The Growth of Seaport Cities, 1790–1825* (1967); and Howard B. Schonberger, *Transportation to the Seaboard: The "Communication Revolution" and American Foreign Policy, 1860–1900* (1971).

35. This argument has a certain unavoidable circularity, since New York enjoyed some of its predominance because of its special links to western trade. Geographical patterns and commercial institutions were mutually reinforcing.

36. Chamberlin, *Chicago and Its Suburbs*, 170.

37. Thomas, *Report*, 25.

38. In a wonderful booster speech before the House of Representatives, Chicago's soon-to-be mayor Carter H. Harrison declared that "Nature . . . wrote on that low divide the first engineer's report in favor of a ship-canal to unite the Mississippi and the lakes." "Speech of Hon. Carter H. Harrison, of Illinois, on the Illinois and Michigan Canal, in the House of Representatives, Tuesday, May 21, 1878."

39. On internal improvements schemes generally, see Howard, *Illinois*, 193–212; the classic study of canal development in the Old Northwest is Harry N. Scheiber, *Ohio Canal Era: A Case Study of Government and the Economy, 1820–1861* (1969). See also Donald J. Pisani, "Promotion and Regulation: Constitutionalism and the American Economy," *JAH* 74 (1987): 740–68.

40. Putnam, *Illinois and Michigan Canal;* Pierce, *History of Chicago*, vol. 1; Andreas, *History of Chicago*, 1:165–73; F. Cyril James, *The Growth of Chicago Banks* (1938; reprint, 1969), 117–89; and Michael P. Conzen and Kay J. Carr, eds., *The Illinois & Michigan Canal National Heritage Corridor: A Guide to Its History and Sources* (1988).

41. By 1852, the *Chicago Tribune*'s annual review of the city's commerce was remarking, "The superior advantage of this market over that of St. Louis, for corn, is well established; and within the next five years that city will receive very little from any point north of the mouth of the Illinois River." *Chicago Tribune*, "The Annual Statement of the Commerce of Chicago for the Year 1852," in "Trade and Growth of Chicago in 1852," *Hunt's Merch. Mag.* 28 (1853): 561. Wheat was more sensitive to shifts in market demand, so farmers shipped to Chicago or St. Louis according to which offered the better price. The *Chicago Tribune* and *Daily Democratic Press* both published annual reviews of commerce under varying titles, usually at the end of December of the relevant year. Unless the publication information is difficult to find or important to my argument, I will cite these below under the following form: "Annual Review for 1852."

42. "Commercial Cities and Towns of the United States: City of Chicago, Illinois," *Hunt's Merch. Mag.* 18 (1848): 164–71; "Commercial Statistics," ibid., 21 (1849): 560–61. One should be very cautious about placing too much trust in early trade statistics. No one institution was responsible for collecting these until the 1850s—Jesse Thomas went from door to door to collect invoices from shippers to estimate Chicago's trade in 1847—and any data gathered were subject to the inevitable booster exaggerations. (Thomas, *Report,* 18.) As the *Tribune* wrote in 1853, "It is a matter of regret, that the published statistics of the Commerce of Chicago previous to 1851, have been, to a considerable extent, a matter of conjecture." "Annual Statement of the Commerce of Chicago for the Year 1852," *Chicago Tribune,* as reprinted in "Trade and Growth of Chicago in 1852," *Hunt's Merch. Mag.* 28 (1853): 558. To their credit, the city newspapers repeatedly offered detailed criticisms of the statistics they published. City trade data improved during the 1850s, especially after the Chicago Board of Trade began to publish its annual reports, but later statistics need to be handled with care as well.

43. Cf. Daniel S. Curtiss, *Western Portraiture, and Emigrants' Guide* (1852), 47–48, quoting *Chicago Tribune,* n.d.

44. Pierce, *History of Chicago,* 1:114–15; Andreas, *History of Chicago,* 1:245–48. See also *Chicago: Her Commerce and Railroads: Two Articles, Chicago Daily Democratic Press* (1852), 17–20.

45. Rockford resolutions, reported in *Chicago Weekly Democrat,* Jan. 20, 1846; Ralph William Marshall, "The Early History of the Galena and Chicago Union Railroad" (M.A. thesis, Univ. of Chicago, 1937), 36–37; Chicago and North Western Railway, *Yesterday and Today: A History of the Chicago and North Western Railway System,* 3d ed. (1910), 11–12.

46. Marshall, "G&CU Railway," 43. A few members from other towns were soon added, but Chicagoans continued to dominate the board.

47. J. Young Scammon, *William B. Ogden,* Fergus Historical Series, no. 17 (1882), 67; Galena and Chicago Union Railroad Company, *Report of William B. Ogden, President of the Company . . . Read at the Annual Meeting of Stockholders, April 5, 1848* (1848), 4–5. Ogden and Scammon left decidedly different accounts of how eastern investors reacted to the proposed railroad. Ogden's report to the company's stockholders described "experienced parties at the East" as being "decidedly friendly to the success of the Galena and Chicago road"; their best judgment, he said, was that "the wisest and surest way to accomplish the speedy extension and completion of the entire route to Galena, was, for the inhabitants along the line of the road, to raise the means themselves. . . ." Scammon's later recollections are a good deal more candid, and suggest the ways in which bankruptcy could be a standard tool for financing a nineteenth-century railroad. He reported that the Boston iron merchant William F. Weld advised the Chicagoans, "Go home, raise what money you can, expend it upon your Road, and when it breaks down, as it surely or in all probability will, come and give it to us, and we will take hold of it and complete it, as we are completing the Michigan Central."

48. Scammon, *Ogden,* 64.

49. Arthur Charles Cole, *The Era of the Civil War, 1848–1870,* vol. 3 of *The Centennial History of Illinois* (1919), 40. (Cole gives no source for this claim, making it difficult to check further.)

50. Ogden, in G&CU, *Report,* 5; Francis Howe, ibid., 33; Andreas, *History of Chicago,* 1:247. For the history of the line generally, see Robert J. Casey and W. A. S. Douglas, *Pioneer Railroad: The Story of the Chicago and North Western System* (1948); see also the Chicago and North Western's *Yesterday and Today.*

51. Pierce, *History of Chicago,* 1:117, n. 220.

52. Scammon, *Ogden,* 66–70. See also William Alan White, "Chicago and Toronto: A Comparative Study in Early Growth" (Ph.D. thesis, Northwestern Univ., 1974), 49–55.

53. Andreas, *History of Chicago,* 1:248–9.

54. "Report of John Van Nortwick, Chief Engineer," in G&CU, *Report,* 16.

55. *Chicago Tribune,* "Annual Statement of Commerce of Chicago," in *Hunt's Merch. Mag.* 28 (1853): 560–61. On the failure of Illinois wheat crops, see "Annual Review of the Business of Chicago for the Year 1852," in *Chicago: Her Commerce and Railroads* (1853), 3.

56. Howard Gray Brownson, "History of the Illinois Central Railroad to 1870," *University of Illinois Studies in the Social Sciences* 1 (1915): 68–69. Like most such pooling agreements, this one proved unstable by the late 1850s, so the Illinois Central had to try

several other arrangements for linking Galena with Chicago before finally settling upon a permanent route. Scammon later claimed that he and Ogden had resisted this partial betrayal of Galena's interests, that they had been overruled by other directors, and that Galena's decline could in part be attributed to its failure to secure the terminus; Scammon, *Ogden,* 64-65.

57. Scammon, *Ogden,* 64-65; Andreas, *History of Chicago,* 1:249; Frederic L. Paxson, "The Railroads of the 'Old Northwest' before the Civil War," *Transactions of the Wisconsin Academy of Sciences, Arts, and Letters* 17 (1914): 243-74; Chicago and North Western, *Yesterday and Today,* 13-37.

58. CBT, *Annual Report for 1900,* 169. I ordinarily cite the Board's reports by listing only the year to which the report's statistics pertained (as opposed to its year of publication, which was generally a year later). Because the format of the reports varied little from year to year, making it easy to locate relevant tables as needed, I rarely give pagination; where it is obvious from the text, or where data are repeatedly contained in many reports, I do not even list the year.

59. The development of these systems can be traced in the various annual reviews of Chicago's commerce published by the *Chicago Tribune* and *Daily Democratic Press;* see also Paxson, "Railroads of the Old Northwest"; and for a summary of the system as it appeared at the end of the Civil War, see Henry M. Flint, *The Railroads of the United States; Their History and Statistics* (1868), 265-69. On railroad growth during this period in general, see John F. Stover, *Iron Road to the West: American Railroads in the 1850s* (1978).

60. Andreas, *History of Chicago,* 1:246; Brownson, "Illinois Central," 17-19. The eastern terminus of the railroad was to have been at the southern end of the Illinois and Michigan Canal, which would have given the railroad at least some access to the lake port.

61. Wm. K. Ackerman, *Early Illinois Railroads,* Fergus Historical Series, no. 23 (1884); Paul Wallace Gates, *The Illinois Central Railroad and Its Colonization Work* (1934); Gates, *Public Land Law Development,* 341-86; Brownson, "Illinois Central," 24-32; Carlton J. Corliss, *Main Line of Mid-America: The Story of the Illinois Central* (1950), 12-20.

62. Illinois Central, *Annual Report,* 1859, 12. Even this figure significantly understates the city's importance, since it ignores the large amount of freight which traveled over the Illinois Central's *main* line only to reach other railroads—like the Galena and Chicago Union—which furnished direct access to Chicago. In 1859, for instance, over 10 percent of the Galena's business came directly from the Illinois Central, most of it presumably moving to or from Chicago. Galena and Chicago Union, *Annual Report,* 1859, 29. Underestimation of the Illinois Central's contribution to the Galena does not end here, since this statistic describes only the *direct* transfers between the two roads; in 1859, Freeport and Dixon, which also had connections with the Central, contributed another 14 percent of the Galena's total business. The Central had a comparable feeder relationship with the Chicago, Burlington and Quincy as well. In 1859, the CB&Q's eastward tonnage from Mendota, where it crossed the Central, accounted for 13 percent of its total. Chicago, Burlington and Quincy, *Annual Report,* 1859, table H. Such figures are difficult to combine accurately, but they suggest that Chicago-bound freight and passengers were accounting for *much* more than a quarter of the Illinois Central's total traffic. By 1863, the president of the company had declared that the Chicago branch had become "the main line of the road"; quoted in Robert Mise Sutton, "The Illinois Central Railroad in Peace and War, 1858-1868" (Ph.D. thesis, Univ. of Illinois, 1948).

63. *Chicago Magazine* 1 (1857): 389.

64. [Caroline Kirkland,] "Illinois in Spring-Time: With a Look at Chicago," *Atlantic Monthly* 2 (1858): 484.

65. "Annual Review of the Trade and Commerce of Chicago for the Year 1850," *Chicago Tribune,* Dec. 28, 1850. Much of this discussion called for lower canal rates to meet increased river competition.

66. "Annual Review of the Commerce of Chicago for the Year 1851," *Chicago Tribune,* as reprinted in "Chicago: Its Trade and Growth in 1851," *Hunt's Merch. Mag.* 26 (1852): 440-41.

67. *Chicago: Her Commerce and Railroads* (1853). In 1853, the pendulum swung still further, with an annual review entitled "The Railroads, History and Commerce of Chicago," [Annual Review for 1853,] *Chicago Daily Democratic Press* (1854).

68. Annual Review for 1852, *Daily Democratic Press*, 24; see also the Annual Review for 1855, ibid., 4.
69. Annual Review for 1854, *Daily Democratic Press*, 5. Cf. the *Tribune* on Dec. 20, 1852, which argued that the railroad would accelerate the natural flow of goods to the city.
70. Brooks, "Chicago and Its Railways," 268.   •
71. The classic treatment of this subject remains Leo Marx, *The Machine in the Garden: Technology and the Pastoral Ideal in America* (1964).
72. I. D. Guyer, *History of Chicago: Its Commercial and Manufacturing Interests and Industry* (1862), 153.
73. Annual Review for 1855, *Daily Democratic Press*, 5. Compare W. F. Rae, *Westward by Rail: A Journey to San Francisco and Back and a Visit to the Mormons* (1871): "If another Queen Scheherazade were compelled to rehearse a tale of enchantment for the gratification of an exacting husband, she might find in the authentic story of the rise of Chicago materials which would produce a result as striking as that caused by a recital of the fabulous doings of Aladdin."
74. *Daily Journal*, Sept. 11, 1849, as quoted in White, "Chicago and Toronto," 48. For a wonderful text that applies these same magical and imperial metaphors to San Francisco and California, see [Henry George,] "What the Railroad Will Bring Us," *Overland Monthly* 1 (1868): 297–306.
75. The modern analogy is space exploration, which has evoked in the second half of the twentieth century many of the same rhetorical tropes and exaggerations that the railroad did in the second half of the nineteenth.
76. To return to an earlier image: Chicago's boosters could write in 1854 that Chicago's factories were "darkening the air with their lofty chimneys and gathering beneath their domes all the tireless forms of known machinery." In the 1850s, clouds of smoke were still an unambiguous sign of progress and improvement. Annual Review for 1854, *Daily Democratic Press*, 4.
77. John M. Binckley, "Chicago of the Thinker," *Lakeside Monthly* 4 (Oct. 1873): 263. Cf. Wright, *Chicago*, xii–xiii: "Nature never makes a city. . . . No human institution is more artificial, success depending upon a conjunction of causes, which, however liberally bestowed by nature, lie dormant until operated by human effort and ingenuity. Art, however, would have a difficult task in localities neglected of nature, and easy upon sites she favored." For an interesting discussion of the merged effects of first and second nature in promoting Chicago's growth, see Appleton Morgan, *The People and the Railways* (1888), 114–17.
78. Kirkland, "Illinois in Spring-time," 485, 476.
79. Few historical analyses have been more misleading about this issue than Robert Fogel's elaborate quantitative argument that the railroad was in no way "indispensable" to American economic growth in the nineteenth century: Robert William Fogel, *Railroads and American Economic Growth: Essays in Econometric History* (1964). According to Fogel, the railroad's contribution to the American economy by 1890 amounted to "well below 5 per cent of gross national product" and could easily have been replaced by alternative technologies based on water transport (p. 223). Leaving aside technical criticisms of Fogel's statistics, and leaving aside questions about whether 5 percent of the GNP—assuming that number is accurate—is really so small, one still suspects that Fogel's argument has almost nothing to do with economic reality as people in the nineteenth century experienced it. Certainly Chicagoans in the 1850s would have been astonished to learn that the railroad was so insignificant a part of their lives.

There are good reasons why Fogel's thesis seems intuitively wrong, for its question about whether the railroads were "indispensable" is misconceived from the outset, and yields an answer of limited historical interest. Perhaps, as Fogel claims, canals really could have carried produce to market without slowing the pace of western development. Perhaps people really could have compensated for the seasonal freezing of waterways by constructing massive warehouse facilities. Perhaps the lack of water for canals in arid regions of the West need not have influenced the pace of settlement there—or perhaps the arid West did not itself contribute much to the American GNP in the nineteenth century, and so can be written out of the analysis altogether. At a gross macroeconomic scale, these counterfactual claims may all—*conceivably*—be plausible. But were one to project them backward into the nineteenth century, so many other aspects of life would have to change to accommodate them that the whole course of American history would be profoundly different, whatever the size of the GNP in that hypothetical world. One feature of Fogel's calculations that is particularly striking to an environmental historian is his tendency to use statistics based on annual averages rather than seasonal minimums and maximums. He seems unconcerned about the seasonal fluctuations that were a basic part of nineteenth-century life, and so he reflects the biases of his own postrailroad era, in which nonagricultural parts of the economy have become much less dependent on seasonal change. These and many other details of ordinary life are quite irrelevant to Fogel's highly aggregated GNP calculations, which suggests just how many red herrings his statistics offer to anyone trying to understand how railroads changed the course of American economic and environmental history. More to the point, no history which seeks to understand Chicago's changing relationship to its hinterland can proceed from Fogel's central premise, for if we imagine away the railroad, we imagine away nineteenth-century Chicago as well.

For an excellent review of the literature surrounding Fogel's work, see David L. Lightner, "Railroads and the American Economy: The Fogel Thesis in Retrospect," *Journal of Transport History,* 3d ser., 4, no. 2 (Sept. 1983): 20–34; see also P. A. David, "Transport Innovation and Economic Growth: Professor Fogel on and off the Rails," *Economic History Review* 22 (1969): 506–25; Jeffrey G. Williamson, "The Railroads and Midwestern Development, 1870–1890: A General Equilibrium History," in David C. Klingaman and Richard K. Vedder, eds., *Essays in Nineteenth Century Economic History: The Old Northwest* (1975), 269–352; and Fogel's response to his critics, "Notes on the Social Saving Controversy," *JEH* 39 (1979): 1–54. A quantitative treatment of railroad growth in the pre-1860 era that matches Fogel's technical sophistication without his reductionism is Albert Fishlow, *American Railroads and the Transformation of the Ante-Bellum Economy* (1965). In a more comic vein, R. Preston McAfee has satirized Fogel's approach by "proving" that American history would have remained unchanged had Columbus never discovered the New World; see his "American Economic Growth and the Voyage of Columbus," *American Economic Review* 73 (1983): 735–40. In fairness to Fogel, I should note that his oversimplifications of the nineteenth-century economy derive in part from his effort to critique the equally simplistic analyses of W. W. Rostow, *The Stages of Economic Growth* (1960).

80. In the discussion that follows for the rest of this chapter, I have relied on a number of standard works on railroad engineering, economics, and history, many of which are old but still indispensable. Among the most useful of these have been Arthur M. Wellington, *The Economic Theory of the Location of Railroads* (1877), 5th ed. (1891); William Z. Ripley, *Railroads: Rates and Regulation* (1912); Ripley, *Railroads: Finance and Organization* (1915); Ripley, ed., *Railway Problems,* rev. ed. (1913); Kent T. Healy, *The Economics of Transportation in America: The Dynamic Forces in Development, Organization, Functioning and Regulation* (1940); Edward Chase Kirkland, *Men, Cities, and Transportation: A Study in New England History, 1820–1900* (1948); George Rogers Taylor, *The Transportation Revolution, 1815–1860,* vol. 4 of *The Economic History of the United States* (1951); John F. Stover, *American Railroads* (1961); Fishlow, *American Railroads;* and Alfred D. Chandler, Jr., ed., *The Railroads: The Nation's First Big Business* (1965). R. D. McKenzie, *The Metropolitan Community* (1933), esp. 127–70, contains useful discussions of the importance of transportation to metropolitan growth. For a general historical geography of transportation in Europe and North America since the sixteenth century, see James E. Vance, Jr., *Capturing the Horizon: The Historical Geography of Transportation since the Transportation Revolution of the Sixteenth Century* (1986). On the cultural consequences of the railroads, see John R. Stilgoe, *Metropolitan Corridor: Railroads and the American Scene* (1983); and James A. Ward, *Railroads and the Character of America, 1820–1887* (1986).

81. Wright, "Internal Improvements," 271.

82. Statistics for the accompanying graphs were drawn from the Annual Review for 1850, *Chicago Tribune,* Dec. 29, 1850 [canal data]; "Annual Review of the Commerce of Chicago for the Year 1851," *Chicago Tribune,* in "Chicago: Its Trade and Growth in 1851," *Hunt's Merch. Mag.* 26 (1852): 436 [harbor data]; Galena and Chicago Union Railroad, *Annual Reports,* 1851, 1852 [1851 tonnage data]; Annual Review for 1856, *Daily Democratic Press,* 52 [G&CU RR 1856 receipts data]. Early seasonal swings in railroad transport were to some extent masked by the rising secular trend that increased a road's receipts from month to month as track mileage increased, whatever

the season. I have therefore supplied G&CU statistics for both 1851 and 1856 to show the somewhat larger seasonal fluctuations of the latter year. The biggest difference between water and rail routes was that the latter never shut down because of freezing.

83. Annual Review for 1852, *Daily Democratic Press,* 15. See also Charles O. Paullin, *Atlas of the Historical Geography of the United States* (1932), plate 138.

84. Pierce, *History of Chicago,* 2:73.

85. "Trade and Growth of Chicago in 1852," *Hunt's Merch. Mag.* 28 (1853): 560; "Chicago: Its Trade and Growth in 1851," ibid., 26 (1852): 428.

86. CBT, *Annual Report,* 1860, 1870.

87. Cleaver, *History of Chicago,* 112.

88. Reverend J. P. Thompson, in Curtiss, *Western Portraiture,* 309.

89. For a superb geographical comparison of stage and rail service out of Chicago in 1850, see Michael Peter Conzen, "Metropolitan Dominance in the American Midwest during the Later Nineteenth Century" (Ph.D. thesis, Univ. of Wisconsin, 1972), 145–64.

90. Until the 1850s, nighttime operation of trains was relatively rare, but that decade saw the practice become common as traffic increased dramatically. Oil headlights had become standard equipment on most locomotives by the Civil War. See John H. White, Jr., *American Locomotives: An Engineering History, 1830–1880,* (1968), 215–17.

91. In the twentieth century, this process of dislocating travelers from the landscape through which they pass has occurred even more dramatically with the advent of air travel. Barry Lopez has written insightfully about this issue in respect to travel through the Arctic, and what he says seems quite relevant to nineteenth-century train travel: "The airplane, like the map, creates a false sense of space; it achieves simplicity and compression, however, not with an enforced perspective but by altering the relationship between space and time. The interior of a plane is artificially lit, protected from weather, full of rarefied air cut with the odor of petroleum distillates and tobacco, and far noisier than the ground below. . . . The plane is a great temptation; but to learn anything of the land, to have any sense of the relevancy of the pertinent maps, you must walk away from the planes. You must get off into the country and sleep on the ground. . . ." Barry Lopez, *Arctic Dreams: Imagination and Desire in a Northern Landscape* (1986), 284–85.

92. British railroads had adopted standardized time as early as 1847. See David S. Landes, *Revolution in Time: Clocks and the Making of the Modern World* (1983), 285–86.

93. *Chicago Tribune,* Nov. 18, 1883, 12. Good evidence of the less catastrophic effects this had on train operations can be found in Robert Harris to H. Hitchcock, May 7, 1869, Robert Harris Out-Letters, CB&Q Archives.

94. "The New Time Standards," *Railway Age* 8 (Nov. 15, 1883): 722; "Standard Time—The Change Successfully Adopted," ibid. (Nov. 22, 1883): 743. The latter article includes a map showing the boundaries of the new zones, which are quite different from the ones in use today. The new standard central time in 1883 was almost identical to local time in St. Louis.

95. *Chicago Tribune,* Nov. 19, 1883, 1.

96. On the shift to standard time, see Stover, *American Railroads,* 157–58; George Rogers Taylor and Irene D. Neu, *The American Railroad Network, 1861–1890,* (1956); Carlton J. Corliss, *The Day of Two Noons* (1941); and Stilgoe, *Metropolitan Corridor,* 203–5. For an account of changing definitions of time in American history, see Michael O'Malley, *Keeping Watch: A History of American Time* (1990), which became available after this book was completed.

97. Fred Cottrell, *Energy and Society: The Relation between Energy, Social Change, and Economic Development* (1955), 21.

98. White, *American Locomotives,* 74–76. It is surprisingly hard to find published horsepower ratings for nineteenth-century railroad locomotives; curiously, horsepower never became as standard for the rating of vehicular steam engines as for that of stationary ones. This was presumably because engineers found it difficult to evaluate a locomotive's performance in the wide range of conditions under which railroads had to operate. Tractive force became the standard measure for engine power in the twentieth century, but nineteenth-century engineers contented themselves with stating the cylinder sizes and hauling capacities of their locomotives.

99. U.S. Bureau of the Census, *Historical Statistics of the United States: Colonial Times to 1970* (1975), pt. 2, ser. Q346–55, Q559–64. I have not tried to convert these cumulative

figures into real dollars, but price indexes suggest that doing so would probably not increase the size of canal investments by more than half. Relative orders of magnitude would remain the same.

100. Even history depends on such things: without the railroads' new interest in gathering statistics, much of the evidence for this book would never have existed.

101. As Alfred Chandler has written, "The railroads were the first American business to work out the modern ways of finance, management, labor relations, competition, and government regulation." Chandler, *American Railroads*, 9. No historian has shed brighter light on these issues; see Alfred D. Chandler, Jr., *The Visible Hand: The Managerial Revolution in American Business* (1977); Chandler, *Scale and Scope: The Dynamics of Industrial Capitalism* (1990); and Chandler, *The Essential Alfred Chandler: Essays toward a Historical Theory of Big Business,* ed. Thomas K. McCraw (1988).

102. For examples of municipal investment in railroad construction, see Kathleen B. Jacklin, "Local Aid to Railroads in Illinois, 1848–1870" (M.A. thesis, Cornell Univ., 1958); James Edward Morgan, "Sources of Capital for Railroads in the Old Northwest before the Civil War" (Ph.D. thesis, Univ. of Wisconsin, 1964); Philip Alan Schilling, "Farmers and Railroads: A Case Study of Farmer Attitudes in the Promotion of the Milwaukee and Mississippi Railroad Company" (M.S. thesis, Univ. of Wisconsin, 1964); and Dykstra, *Cattle Towns.*

103. William Jones, Jr., *An Address to the Merchants of the N. West, Setting Forth the Advantages of the City of Chicago as the Central Mart of the Union* (1856), 3.

104. Wright, *Chicago,* xv. For a comparable view, see Brooks, "Chicago and Its Railways," 269.

105. Wright, *Chicago,* xv.

106. Arthur M. Johnson and Barry E. Supple, *Boston Capitalists and Western Railroads: A Study in the Nineteenth-Century Railroad Investment Process* (1967), 130–31, 134–36, 143–44. On British investment in western railroads, see Ralph W. Hidy and Muriel E. Hidy, "Anglo-American Merchant Bankers and the Railroads of the Old Northwest, 1848–1860," *Bus. Hist. Rev.* 34 (1960): 150–69; and A. W. Currie, "British Attitudes toward Investment in North American Railroads," ibid., 194–215.

107. Because of the quality and public accessibility of its extraordinary archives, no Chicago railroad has received more thorough scholarly attention than the Burlington. The standard history is Richard C. Overton, *Burlington Route: A History of the Burlington Lines* (1965). On the issue of eastern investment, see also Overton, *Burlington West: A Colonization History of the Burlington Railroad* (1941); Johnson and Supple, *Boston Capitalists;* Thomas C. Cochran, *Railroad Leaders, 1854–1890: The Business Mind in Action* (1953); and John Lauritz Larson, *Bonds of Enterprise: John Murray Forbes and Western Development in America's Railway Age* (1984).

108. CB&Q list of shareholders with more than 500 shares, June 30, 1890, in CB&Q Archives, 33 1880 8.17. Most of these shares were held by a few investors, but Burlington stock was also widely distributed among smaller eastern shareholders as well. As of 1887, there were 7,743 New Englanders holding shares of CB&Q stock valued at less than $5,000; see Charles Perkins to Governor William Larrabee of Iowa, June 28, 1887, in CB&Q Archives.

109. Chicago and North Western, *Yesterday and Today,* 68.

110. Charles Perkins to Governor William Larrabee of Iowa, Dec. 2, 1887, CB&Q Archives, 3 P4.13.

111. Chicago Building & Loan Association, *Statistical and Historical Review of Chicago,* 43. For an interesting inside look at the broad-based investment interests of Chicago railroad managers and financiers, see H. H. Porter, *A Short Autobiography, Written for His Children and Grandchildren* (1915).

112. Pierce, *History of Chicago,* 2:55–58. The Michigan Southern and Michigan Central were joined in 1856 by the Pittsburgh, Fort Wayne, and Chicago, which was aligned from the outset with the Pennsylvania Railroad system. It too terminated at Chicago. Stover, *Iron Road to the West,* 124–25.

113. The classic work on this subject after more than seventy-five years remains William Z. Ripley's extraordinarily lucid *Railroads: Rates and Regulation,* first published in 1912. Anyone wishing to understand railroad rates must still begin with this book. Although Ripley could use post-1890 statistics from the Interstate Commerce Commission to calculate railroad costs with a precision simply not possible for earlier years, his figures

suggest that the distribution of operating costs among different categories of railroad expenditure remained virtually constant between 1890 and 1906. There is no reason to believe that the basic principles he defined are any less relevant to the earlier period I discuss in this chapter, especially since the earlier standard text by Wellington, *Economic Theory of the Location of Railways,* makes essentially the same points.

114. W. M. Grosvenor, "The Railroads and the Farms," *Atlantic Monthly* 32 (1873): 606.

115. Robert Harris to C. Ballance, Aug. 29, 1868, Robert Harris Out-Letters, CB&Q Archives.

116. The only effective way for a company to generate nonloan income before actually operating a railroad was to sell land (usually gained from government grants) along its right of way. This was why railroads like the Illinois Central and the Chicago, Burlington and Quincy engaged in extensive colonization work before and after constructing their lines. See Overton, *Burlington West;* and Gates, *Illinois Central Railroad.*

117. Ripley, *Railroads: Rates and Regulation,* 45–46. Fishlow provides a much more sophisticated discussion of interest rates and discounts during the pre-1860 period in his *American Railroads,* 351–57. Because he is primarily interested in capital formation and so tends to examine railroad construction expenses as opposed to operating costs, Fishlow's figures are not directly comparable to Ripley's.

118. Ripley, *Railroads: Rates and Regulation,* 54–55; Wellington, *Economic Theory of the Location of Railways* (5th ed.), 106–82.

119. Ripley, *Railroads: Rates and Regulation,* 55.

120. For an early text that made this argument cogently, see Charles Whiting Baker, *Monopolies and the People* (1889). See also H. T. Newcomb, "The Decline in Railway Rates; Some of Its Causes and Results," *J. Pol. Econ.* 6 (1897–98): 457–75.

121. Colonel Milo Smith, "Information Furnished . . . in Regard to the Commerce of the Mississippi River . . . ," in Nimmo, *Rept. Int. Commerce* (1879), appendix no. 10, p. 102.

122. The only major exception north of St. Louis was Peoria, where shippers could bypass the Chicago market by shipping directly east on the Toledo, Wabash, and Western. But Peoria was an exception to prove the rule, as James Lester Sturm demonstrates in his excellent "Railroads and Market Growth: The Case of Peoria and Chicago, 1850–1900" (M.A. thesis, Univ. of Wisconsin, 1965).

123. Charles Randolph, "Answers to Inquiries in Relation to the Commerce of Chicago . . . ," in Nimmo, *Rept. Int. Commerce* (1877), appendix no. 4, p. 85.

124. CBT, *Annual Reports.* For a summary of the competitive effects of lake transport, see Joseph Nimmo, Jr., "The Economy of Transport by Rail," in Nimmo, *Rept. Int. Commerce* (1877), 109–10 and passim. See also Peoria Board of Trade, *Fifth Annual Report for 1874* (1875), 13–14, which discusses Peoria's competitive disadvantage because of Chicago's access to the lake.

125. CBT, *Annual Reports.*

126. Nimmo, *Rept. Int. Commerce* (1877), 114; see also appendix no. 4, p. 85; appendix no. 5, p. 98; and the foldout graph of lake and rail rates that accompanies the report as a whole. Nimmo's graph extends further forward in time than mine and displays the flattening at least of *official* railroad rate schedules as pooling agreements began to take hold toward the end of the 1870s. One of Nimmo's informants rightly observed that the rate-lowering effect of lake competition spread out from Chicago to affect stations far out in the hinterland: "This competition," wrote J. D. Hayes of Detroit, "goes back into the interior cities and towns until the local rate into Chicago and the expense from there added equal the 'all rail' from the interior to the seaboard." J. D. Hayes, "Statement in Regard to the Development of Manufacturing Industries in Western Towns and Cities," ibid. (1881), appendix no. 8, p. 178. Thorstein Veblen dated the onset of serious lake-rail competition in the eastward movement of grain from Chicago to 1873–74, but the cycle of railroad rates was already in place by then; see Thorstein B. Veblen, "The Price of Wheat since 1867," *J. Pol. Econ.* 1 (1892–93): 88.

127. Like railroads everywhere, the eastern roads tried to solve their competitive problems by price-fixing and were aided in so doing by the eventual development of government regulation. The most sophisticated analysis of competitive rate relationships between Chicago and New York is Paul W. MacAvoy, *The Economic Effects of Regulation: The Trunk-Line Railroad Cartels and the Interstate Commerce Commission before 1900* (1965). For more heated discussions of the causes and effects of government regulation, see Ga-

briel Kolko, *Railroads and Regulation, 1877–1916* (1965); and Albro Martin, *Enterprise Denied: Origins of the Decline of American Railroads, 1897–1917* (1971). On the early political controversies surrounding railroad regulation in the East, see Lee Benson, *Merchants, Farmers, & Railroads: Railroad Regulation and New York Politics, 1850–1887* (1955). For a good example of the Populist attack on railroads, see William Larrabee, *The Railroad Question: A Historical and Practical Treatise on Railroads, and Remedies for Their Abuses* (1893). For a lucid early presentation of the reasons why railroad managers almost inevitably had to resort to some sort of price-fixing mechanism, given their problems with capital costs and competition, see Baker, *Monopolies and the People*, 42–58, which is well summarized in his conclusion: "The railway is essentially a monopoly, not, be it noted, because of any especial wickedness of its managers or owners, but because competition is *impossible* as regards the greater part of its business, and because wherever competition is possible, its effect, as the managers well know, would be to annihilate all profits from the operation of the road" (p. 52).

128. Nimmo, *Rept. Int. Commerce,* (1877), 24.
129. Brooks, "Chicago and Its Railways," 269.
130. Nimmo, *Rept. Int. Commerce* (1881), 106.
131. Robert Harris to C. E. Perkins, Oct. 30, 1867, CB&Q Archives.
132. Robert Harris to A. J. [?] Bell, April 16, 1868, CB&Q Archives.
133. Robert Harris to H. F. Clark, Dec. 26, 1867, CB&Q Archives.
134. Handwritten notes on letter from A. R. Anderson of the Iowa Railroad Commissioners Office to T. J. Potter, General Manager of the CB&Q at Chicago, Aug. 3, 1881, CB&Q Archives, box 33 1880 4.6.
135. Robert Harris to H. H. Porter, March 18, 1869, CB&Q Archives, H 4.1.
136. Julian Ralph, *Our Great West: A Study of the Present Conditions and Future Possibilities of the New Commonwealths and Capitals of the United States* (1893), 12.
137. Karl Marx, *Grundrisse: Foundations of the Critique of Political Economy (Rough Draft),* trans. Martin Nicolaus (1973), 524.
138. Bross, *Chicago and Her Growth,* 14.

3: PRICING THE FUTURE: GRAIN

1. Caton, "Sixty Years," 590. Cf. Caton, "Address Delivered to the Settlers," 165.
2. On the origins of domesticated plants and animals, see Carl O. Sauer, *Agricultural Origins and Dispersals* (1952; reprint, 1969); Peter J. Ucko and G. W. Dimbleby, *The Domestication and Exploitation of Plants and Animals* (1969); John R. Campbell and John F. Lasley, *The Science of Animals That Serve Humanity,* 3d ed. (1985); Robert W. Schery, *Plants for Man,* 2d ed. (1972); Juliet Clutton-Brock, *A Natural History of Domesticated Animals* (1987); Jack R. Kloppenburg, Jr., *First the Seed: The Political Economy of Plant Biotechnology, 1492–2000* (1988); see also the general historical works cited in the next footnote.
3. Allan G. Bogue, *From Prairie to Cornbelt: Farming on the Illinois and Iowa Prairies in the Nineteenth Century* (1963), remains the classic work on this subject. It contains material relevant to much of the discussion in this chapter, as do Fred A. Shannon, *The Farmer's Last Frontier: Agriculture, 1860–1897,* vol. 5 of *The Economic History of the United States* (1945); Paul W. Gates, *The Farmer's Age: Agriculture, 1815–1860,* vol. 3 of *The Economic History of the United States* (1960). For a summary of trends in the Chicago area, see Robert H. Engle, "The Trends of Agriculture in the Chicago Region" (Ph.D. thesis, Univ. of Chicago, 1941); and for a general survey of agricultural history, John T. Schlebecker, *Whereby We Thrive: A History of American Farming, 1607–1972* (1975). The most sophisticated recent study is Jeremy Atack and Fred Bateman, *To Their Own Soil: Agriculture in the Antebellum North* (1987).
4. Bogue, *Prairie to Cornbelt,* 1–7; John Madson, *Where the Sky Began: Land of the Tallgrass Prairie* (1982), 38–40, 116–17. For a useful anthology of contemporary descriptions of the prairie, see Dorothy Anne Dondore, *The Prairie and the Making of Middle America: Four Centuries of Description* (1926); Thomas H. Macbride, "Landscapes of Early Iowa" (1895), reprinted in *Palimpsest* 7 (1926): 283–93; and Charles Aldrich, "The Old Prairie Slough," *Annals of Iowa,* 3d ser., 5 (1901): 27–32. On vegetation, see Edgar Nelson Transeau, "The Prairie Peninsula," *Ecology* 16 (1935): 423–37; Paul D. Kilburn, "The Forest-Prairie Ecotone in Northeastern Illinois," *American Midland Naturalist* 62

(1959): 206–17; Cassandra S. Rodgers and Roger C. Anderson, "Presettlement Vegetation of Two Prairie Peninsula Counties," *Botanical Gazette* 140 (1979): 232–40.

5. Madson, *Where the Sky Began,* 38.

6. Leo Rogin, *The Introduction of Farm Machinery in Its Relation to the Productivity of Labor in the Agriculture of the United States during the Nineteenth Century* (1931), 32–35; Wayne G. Broehl, Jr., *John Deere's Company: A History of Deere & Company and Its Times* (1984).

7. Bogue, *Prairie to Cornbelt,* 67–85.

8. On the spread of tame hay, see Thomas A. Williams, "Timothy in the Prairie Region," in USDA, *Yearbook of the United States Department of Agriculture, 1896* (1897), 147–54; and Jonathan Periam, *The Home and Farm Manual* (1884; reprint, 1984), 132–66; and Gates, *Farmer's Age.*

9. On the importance of fences as a symbol of environmental "improvement," see William Cronon, *Changes in the Land: Indians, Colonists, and the Ecology of New England* (1983).

10. *Illinois in 1837 & 8,* 14. Cf. John Plumbe, Jr., *Sketches of Iowa and Wisconsin, Taken during a Residence of Three Years in Those Territories* (1839), 9.

11. The literature on the ecological consequences of prairie fires is enormous. For useful introductions, see Stephen J. Pyne, *Fire in America: A Cultural History of Wildland and Rural Fire* (1982); and Curtis, *Vegetation of Wisconsin.* For shorter and more monographic treatments, see Richard T. Ward, "Vegetational Change in a Southern Wisconsin Township," *Proceedings of the Iowa Academy of Science* 63 (1956): 321–26; R. Daubenmire, "Ecology of Fire in Grassland," *Advances in Ecological Research* 5 (1968): 209–66; Richard J. Vogl, "Effects of Fires on Grasslands," in T. T. Kozlowski and C. E. Ahlgren, eds., *Fire and Ecosystems* (1974), 139–94; and Virginia M. Kline and Grant Cottam, "Vegetation Response to Climate and Fire in the Driftless Area of Wisconsin," *Ecology* 60 (1979): 861–68. On the threat of prairie fires, see Bessie L. Lyon, "The Menace of the Blue-stem," *Palimpsest* 21 (1940): 247–58.

12. The classic work on the public lands is Gates, *Public Land Law Development;* see also Malcolm J. Rohrbough, *The Land Office Business: The Settlement and Administration of American Public Lands, 1789–1837* (1968).

13. Hildegard Binder Johnson, *Order upon the Land: The U.S. Rectangular Land Survey and the Upper Mississippi Country* (1976); Norman J. Thrower, *Original Survey and Land Subdivision: A Comparative Study of the Form and Effect of Contrasting Cadastral Surveys* (1966). Johnson rightly points out that the grid pattern is not so exact as the word "checkerboard" suggests, but it certainly biased landowners toward rectilinear property boundaries.

14. J. M. Peck, *A Guide for Emigrants, Containing Sketches of Illinois, Missouri, and the Adjacent Parts* (1831), 106.

15. Henry Rowe Schoolcraft, "A Journey up the Illinois River in 1821," from *Travels in the Central Portion of the Mississippi Valley,* reprinted in Milo Milton Quaife, ed., *Pictures of Illinois One Hundred Years Ago* (1918), 96.

16. John G. Clark, *The Grain Trade in the Old Northwest* (1966), 41–42.

17. Harry N. Scheiber, "The Ohio-Mississippi Flatboat Trade: Some Reconsiderations," in David M. Ellis, ed., *The Frontier in American Development: Essays in Honor of Paul Wallace Gates* (1969), 278–79; Erik F. Haites, James Mak, and Gary M. Walton, *Western River Transportation: The Era of Early Internal Development, 1810–1860* (1975), 166.

18. Bogue, *Prairie to Cornbelt,* 8–13; see also the very sophisticated analyses of settlement dynamics in Michael J. O'Brien, ed., *Grassland, Forest, and Historical Settlement: An Analysis of Dynamics in Northeast Missouri* (1984). For contemporary descriptions, see the examples in Quaife, ed., *Pictures of Illinois;* Daniel Harmon Brush, *Growing Up with Southern Illinois, 1820 to 1861,* ed. Milo Milton Quaife (1944).

19. U.S. Censuses, 1830, 1850; Paullin, *Atlas of the Historical Geography,* plates 76–77.

20. The best general survey of early immigration to the upper Mississippi Valley is Mark Wyman, *Immigrants in the Valley: Irish, Germans, and Americans in the Upper Mississippi Country, 1830–1860* (1984); for a case study of German ethnicity in an urban setting, see Kathleen Neils Conzen, *Immigrant Milwaukee, 1836–1860: Accommodation and Community in a Frontier City* (1976).

21. U.S. Census, 1850.

22. Rebecca and Edward Burlend, *A True Picture of Emigration,* ed. Milo Milton Quaife (1848; reprint, 1968), 67.

23. The best study of frontier merchandising activities continues to be Lewis Atherton,

Frontier Merchant in Mid-America, though a broader picture of the overall distribution network of nineteenth-century marketing can be obtained from Glenn Porter and Harold C. Livesay, *Merchants and Manufacturers: Studies in the Changing Structure of Nineteenth-Century Marketing* (1971).

24. Burlend, *True Picture of Emigration,* 67.

25. J. M. D. Burrows, *Fifty Years in Iowa* (1888), in Milo Milton Quaife, ed., *The Early Day of Rock Island and Davenport: The Narratives of J. W. Spencer and J. M. D. Burrows* (1942), 162.

26. Ibid., 182–85.

27. Burlend, *True Picture of Emigration,* 67–68.

28. William Oliver, *Eight Months in Illinois; with Information to Emigrants* (1843; reprint, 1966), 88. On the importance of St. Louis as the chief entrepôt for upstream farming districts, see Plumbe, *Sketches of Iowa and Wisconsin,* 12.

29. The best general survey of grain trading on the Great Lakes and Mississippi River is John G. Clark, *Grain Trade in the Old Northwest;* for later periods, I also benefited from Morton Rothstein's generosity in allowing me to read unpublished chapters of his work on the grain trade. There is a long-standing academic controversy about the aggregate importance of interregional trade in grain and other foodstuffs to the economic development of different parts of the United States. For important contributions to the debate, see Isaac Lippincott, "Internal Trade of the United States, 1700–1860," *Washington University Studies* 4 (1916): 63–150; Albert L. Kohlmeier, *The Old Northwest as the Keystone of the Arch of American Federal Union* (1938); Louis B. Schmidt, "Internal Commerce and the Development of National Economy before 1860," *J. Pol. Econ.* 47 (1939): 798–822; Douglass C. North, "Agriculture in Regional Economic Growth," *Journal of Farm Economics* 41 (1959): 943–51; Watkins, "A Staple Theory of Economic Growth," 141–58; Albert Fishlow, "Antebellum Interregional Trade Reconsidered," *American Economic Review (Supplement)* 54 (1964): 352–64; William K. Hutchinson and Samuel H. Williamson, "The Self-Sufficiency of the Antebellum South: Estimates of the Food Supply," *JEH* 31 (1971): 591–612; Sam B. Hilliard, *Hog Meat and Hoecake: Food Supply in the Old South, 1840–1860* (1972); Hilliard, "Antebellum Interregional Trade: The Mississippi River as an Example," in Ralph E. Ehrenberg, ed., *Pattern and Process: Research in Historical Geography* (1975), 202–14; Diane Lindstrom, *Economic Development in the Philadelphia Region, 1810–1850* (1978); Diane Lindstrom and John Sharpless, "Urban Growth and Economic Structure in Antebellum America," *Research in Economic History* 3 (1978): 161–216. My own view is that extraregional trade was critical at least on the margin to western farmers seeking cash income during early stages of frontier settlement, whatever its total contribution to southern plantation food supply (which has been one of the most contested topics of debate).

30. J. W. Norris, *Norris' Business Directory and Statistics of the City of Chicago for 1846,* ed. Robert Fergus, Fergus Historical Series, no. 25 (1883), 36, 40.

31. Moritz Busch, *Travels between the Hudson & the Mississippi, 1851–1852,* trans. and ed. Norman H. Binger (1971), 233.

32. Oliver, *Eight Months in Illinois,* 89.

33. *Carlinville* (Ill.) *Spectator,* as quoted in *Missouri Republic,* April 29, 1855, as quoted by Belcher, *Rivalry between St. Louis and Chicago,* 53.

34. Anonymous, quoted by Taylor, ed., *Chicago Board of Trade,* 1:155.

35. Percy Tracy Dondlinger, *The Book of Wheat: An Economic History and Practical Manual of the Wheat Industry* (1919): 221–22.

36. *Norris' Business Directory for 1846,* 44–45; Alice E. Smith, *George Smith's Money: A Scottish Investor in America* (1966). George Smith's famous Chicago Marine and Fire Insurance Company was so successful that it supplied a sizable portion of Chicago's circulating currency during the 1840s and early 1850s, behaving as much like a bank as an insurance company. It was able to do this partly because the state legislature had imposed steep restrictions on the ability of Illinois banks to issue notes.

37. Burrows, *Fifty Years in Iowa,* 183.

38. ICPSR, "Historical Demographic, Economic and Social Data: The United States, 1790–1970" (machine-readable dataset of census statistics). Statistical work for this book is based on an eleven-state subset of the master series, containing economic and demographic statistics for Michigan, Indiana, Illinois, Wisconsin, Minnesota, Iowa, Missouri, Kansas, Nebraska, North Dakota, and South Dakota between 1840 and 1900. I shall refer to it hereafter as ICPSR Census Series. The argument here is based on a simple comparison of z-scores for decennial county growth rates between 1840 and

1860. For less geographically oriented versions of this same argument, see Douglass C. North, *The Economic Growth of the United States, 1790–1860* (1961; reprint, 1966), 146–53; and Fishlow, *American Railroads,* 207–15.

39. Gates, *Illinois Central Railroad;* Corliss, *Main Line of Mid-America,* 81–89.

40. ICPSR Census Series; Fishlow, *American Railroads,* 211–12.

41. Bureau of Statistics, Treasury Department, "The Grain Trade of the United States, and the World's Wheat Supply and Trade," in *Monthly Summary of Commerce and Finance of the United States* (January, 1900), 1958–60; CBT, *Annual Reports.*

42. Haites, *Western River Transportation,* 8. The northern route had already surpassed New Orleans in shipments of flour at a much earlier date. See Thomas D. Odle, "The American Grain Trade of the Great Lakes, 1825–1873," *Inland Seas* 8 (1952): 103.

43. Guy A. Lee, "History of the Chicago Grain Elevator Industry, 1840–1890" (Ph.D. thesis, Harvard Univ., 1938), 62. A railroad car was small compared with a canalboat or steamboat that might carry four to ten thousand bushels of grain. Chicago's problem was to combine many small loads into the much larger quantities that could be stored in a warehouse or transported on a ship.

44. *Chicago Democratic Press,* Sept. 13, 1854, as quoted in Taylor, *Chicago Board of Trade,* 1:190–91.

45. U.S. Treasury Department, "Grain Trade of U.S.," 1958.

46. CBT, *Annual Reports;* Annual Review for 1854, *Chicago Daily Democratic Press.*

47. The classic work on Chicago's grain elevators is Guy A. Lee's "History of the Chicago Grain Elevator Industry, 1840–1890," to which I am indebted for several of the central arguments of this chapter. Lee summarized his main points in "The Historical Significance of the Chicago Grain Elevator System," *Ag. Hist.* 11 (Jan. 1937): 16–32.

48. Joseph Dart, "The Grain Elevators of Buffalo," *Publications of the Buffalo Historical Society* 1 (1879): 391–404. Thomas Odle traces the spread of grain elevators around the Great Lakes basin in his "American Grain Trade," 8 (1952): 189–92.

49. Anthony Trollope, *North America* (1862), ed. Donald Smalley and Bradford Allen Booth (1951), 164. Trollope uses "corn" in the English sense, referring to wheat or to grain generally.

50. Taylor, *Chicago Board of Trade,* 1:189. The shift from volume to weight was one step among many toward perceiving grain not as traditional human-scaled *units* but as interchangeable, abstract, and infinitely divisible *flows.*

51. Although elevators grew enormously in size during the second half of the nineteenth century, their essential organization remained relatively unchanged. For illustrations and an excellent technical description of a Chicago grain elevator in the early 1890s, see *Scientific American* 65, no. 17 (Oct. 24, 1891): cover.

52. *Chicago Weekly Democrat,* Sept. 19, 1848.

53. Lee, "Chicago Grain Elevator Industry, 41.

54. Annual Review for 1857, *Chicago Daily Press,* 7–8; U.S. Treasury Department, "Grain Trade of the U.S.," 1958. The comparison is unfair in the sense that Chicago's elevators would never have contained only wheat, but the point about relative grain-handling capacities nonetheless holds.

55. Annual Review for 1857, *Chicago Daily Press,* 8.

56. Ibid. "Two or three hundred" is undoubtedly an exaggeration, but the people involved in such a transfer surely numbered in the dozens.

57. Scheiber, "Ohio-Mississippi Flatboat Trade," 297; Odle, "American Grain Trade," 8 (1952): 248–51.

58. "The City of St. Louis," *Atlantic Monthly* 19 (June 1867): 656. The eventual solution to this problem, devised after the Civil War, was to build elevators with chutes that could be extended and retracted to accommodate any level of the river. See also John B. Appleton, "The Declining Significance of the Mississippi as a Commercial Highway in the Middle of the Nineteenth Century," *Bulletin of the Geographical Society of Philadelphia* 28 (1930): 274–75.

59. Peyton, *Over the Alleghanies,* 325. Peyton visited Chicago in 1848.

60. The Rock Island elevator described above cost $150,000 to construct, on land valued at $90,000, while the Illinois Central's two largest elevators had a combined value of $650,000. Annual Review for 1857, *Chicago Daily Press,* 8.

61. "The City of St. Louis," *Atlantic Monthly* 19 (June 1867): 656; Odle, "American Grain Trade," 8 (1952): 192.

62. Annual Review for 1857, *Chicago Daily Press,* 8.

63. Ibid.; Odle, "American Grain Trade," 8 (1952): 190.
64. Annual Review for 1857, *Chicago Daily Press,* 7.
65. Trollope, *North America,* 164.
66. Annual Review for 1857, *Chicago Daily Press,* 7-8.
67. Colbert, *Chicago,* 48. Given the destruction of pre-1871 records in the fire, Taylor regards Colbert's brief account as one of the most reliable available for the Board's early history. Taylor, *Chicago Board of Trade,* 1:139-41.
68. On the origins of boards of trade in general, see Thomas Odle, "Entrepreneurial Cooperation on the Great Lakes: The Origin of the Methods of American Grain Marketing," *Bus. Hist. Rev.* 38 (1964): 439-55.
69. Colbert, *Chicago,* 50; Taylor, *Chicago Board of Trade,* 1:189-91. The Board urged merchants in Buffalo, Toledo, Milwaukee, and other cities to adopt similar standards for weight-based bushels—all soon did—and also suggested that they join in lobbying against New York's continued use of a half-bushel volume measure for grain transactions. Important as weight-based measures were becoming, New York ignored the appeal and did not use grain elevators until the 1870s. To anticipate my own argument, New York's intransigence about grain elevators resulted only in part from a conservatism encouraged by its preeminent position in the national economy. Because most of the city's grain arrived in the relatively large units represented by canalboats and oceangoing vessels, there was less need for the break-in-bulk capabilities offered by elevators. New Yorkers also faced the special problem of matching their own business practices with those of traders in the British Empire, who strongly favored sale by sample rather than by grade. New York's growing acceptance of the new elevator and grading technologies after 1870 corresponded with the increasing amount of grain entering the city in railroad cars.
70. Taylor, *Chicago Board of Trade,* 1:172-73, 189.
71. Colbert, *Chicago,* 49.
72. U.S. Bureau of the Census, *Historical Statistics,* ser. U279-80, 899, ser. E123-24, 209. The growth of Chicago's grain markets was strongly linked to international exports, about which there is a large literature. For important discussions, see R. F. Crawford, "An Inquiry into Wheat Prices and Wheat Supply," *Journal of the Royal Statistical Society* 58 (1895): 75-120; Egerton R. Williams, "Thirty Years in the Grain Trade," *No. Am. Rev.* 161 (1895): 25-33; William Trimble, "Historical Aspects of the Surplus Food Production of the United States, 1862-1902," *American Historical Association Annual Report for 1918* (1921), 223-39; Wilfred Malenbaum, *The World Wheat Economy, 1885-1839* (1953); Morton Rothstein, "America in the International Rivalry for the British Wheat Market, 1860-1914," *MVHR* 47 (1960): 401-18; Rothstein, "The International Market for Agricultural Commodities, 1850-1873," in David T. Gilchrist and W. David Lewis, eds., *Economic Change in the Civil War Era* (1965), 62-82; Rothstein, "Antebellum Wheat and Cotton Exports: A Contrast in Marketing Organization and Economic Development," *Ag. Hist.* 40 (1966): 91-100; Harry Fornari, *Bread upon the Waters: A History of United States Grain Exports* (1973); C. Knick Harley, "Transportation, the World Wheat Trade, and the Kuznets Cycle, 1850-1913," *Explorations in Economic History* 17 (1980): 218-50; and Jeffrey G. Williamson, "Greasing the Wheels of Sputtering Export Engines: Midwestern Grains and American Growth," ibid., 189-217.
73. CBT, *Annual Reports.* For the effect of the war on Chicago prices, see James E. Boyle, *Chicago Wheat Prices for Eighty-one Years* (1922), 14.
74. Colbert, *Chicago,* 50-51.
75. Ibid., 51; Taylor, *Chicago Board of Trade,* 1:220-21.
76. "The Metropolis of the Prairies," *Harper's New Monthly Magazine* 61 (1880): 726.
77. On grading systems generally, see Dondlinger, *Book of Wheat,* 221-26. So complete was this severing process by the 1860s that Chicago elevators began to issue general receipts for whole trainloads of grain, irrespective of who owned which particular lot; see Henry Crosby Emery, *Speculation on the Stock and Produce Exchanges of the United States* (1896), 38. For a discussion of grain grading in the modern world, see Lowell D. Hill, *Grain Grades and Standards: Historical Issues Shaping the Future* (1990).
78. *Chicago Daily Press and Tribune,* July 19, 1858.
79. Brittania, "Grain Marketing," *Prairie Farmer,* June 1852, 282.
80. Annual Review for 1857, *Chicago Daily Press,* 11.
81. CBT, *Annual Report for 1858,* 11.

82. For an example of this sort of report, see the *Chicago Daily Press and Tribune*, July 19, 1858. See also Taylor, *Chicago Board of Trade*, 1:242–43.
83. Taylor, *Chicago Board of Trade*, 1:227.
84. CBT, *Annual Report for 1858*, 11.
85. CBT, *Annual Report for 1860*, 13.
86. CBT, *Annual Report for 1858*, 10.
87. For the first several years, the chief inspector relied on assistants already employed as inspectors by the elevators to do the work of grading, but this created a clear conflict of interest and invited corruption. In 1860, therefore, the chief inspector began hiring his own team of inspectors, who could not be employees of the elevators and who earned their salaries by charging a fee for each inspection. See William G. Ferris, *The Grain Traders: The Story of the Chicago Board of Trade* (1988), 20–21.
88. "Grain and Flour Inspection," *Prairie Farmer*, July 18, 1861.
89. Ibid.
90. The 1859 charter is reprinted in an appendix to the Board's *Annual Report for 1877*, pp v–ix, and can also be found in Andreas, *History of Chicago*, 2:326.
91. The best modern history of the Board's regulatory apparatus is Jonathan Lurie, *The Chicago Board of Trade, 1859–1905: The Dynamics of Self Regulation* (1979). Lurie focuses on the legal history of the Board's regulatory apparatus in relation to state judicial oversight. More comprehensive but much less analytical histories include Taylor, *Chicago Board of Trade;* and Ferris, *Grain Traders*. For a brief popular survey, see Edward Jerome Dies, *The Wheat Pit* (1925); and James E. Boyle, *The Chicago Board of Trade: What It Is and What It Does* (1921).
92. Emery, *Speculation on Stock and Produce Exchanges*, 38. Emery's book remains a classic on the origins of futures markets in the United States, and his chief arguments about this subject appear in the work of most historians who have followed him.
93. F. H. West, a Milwaukee representative at the National Board of Trade meeting in Buffalo in 1870, addressed "the subject of issuing grain receipts by warehouses and elevators" as follows: "That is a new feature in the commerce of the West. . . . The managers of these elevators have adopted the practice of issuing receipts, and those receipts now enter largely into the commerce of our section of the country. They are in some respects analogous to bank-bills, and pass like bank-bills from hand to hand. In our Western States they are a favorite collateral security with banks; in fact they are nearly all the securities we have to offer for demand loans. . . ." *Proceedings of the Third Annual Meeting of the National Board of Trade, Held in Buffalo, December, 1870* (1871), 44. The commercial institution I describe in the text is more precisely known as a negotiable instrument, or a mercantile instrument of credit; for a survey of its history and development, see Joseph J. Klein, "The Development of Mercantile Instruments of Credit in the United States," *Journal of Accountancy* 12 (1911): 321–45, 422–49, 526–37, 594–607; 13 (1912): 44–50, 122–32, 207–17.
94. Taylor, *Chicago Board of Trade*, 1:135.
95. Richard B. DuBoff, "Business Demand and the Development of the Telegraph in the United States, 1844–1860," *Bus. Hist. Rev.* 54 (1980): 459–79; DuBoff, "The Telegraph and the Structure of Markets in the United States, 1845–1890," *Research in Economic History* 8 (1983): 256.
96. This effect had first been apparent at Buffalo, where the arrival of the telegraph in early 1847 reduced the traveling time of New York market reports from more than four days to just under one. See John Langdale, "The Impact of the Telegraph on the Buffalo Agricultural Commodity Market: 1846–1848," *Professional Geographer* 31 (1979): 165–69. On other effects of the telegraph, see DuBoff, "Telegraph and Structure of U.S. Markets," 253–77; and Allan Pred, *Urban Growth and City-Systems in the United States, 1840–1860* (1980), 151–56.
97. *Chicago Democrat*, Sept. 12, 1848, as quoted by Taylor, *Chicago Board of Trade*, 1:147.
98. On general trends in wheat prices after 1867, see Veblen, "Price of Wheat since 1867," 68–103; and Helen C. Farnsworth, "Decline and Recovery of Wheat Prices in the 'Nineties," *Wheat Studies* 10 (1933–34): 289–352.
99. Andreas, *History of Chicago*, 2:325, 333; Taylor, *Chicago Board of Trade*, 1:241, 260, 267.
100. Robert Sobel, *The Big Board: A History of the New York Stock Market* (1965), 52–53; DuBoff, "Telegraph and Structure of U.S. Markets," 262.
101. Reverend J. P. Thompson, in Curtiss, *Western Portraiture*, 334.

102. The risks of fire, shipwreck, and spoilage continued, so insurance remained a key feature of the grain trade; while grain was in transit, shippers still bore the cost of damage along the way.

103. Odle, "Entrepreneurial Cooperation," 451–53; Odle, "American Grain Trade," 9 (1953): 54–58, 105–9, 162–66.

104. Taylor, *Chicago Board of Trade*, 1:146–47; Julius B. Baer and Olin Glenn Saxon, *Commodity Exchanges and Futures Trading: Principles and Operating Methods* (1949), 3–26; Henry H. Bakken, "Historical Evaluation, Theory and Legal Status of Futures Trading in American Agricultural Commodities," in CBT, *Futures Trading Seminar: History and Development* (1960), 12–15; Emery, *Speculation on Stock and Produce Exchanges*, 38–40; James E. Boyle, *Speculation and the Chicago Board of Trade* (1920), 53–58. Jeffrey Williams argues that "to arrive" contracts were common enough at Buffalo during the late 1840s that they already constituted almost a full futures market, but I side with the older interpretation which sees "to arrive" contracts as only one of the several steps that had to be taken before a futures market could come to full flower in Chicago during the following two decades. Although "to arrive" contracts were certainly in use on the Great Lakes before the advent of grain standardization and regulated trading, the latter enormously increased market volume, which was a crucial element in making full-fledged futures possible. See Jeffrey C. Williams, "The Origin of Futures Markets," *Ag. Hist.* 56 (1982): 306–16; and Williams, *The Economic Functions of Futures Markets* (1986).

105. Small futures markets of one sort or another had existed in the past—a few European cities had been conducting them since at least the 1830s—and other American cities were experimenting with them at the same time as Chicago. But none had become so large and institutionalized as the Chicago Board of Trade by the end of the Civil War. As with the railroads, the shifting scale of the Chicago market made its grain trade look radically different from its predecessors. See CBT, *Futures Trading Seminar*, 12–16; Emery, *Speculation on Stock and Produce Exchanges*, 40–41.

106. Taylor, *Chicago Board of Trade*, 1:192–93.

107. Lee, "Chicago Grain Elevator Industry," 93; Emery, *Speculation on Stock and Produce Exchanges*, 37–38. The actual rules adopted in 1865 specified that buyers or sellers could at any time request a 10 percent margin on any future contract; that grain undelivered at the expiration of a contract would be valued at its market price on the day following; and that contracts would expire at certain uniform times of day.

108. CBT, *Annual Report for 1866*, 9; CBT, *Annual Report for 1869*, 149–50 contains the first publication of the new rules in the *Annual Report;* see also Taylor, *Chicago Board of Trade*, 1:317, 325, 331–32; and FTC, *Report on the Grain Trade* (1920), 2:107–9.

109. Emery, *Speculation on Stock and Produce Exchanges*, 46. For an excellent summary of the preconditions necessary for futures trading, see FTC, *Grain Trade*, 5:23–27.

110. The transaction between Jones and Smith is only the simplest form of such a settlement, since the trade in futures might involve a whole series of speculators who had all bought and sold from each other. Settling these complicated chains of contracts was generally done at the end of a trading day by brokers on behalf of their clients. The system was eventually formalized at Chicago in 1883, with the creation of a clearinghouse whose sole purpose was to "ring-out" differences in futures contracts. For a fuller discussion of clearinghouses and their role in the grain market, see Emery, *Speculation on Stock and Produce Exchanges*, 57–74; FTC, *Grain Trade*, 5:227ff.; and Albert C. Stevens, " 'Futures' in the Wheat Market," *Quarterly Journal of Economics* 2 (1888): 40–44.

111. Morton Rothstein, "Frank Norris and Popular Perceptions of the Market," *Ag. Hist.* 56 (1982): 58.

112. The origin of these two terms is uncertain. The *Oxford English Dictionary* dates them back to at least early-eighteenth-century England, when those who sold short were sometimes called "bearskin jobbers," suggesting an allusion to the old proverb "To sell the bear's skin before one has caught the bear." "Bull" appeared somewhat later, and is more obscure in its origins.

113. Individual traders might be either bulls or bears at any given moment, though the logic and strategies of the two positions were different enough that many traders tended to specialize in one or the other.

114. *Chicago Tribune*, April 17, 1875.

115. Stevens, " 'Futures' in the Wheat Market," 51–55. Stevens gathered weekly statistics on spot and futures sales in wheat at the New York Produce Exchange during the first half of 1887, and found that the dollar volume of futures contracts amounted to about twenty times the volume of spot sales. Although he gathered no such statistics for Chicago, he did assemble them for St. Louis, where the ratio was better than 24 to 1. It seems reasonable to believe that Chicago was in the same ballpark. Indeed, Stevens thought it "well within the limits of probability" that the combined futures trading at St. Louis, Chicago, Toledo, and the major Atlantic ports of the United States during the first half of 1887 "more than equalled the total production of wheat in the world in 1886."

116. To have stated this option so explicitly would have been to declare openly that the futures contract was a wager on the future price of grain, and as such was a "gambling" contract. Gambling contracts were of dubious legal standing even before the Illinois legislature outlawed them in 1874. Because of this, the Board went to great lengths to argue—not always convincingly—that its traders really did intend to complete delivery of the grain they bought and sold. For excellent discussions of this issue, see Lurie, *Chicago Board of Trade;* and Ann Fabian, *Card Sharps, Dream Books, and Bucket Shops: Gambling in Nineteenth-Century America* (1990).

117. At least in the years prior to 1870, corners bore some relation to the seasonal cycling of grain production, since they were easiest to run when grain was in short supply. The *Tribune* explained the phenomenon this way: "It is a singular fact that these corner operations are always made about this time of the year; just before the new crop, and when everybody is expecting lower prices. But there are good and sufficient reasons for the choice of midsummer by the schemers. Money is generally more plentiful at that season, not being wasted to move the crops, or to pay for either spring or fall trade; hence its use can be secured by the combination at less than the average cost of accommodation; then, too, there is less danger of the operation being swamped by excessive receipts, as the farmers are all too much busied with harvesting to be able to spare their men and teams to haul grain from the garner to the railroad station. Besides, the general anticipation of a decline in prices, as a consequence of the gathering in of the new crop, makes it more easy to induce parties to sell at a low figure for the future delivery, especially people in the country, who are not so well read in the details of the 'confidence game' as their city brethren." *Chicago Tribune,* July 1, 1868.

118. For a general discussion of corners and their relationship to the futures market, see FTC, *Grain Trade,* 5:322–29.

119. Andreas, *History of Chicago,* 2:362.

120. Because futures contracts relied so heavily on abundantly available and standardized grain, they were almost always written for one particular grade of medium-quality, "staple" grain. By the 1860s, spring wheat futures contracts were always for No. 2, the most common grade in the market.

121. The corner is briefly described in Ferris, *Grain Traders,* 33–34. While Lyon ran the corner in Chicago, Smith ran a parallel corner by buying up available grain in Milwaukee.

122. *Chicago Tribune,* June 24, 1868.

123. Ibid., June 30, 1868.

124. Ibid., July 1, 1868.

125. Ibid., June 30, 1868. Not all of this $220,000 was clear profit, of course. In order to sustain the corner, its operators had been forced to purchase "spot" wheat at inflated prices themselves, and to hold or ship that grain where other speculators could not get at it. The *Tribune* estimated that the total cost of the June 1868 corner, measured in inflated wheat prices, commissions, storage charges, and so on, was probably about $100,000, so the operators' net gain was perhaps $120,000.

126. Ibid., July 1, 1868.

127. Andreas, *History of Chicago,* 2:362.

128. *Chicago Tribune,* July 1, 1868. Those who criticized such corners usually did so on behalf of small "legitimate" traders, not speculators. Thus, after a corner in August 1872, a Chicago-based agricultural newspaper had this to say: "No one is sorry for the swindlers of Chicago and other cities who have lost. . . . They are *not* the parties who are the real sufferers. It is the country merchants, and other grain buyers who are doing a legitimate business, who are to be pitied; and also, those in the city of Chicago,

who pay cash for the grain they buy. Not the scalpers who have less moral feeling than brutes." "The Great Grain Corner.—Black Tuesday," *Western Rural,* Aug. 31, 1872.
129. *Chicago Tribune,* June 30, 1868.
130. Ibid., June 24, 1868, and market reports for the entire period from June 15 through June 30.
131. Ibid., July 2, 1868.
132. Ibid., July 3, 1868.
133. On traders' fears that a corner might be run again, see ibid., June 30, July 1, 4, 14, 1868.
134. Ibid., July 4, 1868.
135. Ibid., July 14, 1868.
136. Ibid., July 16, 1868.
137. Ibid., July 20, 1868.
138. Ibid., July 25, 1868.
139. See *Chicago Tribune* market reports for Aug. 1868.
140. Taylor, *Chicago Board of Trade,* 1:371.
141. CBT, *Annual Report for 1869,* 164; see also Boyle, *Speculation and the Chicago Board of Trade,* 63; and Taylor, *Chicago Board of Trade,* 1:371.
142. Frank Norris, *The Pit: A Story of Chicago* (1903; reprint, n.d.). On the inaccuracies of Norris's depiction of futures trading, see Charles Kaplan, "Norris's Use of Sources in *The Pit,*" *American Literature* 25 (1953): 75–84; and Rothstein, "Frank Norris and the Market." On the Leiter corner itself, see Edward J. Dies, *The Plunger: A Tale of the Wheat Pit* (1929), 222–37; Harper Leech and John Charles Carroll, *Armour and His Times* (1938), 305–20; and Ferris, *Grain Traders,* 99–115.
143. Lurie, *Chicago Board of Trade,* 46–49, 52–55.
144. For individual examples of such legends, see B. P. Hutchinson, "Speculation in Wheat," *No. Am. Rev.* 153 (1891): 414–19; Charles H. Baker, *Life and Character of William Taylor Baker* (1908); Dies, *Plunger;* William Ferris, "Old Hutch—The Wheat King," *J. Ill. State Hist. Soc.* 41 (1948): 231–43; Dorothy J. Ernst, "Wheat Speculation in the Civil War Era: Daniel Wells and the Grain Trade, 1860–1862," *Wis. Mag. Hist.* 47 (1963–64): 125–35.
145. This was the reason that the Board proposed to "solve" the corner problem by suspending the ordinary boundaries between grades, making them temporarily exchangeable in a way they never ordinarily were, so that cornered speculators could fulfill their contracts with uncorned grain.
146. All these figures are based on 1860 statistics contained in CBT, *Annual Report for 1860,* 13, 21, and are reasonably typical. They assume a price for No. 2 spring wheat of roughly $1.00 and for Rejected of $.90.
147. *Chicago Daily Press and Tribune,* July 19, 1858.
148. Lorenzo D. Whiting of Bureau County, representing the Forty-fifth District, in *Debates and Proceedings of the Constitutional Convention of the State of Illinois* (1870), 1627.
149. William Cary of Jo Daviess County, representing the Fifty-seventh District, in Ill. Const. Debates, 1622, also Samuel S. Hayes's statement, 1630; "Grain and Flour Inspection," *Prairie Farmer,* July 18, 1861.
150. Chicago Joint Committee of the Board of Trade and Mercantile Association, *Produce and Transportation: The Railway and Warehouse Monopolies* (1866), 7.
151. One practical source of conflict was that grain had to be graded *twice,* once at a country elevator or grain dealer and again at a Chicago elevator. Because grading was hardly an exact science, and because country inspectors did not always fully understand the Chicago system, it was not uncommon for two different grade assignments to result. (This was especially true if country buyers were competing with each other for farmers' grain, and wanted to offer the highest possible price for it.) Whenever Chicago grades proved to be lower than country grades, farmers felt they had proof positive that *someone* in Chicago was robbing them. For a helpful article that identified this problem shortly after the new grading system was created, see the letter by A. H. Loomis of Kewanee, Ill., in the *Prairie Farmer,* July 19, 1858.
152. In the same way, farmers who produced grain whose quality was near the *lower* boundary of a grade tended to benefit at the expense of farmers whose grade was near the *upper* boundary of that grade. These effects were exacerbated when the price differentials among different grades were greater.

153. An even murkier problem was posed by elevators that installed machinery to *clean* grain so as to remove dirt and other impurities and raise it to a higher grade. In this case, elevators were legitimately *improving* the grain which had been delivered to them, but there was no easy way to determine whether the income they earned by so doing was commensurate with the work they performed. Cleaning and other processing techniques became increasingly common in the 1880s, and because traders and farmers did not want to see regular elevators earn the resulting profits for themselves, specialized warehouses gradually took over the role of doing this processing directly for paying customers. See Lee, "Chicago Grain Elevator Industry," 266–67.

154. Guy Lee cites the case of a farmer who believed he had been "filched" in this way. Ibid., 76.

155. *Chicago Tribune*, Nov. 22, 1870. The *Tribune*'s proposed solution was to disallow *all* mixing, even within grades, but this amounted to throwing out the baby with the bath.

156. CBT, *Report on Produce and Transportation*, 5–6. This same report was published in the *Chicago Tribune*, Feb. 14, 1866.

157. As long as grading partitioned the market for grain, *someone* was ultimately going to benefit from variation within any given grade. If the elevator operators did not appropriate it in the process of moving grain through Chicago, the millers would finally get its benefits when they milled that grain into flour. The technical difference between the two arrangements was that elevator operators who mixed would tend to bring their grain to the lowest possible level still within its grade, whereas flour millers would tend to produce a flour that reflected the midpoint of a grade.

158. CBT, *Annual Report for 1870*, 44. Many elevators also received grain from the Illinois and Michigan Canal, largely because the canal did not represent significant competition with the railroads.

159. Lee, "Chicago Grain Elevator Industry," 113–28, attempts to reconstruct the various secret agreements among elevators and railroads that allowed them to keep competition to a minimum. One of his conclusions is that Ira Munn, later known for his participation in the famous *Munn* v. *Illinois* court case, was the "kingpin" in a multipartnership combination which controlled about half of Chicago's total elevator space.

160. Ibid., 124–26, 173. Since elevators at Buffalo assessed comparable charges, the total cost to the farmer for elevator storage and handling was more like 10 percent. Cf. "Breadstuffs and Transportation Facilities," *Hunt's Merch. Mag.* 62 (1870): 284–87.

161. "The Storage of Grain in Chicago," *Prairie Farmer*, April 9, 1864.

162. Lee, "Chicago Grain Elevator Industry," 127–28, based on income tax statements from 1863, 1865, and 1867, as reported in the *Chicago Tribune*, Jan. 17, July 18, 1865; May 2, 1867; June 9–13, 1868; and Aug. 26, 1872.

163. "The Storage of Grain in Chicago," *Prairie Farmer*, April 9, 1864.

164. CBT, *Report on Produce and Transportation*, 8.

165. The elevator operators, though themselves members of the Board, were so few in number that the Board mainly looked after the interests of the city's several hundred grain traders.

166. As early as 1858, the major elevator operators had agreed to provide the Board with daily statistics on "the quantity and grade of all grain delivered to each vessel," but this was not the same thing as the amount of grain in *store*. It was also easy to distort such figures. CBT, *Annual Report for 1858*, 12.

167. John L. Tincher of Vermilion County, representing the Thirty-ninth District, in Ill. Const. Debates, 1628.

168. Samuel S. Hayes of Cook County, representing the Fifty-ninth District, in Ill. Const. Debates, 1630.

169. Taylor, *Chicago Board of Trade*, 1:342 and 339–423 generally; Benjamin F. Goldstein, *Marketing: A Farmer's Problem* (1928), 26–31; Lee, "Chicago Grain Elevator Industry," 176, 186.

170. The Board of Trade summarized and evaluated most of these charges in its *Report on Produce and Transportation*.

171. This argument is convincingly made by Harold D. Woodman in his "Chicago Businessmen and the 'Granger Laws,'" *Ag. Hist.* 36 (1962): 16–24; for a discussion of analogous activities among Milwaukee merchants, see Dale Emory Treleven, "Commissions, Corners and Conveyance: The Origins of Anti-Monopolism in Milwaukee,"

(M.A. thesis, Univ. of Wisconsin, 1968); and Treleven, "Railroads, Elevators, and Grain Dealers: The Genesis of Antimonopolism in Milwaukee," *Wis. Mag. Hist.* 51 (1969): 205–22.

172. Unlike their successors the Populists, the Grangers have received nothing like the attention they deserve from recent historians. Many of the most useful works on the movement are very old: Edward Winslow Martin [James Dabney McCabe,] *History of the Grange Movement; or, The Farmer's War against Monopolies* (1873); Jonathan Periam, *The Groundswell: A History of the Origin, Aims, and Progress of the Farmers' Movement* (1874); Arthur E. Paine, *The Granger Movement in Illinois* (1904); Solon J. Buck, *The Granger Movement: A Study of Agricultural Organization and Its Political, Economic and Social Manifestations, 1870–1880* (1913); Ernest Ludlow Bogart and Charles Manfred Thompson, *The Industrial State, 1870–1893*, vol. 4 of *The Centennial History of Illinois* (1920), 82–106; Solon J. Buck, *The Agrarian Crusade: A Chronicle of the Farmer in Politics* (1920); Henrietta M. Larson, *The Wheat Market and the Farmer in Minnesota, 1858–1900* (1926); Chester McArthur Destler, "Agricultural Readjustment and Agrarian Unrest in Illinois, 1880–1896," *Ag. Hist.* 21 (1947): 104–16; and D. Sven Nordin, *Rich Harvest: A History of the Grange, 1867–1900* (1974). On the struggle to impose state regulation on railroads via the "Granger laws," see Grosvenor, "Railroads and Farms," 591–610; Larrabee, *Railroad Question;* Frank H. Dixon, *State Railroad Control, with a History of Its Development in Iowa* (1896); Charles R. Detrick, "The Effects of the Granger Acts," *J. Pol. Econ.* 11 (1902–03), 237–56; Robert T. Daland, "Enactment of the Potter Law," *Wis. Mag. Hist.* 33 (1949): 45–54; George H. Miller, "Origins of the Iowa Granger Law," *MVHR* 40 (1954): 657–80; and George H. Miller, *Railroads and the Granger Laws* (1971).

173. Board resolution, as reported in the *Chicago Express*, Jan. 23, 1867, as quoted in Taylor, *Chicago Board of Trade*, 1:349–50.

174. The warehousemen also promoted an amendment outlawing futures as "void and gambling contracts," apparently to punish members of the Board who had supported elevator regulation. The clause was never enforced, and the legislature repealed it in 1869. Taylor, *Chicago Board of Trade*, 1:348–50; Lee, "Chicago Grain Elevator Industry," 161–64; Goldstein, *Marketing*, 18–26.

175. "Farmers' Convention at Bloomington," *Western Rural*, April 28, 1870, 136; see also Periam, *Groundswell*, 229–30; Periam erroneously gives the year of this meeting as 1869.

176. *Western Rural*, April 28, 1870, 136. Their actual resolution about elevators reads somewhat ambiguously, so the wording I quote here may actually mean that they sought the right to have grain delivered to any elevator they *chose*, not to no elevator at all.

177. "The Chicago Elevators," *Chicago Tribune*, July 28, 1870.

178. Thomas J. Turner of Stephenson County, representing the Fifty-sixth District, in Ill. Const. Debates, 1623–24. Turner appears to have been something of a laughingstock at the convention, and his arguments were not particularly coherent.

179. James McCoy of Whiteside County, representing the Forty-eighth District, in Ill. Const. Debates, 1631.

180. Joseph Medill of Cook County, representing the Fifty-ninth District, in Ill. Const. Debates, 1629.

181. In the Board's original draft, this right to inspect was also given to any "board of trade" that might exist in the community where such elevators stood, but other delegates quickly struck this clause. Ill. Const. Debates, 1693.

182. Article 13, "Warehouses," in Ill. Const. Debates, 1878. See also Goldstein, *Marketing*, 32–39.

183. The Board fought state inspection until the early 1880s, but thereafter accepted it as inevitable. See Taylor, *Chicago Board of Trade*, 1:403, 406–13; Goldstein, *Marketing*, 36, 43–58.

184. Goldstein, *Marketing*, 54–58.

185. For examples of the continuing controversies surrounding elevator charges, see Baker, *Life of William Baker*, 123–30; *Chicago Conference on Trusts* (1900), 202ff.; and U.S. House of Representatives, *Report of the Industrial Commission on Transportation*, 56th Cong., 1st sess., Doc. 476, 4:7ff.

186. Goldstein, *Marketing*, 64–96, contains a useful summary of *Munn*, but the literature on this case is enormous. The best recent surveys of the issues involved are Edmund W. Kitch and Clara Ann Bowler, "The Facts of *Munn* v. *Illinois*," in Philip B. Kurland and

Gerhard Casper, eds., *1978: The Supreme Court Review* (1979), 313–43; and Harry N. Scheiber, "The Road to *Munn:* Eminent Domain and the Concept of Public Purpose in the State Courts," *Perspectives in American History* 7 (1971): 327–402.

187. Goldstein, *Marketing*, 96.
188. "Grain and Flour Inspection," *Prairie Farmer*, July 18, 1861.
189. John Tincher, in Ill. Const. Debates, 1628.
190. Thomas Turner, in Ill. Const. Debates, 1623.
191. Judge Dickey in a speech at the Ottawa convention, as quoted in the *Chicago Tribune*, Feb. 21, 1866.
192. This process, called hedging, eventually emerged as the single most powerful argument that futures trading performs a genuinely useful economic function, and is not just "gambling." But defenders of the futures market did not start to discuss hedging in this way until somewhat later in the century. For an early example, see Stevens, " 'Futures' in the Wheat Market," esp. 48–51; Albert Clark Stevens, "The Utility of Speculation in Modern Commerce," *Political Science Quarterly* 7 (1892): 419–30; and Henry Crosby Emery, "Legislation against Futures," ibid., 10 (1895): 62–86. For later, more technical discussions of the economics of hedging and its practical importance to the grain trade, see Alonzo E. Taylor, "Speculation, Short Selling, and the Price of Wheat," *Wheat Studies* 7 (1931): 231–66; Holbrook Working, "Financial Results of Speculative Holding of Wheat," ibid., 405–37; Truman F. Graf, "Hedging—How Effective Is It?" *Journal of Farm Economics* 35 (1953): 398–413; Holbrook Working, "Hedging Reconsidered," ibid., 544–61; and Williams, *Economic Functions of Futures Markets*.
193. Samuel S. Hayes, in Ill. Const. Debates, 1630. There was a deeper change here as well: the Board symbolized the farmers' growing dependence on cash transactions to sustain the rural economy. "In former years," wrote a reporter for Chicago's *Western Monthly*, "when the producers were less numerous and the aggregate of their surplus but small, the farmer could make his exchanges direct with the grocer, dry goods dealer, or other trader. But, with the systematizings of modern commerce, these duplex operations are no longer convenient or profitable; in other words, they are rendered impossible. 'Cash' is now the only recognized means of purchase for land, improvements, labor, furniture, or goods; and the farmer must sell his grain and live stock for cash." "The Chicago Board of Trade," *Western Monthly* 3 (1870): 406.
194. CBT, *Annual Reports*, 1871–80.
195. William Cary, in Ill. Const. Debates, 1623. On later controversies surrounding speculation at the Board of Trade and elsewhere, see Cedric B. Cowing, *Populists, Plungers, and Progressives: A Social History of Stock and Commodity Speculation, 1890–1936* (1965).
196. "A prerequisite to the development of future trading . . . is homogeneity in the commodity dealt in, such that commercial units are interchangeable. . . . A system of grading much increases the availability of grain in this respect for future trading." FTC, *Grain Trade*, 5:24.
197. Orlando H. Wright, in Ill. Const. Debates, 1636. Wright's confusion is evident even in his misquotation of Board vocabulary: one does not sell long, only short.
198. "Metropolis of the Prairies," 727.
199. CBT, *Annual Report for 1875*, 22.
200. Cf. *Origin, Growth, and Usefulness of the Chicago Board of Trade* (1885), 62: "These figures [of Chicago grain shipments] demonstrate that the Board of Trade of the city of Chicago does not deal in fictions, for if there should be removed from the world's supplies for one year these vast quantities of grain and provisions, want and hunger and famine, most positive and real, would follow, which would be no fictions, but realities of the most deplorable and calamitous character."

4: THE WEALTH OF NATURE: LUMBER

1. Wright, *Chicago*, xiii.
2. Karl Marx, *Capital: A Critique of Political Economy*, vol. 2 (1885; reprint, 1967), 105. David Fernbach translates this phrase as "self-valorizing value" in his edition of *Capital*, vol. 2 (1978), 185, emphasizing the extent to which capital seems to act "with the force of an elemental natural process," a theme I emphasize throughout this book.
3. "What exclusively determines the magnitude of the value of any article is therefore the

amount of labour socially necessary, or the labour-time socially necessary for its production." Karl Marx, *Capital*, vol. 1, trans. Ben Fowkes (1977), 129. Eric Roll, *A History
of Economic Thought*, 4th ed. (1973), surveys changing theories of value since the eighteenth century.

4. I have tried wherever possible in this book to avoid sexist language, but have been
unable to find an adequate replacement for "lumberman," which was the standard
nineteenth-century usage for the capitalists of the lumber trade. "Lumberjack," a
word used much less commonly in the nineteenth century than it is today, referred
only to the workers, who preferred to call themselves "woodsmen," "shanty boys," or
"loggers." On these questions of vocabulary, see Rolland H. Maybee, "Michigan's
White Pine Era, 1840–1900," *Mich. Hist.* 43 (1959): 407–8; Agnes M. Larson, *History of
the White Pine Industry in Minnesota* (1949), 210–13; and Lynwood Carranco, "Terminol-
ogy," in Richard C. Davis, ed., *Encyclopedia of American Forest and Conservation History*
(1983), 640–45.

5. Always understanding, of course, that different human societies can impose quite
different social constructions on "natural" values.

6. Indians had contributed to that wealth by promoting the fires that encouraged the
growth of prairie grasses and the reproduction of white pines, and also by living in
such a way as not to diminish ecological accumulations of forest biomass or prairie
soil. But in ecological terms, the labor theory of value did not apply to their universe
either.

7. I have discussed several technical questions concerning the labor theory of value and
Marx's "mode of production" as they relate to environmental history in my "Modes of
Prophecy and Production: Placing Nature in History," *JAH* 76 (1990): 1122–31.

8. To sample the enormous and much contested historiography of the frontier thesis, see
George Wilson Pierson, "American Historians and the Frontier Hypothesis in 1941,"
Wis. Mag. Hist. 26 (1942): 36–60, 170–85; George Rogers Taylor, ed., *The Turner Thesis
concerning the Role of the Frontier in American History*, rev. ed. (1956); Gene M. Gressley,
"The Turner Thesis: A Problem in Historiography," *Ag. Hist.* 32 (1958): 227–49;
Richard Hofstadter and Seymour Martin Lipset, eds., *Turner and the Sociology of the
Frontier* (1968); Ray Allen Billington, ed., *The Frontier Thesis: Valid Interpretation of Ameri-
can History?* (1966); Billington, *America's Frontier Heritage* (1963); Harry N. Scheiber,
"Turner's Legacy and the Search for a Reorientation of Western History: A Review
Essay," *New Mexico Historical Review* 44 (1969): 231–48; Jerome O. Steffen, "Some
Observations on the Turner Thesis: A Polemic," *Papers in Anthropology* 14 (1973):
16–30; Jackson K. Putnam, "The Turner Thesis and the Westward Movement: A
Reappraisal," *WHQ* 7 (1976): 377–404; Richard Jensen, "On Modernizing Frederick
Jackson Turner: The Historiography of Regionalism," *WHQ* 11 (1980): 307–22; Lim-
erick, *Legacy of Conquest;* Peter Novick, *That Noble Dream: The "Objectivity Question" in the
American Historical Profession* (1988), 86ff.; and Richard White, "Frederick Jackson
Turner," in John R. Wunder, ed., *Historians of the American Frontier: A Bio-Bibliographical
Sourcebook* (1988), 660–81.

9. I have argued that this is likely to be the most enduring and useful aspect of Turner's
frontier thesis in my essays "Revisiting the Vanishing Frontier," and "Turner's First
Stand."

10. The standard guide to Wisconsin's vegetation, and one of the best such state studies in
the country, is Curtis, *Vegetation of Wisconsin.* The general geography of Wisconsin's
shoreline as described in this paragraph can be followed in much more detail on two
maps of the state's presettlement vegetation, both based on the surveyors' notes of the
original government land survey: Robert W. Finley, "The Original Vegetation Cover
of Wisconsin" (Ph.D. thesis, Univ. of Wisconsin, 1951); and G. Cottam and O. L.
Loucks, *Early Vegetation of Wisconsin* (Madison: Wisconsin Geological and Natural History Survey, 1965). A comparable map of Minnesota can be found in M. L. Heinselman
and F. J. Marschner, *The Original Vegetation of Minnesota* (North Central Forest Experiment Station, USDA, U.S. Forest Service, 1974). On Michigan, see Samuel A. Graham,
"Climax Forests of the Upper Peninsula of Michigan," *Ecology* 22 (1941): 355–62. For
a good general guide to the ecology of the north woods, written for lay readers, see
Daniel and Sullivan, *A Sierra Club Naturalist's Guide to the North Woods;* more technical
but very useful is E. Lucy Braun, *Deciduous Forests of Eastern North America* (1950). See

also Eric A. Bourdo's helpful summary description in "The Forest the Settlers Saw," in Susan L. Flader, ed., *The Great Lakes Forest: An Environmental and Social History* (1983), 3–16.

11. Henry David Thoreau, *The Journal of Henry David Thoreau,* ed. Bradford Torrey and Francis H. Allen (1906), 10:33 (Sept. 16, 1857). Elsewhere, Thoreau explained his emotion more fully by saying that "the trees indeed have hearts," and "nothing stands up more free from blame in this world than a pine tree." Ibid., 3:145 (Dec. 20, 1851).

12. Curtiss, *Western Portraiture,* 38; for a similar discussion, see James S. Ritchie, *Wisconsin and Its Resources* (1858), 66–72.

13. Filibert Roth, *Forestry Conditions and Interests of Wisconsin,* USDA Bulletin no. 16 (1898), 31.

14. G. H. Collingwood and Warren D. Brush, *Knowing Your Trees: 51 Tree Edition,* revised and edited by Devereux Butcher (1964), 24–25; Daniel and Sullivan, *North Woods,* 154–56.

15. C. H. Brigham, "The Lumber Region of Michigan," *No. Am. Rev.* 107 (July 1868): 83. By way of comparison, most white pines today are harvested when they reach a diameter of twelve to seventeen inches. Collingwood and Brush, *Knowing Your Trees,* 25.

16. George W. Hotchkiss, *History of the Lumber and Forest Industry of the Northwest* (1898), 752.

17. "Where the Lumber Goes," *NWL,* March 27, 1880, 1.

18. Chas. D. Robinson, "The Lumber Trade of Green Bay," *Transactions of the Wisconsin State Agricultural Society* 5 (1858–59): 401–2. A late version of this same theory, written at a time when the relationship between prairie and forest finally seemed to be breaking down, can be found in "Taming the Prairies," *NWL,* Sept. 6, 1884, 3.

19. "The Future Demand for Lumber," *Wisconsin Lumberman,* Nov. 1873, 50.

20. J. W. Bond, *Minnesota and Its Resources* (1854), 30.

21. "Commercial Cities and Towns of the United States: City of Chicago, Illinois," *Hunt's Merch. Mag.* 18 (1848): 164–71; "Commercial Statistics," ibid., 21 (1849): 560–61.

22. Except for the suggestively anomalous year 1872, which followed the Great Fire, lake shipments accounted for well over 90 percent of Chicago's lumber until the very end of the 1870s. CBT, *Annual Reports.*

23. The literature on logging and the Great Lakes lumber industry in general is so enormous as to defy easy summary. Among the best academic surveys of Great Lakes logging and life in the lumber camps are Frederick Merk, *Economic History of Wisconsin during the Civil War Decade* (1916; reprint, 1971), 59–110; William F. Raney, "Pine Lumbering in Wisconsin," *Wis. Mag. Hist.* 19 (1935): 71–90; Bernhardt J. Kleven, "Wisconsin Lumber Industry" (Ph.D. thesis, Univ. of Minnesota, 1941); Lloyd Francis Dobyns, "The History of Lumbering in Marinette County, Wisconsin" (M.A. thesis, Univ. of Iowa, 1942); George B. Engberg, "Labor in the Lake States Lumber Industry, 1830–1930" (Ph.D. thesis, Univ. of Minnesota, 1949); Larson, *White Pine Industry;* Robert F. Fries, *Empire in Pine: The Story of Lumbering in Wisconsin, 1830–1900* (1951); William G. Rector, "From Woods to Sawmill: Transportation Problems in Logging," *Ag. Hist.* 23 (1949): 239–44; William Gerald Rector, *Log Transportation in the Lake States Lumber Industry, 1840–1918: The Movement of Logs and Its Relationship to Land Settlement, Waterway Development, Railroad Construction, Lumber Production and Prices* (1953); Carl Edward Krog, "Marinette: Biography of a Nineteenth Century Lumbering Town" (Ph.D. thesis, Univ. of Wisconsin, Madison, 1971); Charles E. Twining, *Downriver: Orrin H. Ingram and the Empire Lumber Company* (1975); Malcolm Rosholt, *The Wisconsin Logging Book, 1839–1939* (1980); Charles Twining, "The Apostle Islands and the Lumbering Frontier," *Wis. Mag. Hist.* 66 (1983): 205–20; and Randall E. Rohe, "The Evolution of the Great Lakes Logging Camp, 1830–1930," *Journal of Forest History* 30 (1986): 17–28. Good examples of the more colorful popular literature include Stewart Holbrook, *Holy Old Mackinaw: A Natural History of the American Lumberjack* (1938); Richard G. Lillard, *The Great Forest* (1948); and Maybee, "Michigan's White Pine Era." The standard syntheses of American forest history are now Thomas R. Cox et al., *This Well-Wooded Land: Americans and Their Forests from Colonial Times to the Present* (1985); and Michael Williams, *Americans and Their Forests: A Historical Geography* (1989), which became available after I had written this chapter. For comparison, see also the fine local studies of other regions in Thomas R. Cox, *Mills and Markets: A History of the Pacific Coast*

Lumber Industry to 1900 (1974); Graeme Wynn, *Timber Colony: A Historical Geography of Early Nineteenth Century New Brunswick* (1981); and Richard W. Judd, *Aroostook: A Century of Logging in Northern Maine* (1989).

24. The best data on ethnicity are probably in George Blackburn and Sherman L. Ricards, Jr., "A Demographic History of the West: Manistee County, Michigan, 1860," *JAH* 57 (1970): 613–15, though these do not differentiate workers and other inhabitants. Other evidence can be found in Raney, "Pine Lumbering," 85–86; Fries, *Empire in Pine*, 204; and Larson, *White Pine Industry*, 369–70.

25. Robert Nesbit makes this point in a wonderful passage: "None of this required a special breed of men. That is a delusion of memorialists who have been told they led exciting lives in a setting which is forever gone, or of romantics, regional authors, and eager folklorists. It is the province today of advertising agencies pushing fabricated pancake mix and imitation maple syrup. They should be condemned to a season in a logging camp of the 1870's." Robert C. Nesbit, *Urbanization and Industrialization, 1873–1893*, vol. 3 of *The History of Wisconsin* (1985), 63.

26. Rohe, "Great Lakes Logging Camps," 18–20; Fries, *Empire in Pine*, 25–27.

27. On competition with agriculture, see George B. Engberg, "Lumber and Labor in the Lake States," *Minn. Hist.* 36 (1959): 155. On the problems of bringing heavy logs to market, the classic work is Rector, *Log Transportation*, which is usefully summarized in his article "From Woods to Sawmill"; he has also brought his analysis up to the present in his article "Log Transportation" in Davis, *Encyclopedia of Forest History*, 354–62. For the description that follows, see also Fries, *Empire in Pine*, 24–59; and Larson, *White Pine Industry*, 71–104, 165–219. For a contemporary description, see H. M. Atkins, "Life in the Pineries," in J. W. McClung, *Minnesota as It Is in 1870* (1870), 144–49.

28. The common practice was to cut sections of trunk to be as long as possible, always making sure that the resulting log measured an even number of feet.

29. Elizabeth M. Bachmann discusses the practice of branding logs, which was akin to the more familiar branding of cattle, in her "Minnesota Log Marks," *Minn. Hist.* 26 (1945): 126–37; see also Rector, *Log Transportation*, 110–13. Examples of some Michigan logmarks are given in Maybee, "Michigan's White Pine Era," 415, and in Fries, *Empire in Pine*, chapter headings. Maybee also discusses the shift from axes to saws during the 1870s (p. 407).

30. See virtually any midwinter issue of the *NWL* during the 1870s or early 1880s. Fears about the weather could run in quite contradictory directions, reflecting entrepreneurial anxiety as much as anything else. Among the weather fears noted by a bemused editor of the *NWL* in 1876 were the following: "That for the first two or three months the weather and condition of the snow in the woods are fearful; the snow is too deep; the snow is so mealy that a good road cannot be made of it; there is no snow in the woods." *NWL*, March 4, 1876, 68.

31. Eli Bates to Charles Mears, Jan. 10, 1858, Charles Mears Papers, CHS.

32. Robinson, "Lumber Trade of Green Bay," 403.

33. The "peavey," invented in 1858 by a Maine blacksmith, rapidly became the standard tool of log drives throughout the country. It consisted of a five-foot pole with a sharp metal point at one end and an adjustable hook on the other.

34. Robinson, "Lumber Trade of Green Bay," 403.

35. Rector, *Log Transportation*, 257; Fries, *Empire in Pine*, 45.

36. No one who writes about the lumber industry seems able to resist describing a dramatic logjam, and I fear I have been no exception. The best (and least romantic) account is in Rector, *Log Transportation*, 256–65, but others can be found in Fries, *Empire in Pine*, 45–47; Larson, *White Pine Industry*, 187–89.

37. As late as 1859, Chicago was receiving over 8 percent of its lumber from the Saginaw district. CBT, *Annual Report for 1859;* see also "A Leaf from an Old Chapter," *NWL*, Oct. 12, 1889, 2.

38. The history of these various milling districts is traced in greatest detail in Hotchkiss, *History of the Lumber and Forest Industry of the Northwest.*

39. The best general discussion of booming is again in Rector, *Log Transportation*, 115–46. On the eastern origins of this institution, see the discussions in Richard G. Wood, *A History of Lumbering in Maine, 1820–1861*, University of Maine Studies, no. 33 (1935); David C. Smith, *A History of Lumbering in Maine, 1861–1960*, University of Maine Studies, no. 93 (1972); and Judd, *Aroostook.*

40. See *Annual Report of the Menominee River Boom Company* (1893), 20–21.

41. The evolution of sawmill technology is a good deal more complicated than this discussion suggests. Further details can be found in Hotchkiss, *Lumber Industry of the Northwest,* 649–60; and, more generally, in Cox, *This Well-Wooded Land,* 64–68.

42. Ulao is a rural area in Washington County, Wisconsin, northwest of Milwaukee.

43. Agreement between Zebina Eastman of Chicago, Richard P. Derrickson of Ulao, Washington County, Wisconsin, and James McClellan, Jr. of Chicago, Dec. 1, 1849, in Zebina Eastman Papers, CHS. A brief sketch of Eastman's career as a journalist can be found in Andreas, *History of Cook County,* 804–5; see also his credit history in the R. G. Dun Collection, Baker Library, Harvard Univ.

44. The basic facts of Charles Mears's life and business career can be found in Andreas, *History of Chicago,* 2:692; and in Carrie E. Mears, "Charles Mears, Lumberman," *Mich. His.* 30 (1946): 535–45. Mears's papers are housed at the Michigan Historical Collections of the Univ. of Michigan, and at CHS. Barbara Ellen Benson made extensive use of both collections in her 1976 Indiana Univ. dissertation, "Logs and Lumber: The Development of the Lumber Industry in Michigan's Lower Peninsula, 1837–1870." One other key document surveying Mears's life is the long and bitter autobiographical letter he sent to Isaac G. Lombard on Oct. 29, 1891, in which he outlined his entire credit history. It can be found at CHS.

45. Eli Bates to Charles Mears, Nov. 14, 1849, Mears Papers, CHS; Andreas, *History of Chicago,* 2:692. Probably because he could be difficult to work with, Charles Mears eventually had a succession of different partners. Nathan Mears and Eli Bates would go on to form their own company, Mears, Bates and Company, which owned large interests in lands and mill property at Oconto, Wisconsin. At its height, its estimated worth was over $700,000. See manuscript entries for Mears, Bates and Co. in the R. G. Dun Collection, Baker Library, Harvard Univ. On the backgrounds of Great Lakes lumbermen as a group, see Frederick W. Kohlmeyer, "Northern Pine Lumbermen: A Study in Origins and Migrations," *JEH* 16 (1956): 529–38; and Carl Krog, "Marinette Lumbermen," *Journal of Forest History* 21 (1977): 97–100.

46. Lincoln was originally known as Little Sauble. When Mears paid federal taxes in 1864 on a declared income of $40,975.26, he gave his residence as Lincoln, Michigan, and paid his tax at Grand Rapids, Michigan—but had his form sworn and notarized at the Cook County courthouse in Chicago. See Charles Mears, 1864 U.S. tax form, Mears Papers, CHS.

47. Eli Bates to Charles Mears, Aug. 22, 1852, Mears Papers, CHS. See also Nathan Mears to Charles Mears, Oct. 12, 1852, and April 24, 1853, for examples of the Chicago yard ordering specific mill cuts.

48. Charles Mears to E. H. Denison, June 5, 1867, Mears Papers, CHS. On Nov. 26, 1867, Mears wrote Denison, "You may send the Chicago daily Tribune for six months as it will be needed for the Market Reports."

49. As an example, see the monthly market report issued by Woolner and Garrick, Forwarding and Commission Merchants, Chicago, Sept. 3, 1867, Mears Papers, CHS.

50. See, for instance, Charles Mears to E. H. Townsend, March 12, 1856, and Charles Mears to John Lamieux, Dec. 12, 1856, Mears Papers, CHS.

51. All of the following details on Mears's activities in 1856 come from his diary for that year, which is at CHS. I have generally relied on Carrie Mears's typed transcript of her father's original journal. My spot checks of the transcript suggest that although Carrie corrected misspellings and expanded some contractions, she was otherwise scrupulously accurate in her work.

52. In fairness, it should be noted that there were other years in which Mears spent more time at his Michigan mills, but even when he himself was residing on the east shore of the lake, his activities continued to focus on Chicago's market. In their article "The Timber Industry in Manistee County, Michigan: A Case Study in Local Control," *Journal of Forest History* 18 (1974): 14–21, George M. Blackburn and Sherman L. Ricards argue that most lumbering in Manistee (and, by inference, other Michigan areas as well) was done with local capital. My own sense is that Chicago capital played a much larger role than they suggest, but our disagreement may be more semantic than real. I tend to count someone like Charles Mears among the Chicago capitalists; I suspect they would be inclined to count him among the "local" Michigan ones. The

more important point is the degree to which Chicago and Michigan operations were integrated, something that clearly became more common with time.

53. Charles Mears to William J. Croxen [sp?], May 3, 1875, Mears Papers, CHS.

54. Charles Mears, Transcript of Diary for 1856, Mears Papers, 1856. These purchases occurred on Aug. 25; Sept. 15, 19; Oct. 6, 20; and Nov. 13, 17, 19.

55. Mears to E. H. Denison, Oct. 6, 1867, Mears Papers, CHS.

56. The $100 wage was typical of 1859; by the end of the Civil War inflation, it had risen to $300 per year. The Mears Papers at CHS contain numerous examples of labor contracts for this period. The one from which I've drawn this paragraph's description is the contract Jacob Klim signed with Mears on July 8, 1859.

57. Labor contract of Samuel Everetts with Charles Mears, Oct. 6, 1857, Mears Papers, CHS.

58. Mears to E. H. Denison, June 5, 1867, Mears Papers, CHS.

59. Mears to Peter D. Fraser, July 4, 1858, Mears Papers, CHS. Mears prided himself on being the employer who "paid less than any one else on the shore"—perhaps about 20 percent less than any of his neighbors. Mears to Fraser, May 20, 1858.

60. Mears to William Sprigg, Oct. 30, 1857, Mears Papers, CHS.

61. Not that Chicago's wages were always the lowest in the area; quite the contrary. In 1867, Mears reported to the Chicago office that he thought Chicago was "paying 30% more than Milwaukee" for workers, and wondered whether there was "to be an effort made to reduce wages in the yards" in Chicago to bring them into line. Mears to E. H. Denison, July 19, 1867, Mears Papers, CHS.

62. William Sprigg to Mears, Dec. 18, 1857, Mears Papers, CHS.

63. Mears to P. D. Fraser, Dec. 21, 1857, Mears Papers, CHS.

64. Mears to William Sprigg, Oct. 30, 1857, Mears Papers, CHS.

65. Mears to P. D. Fraser, Dec. 21, 1857, Mears Papers, CHS. That this practice was not limited to panic years can be seen from Mears's contract of Dec. 6, 1871, with Michael McDonald, in which McDonald cut wood on Mears's land in return for payments in kind from Mears's store in Pentwater.

66. For a general discussion of this topic that is not limited to lumbering, see Margaret Walsh, *The Manufacturing Frontier: Pioneer Industry in Antebellum Wisconsin, 1830–1860* (1972).

67. William Sprigg in Duck Lake to Charles Mears, Nov. 16, 1858, Mears Papers, CHS.

68. Mears to William Sprigg, Nov. 18, 1858, Mears Papers, CHS. Employers suspected incendiarism even when it hadn't occurred; certainly this was true of Mears. He suffered several major fires at his mills and at his Chicago office, and always suspected— sometimes to the point of hiring a detective to investigate—employees. See Mears to H. C. Flagg, Dec. 11, 1865; John Baldwin [?] to Mears, Dec. 9, 1867; Mears to John Smith, July 26, 1875; and John S. Turns to Mears, Nov. 18, 19, 1889. In this last letter, Turns refers to "four or five mysterious and as many people think incendiary fires" at the Mears mills since he began work there.

69. See *NWL*.

70. See, for instance, Charles Mears to John Lamieux, Feb. 10, 1857; Mears to E. H. Denison, Dec. 11, 12, 13, 1867; and Mears to W. J. Croxen, Aug. 9, 1875, all in Mears Papers, CHS. Mears regularly ran his boats late in the year, sometimes during such dangerous weather that he had trouble finding crews: one December, he complained that "the many frightful disasters on the Lakes . . . scared most of the Sailors out of their wits," with the result that few were willing to sign up with him. Mears to John Wallace, Dec. 6, 1871. Reports of shipwrecks were standard fare in the pages of the *NWL*.

71. For a glimpse of what this struggle for money and credit looked like for one individual, see the rather pathetic letter in which Charles Mears, writing near the end of his life, narrated his own credit history to Isaac G. Lombard, whose bank had just refused Mears a loan. Mears to Lombard, Oct. 29, 1891, Mears Papers, CHS.

72. Holt and Balcolm in Chicago to Holt and Balcolm in Oconto, Wisconsin, Sept. 25, 1877, in the Chicago Letter Books of the Holt Lumber Company, SHSW, Green Bay Record Center. (Hereafter cited as Holt Lumber Company Papers, SHSW.)

73. Charles Mears to John Lamieux, Dec. 26, 1856; Mears to E. H. Townsend, March 12, 1856; Mears to Peter D. Fraser, July 4, 1858; Mears to E. H. Denison, June 22, 1867, Sept. 20, 1867, Oct. 3, 1867, Mears Papers, CHS. Mears also tried occasionally to sell furs and fruit even when his lumber business was profitable.

74. Mears (in Chicago) to H. C. Flagg, Nov. 21, 1866, Mears Papers, CHS. For other examples, see Mears to William Sprigg, Oct. 9, 1859; Mears to Peter D. Fraser, July 4, 1858. Although one might assume that the general movement of capital was from the place where goods were being sold to the place where they were being bought, there was no clear tendency for Mears to move money mainly to or from Chicago; indeed, he seems mainly to have wanted money sent wherever he himself was residing.

75. Holt and Balcolm in Chicago to Holt and Balcolm in Oconto, Wisconsin, Sept. 25, 1877, Holt Lumber Company Papers, SHSW.

76. Nathan Mears (in Chicago) to Charles Mears, Oct. 12, 1852, Mears Papers, CHS.

77. As will become clear below, many firms during the pre-1877 period suffered because they lacked this interstate character, precisely because they could not shift capital around in this way.

78. Mears to William Sprigg, Oct. 9, 1859, Mears Papers, CHS.

79. Mears to H. C. Flagg, Dec. 11, 1865, Mears Papers, CHS. For other examples, see Mears to William Sprigg, Oct. 9, 1859, and Mears to Flagg, Nov. 21, 1866.

80. *NWL*, June 2, 1877, 1.

81. In these wholesale markets, most of the stock was sold before it arrived in the city.

82. *NWL*, May 18, 1878, 1.

83. Good summary descriptions of the cargo market in action can be found in *NWL*, May 18, 1878, 1; and "Metropolis of the Prairies," 729–30. More technical details of its operation can be learned from the many criticisms that were directed against it beginning in the late 1870s. See subsequent notes for references to these critiques.

84. "Sound Advice from Chicago," *Wisconsin Lumberman*, June 1874, 236.

85. See, for example, *NWL*, Feb. 24, 1877, 2; and Feb. 22, 1879, 4. In terms of actual volume handled as opposed to stocks maintained, Milwaukee's lumber trade was even less competitive. See "The Lumber Trade of Milwaukee," *Wisconsin Lumberman*, Nov. 1873, 52.

86. *NWL*, Aug. 18, 1883, 2. Milwaukeeans by the 1870s were attributing their city's second-class status to discriminatory railroad rates. See "The Lumber Trade of Milwaukee," *Wisconsin Lumberman*, Nov. 1873, 52–53.

87. "Chicago as Lumber Market," *Wisconsin Lumberman*, Dec. 1874, 201.

88. *NWL*, Sept. 15, 1888, 3.

89. "Chicago Lumber Trade," *Wisconsin Lumberman*, Oct. 1873, 12.

90. [James Parton,] "Chicago," *Atlantic Monthly* 19 (March 1867): 331.

91. *NWL*, April 19, 1879, 3.

92. Muskegon shipped 54 million board feet in 1859, while Green Bay shipped 43 million; Chicago's total receipts were 303 million board feet. CBT, *Annual Report for 1859.*

93. "Metropolis of the Prairies," 729.

94. *NWL*, Feb. 22, 1879, 4.

95. "A Visit to the States: The Metropolis of the Lakes," (London) *Times,* Oct. 21, 1887, 4.

96. "Metropolis of the Prairies," 729.

97. For illustrations of small parts of the district, see ibid., 727; Stone, "Chicago before the Fire," 676; and the photographic collections of CHS. The image that probably best gives a sense of the district is the one that appeared in *Harper's Weekly* on Oct. 20, 1883.

98. The best brief description of these yards in action is in "Metropolis of the Prairies," 729–30; the original plat map of the Chicago South Branch Canal Company, which laid out these lumber canals, is at CHS.

99. Even manufacturers like Mears who owned their own yard tended to ship lumber to Chicago immediately after it was cut, on the assumption that any drying that might be done would occur at the yard. Cf. Isaac Stephenson, *Recollections of a Long Life, 1829–1915* (1915), 82–83.

100. See, for example, the letter from an Iowa dealer in *NWL*, Aug. 27, 1881, 4. Subsequent controversies about dry versus green lumber in relation to railroad rates are examined below.

101. Generally, the nearer one got to newly settled rural areas, the easier it was to sell lower-grade lumber. This is nicely suggested by the following conversation between a Duluth manufacturer and his Chicago visitor in 1882. Explaining that Duluth dealers preferred to sell their product along the far western reaches of the Northern Pacific line in Dakota Territory and beyond, the manufacturer said, "We prefer the markets in that region, for we can sell poorer grades in a new country. Out on the Northern

Pacific they are happy if they can get any kind of lumber. They know little about grades,—lumber is lumber,—and anything pleases them." As the Chicagoan soon discovered, Duluth accordingly graded its "best" wood much more generously than Chicago. "The Lake Superior District," *NWL*, Jan. 7, 1882, 3. Still, by the standards of the twentieth century, even "common" lumber during this period was fine, relatively knotless wood of wide dimensions, since the trees from which it came were old-growth timber the likes of which was gone from the Great Lakes region by the 1920s. All grading standards were necessarily relative, however rigidly they partitioned the market.

102. Grades also began to affect the way mills cut lumber. As Lake Michigan sawmills adopted mass-produced circular and band saws in the years following the Civil War, their output tended to become more similar as well, with production standards geared toward meeting urban grading schemes. One of Chicago's most prominent lumbermen, A. G. Van Schaick, made this point in 1878 when he wrote, "At this time saws and rotary mills located hundreds of miles apart duplicate each other's sawing without apparent intention, and from the adoption of improved and new styles of machinery the sawing of our mills yearly tends toward a common standard." *NWL*, Feb. 23, 1878, 4.

103. Charles E. Twining to William Cronon, Aug. 24, 1989, personal communication.

104. Unsurprisingly, when a futures market in lumber finally did develop in Chicago, at the Board of Trade, it involved that most standardized and homogeneous of twentieth-century building materials—plywood.

105. "Either because it [lumber] has been considered too bulky for such purpose, or the expense of storing and handling it has been thought too great, or the liability to deterioration has been deemed to involve too large an element of risk, or for some other reason, it has always been treated as a product to be dealt in only legitimately, sales being followed up by actual deliveries, and purchases being always made with such expectation." "Lumber as a Speculative Commodity," *NWL*, May 15, 1880, 3.

106. For a brief survey of Chicago's various lumber organizations, see Hotchkiss, *Lumber Industry of the Northwest*, 678–84; the discussions by Hotchkiss in *Chicago: Commerce, Manufactures, Banking and Transportation Facilities* (1884), 164–84; and in *Industrial Chicago*, vol. 3, *The Manufacturing Interests* (1894), 1–580. Despite the relative weakness of their enforcement mechanisms, the formal grading rules of the Lumbermen's Exchange did play an important part in maintaining the rough consensus among wholesalers about how lumber should be graded.

107. See, for instance, *NWL*, Feb. 23, 1878, 3, 4; July 13, 1878, 2; Oct. 11, 1879, 4; Feb. 28, 1880, 2.

108. The best brief survey of this topic is Fred W. Kohlmeyer, "Lumber Distribution and Marketing," in Davis, *Encyclopedia of Forest History*, 365–70. Historically, Mississippi Valley standards had evolved from those of Chicago, so in an indirect sense Chicago did contribute to the eventual adoption of uniform grading standards.

109. Carl W. Condit, "Buildings and Construction," in Melvin Kranzberg and Carroll W. Pursell, Jr., eds., *Technology in Western Civilization*, vol. 1 (1967), 370. See also Walker Field, "A Re-examination into the Invention of the Balloon Frame," *Journal of the Society of Architectural Historians* 2, no. 4 (Oct. 1942): 3–29, which discusses the forerunners of Taylor's church; and Frank Alfred Randall, *History of the Development of Building Construction in Chicago* (1949). A brief biographical sketch of Taylor can be found in Andreas, *History of Cook County*, 145. St. Mary's Church is illustrated ibid., 237.

110. Periam, *Home and Farm Manual*, 385.

111. Later builders would solve this flaw of the original balloon-frame design by nailing horizontal pieces of wood in the spaces between studs to block the building's vertical airflow. The need for such stops has largely disappeared in twentieth-century wooden buildings as carpenters have adopted the modified version of the balloon frame known as the "platform" or "western" frame building. In these structures, the horizontal ribband which originally connected the second floor's joists to the notched two-story studs of the balloon frame has been replaced by joist headers sitting directly atop studs which are only one story high. The joist header supports the load of the floor above it, and incidentally blocks vertical air flow. Interestingly, the platform frame also has the virtue that it no longer requires that studs extend for the full height of the building; as a result, the smaller lumber that has typified twentieth-century milling does not pose

problems for carpenters. For a good brief explanation of these different framing systems, see Charles Wing, *From the Walls In* (1979), 51–60.

112. For a suggestion of how the fire affected Chicago's lumber supply hinterland, see
James Thomas Craig, "Muskegon and the Great Chicago Fire," *Mich. Hist.* 28 (1944):
610–23.

113. "Metropolis of the Prairies," 729.

114. Parton, "Chicago," 333.

115. Robert Harris to N. D. Munson, Jan. 4, 1868, CB&Q Archives.

116. Parton, "Chicago," 333–34. See also *NWL*, April 15, 1882, 7.

117. "Metropolis of the Prairies," 730. On the firms involved in this trade, see the series of
articles entitled "Wood Conversion in Chicago: Sash, Doors, Blinds and Planing" in
NWL, Jan. 15, 22, 29, Feb. 5, 1876.

118. Note that the figures I cite here are only for lumber; they do not include the 168
million shingles and the 32 million pieces of lath shipped from the city in 1860. CBT,
Annual Report for 1860.

119. CBT, *Annual Reports,* 1870, 1880.

120. In 1870, for instance, less than 10 percent of Chicago's lumber shipments left the city
on eastbound railroads. CBT, *Annual Report for 1870.*

121. From other locations, such as some towns in northern Wisconsin, the differential
worked by *adding* cents to the Chicago rate, thus making it *more* expensive to ship from
the pineries than from Chicago. The Bogue award controversy centered on this issue.

122. The clearest discussion of the Bogue award, which quickly became controversial because of its apparent discrimination against the city of Eau Claire, Wisconsin, can be
found in the report of the Interstate Commerce Commission, dated June 17, 1892, on
the case of the *Eau Claire Board of Trade* v. *the Chicago, Milwaukee & St. Paul Railway
Company, et al.* Bogue's own letter of arbitration, dated May 10, 1884, is quoted in full
on pp. 7–8 of this document. Portions of the ICC ruling can be found in Ripley, ed.,
Railway Problems, 231–51. One should note that although the ICC in 1892 lowered
Bogue's differential for Eau Claire after finding it to be discriminatory, and "radically
unsound" in principle, it nonetheless praised the wisdom of Bogue's overall system of
Chicago-centered differentials for having been "observed by so many roads and
proved fairly acceptable to so many communities." The ICC added, "Its correction at
this time in a single particular is no discredit to its general excellence" (p. 13).

123. Bogue Award, as reprinted in Interstate Commerce Commission, Eau Claire ruling,
June 17, 1892, 7.

124. Eau Claire was the most vocal instance of this. See its complaint in the 1892 ICC
ruling, cited above.

125. George W. Hotchkiss, "Lumber," in *Chicago: Commerce Manufactures, Banking and Transportation Facilities,* 168.

126. At the end of 1884, Chicago had 623,910,097 board feet of lumber stored; CBT,
Annual Report for 1884. If we assume that the average sawlog at that time contained
about 200 board feet and that there were perhaps eight to ten such logs in a large tree,
we arrive at the rough numbers given in the text. The figure on average yield per
sawlog is from "Depleted Forests," *NWL,* Feb. 7, 1880, 5.

127. CBT, *Annual Reports.*

128. "The Chicago Wholesale Trade," *NWL,* Sept. 19, 1891, 2.

129. Charles Mears to Isaac G. Lombard, Oct. 29, 1891, original and typescript copy in
Mears Papers, CHS. Details of Mears's harbor-dredging schemes can be found in
several of his letters for 1891.

130. *Oxford English Dictionary;* Mitford M. Mathews, ed., *A Dictionary of Americanisms on Historical Principles* (1951). Again: drummers in the lumber trade were almost universally
men, hence my use of the male pronoun in this sentence. For a fascinating discussion
of drummers and many other aspects of lumber retailing, see Met L. Saley, *Realm of the
Retailer: The Retail Lumber Trade, Its Difficulties and Successes, Its Theory and Practice, with
Practical Yard Ideas* (1902).

131. A concise statement of this argument can be found in "Retail Lumber Dealers' Association," *NWL,* May 25, 1878, 2–3.

132. "Freights," *NWL,* May 13, 1876, 156.

133. Attacks on drummers were a standard feature of the lumber trade journals during the
1870s and were written as much from the perspective of wholesalers as from that of

retailers. Because of the drummers' tendency to cut prices to a bare minimum to acquire orders and earn their commissions, even wholesalers had reservations about using them. Good examples of antidrummer critiques can be found in the *Wisconsin Lumberman,* June 1874, 248; and *NWL,* Oct. 13, 1877, 4; Nov. 10, 1877, 2; Sept. 14, 1878, 2; Oct. 12, 1878, 2, 5; and May 1, 1880, 2. Although the wholesalers were probably right that drummers had an incentive to misrepresent market conditions, arguing with their employers for permission to offer lower prices in order to increase the number of their commissions, it nonetheless seems clear that the ultimate cause of price declines during this period was overproduction. I discuss drummers in other wholesale lines in chapter 7.

134. Letter from "Lux" in Watseka, Ill., in *NWL,* Nov. 24, 1877, 4.
135. Letter from "E. J. R.," *NWL,* Aug. 25, 1877, 4.
136. "The Grange Monopoly," *Wisconsin Lumberman,* Feb. 1874, 294.
137. An example of the way Grange members were encouraged to view retailers can be found in an attack on retail yards published in the catalog of George Woodley, a Chicago wholesaler who specialized in selling to Grange agencies. "I feel humiliated," wrote Woodley, using familiar republican rhetoric, "to know that in this, our boasted Land of Liberty, a few thousand lumber dealers can openly conspire together for the purpose of compelling the hundreds of thousands of the producers and citizens of our country to pay a large tax on their lumber. . . . Our forefathers fought, bled, and died in opposition [to] a tax on tea, which in comparison with this iniquity, sinks into utter insignificance. Is the spirit of 1776 totally extinguished in our bosoms?" Woodley's "Fourth Annual Catalogue," dated Feb. 1, 1878, as quoted in *NWL,* March 23, 1878, 3. (The conspiracy to which Woodley referred was the formation of the NALD, discussed below.) For the story of another Chicago wholesaler who also sold direct to the Grange, without resorting to such rhetoric, see my discussion of Montgomery Ward in chapter 7.
138. "The Grange Monopoly," *Wisconsin Lumberman,* Feb. 1874, 294. I discuss this issue of retail-wholesale conflict in relation to farmers' movements again in chapter 7.
139. Letter from "E. J. R.," *NWL,* Aug. 25, 1877, 4.
140. "Another Organization Wanted," *NWL,* Sept. 1, 1877, 2.
141. According to Judson, his purpose was "to unite the dealers of Illinois and the adjacent states supplied largely from Chicago, in a protective association, having for its immediate object the adjustment of an evil which is injurious to business. . . ." *NWL,* Oct. 13, 1877, 2. One can suspect that he also thought the organization might promote goodwill—and even a few subscriptions—for the *Northwestern Lumberman.* That this was not an idle hope is suggested by the fact that the same agent who was hired to attract members to the NALD was also in charge of selling subscriptions to the *Lumberman. NWL,* Aug. 31, 1878, 1.
142. For documents and minutes pertaining to the formation of the organization, see *NWL,* Sept. 8, 1877, 2; Sept. 22, 1877, 2; Nov. 10, 1877, 2–3; June 28, 1879, 3.
143. *NWL,* June 8, 1878, 4. I will use the acronym NALD even when referring to the earlier period when the organization had another name.
144. *NWL,* Nov. 10, 1877, 3.
145. Initially, fines were $10 per carload of common lumber, $15 per carload of better grades, and 20 percent of the value of sash, door, and blind shipments. (These and other details come from the minutes of the first meeting as printed in *NWL,* Nov. 10, 1877, 3.) By June 1878, these numbers had dropped to $5, $8, and 10 percent, respectively.
146. Judson held the secretary's post until July 1880, by which time the organization had lost most of its original fervor. *NWL,* July 17, 1880, 3–5. Not surprisingly, the *Lumberman* came under criticism during his tenure, especially from wholesalers, for being too closely affiliated with the NALD. In 1878, for instance, the *Inter-Ocean,* one of Chicago's major dailies, wrote, that "The NORTHWESTERN LUMBERMAN, of this city, published ostensibly in the interests of the lumber trade at large, but more really playing into the hands of country retailers, to put it mildly, is a journalistic mountebank and quack." *NWL,* Oct. 5, 1878, 2. The *Inter-Ocean*'s criticisms were in fact much too strong, since the *Lumberman* made a clear effort to speak on behalf of as many interests in the industry as it could—if only to assure itself the widest possible subscription base. The only group it never defended was organized labor, which its editors apparently did not regard as fertile ground for subscriptions.

147. In order to warn wholesalers about the potential influence of its membership in the event of a boycott, the NALD in 1878 began to publish its membership list regularly in the pages of the *Northwestern Lumberman.* The first such list was in *NWL,* June 15, 1878, 6; the NALD's reasons for printing it are given in *NWL,* May 25, 1878, 2–3.

148. NALD membership list, *NWL,* Jan. 31, 1880, 22–23.

149. *NWL,* June 1, 1878, 2.

150. *NWL,* July 12, 1879, 2.

151. *NWL,* July 17, 1880, 3.

152. Compare articles on NALD in *NWL,* Sept. 2, 1882, 5; May 12, 1883, 4; June 21, 1884, 2; May 15, 1886, 3; and Oct. 9, 1886.

153. "The Chicago Auction Market," *NWL,* Jan. 18, 1879, 2–3.

154. "A Remedy," *NWL,* Aug. 25, 1877, 2.

155. "Sound Advice from Chicago," *Wisconsin Lumberman,* June 1874, 236.

156. "A Remedy," *NWL,* Aug. 25, 1877, 2.

157. Cf. "The Chicago Cargo Market," *NWL,* April 19, 1879, 3: "They are without the money to carry it [business] on successfully, and so they endeavor to supply the deficiency by borrowing. This expedient soon creates a host of obligations which must be met as they become due, and the only way that can be done is to cut as much lumber as possible, rush it off to the Chicago market, and sell it for whatever the buyer feels willing to pay. What is the result? Simply that each season they have to cut a larger amount and sell it at a lower price. . . ."

158. "The Chicago Auction Market," *NWL,* Jan. 18, 1879, 3.

159. Data from CBT, *Annual Reports.* Useful compilations of time series for lumber production at various points on Lake Michigan, derived from the *Northwestern Lumberman*'s annual reviews, can be found in James B. Smith, "Lumbertowns in the Cutover: A Comparative Study of the Stage Hypothesis of Urban Growth" (Ph.D. thesis, Univ. of Wisconsin, Madison, 1973). All percentages in this paragraph are calculated from CBT data in combination with *NWL* annual reviews.

160. It is worth remembering that *all* lumber production and sales statistics for this period—like nineteenth-century commodity statistics generally—were gathered privately by trade journals and organizations, and have very large margins of error. Census data were little better, and may have been, if the lumber press is to believed, a lot worse. The *Northwestern Lumberman* regularly discussed the difficulties of acquiring good trade information, and published a number of useful critiques of the efforts by early foresters to quantify timber supply and production in the Great Lakes region. See, for instance, *NWL,* Sept. 20, 1879, 3–4; Nov. 8, 1879, 5; Jan. 27, 1883, 4; March 10, 1883, 5; and Sept. 15, 1888, 2. The percentages I offer in this paragraph nonetheless almost surely convey the right orders of magnitude concerning the relative mutual dependency of Chicago and the Lake Michigan lumber towns.

161. Interestingly, Chicago's own *Northwestern Lumberman*—trying to live up to its claim of being regional rather than local in its interests—supported the manufacturers as strongly as it did the retailers in their criticisms of the city's market. Its regular analyses of how Chicago's wholesalers and cargo market depressed prices and profits helped confirm the manufacturers' hostile attitude toward the city. Typical of its editorials was this prophetic prediction in 1877: "All the signs indicate that the Chicago wholesale lumber market will, at no very distant day become a thing of the past. Viewed in no matter what light, it seems to be a nuisance and a curse to the trade, not only of the Northwest, but the country at large." "A Wholesale Evil," *NWL,* Nov. 3, 1877, 2.

162. A good early example of this attitude can be found in "The Middle Men," *Wisconsin Lumberman,* Sept. 1874, 565–67.

163. *Michigan Lumberman* [1873?], reprinted in "Chicago Lumber Trade," *Wisconsin Lumberman,* Oct. 1873, 13.

164. James Glasgow, "Muskegon, Michigan: The Evolution of a Lake Port" (Ph.D. thesis, Univ. of Chicago, 1939), 45–46; and Krog, "Marinette," 60. Reliable maps for U.S. rail systems in any given year of the nation's history are surprisingly difficult to locate, and an atlas of them remains badly needed in historical geography. The best contemporary sources are probably the annual editions of *Poor's Manual of Railroads.* For a suberb collection of maps showing the annual extension of Wisconsin's railroads, see Richard L. Canuteson, "The Railway Development of Northern Wisconsin" (M.A. thesis, Univ. of Wisconsin, 1930).

165. *NWL,* Aug. 25, 1877, 2.

166. In 1881, the *Northwestern Lumberman* reported, "One extreme case of which we have learned, and which occurred at a market competing with Chicago, was that of four cars loaded with lumber, billed at 24,000 pounds each, but which, on being placed upon the scales, were found to be so heavy that the scales would not weigh them, and upon the lumber being weighed by the wagon load an excess of over 62,000 pounds was discovered, the extra charges on which exceeded $200." "Lumber Is Shipped by Weight," *NWL*, March 12, 1881, 2.

167. One minor consequence was a whole new terrain for conflict between lumbermen and railroads over whether measured weights for lumber cars were accurate. The angry letter William A. Holt sent to the Michigan, Lake Shore, and Western Railroad on Sept. 7, 1886, was typical of the genre: "Any lumberman or any one else familiar with the facts will tell you that no *dry lumber ever yet* weighed what you claim." Holt Lumber Company Papers, SHSW.

168. *NWL*, Sept. 15, 1877, 2–3; March 12, 1881, 2. The organization that standardized shipments by weight was the Northwestern Weighing Association, based in Chicago.

169. *NWL*, Sept. 15, 1877, 2.

170. *NWL*, Aug. 25, 1877, 2.

171. "Lake Michigan Trade—An Impending Change," *NWL*, March 13, 1886, 2.

172. *NWL*, April 30, 1881, 3; see also June 28, 1884, 2.

173. Cf. "The Cargo Market and the Yard Trade," *NWL*, July 9, 1887, 3.

174. Their problem was exacerbated by the increasing presence of lumber buyers from the Northeast, who were looking to midwestern white pine as eastern supplies diminished. See *NWL*, Oct. 9, 1886, 2; Sept. 10, 1887, 3; Oct. 1, 1887, 2; Dec. 3, 1887, 2; April 19, 1890, 2; July 5, 1890, 2; Sept. 19, 1891, 2.

175. *NWL*, April 21, 1883, 5.

176. "The New Menominee Departure," *NWL*, March 19, 1887, 16. See also March 20, 1886, 2; Nov. 13, 1886, 3. See also " 'The Future of the Chicago Lumber Trade,' " written by one of the Menominee millmen, in *NWL*, March 21, 1885, 6–7, and its sequel on April 4, 1885, 16.

177. Useful surveys of the Iowa sawmills can be found in George Bernhardt Hartman, "The Iowa Sawmill Industry," *Iowa Journal of History and Politics* 40 (1942): 52–93; Lyda Belthuis, "The Lumber Industry in Eastern Iowa," ibid., 46 (1948): 115–55; George W. Sieber, "Sawmilling on the Mississippi: The W. J. Young Lumber Company, 1858–1900" (Ph.D. thesis, Univ. of Iowa, 1960); George W. Sieber, "Railroads and Lumber Marketing, 1858–78: The Relationship between an Iowa Sawmill Firm and the Chicago and Northwestern Railroad," *Annals of Iowa*, 3d ser., 39 (1967): 33–46.

178. Weyerhaeuser's activities in the upper Mississippi Valley are recounted in Ralph W. Hidy, Frank Ernest Hill, and Allan Nevins, *Timber and Men: The Weyerhaeuser Story* (1963); but see also Matthew G. Norton, *The Mississippi River Logging Company: An Historical Sketch* (1912); Roujet D. Marshall, *Autobiography*, ed. Gilson G. Glasier (1923); Bernhardt J. Kleven, "The Mississippi River Logging Company," *Minn. Hist.* 27 (1946): 190–202; Robert F. Fries, "The Mississippi River Logging Company and the Struggle for the Free Navigation of Logs, 1865–1900," *MVHR* 35 (1948): 429–48; Paul Wallace Gates, "Weyerhaeuser and the Chippewa Logging Industry," in O. Fritiof Ander, ed., *The John H. Hauberg Historical Essays*, Augustana Library Publications, no. 26 (1954), 50–64; Twining, *Downriver;* and Malcolm Rosholt, *Lumbermen on the Chippewa* (1982).

179. As early as September 1874, the *Wisconsin Lumberman* was reporting, "Many prominent pine land owners are investigating the pineries of the southern states with a view to investment of capital," though its editor still had no hesitation in asserting, "Yellow pine cannot supply the place of white pine. . . ." "Southern Pine Lands," *Wisconsin Lumberman*, Sept. 1874, 565.

180. *NWL*, May 12, 1877, 1.

181. For contemporary discussions of yellow pine for use in buildings, see *NWL*, May 6, 1882, 4–5; July 12, 1884, 2–3.

182. George Hotchkiss saw 1884 as the real beginning of the yellow pine invasion of Chicago's territory, and *NWL* articles from the period bear him out. Hotchkiss, *Lumber Industry of the Northwest*, 680. Although separate statistics for yellow pine are difficult to come by, it appears that approximately 20 million board feet of it arrived in Chicago in 1884, of which more than half—12 million—was used in the city itself, mainly for flooring. *NWL*, July 12, 1884, 2.

183. For an antiquarian survey of the Kansas City trade, see Chas. P. Deatherage, *The Early History of the Lumber Trade of Kansas City* (1924).

184. *NWL,* Nov. 6, 1886, 1.

185. "Piece Stuff in the Chicago Market," *NWL,* Feb. 8, 1890, 2.

186. "Territorial Limitation in the Lumber Trade," *NWL,* Feb. 22, 1890, 2.

187. "Logging Roads," *NWL,* March 25, 1882, 7.

188. *NWL,* Feb. 18, 1882, 8; Jan. 10, 1885, 2–4; March 1, 1890, 2; April 12, 1890, 2; Dec. 19, 1891, 2. The article "Chicago's Hardwood Supply," *NWL,* June 14, 1884, 2–3, is particularly helpful in identifying the supply regions for the different species of hardwoods sold in Chicago.

189. The statistics in this paragraph are all calculated from CBT, *Annual Reports.* Note that the only year prior to 1880 in which more than 10 percent of Chicago's lumber came to it by rail was 1872, when the city was rebuilding after the Great Fire of the year before. The ability of local urban demand to pull in railroad shipments from afar was symptomatic of the trend that soon developed in the industry as a whole.

190. Marx, *Grundrisse,* 524.

191. "Territorial Limitation in the Lumber Trade," *NWL,* Feb. 22, 1890, 2.

192. George S. Kaime, "Where Our Lumber Comes From," *Western Monthly* 3 (1870): 191. Kaime was speaking broadly about the entire nation's supply of timber, not just that of the Great Lakes, but his general attitude applied to the regional supply as well.

193. An important article on this early period of forest conservation is Donald J. Pisani's "Forests and Conservation, 1865–1890," *JAH* 72 (1985): 340–59.

194. James Little, "The Timber Supply," *NWL,* July 29, 1876, 243. The rest of Little's article, which was published in sections, can be found in the July 22 and Aug. 5 issues.

195. For examples, see *NWL,* Jan. 27, 1883, 4; March 10, 1883, 5; May 19, 1883, 5; April 5, 1884, 2; and Sept. 15, 1888, 2.

196. "Where Will the Uppers Come From?" *NWL,* Sept. 27, 1879, 4. On stumpage increases, see *NWL,* Nov. 6, 1886, 1; Jan. 29, 1887, 2; and Oct. 4, 1890, 2. Interestingly, the competition of yellow pine put a ceiling on how high the price of white pine timber and stumpage could rise before consumers would start purchasing the other wood. This was an important reason why many Lake Michigan manufacturers and wholesalers found it increasingly difficult to make a profit by the late 1880s.

197. "Depleted Forests," *NWL,* Feb. 7, 1880, 5; "Ten Years Ago," Dec. 10, 1881, 2. The average number of board feet per log received at Saginaw in 1870 was 229 feet, a number that had fallen to 143 feet by 1879. In 1893, the average log at Menominee contained only 117 feet. *Annual Report of the Menominee River Boom Co., 1893* (1893), 24.

198. "The Decline in Quality—Its Effect on Values," *NWL,* Sept. 1, 1883, 5.

199. "Where Will the Uppers Come From?" *NWL,* Sept. 27, 1879, 4.

200. Ibid.

201. "Low Grade White Pine," *NWL,* Oct. 4, 1890, 2.

202. "Ten Years Ago," *NWL,* Dec. 10, 1881, 2.

203. "An Important Movement," *NWL,* Jan. 29, 1887, 2.

204. For statistics, see R. V. Reynolds and A. H. Pierson, *Forest Products Statistics of the Lake States,* USDA Statistical Bulletin no. 68 (1939). For details of how this process affected hinterland lumber towns, see Krog, "Marinette"; and H. J. Hirshheimer, "The Passing of the Sawmills and the Growth of Manufactures in La Crosse, 1880–1905," *La Crosse County Historical Sketches,* ser. 3, *The Lumber Industry* (1937), 69–99.

205. These fires and their surrounding history are brilliantly described in Pyne, *Fire in America,* 199–218.

206. For an accessible discussion of these changes, see Clifford Ahlgren and Isabel Ahlgren, *Lob Trees in the Wilderness* (1984), 93–124; see also Daniel and Sullivan, *North Woods,* 204–10.

207. *Report of the Forestry Commission of the State of Wisconsin* (1898), 18.

208. On the problems of the Cutover, see Alvah L. Sawyer, "The Forests of the Upper Peninsula and Their Place in History," *Mich. Hist.* 3 (1919): 367–83; Russell Watson, "Forest Devastation in Michigan: A Study of Some of Its Deleterious Economic Effects," *Journal of Forestry* 21 (1923): 425–51; William N. Sparhawk and Warren D. Brush, *The Economic Aspects of Forest Destruction in Northern Michigan,* USDA Technical Bulletin no. 92 (1929); Leo Alilunas, "Michigan's Cut-Over 'Canaan,' " *Mich. Hist.* 26 (1942): 188–201; Orman S. Danford, "The Social and Economic Effects of Lumbering on Michigan, 1835–1890," ibid., 346–64; *1848–1948: A History of the Wisconsin Paper*

Industry (1948); Maurice Lloyd Branch, "The Paper Industry in the Lake States Region, 1834–1947" (Ph.D. thesis, Univ. of Wisconsin, 1954); Vernon Carstensen, *Farms or Forests: Evolution of a State Land Policy for Northern Wisconsin, 1850–1932* (1958); Erling D. Solberg, *New Laws for New Forests: Wisconsin's Forest-Fire, Tax, Zoning, and County-Forest Laws in Operation* (1961); Arlan Helgesen, *Farms in the Cutover: Agricultural Settlement in Northern Wisconsin* (1962); Charles Gordon Mehaffey, "Changing Images of the Cutover: A Historical Geography of Resource Utilization in the Lake Superior Region, 1840–1930" (Ph.D. thesis, Univ. of Wisconsin, Madison, 1978); Ronald N. Johnson and Gary D. Libecap, "Efficient Markets and Great Lakes Timber: A Conservation Issue Reexamined," *Explorations in Economic History* 17 (1980): 372–85; and Flader, *Great Lakes Forest.* On the legacy of place-names that still mark the north woods from lumbering days, see Randall E. Rohe, "Place-names: Relics of the Great Lakes Lumber Era," *Journal of Forest History* 28 (1984): 126–35. Finally, I cannot close this chapter without acknowledging the extraordinary work of James Willard Hurst in *Law and Economic Growth: The Legal History of the Lumber Industry in Wisconsin, 1836–1915* (1964). Although my focus in this chapter on Chicago has prevented me from making direct use of Hurst's book, his analysis of the legal conditions under which lumber and other commodity markets evolved in the second half of the nineteenth century underpins my entire argument. He addresses state regulatory responses to the Cutover, and all other aspects of lumbering as well. For a more general discussion of these same issues, see James Willard Hurst, *Law and Markets in United States History: Different Modes of Bargaining among Interests* (1982).

209. "Steady Prices—Sure Profits," *NWL,* May 11, 1889, 2.
210. "A Trade Evolution," *NWL,* April 12, 1890, 2.
211. "The Growth of Cities," *NWL,* July 19, 1890, 2.
212. Brigham, "Lumber Region of Michigan," 97–98.
213. Stephenson, *Recollections of a Long Life,* 205. For a comparable view, see John Emmett Nelligan, *The Life of a Lumberman* (1929), 29: "It was almost a crime against Nature to cut it, but we lumbermen were never concerned with crimes against Nature. We heard only the demand for lumber, more lumber, and better lumber." This theme of American abundance as a windfall of the wealth of nature is explored in Walter Prescott Webb, *The Great Frontier* (1952); and David M. Potter, *People of Plenty: Economic Abundance and the American Character* (1954). I discuss this theme of abundance in relation to Frederick Jackson Turner in my "Revisiting the Vanishing Frontier." For discussions that relate directly to lumbering, see D. C. Everest, "A Reappraisal of the Lumber Barons," *Wis. Mag. Hist.* 36 (1952): 17–22; and Charles E. Twining, "Plunder and Progress: The Lumbering Industry in Perspective," ibid., 47 (1963): 116–24.

5: ANNIHILATING SPACE: MEAT

1. "Visit to the States," 4.
2. G. W. S. Patterson, *The World's Fair and My Trip round the World* (1894), 70–71.
3. "Metropolis of the Prairies," 730.
4. Rudyard Kipling, *From Sea to Sea: Letters of Travel* (1899), 2:153.
5. Upton Sinclair, *The Jungle* (1906; reprint, 1960), 40.
6. The most comprehensive modern history of the yards is Louise Carroll Wade, *Chicago's Pride: The Stockyards, Packingtown, and Environs in the Nineteenth Century* (1987); on their origin and construction, see pp. 47–60. For an anecdotal contemporary survey, see W. Jos. Grand, *Illustrated History of the Union Stockyards* (1896). See also Howard Copeland Hill, "The Development of Chicago as a Center of the Meat Packing Industry," *MVHR* 10 (1923–24): 253–73.
7. "Visit to the States," 4.
8. Colbert, *Chicago,* 59–60; Pierce, *History of Chicago,* 2:92; Wade, *Chicago's Pride,* 6–7, 25–28.
9. Jack Wing, *The Great Union Stock Yards of Chicago* (1865), 10–11.
10. Colbert, *Chicago,* 60.
11. Wing, *Union Stock Yards,* 12; Joseph G. Knapp, "A Review of Chicago Stock Yards History," *University [of Chicago] Journal of Business* 2 (1923–24): 331–46; "The Union Stockyards, December 25, 1865," *Chicago History* 7 (1965–66): 289–96; Wade, *Chicago's Pride,* 47–50. The nine railroad companies that sponsored the prospectus were the

Chicago, Burlington and Quincy; the Chicago and Northwestern; the Chicago and Milwaukee; the Chicago and Rock Island; the Chicago and Alton; the Michigan Southern; the Michigan Central; the Illinois Central; and the Pittsburgh, Fort Wayne, and Chicago. They did not hold their stock for long. See Porter, *Short Autobiography,* 21–22.

12. Parton, "Chicago," 332.

13. The directors of the stockyard company at least in theory intended to make their profits mainly by selling hay and corn as feed; yard charges were otherwise set at rates designed mainly to recover capital costs. Parton, "Chicago," 333.

14. Wing, *Union Stock Yards;* Wade, *Chicago's Pride,* 50–54; Colbert, *Chicago,* 60.

15. Wing, *Union Stock Yards,* 24.

16. Ibid., 29.

17. Parton, "Chicago," 333.

18. Ibid.

19. George Catlin, *Letters and Notes on the Manners, Customs, and Conditions of the North American Indians* (1844; reprint, 1973), 2:17.

20. On the fire history of the prairies, the best brief synthesis is Pyne, *Fire in America,* 84–99.

21. The best popular account of the tallgrass prairie, beautifully written and scientifically quite accurate, is Madson's superb *Where the Sky Began.* Among the classic prairie studies are Curtis, *Vegetation of Wisconsin;* J. E. Weaver, *North American Prairie* (1954); and J. E. Weaver and T. J. Fitzpatrick, "The Prairie," *Ecological Monographs* 4 (1934): 109–295. James C. Malin, *The Grassland of North America: Prolegomena to Its History with Addenda and Postscript* (1947; reprinted with postscript, 1967), deals with the history of grasslands generally; for an anthology of contemporary descriptions, see Dondore, *Prairie and Middle America;* and for a popular science discussion of grassland ecosystems worldwide, see Paul B. Sears, *Lands beyond the Forest* (1969). See also the able review essay by Paul G. Risser, "Grasslands," in Brian F. Chabot and Harold A. Mooney, eds., *Physiological Ecology of North American Plant Communities* (1985), 232–56; and the equally useful essay by Phillip L. Sims, "Grasslands," in Michael G. Barbour and William Dwight Billings, eds., *North American Terrestrial Vegetation* (1988), 265–86. On the effects of agriculture, see J. E. Weaver, "Some Ecological Aspects of Agriculture in the Prairie," *Ecology* 8 (1927): 1–17. For discussions of prairie remnants, see Donald Christisen, "A Vignette of Missouri's Native Prairie," *Mo. Hist. Rev.* 61 (1967): 166–86; Richard Brewer, "Death by the Plow," *Natural History,* Aug.–Sept. 1970, 28–35, 110; W. J. Beecher, "The Lost Illinois Prairie," *Chicago History,* n.s. 2, no. 3 (Spring–Summer 1973): 166–72.

22. An excellent popular account of these western grasslands can be found in Lauren Brown, *Audubon Nature Society Guides: Grasslands* [1985]. The floristics of Great Plains grasses and forbs are usefully summarized in Great Plains Flora Association, *Atlas of the Flora of the Great Plains* (1977). A thorough but somewhat dated ecological description is J. E. Weaver and F. W. Albertson, *Grasslands of the Great Plains: Their Nature and Use* (1956); the classic historical account is Walter Prescott Webb, *The Great Plains* (1931), which should be read in conjunction with Malin, *Grassland of North America.*

23. Donald Worster explores some of the consequences of agricultural settlement on the plains in his *Dust Bowl: The Southern Plains in the 1930s* (1979). Useful agricultural history surveys which explore these issues include Gilbert Fite, *The Farmer's Frontier, 1865–1900* (1966); Everett Dick, *The Sod-House Frontier, 1854–1890: A Social History of the Northern Plains from the Creation of Kansas and Nebraska to the Admission of the Dakotas* (1937); and Shannon, *Farmer's Last Frontier.*

24. Charles Wentworth Dilke, *Greater Britain: A Record of Travel in English-Speaking Countries during 1866–7* (1869), 114.

25. Bison population statistics are necessarily based on only the crudest of estimates. The fullest discussion of the relevant sources for such estimates is Frank Gilbert Roe, *The North American Buffalo: A Critical Study of the Species in Its Wild State,* 2d ed. (1970), 489–520. Two earlier surveys that remain important as documents are Joel A. Allen, "The American Bison, Living and Extinct," *Memoirs of the Museum of Comparative Zoology* (Harvard University), 4, no. 10 (1876): 1–246; and William T. Hornaday, *The Extermination of the American Bison* (1887). Dan Flores has been reevaluating the environmental history of bison on the plains, but has not yet published his work.

26. On the effects of the bison herds on prairie vegetation, see Floyd Larson, "The Role of

the Bison in Maintaining the Short Grass Plains," *Ecology* 21 (1940): 113–21. For a more general discussion of grazing effects on the plains, see Weaver, *North American Prairie*, 271–96.

27. Classic firsthand descriptions of these herds include Catlin, *Letters and Notes*, 1:247–64; and Richard Irving Dodge, *The Plains of the Great West and Their Inhabitants* (1877; reprint, 1959), 119–47.

28. Catlin, *Letters and Notes*, 1:249.

29. Edwin James, *Account of an Expedition from Pittsburgh to the Rocky Mountains* (1823; reprint, 1966), 470.

30. Roe, *North American Buffalo*, provides an abundant stock of quotations from early travelers' accounts, as does one of the earliest scientific treatises on the animal, Allen's "American Bison." For a more recent popular account similarly stocked with extracts, see Tom McHugh, *The Time of the Buffalo* (1972). For Rundle's words, see ibid., 14.

31. Hays, *The Herd on the Move*, original oil painting in the Gilcrease Art Gallery, Tulsa, Okla.; a lithographic version is reproduced in Larry Barsness, *The Bison in Art: A Graphic Chronicle of the American Bison* (1977), 60–61.

32. Catlin, *Letters and Notes*, 1:256. In a remarkable passage, Catlin predicted the destruction of the herds forty years before it happened, recording a prophetic vision in which "Hundreds and thousands [of the animals] were strewed upon the plains—they were flayed, and their reddened carcasses left; and about them bands of wolves, and dogs, and buzzards were seen devouring them." He continued, "I cast my eyes into the towns and cities of the East, and there I beheld buffalo robes hanging at almost every door for traffic; and I saw also the curling smokes of a thousand *Stills*—and I said, 'Oh insatiable man, is thy avarice such! wouldst thou tear the skin from the back of the last animal of this noble race, *and rob thy fellow-man of his meat, and for it give him poison!*'" Catlin went on to make the first American proposal for a national park that would preserve Great Plains Indians and bison alike. Ibid., 259–60; the national park proposal is on pp. 260–64.

33. McHugh, *Time of Buffalo*, 247–53, summarizes such episodes.

34. E. Douglas Branch, *The Hunting of the Buffalo* (1929; reprint, 1962), 151–53.

35. Dodge, *Plains of the Great West*, 119–47, is probably the best firsthand account of this period. Dodge's careful statistical estimates of waste and total kill during the 1870s can be found on pp. 131–44; the quotation is on p. 134.

36. Ibid., 136.

37. Ibid., 133.

38. Catlin, *Letters and Notes*, 1:261.

39. Dodge, *Plains*, 132.

40. For a few years after the animals disappeared, there remained a substantial market in their sun-bleached bones. Bone collectors gathered bison skeletons by the ton and shipped them back to eastern cities, where they were ground up for phosphorous fertilizer to be used on farms where the initial fertility of forest and prairie soil had waned. Bison bones were an important source of early income for many families struggling to set up farms on the plains.

41. Joseph G. McCoy, *Historic Sketches of the Cattle Trade of the West and Southwest* (1874; reprint, 1966), 40.

42. Ibid., 44.

43. Ibid., 52–53

44. There is no alternative gender-neutral vocabulary to describe "cowboys" or "cattlemen," but, like the sexism in the language of lumbering, the sexism of these terms reflects the overwhelmingly male composition of the range industry labor force. Women played important roles in the cattle towns—prostitution was one of the key attractions of the drovers' hotels that operated in such places—and they became more important and their numbers grew as the industry shifted toward permanent ranches as centers of cattle production. There, an integrated family economy emerged in which women's work was no less significant than men's. But for the period of Chicago's early dominance of the livestock industry on the western plains, men were the major players in the economy, at least until the animals reached the feedlots of Illinois and Iowa.

45. Still the best account of the cattle drives is Andy Adams, *The Log of a Cowboy: A Narrative of the Old Trail Days* (1903; reprint, 1964); see also "Where the Beef Comes From,"

Lippincott's Magazine 24 (1879): 573–79; Charles A. Siringo, *A Texas Cowboy; or, Fifteen Years on the Hurricane Deck of a Spanish Pony* (1885; reprint 1979).

46. For a study that emphasizes this aspect of the long drives, see Jimmy M. Skaggs, *The Cattle-Trailing Industry: Between Supply and Demand, 1866–1890* (1973).

47. In addition to resenting the destruction that Texas cattle visited upon their fields, Kansas farmers fought the cattle drives for a subtler ecological reason. The mild southern winters allowed Texas longhorns to serve as hosts for ticks which could not survive the cold farther north; the ticks in turn were the vectors for transmitting minute parasites known as piroplasms. Texas longhorns were generally immune to the effects of these microorganisms, but northern cattle and milch cows were not. Once infected, they developed high fevers, and their livers and spleens became enlarged; up to 90 percent of those with acute cases soon died. By the 1860s, farmers in Kansas and other northern areas were referring to the disease as Texas fever, and urging legislatures to ban the importation of southern animals. Quarantine lines were eventually created to support such a ban, and the gradual westward migration of the lines forced each of the major Kansas cattle towns out of the livestock business. On the history of tick fever and efforts to control it, see the useful survey by T. W. Cole and Wm. M. MacKellar, "Cattle Tick Fever," in USDA, *The Yearbook of Agriculture 1956: Animal Diseases* (1956), 310–12; on its relation to the Kansas cattle drives, the classic account is still Dykstra, *Cattle Towns.* See also James W. Whitaker, *Feedlot Empire: Beef Cattle Feeding in Illinois and Iowa, 1840–1900* (1975), 59–63; and H. Craig Miner, *Wichita: The Early Years, 1865–80* (1982); and Miner, *West of Wichita: Settling the High Plains of Kansas, 1865–1890* (1986).

48. The best general account of ranching on the northern plains remains Ernest Staples Osgood, *The Day of the Cattleman* (1929; reprint, n.d.). See also Maurice Frink, W. Turrentine Jackson, and Agnes Wright Spring, *When Grass Was King: Contributions to the Western Range Cattle Industry Study* (1956); Lewis Atherton, *The Cattle Kings* (1961; reprint, 1972); and Gene M. Gressley, *Bankers and Cattlemen* (1966).

49. Granville Stuart, *Forty Years on the Frontier, as Seen in the Journals and Reminiscences of Granville Stuart, Gold-Miner, Trader, Merchant, Rancher and Politician,* ed. Paul C. Phillips (1925), 2:187–88.

50. Osgood, *Day of the Cattleman,* 176–215.

51. Weaver, *North American Prairie,* 273–86; Weaver, *Prairie Plants and Their Environment: A Fifty-Year Study in the Midwest* (1968), 195–207; Charles Clinton Smith, "The Effect of Overgrazing and Erosion upon the Biota of the Mixed-Grass Prairie of Oklahoma," *Ecology* 21 (1940): 381–97; and R. M. Moore and E. F. Biddiscombe, "The Effects of Grazing on Grasslands," in C. Barnard, ed., *Grasses and Grasslands* (1964), 221–35.

52. The separation of herds could be legal instead of physical, as when several owners collectively conducted a "roundup" to brand their animals with distinctive marks. Once branded, animals could graze together as a single physical herd without their owners having to worry about securing property rights. But where grazing resources were scarce, such legal separation ultimately proved inadequate, and the physical separation of fencing became necessary.

53. I have written at some length about the ecological and cultural implications of fencing in my *Changes in the Land,* 130–38.

54. The classic account of fencing on the Great Plains is Webb, *Great Plains,* 280–318; the subject is treated at much greater length in Henry D. McCallum and Frances T. McCallum, *The Wire That Fenced the West* (1965); see also Earl W. Hayter, *The Troubled Farmer, 1850–1900: Rural Adjustment to Industrialism* (1968), 85–103, 228–45; and Joseph M. McFadden, "Monopoly in Barbed Wire: The Formation of the American Steel and Wire Company," *Bus. Hist. Rev.* 52 (1978): 465–89. It is probably no accident that Glidden manufactured his invention in DeKalb, Illinois, some fifty miles west of the transportation center that would spread it far and wide across the West: Chicago.

55. Pyne, *Fire in America,* 84–99.

56. The best discussion of midwestern agriculture in this period remains Bogue, *Prairie to Cornbelt.* On livestock, see pp. 86–122.

57. The midwestern cattle kings have been well described in Paul Wallace Gates, "Hoosier Cattle Kings," *Indiana Magazine of History* 44 (1948): 1–24; Gates, "Cattle Kings in the Prairies," *MVHR* 35 (1948): 379–412; Helen M. Cavanagh, *Funk of Funk's Grove: Farmer, Legislator, and Cattle King of the Old Northwest, 1797–1865* (1952); Margaret Beat-

tie Bogue, *Patterns from the Sod: Land Use and Tenure in the Grand Prairie, 1850–1900* (1959), 48–112; and Allan Bogue, *Prairie to Cornbelt,* 86–102.

58. Margaret Bogue, *Patterns from the Sod,* 68–69.

59. Allan Bogue, *Prairie to Cornbelt,* 96–102.

60. J. Shaw to Seth Bird, March 7, 1838, Shaw Family Papers, Newberry Library.

61. On breeding, see Gates, *Farmer's Age.*

62. The best survey of this subject is Whitaker, *Feedlot Empire;* but see also John A. Hopkins, Jr., *Economic History of the Production of Beef Cattle in Iowa* (1928); and Rudolf Alexander Clemen, *The American Livestock and Meat Industry* (1923), 47–91, 190–210. For a good contemporary description of this breeder-feeder system in action, see Paul de Rousiers, *American Life,* trans. A. J. Herbertson (1892), 39–56.

63. Indians were by no means passive in their use of grazing animals on the plains. Although bison were not particularly tractable as herd animals, after the seventeenth century the Plains tribes kept substantial herds of horses and conducted a major south–north trade which bore some resemblance to the later Euroamerican livestock industry. See Richard White, "The Winning of the West: The Expansion of the Western Sioux in the Eighteenth and Nineteenth Centuries," *JAH* 55 (1978): 319–43.

64. Allan Bogue, *Prairie to Corn Belt,* 102.

65. On the history of early packing, see Clemen, *Livestock and Meat,* 110–34; and Lynn Ramsay Edminster's still valuable survey "Meat Packing and Slaughtering," in Edwin R. A. Seligman, ed., *Encyclopaedia of the Social Sciences* (1933), 242–49. Joy Morton, founder of Chicago's Morton Salt Company, would make a fortune for himself by servicing this rural and urban demand for salt; see James D. Norris and James Livingston, "Joy Morton and the Conduct of Modern Business Enterprise," *Chicago History* 10, no. 1 (Spring 1981): 13–25.

66. On Chicago's participation in the English trade, see Colbert, *Chicago,* 59; it is not wholly accurate, however, as evidenced by Charles T. Leavitt, "Some Economic Aspects of the Western Meat-Packing Industry, 1830–1860," *Journal of Business* 4 (1931): 86–87. For an early account of beef packing for the English market in Chicago, see "Beef Packing in Chicago by Wadsworth, Dyer & Co.," *Prairie Farmer* 8 (1848): 336–37.

67. For a comprehensive survey of nineteenth-century pork-packing techniques, see *Directory and Hand-Book of the Meat and Provision Trades and Their Allied Industries for the United States and Canada* (1895), 273–380; see also Institute of American Meat Packers, *The Packing Industry* (1924).

68. Clemen, *Livestock and Meat,* 58–59.

69. Charles Townsend Leavitt, "The Meat and Dairy Livestock Industry" (Ph.D. thesis, Univ. of Chicago, 1931), 149–56; see also James W. Thompson, *History of Livestock Raising in the United States, 1607–1860,* USDA, Bureau of Agricultural Economics, Agricultural History Series, no. 5 (1942); and Clemen, *Livestock and Meat,* 21–68.

70. The best modern study of pork packing as a frontier industry is Margaret Walsh, *The Rise of the Midwestern Meat Packing Industry* (1982); see also her summary articles "Pork Packing as a Leading Edge of Midwestern Industry, 1835–1875," *Ag. Hist.* 51 (1977): 702–17, "The Spatial Evolution of the Mid-western Pork Industry, 1835–75," *Journal of Historical Geography* 4 (1978): 1–22, and "From Pork Merchant to Meat Packer: The Midwestern Meat Industry in the Mid Nineteenth Century," *Ag. Hist.* 56 (1982): 127–37, 167–71. For an early description of rural pork packing, see Oliver, *Eight Months in Illinois,* 34–36.

71. Charles Wayland Towne and Edward Norris Wentworth, *Pigs: From Cave to Corn Belt* (1950), 7; Allan Bogue, *Prairie to Cornbelt,* 104.

72. With time, the reciprocal movement of corn and pork sale prices and volumes, often on a two- to three-year cycle, became a predictable feature of the agricultural commodity markets. As such, it is direct evidence of the degree to which even early agricultural settlements in the Midwest oriented their production toward the market. See, for instance, Mordecai Ezekiel, "The Cobweb Theorem," *Quarterly Journal of Economics* 52 (1937–38): 255–80; Towne and Wentworth, *Pigs,* 201; Allan Bogue, *Prairie to Cornbelt,* 112; Walsh, *Meat Packing Industry,* 11–12.

73. Samuel B. Ruggles, as quoted by Parton, "Chicago," 331. This popular remark was widely quoted by those who wrote about Chicago pork packing. See, for instance, Wright, *Chicago,* 213.

74. For maps of the evolution of packing operations in various towns, see Walsh, *Meat Packing Industry*, 16, 42, 76.

75. Burrows, *Fifty Years in Iowa*, 233–34. On the early history of Iowa packing, see H. H. McCarty and C. W. Thompson, "Meatpacking in Iowa," *Iowa Studies in Business* 12 (June 1933).

76. The development of a market in salt, often extended over relatively long distances, was an intimate adjunct of frontier meat-packing. See, for instance, John A. Jakle, "Salt on the Ohio Valley Frontier, 1770–1820," *Annals Assoc. Am. Geog.* 59 (1969): 687–709; Janet Bruce, "Of Sugar and Salt and Things in the Cellar and Sun: Food Preservation in Jackson County in the 1850s," *Mo. Hist. Rev.* 75 (1981): 417–47; and Robert P. Multhauf, *Neptune's Gift: A History of Common Salt* (1978).

77. Frances Trollope, *Domestic Manners of the Americans* (1832), ed. Donald Smalley (1949), 88.

78. Frederick Law Olmsted, *A Journey through Texas: or, A Saddle-Trip on the Southwestern Frontier* (1857; reprint, 1978), 12.

79. Siegfried Giedion, *Mechanization Takes Command: A Contribution to Anonymous History* (1948), 214–18; Richard G. Arms, "From Disassembly to Assembly: Cincinnati: The Birthplace of Mass-production," *Bulletin of the Historical and Philosophical Society of Cincinnati* 17 (1959): 195–203; Carl M. Becker, "Evolution of the Disassembly Line: The Horizontal Wheel and the Overhead Railway Loop," ibid., 26 (1968): 276–82. To compare the Cincinnati system with later pork-packing at Chicago, see "Hog Killing at the Chicago Stock Yards," *Scientific American* 65 (Nov. 7, 1891): 291.

80. Olmsted, *Journey through Texas*, 9.

81. Victor S. Clark, *History of Manufactures in the United States*, (1929), 1:483–84.

82. CBT, *Annual Report for 1900*, 45.

83. Walsh, *Meat Packing Industry*, 57.

84. On the structural reasons for Cincinnati's relative decline during the years surrounding the Civil War, see Sherry O. Hessler, " 'The Great Disturbing Cause' and the Decline of the Queen City," *Bulletin of the Historical and Philosophical Society of Cincinnati* 20 (1962): 169–85. An early prediction that Chicago would eventually surpass Cincinnati can be found in Thomas, *Report*, iii–iv.

85. CBT, *Annual Report for 1900*, 45.

86. Elmer A. Riley, *The Development of Chicago and Vicinity as a Manufacturing Center Prior to 1880* (1911), 126–27, argues that the influence of the Civil War on Chicago's meat-packing industry has been exaggerated. Hill, "Chicago as a Meat Packing Center," agrees with him. Both men frame their argument principally in terms of beef, however, and there seems little reason to doubt that the Civil War accelerated the city's pork sales. Walsh, *Meat Packing Industry*, 57–60, takes this position, as do I.

87. U.S. Census of Manufactures, 1860 and 1870; Manuscript Schedules for 1870 Census of Manufactures, Illinois State Library.

88. Henry Hall, "The Ice Industry in the United States, with a Brief Sketch of Its History and Estimates of Production in the Different States," in U.S. Department of the Interior, Census Office, *Tenth Census of the United States, 1880* (1888), 22:1–5. The only book-length study of this important nineteenth-century industry is Richard O. Cummings, *The American Ice Harvests: A Historical Study in Technology, 1800–1918* (1949); relevant chapters are also contained in Oscar Edward Anderson, Jr., *Refrigeration in America: A History of a New Technology and Its Impact* (1953), 3–36.

89. Cummings, *Ice Harvests*, 58.

90. Pierce, *History of Chicago*, 2:98. Cincinnati firms were experimenting with ice-cooled packing plants at this same time, with the packer John L. Schooley leading the way in innovative technologies. See Cummings, *Ice Harvests*, 60.

91. *Annual Report of the Packing of the West* (1876), 30.

92. CBT, *Annual Reports*, 1859–80. A subtler but even more suggestive measure of the impact of summer packing was the decision of the Board in 1881 to cease publication of monthly statistics for live-hog receipts, presumably because there was no longer enough variation in them to matter to business.

93. In this, Chicago's meat markets (for pork *and* beef) were like its lumber market in being conducted much more continuously than in other locations. Even in cities like Boston or New York, meat was generally traded on specially designated days of the week, whereas Chicago dealers were willing to buy at any time. As early as 1858, the

Board of Trade was noting, "In no other city on this continent is there a *daily cattle market* which has been as regularly represented throughout the year as our grain and provision markets . . . and this enables the drover to sell out almost as soon as he arrives, without the delays or hindrances which annoy and harrass [*sic*] the drovers in the East, if circumstances should delay them beyond the special market day." Chicago's market in livestock, like its grain and lumber markets, was also a *cash* market, with all the benefits that implied for shippers. CBT, *Annual Report for 1858*, 24.

94. CBT, *Annual Report for 1882*, 29.

95. CBT, *Annual Report for 1871*, 66, 147.

96. Rudolf A. Clemen, *George H. Hammond (1838–1886): Pioneer in Refrigerator Transportation* (1946), 13–16. There is some controversy about the date of the first shipment of refrigerated beef; some sources place it as early as 1865 and others as late as 1871. See Hill, "Chicago as Meat Packing Center," 271. An early reference to refrigeration in Chicago can be found in Brooks, "Chicago and Its Railways," 276–77.

97. On Swift's career, see Louis F. Swift with Arthur Van Vlissingen, Jr., *The Yankee of the Yards: The Biography of Gustavus Franklin Swift* (1927); Louise A. Neyhart, *Giant of the Yards* (1952); Louis Unfer, "Swift and Company: The Development of the Packing Industry, 1875 to 1912" (Ph.D. thesis, Univ. of Illinois, 1951); Bertram B. Fowler, *Men, Meat and Miracles* (1952); and Clemen, *Livestock and Meat*, 225–51.

98. Swift and Van Vlissingen, *Yankee of the Yards*, 127–28.

99. Giedion, *Mechanization Takes Command*, 219–22, provides a useful survey but is unreliable on several facts; Clemen, *Livestock and Meat*, 217–22; J. Ogden Armour, *The Packers, the Private Car Lines, and the People* (1906), 19–21.

100. For the more general institutional history of private freight cars and their relationship to railroad management, see L. D. H. Weld, *Private Freight Cars and American Railways*, Columbia University Studies in History, Economics, and Public Law, vol. 31 [1908], 3–185.

101. CBT, *Annual Report for 1884*, 43.

102. FTC, *Report on the Meat-Packing Industry*, Summary and pt. 1 (1919), 139.

103. Unfer, "Swift and Company," 41.

104. Lee E. Lawrence, "The Wisconsin Ice Trade," *Wis. Mag. Hist.* 48 (1965): 257–67. In addition to the Chicago packers, the Milwaukee breweries were major customers of the state's ice trade. On Swift's ice sources, see Unfer, "Swift and Company," 36.

105. In addition to Anderson, *Refrigeration*, see J. F. Nickerson, "The Development of Refrigeration in the United States," *Ice and Refrigeration* 49, no. 4 (Oct. 1, 1915): 170–77.

106. Swift and Van Vlissingen, *Yankee of the Yards*, 191.

107. Trunk Line Executive Committee, *Report upon the Relative Cost of Transporting Live Stock and Dressed Beef* (1883), 73–74.

108. The most important work on the emergence of modern managerial organization in the meat-packing firms is that of Mary Yeager, *Competition and Regulation: The Development of Oligopoly in the Meat Packing Industry* (1981); see also her useful summary in Mary Yeager Kujovich, "The Refrigerator Car and the Growth of the American Dressed Beef Industry," *Bus. Hist. Rev.* 44 (1970): 460–82. Her work, like my own, follows that of Alfred D. Chandler, Jr., who deals with Armour's role in meat-packing in his *Visible Hand*, 391–402; see also his seminal essay "The Beginnings of 'Big Business' in American Industry," *Bus. Hist. Rev.* 33 (Spring 1959): 131, which uses Swift as a key example; and the various collected essays in Chandler, *The Essential Alfred Chandler: Essays toward a Historical Theory of Big Business*, ed. Thomas K. McCraw (1988). For the effects of these changes on labor, see David Brody, *The Butcher Workmen: A Study of Unionization* (1964), 1–12.

109. Swift and Van Vlissingen, *Yankee of the Yards*, 69.

110. Clemen, *Livestock and Meat Industry*, 235.

111. Fred C. Croxton, "Beef Prices," *J. Pol. Econ.* 8 (1905): 201–16; U.S. Bureau of the Census, *Historical Statistics*, ser. E189–190, 1:213.

112. Trunk Line Executive Committee, *Cost of Transporting Live Stock and Dressed Beef*, 6–9. Clemen gives the modern figure as 55.6 percent in Rudolf A. Clemen, *By-products in the Packing Industry* (1927), 10.

113. Testimony of G. Baurmann (Chicago dressed beef dealer), Feb. 1, 1889, in U.S. Senate, *Testimony Taken by the Select Committee on the Transportation and Sale of Meat Products*, 51st Cong., 1st sess., 1889–90, Sen. Rept. 829 (Serial ?705), 184 (hereafter cited as the

Vest Report). The testimony at the select committee's hearings, which were held in several major western cities, is invaluable in exploring the complex interregional changes that went on during the early years of the dressed beef trade.

114. Swift and Van Vlissingen, *Yankee of the Yards,* 75–76.

115. The best and most comprehensive analysis of relations between the packers and the railroads is Yeager, *Competition and Regulation;* and Yeager Kujovich, "Refrigerator Car." The key contemporary document surveying these linkages is New York State Assembly, *Proceedings of the Special Committee Appointed to Investigate Alleged Abuses in the Management of Railroads Chartered by the State of New York,* 8 vols., Assembly Doc. 38, 1879–80, which is generally referred to as the Hepburn Report. For its political context, see Benson, *Merchants, Farmers, & Railroads;* see also Wilford L. White, "The Refrigerator Car and the Effect upon the Public of Packer Control of Refrigerator Lines," *Southwestern Political and Social Science Quarterly* 10 (1930): 388–400.

116. The express car as a railroad innovation was the necessary predecessor of the refrigerator car. Express companies emerged as a way of guaranteeing fast shipments for valuable or perishable commodities. Since travel between any two long-distance points might require movement on several different railroads, express companies contracted for rapid transfer between lines (ordinarily the worst bottleneck for long-distance freight) to guarantee their customers the highest possible rate of movement. Without such preexisting institutional arrangements, the refrigerator car would have been impossible.

117. Yeager, *Competition and Regulation,* 30–41. On the effectiveness of these and subsequent railroad efforts at pooling, using the grain trade as a case study, see MacAvoy, *Economic Effects of Regulation.*

118. This was also the conclusion of the Vest Report, 2.

119. Testimony of Thomas Brown, Jr. (Chicago livestock commission merchant), Sept. 2, 1889, Vest Report, 219.

120. Ripley, *Railroads: Rates and Regulations,* 140.

121. Swift and Van Vlissingen, *Yankee of the Yards,* 184–85.

122. CBT, *Annual Report for 1885,* 105.

123. Yeager, *Competition and Regulation,* 89–100.

124. *Proceedings and Circulars of the Standing Committee of the Joint Executive Committee,* March 30, 1883, Circular no. 472, 27.

125. Armour and Co. to Commissioner Fink, May 11, 1883, in Trunk Line Executive Committee, *Cost of Transporting Live Stock and Dressed Beef,* appendix 19, 131. See also Armour's testimony in Vest Report, 461–62.

126. Trunk Line Executive Committee, *Cost of Transporting Live Stock and Dressed Beef,* 17.

127. Ripley, *Railroads: Rates and Regulations,* 139–40; Clemen, *Livestock and Meat Industry,* 240–41.

128. Testimony of William Peters (Allegheny City butcher), Nov. 23, 1889, Vest Report, 169.

129. Testimony of George Beck (Detroit butcher), Nov. 22, 1888, Vest Report, 133.

130. Testimony of Warren Buckmaster (Akron, Ohio, butcher), Nov. 22, 1888, Vest Report, 150–51. Clemen, *Livestock and Meat Industry,* 242, mistakenly gives the date of the organization's founding as May 1886.

131. A valuable analysis of branch house operation is Porter and Livesay, *Merchants and Manufacturers,* 168–73. For an interesting example of a non-meat-packing Chicago firm's reason for adopting branch houses, see Richard Teller Crane, *The Autobiography of Richard Teller Crane* (1927), 82–85.

132. Testimony of Warren Buckmaster, Vest Report, 145.

133. Armour made this one of his central arguments in defending his company before the Vest Committee: "I wish to call the attention of the committee," he said, "to a fact which seems to be very generally overlooked, and that is, that fresh meat is a perishable commodity. It must be handled with the greatest judgment and care, and to keep it in good marketable condition the very best possible methods and appliances must be used to preserve it from the time that the animal is killed, during the chilling process and transportation, and until the carcass is distributed for consumption. A small mistake in handling it results in great loss. From the time the animal is slaughtered until the meat is marketed to the consumer only a short time can intervene. It is very apparent, therefore, that a supply can not be accumulated by the jobber of fresh

meats, either at the point where he slaughters or at his refrigerator, where he sells to the retailer, for the purpose of controlling the market. He must dispose of his meat as soon as it is ripe enough, and to retain his markets and keep his customers he must be ready, day after day and every day, to supply the trade which he caters to." Testimony of Philip D. Armour, Nov. 30, 1889, Vest Report, 426–27.

134. Swift and Van Vlissingen, *Yankee of the Yards,* 67.

135. Testimony of William Peters, Vest Report, 171.

136. Testimony of Levi Samuels (New York wholesale butcher), Nov. 22, 1888, Vest Report, 118.

137. This process went furthest in major eastern cities other than New York, and in the Midwest generally. Smaller eastern towns continued to conduct slaughtering on a modest scale for home consumption, largely as an outlet for local dairy cattle. See, for instance, *Report of the Commissioner of Corporations on the Beef Industry,* (1905), xxii.

138. Numerous witnesses made this claim before the Senate's select committee in 1889. See, for instance, Vest Report, 146.

139. Testimony of Jefferson Reynolds (New Mexican stock raiser), Nov. 23, 1889, Vest Report, 175.

140. This was the conclusion of the Select Committee on the Transportation and Sale of Meat Products in its final report (Vest Report, 2): "a few enterprising men at Chicago, engaged in the packing and dressed beef business, are able through their enormous capital to centralize and control the beef business at that point. So far has this centralizing process continued that for all practical purposes the market at that city dominates absolutely the price of beef cattle in the whole country." California was the chief exception for livestock sales, but even there dressed beef was beginning to appear.

141. Testimony of Levi Samuels, Vest Report, 121.

142. CBT, *Annual Report for 1889,* 140. Included in this percentage are the outputs of the Fairbank Canning Company (owned by Nelson Morris) and Libby, McNeil and Libby (in which Swift owned a controlling interest).

143. The classic account of oligopoly in the packing industry is again Yeager, *Competition and Regulation.* My own discussion hardly begins to suggest the complexity of this topic, and interested readers are urged to refer to Yeager's fine book.

144. Testimony of G. Baurmann, Vest Report, 184. Armour admitted his involvement in such pooling agreements in his testimony before the Vest Committee. Vest Report, 481.

145. Testimony of Silvanus Wilcox (Elgin, Illinois, dairy farmer), Sept. 2, 1889, Vest Report, 190–91.

146. Testimony of John A. Evans (Iowa farmer), Sept. 7, 1889, Vest Report, 266.

147. Testimony of Martin Flynn (Iowa farmer), Sept. 7, 1889, Vest Report, 255–56.

148. Testimony of John B. Sherman (Chicago Union Stockyards general manager), Sept. 4, 1889, Vest Report, 244.

149. Testimony of Martin Flynn, Vest Report, 255.

150. "The Union Stock Yards," *Western Rural,* March 8, 1879, 76.

151. Testimony of G. Baurmann, Vest Report, 184.

152. Vest Report, 6, 12, 33.

153. Ibid., 2.

154. CBT, *Annual Report for 1890,* 89, reports the USDA's estimated number of Great Plains cattle for 1890 as about 8.5 million, down from its speculative peak in the late 1880s.

155. Weld, *Private Freight Cars and American Railways,* 18–20, 58–65; Giedion, *Mechanization Takes Command,* 227; Leech and Carroll, *Armour,* 154–61.

156. CBT, *Annual Report for 1891,* 34.

157. Leech and Carroll, *Armour,* 305–20. Leiter's corner was not finally broken until May 1898, by which time Armour was helping him and his father close out the young man's debts. As I note in Chapter 3, the Leiter corner became the basis for Frank Norris's novel *The Pit,* first published in 1903.

158. Arthur Warren, "Philip D. Armour: His Manner of Life, His Immense Enterprises in Trade and Philanthropy," *McClure's Magazine* 2 (1893–94): 262. For a useful thumbnail sketch of Armour and Company's corporate history under Philip Armour and its later decline under his son J. Ogden Armour, see Gras and Larson, eds., *Casebook in American Business History,* 623–44.

159. Sinclair, *The Jungle,* 135; Swift and Van Vlissingen, *Yankee of the Yards,* 11–12.

160. The classic work on progressive conservation is Samuel D. Hays, *Conservation and the Gospel of Efficiency: The Progressive Conservation Movement, 1890–1920* (1959). Because Hays deals mainly with professional conservationists within the federal bureaucracies, his readers can fail to realize that corporate America originated this impulse toward conservation, efficiency, and waste prevention. Government figures like Pinchot and Roosevelt saw themselves applying "business principles" to promoting and conserving the public good.

161. See, for instance, Cleaver, *History of Chicago,* 109. Cleaver was one of Chicago's largest manufacturers of pork by-products in the 1850s.

162. The story of Chicago's water supply is well told in J. H. Rauch, *The Sanitary Problems of Chicago, Past and Present* (1879); Louis P. Cain, "Raising and Watering a City: Ellis Sylvester Chesbrough and Chicago's First Sanitation System," *Technology and Culture* 13 (1972): 353–72; Louis P. Cain, *Sanitation Strategy for a Lakefront Metropolis: The Case of Chicago* (1978); and James C. O'Connell, "Technology and Pollution: Chicago's Water Policy, 1833–1930" (Ph.D. thesis, Univ. of Chicago, 1980). See also Bessie Louise Pierce, *A History of Chicago,* vol. 3, *The Rise of a Modern City, 1871–1893* (1957), 310–13. The Sanitary District of Chicago succeeded in permanently reversing the flow of the river during all weather conditions by the end of the century. Downstate reactions to the effects of "the grand sewer of Chicago nastiness" are explored in William Booth Philip, "Chicago and the Down State: A Study of Their Conflicts, 1870–1934" (Ph.D. thesis, Univ. of Chicago, 1940), 200–233.

163. Quoted by Wade, *Chicago's Pride,* 132, from *Chicago Tribune,* Jan. 26, Feb. 8, 9, 26, 1879. On the disposal of toxic industrial wastes in the Chicago area, see Craig E. Colten, "Industrial Wastes in Southeast Chicago: Production and Disposal, 1870–1970," *Environmental Review* 10 (1986): 93–105.

164. Frank W. Gunsaulus, "Philip D. Armour: A Character Sketch," *North American Monthly Review of Reviews* 23 (1901): 172.

165. A comprehensive list of the more than six hundred products Chicago packers were handling by the second decade of the twentieth century can be found in FTC, *Report on the Meat-Packing Industry,* 1:95–102. A more vivid description of these by-products is in Sinclair, *The Jungle,* 44–45, 100–102.

166. Julian Ralph, *Harper's Chicago and the World's Fair* (1893), 78–79. See also the testimony of G. Baurmann, Vest Report, 184.

167. "Showing the Proportion the Products of 290 Steers bear to the Gross Weight of said Steers on hoof in Chicago and at the Seaboard . . . computed from Statement Furnished by Mr. Hammond," in Trunk Line Executive Committee, *Cost of Transporting Live Stock and Dressed Beef,* appendix 2, 112; see also Clemen, *By-products in the Packing Industry,* for a detailed survey of by-product yields and manufacturing processes.

168. Unsurprisingly, this was not the butchers' view of themselves. When asked whether he made use of all parts of the cattle he slaughtered, whether there was "any waste at all," a Pennsylvania butcher named William Peters replied, "No sir; there is no waste. I make use of everything. If we would not make use of everything we would be badly left." Testimony, Vest Report, 172. But however hard he might work to sell bones, hides, entrails, blood, offal, and manure to his local customers, a man like Peters was still limited by the traditional character of his immediate market. The Chicago packers, on the other hand, could more or less create new markets for by-products as such products emerged from the labs, relying on their ability to sell on a national and even international scale.

169. Table constructed from testimony of Philip D. Armour, Vest Report, 424. Armour's rounding errors produce results that are slightly different from an exact calculation; in this table, I have retained his original estimates, except for his estimate of final profit—"about 60 cents"—which I have replaced with the more accurate 59 cents.

170. Sinclair, *The Jungle,* 97.

171. The packers also reduced their reliance on hogs for garbage disposal, another sign that they were putting wastes to other uses. Testimony of William Peters, Vest Report, 169–70.

172. Testimony of William Peters, Vest Report, 169–70.

173. Testimony of G. Baurmann, Vest Report, 185–86; Sinclair, *The Jungle,* 136–37. Sinclair made much of the presence of ground-up rats and feces in such sausages, but one can reasonably doubt that this was the most important part of the problem.

174. On the writing of Sinclair's book, see Christine Scriabine, "Upton Sinclair and the

Writing of *The Jungle*," *Chicago History* 10, no. 1 (Spring 1981): 26–37. On the hazards of *rural* butchering, see Ch. Wardell Stiles, "The Country Slaughterhouse as a Factor in the Spread of Disease," in USDA, *Yearbook of the United States Department of Agriculture, 1896* (1897), 155–66.

175. Sinclair, *The Jungle*, 136–37.

176. Another example of meat muckraking is Charles Edward Russell, *The Greatest Trust in the World* (1905).

177. *Report of the Commissioner of Corporations on the Beef Industry*, 22. Even the Federal Trade Commission, which was otherwise quite critical of the packers for their oligopolistic economic power, agreed that they had improved the nation's food supply: "In the shipment of live stock, freight was paid on a vast aggregate tonnage of waste product, while in the shipments of dressed beef and other packing-house products in a refrigerator car, only the useful products are shipped and a large saving in freight charges is effected. Meat was delivered to the consumer in better condition after the introduction of the refrigerator car also, because the cattle then slaughtered nearer to the point of production, were in better condition, not having had to endure the additional 1,000-mile journey from Chicago to the seaboard." FTC, *Report on the Meat-Packing Industry*, 1:138.

178. Testimony of Philip D. Armour, Vest Report, 423.

179. On the development of the international meat trade during this period, see J. P. Sheldon, "Report on the American and Canadian Meat Trade," *Journal of the Royal Agricultural Society of England*, 2d ser., 13 (1877): 295–355; H. E. Alvord, "The American Cattle Trade," ibid., 356–74; P. G. Craigie, "Twenty Years' Changes in Our Foreign Meat Supplies," ibid., 465–500; J. D. Whelpley, "American Control of England's Food Supply," *No. Am. Rev.* 174 (1902): 796–806; James Troubridge Critchell and Joseph Raymond, *A History of the Frozen Meat Trade* (1912); Wm. David Zimmerman, "Live Cattle Export Trade between United States and Great Britain, 1868–1885," *Ag. Hist.* 36 (1962): 46–52; Richard Perren, "The North American Beef and Cattle Trade with Great Britain, 1870–1914," *Econ. Hist. Rev.*, 2d ser., 24 (1971): 430–44; Perren, *The Meat Trade in Britain, 1840–1914* (1978).

180. Vest Report, 2.

181. Kipling, *From Sea to Sea*, 151.

182. This is one of the major conclusions that Alfred Chandler and his students have been emphasizing in their work for the past thirty years. See Chandler, *Visible Hand;* and Chandler, *Strategy and Structure*.

183. Swift and Van Vlissingen, *Yankee of the Yards*, 131–32.

184. For a review of packing company investments in widely scattered facilities up until 1919, see FTC, *Report on the Meat-Packing Industry*, 1:121–33. For a case study of a non-Chicago firm that succeeded at operating in the city's hinterland, see Lawrence O. Cheever, "John Morrell & Co.," *Palimpsest* 47 (1966): 145–92. On Kansas City, see G. K. Renner, "The Kansas City Meat Packing Industry before 1900," *Mo. Hist. Rev.* 55 (1961): 18–29; and for comparison, see Frank S. Popplewell, "St. Joseph, Missouri, as a Center of the Cattle Trade," ibid., 32 (1938): 443–57. For the biography of a prominent Omaha packer, see W. Kane, *The Education of Edward Cudahy* (1941).

185. Bureau of Statistics, U.S. Treasury Department, "The Provision Trade of the United States," *Monthly Summary of Commerce and Finance of the United States*, Feb. 1900 (1900), 2291–98, 2303–5; CBT, *Annual Report for 1900*, 45.

186. A good analysis of the rise and fall of Chicago's locational advantages in the meat-packing industry is Robert Aduddell and Louis Cain, "Location and Collusion in the Meat Packing Industry," in Louis Cain and Paul J. Uselding, eds., *Business Enterprise and Economic Change: Essays in Honor of Harold F. Williamson* (1973), 85–117. See also McCarty and Thompson, "Meat Packing in Iowa," 76–126.

187. For a thorough analysis of Chicago's supply hinterland at the beginning of the 1930s, see Edward A. Duddy, *The Supply Area of the Chicago Livestock Market* (1931).

188. A brief summary of the stockyards' twentieth-century decline can be found in Glen E. Holt and Dominic A. Pacyga, *Chicago: A Historical Guide to the Neighborhoods, The Loop and South Side* (1979), 28–37.

189. The corporations shifted as much as the products they sold: Armour was finally acquired by the Greyhound Corporation in 1969, and Swift (its name changed to Esmark because of the diminished significance of meat among its products) by Beatrice in

1984. See, for instance, "Armour, Swift, Wilson: Why the Old Brands Are Fading," *New York Times*, Dec. 21, 1980. For thumbnail sketches of these corporate histories, see Milton Moskowitz, Michael Katz, and Robert Levering, *Everybody's Business, An Almanac: The Irreverent Guide to Corporate America* (1980).

6: GATEWAY CITY

1. John J. Flinn, *Chicago, the Marvelous City of the West: A History, an Encyclopedia, and a Guide, 1891* (1890), 222. Flinn's unwillingness to try to explain the view "from the balcony" makes an interesting contrast with Dies, *Wheat Pit,* 7–9, which described "the wheat pit" as "a strange, mysterious giant in the center of a warfare handed down by the ages," "perhaps the most romantic figure in the whole world of commerce," and then proposed "to draw back the veil of mystery and step behind the scenes" so that visitors could better understand "the science of grain marketing."

2. Robert Herrick, *The Gospel of Freedom* (1898), 101.

3. Some species increased their abundance not because people placed high prices on them and encouraged their growth but because they adapted themselves so well to the artificial habitats human beings created for them. The organisms we label "weeds," "vermin," and "pests" are among the most successful that fall into this group.

4. All ecosystems export certain gases as part of their ordinary mechanisms of respiration and decay, and they also lose nutrients at a predictable rate to the watersheds which drain them. Migrating animal species transport materials from one location to another, and depend on a long chain of widely separated local habitats as they pursue their annual reproductive cycles. But there are few analogues in first nature for the long-distance movement of "valuable" resources that characterizes the human economy of second nature.

5. For a description of the bankruptcy data on which much of this section is based, see the methodological appendix. Note that the bankrupts and creditors I tally here all went bankrupt under the *federal* bankruptcy law of 1867; state laws constituted a less uniform but often more popular route to bankruptcy during this period.

6. The records of Garden City's bankruptcy are in the National Archives Regional Record Center in Chicago, Bankruptcy Court case no. 2501, box 317. For its credit history, see *The Mercantile Agency Reference Book,* Jan. 1872; and *Bradstreet's Commercial Reports,* July 1873. Additional information can be found in the R. G. Dun Company Archives in the Baker Library of the Harvard Business School, indexed at vol. 9, p. 147, in Baker vol. 35.

7. R. G. Dun Archives, Baker Library, vol. 13, p. 213, Baker vol. 39; National Archives Regional Record Center, Chicago, Bankruptcy Court case no. 2456, box 315.

8. R. G. Dun Archives, Baker Library, vol. 10, p. 258, Baker vol. 36; the quotation is dated Sept. 17, 1872.

9. Freeland Gardner's case is in the National Archives Regional Record Center, Chicago, Bankruptcy Court case no. 2472, box 316; his son Horatio's case is case no. 2463, box 315.

10. R. G. Dun Archives, Baker Library, vol. 10, pp. 71, 102, Baker vol. 36; National Archives Regional Record Center, Chicago, Bankruptcy Court case no. 2620, box 322.

11. One problem with these creditor maps is that their visual impact is heavily affected by the size of the county in which particular creditors lived. This creates difficulties when the creditor county is small, as in the important case of New York City. New York was Chicago's most significant trading partner for many lines of trade, and yet creditor maps inevitably obscure its importance because the city occupied such a small geographical area.

12. Nimmo, *Rept. Int. Commerce* (1879), 48.

13. Charles H. Randolph, quoted ibid., 49.

14. Nimmo, *Rept. Int. Commerce* (1881), 103.

15. The early classics of central place theory were almost entirely by German geographers trying to elaborate the insights of von Thünen, *Isolated State.* The most important works are Alfred Weber, *Theory of the Location of Industries* (1909), trans. Carl J. Friedrich (1929); Walter Christaller, *Central Places in Southern Germany* (1933), trans. Carlisle W. Baskin (1966); August Lösch, "The Nature of Economic Regions," *Southern Economic Journal* 5 (1938): 71–78; Lösch, *The Economics of Location* (1939), trans. William H.

Woglom (1954); Edward Ullman, "A Theory of Location for Cities," *American Journal of Sociology* 46 (1940–41): 853–64; Edgar M. Hoover, *The Location of Economic Activity* (1948); and Walter Isard, *Location and Space-Economy: A General Theory Relating to Industrial Location, Market Areas, Land Use, Trade, and Urban Structure* (1956). A useful brief synthesis of the industrial aspects of this body of theory is William Alonso, "Location Theory," in John Friedmann and William Alonso, eds., *Regional Development and Planning: A Reader* (1964), 78–106; for a synthesis that concentrates on retail geography, see Brian J. L. Berry, *The Geography of Market Centers and Retail Distribution* (1967). Interestingly, some of the most successful applications of central place theory to real empirical examples have been conducted in Chicago's hinterland, in places like Iowa, southwestern Wisconsin, and the southern Canadian prairies. See, for example, John E. Brush and Howard E. Bracey, "Rural Service Centers in Southwestern Wisconsin and Southern England," *Geographical Review* 45 (1955): 559–69; Brian J. L. Berry, H. Gardiner Barnum, and Robert J. Tennant, "Retail Location and Consumer Behaviour," *Papers and Proceedings of the Regional Science Association* 9 (1962): 65–106; H. A. Stafford, Jr., "The Functional Bases of Small Towns," *Economic Geography* 39 (1963): 165–75; and Gerald Hodge, "The Prediction of Trade Center Viability in the Great Plains," *Papers and Proceedings of the Regional Science Association* 14 (1965): 87–115. Also suggestive is Richard E. Preston, "The Structure of Central Place Systems," *Economic Geography* 47 (1971): 136–55, which deals with the urban hierarchy of the modern state of Washington.

16. The classic essay on city systems is Brian J. L. Berry, "Cities as Systems within Systems of Cities," *Papers and Proceedings of the Regional Science Association* 13 (1964): 147–63, also reprinted in Friedmann and Alonso, *Regional Development and Planning,* 116–37. See also L. S. Bourne and J. W. Simmons, eds., *Systems of Cities: Readings on Structure, Growth, and Policy* (1968).

17. U.S. Bureau of the Census, *Historical Statistics,* ser. A43-56, 1:11. See also Beverly Duncan and Stanley Lieberson, *Metropolis and Region in Transition* (1970), 52, 57, 75, and passim, for useful graphical representations of these and related data. There is a large literature on the logarithmic rank ordering of urban places. Among the classic essays are Mark Jefferson, "The Law of the Primate City," *Geographical Review* 29 (1939): 226–32; Colin Clark, "The Economic Functions of a City in Relation to Its Size," *Econometrica* 13 (1945): 97–113; Carl H. Madden, "On Some Indications of Stability in the Growth of Cities in the United States," *Economic Development and Cultural Change* 4 (1956): 236–52; Martin J. Beckmann, "City Hierarchies and the Distribution of City Size," ibid., 6 (1958): 243–48; Brian J. L. Berry, "City Size Distributions and Economic Development," ibid., 9 (1961): 573–88; Fred Lukermann, "Empirical Expressions of Nodality and Hierarchy in a Circulation Manifold," *East Lakes Geographer* 2 (Aug. 1966): 17–44; and Harry W. Richardson, "Theory of the Distribution of City Sizes: Review and Prospects," *Regional Studies* 7 (1973): 239–51. A somewhat dated but still useful survey of the subject can be found in Brian J. L. Berry and Frank E. Horton, *Geographic Perspectives on Urban Systems, with Integrated Readings* (1970), 64–93.

18. On rural consumer travel and small-town hinterlands, see Norman T. Moline, *Mobility and the Small Town, 1900–1930: Transportation Change in Oregon, Illinois,* University of Chicago Department of Geography Research Paper no. 132 (1971); and Edwin N. Thomas, Richard A. Mitchell, and Donald A. Blome, "The Spatial Behavior of a Dispersed Non-farm Population," *Papers and Proceedings of the Regional Science Association* 9 (1962): 107–33.

19. For reasons that have to do with the history of American federalism, the very highest-ranking cities in the United States are often not the capitals of their states. Rural citizens who dominate state legislatures have often been reluctant to allow economic metropolises to become centers of formal political power as well. State capitals in newly created cities were also an immensely attractive real estate speculation for politicians who knew where to buy up property before anyone else, giving them a strong vested interest in moving the seat of state government onto virgin urban soil. Chicago and Springfield have a long history of conflict, stretching well back into the nineteenth century, and in this respect have much in common with New York City and Albany, or Los Angeles or San Francisco and Sacramento. A valuable discussion of this subject in Illinois is Philip, "Chicago and the Down State."

20. Like governments, colleges and universities are an interesting exception that proves

this general rule. They too express a national hierarchy, with institutions at the upper ranks drawing their students from ever wider geographical fields. But because the American campus developed within a romantic tradition that stressed the virtues of cloistered retreat in nurturing the life of the mind, many elite urban parents chose to send their children to schools well away from metropolitan centers. Such institutions were thus displaced from the urban locales that financed them, whether through individual tuitions, philanthropic donations, or church or state support. There is thus no reliable correlation between the status rank of a college or university and its geographical location within the urban hierarchy.

21. Vance, *The Merchant's World: The Geography of Wholesaling* remains the classic on this subject, and offers an important historical critique of the ahistorical models that characterize other central place theorists. My historical treatment of central place theory in this chapter has more in common with Vance than with his colleagues who favor formal mathematical treatments of the same subject.

22. David R. Meyer, "A Dynamic Model of the Integration of Frontier Urban Places into the United States System of Cities," *Economic Geography* 56 (1980): 122–26, offers cogent arguments about the importance of increasing specialization to the rank ordering of urban places. On Chicago's early retail trade, before the city became a major wholesaler, see Frueh, "Retail Merchandising in Chicago."

23. In this way, modern central place theorists echo the Cincinnati booster S. H. Goodin, whom I discussed in chapter 1.

24. Critiques of central place theory and more historical approaches to urbanization have been offered by several American and British geographers and social scientists whose work parallels my own. In addition to Vance, *Merchant's World,* and the various Canadian scholars whose work I cited in the notes to chapter 1, see Eric E. Lampard, "The History of Cities in the Economically Advanced Areas," *Economic Development and Cultural Change* 3 (1955): 81–136; Harvey S. Perloff et al., *Regions, Resources, and Economic Growth* (1960); Eugene Smolensky and Donald Ratajczak, "The Conception of Cities," *Explorations in Entrepreneurial History* 2 (1964): 90–131; Julius Rubin, "Urban Growth and Regional Development," in Gilchrist, ed., *Growth of Seaport Cities,* 3–21; A. F. Burghardt, "A Hypothesis about Gateway Cities," *Annals Assoc. Am. Geog.* 61 (1971): 269–85; Michael P. Conzen, *Frontier Farming in an Urban Shadow: The Influence of Madison's Proximity on the Agricultural Development of Blooming Grove, Wisconsin* (1971); Conzen, "Metropolitan Dominance"; John R. Borchert, "America's Changing Metropolitan Regions," *Annals Assoc. Am. Geog.* 62 (1972): 352–73; Michael P. Conzen, "A Transport Interpretation of the Growth of Urban Regions: An American Example," *Journal of Historical Geography* 1 (1975): 361–82; Edward K. Muller, "Selective Urban Growth in the Middle Ohio Valley, 1800–1860," *Geographical Review* 66 (1976): 178–99; Muller, "Regional Urbanization and the Selective Growth of Towns in North American Regions," *Journal of Historical Geography* 3 (1977): 21–39; Woodrow Borah, Jorge Hardoy, and Gilbert A. Stelter, eds., *Urbanization in the Americas: The Background in Comparative Perspective* (1980); Meyer, "Dynamic Model of the Integration of Frontier Urban Places," 120–40; Michael P. Conzen, "The American Urban System in the Nineteenth Century," in T. Herbert and R. J. Johnston, eds., *Geography and the Urban Environment: Progress in Research and Applications,* vol. 4 (New York: John Wiley, 1981), 295–347; F. A. Dahms, "The Evolution of Settlement Systems: A Canadian Example, 1851–1970," *J. Urban Hist.* 7 (1981): 169–204; David R. Meyer, "Emergence of the American Manufacturing Belt: An Interpretation," *Journal of Historical Geography* 2 (1983): 145–74; Carl Abbott, "Frontiers and Sections: Cities and Regions in American Growth," *American Quarterly* 37 (1985): 395–410; Timothy R. Mahoney, "Urban History in a Regional Context: River Towns on the Upper Mississippi, 1840–1860," *JAH* 72 (1985): 318–39; Michael Timberlake, ed., *Urbanization in the World-Economy* (1985); Michael P. Conzen, "The Progress of American Urbanism, 1860–1930," in Robert D. Mitchell and Paul A. Groves, eds., *North America: The Historical Geography of a Changing Continent* (1987), 347–70; David R. Meyer, "The National Integration of Regional Economies, 1860–1920," ibid., 321–46; Paul Bairoch, *Cities and Economic Development: From the Dawn of History to the Present,* trans. Christopher Braider (1988); and Timothy R. Mahoney, *River Towns in the Great West: The Structure of Provincial Urbanization in the American Midwest, 1820–1870* (1990). The work of Allan R. Pred is also important in this area: see his *The External Relations of Cities during "Industrial Revolution," with a Case Study of Goteborg, Sweden: 1868–*

1890, University of Chicago Department of Geography Research Paper no. 76 (1962); *The Spatial Dynamics of U.S. Urban Industrial Growth, 1800–1914: Interpretive and Theoretical Essays* (1966); *Urban Growth and the Circulation of Information: The United States System of Cities, 1790–1840* (1973); and *Urban Growth and City-Systems.* For a suggestive discussion of these issues in an international context, see Edward J. Taaffe, Richard L. Morrill, and Peter R. Gould, "Transport Expansion in Underdeveloped Countries: A Comparative Analysis," *Geographical Review* 53 (1963): 503–29; and the synthesis in Robert E. Dickinson, *City and Region: A Geographical Interpretation* (1964). McKenzie, *Metropolitan Community,* is still useful as well. Finally, the work of Immanuel Wallerstein, although couched in a vocabulary different from that of much of the literature I have just cited, speaks to many of the same issues, and has direct applicability to the overall argument of this book. See Wallerstein, *The Modern World-System: Capitalist Agriculture and the Origins of the European World-Economy in the Sixteenth Century* (1974); Wallerstein, *The Modern World-System II: Mercantilism and the Consolidation of the European World-Economy, 1600–1750* (1980); Wallerstein, *The Modern World-System III: The Second Era of Great Expansion of the Capitalist World-Economy, 1730–1840s* (1989); Wallerstein, *The Capitalist World-Economy: Essays* (1979). For an important critique, see Steve J. Stern, "Feudalism, Capitalism, and the World-System in the Perspective of Latin America and the Caribbean," *AHR* 93 (1988): 829–72. I have also benefited throughout from the work of David Harvey: see *Social Justice and the City* (1973; reprint, 1975);, *The Urbanization of Capital: Studies in the History and Theory of Capitalist Urbanization* (1985); *Consciousness and the Urban Experience: Studies in the History and Theory of Capitalist Urbanization* (1985).

25. Timothy Mahoney provides graphic evidence of this rearrangement in his "Urban History in a Regional Context," 321–27.

26. Technically, this exaggerated metropolitan status is reflected in the nonlinear distribution of the Midwest's highest-order cities on a log-log plotting of their population size versus their population rank. Using county populations as a surrogate for settlement size (the census did not record populations of individual communities until late in the nineteenth century), plots for 1850, 1870, and 1890 show a distinct jump in population size for settlements above the rank of about 10; moreover, the top-ranked metropolis (St. Louis, and then Chicago) stands distinctly outside the expected linear distribution for the settlement system as a whole. A comparably nonlinear distribution, with an even more dramatic jump for the top two metropolitan centers, occurs if one performs a log-log plot of the total per-county debt of the 1873–74 bankrupts against the rank of each county by total debt size.

27. Cf. Charles M. Gates, "Boom Stages in American Expansion," *Bus. Hist. Rev.* 33 (1959): 32–42.

28. Binckley, "Chicago of the Thinker," 262.

29. Burghardt, "Hypothesis about Gateway Cities."

30. Unless otherwise noted, all statistics cited in the following pages derive from the midwestern county bankruptcy dataset described in the appendix. It is important to remember that the many gaps in this map and the ones that follow—unshaded counties which do not appear to have held debts or credits—simply represent areas where no one became involved in federal bankruptcy proceedings between August 1873 and April 1874. One can reasonably assume that the debt patterns of such counties, almost all of which were rural areas, were similar to those of their neighbors.

31. In reading these bankruptcy maps, remember that there are two ways they can represent relations of debt and credit. On the one hand, they can show where all the bankrupts lived who owed money to the creditors of a particular place. In this text, I consistently refer to these as maps of "debtor counties." On the other, they can show where all the creditors lived to whom the bankrupts of a particular place owed money. I refer to these as maps of "creditor counties."

32. Larson, *Wheat Market and the Farmer in Minnesota;* Gras, "Significance of the Twin Cities"; John R. Borchert, *America's Northern Heartland* (1987).

33. The western limit of the dataset is the first tier of Great Plains states, so by definition it contains no bankrupts farther to the west. Abundant anecdotal evidence suggests that Chicago's trading hinterland extended far to the west of the Great Plains.

34. New York's debt hinterland west of the Great Lakes was more diffuse than Chicago's, but no less extensive. Philadelphia and Boston showed comparably extensive debt distributions, but their debtors were much more scattered.

35. P. R. Earling, *Whom to Trust: A Practical Treatise on Mercantile Credit* (1890), 45.

36. Ibid., 46.

37. Flinn, *Chicago*, 367–79. On the importance of these sorts of information flows to metropolitan status, see McKenzie, *Metropolitan Community*, 98–110 and passim; and David Paul Nord, "The Public Community: The Urbanization of Journalism in Chicago," *J. Urban Hist.* 11 (1985): 411–41.

38. Ralph, *Our Great West*, 11.

39. Earling, *Whom to Trust*, 49.

40. For much the same reason, Atherton, *Frontier Merchant*, 40–41, notes that the average amount of capital invested in a New York or Massachusetts retail store in 1840 was nearly half as much as in western states like Missouri or Arkansas.

41. I should offer several caveats at this point. First, although I refer in this paragraph to Chicago for the sake of simplicity, I am actually citing figures for Cook County; the two are not significantly different in this context. Second, the calculation I offer comparing Chicago's out-of-region debts as a percentage of its out-of-county debts with the mean out-of-county and out-of-region debt percentages for counties in the region as a whole is just what it says: a measure of the *county's* behavior, *not* the behavior of individual bankrupts. For *bankrupts* in the region, 66 percent of out-of-county debts were also outside the region; lower than the figure for Chicago alone, but not so dramatically. The reason for the large difference between this number and the one I cite in the text is that a comparison of *counties* allocates each place—even a large city with thousands of creditors—only one contribution to the final mean, so the influence of a Chicago or a St. Louis is heavily discounted in the resulting percentage. Since I am trying to contrast places rather than people, this is the relevant comparison.

   Note, incidentally, that out-of-county, out-of-state, and out-of-region debt percentages do not sum to 100 percent, since the categories overlap each other. Also, statistics for out-of-region debt shares in thinly populated counties are somewhat misleading. They tend to fluctuate wildly from place to place, ranging from zero percent all the way up to 100 percent, being much more influenced by the special circumstances of individual bankrupts than the comparable figures for large cities. A single Illinois farmer who had financed his farm by borrowing from family members living in Massachusetts could make his county look much more heavily involved in extraregional trade than the nearly two thousand debts that bankrupt Chicagoans owed outside the region. This is a problem with the bankruptcy statistics in general: the smaller the number of people they represent, the more anecdotal (and accidental) the evidence becomes. In the text, I therefore try to base my argument only on the most aggregated bankruptcy statistics for Chicago and its region.

42. The classic account of the Chicago–St. Louis trade rivalry is Wyatt Winton Belcher, *The Economic Rivalry between St. Louis and Chicago.* Although it contains much useful information on the structural underpinnings of the two cities' economies, it casts its explanation far too much in terms of the "energies" and "attitudes" of merchants in the two cities, attributing St. Louis's decline primarily to complacency and want of entrepreneurial energy. My own explanation is much more structural: given the forces arrayed against them, it is hard to see how the St. Louis merchants could have held their own relative to Chicago. On this point, see the various reports in Nimmo, *Rept. Int. Commerce;* White, "Chicago and Toronto," 40–48; and J. Christopher Schnell, "Chicago versus St. Louis," 245–65. For more general comparisons of shifting trade balances between water and rail transport networks, see George G. Tunell, "The Diversion of the Flour and Grain Traffic from the Great Lakes to the Railroads," *J. Pol. Econ.* 5 (1897): 340–75, 413–20; Appleton, "Declining Significance of the Mississippi," 267–84; Samuel H. Williamson, "The Growth of the Great Lakes as a Major Transportation Resource, 1870–1911," *Research in Economic History* 2 (1977): 173–248; and Jerome K. Laurent, "Trade, Transport and Technology: The American Great Lakes, 1866–1910," *Journal of Transport History,* 3d ser. 4 (1983): 1–24. See also the interesting discussion in Morgan, *The People and the Railways,* 111–21.

43. Jay Gitlin's forthcoming Yale dissertation, "The Bourgeois Frontier: French Creole Communities in the American Midwest, 1770–1840," does a superb job of tracing the mercantile activities of St. Louis's earlier fur-trading era. An article which gives a sense of its contents is Gitlin, "Managing the 'Tribe of Couteau,' 1810–1850," *WHQ,* forthcoming.

44. Appleton, "Declining Significance of the Mississippi," 274.

45. Mahoney, "Urban History in a Regional Context," 321–27.
46. The history of railroad construction to the river can be tracked in Paxson, "Railroads of the 'Old Northwest,' " 247–74.
47. Appleton, "Declining Significance of the Mississippi," 267–71.
48. *Daily Democratic Press,* Feb. 24, 1854, as quoted in White, "Chicago and Toronto," 44.
49. "Statement Prepared by Mr. Geo[r]ge Frazee, Surveyor of Customs at Burlington, Iowa, in Regard to the Conditions Governing the Course of the Commerce of the Northwestern States," in appendix no. 17, Nimmo, *Rept. Int. Commerce* (1879), 170. The combined effects of Chicago's trade advantages were nicely summarized in appendix no. 10 of the same report (p. 98) by Milo Smith of Iowa: "The reasons for the great decline in river business are obvious. First, the change in the manner of doing the produce business of the West requires it to be done in the shortest possible time, and the roads crossing the river at all the important points penetrate the country where the bulk of the grain is raised, gather it up in car loads, and, when once in the train, no more time is consumed in reaching the market in Chicago than would be by stopping for reshipment at the river crossing, while Chicago is a market at all times of the year, ample to take everything that is raised west of that point, and with unequaled facilities for handling it expeditiously. There is no town on the Mississippi River possessing these advantages. They can only take what is required for home consumption. All towns on the river above New Orleans are but way stations, as it were, on the railroads and river, while Chicago, at the head of lake navigation, becomes the transshipping point for all Western products, and a market that can be relied upon, easily reached, and from which rapid returns are made to the seller, thus enabling him to do a large amount of business on a small capital."
50. "Contests for the Trade of the Mississippi Valley," *DeBow's Review* 3, no. 2 (Feb. 1847): 98–111; Guy Stevens Callender, *Selections from the Economic History of the United States, 1765–1860* (1909), 337–44; Isaac Lippincott, "A History of River Improvement," *J. Pol. Econ.* 22 (1914): 644; Appleton, "Declining Significance of the Mississippi," 276–84; Belcher, *Rivalry between St. Louis and Chicago,* 96–113. See also Fishlow, "Antebellum Interregional Trade," 352–64.
51. Philadelphia's relative decline as a commercial center should in no way be taken to indicate an *absolute* decline of its overall economy; quite the opposite. In one of the most sophisticated city-hinterland studies yet written by an American historian, Diane Lindstrom has demonstrated that the city and its region shifted increasingly toward manufacturing and agricultural export during the first half of the nineteenth century, and that its involvement with eastern markets rose during the same period. See Lindstrom, *Economic Development in the Philadelphia Region.* Because the mountains and its poor harbor limited its extraregional trading possibilities, the city relied on intraregional demand and on the wholesaling services of cities like New York that were better positioned to conduct long-distance trade. Given Philadelphia's special circumstances, Lindstrom pays little attention to commerce and wholesaling, and may generalize too much about their insignificance in other places. As the Chicago booster Albert H. Walker remarked in 1873, "Two branches of human employment . . . constitute the basis of a modern city. They are Manufactures and Commerce. . . . Chicago has heretofore been chiefly a commercial city. . . ." Albert H. Walker, "The Future of Chicago," in Chamberlin, *Chicago and Its Suburbs,* 178.
52. Atherton, *Frontier Merchant,* 80–91. See also Gilchrist, ed., *Growth of Seaport Cities.* When the Pennsylvania Railroad did finally give Philadelphia a set of western rail connections, they branched at Pittsburgh: one led to St. Louis and the other—to Chicago.
53. Reavis, *Change of National Empire,* 47.
54. Lippincott, "History of River Improvement"; Belcher, *Rivalry between St. Louis and Chicago,* 193–97; and for a useful general discussion of railroads versus waterway improvements in the post–Civil War era, see Schonberger, *Transportation to the Seaboard.*
55. Abraham Lincoln was among the lawyers who defended the railroad and bridge company. Pierce, *History of Chicago,* 2:41–42.
56. St. Louis Chamber of Commerce, *Fifth Annual Report* (1860), 5.
57. Stover, *American Railroads,* 174.
58. Overton, *Burlington Route,* 19–21, 53–56, 91–92; Belcher, *Rivalry between St. Louis and Chicago,* 72–95.

59. For general surveys of St. Louis's efforts to construct railroads for itself, see Belcher, *Rivalry between St. Louis and Chicago,* 72–95; and Schnell's important critique "Chicago versus St. Louis," 245–65.

60. CBT, *Annual Report for 1861.*

61. Paxson, "Railroads of the 'Old Northwest,' " 261–63; Belcher, *Rivalry between St. Louis and Chicago,* 92–95.

62. "The City of St. Louis," *Atlantic Monthly* 19 (June 1867): 662. On the general effects of the war on the western economy, see Ralph Andreano, ed., *The Economic Impact of the American Civil War* (1962), esp. 48–63.

63. "Statement Prepared by Geo[r]ge Frazee," in Nimmo, *Rept. Int. Commerce* (1879), 167.

64. U.S. Census Bureau, *Census of Population, 1870.*

65. "St. Louis," *Harper's New Monthly Magazine* 68 (March 1884): 501. On St. Louis and the census, see Jeanette C. Lauer and Robert H. Lauer, "St. Louis and the 1880 Census: The Shock of Collective Failure," *Mo. Hist. Rev.* 76 (1982): 151–63.

66. Nimmo, *Rept. Int. Commerce* (1881), 126–27.

67. Wright, *Chicago,* 33, quoting an Omaha correspondent to the *Cincinnati Commercial* as quoted by the *Chicago Times.*

68. *St. Louis Intelligencer* quoted in the *Chicago Daily Democratic Press,* Sept. 21, 1855, as quoted by Belcher, *Rivalry between St. Louis and Chicago,* 124.

69. "Statement Prepared by Geo[r]ge Frazee," in Nimmo, *Rept. Int. Commerce* (1879), 171.

70. W. L. Fawcette, "Currency and Banking in Chicago," *Lakeside Monthly* 9 (Feb. 1873): 133. On the general history of Chicago's banks and their metropolitan influence, see Don Marcus Dailey, "The Development of Banking in Chicago before 1890" (Ph.D. thesis, Northwestern Univ., 1934); Dailey, "The Early Development of the Note-Brokerage Business in Chicago," *J. Pol. Econ.* 46 (1938): 202–17; and James, *Growth of Chicago Banks.*

71. Michael P. Conzen, "The Maturing Urban System in the United States, 1840–1910," *Annals Assoc. Am. Geog.* 67 (1977): 88–108; see also Conzen, "Capital Flows and the Developing Urban Hierarchy: State Bank Capital in Wisconsin, 1854–1895," *Economic Geography* 51 (1975): 321–38.

72. Conzen, "Maturing Urban System," 96.

73. James, *Growth of Chicago Banks,* 1:444–45.

74. *Chicago: Commerce, Manufactures, Banking and Transportation Facilities,* 15. On New York's national financial functions, see Margaret G. Myers, *The New York Money Market,* vol. 1, *Origins and Development* (1931).

75. Conzen created these lower-order regional maps by suppressing part of New York's overwhelming dominance of national banking correspondent relations. New York institutions did business with nearly every major bank in the country, so at the highest level there was really just one financial hinterland in the country. Only by statistically discounting this New York influence (and discounting some of Chicago's national role as well) does one begin to see the second- and third-order regional centers that expressed the national system of cities.

76. Conzen, "Maturing Urban System," 98–108.

77. Nimmo, *Rept. Int. Commerce* (1881), 126–27, delimits St. Louis's *trading* hinterland in 1880.

78. The classic work on this subject is Burghardt, "A Hypothesis about Gateway Cities," 269–85. For a contemporary description of Chicago and other western cities that conveys a strong sense of this gateway role, see de Rousiers, *American Life,* 19–156.

79. Nineteenth-century San Francisco is the exception to prove the rule: it sat at the *western* edge of an elongated *eastern* hinterland stretching beyond the Sierra Nevada into the Great Basin, but was in all other respects a classic gateway city.

80. Thomas, *Report,* iii.

81. Nimmo, *Rept. Int. Commerce* (1881), 105; see also ibid. (1879), 47; and *Report of a Committee of the Board of Trade, Chicago, on the Question of the Advantages of That City as a Location for a Branch Mint, for the Refining and Coinage of Silver and Gold* (1875), 2.

82. For an interesting example, see the discussion of how Chicago banks financed the western cattle trade in John Clay, *My Life on the Range* (1924; reprint, 1962).

83. "Answers to Inquiries in Relation to Commercial Movements to and from the State of Iowa . . . by Col. Milo Smith, of Clinton, Iowa," in Nimmo, *Rept. Int. Commerce* (1877), 95.

7: THE BUSY HIVE

1. See Thomas, *Report,* 14–15, for a list of the city's trades in 1847. On primary manufacturing of this sort, see Walsh, *Manufacturing Frontier.*
2. U.S. Census, 1860–80; Wesley G. Skogan, *Chicago since 1840: A Time-series Data Handbook* (1976). For handy maps and statistics tracing Chicago's ethnic populations, see *Historic City: The Settlement of Chicago* (1976), with its accompanying volume of census statistics, *The People of Chicago: Who We Are and Who We Have Been* (1976).
3. Before the railroad construction booms of the 1870s and 1880s increased competition and drove down transport rates still further, many heavy, bulky manufactured goods of this kind also enjoyed a locational advantage that favored the Midwest over the Northeast. Early historical explanations of American manufacturing and urban growth emphasized the importance of export and *inter*regional trade demand in encouraging the spread of factories. It now seems clear that *intra*regional demand was at least as important, especially in secondary manufacturing. See Lindstrom, *Economic Development in the Philadelphia Region.*
4. Chicago's nearest-ranking industrial competitors were Cincinnati with 53,508 factory workers and St. Louis with 38,500. In this paragraph, I follow David R. Meyer in "Midwestern Industrialization and the American Manufacturing Belt in the Nineteenth Century," *JEH* 49 (1989): 921–37; the statistics I have just cited are on p. 931. See also Albert W. Niemi, Jr., *State and Regional Patterns in American Manufacturing, 1860–1900* (1974); Donald L. Kemmerer, "Financing Illinois Industry, 1830–1890," *Bulletin of the Business History Society* 27 (1953): 97–111; and Mary Oona Marquardt, "Sources of Capital of Early Illinois Manufacturers, 1840–1880" (Ph.D. thesis, Univ. of Illinois, 1960).
5. *U.S. Census of Manufactures,* 1880. A striking instance of the varying success of midwestern factories in competing with older firms in the Northeast is the clothing industry. In 1880, Chicago made $17 million worth of men's clothing but less than $2 million worth of women's clothing—presumably because the market for fashionable female clothing was much more heavily dominated by northeastern firms. For a helpful descriptive survey of Chicago's factories shortly after the Great Fire, see S. S. Schoff, *The Industrial Interests of Chicago* (1873).
6. "Statement in Regard to the Development of Manufacturing Industries in Western Towns and Cities, Prepared by J. D. Hayes, Esq., of Detroit, Mich., April 7, 1881" in Nimmo, *Rept. Int. Commerce* (1881), 179.
7. Riley, *Development of Chicago and Vicinity as a Manufacturing Center,* 101–9. Details of the earlier history of the iron industry in Chicago, when rolling mills and boilermakers depended almost entirely on pig iron imported from elsewhere, can be found in Joseph T. Ryerson, "Recollections of His First Journey, Philadelphia to Chicago, and Impressions of Chicago—1842," and in the unpublished corporate history of the Ryerson Company, both held in the company archives in Chicago. See also George W. Cope, *The Iron and Steel Interests of Chicago* (1890). For the role of Chicago capitalists in developing a later iron supply hinterland for the city, see David A. Walker, *Iron Frontier: The Discovery and Early Development of Minnesota's Three Ranges* (1979).
8. *U.S. Census of Manufactures,* 1880.
9. On McCormick's career, see William T. Hutchinson, *Cyrus Hall McCormick,* vol 1, *Seed-Time, 1809–1856* (1930); Hutchinson, *Cyrus Hall McCormick,* vol. 2, *Harvest, 1856–1884* (1935); and Cyrus McCormick, *The Century of the Reaper* (1931).
10. Before the move to Chicago, many of McCormick's reapers had been manufactured by independent factories which contracted to handle the production of a particular area. These subcontracting arrangements made it hard to maintain quality control, however, and McCormick abandoned them after establishing his own base of operations in Chicago.
11. Hutchinson, *McCormick,* 1:250–52; William Cronon, "To Be the Central City," *Chicago History* 10 (1981): 130–40.
12. On reasons for the relatively slow adoption of reaping technology in American agriculture, see Paul A. David, "The Mechanization of Reaping in the Ante-Bellum Midwest," in Henry Rosovsky, ed., *Industrialization in Two Systems: Essays in Honor of Alexander*

Gerschenkron (1966), 3–39, which stresses rising labor costs during the 1850s relative to reaper costs as being more important than regional shifts in explaining adoption of the technology; William N. Parker and Judith L. V. Klein, "Productivity Growth in Grain Production in the United States, 1840–60 and 1900–10," in Conference on Research in Income and Wealth, *Output, Employment, and Productivity in the United States after 1800,* Studies in Income and Wealth, vol. 30 (1966), 523–82; Alan L. Olmstead, "The Mechanization of Reaping and Mowing in American Agriculture, 1833–1870," *JEH* 35 (1975): 327–52, which lays greater emphasis on gradual improvements in McCormick's basic design as being more critical to eventual adoption. Both authors underrate the geographical fact of Chicago's expanding market hinterland. See also Herbert A. Kellar, "The Reaper as a Factor in the Development of the Agriculture of Illinois, 1834–1865," *Transactions of the Illinois State Historical Society* 34 (1927): 105–14; and a useful critique of Olmstead, Lewis R. Jones, " 'The Mechanization of Reaping and Mowing in American Agriculture, 1833–1870': Comment," *JEH* 37 (1977): 451–55.

13. The history of reaping technology is traced in Rogin, *Introduction of Farm Machinery,* 69–153.

14. McCormick's success as a manufacturer, like that of many of his industrial peers in the second half of the nineteenth century, rested more on his marketing prowess than on any special genius he might have had as a manufacturer. His production techniques were rather old-fashioned by the standards of the day, relying much more heavily on artisanal craft methods than on newer mass production arrangements. See David A. Hounshell, *From the American System to Mass Production, 1800–1932: The Development of Manufacturing Technology in the United States* (1984), 152–87, on this point.

15. Hutchinson, *McCormick,* 1:327–76, does a good job of surveying the reaper maker's distribution techniques. See also Porter and Livesay, *Merchants and Manufacturers,* 192.

16. *McCormick Reaper Centennial Source Material* [1931], 55.

17. Typical was McCormick's contract with the firm of Fiske and Elliott in Iowa City in 1860. The agent received a 12 percent discount on reaper prices and up to $25 for advertising in return for handling equipment sales in five adjacent counties "and westward as much as [the firm] can canvas." Contract with Fiske & Elliott, Iowa City, Johnson County, Iowa, 1860, Agency Records, McC 3X 3M7D6, McCormick Collections, SHSW. Some agents handled a large enough business to contract subagents themselves, in effect becoming wholesalers for the McCormick company. See, for instance, the records of A. R. Metcalf in Constantine, Michigan, and J. B. Fairbanks & Sons in Concord, Illinois, in the Agency Records files.

18. A useful discussion of McCormick's relations with his agents can be found in Forrest Dean Flippo, "The McCormick Reaper and the Development of United States Wheat Production in the Ante-bellum Years" (M.S. thesis, Univ. of Wisconsin, 1964), 33ff. McCormick's agency system was an early version of a distribution mechanism that became increasingly common among manufacturers of expensive nonconsumer machinery in the decades to come. See Arthur H. Cole, "Marketing Nonconsumer Goods before 1917: An Exploration of Secondary Literature," *Bus. Hist. Rev.* 33 (1959): 420–28.

19. Olmstead points out that the McCormick Harvesting Machine Company has sometimes been lauded for its 6 percent interest rate, which superficially seems so generous as to be below the company's own borrowing costs; in fact, one has to add to the direct interest charge the $5 differential between the cash and the credit prices. When one does so, the 6 percent interest rate becomes 19 percent—not nearly so generous, but still below the rates charged by other farm equipment manufacturers. Olmstead, "Mechanization of Reaping," 332–33.

20. McCormick Reaper Sales, 1849–1872, 3M16J2, McCormick Archives, SHSW.

21. Ibid. *Production* figures for the McCormick reaper are conveniently tabulated in Hounshell, *American System to Mass Production,* 161, though these sometimes differ in surprising ways from the *sales* figures I cite from the McCormick Archives. I suspect that the company's statistics on this subject may have been fairly imprecise.

22. McCormick Reaper Sales, 1849–1872, 3M16J2, McCormick Archives, SHSW.

23. McCormick was by no means the only reaper manufacturer in the country during the 1850s. After he lost control of his original patent in 1848, eastern manufacturers produced thousands of similar machines, especially in the prosperous agricultural

regions of upstate New York. McCormick was nonetheless the largest and best-known manufacturer in the country, and the most important in the West.

24. Burrows, *Fifty Years in Iowa* (1888). Burrows's autobiography is perhaps the most remarkable ever written by a western merchant about the period 1830–60, and deserves to be much better known than it is. The classic scholarly work that places Burrows in his larger setting is Atherton, *Frontier Merchant.*

25. Burrows, *Fifty Years in Iowa,* 149–50.

26. Three years after he arrived in Davenport, Burrows hired R. M. Prettyman to handle the storekeeping end of his business. Prettyman became Burrows's partner in 1844, and the two appear to have divided the business so that Burrows concentrated on produce and Prettyman on the general retail store. Ibid., 150–53, 181–82.

27. Ibid., 200–201.

28. Ibid., 152–53.

29. Burrichter & Hellman of Galena, Illinois, to Charles J. Brewster (a merchant in Fort Madison, Iowa), May 29, 1856, in Brewster Papers, SHSI.

30. Burrows, *Fifty Years in Iowa,* 182–85.

31. Ibid., 202–5.

32. Interestingly, a heavy snowfall could actually make it *easier* for rural customers to visit nearby towns in the winter, by improving sleighing conditions. See, for instance, George Kepner to Henry C. Potter Company, Dec. 2, 1865, in George W. Kepner Papers, MsC16, UISC.

33. Burrows, *Fifty Years in Iowa,* 154.

34. Ibid., 233–34.

35. Many banknotes also had to be physically redeemed at the location from which they were issued, adding a significant transportation cost for anyone who wanted to convert them. It was far easier to redeem a banknote in New York than in the Okefenokee Swamp of Georgia—which was a good reason to issue such "wildcat" notes in the middle of the swamp if one wanted to keep them in circulation! For a fascinating account of frontier currency operations, see Alice E. Smith, *George Smith's Money.* For general surveys of banking and currency in the nineteenth century, see F. Cyril James, *Growth of Chicago Banks;* Robert P. Sharkey, *Money, Class, and Party: An Economic Study of Civil War and Reconstruction* (1959); Hammond, *Banks and Politics in America;* Irwin Unger, *The Greenback Era: A Social and Political History of American Finance, 1865–1879* (1964); Walter T. K. Nugent, *The Money Question during Reconstruction* (1967); Margaret G. Myers, *A Financial History of the United States* (1970); Richard Sylla, "The United States, 1863–1913," in Rondo Cameron, ed., *Banking and Economic Development: Some Lessons of History* (1972), 232–62; John A. James, *Money and Capital Markets in Postbellum America* (1978).

36. The fact that metropolitan banknotes circulated much nearer to par than notes issued elsewhere was yet another advantage that the residents of a major city gained by living at the top of the urban hierarchy.

37. Requests for "New York or Chicago Exchange" are common in nineteenth-century invoice books. See, for example, the account books of Frank S. Whitaker, a hardware store dealer in Nortonville, Kansas, where invoices for the Atchison, Kansas, wholesaler A. J. Harwi (c. 1900) announce that they are "Payable in New York or Chicago Exchange" (Frank S. Whitaker Collection, Kansas State Historical Museum); or the invoice collections of the Emery Grocery in Cedar Rapids, Iowa (c. 1880), where the printed invoice of T. M. Sinclair & Co., a Cedar Rapids pork packer, announces that its recipient should "Remit in New York or Chicago Exchange, at par, or by P. O. Order or Express, charges prepaid." Emery Grocery Papers, Ac25a, SHSI. Although these date from a later period, they are entirely typical (save for the addition of Chicago) of earlier mercantile practices. On the use of banknotes as currency during the first half of the nineteenth century, see Atherton, *Frontier Merchant in Mid-America,* 136–42.

38. Burrows, *Fifty Years in Iowa,* 141–44.

39. Ibid., 190–95, 237–40.

40. Ibid., 234–36, 241–44, 273–91. Burrows's scheme of issuing his own notes eventually led to his downfall in 1859. Under the straitened conditions that followed the panic of 1857, when credit was extremely tight, the Davenport bank, Cook and Sargent, itself fell on hard times. Burrows and the bank worked out a rather underhanded arrangement for "swapping notes" whereby each agreed to redeem notes only with each

other's notes—a circular arrangement from which their customers had trouble escaping.

41. Ibid., 162. For a survey of the credit mechanisms that permitted merchants to do business during this and earlier periods, see Klein, "Development of Mercantile Instruments of Credit."

42. William K. Brown, farmer, to Charles J. Brewster, Jan. 29, 1858, in Brewster Papers, SHSI. The worst fear of the letter writer, suggested in his plea "dont put me to any cost," was that Brewster might begin a legal proceeding to recover the debt, and that a court's judgment would eventually lead to the loss of his mortgage, farm, and home.

43. W. M. Wyeth & Co. of St. Joseph, Missouri, to Francis E. Newton, general hardware merchant in Lincoln, Nebraska, June 2, 1880, in Francis E. Newton Papers (Wilson & Newton, general hardware dealers), MS444, Nebraska State Historical Society. This letter is from the postrailroad period, but it is little different from letters of Burrows's era.

44. Ryerson, "Recollections," unpaginated typescript 3 pages from end.

45. On this point, see Curtiss, *Western Portraiture*, 52; and Colbert, *Chicago*, 74.

46. Flint, *Railroads of the United States*, 267.

47. George Frazee gave a superb summary of these effects: "Formerly the dealer was under the necessity of purchasing as many goods as he supposed he could dispose of in six months. In the winter the river was closed by the ice. In summer, for the greater part, it was apt to be too low for easy navigation. The spring and fall were the only seasons in which he could rely upon a reasonably certain transportation of his goods at a not excessive cost. Besides, such dealers as purchased in the East, were compelled to make long and tedious journeys at the expense of much time and money, and their goods were a long time in transit at heavy charges for freight, even when freights were lowest. Those who bought in western cities, paid the jobber there for doing what the purchaser in the East did for himself, and a profit in addition. And when the retailer at last received his goods, he was compelled as a rule to sell upon credit more or less extended, and dependent usually upon the result of current or future crops.

"Under all these burdens of actual expense and necessary uncertainty, it followed inevitably that the consumer was required to pay a price for everything he purchased calculated to cover all contingencies. Prices of all commodities brought from a distance were *high,* while the products of home industry were exceedingly *low*; and they were low because during half the year they could not be transported to any market, and all markets were so distant, and to be reached only by such circuitous and expensive routes, that the most favorable results could bring but a small return to the producer. Railroads have changed all this to the lasting advantage of all our communities, and without railroads the change could never have been made." "Statement Prepared by Geo[r]ge Frazee," in Nimmo, *Rept. Int. Commerce* (1879), 168.

48. "Answers . . . by Col. Milo Smith, of Clinton, Iowa," in Nimmo, *Rept. Int. Commerce* (1879), 98–99.

49. Burrows, *Fifty Years in Iowa*, 270–71.

50. Ibid., 271.

51. Ibid., 293.

52. For a general survey of these phenomena, see Vance, *Merchant's World.*

53. Atherton, *Frontier Merchant in Mid-America*, 70.

54. Curtiss, *Western Portraiture*, 52.

55. Charles Randolph, "Answers to Inquiries in Relation to the Commerce of Chicago," in Nimmo, *Rept. Int. Commerce* (1877), 82.

56. Brewster's reliance on Philadelphia as a wholesaling center was consistent with the behavior of other Mississippi Valley merchants in the 1840s, but was undoubtedly also strengthened by the fact that he arrived in that city as a twelve-year-old immigrant from Ireland and lived there until migrating west at the age of twenty-three. For a sketch of Brewster's career, see John E. Pilcher, "Charles Brewster of Fort Madison: A Profile in Enterprise, 1845–1875," *Annals of Iowa*, 3d ser., 44 (1979): 602–26.

57. This transition toward Chicago financial institutions happened to most Iowa banks during the late 1850s and early 1860s as their customers used increasing numbers of sight drafts drawn on banks in Chicago as opposed to New York. See, for instance, the records of Culbertson and Reno, a small bank in Iowa City. In 1856, as this shift was in its early stages, it made thirteen transactions, worth $2,801, with Chicago banks, and

twenty-six, worth $9,587, with New York; only three were with St. Louis. Account Book, Culbertson and Reno Papers, MsC 29, UISC. See also Erling A. Erickson, *Banking in Frontier Iowa, 1836–1865* (1971).

58. Bills and Receipts Folders, Charles J. Brewster Papers, B47, SHSI. There is some risk in drawing these inferences from what is undoubtedly an incomplete collection of invoices and receipts, but the pattern of these surviving records is so strong, and is confirmed by so much other evidence, that the argument I offer in the text is almost surely correct as a broad generalization.

59. Vigo Bardollet in St. Louis to Charles J. Brewster, March 4, 1864, Charles Brewster Papers, SHSI.

60. Potter Palmer advertisement, *Chicago Tribune,* Nov. 9, 1861.

61. George W. Kepner to Henry C. Potter Co., Aug. [?] 5, 1865, in Kepner Papers, UISC.

62. On Palmer's marketing activities, see Robert W. Twyman, "Potter Palmer: Merchandising Innovator of the West," *Explorations in Entrepreneurial History* 4 (1951–52): 58–72; see also Lloyd Wendt and Herman Kogan, *Give the Lady What She Wants! The Story of Marshall Field & Company* (1952). For surveys of Chicago's merchandisers and wholesalers by the 1880s, see *Chicago's First Half Century,* 86–97; and *Chicago: Commerce, Manufactures, Banking and Transportation Facilities,* 122–53.

63. On the life of the traveling salesman, see Timothy B. Spears, "A Grip on the Land," *Chicago History* 17, nos. 3–4 (Fall–Winter 1988–89): 4–25.

64. *Chicago Exposition Gazeteer and Jobbers' Record,* Sept. 3, 1879, published for the 1879 Industrial Exposition of Chicago.

65. Colbert, *Chicago,* 74.

66. "The Best Kind of Drummer," *Milwaukee Journal of Commerce,* as reprinted in the *Wisconsin Lumberman,* June 1874, 248. Lumber wholesalers, selling relatively uniform products in a market where one firm's products were much like another's, were especially ambivalent about what they called "the evil of drummers." In November 1878, the Chicago Lumbermen's Exchange tried to impose a moratorium on their use, but the experiment ended ignominiously within a few weeks when it became clear that many wholesalers were unwilling to abandon so effective a competitive tool. For key articles that give a sense of the drummer controversy in the lumber trade, see *NWL,* Oct. 13, 1877; Nov. 10, 1877; Sept. 14, 1878; Oct. 12, 1878; Nov. 12, 1878; Nov. 30, 1878; Dec. 7, 1878; and May 1, 1880. See also the useful volume by Saley, *Realm of the Retailer,* which surveys marketing techniques in the lumber industry in general.

67. Correspondence and Invoice files, Francis E. Newton Papers, MS444, Nebraska State Historical Society.

68. Hayden Hardware Store Papers, Wis MSS OI, SHSW. The store bought virtually its entire stock from just five firms, two in Chicago and three in Milwaukee.

69. Invoice Books, Darwin Clark Collections, MSS 19, SHSW.

70. See, for instance, the account books of Frank S. Whitaker, a hardware store owner in Nortonville, Kansas, in the 1880s and 1890s (Kansas State Historical Museum). Few of his major transactions were with Chicago; instead, he relied for more than half of his orders on a nearby wholesaler in Atchison (who probably bought in turn from Chicago firms).

71. Charles B. Sawyer Invoice Book, 1871, CHS. Sawyer's warehouse was destroyed in the Great Fire, so his account books come to an abrupt end on October 7, 1871. The claims in this paragraph are based on a computer tabulation of all Sawyer's invoices for 1871, and on maps of his total and average sales by county.

72. See Invoices, Henry Veith Collection, MS3610, Nebraska State Historical Society, 1873–79. These trading relationships were made still more complicated by the fact that some of Veith's wholesalers in Lincoln had strong ties to the Chicago firms that supplied them; moreover, some of his Chicago suppliers were agents in turn for wholesalers in New York and other eastern cities.

73. See, for instance, George W. Kepner to Henry C. Potter Co., Dec. 11, 1865, in Kepner Collection, UISC.

74. Marshall Lefferts, "The Electric Telgraph: Its Influence and Geographical Distribution," *Bulletin of the American Geographical and Statistical Society* 2 (1857): 259; DuBoff, "The Telegraph and the Structure of Markets," 253–77. The telegraph also enabled railroads to run more efficiently, by making it possible to send out scheduling information for dispatching trains. The Chicago, Burlington and Quincy began telegraph

dispatching in the fall of 1864; five years later, it suffered its first train wreck as a result of a telegrapher's dispatching error. Robert Harris to J. N. Denison, Jan. 28, 1869, CB&Q Archives, H.4.1.

75. George W. Kepner to Henry C. Potter Co., Nov. 16, 1865, in Kepner Collection, UISC.

76. Wayne E. Fuller, *The American Mail: Enlarger of the Common Life* (1972), 167.

77. "Available Record of Chicago Daily Newspaper Circulation" and "History of the Chicago Tribune Circulation Department," in the Tribune Company Archives. On the operation of a major Chicago daily in the early 1890s, see *Chicago Daily News*, Oct. 12, 1891, also subsequently published as a pamphlet, n.d. See also Philip Kinsley, *The Chicago Tribune: Its First Hundred Years* (1943). On the eagerness of hinterland readers to obtain metropolitan newspapers, even from New York, see the letter from John H. Leavitt in Waterloo, Iowa, to his father, Roger Hooker Leavitt, in western Massachusetts, June 19, 1860, as reprinted in the *Waterloo Daily Courier*, June 20, 1930, copy in the Chicago, Milwaukee, St. Paul and Pacific Railroad Collection, SHSW.

78. Overton, *Burlington Route*, 201.

79. *Chicago Tribune*, March 12, 1884.

80. Ibid., March 13, 1884. The reach of Chicago newspapers and other periodicals extended even farther the next year, after Congress reduced postage rates for bulk mail from two cents per pound to one cent, making it possible to send approximately eight papers for the same price that less than a decade earlier it had cost to send only two. Fuller, *American Mail*, 133.

81. On Ward's life and career, see Nina Baker, *Big Catalogue: The Life of Aaron Montgomery Ward* (1956); Daniel J. Boorstin, "A. Montgomery Ward's Mail-Order Business," *Chicago History*, n.s., 2 (1973): 142–52; Boorstin, *The Americans: The Democratic Experience* (1973), 118–29; Cecil C. Hoge, Sr., *The First Hundred Years Are the Toughest: What We Can Learn from the Century of Competition between Sears and Wards* (1988). Still in many ways the most useful survey of the early mail order industry in Chicago is Rae Elizabeth Rips, "An Introductory Study of the Role of the Mail Order Business in American History, 1872–1914" (Master's thesis, Univ. of Chicago, 1938). The best study of a Chicago mail order company is Boris Emmet and John E. Jeuck, *Catalogues and Counters: A History of Sears, Roebuck & Company* (1950); this should be supplemented with the relevant chapters of Chandler, *Strategy and Structure.*

82. "The Middle-Man," in George F. Root, *The Trumpet of Reform: A Collection of Songs, Hymns, Chants and Set Pieces for the Grange, the Club and all Industrial & Reform Associations* (1874), 22.

83. *Western Rural*, Sept. 4, 1875.

84. "Grangers Beware!" *Chicago Tribune*, Nov. 8, 1873.

85. "Montgomery, Ward & Co.," *Chicago Tribune*, Dec. 24, 1873.

86. Ibid.

87. In addition to the catalogs themselves, which are the ultimate statistical and descriptive source on Ward's growth, this paragraph is based on the summaries in Rips, "Mail Order Business," 15–22; and Hoge, *First Hundred Years*, 12–40. The most widely available reprints of nineteenth-century Ward and Sears catalogs are *Montgomery Ward & Co. Catalogue and Buyers Guide, No. 57, Spring and Summer 1895* (reprint, 1969); and *Sears, Roebuck and Co. Catalogue No. 104, 1897* (reprint, 1968).

88. Montgomery Ward & Co. "Beehive" catalog cover, c. 1900. The image is reprinted in color as the cover of *Chicago History*, n.s. 2, no. 3 (Spring–Summer 1973), and even more accurately in Perry Duis, *Chicago: Creating New Traditions* (1976), 109.

89. Mrs. S. Gilbert, Benkleman, Nebraska, quoted in Hoge, *First Hundred Years*, 16.

8: WHITE CITY PILGRIMAGE

1. The Chicago World's Fair has been so studied by scholars that it has become almost an academic industry in its own right. The best recent works include Thomas S. Hines, *Burnham of Chicago: Architect and Planner* (1974); David F. Burg, *Chicago's White City of 1893* (1976); R. Reid Badger, *The Great American Fair: The World's Columbian Exposition & American Culture* (1979); Mario Manieri-Elia, "Toward an 'Imperial City': Daniel H. Burnham and the City Beautiful Movement," in Giorgio Ciucci et al., *The American City from the Civil War to the New Deal* (1979), 1–142; Alan Trachtenberg, *The Incorporation of*

America: Culture and Society in the Gilded Age (1982), 208–34; Robert W. Rydell, *All the World's a Fair: Visions of Empire at American International Expositions, 1876–1916* (1984); Frank A. Cassell and Marguerite E. Cassell, "The White City in Peril: Leadership and the World's Columbian Exposition," *Chicago History* 12, no. 3 (Fall 1983): 10–27. The indispensable primary historical source on the fair, comprehensive in its official narrative of exhibits and activities, is Rossiter Johnson, ed., *A History of the World's Columbian Exposition Held in Chicago in 1893,* 4 vols. (1897); see also Moses P. Handy, ed., *The Official Directory of the World's Columbian Exposition: A Reference Book* (1893); and Hubert Howe Bancroft, *The Book of the Fair: A Historical and Descriptive Presentation of the World's Science, Art, and Industry, as Viewed through the Columbian Exposition at Chicago in 1893* (1894). The most readily available modern photographic collection offering a general visual sense of the fair is Stanley Appelbaum, *The Chicago World's Fair of 1893: A Photographic Record* (1980).

2. *Rand, McNally & Co.'s Handbook of the World's Columbian Exposition* (1893), 26; John J. Flinn, *Official Guide to the World's Columbian Exposition* (1893), 30–34.

3. Noble Canby, "The Great Exposition at Chicago," *Chautauquan* 15 (1892): 460–68, is a good example of the pre-fair periodical literature, as is H. C. Bunner, "The Making of the White City," *Scribner's Magazine* 12 (Oct. 1892): 398–418; and Franklin MacVeagh, "Chicago's Part in the World's Fair," ibid., 551–57. On final costs, see Badger, *Great American Fair,* 140.

4. Montgomery Schuyler, one of the nation's leading architecture critics, noticed this feature of Chicago culture while summing up the accomplishments of the exposition. "In this country," he wrote, "mere bigness counts for more than anywhere else, and in Chicago, the citadel of the superlative degree, it counts for more, perhaps, than it counts for elsewhere in this country. To say of anything that it is the 'greatest' thing of its kind in the world is a very favorite form of advertisement in Chicago. One cannot escape hearing it and seeing it there a dozen times a day, nor from noting the concomitant assumption that the biggest is the best." Montgomery Schuyler, "Last Words about the World's Fair," *Architectural Record* 3 (Jan.–March 1894): 297.

5. James W. Shepp and Daniel B. Shepp, *Shepp's World's Fair Photographed* (1893), 5.

6. William James to Henry James, Sept. 22, 1893, as quoted in Badger, *Great American Fair,* 97. Turnabout is fair play: for a satirical critique of people like James who chose *not* to visit the exposition, see Robert Grant, "People Who Did Not Go to the Fair," *Cosmopolitan* 16 (Dec. 1893): 158–64.

7. James Fullarton Muirhead, *The Land of Contrasts: A Briton's View of His American Kin* (1898), 205.

8. Patterson, *World's Fair,* 69.

9. Eugene V. Debs, as quoted in Trachtenberg, *Incorporation of America,* 218, 222; William Dean Howells, "Letter of an Altrurian Traveller, Chicago, Sept. 28, 1893," *Cosmopolitan* 16 (Dec. 1893): 218–32.

10. Characteristically, Chicagoans and others responded to these worrisome attendance rates by complaining that the railroads were charging excessive passenger fares for travelers trying to reach the fair. Newspapers in Chicago and elsewhere during the second half of 1893 were filled with articles reporting on the controversy between railroad companies and those who argued that exposition attendance would dramatically increase if only there were special excursion fares to the White City. For examples, see the *Kansas City Journal,* May 25, 1893; *Chicago Herald,* June 3, 1893; *Kansas City Journal,* Aug. 5, 1893; *Chicago Tribune,* Aug. 6, 1893; *Chicago Inter Ocean,* Aug. 21, Sept. 1, 1893; *Chicago Journal,* Sept. 7, 1893 (a rare prorailroad piece); *Chicago Times,* Sept. 14, 1893; *Chicago Tribune,* Sept. 25, 1893; *Chicago Times,* Oct. 28, 1893 (in which an attorney argued that the railroads ought to be liable to pay damages to Chicago hotelkeepers unable to fill all their rooms); *Chicago Tribune,* Nov. 1, 1893 (an excellent overall review claiming that the fair lost several million dollars as a result of high railroad fares). An interesting review of how one railroad, the CB&Q, benefited from fair-bound passengers, can be found in the *Railroad Gazette,* Jan. 19, 1894.

11. Johnson, ed., *History of the Columbian Exposition,* 1:475; "Attendance at the Fair," *Chicago Tribune,* Nov. 1, 1893.

12. Johnson, *History of the Columbian Exposition,* 1:453–56.

13. Ibid., 449–50.

14. Ibid., 438.

15. Most registration books frrom individual state exhibits at the exposition have not survived, but the few remaining examples suggest that different exhibits at the fair drew from very different hinterlands. See, for instance, the Register of the Illinois Women's Exposition Board, May 17–July 22, 1893, Newberry Library MS +R 1832 .4312, in which four-fifths of the registrants were from Illinois; and the Visitors Register to the Wisconsin State Building (CHS), in which Wisconsinites accounted for well over 90 percent of all registrants. Contrast these two state registers with the Register of the Columbian Pickwick Rooms at the Great White Horse Inn (CHS), a posh restaurant offering British atmosphere. Although wealthy Chicagoans were the largest single group to eat in these expensive dining rooms, visitors from the city's western hinterland were outnumbered by easterners and foreigners, most from major metropolitan centers. (In all cases, I have relied on rough samples—generally one randomly chosen address for each page of the registration book—as the basis for these observations.)

16. Mary E. Stewart, Record of the World's Columbian Exposition, Isaac N. and Mary E. Stewart Papers, MSS C5, vol. 4, SHSW.

17. Teresa Dean, *White City Chips* (1895), 171. Dean's is among the best texts for getting a sense of how ordinary visitors reacted to the fair.

18. Ibid., 95–100.

19. *My Record of the World's Columbian Exposition* (1893); for a filled-in example of how a hinterland tourist actually used such a diary, see the Isaac N. and Mary E. Stewart Papers, Wis Mss C5, vol. 4, SHSW.

20. Quondam [Charles M. Stevens], *The Adventures of Uncle Jeremiah and Family at the Great Fair, Their Observations and Triumphs* (1893), 28. The reference is to Jesus bringing sight to a blind man in Mark 8:24.

21. Henry Adams, *The Education of Henry Adams* (1906), in *Henry Adams: Novels, Mont Saint Michel, The Education* (1983), 1031. On Adams's visit, see Paul C. Nagel, "Twice to the Fair," *Chicago History* 11, no. 1 (Spring 1985): 4–19

22. William T. Stead, "My First Visit to America: An Open Letter to My Readers," *Review of Reviews* (London ed.), 9 (1894): 414. Adams was probably aware of the analogy himself, saying at one point that "all traders' taste smelt of bric-a-brac; Chicago tried at least to give her taste a look of unity." Adams, *Education*, 1031. Russell Lewis explores this association between department stores and world's fairs in "Everything under One Roof: World's Fairs and Department Stores in Paris and Chicago," *Chicago History* 12, no. 3 (Fall 1983): 28–47.

23. Adams, *Education*, 1034.

24. Shepp, *World's Fair Photographed*, 7.

25. The fire produced an outpouring of popular histories and relief-oriented promotional publications second only to the Columbian Exposition in Chicago's history. The best among these are probably Elias Colbert and Everett Chamberlin, *Chicago and the Great Conflagration* (1871); Alfred L. Sewall, *The Great Calamity* (1871); and James W. Sheahan and George P. Upton, *The Great Conflagration: Chicago: Its Past, Present and Future* (1872). For a modern anthology of reprinted narratives and photographs, see David Lowe, comp., *The Great Chicago Fire in Eyewitness Accounts and 70 Contemporary Photographs and Illustrations* (1979); and Mabel McIlvaine, ed., *Reminiscences of Chicago during the Great Fire* (1915). Recent analytical histories of the fire include Christine Meisner Rosen, *The Limits of Power: Great Fires and the Process of City Growth in America* (1986), which is summarized in part in Rosen, "Infrastructural Improvement in Nineteenth-Century Cities: A Conceptual Framework and Cases," *J. Urban Hist.* 12 (1986): 211–56; John J. Pauly, "The Great Chicago Fire as a National Event," *American Quarterly* 36 (1984): 668–83; and Karen Sawislak, "Smoldering City," *Chicago History* 17, nos. 3–4 (Fall–Winter 1988–89): 70–101. Sawislak's forthcoming dissertation from Yale University, "Smoldering City: Class, Ethnicity, and Politics in Chicago, 1867–1877," examines class conflict in the relief efforts following the fire. The best full-scale treatment of the Great Fire as the central myth of nineteenth-century Chicago history is Ross Miller, *American Apocalypse: The Great Fire and the Myth of Chicago* (1990), which became available only after my own text was completed.

26. For an early example, see "Chicago," *Scribner's Monthly* 10, no. 5 (Sept. 1875): 3. On the use of the phoenix image in booster rhetoric generally, see Hamer, *New Towns in the New World*, 171–72, 215.

27. William Bross, "Statement of Ex-Lieut. Gov. Bross of the Chicago Tribune," *Chicago*

Tribune, Oct. 14, 1871, as quoted in Bross, *History of Chicago,* 101. See also Brooks, "Chicago and Its Railways," 265: "The hope of the city was seen to lie immediately in its railway system. It was in the railways alone that was found living assurance in the dead ashes of the metropolis; it was the 'great civilizer,' the locomotive, whose breath was anew to 'create a soul under the ribs of death.' The ascending smoke from a thousand speeding engines formed in fancy above the desolated city a pillar of cloud by day and of fire by night; and, no doubt, some poetic imagination may have pictured its curling volumes shaping themselves in the upper air into form of fabled Phoenix, *volant*—the new city's shield and coat of arms."

28. See Rosen, *Limits of Power,* 92–176.

29. Andrew Shuman, "One Year After," *Lakeside Monthly* 8 (Oct. 1871): 241–43, 246. Progress was not so smoothly continuous as my shorthand description in the text suggests. The imposition of building codes and fire limits involved a long political struggle among the different groups that would be helped and harmed thereby. The 1873 panic brought a temporary halt to large-scale reconstruction efforts, and another major fire, on July 14, 1874, meant additional struggles over building restrictions. The general trends nonetheless pointed in the direction of taller, more expensive, non-wooden structures in the downtown district, with wooden working-class housing, single-family residences, and fire-prone industries moving farther out toward the periphery. For a thorough analysis of changing property values in the wake of the fire, see Hoyt, *Land Values in Chicago,* 101–95.

30. Carl W. Condit, *The Chicago School of Architecture: A History of Commercial and Public Building in the Chicago Area, 1875–1925* (1964); "Architecture and the City," special theme issue of *Chicago History* 12, no. 4 (Winter 1983–84): 1–72; and John Zukowsky, ed., *Chicago Architecture, 1872–1922: Birth of a Metropolis* (1987). For a visual sense of the emerging Chicago cityscape of the late nineteenth century, see David Lowe, *Lost Chicago* (1978); and for an excellent guidebook that surveys the city's modern neighborhoods and discusses their historical backgrounds, see Dominic A. Pacyga and Ellen Skerrett, *Chicago, City of Neighborhoods: Histories and Tours* (1986).

31. *Chicago: Commerce, Manufactures, Banking and Transportation Facilities,* 8.

32. On the environmental and social problems of the packing district, the classic contemporary description remains Sinclair, *The Jungle;* but see also Charles J. Bushnell, *The Social Problem at the Chicago Stock Yards* (1902); Robert A. Slayton, *Back of the Yards: The Making of a Local Democracy* (1986); and Wade, *Chicago's Pride.* For a general survey of working-class life in Chicago, see Kenneth Lyle Kann, "Working Class Culture and the Labor Movement in Nineteenth Century Chicago" (Ph.D. thesis, Univ. of California, Berkeley, 1977).

33. *Chicago Times,* May 4, 1873, as reprinted in *Our Suburbs: A Resumé of the Origin, Progress and Present Status of Chicago's Environs* [1873],3.

34. On the shoreline suburbs, the standard work is Michael H. Ebner, *Creating Chicago's North Shore: A Suburban History* (1988). A still useful survey of their early growth is Chamberlin, *Chicago and Its Suburbs.* See also the studies by Jerome D. Fellmann, "Prebuilding Growth Patterns of Chicago," *Annals Assoc. Am. Geog.* 47 (March 1957): 59–82; Barbara Mercedes Posadas, "Community Structures of Chicago's Northwest Side: The Transition from Rural to Urban, 1830–1889" (Ph.D. thesis, Northwestern Univ., 1976); Carl Abbott, " 'Necessary Adjuncts to Its Growth': The Railroad Suburbs of Chicago, 1854–1875." *J. Ill. State Hist. Soc.* 73 (1980): 117–31; Gwendolyn Wright, *Moralism and the Model Home: Domestic Architecture and Cultural Conflict in Chicago, 1873–1913* (1980); Michael H. Ebner, " 'In the Suburbes of Toun': Chicago's North Shore to 1871," *Chicago History* 11, no. 2 (Summer 1982): 66–77; the special suburban theme issue of *Chicago History* 13, no. 2 (Summer 1984); and Ann Durkin Keating, *Building Chicago: Suburban Developers & the Creation of a Divided Metropolis* (1988). The best one-volume synthesis of American suburban history nationwide is Kenneth T. Jackson, *Crabgrass Frontier: The Suburbanization of the United States* (1985); on the aesthetics and ideology of the romantic suburb, see David Schuyler, *The New Urban Landscape: The Redefinition of City Form in Nineteenth-Century America* (1986); and James L. Machor, *Pastoral Cities: Urban Ideals and the Symbolic Landscape of America* (1987); see also Henry C. Binford, *The First Suburbs: Residential Communities on the Boston Periphery, 1815–1860* (1985); Robert Fishman, *Bourgeois Utopias: The Rise and Fall of Suburbia* (1987). I do not mean to suggest that no middle-class residents remained near the downtown, for the

suburban flight of residents from the heart of the Loop was accompanied by the emergence of downtown apartment buildings, if not in the commercial office buildings proper then in their near vicinity. See Carroll William Westfall, "Home at the Top: Domesticating Chicago's Tall Apartment Buildings," *Chicago History* 14, no. 1 (Spring 1985): 20–39.

35. Olmsted, Vaux & Co., *Preliminary Report upon the Proposed Suburban Village at Riverside, near Chicago* (1868), 26.

36. *Riverside in 1871, with a Description of Its Improvements* [1871],21.

37. *Dedication of the New Board of Trade Building . . . Dedicatory and Banquet Addresses* (1885), 7.

38. Stone, "Chicago before the Fire," 675. One French visitor to the fair felt the presence of the fire so vividly that he wrote, "That month of October, 1871, was more than near to me; it seemed as if I could touch it, as if I were still in it." Paul Bourget, *Outre-mer: Impressions of America* (1895), 116.

39. Daniel Burnham eventually took his ideas from the exposition and applied them to a grand plan for redesigning the entire city. Anyone reading it today cannot help being struck by its effort to impose White City ideals on the real city of Chicago. See Daniel H. Burnham and Edward H. Bennett, *Plan of Chicago,* ed. Charles Moore (1909); and *The Plan of Chicago: 1909–1979* (1979).

40. Muirhead, *Land of Contrasts,* 207.

41. Schuyler, "Last Words about the Fair," 300.

42. Ralph, *Harper's Chicago and the World's Fair,* 1.

43. "The demonstration was a signal and unprecedented triumph, not alone of Chicago, but for the new empire of the west, of which Chicago is the foreordained metropolis." John J. Ingalls, "Lessons of the Fair," *Cosmopolitan* 16 (Dec. 1893): 143.

44. Paul Bourget, "A Farewell to the White City," *Cosmopolitan* 16 (Dec. 1893): 135–36.

45. On elite Chicagoans' attempts to create a higher culture for themselves in the decades following the fire, see Helen Lefkowitz Horowitz, *Culture & the City: Cultural Philanthropy in Chicago from the 1880s to 1917* (1976).

46. Mable L. Treseder, "A Visitor's Trip to Chicago in 1893," typescript of original diary edited by Sheldon Treseder Gardner, 1943, Treseder MS E902/TR, SHSW, 30.

47. Dean, *White City Chips,* 109. For a description of the Potter Palmer mansion that so impressed Treseder, see John Drury, *Old Chicago Houses* (1941), 128–31.

48. Treseder, "Visitor's Trip to Chicago in 1893," SHSW, 27.

49. Ibid., 31–32.

50. *Chicago Post,* Aug. 23, 1893.

51. For an interesting contrast with *Uncle Jeremiah,* one that presents the fair and Chicago in much more innocent, "gee whiz" terms, see Tudor Jenks, *The Century World's Fair Book for Boys and Girls, Being the Adventures of Harry and Philip with Their Tutor, Mr. Douglass, at the World's Columbian Exposition* (1893).

52. George Eugene Sereiko, "Chicago and Its Book Trade, 1871–1893" (Ph.D. thesis, Case Western Reserve Univ., 1973), 168–69.

53. Quondam, *Uncle Jeremiah at the Great Fair,* 12–14. On the role of the confidence man as a central icon of nineteenth-century culture, see Karen Halttunen, *Confidence Men and Painted Women: A Study of Middle-Class Culture in America, 1830–1870* (1982).

54. Quondam, *Uncle Jeremiah at the Great Fair,* 28.

55. Ibid., 28, 82, 175.

56. Ibid., 82.

57. Ibid., 73–74.

58. Ibid., 63–64.

59. Ibid., 221–27, quotation on 227.

60. Ibid., 38–42, 63–68.

61. *Chicago Post,* Aug. 23, 1893. Cf. "World's Fair Extortions," *Prairie Farmer,* May 13, 1893, 8.

62. Johnson, *History of the Columbian Exposition,* 1:368–74.

63. *Rand, McNally & Co.'s A Week at the Fair, Illustrating the Exhibits and Wonders of the World's Columbian Exposition* (1893), 19.

64. William Thomas Stead, *If Christ Came to Chicago* (1894; reprint, 1978), 259–60; see also 241, which notes that some of the larger, more respectable wholesaling establishments complained to Stead that "they have great difficulty in entertaining their country customers because they cannot take them around to gambling houses."

65. "Preface," *Sporting and Club House Directory, Chicago, Containing a Full and Complete List of All First Class Club and Sporting Houses* (1889). On the history of Chicago's vice district, see Herbert Asbury, *Gem of the Prairie: An Informal History of the Chicago Underworld* (1940); and Stephen Longstreet, *Chicago: An Intimate Portrait of People, Pleasures, and Power: 1860–1919* (1973). See also Nell Kimball, *Nell Kimball: Her Life as an American Madam, by Herself,* ed. Stephen Longstreet (1970).

66. [Harold Richard Vynne,] *Chicago by Day and Night: The Pleasure Seeker's Guide to the Paris of America* (1892). The book included a discussion of the fair in its final pages, suggesting its target audience.

67. Ibid., 21.

68. Ibid., 23.

69. Ibid., 28.

70. Ibid., 49–50.

71. Ibid., 132.

72. Ibid., 125–26.

73. Stead, *If Christ Came to Chicago,* 250.

74. Ibid., 256–57. This practice was apparently common (or infamous) enough that the City Council went to the trouble of passing an ordinance expressly forbidding it.

75. See, for instance, *Chicago's Dark Places: Investigations by a Corps of Specially Appointed Commissioners,* 5th ed. (1891), 132.

76. On the general phenomenon of female migration to Chicago in the late nineteenth and early twentieth centuries, see Joanne Meyerowitz, "Women and Migration: Autonomous Female Migrants to Chicago, 1880–1930," *J. Urban Hist.* 13 (1987): 147–68; and on working-class women in Chicago generally, see Meyerowitz, *Women Adrift: Independent Wage Earners in Chicago, 1880–1930* (1988). On Chicago's entertainment markets and public spaces more generally, see Perry Duis, "Whose City?: Public and Private Places in Nineteenth-Century Chicago," *Chicago History* 12, no. 1 (Spring 1983): 12–27; 12, no. 2 (Summer 1983): 2–23. There is a large literature on urban prostitution; Christine Stansell, *City of Women: Sex and Class in New York, 1789–1860* (1986), suggests the range of issues relevant to Chicago.

77. Philip, "Chicago and the Down State," 11, 270. Cf. "Chicago Gamblers Scotched," *Prairie Farmer,* May 24, 1890, 328.

78. See, for instance, "A Humiliating Spectacle," *Western Rural,* April 15, 1876; and also Sidney Corning Eastman, *An Open Letter to the Members of the Union League Club of Chicago* [1887], 14, written shortly after Haymarket: *"It is generally conceded that the aldermanic boards of all of our large cities are corrupt. It is only the small towns that can lay claim to honest government; and this state of affairs grows daily worse. . . . The growth from a small town to a city seems invariably to bring with it dishonest administration."*

79. A wonderful exposé cataloging the nearly infinite ways that subscription salesmen could dupe rural customers is [Bates Harrington,] *How 'Tis Done: A Thorough Ventilation of the Numerous Schemes Conducted by Wandering Canvassers, Together with the Various Advertising Dodges for the Swindling of the Public* (1890). The story of how Chicago pioneered in the subscription sale of county atlases and histories throughout the midcontinent is fascinating, and Bates is a key text for studying it. For scholarly discussions of the subscription atlas and county history trades that Harrington emphasizes in his exposé, see Norman J. W. Thrower, "The County Atlas of the United States," *Surveying and Mapping* 21 (1961): 365–73; Michael P. Conzen, ed., "Maps and the City," special theme issue of *Chicago History* 13, no. 1 (Spring 1984): 1–72; and Conzen, *Chicago Mapmakers: Essays on the Rise of the City's Map Trade* (1984). For a fascinating inside look at how one Chicago publisher operated its subscription county history business in the Pacific Northwest, see the papers of Nathan Henry Wilson, salesman for the Lewis Publishing Company, in UISC.

80. For examples of the many attacks on the Board, see *Western Rural,* June 28, 1873; Nov. 21, Dec. 26, 1874; Jan. 16, 1875; April 1, 1876; March 3, 1877; June 1, 1878 (a particularly strong attack); and June 28, 1878.

81. R. K. Slosson, "Farmer and Board of Trade—No. 7," *Western Rural,* June 1, 1878. Had the farmers looked into Vynne's guide to Chicago's underworld, they would have found further proof of this point, for he included the Board in his chapter on gambling entertainments, saying, "While the claim is always made that only legitimate business is transacted on the Board of Trade the statement cannot be disputed that it presents

the greatest opportunity for high gambling in the whole world." Vynne, *Chicago by Day and Night,* 106.

82. "Grand College of Vice," *Western Rural,* June 29, 1878. For rural fears of tramps, see ibid., June 10, Aug. 26, 1876; April 14, May 12, June 16, June 30, Oct. 13, Oct. 20, 1877; for a more sympathetic view, see Walter A. Wyckoff, *A Day with a Tramp and Other Days* (1901); and Wyckoff, *The Workers: An Experiment in Reality* (1898). It is always worth remembering the paradox that several agricultural newspapers like the *Rural,* although speaking on behalf of hinterland farmers, were themselves published in Chicago. This appears not to have diminished their authority, and perhaps they knew whereof they spoke.

83. "Legislation and Large Cities," *Western Rural,* Nov. 30, 1878.

84. Such essays drew on a long agrarian tradition of anti-urbanism in American thought stretching back to Jefferson, and on romanticism generally. The literature on this subject is very large. Key texts include George Arthur Dunlap, *The City in the American Novel, 1789–1900: A Study of American Novels Portraying Contemporary Conditions in New York, Philadelphia, and Boston* (1934); Eugene Arden, "The Evil City in American Fiction," *New York History* 35 (1954): 259–79; Anselm L. Strauss, *Images of the American City* (1961); Morton White and Lucia White, *The Intellectual versus the City: From Thomas Jefferson to Frank Lloyd Wright* (1962); David R. Weimer, ed., *City and Country in America* (1962); Leo Marx, *Machine in the Garden;* R. Richard Wohl, "The 'Country Boy' Myth and Its Place in American Urban Culture: The Nineteenth-Century Contribution," *Perspectives in American History* 3 (1969): 75–156; Williams, *The Country and the City;* William A. Bullough, " 'It Is Better to Be a Country Boy': The Lure of the Country in Urban Education in the Gilded Age," *Historian* 35 (1973): 183–95; Thomas Bender, *Toward an Urban Vision: Ideas and Institutions in Nineteenth Century America* (1975); Adrienne Siegel, *The Image of the American City in Popular Literature, 1820–1870* (1981); David E. Shi, *The Simple Life: Plain Living and High Thinking in American Culture* (1985); Schuyler, *New Urban Landscape;* and Jackson, *Crabgrass Frontier.* For a useful perspective on this tradition in relation to Chicago, see Carl S. Smith, *Chicago and the American Literary Imagination, 1880–1920* (1984).

85. "Don't Leave the Farm," *Bulletin of the Executive Committee of the State Grange of Wisconsin* 4, no. 8 (Aug. 1878): n.p.

86. R.A.C. (Osborn, Mo.), "Country vs. City Life," *Western Rural,* Feb. 26, 1876.

87. "To Our Young Men," *Western Rural,* March 10, 1877.

88. "The City in Winter," *Western Rural,* Dec. 1, 1877, is an interesting piece noting that winter was a period of high unemployment and great suffering in the city, and that country boys who sat dreaming of urban pleasures by the warm fire of their parents' farmhouse would do well to remember that they might have no fire at all if they left home.

89. "Stay in the Country," *Western Rural,* May 19, 1870. Cf. "Why Boys Leave the Farm," *Prairie Farmer,* March 1, 1890, 129. Note the gender implications in these arguments. Although rural parents were clearly horrified at the "fate worse than death" that prostitution might mean for country girls who lost themselves in the city, the largest share of this anti-urban literature about rural children in the city addressed males rather than females. Either because boys were more likely to leave home, or more likely to get themselves into trouble once they left—or because the sentimental imagination expected them to—young men bore the brunt of this prescriptive literature much more than young women.

90. "The Farm Preferable to City Life," *Western Rural,* Oct. 17, 1874. This appeal to the young person of "average" talents seems strikingly off target as an argument against ambitions of self-improvement—one wonders how many of those who heard it thought of themselves as "average."

91. "The City in Winter," *Western Rural,* Dec. 1, 1877.

92. "To Our Young Men," *Western Rural,* March 10, 1877.

93. W.M.K. (Oneida, Ill.), " 'Stick to the Farm, Boys,' " *Western Rural,* May 30, 1874. W.M.K. elaborated these arguments in a later response to his critics, also called " 'Stick to the Farm, Boys,' " ibid., Sept. 19, 1874. On the nature of rural labor in the antebellum Midwest, see David E. Schob, *Hired Hands and Plow Boys: Farm Labor in the Midwest, 1815–1860* (1975).

94. Frederick Lockley, "The Retail Trade as a Medium of Distribution," *Western Monthly* 2

(1869): 263, 264. Lockley acknowledged that transportation could increase value by moving a product "from its producer to a market," so the railroads might be exempt from this particular argument; still, most agrarian protesters undoubtedly agreed that the railroads took far more money than they deserved.

95. H. C. Wheeler (DuPage, Ill.), "Scraps of History," *Western Rural,* Nov. 15, 1873.

96. *Bulletin of the Executive Committee of the State Grange of Wisconsin* 1, no. 3 (March 1875): 8, quoting Henry Bronson.

97. I have surveyed Granger literature in the notes to chapter 3; the literature on Populism is so enormous that I cannot do it justice here. Key works include John D. Hicks, *The Populist Revolt: A History of the Farmers' Alliance and the People's Party* (1931); Richard Hofstadter, *The Age of Reform: From Bryan to F.D.R.* (1955); Norman Pollack, *The Populist Response to Industrial America* (1962); Allen Weinstein, *Prelude to Populism: Origins of the Silver Issue, 1867–1878* (1970); James Edward Wright, *The Politics of Populism: Dissent in Colorado* (1974); Peter H. Argersinger, *Populism and Politics: William Alfred Peffer and the People's Party* (1974); Lawrence Goodwyn, *Democratic Promise: The Populist Moment in America* (1976); Scott G. McNall, *The Road to Rebellion: Class Formation and Kansas Populism, 1865–1900* (1988).

98. Although not himself an agrarian protester, the secretary of agriculture in 1893, J. M. Rusk, summarized this perspective nicely in "American Farming a Hundred Years Hence," *No. Am. Rev.* 436 (March 1893): 257–64.

99. Dudley W. Adams, "An Address Delivered before the Patrons of Husbandry of Muscatine and Union Counties, October 1872," *The Order of the Patrons of Husbandry,* Bryan Fund Publications, no. 8 [1872], 4.

100. Ibid., 7.

101. Periam, *Groundswell,* 50. Another general Granger text that offers these arguments is Edward Winslow Martin [James Dabney McCabe,] *History of the Grange Movement,* 450–70.

102. "Master's Address," *Proceedings of the Twelfth Annual Session of the Wisconsin State Grange,* held at Madison, Dec. 11–14, 1883 (1884), 12.

103. E. E. Bryant, "Co-operation among Farmers," *Transactions of the Wisconsin State Agricultural Society* 11 (1872–73): 279. For later examples, cf. "Farmers Should Combine," *Prairie Farmer,* March 15, 1890, 169; and "Unity," ibid., March 29, 1890, 193.

104. On the subsequent history of farm cooperatives, see Theodore Saloutos and John D. Hicks, *Agricultural Discontent in the Middle West, 1900–1939* (1951); Murray R. Benedict, *Farm Policies of the United States, 1790–1950: A Study of Their Origins and Development* (1953); and Gilbert C. Fite, *American Farmers: The New Minority* (1981).

105. [L. G. Kniffen,] "The State Agent," *Proceedings of the Seventh Annual Meeting of the Wisconsin State Grange,* held at Milwaukee, Jan. 21–24, 1879 (1879), 16.

106. For an interesting defense of retailers, see Stephe Smith, *Grains for the Grangers, Discussing All Points Bearing upon the Farmers' Movement for the Emancipation of White Slaves from the Slave-Power of Monopoly* (1873; reprint, 1889), 133–34.

107. For a sardonic explanation of the reasons for such losses, see "The Moan of a Middleman" (originally published in the *New York Tribune*), *Western Rural,* Dec. 27, 1873.

108. John G. Otis, "State Agent's Report," *Third Annual Session, Kansas State Grange,* held at Topeka, Feb. 16–20 (1875), 9. The reports of state agents often say much between the lines about the Grange's chastening encounter with the distribution system, but Otis's is perhaps the most forthright about the wholesalers and retailers, who usually play only the roles of villainous "monopolies" in this literature.

109. The cooperative stores that eventually succeeded were based largely on the "Rochdale System," in which customers bought memberships in a store, paid ordinary retail prices for the goods they purchased, and then received a division of the profits according to how much they had bought during the year. One big advantage of this arrangement was that it did not antagonize local retailers by responding with cutthroat competition when Grange merchandise was priced at cost. Cooperatives of this sort did quite well in some areas, precisely because they succeeded in reproducing existing wholesale-retail networks. Grange members who used them in effect became stockholders in the store, mimicking the corporate organization which the Grange cooperatives both criticized and embraced. See Buck, *Granger Movement,* 238–78, for a discussion of this subject.

110. An extraordinary contemporary essay that grapples with the positive and negative aspects of these various commercial and political changes is D. A. Wasson, "The

Modern Type of Oppression," *No. Am. Rev.* 245 (Oct. 1874): 253–85. For a suggestive collection by modern historians on similar issues, see Steven Hahn and Jonathan Prude, eds., *The Countryside in the Age of Capitalist Transformation: Essays in the Social History of Rural America* (1985).

111. Census figures cited in Henry J. Fletcher, "The Doom of the Small Town," *Forum* 19 (April 1895): 215.

112. Ibid., 214, 222. On the general reasons for urban growth at the expense of rural areas, see the classic study of Adna Ferrin Weber, *The Growth of Cities in the Nineteenth Century: A Study in Statistics* (1899; reprint, 1963).

113. Wyckoff, *Day with a Tramp,* 61, 79. See also the fascinating discussion of urban-rural exploitation in the text of a contemporary socialist, A. M. Simons, *The American Farmer* (1906), 63–73. Early-twentieth-century "rural sociologists" were much concerned about the problems of rural life. For a sense of the kinds of arguments they offered, see the classic *Report of the Commission on Country Life,* 60th Cong., 2d sess., 1910, Sen. Doc. 705; Wilbert L. Anderson, *The Country Town: A Study of Rural Evolution* (1906). Scholarly treatments include Lewis E. Atherton, "The Midwestern Country Town—Myth and Reality," *Ag. Hist.* 26 (1952): 73–80; Atherton, *Main Street on the Middle Border;* and Hudson, *Plains Country Towns.*

114. Wyckoff, *Day with a Tramp,* 84.

115. Rusk, "American Farming a Hundred Years Hence," 264. For a fascinating earlier discussion of rural decline (focused more on the Northeast than on the West) which shows the linkages between rural "improvement" and suburban ideals, see Nathaniel Hillyer Egleston, *Villages and Village Life, with Hints for Their Improvement* (1878).

116. *Pawnee Banner,* Crete Union, Neb., as described in the Lincoln, Neb., *Daily State Journal,* Sept. 14, 1883.

117. Ignatius Donnelly, *Caesar's Column: A Story of the Twentieth-Century* (1891), ed. Walter B. Rideout (1960), 18.

118. Henry Blake Fuller, *The Cliff-dwellers* (1893; reprint, 1973), 229; ellipses in original.

119. Ibid., 32.

120. Ibid., 4.

121. Ibid., 6.

122. Stead, *If Christ Came to Chicago,* 410–11.

123. Howells, "Letters of an Altrurian Traveller," 232.

124. Stead, "My First Visit to America," 414–15.

125. Stead, *If Christ Came to Chicago,* 421–42.

126. Stone, "Chicago," 679.

127. Ralph, *Our Great West,* 21–22. On the history of Chicago's unusually extensive park system, see Glen E. Holt, "Private Plans for Public Spaces: The Origins of Chicago's Park System, 1850–1875," *Chicago History* 8, no. 3 (Fall 1979): 173–84.

128. Quondam, *Uncle Jeremiah at the Great Fair,* 46. For one example of the White City's subsequent influence on Chicago architecture, see Ann Lorenz Van Zanten, "The Marshall Field Annex and the New Urban Order of Daniel Burnham's Chicago," *Chicago History* 11, no. 3 (Fall–Winter 1982): 130–41.

129. Adams, *Education,* 1034.

130. "Agriculture and Commerce of Missouri," *Prairie Farmer* 9 (May 1849): 149. See also John Wentworth, "A Lecture Delivered before the Sunday Lecture Society, May 7, 1876," in McIlvaine, ed., *Reminiscences of Early Chicago,* 55–56: "God made Lake Michigan and the country to the west of it; and, when we come to estimate who have done the most for Chicago, the glory belongs first to the enterprising farmers who raised a surplus of produce and sent it here for shipment; and second, to the hardy sailors who braved the storms of our harborless lakes to carry it to market. All other classes were the incidents, and not the necessities, of our embryo city. Chicago is but the index of the prosperity of our agricultural classes."

EPILOGUE

1. Aldo Leopold, *A Sand County Almanac and Sketches Here and There* (1949), 203, 205, 207.

2. Ralph, *Our Great West,* 28.

3. Robert Harris to George H. Burrows (Toledo), June 15, 1869, Robert Harris Out-Letters, H.4.1, CB&Q Archives.

4. Woodman, "Chicago Businessmen and the 'Granger' Laws," 16–24; a similar phe-

nomenon happened in Milwaukee, and is ably traced in Treleven, "Railroads, Elevators, and Grain Dealers," 205–22. The Chicago-based *Western Rural* conducted a massive lobbying campaign against the city's high elevator charges during 1876–77, arguing on behalf of farmers and city merchants alike. For examples of the articles which
appear in virtually every issue at the peak of the controversy, see Jan. 22, Feb. 19, Feb.
26, March 18, May 27, June 3, Aug. 26, 1876; and Feb. 24, May 5, 1877.

5. Robert Harris to J. N. Denison, May 13, 1869, Harris Out-Letters, CB&Q Archives,
   summarizes these problems nicely.
6. Stead, *If Christ Came to Chicago,* 188.
7. Ralph, *Our Great West,* 26.
8. *Clinton Age,* Aug. 18, 1893. For another example of Iowans' grievances against Chicago, see "Chicago against Iowa Interests," *Iowa State Register,* Feb. 9, 1884.
9. The Chicago newspapers conducted a running controversy about the city's grade
   crossings during the early 1890s. The *Herald,* May 30, 1893, estimated that 90 percent
   of the city's through traffic just transferred between stations, adding nothing to Chicago except traffic jams. More interestingly, the paper resorted to the familiar metaphors of urban youth and adulthood to argue that the time had come for the city to
   shed its adolescent dependence on downtown railroad transfers: "Can you imagine
   what the downtown district would be . . . with half the street cars, with one-fourth of
   the baggage wagons, with a tithe of the freight vans? . . . It will be no lessening of life,
   no loss of hours, no missing of opportunity. It will simply be the proper rise of a
   growing city from the heaviest load youth and swift growth could heap upon it to the
   freedom of a giant who knew his strength, and was not afraid all would vanish in a
   night."
10. Herrick, *Memoirs of an American Citizen,* 139–40.
11. In 1869, the manager of the Chicago, Burlington and Quincy could declare that west-
    ern lumber dealers in places like Kansas City, Leavenworth, and St. Joseph need not
    be given any special favors in buying lumber from Chicago because they had no choice
    but to do so: "they get from Chicago their lumber because they cannot ge[t] it any
    other way. . . ." Even ten or fifteen years later, this was no longer true. Robert Harris to
    N. D. Munson, Jan. 4, 1868, Harris Out-Letters, CB&Q Archives.
12. The classic discussion of this subject is Charles Byron Kuhlmann, *The Development of the
    Flour-Milling Industry in the United States with Special Reference to the Industry in Minneapolis*
    (1929); for the history of milling technology, see John Storck and Walter Dorwin
    Teague, *Flour for Man's Bread: A History of Milling* (1952). See also George D. Rogers,
    "History of Flour Manufacture in Minnesota," *Minnesota Historical Society Collections* 10,
    pt. 1 (1900–04): 35–55; Frank Andrews, *Grain Movement in the Great Lakes Region,*
    USDA, Bureau of Statistics, Bulletin no. 81 (1910); and Charles B. Kuhlmann, "The
    Influence of the Minneapolis Flour Mills upon the Economic Development of Min-
    nesota and the Northwest," *Minn. Hist.* 6 (1925): 141–54. For comparison, see Alice
    Lanterman, "The Development of Kansas City as a Grain and Milling Center," *Mo.
    Hist. Rev.* 42 (1947): 20–33. For a map of the grain hinterlands of different cities in
    1901, see U.S. House of Representatives, *Report of the Industrial Commission on the Distri-
    bution of Farm Products,* 56th Cong., 2d sess., 1901, Doc. 494, 6:44–45. On the changing
    agriculture of the wheat-growing districts, see Ray Stannard Baker, "The Movement
    of Wheat," *McClure's Magazine* 14 (1899): 124–37; William Allen White, "The Business
    of a Wheat Farm," *Scribner's Magazine* 22 (1897): 530–48; C. W. Thompson, "The
    Movement of Wheat-Growing: A Study of a Leading State," *Quarterly Journal of Econom-
    ics* 18 (1903–04): 570–84; John Giffin Thompson, "The Rise and Decline of the Wheat
    Growing Industry in Wisconsin," *Bulletin of the University of Wisconsin,* no. 292, *Economic
    and Political Science Series* 5, no. 3 (1909): 295–544; James Mavor, "The Economic
    Results of the Specialist Production and Marketing of Wheat," *Political Science Quarterly*
    26 (1911): 659–75; Edward Van Dyke Robinson, *Early Economic Conditions and the Devel-
    opment of Agriculture in Minnesota,* University of Minnesota Studies in the Social
    Sciences, no. 3 (1915); W. O. Blanchard, *The Geography of Southwestern Wisconsin,* Wis-
    consin Geological and Natural History Survey, Bulletin no. 65 (1924), 66–97; Larson,
    The Wheat Market and the Farmer in Minnesota; Holbrook Working, "Wheat Acreage and
    Production in the United States since 1866: A Revision of Official Estimates," *Wheat
    Studies* 2 (1926): 237–64; James C. Malin, *Winter Wheat in the Golden Belt of Kansas: A
    Study in Adaptation to Subhumid Geographical Environment* (1944); Theodore Saloutos,

"The Spring-Wheat Farmer in a Maturing Economy, 1870–1920," *JEH* 6 (1946): 173–90; Richard Bardolph, "Illinois Agriculture in Transition, 1820–1870," *J. Ill. State Hist. Soc.* 41 (1948): 244–64; Merrill E. Jarchow, "King Wheat," *Minn. Hist.* 29 (1948): 1–28; Eric E. Lampard, *The Rise of the Dairy Industry in Wisconsin: A Study in Agricultural Change, 1820–1920* (1963); Hiram M. Drache, *The Day of the Bonanza: A History of Bonanza Farming in the Red River Valley of the North* (1964); and Franklin M. Fisher and Peter Temin, "Regional Specialization and the Supply of Wheat in the United States, 1867–1914," *Review of Economics and Statistics* 52 (1970): 134–49.

13. Burghardt, "Hypothesis about Gateway Cities," 269–85.

14. As the railroad network and central place hierarchy filled in, the railroads had increasing incentives to promote traffic not just at the gateway but at other major cities as well. See, for instance, the letter of Robert Harris to J. I. McCune, April 3, 1868, Harris Out-Letters, CB&Q Archives, which gives his views about why the CB&Q ought to begin promoting development at Kansas City.

15. "Answers to Inquiries in Relation to the Commerce of Chicago . . . by Charles Randolph, Secretary of the Board of Trade of Chicago, 1876," appendix no. 4 in Nimmo, *Rept. Int. Commerce* (1877), 82.

16. On the role of transport technologies in the timing of American urban growth, see John R. Borchert, "American Metropolitan Evolution," *Geographical Review* 57 (1967): 301–32; and Vance, *Capturing the Horizon.* On Los Angeles and the automobile, see Robert M. Fogelson, *The Fragmented Metropolis: Los Angeles, 1850–1930* (1967); and Scott L. Bottles, *Los Angeles and the Automobile: The Making of the Modern City* (1987).

17. Cf. *A Business Tour of Chicago* (1887), 32, which describes the gradual diversion of grain from Chicago and then concludes, "But this city has really been the market for it all, and never demonstrated her ability to care for and control the produce business of the great west better than during the recent years whose figures show the apparent falling off which has been noted. Chicago has carried the whole of the visible supply of wheat and other cereals, and our moneyed men have furnished the capital required to hold the greater part of it."

18. Perhaps the best proofs of this shifting set of geographical labels are the ongoing arguments about the title of this book that I have had with one western historian colleague who has tried to convince me that Chicago's hinterland was not "the West" at all. My own belief is that most nineteenth-century Americans would have been mystified by such a claim. When Julian Ralph chose to open his 1893 book *Our Great West* with two chapters on Chicago—the only city to receive such double treatment—I doubt that any of his readers gave a second thought to why he did so. In their eyes, few things could have seemed more "natural." See Peter Gould and Rodney White, *Mental Maps* (1974); and James R. Shortridge, *The Middle West: Its Meaning in American Culture* (1989).

19. The classic works on this subject are Williams, *The Country and the City;* and Marx, *Machine in the Garden.* For a little-known essay which surveys this subject in a suggestive way, see Leo Marx, "Pastoral Ideas and City Troubles," *Journal of General Education* 20 (Jan. 1969): 251–71. I am indebted to Sidney Bremer for this reference.

20. Frederick Law Olmsted, "Public Parks and the Enlargement of Towns" (1870), reprinted in S. B. Sutton, ed., *Civilizing American Cities: A Selection of Frederick Law Olmsted's Writings on City Landscape* (1971), 81.

21. Edward A. Duddy, "Aaron Montgomery Ward," in Dumas Malone, ed., *Dictionary of American Biography* (1936), 414.

22. *Business Tour of Chicago,* 61.

23. *In Lake Land* (1902), 26–27.

24. *Business Tour of Chicago,* 61.

25. A. A. Mosher, "The Wisconsin Lakes," *Outing* 16 (1890): 177.

26. Although one would never ordinarily read them as tales of an urban hinterland, Hemingway's early Nick Adams stories are just that. The most famous is Ernest Hemingway, "Big Two-Hearted River," in *The Fifth Column and the First Forty-nine Stories* (1939), 307–30.

27. Robert W. Heiple and Emma B. Heiple, *A Heritage History of Beautiful Green Lake Wisconsin* (1976), 115–19.

28. Ibid., 248.

Bibliography

MANUSCRIPT COLLECTIONS

Aulls, Silas D. Correspondence. Kansas State Historical Museum, Topeka.
Bankruptcy Court Cases. Federal District Court Records. National Archives Regional Record Center, Chicago.
Bankruptcy Court Cases. Federal District Court Records. National Archives Regional Record Center, Kansas City.
Brewster, Charles J. Papers. SHSI.
Calhoun, John. Subscription Book for the *Chicago Democrat*, Dec. 3, 1834. CHS.
Carter, Thomas Butler. Manuscript Autobiography and Letters. CHS.
Chandler, Daniel Lyman. Letters. Newberry Library, Chicago.
Chicago and Northwestern Railroad Collection. Letters and Traffic Records. SHSW.
Chicago, Burlington and Quincy Railroad. Letters, Traffic Records, Scrapbooks, Miscellaneous Papers. Newberry Library, Chicago.
Chicago, Milwaukee, St. Paul and Pacific Railroad Collection, SHSW.
Chicago Tribune. Circulation Records for Chicago Newspapers. Tribune Company Archives.
Clark, Darwin. Invoices. SHSW.
Columbian Pickwick Rooms at the Great White Horse Inn, World's Columbian Exposition. Register Book. CHS.
Culbertson and Reno, Bankers, Iowa City. Account Book. UISC.
Dun, R. G., and Company. Manuscript Credit Reports. Baker Library, Harvard Business School, Cambridge.
Eastman, Zebina. Letters, Contracts, and Subscription Books. CHS.
Emery Grocery, Cedar Rapids, Iowa. Account Books. SHSI.
Gillett and Hadley, Wholesale Grocers. Invoice Book. Kansas State Historical Museum, Topeka.
Harding, Lester. Letters. Lackawanna Historical Society, Scranton, Penn. (copies in CHS).
Hayden Hardware. Account Books. SHSW.
Holt Lumber Company. Letters and Account Books. Green Bay Record Center, SHSW.
Illinois Women's Exposition Board, World's Columbian Exposition. Register Book. Newberry Library, Chicago.
Kepner, George W. Papers. UISC.
McCormick Collection. Contracts, Production Records. SHSW.
Mears, Charles E. Letters and Diaries. CHS.
Morrell and Company. Correspondence. UISC.
Newton, Francis E. Letters and Account Books. Nebraska State Historical Society, Lincoln.

Ryerson, Joseph T. Typescript Autobiographical Material. Joseph T. Ryerson & Son, Inc.,
    Company Archives, Chicago.
Sawyer, Charles B. Invoice Books. CHS.
Shaw Family Papers. Letters. Newberry Library, Chicago.
Smith, E. S. Papers. SHSI.
Snow and Huber, Pella, Iowa. Account Books. UISC.
Stewart, Mary E. "Record of the World's Columbian Exposition." SHSW.
Stone, John. Account Book. SHSI.
Treseder, Mable L. "A Visitor's Trip to Chicago in 1893." SHSW.
Veith, Henry. Invoices. Nebraska State Historical Society, Lincoln.
Whitaker, Frank S. Account Books. Kansas State Historical Museum, Topeka.
Wilson, Nathan Henry. Papers. UISC.
Wisconsin State Building, World's Columbian Exposition. Register Book. SHSW.

                                    PERIODICALS

Annual Reviews of Commerce. *Chicago Tribune* and *Chicago Daily Democratic Press.* 1850–60.
Bradstreet's Commercial Reports. New York: J. M. Bradstreet & Son, July 1873.
Chicago & Northwestern Railway. *Annual Reports.* 1857–70.
Chicago Board of Trade. *Annual Reports,* 1858–1901.
Chicago, Burlington and Quincy Railroad. *Annual Reports.* 1852–70.
Chicago Democratic Press.
Chicago Exposition Gazeteer and Jobbers' Record, 1879.
Chicago Magazine. 1857.
Chicago Tribune. 1849–1900.
DeBow's Review. 1840–60.
Galena and Chicago Union Railroad. *Annual Reports.* 1848–60.
Hunts' Merchants' Magazine and Commercial Review, 1840–60.
Illinois Central Railroad. *Annual Reports.* 1852–70.
Lakeside Monthly. 1870–73.
Menominee River Boom Company. *Annual Reports.* 1891–95.
The Mercantile Agency Reference Book. New York: Dun Barlow. Jan. 1872.
Montgomery Ward and Company. *Catalogs.* 1874–1901.
New York Produce Exchange. *Annual Reports.* 1870–1900.
Niles' Weekly Register. 1814.
Northwestern Lumberman. 1876–91.
Peoria Board of Trade. *Annual Reports.* 1871–75.
Poor's Manual of Railroads.
Prairie Farmer. 1848–1900.
St. Louis Chamber of Commerce, *Annual Reports.*
Sears, Roebuck and Company. *Catalogs.*
U.S. Censuses of Population, Agriculture, and Manufactures. 1840–1900. (In original
    printed reports and in machine-readable datasets of the ICPSR.)
U.S. Department of Agriculture. *Yearbooks.* 1885–1960.
Western Monthly.
Western Rural. 1866–80.
Wisconsin Lumberman. 1870–80.
Wisconsin State Agricultural Society. *Transactions.* 1870–90.
Wisconsin State Grange. *Proceedings* and *Bulletins of the Executive Committee.* 1872–90.

                                       BOOKS

Abbott, Carl. *Boosters and Businessmen: Popular Economic Thought and Urban Growth in the Antebel-
    lum Middle West.* Westport, Conn.: Greenwood Press, 1981.
A Business Tour of Chicago. Chicago: E. E. Barton, 1887.
Ackerman, Wm. K. *Early Illinois Railroads.* Fergus Historical Series, no. 23. Chicago, 1884.
Adams, Andy. *The Log of a Cowboy: A Narrative of the Old Trail Days.* 1903. Reprint. Lincoln:
    Univ. of Nebraska Press, 1964.
Adams, Henry. *Novels, Mont Saint Michel, The Education.* New York: Library of America,
    1983.

Ahlgren, Clifford, and Isabel Ahlgren. *Lob Trees in the Wilderness*. Minneapolis: Univ. of Minnesota Press, 1984.

Albion, Robert Greenhalgh. *The Rise of New York Port, 1815–1860*. New York: Charles Scribner's Sons, 1939.

Anderson, Oscar Edward, Jr. *Refrigeration in America: A History of a New Technology and Its Impact*. Princeton: Princeton Univ. Press, 1953.

Anderson, Wilbert L. *The Country Town: A Study of Rural Evolution*. New York: Baker & Taylor, 1906.

Andreano, Ralph, ed. *The Economic Impact of the American Civil War*, Cambridge, Mass.: Schenkman, 1962.

Andreas, Alfred T. *History of Chicago from the Earliest Period to the Present Time*. 3 vols. Chicago: Alfred T. Andreas, 1884–86.

———. *History of Cook County, Illinois from the Earliest Period to the Present Time*. Chicago: A. T. Andreas, 1884.

Andrews, Frank. *Grain Movement in the Great Lakes Region*. USDA, Bureau of Statistics, Bulletin no. 81. Washington, D.C.: GPO, 1910.

Appelbaum, Stanley. *The Chicago World's Fair of 1893: A Photographic Record*. New York: Dover Publications, 1980.

Archer, William. *America To-day: Observations and Reflections*. London: William Heinemann, 1900.

Argersinger, Peter H. *Populism and Politics: William Alfred Peffer and the People's Party*. Lexington: Univ. Press of Kentucky, 1974.

Armitage, Susan, and Elizabeth Jameson, eds. *The Women's West*. Norman: Univ. of Oklahoma Press, 1987.

Armour, J. Ogden. *The Packers, the Private Car Lines, and the People*. Philadelphia: Henry Altemus, 1906.

Artibise, Alan F. J. *Winnipeg: A Social History of Urban Growth, 1874–1914*. Montreal: McGill-Queen's Univ. Press, 1975.

———, ed. *Town and City: Aspects of Western Canadian Urban Development*. Regina, Saskatchewan: Canadian Plains Research Center, 1981.

Asbury, Herbert. *Gem of the Prairie: An Informal History of the Chicago Underworld*. New York: Alfred A. Knopf, 1940.

Atack, Jeremy, and Fred Bateman. *To Their Own Soil: Agriculture in the Antebellum North*. Ames: Iowa State Univ. Press, 1987.

Atherton, Lewis. *The Cattle Kings*. 1961. Reprint. Lincoln: Univ. of Nebraska Press, 1972.

———. *The Frontier Merchant in Mid-America*. 1939. Reprint. Columbia: Univ. of Missouri Press, 1971.

———. *Main Street on the Middle Border*. Bloomington: Indiana Univ. Press, 1954.

Badger, R. Reid. *The Great American Fair: The World's Columbian Exposition & American Culture*. Chicago: Nelson Hall, 1979.

Baer, Julius B., and Olin Glenn Saxon. *Commodity Exchanges and Futures Trading: Principles and Operating Methods*. New York: Harper & Brothers, 1949.

Bairoch, Paul. *Cities and Economic Development: From the Dawn of History to the Present*. Translated by Christopher Braider. Chicago: Univ. of Chicago Press, 1988.

Baker, Charles H. *Life and Character of William Taylor Baker*. New York: Premier Press, 1908.

Baker, Charles Whiting. *Monopolies and the People*. New York: G. P. Putnam's Sons, 1889.

Baker, Nina. *Big Catalogue: The Life of Aaron Montgomery Ward*. New York: Harcourt, Brace, 1956.

Bancroft, Hubert Howe. *The Book of the Fair: A Historical and Descriptive Presentation of the World's Science, Art, and Industry, as Viewed through the Columbian Exposition at Chicago in 1893*. San Francisco: H. H. Bancroft, 1894.

Barbour, Michael G., and William Dwight Billings. *North American Terrestrial Vegetation*. New York: Cambridge Univ. Press, 1988.

Barnard, C., ed. *Grasses and Grasslands*. London: Macmillan, 1964.

Barsness, Larry. *The Bison in Art: A Graphic Chronicle of the American Bison*. Flagstaff: Northland Press in cooperation with the Amon Carter Museum of Western Art, 1977.

Belcher, Wyatt Winton. *The Economic Rivalry between St. Louis and Chicago, 1850–1880*. New York: Columbia Univ. Press, 1947.

Bender, Thomas. *Toward an Urban Vision: Ideas and Institutions in Nineteenth Century America*. Baltimore: Johns Hopkins Univ. Press, 1975.

Benedict, Murray R. *Farm Policies of the United States, 1790–1950: A Study of Their Origins and Development.* New York: Twentieth-Century Fund, 1953.

Benson, Lee. *Merchants, Farmers, & Railroads: Railroad Regulation and New York Politics, 1850–1887.* Cambridge: Harvard Univ. Press, 1955.

———. *Turner and Beard: American Historical Writing Reconsidered.* New York: Free Press, 1960.

Benton, Colbee C. *A Visitor to Chicago in Indian Days: "Journal to the 'Far-Off West.'"* Chicago: Caxton Club, 1957.

Berger, Carl. *The Writing of Canadian History: Aspects of English-Canadian Historical Writing, 1900 to 1970.* Toronto: Oxford Univ. Press, 1976.

Berkeley, George. "Verses on the Prospect of Planting Arts and Learning in America." In *The Works of George Berkeley,* edited by Alexander Campbell Fraser. Oxford: Clarendon Press, 1901.

Berry, Brian J. L. *The Geography of Market Centers and Retail Distribution.* Englewood Cliffs, N.J.: Prentice-Hall, 1967.

Berry, Brian J. L., and Frank E. Horton. *Geographic Perspectives on Urban Systems, with Integrated Readings.* Englewood Cliffs, N.J.: Prentice-Hall, 1970.

Billington, Ray Allen. *America's Frontier Heritage.* New York: Holt, Rinehart, and Winston, 1963.

———, ed. *The Frontier Thesis: Valid Interpretation of American History?* New York: Holt, Rinehart, and Winston, 1966.

Binford, Henry C. *The First Suburbs: Residential Communities on the Boston Periphery, 1815–1860.* Chicago: Univ. of Chicago Press, 1985.

Black Hawk. *An Autobiography.* 1833. Edited by Donald Jackson. Urbana: Univ. of Illinois Press, 1955.

Blanchard, W. O. *The Geography of Southwestern Wisconsin.* Wisconsin Geological and Natural History Survey, Bulletin no. 65. Madison, 1924.

Bogart, Ernest Ludlow, and Charles Manfred Thompson. *The Industrial State, 1870–1893.* Vol. 4 of *The Centennial History of Illinois.* Springfield: Illinois Centennial Commission, 1920.

Bogue, Allan G. *From Prairie to Cornbelt: Farming on the Illinois and Iowa Prairies in the Nineteenth Century.* Chicago: Univ. of Chicago Press, 1963.

Bogue, Margaret Beattie. *Patterns from the Sod: Land Use and Tenure in the Grand Prairie, 1850–1900.* Springfield: Illinois State Historical Library, 1959.

Bond, J. W. *Minnesota and Its Resources.* New York: Redfield, 1854.

Boorstin, Daniel J. *The Americans: The Democratic Experience.* New York: Random House, 1973.

———. *The Americans: The National Experience.* New York: Random House, 1965.

Borah, Woodrow, Jorge Hardoy, and Gilbert A. Stelter, eds. *Urbanization in the Americas: The Background in Comparative Perspective.* Ottawa: National Museum of Man, 1980.

Borchert, John R. *America's Northern Heartland.* Minneapolis: Univ. of Minnesota Press, 1987.

Bottles, Scott L. *Los Angeles and the Automobile: The Making of the Modern City.* Berkeley: Univ. of California Press, 1987.

Bourget, Paul. *Outre-mer: Impressions of America.* New York: Charles Scribner's Sons, 1895.

Bourne, L. S., and J. W. Simmons, eds. *Systems of Cities: Readings on Structure, Growth, and Policy.* New York: Oxford Univ. Press, 1968.

Boutmy, Emile. *Studies in Constitutional Law: France—England—United States.* London: Macmillan, 1891.

Boyle, James E. *The Chicago Board of Trade: What It Is and What It Does.* Chicago: Edgar A. Russell, 1921.

———. *Chicago Wheat Prices for Eighty-one Years.* 1922.

———. *Speculation and the Chicago Board of Trade.* New York: Macmillan, 1920.

Branch, E. Douglas. *The Hunting of the Buffalo.* 1929. Reprint. Lincoln: Univ. of Nebraska Press, 1962.

Braun, E. Lucy. *Deciduous Forests of Eastern North America.* Philadelphia: Blakiston, 1950.

Bremer, Fredrika. *The Homes of the New World: Impressions of America.* 1853. Reprint. New York: Johnson Reprint, 1968.

Bretz, J. Harlen. *Geology of the Chicago Region.* Illinois State Geological Survey, Bulletin no. 65. Urbana, 1939.

Brody, David. *The Butcher Workmen: A Study of Unionization.* Cambridge: Harvard Univ. Press, 1964.

Broehl, Wayne G., Jr. *John Deere's Company: A History of Deere & Company and Its Times.* Garden City, N.Y.: Doubleday, 1984.

Bross, William. *Chicago and the Sources of Her Past and Future Growth.* Chicago: Jansen, McClurg, 1880.

———. *History of Chicago.* Chicago: Jansen, McClurg, 1876.

Brown, C. Exera. *Brown's Gazeteer of the Chicago and Northwestern Railway, and Branches, and of the Union Pacific Railroad: A Guide and Business Directory.* Chicago, 1869.

Brown, Henry. *The Present and Future Prospects of Chicago: An Address Delivered before the Chicago Lyceum, January 20, 1846.* Fergus Historical Series, no. 9. Chicago, 1876.

Brown, Lauren. *Audubon Nature Society Guides: Grasslands.* New York: Alfred A. Knopf, [1985].

Brush, Daniel Harmon. *Growing Up with Southern Illinois, 1820 to 1861.* Edited by Milo Milton Quaife. Chicago: Lakeside Press, 1944.

Buck, Solon J. *The Agrarian Crusade: A Chronicle of the Farmer in Politics.* New Haven: Yale Univ. Press, 1920.

———. *The Granger Movement: A Study of Agricultural Organization and Its Political, Economic and Social Manifestations, 1870–1880.* Cambridge: Harvard Univ. Press, 1913.

Buckingham, J. S. *The Eastern and Western States of America.* London: Fisher, n.d.

Burg, David F. *Chicago's White City of 1893.* Lexington: Univ. Press of Kentucky, 1976.

Burlend, Rebecca and Edward. *A True Picture of Emigration.* 1848. Edited by Milo Milton Quaife. New York: Citadel Press, 1968.

Burnham, Daniel H., and Edward H. Bennett. *Plan of Chicago.* Edited by Charles Moore. Chicago: Commercial Club of Chicago, 1909.

Burrows, J. M. D. *Fifty Years in Iowa.* 1888. Reprint. *The Early Day of Rock Island and Davenport: The Narratives of J. W. Spencer and J. M. D. Burrows.* Edited by Milo Milton Quaife. Chicago: Lakeside Press, 1942.

Busch, Moritz. *Travels between the Hudson & the Mississippi, 1851–1852.* Translated and edited by Norman H. Binger. Lexington: Univ. Press of Kentucky, 1971.

Bushnell, Charles J. *The Social Problem at the Chicago Stock Yards.* Chicago: Univ. of Chicago Press, 1902.

Cain, Louis P. *Sanitation Strategy for a Lakefront Metropolis: The Case of Chicago.* DeKalb: Northern Illinois Univ. Press, 1978.

Cameron, Rondo, ed. *Banking and Economic Development: Some Lessons of History.* New York: Oxford Univ. Press, 1972.

Campbell, John R., and John F. Lasley. *The Science of Animals That Serve Humanity.* 3d ed. New York: McGraw-Hill, 1985.

Careless, J. M. S. *Frontier and Metropolis: Regions, Cities, and Identities in Canada before 1914.* Toronto: Univ. of Toronto Press, 1989.

Carstensen, Vernon. *Farms or Forests: Evolution of a State Land Policy for Northern Wisconsin, 1850–1932.* Madison: Univ. of Wisconsin College of Agriculture, 1958.

Casey, Robert J., and W. A. S. Douglas. *Pioneer Railroad: The Story of the Chicago and North Western System.* New York: Whittlesey House, 1948.

Catlin, George. *Letters and Notes on the Manners, Customs, and Conditions of the North American Indians.* 1844. Reprint. New York: Dover Publications, 1973.

Cavanagh, Helen M. *Funk of Funk's Grove: Farmer, Legislator, and Cattle King of the Old Northwest, 1797–1865.* Bloomington, Ill.: Pantagraph Print, 1952.

Chabot, Brian F., and Harold A. Mooney, eds. *Physiological Ecology of North American Plant Communities.* New York: Chapman and Hall, 1985.

Chamberlin, Everett. *Chicago and Its Suburbs.* Chicago: T. A. Hungerford, 1873.

Chandler, Alfred D., Jr. *The Essential Alfred Chandler: Essays toward a Historical Theory of Big Business,* edited by Thomas K. McCraw. Cambridge: Harvard Business School Press, 1988.

———. *Scale and Scope: The Dynamics of Industrial Capitalism.* Cambridge: Harvard Univ. Press, 1990.

———. *Strategy and Structure: Chapters in the History of the Industrial Enterprise.* Cambridge: MIT Press, 1962.

———. *The Visible Hand: The Managerial Revolution in American Business.* Cambridge: Harvard Univ. Press, 1977.

———, ed. *The Railroads: The Nation's First Big Business.* New York: Harcourt, Brace & World, 1965.

Chicago and North Western Railway. *Yesterday and Today: A History of the Chicago and North Western Railway System.* 3d ed. Chicago: Chicago and Northwestern Railway, 1910.

Chicago and North-Western Railway Company. Traffic Department. *The Indian, the Northwest, 1600 . . . 1900: the Red Man, the War Man, the White Man, and the North-Western Line.* Chicago: Chicago and North-Western Railway, 1901.

[Chicago Board of Trade.] *Dedication of the New Board of Trade Building . . . Dedicatory and Banquet Addresses.* Chicago, 1885.

Chicago Board of Trade. *Futures Trading Seminar: History and Development.* Madison, Wis.: Mimir Publishers, 1960.

Chicago Building & Loan Association. *Statistical and Historical Review of Chicago.* Chicago: Chicago City Directory Publishing House, 1869.

Chicago: Commerce, Manufactures, Banking and Transportation Facilities. Chicago: S. Ferd Howe, 1884.

Chicago Conference on Trusts. Chicago: Civic Federation, 1900.

Chicago's Dark Places: Investigations by a Corps of Specially Appointed Commissioners. 5th ed., rev. Chicago: Craig Press and Women's Temperance Publishing Association, 1891.

Chicago's First Half Century: The City as It Was Fifty Years Ago, and as It Is To-Day. Chicago: Inter Ocean, 1883.

Chicago Joint Committee of the Board of Trade and Mercantile Association. *Produce and Transportation: The Railway and Warehouse Monopolies.* Chicago: Evening Journal Job Printing House, 1866.

Chicago, Milwaukee & St. Paul Railway. *In Lake Land.* Chicago: Chicago, Milwaukee & St. Paul Railway, 1902.

Christaller, Walter. *Central Places in Southern Germany.* 1933. Translated by Carlisle W. Baskin. Englewood Cliffs, N.J.: Prentice-Hall, 1966.

Ciucci, Giorgio, et al. *The American City from the Civil War to the New Deal.* Cambridge: MIT Press, 1979.

Clark, John G. *The Grain Trade in the Old Northwest.* Urbana: Univ. of Illinois Press, 1966.

Clark, Victor S. *History of Manufactures in the United States.* Washington, D.C.: Carnegie Institution, 1929.

Clay, John. *My Life on the Range.* 1924. Reprint. Norman: Univ. of Oklahoma Press, 1962.

Cleaver, Charles. *Early-Chicago Reminiscences.* Fergus Historical Series, no. 19. Chicago, 1882.

———. *History of Chicago from 1833 to 1892.* Chicago: privately printed, 1892.

Clemen, Rudolf Alexander. *The American Livestock and Meat Industry.* New York: Ronald Press, 1923.

———. *By-products in the Packing Industry.* Chicago: Univ. of Chicago Press, 1927.

———. *George H. Hammond (1838–1886): Pioneer in Refrigerator Transportation.* New York: Newcomen Society, 1946.

Clifton, James A. *The Prairie People: Continuity and Change in Potawatomi Indian Culture, 1665–1965.* Lawrence: Regents Press of Kansas, 1977.

Clutton-Brock, Juliet. *A Natural History of Domesticated Animals.* Austin: Univ. of Texas Press, 1987.

Cochran, Thomas C. *Railroad Leaders, 1854–1890: The Business Mind in Action.* Cambridge: Harvard Univ. Press, 1953.

Colbert, E[lias]. *Chicago: Historical and Statistical Sketch of the Garden City.* Chicago: P. T. Sherlock, 1868.

Colbert, Elias, and Everett Chamberlin. *Chicago and the Great Conflagration.* Cincinnati: C. F. Vent, 1871.

Cole, Arthur Charles. *The Era of the Civil War, 1848–1870.* Vol. 3 of *The Centennial History of Illinois.* Springfield: Illinois Centennial Commission, 1919.

Collingwood, G. H., and Warren D. Brush. *Knowing Your Trees: 51 Tree Edition.* Revised and edited by Devereux Butcher. Washington, D.C.: American Forestry Association, 1964.

Condit, Carl W. *The Chicago School of Architecture: A History of Commercial and Public Building in the Chicago Area, 1875–1925.* Chicago: Univ. of Chicago Press, 1964.

Conzen, Kathleen Neils. *Immigrant Milwaukee, 1836–1860: Accommodation and Community in a Frontier City.* Cambridge: Harvard Univ. Press, 1976.

Conzen, Michael P. *Chicago Mapmakers: Essays on the Rise of the City's Map Trade.* Chicago: CHS, 1984.

———. *Frontier Farming in an Urban Shadow: The Influence of Madison's Proximity on the Agricultural Development of Blooming Grove, Wisconsin.* Madison: SHSW, 1971.

Conzen, Michael P., and Kay J. Carr, eds. *The Illinois & Michigan Canal National Heritage Corridor: A Guide to Its History and Sources*. DeKalb: Northern Illinois Univ. Press, 1988.

Cook, Ramsay. *The Maple Leaf Forever: Essays on Nationalism and Politics in Canada*. Toronto: Macmillan, 1971.

Cooper, James Fenimore. *Home as Found*. 1838. Reprint. New York: Capricorn Books, 1961.

Cope, George W. *The Iron and Steel Interests of Chicago*. Chicago: Rand, McNally, 1890.

Corliss, Carlton J. *The Day of Two Noons*. Washington, D.C.: Association of American Railroads, 1941.

———. *Main Line of Mid-America: The Story of the Illinois Central*. New York: Creative Age Press, 1950.

Cottam, G., and O. L. Loucks. *Early Vegetation of Wisconsin*. Madison: Wisconsin Geological and Natural History Survey, 1965.

Cottrell, Fred. *Energy and Society: The Relation between Energy, Social Change, and Economic Development*. New York: McGraw-Hill, 1955.

Cowing, Cedric B. *Populists, Plungers, and Progressives: A Social History of Stock and Commodity Speculation, 1890–1936*. Princeton: Princeton Univ. Press, 1965.

Cox, Thomas R. *Mills and Markets: A History of the Pacific Coast Lumber Industry to 1900*. Seattle: Univ. of Washington Press, 1974.

Cox, Thomas R., et al. *This Well-Wooded Land: Americans and Their Forests from Colonial Times to the Present*. Lincoln: Univ. of Nebraska Press, 1985.

Crane, Richard Teller. *The Autobiography of Richard Teller Crane*. Chicago: Crane, 1927.

Critchell, James Troubridge, and Joseph Raymond. *A History of the Frozen Meat Trade*. London: Constable, 1912.

Cronon, William. *Changes in the Land: Indians, Colonists, and the Ecology of New England*. New York: Hill and Wang, 1983.

Cummings, Richard O. *The American Ice Harvests: A Historical Study in Technology, 1800–1918*. Berkeley: Univ. of California Press, 1949.

Curtis, John T. *The Vegetation of Wisconsin: An Ordination of Plant Communities*. Madison: Univ. of Wisconsin Press, 1971.

Curtiss, Daniel S. *Western Portraiture, and Emigrants' Guide*. New York: J. H. Colton, 1852.

Cutler, Irving. *Chicago: Metropolis of the Mid-Continent*. 2d ed. Dubuque, Iowa: Kendall/Hunt, 1976.

Daniel, Glenda, and Jerry Sullivan. *A Sierra Club Naturalist's Guide to the North Woods of Michigan, Wisconsin, Minnesota and Southern Ontario*. San Francisco: Sierra Club Books, 1981.

Davis, Richard C., ed. *Encyclopedia of American Forest and Conservation History*. New York: Macmillan, 1983.

Dean, Teresa. *White City Chips*. Chicago: Warren, 1895.

Deatherage, Chas. P. *The Early History of the Lumber Trade of Kansas City*. Kansas City: Retail Lumberman, 1924.

Debates and Proceedings of the Constitutional Convention of the State of Illinois. Springfield: State of Illinois, 1870.

de Rousiers, Paul. *American Life*. Translated by A. J. Herbertson. Paris and New York: Firmin-Didot, 1892.

Dick, Everett. *The Sod-House Frontier, 1854–1890: A Social History of the Northern Plains from the Creation of Kansas and Nebraska to the Admission of the Dakotas*. New York: D. Appleton-Century, 1937.

Dickinson, Robert E. *City and Region: A Geographical Interpretation*. London: Routledge & Kegan Paul, 1964.

Dies, Edward J. *The Plunger: A Tale of the Wheat Pit*. New York: Covici-Friede, 1929.

———. *The Wheat Pit*. Chicago: Argyle Press, 1925.

Dilke, Charles Wentworth. *Greater Britain: A Record of Travel in English-Speaking Countries during 1866–7*. Philadelphia: J. B. Lippincott, 1869.

Directory and Hand-Book of the Meat and Provision Trades and Their Allied Industries for the United States and Canada. New York: National Provisioner, 1895.

Dixon, Frank H. *State Railroad Control, with a History of Its Development in Iowa*. New York: Thomas Y. Crowell, 1896.

Dodge, Richard Irving. *The Plains of the Great West and Their Inhabitants*. 1877. Reprint. New York: Archer House, 1959.

Dondlinger, Percy Tracy. *The Book of Wheat: An Economic History and Practical Manual of the Wheat Industry*. New York: Orange Judd, 1919.

Dondore, Dorothy Anne. *The Prairie and the Making of Middle America: Four Centuries of Description.* Cedar Rapids, Iowa: Torch Press, 1926.

Donnelly, Ignatius. *Caesar's Column: A Story of the Twentieth-Century.* 1891. Edited by Walter B. Rideout. Cambridge: Harvard Univ. Press, 1960.

Doyle, Don Harrison. *The Social Order of a Frontier Community: Jacksonville, Illinois, 1825–1870.* Urbana: Univ. of Illinois Press, 1978.

Drache, Hiram M. *The Day of the Bonanza: A History of Bonanza Farming in the Red River Valley of the North.* Fargo: North Dakota Institute for Regional Studies, 1964.

Dreiser, Theodore. *Dawn: A History of Myself.* New York: Horace Liveright, 1931.

———. *The "Genius".* 1915. Reprint. Cleveland: World, 1954.

Drury, John. *Old Chicago Houses.* Chicago: Univ. of Chicago Press, 1941.

Duddy, Edward A. *The Supply Area of the Chicago Livestock Market.* Chicago: Univ. of Chicago Press, 1931.

Duis, Perry. *Chicago: Creating New Traditions.* Chicago: CHS, 1976.

Duncan, Beverly, and Stanley Lieberson. *Metropolis and Region in Transition.* Beverly Hills: Sage, 1970.

Dunlap, George Arthur. *The City in the American Novel, 1789–1900: A Study of American Novels Portraying Contemporary Conditions in New York, Philadelphia, and Boston.* Philadelphia: Univ. of Pennsylvania, 1934.

Dykstra, Robert R. *The Cattle Towns.* New York: Alfred A. Knopf, 1968.

Earling, P. R. *Whom to Trust: A Practical Treatise on Mercantile Credit.* Chicago: Rand McNally, 1890.

Eastman, Sidney Corning. *An Open Letter to the Members of the Union League Club of Chicago.* Chicago: Clark & Longley, [1887].

Ebner, Michael H. *Creating Chicago's North Shore: A Suburban History.* Chicago: Univ. of Chicago Press, 1988.

Edmunds, R. David. *The Potawatomis: Keepers of the Fire.* Norman: Univ. of Oklahoma Press, 1978.

Egleston, Nathaniel Hillyer. *Villages and Village Life, with Hints for Their Improvement.* New York: Harper & Brothers, 1878.

1848–1948: A History of the Wisconsin Paper Industry. Chicago: Howard, 1948.

Ellis, David M., ed. *The Frontier in American Development: Essays in Honor of Paul Wallace Gates.* Ithaca: Cornell Univ. Press, 1969.

Emerson, Ralph Waldo. *Essays and Lectures.* New York: Library of America, 1983.

———. *The Letters of Ralph Waldo Emerson.* Edited by Ralph L. Rusk. New York: Columbia Univ. Press, 1939.

Emery, Henry Crosby. *Speculation on the Stock and Produce Exchanges of the United States.* New York: Columbia Univ. Press, 1896.

Emmet, Boris, and John E. Jeuck. *Catalogues and Counters: A History of Sears, Roebuck & Company.* Chicago: Univ. of Chicago Press, 1950.

Erickson, Erling A. *Banking in Frontier Iowa, 1836–1865.* Ames: Iowa State Univ. Press, 1971.

Fabian, Ann. *Card Sharps, Dream Books, and Bucket Shops: Gambling in Nineteenth-Century America.* Ithaca: Cornell Univ. Press, 1990.

Faragher, John Mack. *Sugar Creek: Life on the Illinois Prairie.* New Haven: Yale Univ. Press, 1986.

Federal Trade Commission. *Report on the Grain Trade.* Washington, D.C.: GPO, 1920.

Federal Trade Commission, *Report on the Meat-Packing Industry.* Washington, D.C.: GPO, 1919.

Fergus, Robert. *Fergus' Directory of the City of Chicago, 1839.* Fergus Historical Series, no. 2. Chicago, 1876.

Ferris, William G. *The Grain Traders: The Story of the Chicago Board of Trade.* East Lansing: Michigan State Univ. Press, 1988.

Fishlow, Albert. *American Railroads and the Transformation of the Ante-Bellum Economy.* Cambridge: Harvard Univ. Press, 1965.

Fishman, Robert. *Bourgeois Utopias: The Rise and Fall of Suburbia.* New York: Basic Books, 1987.

Fite, Gilbert C. *American Farmers: The New Minority.* Bloomington: Indiana Univ. Press, 1981.

———. *The Farmer's Frontier, 1865–1900.* New York: Holt, Rinehart, and Winston, 1966.

Flader, Susan L., ed. *The Great Lakes Forest: An Environmental and Social History.* Minneapolis: Univ. of Minnesota Press, 1983.

Flinn, John J. *Chicago, the Marvelous City of the West: A History, an Encyclopedia, and a Guide, 1891.* Chicago: Flinn & Sheppard, 1890.

———. *Official Guide to the World's Columbian Exposition.* Chicago: Columbian Guide, 1893.

Flint, Henry M. *The Railroads of the United States; Their History and Statistics.* Philadelphia: John E. Potter, 1868.

Fogel, Robert William. *Railroads and American Economic Growth: Essays in Econometric History.* Baltimore: Johns Hopkins Univ. Press, 1964.

Fogelson, Robert M. *The Fragmented Metropolis: Los Angeles, 1850–1930.* Cambridge: Harvard Univ. Press, 1967.

Fornari, Harry. *Bread upon the Waters: A History of United States Grain Exports.* Nashville: Aurora, 1973.

Fowler, Bertram B. *Men, Meat and Miracles.* New York: Julian Messner, 1952.

Frank, Waldo. *Our America.* New York: Boni and Liveright, 1919.

Friedmann, John, and William Alonso, eds. *Regional Development and Planning: A Reader.* Cambridge: MIT Press, 1964.

Fries, Robert F. *Empire in Pine: The Story of Lumbering in Wisconsin, 1830–1900.* Madison: SHSW, 1951.

Frink, Maurice, W. Turrentine Jackson, and Agnes Wright Spring. *When Grass Was King: Contributions to the Western Range Cattle Industry Study.* Boulder: Univ. of Colorado Press, 1956.

Fuller, Henry Blake. *The Cliff-dwellers.* 1893. Reprint. New York: Holt, Rinehart, and Winston, 1973.

Fuller, S. M. *Summer on the Lakes in 1843.* New York: Little, Brown, 1844.

Fuller, Wayne E. *The American Mail: Enlarger of the Common Life.* Chicago: Univ. of Chicago Press, 1972.

Galena and Chicago Union Railroad Company. *Report of William B. Ogden, President of the Company . . . Read at the Annual Meeting of Stockholders, April 5, 1848.* Chicago, 1848.

Garland, Hamlin. *A Daughter of the Middle Border.* New York: Macmillan, 1921.

———. *Rose of Dutcher's Cooley.* Chicago: Stone & Kimball, 1895.

———. *A Son of the Middle Border.* New York: Grosset & Dunlap, 1917.

Gates, Paul Wallace. *The Farmer's Age: Agriculture, 1815–1860.* Vol. 3 of *The Economic History of the United States.* New York: Holt, Rinehart, and Winston, 1960.

———. *History of Public Land Law Development.* Washington, D.C.: GPO, 1968.

———. *The Illinois Central Railroad and Its Colonization Work.* Cambridge: Harvard Univ. Press, 1934.

Giedion, Siegfried. *Mechanization Takes Command: A Contribution to Anonymous History.* New York: Oxford Univ. Press, 1948.

Gilchrist, David T., ed. *The Growth of Seaport Cities, 1790–1825.* Charlottesville: Univ. Press of Virginia for the Eleutherian Mills-Hagley Foundation, 1967.

Gilpin, William. *The Cosmopolitan Railway: Compacting and Fusing Together All the World's Continents.* San Francisco: History, 1890.

———. *Mission of the North American People, Geographical, Social, and Political.* 2d ed. Philadelphia: J. B. Lippincott, 1874.

Glaab, Charles N. *Kansas City and the Railroads: Community Policy in the Growth of a Regional Metropolis.* Madison: Univ. of Wisconsin Press, 1962.

Glaab, Charles N., and A. Theodore Brown. *A History of Urban America.* 3d ed. New York: Macmillan, 1983.

Goldstein, Benjamin F. *Marketing: A Farmer's Problem.* New York: Macmillan, 1928.

Gould, Peter, and Rodney White. *Mental Maps.* Baltimore: Penguin Books, 1974.

Grand, W. Jos. *Illustrated History of the Union Stockyards.* Chicago: Thos. Knapp, 1896.

Gras, N. S. B. *An Introduction to Economic History.* New York: Harper & Brothers, 1922.

Gras, N. S. B., and Henrietta M. Larson, eds., *Casebook in American Business History.* New York: Appleton-Century-Crofts, 1939.

Great Plains Flora Association. *Atlas of the Flora of the Great Plains.* Ames: Iowa State Univ. Press, 1977.

Griffin, Susan. *Woman and Nature: The Roaring Inside Her.* New York: Harper & Row, 1978.

Guyer, I. D. *History of Chicago; Its Commercial and Manufacturing Interests and Industry.* Chicago: Church, Goodman and Cushing, 1862.

Haeger, John Denis. *The Investment Frontier: New York Businessmen and the Economic Development of the Old Northwest.* Albany: State Univ. of New York Press, 1981.

Hagan, William T. *The Sac and Fox Indians*. Norman: Univ. of Oklahoma Press, 1958.

Hahn, Steven, and Jonathan Prude. *The Countryside in the Age of Capitalist Transformation: Essays in the Social History of Rural America*. Chapel Hill: Univ. of North Carolina Press, 1985.

Haites, Erik F., James Mak, and Gary M. Walton. *Western River Transportation: The Era of Early Internal Development, 1810–1860*. Baltimore: Johns Hopkins Univ. Press, 1975.

Halttunen, Karen. *Confidence Men and Painted Women: A Study of Middle-Class Culture in America, 1830–1870*. New Haven: Yale Univ. Press, 1982.

Hamer, David. *New Towns in the New World: Images and Perceptions of the Nineteenth-Century Urban Frontier*. New York: Columbia Univ. Press, 1990.

Hammond, Bray. *Banks and Politics in America from the Revolution to the Civil War*. Princeton: Princeton Univ. Press, 1957.

Handy, Moses P., ed. *The Official Directory of the World's Columbian Exposition: A Reference Book*. Chicago: W. B. Conkey, 1893.

[Harrington, Bates.] *How 'Tis Done: A Thorough Ventilation of the Numerous Schemes Conducted by Wandering Canvassers, Together with the Various Advertising Dodges for the Swindling of the Public*. Syracuse, N.Y.: W. I. Pattison, 1890.

Harrison, Carter H. *Speech of Hon. Carter H. Harrison, of Illinois, on the Illinois and Michigan Canal, in the House of Representatives, Tuesday, May 21, 1878*. (n.p., n.d.)

Hartsough, Mildred Lucile. *The Twin Cities as a Metropolitan Market: A Regional Study of the Economic Development of Minneapolis and St. Paul*. Minneapolis: Univ. of Minnesota Press, 1925.

Harvey, David. *Consciousness and the Urban Experience: Studies in the History and Theory of Capitalist Urbanization*. Baltimore: Johns Hopkins Univ. Press, 1985.

———. *Social Justice and the City*. 1973. Reprint. Baltimore: Johns Hopkins Univ. Press, 1975.

———. *The Urbanization of Capital: Studies in the History and Theory of Capitalist Urbanization*. Baltimore: Johns Hopkins Univ. Press, 1985.

Hays, Samuel D. *Conservation and the Gospel of Efficiency: The Progressive Conservation Movement, 1890–1920*. Cambridge: Harvard Univ. Press, 1959.

Hayter, Earl W. *The Troubled Farmer, 1850–1900: Rural Adjustment to Industrialism*. DeKalb: Northern Illinois Univ. Press, 1968.

Healy, Kent T. *The Economics of Transportation in America: The Dynamic Forces in Development, Organization, Functioning and Regulation*. New York: Ronald Press, 1940.

Heinselman, M. L., and F. J. Marschner. *The Original Vegetation of Minnesota*. North Central Forest Experiment Station, USDA, U.S. Forest Service, 1974.

Heiple, Robert W., and Emma B. Heiple. *A Heritage History of Beautiful Green Lake Wisconsin*. Green Lake, Wis.: Privately printed, 1976.

Helgesen, Arlan. *Farms in the Cutover: Agricultural Settlement in Northern Wisconsin*. Madison: SHSW, 1962.

Hemingway, Ernest. *The Fifth Column and the First Forty-nine Stories*. New York: Charles Scribner's Sons, 1939.

Herrick, Robert. *The Gospel of Freedom*. New York: Macmillan, 1898.

———. *Memoirs of an American Citizen*. 1905. Edited by Daniel Aaron. Cambridge: Harvard Univ. Press, 1963.

Hicks, John D. *The Populist Revolt: A History of the Farmers' Alliance and the People's Party*. Minneapolis: Univ. of Minnesota Press, 1931.

Hidy, Ralph W., Frank Ernest Hill, and Allan Nevins. *Timber and Men: The Weyerhaeuser Story*. New York: Macmillan, 1963.

Hill, Lowell D. *Grain Grades and Standards: Historical Issues Shaping the Future*. Urbana: Univ. of Illinois Press, 1990.

Hilliard, Sam B. *Hog Meat and Hoecake: Food Supply in the Old South, 1840–1860*. Carbondale: Southern Illinois Univ. Press, 1972.

Hines, Thomas S. *Burnham of Chicago: Architect and Planner*. New York: Oxford Univ. Press, 1974.

Historic City: The Settlement of Chicago. Chicago: Department of Development and Planning, 1976.

Hoffman, Charles Fenno. *A Winter in the West: Letters Descriptive of Chicago and Vicinity in 1833–4*. 1835. Reprint. Fergus Historical Series, no. 20, Chicago, 1882.

Hofstadter, Richard. *The Age of Reform: From Bryan to F.D.R.* New York: Alfred A. Knopf, 1955.

———. *The Progressive Historians: Turner, Beard, Parrington*. New York: Alfred A. Knopf, 1968.

Hofstadter, Richard, and Seymour Martin Lipset, eds. *Turner and the Sociology of the Frontier.* New York: Basic Books, 1968.

Hoge, Cecil C., Sr. *The First Hundred Years Are the Toughest: What We Can Learn from the Century of Competition between Sears and Wards.* Berkeley, Calif.: Ten Speed Press, 1988.

Holbrook, Stewart. *Holy Old Mackinaw: A Natural History of the American Lumberjack.* New York: Macmillan, 1938.

Holt, Glen E., and Dominic A. Pacyga. *Chicago: A Historical Guide to the Neighborhoods, The Loop and South Side.* Chicago: CHS, 1979.

Hoover, Edgar M. *The Location of Economic Activity.* New York: McGraw-Hill, 1948.

Hopkins, John A., Jr. *Economic History of the Production of Beef Cattle in Iowa.* Iowa City: SHSI, 1928.

Hornaday, William T. *The Extermination of the American Bison.* Washington, D.C.: GPO, 1887.

Horowitz, Helen Lefkowitz. *Culture & the City: Cultural Philanthropy in Chicago from the 1880s to 1917.* Lexington: Univ. Press of Kentucky, 1976.

Horsman, Reginald. *Race and Manifest Destiny: The Origins of American Racial Anglo-Saxonism.* Cambridge: Harvard Univ. Press, 1981.

Hotchkiss, George W. *History of the Lumber and Forest Industry of the Northwest.* Chicago: George W. Hotchkiss, 1898.

Hough, Jack L. *The Geology of the Great Lakes.* Urbana: Univ. of Illinois Press, 1958.

Hounshell, David A. *From the American System to Mass Production, 1800–1932: The Development of Manufacturing Technology in the United States.* Baltimore: Johns Hopkins Univ. Press, 1984.

Howard, Robert P. *Illinois: A History of the Prairie State.* Grand Rapids: William P. Eerdmans, 1972.

Hoyt, Homer. *One Hundred Years of Land Values in Chicago: The Relationship of the Growth of Chicago to the Rise in Its Land Values, 1830–1933.* Chicago: Univ. of Chicago Press, 1933.

Hubbard, Gurdon Saltonstall. *The Autobiography of Gurdon Saltonstall Hubbard, Pa-pa-ma-ta-be, "The Swift Walker."* Chicago: Lakeside Press, 1911.

Hudson, John C. *Plains Country Towns.* Minneapolis: Univ. of Minnesota Press, 1985.

Hurst, James Willard. *Law and Economic Growth: The Legal History of the Lumber Industry in Wisconsin, 1836–1915.* Cambridge: Harvard Univ. Press, 1964.

————. *Law and Markets in United States History: Different Modes of Bargaining among Interests.* Madison: Univ. of Wisconsin Press, 1982.

Hutchinson, William T. *Cyrus Hall McCormick.* 2 vols. New York: Appleton-Century, 1930–35.

Illinois in 1837 & 8. Philadelphia: S. Augustus Mitchell, 1838.

Industrial Chicago. Chicago: Goodspeed, 1894.

Innis, Harold A. *Problems of Staple Production in Canada.* Toronto: Ryerson Press, 1933.

Institute of American Meat Packers. *The Packing Industry.* Chicago: Univ. of Chicago Press, 1924.

Interstate Commerce Commission. *Report on the Case of the Eau Claire Board of Trade vs. The Chicago, Milwaukee & St. Paul Railway Company,* et al. June 17, 1892.

Isard, Walter. *Location and Space-Economy: A General Theory Relating to Industrial Location, Market Areas, Land Use, Trade, and Urban Structure.* Cambridge: MIT Press; New York: John Wiley, 1956.

Jackson, Kenneth T. *Crabgrass Frontier: The Suburbanization of the United States.* New York: Oxford Univ. Press, 1985.

Jacobs, Wilbur R., ed. *The Historical World of Frederick Jackson Turner with Selections from His Correspondence.* New Haven: Yale Univ. Press, 1968.

James, Edwin. *Account of an Expedition from Pittsburgh to the Rocky Mountains.* 1823. Reprint. Readex Microprint, 1966.

James, F. Cyril. *The Growth of Chicago Banks.* 1938. Reprint. New York: Harper & Row, 1969.

James, John A. *Money and Capital Markets in Postbellum America.* Princeton: Princeton Univ. Press, 1978.

Jenks, Tudor. *The Century World's Fair Book for Boys and Girls, Being the Adventures of Harry and Philip with Their Tutor, Mr. Douglass, at the World's Columbian Exposition.* New York: Century, 1893.

Johnson, Arthur M., and Barry E. Supple. *Boston Capitalists and Western Railroads: A Study in the Nineteenth-Century Railroad Investment Process.* Cambridge: Harvard Univ. Press, 1967.

Johnson, Hildegard Binder. *Order upon the Land: The U.S. Rectangular Land Survey and the Upper Mississippi Country.* New York: Oxford Univ. Press, 1976.

Johnson, Rossiter, ed. *A History of the World's Columbian Exposition Held in Chicago in 1893.* 4 vols. New York: D. Appleton, 1897.

Jones, William, Jr. *An Address to the Merchants of the N. West, Setting Forth the Advantages of the City of Chicago as the Central Mart of the Union.* Chicago, 1856.

Judd, Richard W. *Aroostook: A Century of Logging in Northern Maine.* Orono: Univ. of Maine Press, 1989.

Kane, W. *The Education of Edward Cudahy.* Chicago: Effingham County Printing, 1941.

Karnes, Thomas L. *William Gilpin: Western Nationalist.* Austin: Univ. of Texas Press, 1970.

Keating, Ann Durkin. *Building Chicago: Suburban Developers & the Creation of a Divided Metropolis.* Columbus: Ohio State Univ. Press, 1988.

Kenny, D. J. *Historical, Statistical, and Descriptive: Chicago: Identifying Those Firms Who Have Contributed Most to Its Prosperity and Grandeur.* Chicago, 1886.

Kimball, Nell. *Nell Kimball: Her Life as an American Madam, by Herself.* Edited by Stephen Longstreet. New York: Macmillan, 1970.

Kinsley, Philip. *The Chicago Tribune: Its First Hundred Years.* New York: Alfred A. Knopf, 1943.

Kinzie, Mrs. John H. *Wau-Bun: The "Early Day" in the North-West.* 1856. Edited by Louise Phelps Kellogg. Menasha, Wis.: National Society of Colonial Dames in Wisconsin, 1948.

Kipling, Rudyard. *From Sea to Sea: Letters of Travel.* New York: Doubleday & McClure, 1899.

Kirkland, Edward Chase. *Men, Cities, and Transportation: A Study in New England History, 1820–1900.* Cambridge: Harvard Univ. Press, 1948.

Kloppenburg, Jack R., Jr. *First the Seed: The Political Economy of Plant Biotechnology, 1492–2000.* New York: Cambridge Univ. Press, 1988.

Kohlmeier, Albert L. *The Old Northwest as the Keystone of the Arch of American Federal Union.* Bloomington, Ind.: Principia Press, 1938.

Kolko, Gabriel. *Railroads and Regulation, 1877–1916.* Princeton: Princeton Univ. Press, 1965.

Kolodny, Annette. *The Lay of the Land: Metaphor as Experience and History in American Life and Letters.* Chapel Hill: Univ. of North Carolina Press, 1975.

Kozlowski, T. T., and C. E. Ahlgren, eds. *Fire and Ecosystems.* New York: Academic Press, 1974.

Kranzberg, Melvin, and Carroll W. Pursell, Jr., eds. *Technology in Western Civilization.* New York: Oxford Univ. Press, 1967.

Kuhlmann, Charles Byron. *The Development of the Flour-Milling Industry in the United States with Special Reference to the Industry in Minneapolis.* Boston: Houghton Mifflin, 1929.

Lampard, Eric E. *The Rise of the Dairy Industry in Wisconsin: A Study in Agricultural Change, 1820–1920.* Madison: Univ. of Wisconsin Press, 1963.

Landes, David S. *Revolution in Time: Clocks and the Making of the Modern World.* Cambridge: Harvard Univ. Press, 1983.

Larrabee, William. *The Railroad Question: A Historical and Practical Treatise on Railroads, and Remedies for Their Abuses.* Chicago: Schulte, 1893.

Larson, Agnes M. *History of the White Pine Industry in Minnesota.* Minneapolis: Univ. of Minnesota Press, 1949.

Larson, Henrietta M. *The Wheat Market and the Farmer in Minnesota, 1858–1900.* New York: Columbia Univ. Press, 1926.

Larson, John Lauritz. *Bonds of Enterprise: John Murray Forbes and Western Development in America's Railway Age.* Cambridge: Harvard Business School Press, 1984.

Latrobe, Charles Joseph. *The Rambler in North America, 1832–1833.* New York: Harper & Brothers, 1835.

Leech, Harper, and John Charles Carroll. *Armour and His Times.* New York: D. Appleton-Century, 1938.

Leopold, Aldo. *A Sand County Almanac and Sketches Here and There.* New York: Oxford Univ. Press, 1949.

Lewis, Lloyd. *John S. Wright: Prophet of the Prairies.* Chicago: Prairie Farmer, 1941.

Lillard, Richard G. *The Great Forest.* New York: Alfred A. Knopf, 1948.

Limerick, Patricia Nelson. *The Legacy of Conquest: The Unbroken Past of the American West.* New York: W. W. Norton, 1987.

Lindstrom, Diane. *Economic Development in the Philadelphia Region, 1810–1850.* New York: Columbia Univ. Press, 1978.

Livingood, James W. *The Philadelphia-Baltimore Trade Rivalry, 1780–1860.* Harrisburg: Pennsylvania Historical and Museum Commission, 1947.

Longstreet, Stephen. _Chicago: An Intimate Portrait of People, Pleasures, and Power: 1860–1919._ New York: David McKay, 1973.

Lopez, Barry. _Arctic Dreams: Imagination and Desire in a Northern Landscape._ New York: Charles Scribner's Sons, 1986.

Lösch, August. _The Economics of Location._ 1939. Translated by William H. Woglom. New Haven: Yale Univ. Press, 1954.

Lowe, David. _Lost Chicago._ Boston: Houghton Mifflin, 1978.

————, comp. _The Great Chicago Fire in Eyewitness Accounts and 70 Contemporary Photographs and Illustrations._ New York: Dover Publications, 1979.

Lurie, Jonathan. _The Chicago Board of Trade, 1859–1905: The Dynamics of Self Regulation._ Urbana: Univ. of Illinois Press, 1979.

MacAvoy, Paul W. _The Economic Effects of Regulation: The Trunk-Line Railroad Cartels and the Interstate Commerce Commission before 1900._ Cambridge: MIT Press, 1965.

MacCormack, Carol P., and Marilyn Strathern. _Nature, Culture and Gender._ Cambridge: Cambridge Univ. Press, 1980.

Machor, James L. _Pastoral Cities: Urban Ideals and the Symbolic Landscape of America._ Madison: Univ. of Wisconsin Press, 1987.

Madson, John. _Where the Sky Began: Land of the Tallgrass Prairie._ Boston: Houghton Mifflin, 1982.

Mahoney, Timothy R. _River Towns in the Great West: The Structure of Provincial Urbanization in the American Midwest, 1820–1870._ New York: Cambridge Univ. Press, 1990.

Malenbaum, Wilfred. _The World Wheat Economy, 1885–1939._ Cambridge: Harvard Univ. Press, 1953.

Malin, James C. _The Grassland of North America: Prolegomena to Its History with Addenda and Postscript._ 1947. Reprint. Gloucester, Mass.: Peter Smith, 1967.

————. _Winter Wheat in the Golden Belt of Kansas: A Study in Adaptation to Subhumid Geographical Environment._ Lawrence: Univ. of Kansas Press, 1944.

Marshall, Roujet D. _Autobiography._ Edited by Gilson G. Glasier. Madison, Wis.: Democrat Printing, 1923.

Martin, Albro. _Enterprise Denied: Origins of the Decline of American Railroads, 1897–1917._ New York: Columbia Univ. Press, 1971.

Martin, Edward Winslow [James Dabney McCabe]. _History of the Grange Movement; or, The Farmer's War against Monopolies._ Chicago: National, 1873.

Martin, Lawrence. _The Physical Geography of Wisconsin._ 1932. 3d ed. Madison: Univ. of Wisconsin Press, 1965.

Martineau, Harriet. _Society in America._ Paris, 1837.

Marx, Karl. _Capital: A Critique of Political Economy._ New York: International, 1967.

————. _Grundrisse: Foundations of the Critique of Political Economy (Rough Draft)._ Translated by Martin Nicolaus. Harmondsworth, England: Penguin, 1973.

Marx, Leo. _The Machine in the Garden: Technology and the Pastoral Ideal in America._ New York: Oxford Univ. Press, 1964.

Masters, D. C. _The Rise of Toronto, 1850–1890._ Toronto: Univ. of Toronto Press, 1947.

Mayer, Harold M. _The Port of Chicago and the St. Lawrence Seaway._ Univ. of Chicago Department of Geography Research Paper no. 49. Chicago, 1957.

Mayer, Harold M., and Richard C. Wade. _Chicago: Growth of a Metropolis._ Chicago: Univ. of Chicago Press, 1969.

McCallum, Henry D., and Frances T. McCallum. _The Wire That Fenced the West._ Norman: Univ. of Oklahoma Press, 1965.

McClung, J. W. _Minnesota as It Is in 1870._ St. Paul, 1870.

McCormick, Cyrus. _The Century of the Reaper._ Boston: Houghton Mifflin, 1931.

McCormick Reaper Centennial Source Material. Chicago: International Harvester, [1931].

McCoy, Joseph G. _Historic Sketches of the Cattle Trade of the West and Southwest._ 1874. Reprint. Readex Microprint, 1966.

McHugh, Tom. _The Time of the Buffalo._ New York: Alfred A. Knopf, 1972.

McIlvaine, Mabel, ed. _Reminiscences of Early Chicago._ Chicago: Lakeside Press, 1912.

————, ed. _Reminiscences of Chicago during the Great Fire._ Chicago: Lakeside Press, 1915.

McKenzie, R. D. _The Metropolitan Community._ New York: McGraw-Hill, 1933.

McNall, Scott G. _The Road to Rebellion: Class Formation and Kansas Populism, 1865–1900._ Chicago: Univ. of Chicago Press, 1988.

Merchant, Carolyn. _The Death of Nature: Women, Ecology, and the Scientific Revolution._ New York: Harper & Row, 1980.

Merk, Frederick. *Economic History of Wisconsin during the Civil War Decade.* 1916. Reprint. Madison: SHSW, 1971.

Meyerowitz, Joanne. *Women Adrift: Independent Wage Earners in Chicago, 1880–1930.* Chicago: Univ. of Chicago Press, 1988.

Miller, George H. *Railroads and the Granger Laws.* Madison: Univ. of Wisconsin Press, 1971.

Miller, Perry. *Nature's Nation.* Cambridge: Harvard Univ. Press, 1967.

Miller, Ross. *American Apocalypse: The Great Fire and the Myth of Chicago.* Chicago: Univ. of Chicago Press, 1990.

Miner, H. Craig. *West of Wichita: Settling the High Plains of Kansas, 1865–1890.* Lawrence: Univ. Press of Kansas, 1986.

———. *Wichita: The Early Years, 1865–80.* Lincoln: Univ. of Nebraska Press, 1982.

Mitchell, Robert D., and Paul A. Groves, eds. *North America: The Historical Geography of a Changing Continent.* Totowa, N.J.: Rowman & Littlefield, 1987.

Moline, Norman T. *Mobility and the Small Town, 1900–1930: Transportation Change in Oregon, Illinois.* Univ. of Chicago Department of Geography Research Paper no. 132. Chicago, 1971.

Morgan, Appleton. *The People and the Railways.* New York: Belford, Clarke, 1888.

Moskowitz, Milton, Michael Katz, and Robert Levering. *Everybody's Business, An Almanac: The Irreverent Guide to Corporate America.* New York: Harper & Row, 1980.

Muirhead, James Fullarton. *The Land of Contrasts: A Briton's View of His American Kin.* Boston: Lamson, Wolffe, 1898.

Multhauf, Robert P. *Neptune's Gift: A History of Common Salt.* Baltimore: Johns Hopkins Univ. Press, 1978.

Mumford, Lewis. *The City in History: Its Origins, Its Transformations, and Its Prospects.* New York: Harcourt, Brace & World, 1961.

———. *The Culture of Cities.* New York: Harcourt, Brace, 1938.

Myers, Margaret G. *A Financial History of the United States.* New York: Columbia Univ. Press, 1970.

———. *The New York Money Market.* New York: Columbia Univ. Press, 1931.

My Record of the World's Columbian Exposition. Chicago: copyright Mrs. Henry Ellsworth Hayden, 1893.

Nelligan, John Emmett. *The Life of a Lumberman.* N.p., 1929.

Nesbit, Robert C. *Urbanization and Industrialization, 1873–1893.* Vol. 3 of *The History of Wisconsin.* Madison: SHSW, 1985.

New York State Assembly. *Proceedings of the Special Committee Appointed to Investigate Alleged Abuses in the Management of Railroads Chartered by the State of New York.* Assembly Doc. 38, 1879–80. (The "Hepburn Report.")

Neyhart, Louise A. *Giant of the Yards.* Boston: Houghton Mifflin, 1952.

Niemi, Albert W., Jr. *State and Regional Patterns in American Manufacturing, 1860–1900.* Westport, Conn.: Greenwood Press, 1974.

Nimmo, Joseph, Jr. *Report on the Internal Commerce of the United States.* U.S. Treasury Department, Bureau of Statistics. Washington, D.C.: GPO, 1877–81.

Nordin, D. Sven. *Rich Harvest: A History of the Grange, 1867–1900.* Jackson: Univ. Press of Mississippi, 1974.

Norris, Frank. *The Pit: A Story of Chicago.* 1903. Reprint. New York: Grove Press, n.d.

Norris, J. W. *Norris' Business Directory and Statistics of the City of Chicago for 1846.* Edited by Robert Fergus. Fergus Historical Series, no. 25. Chicago, 1883.

North, Douglass C. *The Economic Growth of the United States, 1790–1860.* 1961. Reprint. New York: W. W. Norton, 1966.

Norton, Matthew G. *The Mississippi River Logging Company: An Historical Sketch.* N.p., 1912.

Norwood, Vera, and Janice Monk, eds. *The Desert Is No Lady: Southwestern Landscapes in Women's Writing and Art.* New Haven: Yale Univ. Press, 1987.

Novick, Peter. *That Noble Dream: The "Objectivity Question" in the American Historical Profession.* New York: Cambridge Univ. Press, 1988.

Nugent, Walter T. K. *The Money Question during Reconstruction.* New York: W. W. Norton, 1967.

O'Brien, Michael J., ed. *Grassland, Forest, and Historical Settlement: An Analysis of Dynamics in Northeast Missouri.* Lincoln: Univ. of Nebraska Press, 1984.

Odum, Howard W. *American Regionalism: A Cultural-Historical Approach to National Integration.* New York: Henry Holt, 1938.

Oliver, William. *Eight Months in Illinois; with Information to Emigrants.* 1843. Reprint. Readex Microprint, 1966.

Olmsted, Frederick Law. *A Journey through Texas: or, A Saddle-Trip on the Southwestern Frontier.* 1857. Reprint. Austin: Univ. of Texas Press, 1978.

———. *Civilizing American Cities: A Selection of Frederick Law Olmsted's Writings on City Landscape.* Edited by S. B. Sutton. Cambridge: MIT Press, 1971.

Olmsted, Vaux & Co. *Preliminary Report upon the Proposed Suburban Village at Riverside, near Chicago.* New York: Sutton, Bowne, 1868.

O'Malley, Michael. *A History of American Time.* New York: Viking, 1990.

Origin, Growth, and Usefulness of the Chicago Board of Trade. New York: Historical, 1885.

Osgood, Ernest Staples. *The Day of the Cattleman.* 1929. Reprint. Chicago: Univ. of Chicago Press, n.d.

Our Suburbs: A Resumé of the Origin, Progress and Present Status of Chicago's Environs. Chicago: Blue Island Land and Building, [1873].

Overton, Richard C. *Burlington Route: A History of the Burlington Lines.* New York: Alfred A. Knopf, 1965.

———. *Burlington West: A Colonization History of the Burlington Railroad.* Cambridge: Harvard Univ. Press, 1941.

Owram, Doug. *Promise of Eden: The Canadian Expansion Movement and the Idea of the West, 1856–1900.* Toronto: Univ. of Toronto Press, 1980.

Pacyga, Dominic A., and Ellen Skerrett. *Chicago, City of Neighborhoods: Histories and Tours.* Chicago: Loyola Univ. Press, 1986.

Paine, Arthur E. *The Granger Movement in Illinois.* Urbana: Univ. of Illinois Press, 1904.

Patterson, G. W. S. *The World's Fair and My Trip round the World.* Auckland, New Zealand: H. Brett, 1894.

Paullin, Charles O. *Atlas of the Historical Geography of the United States.* Washington, D.C.: Carnegie Institution, 1932.

Peck, J. M. *A Guide for Emigrants, Containing Sketches of Illinois, Missouri, and the Adjacent Parts.* Boston: Lincoln and Edmands, 1831.

Periam, Jonathan. *The Groundswell: A History of the Origin, Aims, and Progress of the Farmers' Movement.* Chicago: Hannaford & Thompson, 1874.

———. *The Home and Farm Manual.* 1884. Reprint. New York: Greenwich House, 1984.

Perloff, Harvey S., et al. *Regions, Resources, and Economic Growth.* Baltimore: Johns Hopkins Univ. Press, 1960.

Perren, Richard. *The Meat Trade in Britain, 1840–1914.* London: Routledge & Kegan Paul, 1978.

Peyton, John Lewis. *Over the Alleghanies and across the Prairies.* 1848. 2d ed. London: Simpkin, Marshall, 1870.

Pierce, Bessie Louise. *A History of Chicago.* 3 vols. New York: Alfred A. Knopf, 1937–57.

———. *As Others See Chicago: Impressions of Visitors, 1673–1933.* Chicago: Univ. of Chicago Press, 1933.

Plumbe, John, Jr. *Sketches of Iowa and Wisconsin, Taken during a Residence of Three Years in Those Territories.* St. Louis: Chambers, Harris & Knapp, 1839.

Pollack, Norman. *The Populist Response to Industrial America.* Cambridge: Harvard Univ. Press, 1962.

Pomeroy, Earl. *The Pacific Slope: A History of California, Oregon, Washington, Idaho, Utah, and Nevada.* New York: Alfred A. Knopf, 1966.

Porter, Glenn, and Harold C. Livesay. *Merchants and Manufacturers: Studies in the Changing Structure of Nineteenth-Century Marketing.* Baltimore: Johns Hopkins Univ. Press, 1971.

Porter, H. H. *A Short Autobiography, Written for His Children and Grandchildren.* Chicago: Privately printed, 1915.

Potter, David M. *People of Plenty: Economic Abundance and the American Character.* Chicago: Univ. of Chicago Press, 1954.

Pred, Allan R. *The External Relations of Cities during "Industrial Revolution," with a Case Study of Göteborg, Sweden: 1868–1890.* Univ. of Chicago Department of Geography Research Paper no. 76. Chicago, 1962.

———. *The Spatial Dynamics of U.S. Urban Industrial Growth, 1800–1914: Interpretive and Theoretical Essays.* Cambridge: MIT Press, 1966.

———. *Urban Growth and City-Systems in the United States, 1840–1860.* Cambridge: Harvard Univ. Press, 1980.

——. *Urban Growth and the Circulation of Information: The United States System of Cities, 1790–1840*. Cambridge: Harvard Univ. Press, 1973.

Putnam, James William. *The Illinois and Michigan Canal: A Study in Economic History*. Chicago: Univ. of Chicago Press, 1918.

Pyne, Stephen J. *Fire in America: A Cultural History of Wildland and Rural Fire*. Princeton: Princeton Univ. Press, 1982.

Quaife, Milo Milton. *Checagou: From Indian Wigwam to Modern City, 1673–1835*. Chicago: Univ. of Chicago Press, 1933.

——. *Chicago and the Old Northwest, 1673–1835: A Study of the Evolution of the Northwestern Frontier, Together with a History of Fort Dearborn*. Chicago: Chicago Univ. Press, 1913.

——, ed. *Pictures of Illinois One Hundred Years Ago*. Chicago: Lakeside Press, 1918.

Quimby, George Irving. *Indian Life in the Upper Great Lakes: 11,000 B.C. to A.D. 1800*. Chicago: Univ. of Chicago Press, 1960.

Quondam [Charles M. Stevens]. *The Adventures of Uncle Jeremiah and Family at the Great Fair, Their Observations and Triumphs*. Chicago: Laird & Lee, 1893.

Rae, W. F. *Westward by Rail: A Journey to San Francisco and Back and a Visit to the Mormons*. London: Longman, Green, 1871.

Ralph, Julian. *Harper's Chicago and the World's Fair*. New York: Harper & Brothers, 1893.

——. *Our Great West: A Study of the Present Conditions and Future Possibilities of the New Commonwealths and Capitals of the United States*. New York: Harper & Brothers, 1893.

Randall, Frank Alfred. *History of the Development of Building Construction in Chicago*. Urbana: Univ. of Illinois Press, 1949.

Rand, McNally & Co.'s A Week at the Fair, Illustrating the Exhibits and Wonders of the World's Columbian Exposition. Chicago: Rand, McNally, 1893.

Rand, McNally & Co.'s Handbook of the World's Columbian Exposition. Chicago: Rand, McNally, 1893.

Rauch, J. H. *The Sanitary Problems of Chicago, Past and Present*. Cambridge: Riverside Press, 1879.

Reavis, L[ogan] U[riah]. *A Change of National Empire; or, Arguments in Favor of the Removal of the National Capital from Washington City to the Mississippi Valley*. St. Louis: J. F. Torrey, 1869.

Rector, William Gerald. *Log Transportation in the Lake States Lumber Industry, 1840–1918: The Movement of Logs and Its Relationship to Land Settlement, Waterway Development, Railroad Construction, Lumber Production and Prices*. Glendale, Calif.: Arthur H. Clark, 1953.

Remini, Robert V. *Andrew Jackson and the Bank War: A Study in the Growth of Presidential Power*. New York: W. W. Norton, 1967.

Report of the Commissioner of Corporations on the Beef Industry. Washington, D.C.: GPO, 1905.

Report of the Commission on Country Life. 60th Cong., 2d sess., 1910. Sen. Doc. 705.

Report of the Forestry Commission of the State of Wisconsin. Madison: Democrat Printing, 1898.

Reps, John W. *The Making of Urban America: A History of City Planning in the United States*. Princeton: Princeton Univ. Press, 1965.

Reynolds, R. V., and A. H. Pierson. *Forest Products Statistics of the Lake States*. USDA Statistical Bulletin no. 68. Washington: GPO, 1939.

Ridgley, Douglas C. *The Geography of Illinois*. Chicago: Univ. of Chicago Press, 1921.

Riley, Elmer A. *The Development of Chicago and Vicinity as a Manufacturing Center Prior to 1880*. Chicago: Univ. of Chicago, 1911.

Riley, Glenda. *The Female Frontier: A Comparative View of Women on the Prairie and the Plains*. Lawrence: Univ. Press of Kansas, 1988.

Ripley, William Z. *Railroads: Finance and Organization*. New York: Longmans, Green, 1915.

——. *Railroads: Rates and Regulation*. New York: Longmans, Green, 1912.

——, ed. *Railway Problems*. Rev. ed. New York: Ginn, 1913.

Ritchie, James S. *Wisconsin and Its Resources*. Philadelphia: Charles Desilver, 1858.

Riverside in 1871, with a Description of Its Improvements. Chicago: Riverside Improvement Co., [1871].

Robinson, Edward Van Dyke. *Early Economic Conditions and the Development of Agriculture in Minnesota*. Univ. of Minnesota Studies in the Social Sciences, no. 3. Minneapolis, 1915.

Roe, Frank Gilbert. *The North American Buffalo: A Critical Study of the Species in Its Wild State*. 2d ed. Toronto: Univ. of Toronto Press, 1970.

Rogin, Leo. *The Introduction of Farm Machinery in Its Relation to the Productivity of Labor in the Agriculture of the United States during the Nineteenth Century*. Berkeley: Univ. of California Press, 1931.

Rohrbough, Malcolm J. *The Land Office Business: The Settlement and Administration of American Public Lands, 1789–1837.* New York: Oxford Univ. Press, 1968.

———. *The Trans-Appalachian Frontier.* New York: Oxford Univ. Press, 1978.

Roll, Eric. *A History of Economic Thought.* 4th ed. London: Faber and Faber, 1973.

Root, George F. *The Trumpet of Reform: A Collection of Songs, Hymns, Chants and Set Pieces for the Grange, the Club and all Industrial & Reform Associations.* Cincinnati: John Church; Chicago: George F. Root & Sons, 1874.

Rosen, Christine Meisner. *The Limits of Power: Great Fires and the Process of City Growth in America.* New York: Cambridge Univ. Press, 1986.

Rosholt, Malcolm. *Lumbermen on the Chippewa.* Rosholt, Wis.: Rosholt House, 1982.

———. *The Wisconsin Logging Book, 1839–1939.* Rosholt, Wis.: Rosholt House, 1980.

Rostow, W. W. *The Stages of Economic Growth.* New York: Cambridge Univ. Press, 1960.

Roth, Filibert. *Forestry Conditions and Interests of Wisconsin.* USDA Bulletin no. 16. Washington, D.C.: GPO, 1898.

Russell, Charles Edward. *The Greatest Trust in the World.* New York: Ridgway-Thayer, 1905.

Rydell, Robert W. *All the World's a Fair: Visions of Empire at American International Expositions, 1876–1916.* Chicago: Univ. of Chicago Press, 1984.

Saley, Met L. *Realm of the Retailer: The Retail Lumber Trade, Its Difficulties and Successes, Its Theory and Practice, with Practical Yard Ideas.* Chicago: American Lumberman, 1902.

Saloutos, Theodore, and John D. Hicks. *Agricultural Discontent in the Middle West, 1900–1939.* Madison: Univ. of Wisconsin Press, 1951.

Sauer, Carl O. *Agricultural Origins and Dispersals.* 1952. Reprint. Cambridge: MIT Press, 1969.

Scammon, J. Young. *William B. Ogden.* Fergus Historical Series, no. 17. Chicago, 1882.

Scheiber, Harry N. *Ohio Canal Era: A Case Study of Government and the Economy, 1820–1861.* Athens: Ohio Univ. Press, 1969.

Schery, Robert W. *Plants for Man.* 2d ed. Englewood Cliffs, N.J.: Prentice-Hall, 1972.

Schlebecker, John T. *Whereby We Thrive: A History of American Farming, 1607–1972.* Ames: Iowa State Univ. Press, 1975.

Schlissel, Lillian, Vicki L. Ruiz, and Janice Monk, eds. *Western Women: Their Land, Their Lives.* Albuquerque: Univ. of New Mexico Press, 1988.

Schmidt, Alfred. *The Concept of Nature in Marx.* London: New Left Books, 1971.

Schob, David E. *Hired Hands and Plow Boys: Farm Labor in the Midwest, 1815–1860.* Urbana: Univ. of Illinois Press, 1975.

Schoff, S. S. *The Industrial Interests of Chicago.* Chicago: Knight & Leonard, 1873.

Schonberger, Howard B. *Transportation to the Seaboard: The "Communication Revolution" and American Foreign Policy, 1860–1900.* Westport, Conn.: Greenwood Press, 1971.

Schuyler, David. *The New Urban Landscape: The Redefinition of City Form in Nineteenth-Century America.* Baltimore: Johns Hopkins Univ. Press, 1986.

Scott, J. W. *A Presentation of Causes Tending to Fix the Position of the Future Great City of the World in the Central Plain of North America: Showing That the Centre of the World's Commerce, Now Represented by the City of London, Is Moving Westward to the City of New York, and Thence, within One Hundred Years, to the Best Position on the Great Lakes.* 2d ed. Toledo, 1876.

Sears, Paul B. *Lands beyond the Forest.* Englewood Cliffs, N.J.: Prentice-Hall, 1969.

Sewall, Alfred L. *The Great Calamity.* Chicago: A. L. Sewall, 1871.

Shannon, Fred A. *The Farmer's Last Frontier: Agriculture, 1860–1897.* Vol. 5 of *The Economic History of the United States.* New York: Farrar & Rinehart, 1945.

Sharkey, Robert P. *Money, Class, and Party: An Economic Study of Civil War and Reconstruction.* Baltimore: Johns Hopkins Univ. Press, 1959.

Sheahan, James W., and George P. Upton. *The Great Conflagration: Chicago: Its Past, Present and Future.* Chicago: Union, 1872.

Shepp, James W., and Daniel B. Shepp. *Shepp's World's Fair Photographed.* Chicago: Globe Bible, 1893.

Shi, David E. *The Simple Life: Plain Living and High Thinking in American Culture.* New York: Oxford Univ. Press, 1985.

Shirreff, Patrick. *A Tour through North America.* Edinburgh: Oliver and Boyd, 1835.

Shortridge, James R. *The Middle West: Its Meaning in American Culture.* Lawrence: Univ. Press of Kansas, 1989.

Siegel, Adrienne. *The Image of the American City in Popular Literature, 1820–1870.* Port Washington, N.Y.: Kennikat Press, 1981.

Simons, A. M. *The American Farmer.* Chicago: Charles H. Kerr, 1906.

Sims, P. K., and G. B. Morey, eds. *Geology of Minnesota.* St. Paul: Minnesota Geological Survey, 1972.

Sinclair, Upton. *The Jungle.* 1906. Reprint. New York: Signet New American Library, 1960.

Siringo, Charles A. *A Texas Cowboy; or, Fifteen Years on the Hurricane Deck of a Spanish Pony.* 1885. Reprint. Lincoln: Univ. of Nebraska Press, 1979.

Skaggs, Jimmy M. *The Cattle-Trailing Industry: Between Supply and Demand, 1866–1890.* Lawrence: Univ. Press of Kansas, 1973.

Skogan, Wesley G. *Chicago since 1840: A Time-series Data Handbook.* Urbana: Univ. of Illinois Institute of Government and Public Affairs, 1976.

Slayton, Robert A. *Back of the Yards: The Making of a Local Democracy.* Chicago: Univ. of Chicago Press, 1986.

Slotkin, Richard. *The Fatal Environment: The Myth of the Frontier in the Age of Industrialization, 1800–1890.* New York: Atheneum, 1985.

———. *Regeneration through Violence: The Mythology of the American Frontier, 1600–1860.* Middletown: Wesleyan Univ. Press, 1973.

Smith, Alice E. *George Smith's Money: A Scottish Investor in America.* Madison: SHSW, 1966.

Smith, Carl S. *Chicago and the American Literary Imagination, 1880–1920.* Chicago: Univ. of Chicago Press, 1984.

Smith, David C. *A History of Lumbering in Maine, 1861–1960.* University of Maine Studies, no. 93. Orono: Univ. of Maine Press, 1972.

Smith, Henry Nash. *Virgin Land: The American West as Symbol and Myth.* Cambridge: Harvard Univ. Press, 1950.

Smith, Neil. *Uneven Development: Nature, Capital and the Production of Space.* New York: Basil Blackwell, 1984.

Smith, Stephe. *Grains for the Grangers, Discussing All Points Bearing upon the Farmers' Movement for the Emancipation of White Slaves from the Slave-Power of Monopoly.* 1873. Reprint. Philadelphia: Keystone, 1889.

Sobel, Robert. *The Big Board: A History of the New York Stock Market.* New York: Free Press, 1965.

Solberg, Erling D. *New Laws for New Forests: Wisconsin's Forest-Fire, Tax, Zoning, and County-Forest Laws in Operation.* Madison: Univ. of Wisconsin Press, 1961.

Sparhawk, William N., and Warren D. Brush. *The Economic Aspects of Forest Destruction in Northern Michigan.* USDA Technical Bulletin no. 92. Washington, D.C.: USDA, 1930.

Spirn, Anne Whiston. *The Granite Garden: Urban Nature and Human Design.* New York: Basic Books, 1984.

Sporting and Club House Directory, Chicago, Containing a Full and Complete List of All First Class Club and Sporting Houses. Chicago: Ross & St. Clair, 1889.

Stansell, Christine. *City of Women: Sex and Class in New York, 1789–1860.* New York: Alfred A. Knopf, 1986.

Stead, William Thomas. *If Christ Came to Chicago.* 1894. Reprint. Chicago: Chicago Historical Bookworks, 1978.

Stephenson, Isaac. *Recollections of a Long Life, 1829–1915.* Chicago: Privately printed, 1915.

Stewart, George R. *American Place-Names.* New York: Oxford Univ. Press. 1970.

Stilgoe, John R. *Metropolitan Corridor: Railroads and the American Scene.* New Haven: Yale Univ. Press, 1983.

Still, Bayrd. *Milwaukee: The History of a City.* Madison: SHSW, 1948.

Storck, John, and Walter Dorwin Teague. *Flour for Man's Bread: A History of Milling.* Minneapolis: Univ. of Minnesota Press, 1952.

Stover, John F. *American Railroads.* Chicago: Univ. of Chicago Press, 1961.

———. *Iron Road to the West: American Railroads in the 1850s.* New York: Columbia Univ. Press, 1978.

Strauss, Anselm L. *Images of the American City.* New York: Free Press, 1961.

Stuart, Granville. *Forty Years on the Frontier, as Seen in the Journals and Reminiscences of Granville Stuart, Gold-Miner, Trader, Merchant, Rancher and Politician.* Edited by Paul C. Phillips. Cleveland: Arthur H. Clark, 1925.

Sullivan, Louis H. *The Autobiography of an Idea.* 1924. Reprint. New York: Dover Publications, 1956.

Swift, Louis F., with Arthur Van Vlissingen, Jr. *The Yankee of the Yards: The Biography of Gustavus Franklin Swift.* Chicago: A. W. Shaw, 1927.

Taylor, Charles H., ed. *History of the Board of Trade of the City of Chicago.* Chicago: Robert O. Law, 1917.

Taylor, George Rogers. *The Transportation Revolution, 1815–1860.* Vol. 4 of *The Economic History of the United States.* New York: Rinehart, 1951.

———, ed. *The Turner Thesis concerning the Role of the Frontier in American History.* Rev. ed. Boston: D. C. Heath, 1956.

Taylor, George Rogers, and Irene D. Neu. *The American Railroad Network, 1861–1890.* Cambridge: Harvard Univ. Press, 1956.

Thomas, Jesse B. *Report of Jesse B. Thomas as a Member of the Executive Committee Appointed by the Chicago Harbor and River Convention, of the Statistics concerning the City of Chicago.* Chicago: R. L. Wilson, 1847.

Thompson, James W. *History of Livestock Raising in the United States, 1607–1860.* USDA, Bureau of Agricultural Economics, Agricultural History Series, no. 5. Washington, D.C.: USDA, 1942.

Thomson, Betty Flanders. *The Shaping of America's Heartland: The Landscape of the Middle West.* Boston: Houghton Mifflin, 1977.

Thoreau, Henry David. *The Journal of Henry David Thoreau.* Edited by Bradford Torrey and Francis H. Allen. Boston: Houghton Mifflin, 1906.

Thrower, Norman J. *Original Survey and Land Subdivision: A Comparative Study of the Form and Effect of Contrasting Cadastral Surveys.* Chicago: Association of American Geographers, 1966.

Timberlake, Michael, ed. *Urbanization in the World-Economy.* Orlando: Academic Press, 1985.

Towne, Charles Wayland, and Edward Norris Wentworth. *Pigs: From Cave to Corn Belt.* Norman: Univ. of Oklahoma Press, 1950.

Trachtenberg, Alan. *The Incorporation of America: Culture and Society in the Gilded Age.* New York: Hill and Wang, 1982.

"Treaty between the United States of America and the United Nation of the Chippewa, Ottowa, and Potawatamie Indians. Concluded September 26, 1833—Ratified February 21, 1835." N.p., nd.

Trigger, Bruce G., ed. *Northeast.* Vol. 15 of *Handbook of North American Indians,* edited by William C. Sturtevant. Washington, D.C.: Smithsonian Institution, 1978.

Trollope, Anthony. *North America.* 1862. Edited by Donald Smalley and Bradford Allen Booth. New York: Alfred A. Knopf, 1951.

Trollope, Frances. *Domestic Manners of the Americans.* 1832. Edited by Donald Smalley. New York: Alfred A. Knopf, 1949.

Trunk Line Executive Committee. *Report upon the Relative Cost of Transporting Live Stock and Dressed Beef.* New York: Russell Brothers, 1883.

Turner, Frederick Jackson. *The Frontier in American History.* 1920. Reprint. New York: Holt, Rinehart, and Winston, 1962.

———. *Rise of the New West, 1819–1829.* New York: Harper & Brothers, 1906.

Twining, Charles E. *Downriver: Orrin H. Ingram and the Empire Lumber Company.* Madison: SHSW, 1975.

Ucko, Peter J., and G. W. Dimbleby. *The Domestication and Exploitation of Plants and Animals.* Chicago: Aldine, 1969.

Unger, Irwin. *The Greenback Era: A Social and Political History of American Finance, 1865–1879.* Princeton: Princeton Univ. Press, 1964.

U.S. Bureau of the Census. *Historical Statistics of the United States: Colonial Times to 1970.* Washington, D.C.: GPO, 1975.

U.S. House of Representatives. *Report of the Industrial Commission on Transportation.* 56th Cong., 1st sess., Doc. 476. Washington, D.C.: GPO, 1900.

U.S. Senate, *Testimony Taken by the Select Committee on the Transportation and Sale of Meat Products.* 51st Cong., 1st sess., 1889–90. Sen. Rept. 829. Serial 2705. (The "Vest Report.")

Vance, James E., Jr. *Capturing the Horizon: The Historical Geography of Transportation since the Transportation Revolution of the Sixteenth Century.* New York: Harper & Row, 1986.

———. *The Merchant's World: The Geography of Wholesaling.* Englewood Cliffs, N.J.: Prentice-Hall, 1970.

Vance, William L. *America's Rome.* 2 vols. New Haven: Yale Univ. Press, 1989.

von Thünen, Johann Heinrich. *Von Thünen's Isolated State.* 1826, 1842. Translated by Carla M. Wartenberg, edited by Peter Hall. New York: Pergamon Press, 1966.

[Vynne, Harold Richard.] *Chicago by Day and Night: The Pleasure Seeker's Guide to the Paris of America.* Chicago: Thomson and Zimmerman, 1892.

Wade, Louise Carroll. *Chicago's Pride: The Stockyards, Packingtown, and Environs in the Nineteenth Century.* Chicago: Univ. of Chicago Press, 1987.

Wade, Richard C. *The Urban Frontier: The Rise of Western Cities, 1790–1830.* Cambridge: Harvard Univ. Press, 1959.

Walker, David A. *Iron Frontier: The Discovery and Early Development of Minnesota's Three Ranges.* St. Paul: Minnesota Historical Society, 1979.

Wallerstein, Immanuel. *The Capitalist World-Economy: Essays.* Cambridge: Cambridge Univ. Press, 1979.

———. *The Modern World-System: Capitalist Agriculture and the Origins of the European World-Economy in the Sixteenth Century.* New York: Academic Press, 1974.

———. *The Modern World-System II: Mercantilism and the Consolidation of the European World-Economy, 1600–1750.* New York: Academic Press, 1980.

———. *The Modern World System III: The Second Era of Great Expansion of the Capitalist World-Economy, 1730–1840s.* San Diego: Academic Press, 1989.

Walsh, Margaret. *The Manufacturing Frontier: Pioneer Industry in Antebellum Wisconsin, 1830–1860.* Madison: SHSW, 1972.

———. *The Rise of the Midwestern Meat Packing Industry.* Lexington: Univ. Press of Kentucky, 1982.

Ward, James A. *Railroads and the Character of America, 1820–1887.* Knoxville: Univ. of Tennessee Press, 1986.

Warner, Charles Dudley. *Studies in the South and West with Comments on Canada.* New York: Harper & Brothers, 1889.

Weaver, J. E. *North American Prairie.* Lincoln, Neb.: Johnsen, 1954.

———. *Prairie Plants and Their Environment: A Fifty-Year Study in the Midwest.* Lincoln: Univ. of Nebraska Press, 1968.

Weaver, J. E., and F. W. Albertson. *Grasslands of the Great Plains: Their Nature and Use.* Lincoln, Neb.: Johnsen, 1956.

Webb, Walter Prescott. *The Great Frontier.* Austin: Univ. of Texas Press, 1952.

———. *The Great Plains.* New York: Ginn, 1931.

Weber, Adna Ferrin. *The Growth of Cities in the Nineteenth Century: A Study in Statistics.* 1899. Reprint. Ithaca: Cornell Univ. Press, 1963.

Weber, Alfred. *Theory of the Location of Industries.* 1909. Translated by Carl J. Friedrich. Chicago: Univ. of Chicago Press, 1929.

Weimer, David R., ed. *City and Country in America.* New York: Appleton-Century-Crofts, 1962.

Weinstein, Allen. *Prelude to Populism: Origins of the Silver Issue, 1867–1878.* (New Haven: Yale Univ. Press, 1970.

Weld, L. D. H. *Private Freight-Cars and American Railways.* Columbia University Studies in History, Economics, and Public Law, 31, no. 1. New York [1908].

Wellington, Arthur M. *The Economic Theory of the Location of Railroads.* 1st ed. New York: Railroad Gazette, 1877. 5th ed. New York: Railroad Gazette, 1891.

Wendt, Lloyd, and Herman Kogan. *Give the Lady What She Wants! The Story of Marshall Field & Company.* Chicago: Rand McNally, 1952.

Whitaker, James W. *Feedlot Empire: Beef Cattle Feeding in Illinois and Iowa, 1840–1900.* Ames: Iowa State Univ. Press, 1975.

White, John H., Jr. *American Locomotives: An Engineering History, 1830–1880.* Baltimore: Johns Hopkins Univ. Press, 1968.

White, Morton, and Lucia White. *The Intellectual versus the City: From Thomas Jefferson to Frank Lloyd Wright.* Cambridge: Harvard Univ. Press and MIT Press, 1962.

White, Richard. *Empires, Indians, and Republics: The Middle Ground of the Pays d'en Haut, 1600–1850.* New York: Cambridge Univ. Press, 1991.

Williams, Jeffrey C. *The Economic Functions of Futures Markets.* New York: Cambridge Univ. Press, 1986.

Williams, Michael. *Americans and Their Forests: A Historical Geography.* Cambridge: Cambridge Univ. Press, 1989.

Williams, Raymond. *The Country and the City.* Oxford: Oxford Univ. Press, 1973.

Wing, Charles. *From the Walls In.* Boston: Little, Brown, 1979.

Wing, Jack. *The Great Union Stock Yards of Chicago.* Chicago: Religo-Philosophical Publishing Association, 1865.

Wood, Richard G. *A History of Lumbering in Maine, 1820–1861.* University of Maine Studies, no. 33. Orono: Univ. of Maine Press, 1935.

Worster, Donald. *Dust Bowl: The Southern Plains in the 1930s.* New York: Oxford Univ. Press, 1979.

Wright, Gwendolyn. *Moralism and the Model Home: Domestic Architecture and Cultural Conflict in Chicago, 1873–1913*. Chicago: Univ. of Chicago Press, 1980.

Wright, H. E., and David G. Frey, eds. *The Quaternary of the United States*. Princeton: Princeton Univ. Press, 1965.

Wright, James Edward. *The Politics of Populism: Dissent in Colorado*. New Haven: Yale Univ. Press, 1974.

Wright, John S. *Chicago: Past, Present, Future Relations to the Great Interior, and to the Continent*. Chicago, 1870.

Wunder, John R., ed. *Historians of the American Frontier: A Bio-Bibliographical Sourcebook*. Westport, Conn.: Greenwood Press, 1988.

Wyckoff, Walter A. *A Day with a Tramp and Other Days*. New York: Charles Scribner's Sons, 1901.

———. *The Workers: An Experiment in Reality*. New York: Charles Scribner's Sons, 1898.

Wyman, Mark. *Immigrants in the Valley: Irish, Germans, and Americans in the Upper Mississippi Country, 1830–1860*. Chicago: Nelson-Hall, 1984.

Wynn, Graeme. *Timber Colony: A Historical Geography of Early Nineteenth Century New Brunswick*. Toronto: Univ. of Toronto Press, 1981.

Yeager, Mary. *Competition and Regulation: The Development of Oligopoly in the Meat Packing Industry*. Greenwich, Conn.: JAI Press, 1981.

Zukowsky, John, ed. *Chicago Architecture, 1872–1922: Birth of a Metropolis*. Munich: Prestel-Verlag in association with the Art Institute of Chicago, 1987.

ARTICLES AND CHAPTERS

Abbott, Carl. "Civic Pride in Chicago, 1844–1860." *J. Ill. State Hist. Soc.* 63 (1970): 399–421.

———. "Frontiers and Sections: Cities and Regions in American Growth." *American Quarterly* 37 (1985): 395–410.

———. "'Necessary Adjuncts to Its Growth': The Railroad Suburbs of Chicago, 1854–1875." *J. Ill. State Hist. Soc.* 73 (1980): 117–31.

Adams, Donald R., Jr. "The Role of Banks in the Economic Development of the Old Northwest." In *Essays in Nineteenth Century Economic History: The Old Northwest*, edited by David C. Klingaman and Richard K. Vedder. Athens: Ohio Univ. Press, 1975.

Aduddell, Robert, and Louis Cain. "Location and Collusion in the Meat Packing Industry." In *Business Enterprise and Economic Change: Essays in Honor of Harold F. Williamson*, edited by Louis Cain and Paul J. Uselding. Kent: Kent State Univ. Press, 1973.

Aldrich, Charles. "The Old Prairie Slough." *Annals of Iowa*, 3d ser., 5 (1901): 27–32.

Alilunas, Leo. "Michigan's Cut-Over 'Canaan.'" *Mich. Hist.* 26 (1942): 188–201.

Allen, Joel A. "The American Bison, Living and Extinct." *Memoirs of the Museum of Comparative Zoology* (Harvard University), 4, no. 10 (1876): 1–246.

Alvord, H. E. "The American Cattle Trade." *Journal of the Royal Agricultural Society of England*, 2d ser., 13 (1877): 356–74.

Appleton, John B. "The Declining Significance of the Mississippi as a Commercial Highway in the Middle of the Nineteenth Century." *Bulletin of the Geographical Society of Philadelphia* 28 (1930): 47–64.

"Architecture and the City." Special theme issue of *Chicago History* 12, no. 4 (Winter 1983–84): 1–72.

Arden, Eugene. "The Evil City in American Fiction." *New York History* 35 (1954): 259–79.

Arms, Richard G. "From Disassembly to Assembly: Cincinnati: The Birthplace of Mass-production." *Bulletin of the Historical and Philosophical Society of Cincinnati* 17 (1959): 195–203.

Artibise, Alan F. J. "Boosterism and the Development of Prairie Cities, 1871–1913." In *Town and City: Aspects of Western Canadian Urban Development*, edited by Alan F. J. Artibise. Regina, Saskatchewan: Canadian Plains Research Center, 1981.

Atherton, Lewis E. "The Midwestern Country Town—Myth and Reality." *Ag. Hist.* 26 (1952): 73–80.

Bachmann, Elizabeth M. "Minnesota Log Marks." *Minn. Hist.* 26 (1945): 126–37.

Baker, Ray Stannard. "The Movement of Wheat." *McClure's Magazine* 14 (1899): 124–37.

Balestier, Joseph N. *The Annals of Chicago: A Lecture Delivered before the Chicago Lyceum, January 21, 1840*. 1840. Reprint. Fergus Historical Series, no. 1. Chicago, 1876.

Bardolph, Richard. "Illinois Agriculture in Transition, 1820–1870." *J. Ill. State Hist. Soc.* 41 (1948): 244–64.

Becker, Carl M. "Evolution of the Disassembly Line: The Horizontal Wheel and the Over-head Railway Loop." *Bulletin of the Historical and Philosophical Society of Cincinnati* 26 (1968): 276–82.

Beckmann, Martin J. "City Hierarchies and the Distribution of City Size." *Economic Development and Cultural Change* 6 (1958): 243–48.

Beecher, W. J. "The Lost Illinois Prairie." *Chicago History,* n.s., 2, no. 3 (Spring–Summer 1973): 166–72.

Belthuis, Lyda. "The Lumber Industry in Eastern Iowa." *Iowa Journal of History and Politics* 46 (1948): 115–55.

Berry, Brian J. L. "Cities as Systems within Systems of Cities." *Papers and Proceedings of the Regional Science Association* 13 (1964): 147–63.

———. "City Size Distributions and Economic Development." *Economic Development and Cultural Change* 9 (1961): 573–88.

Berry, Brian J. L., H. Gardiner Barnum, and Robert J. Tennant. "Retail Location and Consumer Behaviour." *Papers and Proceedings of the Regional Science Association* 9 (1962): 65–106.

Betts, Raymond F. "The Allusion to Rome in British Imperialist Thought of the Late Nineteenth and Early Twentieth Centuries." *Victorian Studies* 15 (1971): 149–59.

Binckley, John M. "Chicago of the Thinker." *Lakeside Monthly* 4 (Oct. 1873): 258–67.

Blackburn, George, and Sherman L. Ricards, Jr. "A Demographic History of the West: Manistee County, Michigan, 1860." *JAH* 57 (1970): 613–15.

———. "The Timber Industry in Manistee County, Michigan: A Case Study in Local Control." *Journal of Forest History* 18 (1974): 14–21.

Boorstin, Daniel J. "A. Montgomery Ward's Mail-Order Business." *Chicago History,* n.s. 2 (1973): 142–52.

Borchert, John R. "American Metropolitan Evolution." *Geographical Review* 57 (1967): 301–32.

———. "America's Changing Metropolitan Regions." *Annals Assoc. Am. Geog.* 62 (1972): 352–73.

Bourget, Paul. "A Farewell to the White City." *Cosmopolitan* 16 (Dec. 1893): 133–40.

Bremer, Sidney H. "Lost Continuities: Alternative Urban Visions in Chicago Novels, 1890–1915." *Soundings* 64 (1981): 29–51.

Brewer, Richard. "Death by the Plow." *Natural History,* Aug.–Sept. 1970, 28–35, 110.

Brigham, C. H. "The Lumber Region of Michigan." *No. Am. Rev.* 107 (July 1868): 77–103.

Brooks, D. C. "Chicago and Its Railways." *Lakeside Monthly* 8 (1872): 264–80.

Brownson, Howard Gray. "History of the Illinois Central Railroad to 1870." *University of Illinois Studies in the Social Sciences* 1 (1915): 1–182.

Bruce, Janet. "Of Sugar and Salt and Things in the Cellar and Sun: Food Preservation in Jackson County in the 1850s." *Mo. Hist. Rev.* 75 (1981): 417–47.

Brush, John E., and Howard E. Bracey. "Rural Service Centers in Southwestern Wisconsin and Southern England." *Geographical Review* 45 (1955): 559–69.

Bullough, William A. " 'It Is Better to Be a Country Boy': The Lure of the Country in Urban Education in the Gilded Age." *Historian* 35 (1973): 183–95.

Bunner, H. C. "The Making of the White City." *Scribner's Magazine* 12 (Oct. 1892): 398–418.

Bureau of Statistics, U.S. Treasury Department. "The Grain Trade of the United States, and the World's Wheat Supply and Trade." In *Monthly Summary of Commerce and Finance of the United States.* Washington, D.C.: GPO, Jan. 1900.

———. "The Provision Trade of the United States." In *Monthly Summary of Commerce and Finance of the United States.* Washington, D.C.: GPO, Feb. 1900.

Burghardt, A. F. "A Hypothesis about Gateway Cities." *Annals Assoc. of Am. Geog.* 61 (1971): 269–85.

Cain, Louis P. "Raising and Watering a City: Ellis Sylvester Chesbrough and Chicago's First Sanitation System." *Technology and Culture* 13 (1972): 353–72.

———. "From Mud to Metropolis: Chicago before the Fire." *Research in Economic History* 10 (1986): 93–129.

Canby, Noble. "The Great Exposition at Chicago." *Chautauquan* 15 (1892): 460–68.

Careless, J. M. S. "Frontierism, Metropolitanism, and Canadian History." *Canadian Historical Review* 35 (1954): 1–21.

Cassell, Frank A., and Marguerite E. Cassell. "The White City in Peril: Leadership and the World's Columbian Exposition." *Chicago History* 12, no. 3 (Fall 1983): 10–27.

Caton, John Dean. "An Address Delivered at the Reception to the Settlers of Chicago prior to 1840, by the Calumet Club of Chicago, May 27, 1879." In *Reminiscences of Early Chicago*, edited by Mabel McIlvaine. Chicago: Lakeside Press, 1912.

———. " 'Tis Sixty Years Since' in Chicago," *Atlantic Monthly* 71 (May 1893): 588–97.

Chandler, Alfred D., Jr. "The Beginnings of 'Big Business' in American Industry." *Bus. Hist. Rev.* 33 (Spring 1959): 131.

Cheever, Lawrence O. "John Morrell & Co." *Palimpsest* 47 (1966): 145–92.

"Chicago," *The Land We Love* 6 (1868), 469–76.

"Chicago in 1856." *Putnam's Monthly* 7 (1856): 606–13.

Christisen, Donald. "A Vignette of Missouri's Native Prairie." *Mo. Hist. Rev.* 61 (1967): 166–86.

Clark, Colin. "The Economic Functions of a City in Relation to Its Size." *Econometrica* 13 (1945): 97–113.

Clifton, James A. "Chicago, September 14, 1833: The Last Great Indian Treaty in the Old Northwest." *Chicago History* 9, no. 2 (Summer 1980): 86–97.

Cole, Arthur H. "Cyclical and Sectional Variations in the Sale of Public Lands, 1816–1860." *Review of Economics and Statistics* 9 (1927): 41–53.

———. "Marketing Nonconsumer Goods before 1917: An Exploration of Secondary Literature." *Bus. Hist. Rev.* 33 (1959): 420–28.

Colten, Craig E. "Industrial Wastes in Southeast Chicago: Production and Disposal, 1870–1970." *Environmental Review* 10 (1986): 93–105.

Conzen, Michael P. "The American Urban System in the Nineteenth Century." In *Geography and the Urban Environment: Progress in Research and Applications*, edited by D. T. Herbert and R. J. Johnston. Vol. 4. New York: John Wiley, 1981.

———. "Capital Flows and the Developing Urban Hierarchy: State Bank Capital in Wisconsin, 1854–1895." *Economic Geography* 51 (1975): 321–38.

———. "The Maturing Urban System in the United States, 1840–1910." *Annals Assoc. Am. Geog.* 67 (1977): 88–108.

———. "A Transport Interpretation of the Growth of Urban Regions: An American Example." *Journal of Historical Geography* 1 (1975): 361–82.

———, ed. "Maps and the City." *Chicago History* 13, no. 1 (Spring 1984): 1–72.

Craig, James Thomas. "Muskegon and the Great Chicago Fire." *Mich. Hist.* 28 (1944): 610–23.

Craigie, P. G. "Twenty Years' Changes in Our Foreign Meat Supplies." *Journal of the Royal Agricultural Society of England,* 2d ser. 23 (1887): 465–500.

Crawford, R. F. "An Inquiry into Wheat Prices and Wheat Supply." *Journal of the Royal Statistical Society* 58 (1895): 75–120.

Cronon, William. "Modes of Prophecy and Production: Placing Nature in History." *JAH* 76 (1990): 1122–31.

———. "Revisiting the Vanishing Frontier: The Legacy of Frederick Jackson Turner." *WHQ* 18 (1987): 157–76.

———. "To Be the Central City." *Chicago History* 10 (1981): 130–40.

———. "Turner's First Stand: The Significance of Significance in American History." In *Writing Western History: Essays on Classic Western Historians*, edited by Richard Etulain. Albuquerque: Univ. of New Mexico Press, 1991.

Croxton, Fred C. "Beef Prices." *J. Pol. Econ.* 8 (1905): 201–16.

Currie, A. W. "British Attitudes toward Investment in North American Railroads." *Bus. Hist. Rev.* 34 (1960): 194–215.

Dahms, F. A. "The Evolution of Settlement Systems: A Canadian Example, 1851–1970." *J. Urban Hist.* 7 (1981): 169–204.

Dailey, Don M. "The Early Development of the Note-Brokerage Business in Chicago." *J. Pol. Econ.* 46 (1938): 202–17.

Daland, Robert T. "Enactment of the Potter Law." *Wis. Mag. Hist.* 33 (1949): 45–54.

Danford, Orman S. "The Social and Economic Effects of Lumbering on Michigan, 1835–1890." *Mich. Hist.* 26 (1942): 346–64.

Dart, Joseph. "The Grain Elevators of Buffalo." *Publications of the Buffalo Historical Society* 1 (1879): 391–404.

Daubenmire, R. "Ecology of Fire in Grassland." *Advances in Ecological Research,* 5 (1968): 209–66.

David, Paul A. "The Mechanization of Reaping in the Ante-Bellum Midwest." In *Industrial-*

ization in Two Systems: Essays in Honor of Alexander Gerschenkron, edited by Henry Rosovsky. New York: John Wiley, 1966.

———. "Transport Innovation and Economic Growth: Professor Fogel on and off the Rails." *Economic History Review* 22 (1969): 506–25.

Davis, Margaret B. "Palynology and Environmental History during the Quaternary Period." *American Scientist* 57 (1969): 317–32.

Destler, Chester McArthur. "Agricultural Readjustment and Agrarian Unrest in Illinois, 1880–1896." *Ag. Hist.* 21 (1947): 104–16.

Detrick, Charles R. "The Effects of the Granger Acts." *J. Pol. Econ.* 11 (1902–03): 237–56.

Devoto, Bernard. "Geopolitics with the Dew on It." *Harper's Magazine* 188 (March 1944): 313–23.

Doucet, Michael J. "Urban Land Development in Nineteenth-Century North America." *JUH* 8 (1982): 299–342.

DuBoff, Richard B. 'Business Demand and the Development of the Telegraph in the United States, 1844–1860." *Bus. Hist. Rev.* 54 (1980): 459–79.

———. "The Telegraph and the Structure of Markets in the United States, 1845–1890." *Research in Economic History* 8 (1983): 253–77.

Duis, Perry. "Whose City?: Public and Private Places in Nineteenth-Century Chicago." *Chicago History* 12, no. 1 (Spring 1983): 12–27; no. 2 (Summer 1983): 2–23.

Ebner, Michael H. " 'In the Suburbes of Town': Chicago's North Shore to 1871." *Chicago History* 11, no. 2 (Summer 1982): 66–77.

Edminster, Lynn Ramsay. "Meat Packing and Slaughtering." In *Encyclopaedia of the Social Sciences,* edited by Edwin R. A. Seligman. New York: Macmillan, 1933.

Einhorn, Robin L. "A Taxing Dilemma: Early Lake Shore Protection." *Chicago History* 18, no. 3 (Fall 1989): 34–51.

Ellis, David Maldwyn. "New York and the Western Trade, 1850–1910." *New York History* 33 (1952): 379–96.

Emery, Henry Crosby. "Legislation against Futures." *Political Science Quarterly* 10 (1895): 62–86.

Engberg, George B. "Lumber and Labor in the Lake States." *Minn. Hist.* 36 (1959): 153–66.

Ernst, Dorothy J. "Wheat Speculation in the Civil War Era: Daniel Wells and the Grain Trade, 1860–1862." *Wis. Mag. Hist.* 47 (1963–64): 125–35.

Everest, D. C. "A Reappraisal of the Lumber Barons." *Wis. Mag. Hist.* 36 (1952): 17–22.

Ezekiel, Mordecai. "The Cobweb Theorem." *Quarterly Journal of Economics* 52 (1937–38): 255–80.

Farnsworth, Helen C. "Decline and Recovery of Wheat Prices in the 'Nineties." *Wheat Studies* 10 (1933–34): 289–352.

Fellmann, Jerome D. "Pre-building Growth Patterns of Chicago." *Annals Assoc. Am. Geog.* 47 (1957): 59–82.

Ferris, William. "Old Hutch—The Wheat King." *J. Ill. State Hist. Soc.* 41 (1948): 231–43.

Field, Walker. "A Re-examination into the Invention of the Balloon Frame." *Journal of the Society of Architectural Historians* 2, no. 4 (Oct. 1942): 3–29.

Fisher, Franklin M., and Peter Temin. "Regional Specialization and the Supply of Wheat in the United States, 1867–1914." *Review of Economics and Statistics* 52 (1970): 134–49.

Fishlow, Albert. "Antebellum Interregional Trade Reconsidered." *American Economic Review (Supplement)* 54 (1964): 352–64.

Fletcher, Henry J. "The Doom of the Small Town." *Forum* 19 (April 1895): 214–23.

Fogel, Robert William. "Notes on the Social Saving Controversy." *JEH* 39 (1979): 1–54.

Frazier, Arthur H. "The Military Frontier: Fort Dearborn." *Chicago History* 9, no. 2 (Summer 1980): 80–85.

Fries, Robert F. "The Mississippi River Logging Company and the Struggle for the Free Navigation of Logs, 1865–1900." *MVHR* 35 (1948): 429–48.

Frueh, Erne Rene. "Retail Merchandising in Chicago, 1833–1848." *J. Ill. State Hist. Soc.* 32 (1939): 149–72.

Gates, Charles M. "Boom Stages in American Expansion." *Bus. Hist. Rev.* 33 (1959): 32–42.

———. "The Concept of the Metropolis in the American Western Movement." *MVHR* 49 (1962–63): 299–300.

———. "The Role of Cities in the Westward Movement." *MVHR* 37 (1950–51): 277–78.

Gates, Paul Wallace. "Cattle Kings in the Prairies." *MVHR* 35 (1948): 379–412.

———. "Hoosier Cattle Kings." *Indiana Magazine of History* 44 (1948): 1–24.

————. "Weyerhaeuser and the Chippewa Logging Industry." In *The John H. Hauberg Historical Essays*, edited by O. Fritiof Ander. Augustana Library Publications, no. 26. Rock Island, Ill.: Augustana Book Concern, 1954.

[George, Henry.] "What the Railroad Will Bring Us." *Overland Monthly* 1 (1868): 297–306.

Gerwing, Anselm J. "The Chicago Indian Treaty of 1833." *J. Ill. State Hist. Soc.* 57 (1964): 117–42.

Glaab, Charles N. "Historical Perspective on Urban Development Schemes." In *Urban Research and Policy Planning*, edited by Leo F. Schnore and Henry Fagin. Beverly Hills: Sage, 1967.

————. "Jesup W. Scott and a West of Cities." *Ohio History* 73 (1964): 3–12, 56.

————. "Visions of Metropolis: William Gilpin and Theories of City Growth in the American West." *Wis. Mag. Hist.* 45 (1961): 21–31.

Goodin, S. H. "Cincinnati—Its Destiny." In *Sketches and Statistics of Cincinnati in 1851*, edited by Charles Cist. Cincinnati: William H. Moore, 1851.

Graf, Truman F. "Hedging—How Effective Is It?" *Journal of Farm Economics* 35 (1953): 398–413.

Graham, Samuel A. "Climax Forests of the Upper Peninsula of Michigan." *Ecology* 22 (1941): 355–62.

Grant, Robert. "People Who Did Not Go to the Fair." *Cosmopolitan* 16 (Dec. 1893): 158–64.

Gras, Norman S. B. "The Significance of the Twin Cities in Minnesota History." *Minn. Hist.* 7 (1926): 3–17.

Gressley, Gene M. "The Turner Thesis: A Problem in Historiography." *Ag. Hist.* 32 (1958): 227–49.

Grosvenor, W. M. "The Railroads and the Farms," *Atlantic Monthly* 32 (1873): 591–610.

Gunsaulus, Frank W. "Philip D. Armour: A Character Sketch." *North American Monthly Review of Reviews* 23 (1901): 167–76.

Hall, James. "The Commercial Growth and Greatness of the West: As Illustrating the Dignity and Usefulness of Commerce." *Hunt's Merch. Mag.* 17 (1847): 495–503.

Harley, C. Knick. "Transportation, the World Wheat Trade, and the Kuznets Cycle, 1850–1913." *Explorations in Economic History* 17 (1980): 218–50.

Hartman, Bernhardt. "The Iowa Sawmill Industry." *Iowa Journal of History and Politics* 40 (1942): 52–93.

Hessler, Sherry O. " 'The Great Disturbing Cause' and the Decline of the Queen City." *Bulletin of the Historical and Philosophical Society of Cincinnati* 20 (1962): 169–85.

Hidy, Ralph W., and Muriel E. Hidy. "Anglo-American Merchant Bankers and the Railroads of the Old Northwest, 1848–1860." *Bus. Hist. Rev.* 34 (1960): 150–69.

Hill, Howard Copeland. "The Development of Chicago as a Center of the Meat Packing Industry." *MVHR* 10 (1923–24): 253–73.

Hilliard, Sam B. "Antebellum Interregional Trade: The Mississippi River as an Example." In *Pattern and Process: Research in Historical Geography*, edited by Ralph E. Ehrenberg. Washington, D.C.: Howard Univ. Press, 1975.

Hirshheimer, H. J. "The Passing of the Sawmills and the Growth of Manufactures in La Crosse, 1880–1905." La Crosse County Historical Sketches, ser. 3, *The Lumber Industry*, 2d ed. La Crosse, 1937. 69–99.

Hodge, Gerald. "The Prediction of Trade Center Viability in the Great Plains." *Papers and Proceedings of the Regional Science Association* 14 (1965): 87–115.

"Hog Killing at the Chicago Stock Yards." *Scientific American* 65 (Nov. 7, 1891): 291.

Holt, Glen E. "Private Plans for Public Spaces: The Origins of Chicago's Park System, 1850–1875." *Chicago History* 8, no. 3 (Fall 1979): 173–84.

Hough, Jack L. "The Prehistoric Great Lakes of North America." *American Scientist* 51 (1963): 84–109.

Howells, William Dean. "Letter of an Altrurian Traveller, Chicago, Sept. 28, 1893." *Cosmopolitan* 16 (Dec. 1893): 218–32.

Hunter, Louis C. "Studies in the Economic History of the Ohio Valley: Seasonal Aspects of Industry and Commerce Before the Age of Big Business." *Smith College Studies in History* 19, nos. 1–2 (Oct. 1933–Jan. 1934): 1–49.

Hutchinson, B. P. "Speculation in Wheat." *No. Am. Rev.* 153 (1891): 414–19.

Hutchinson, William K., and Samuel H. Williamson. "The Self-Sufficiency of the Antebellum South: Estimates of the Food Supply." *JEH* 31 (1971): 591–612.

Ingalls, John J. "Lessons of the Fair." *Cosmopolitan* 16 (Dec. 1893): 141–49.

Innis, Harold A. "Significant Factors in Canadian Economic Development." *Canadian Historical Review* 18 (1937): 374–84.

Jakle, John A. "Salt on the Ohio Valley Frontier, 1770–1820." *Annals Assoc. Am. Geog.* 59 (1969): 687–709.

"James Thompson's Plat of Chicago: A 150-Year Perspective." *Chicago History* 9, no. 2 (Summer 1980): 66–67.

Jarchow, Merrill E. "King Wheat." *Minn. Hist.* 29 (1948): 1–28.

Jefferson, Mark. "The Law of the Primate City." *Geographical Review* 29 (1939): 226–32.

Jensen, Richard. "On Modernizing Frederick Jackson Turner: The Historiography of Regionalism." *WHQ* 11 (1980): 307–22.

Johnson, Ronald N., and Gary D. Libecap. "Efficient Markets and Great Lakes Timber: A Conservation Issue Reexamined." *Explorations in Economic History* 17 (1980): 372–85.

Jones, Lewis R. " 'The Mechanization of Reaping and Mowing in American Agriculture, 1833–1870': Comment." *JEH* 37 (1977): 451–55.

Kaime, George S. "Where Our Lumber Comes From," *Western Monthly* 3 (1870): 188–91.

Kaplan, Charles. "Norris's Use of Sources in *The Pit.*" *American Literature* 25 (1953): 75–84.

Kellar, Herbert A. "The Reaper as a Factor in the Development of the Agriculture of Illinois, 1834–1865." *Transactions of the Illinois State Historical Society* 34 (1927): 105–14.

Kemmerer, Donald L. "Financing Illinois Industry, 1830–1890." *Bulletin of the Business History Society* 27 (1953): 97–111.

Kilburn, Paul D. "The Forest-Prairie Ecotone in Northeastern Illinois." *American Midland Naturalist* 62 (1959): 206–17.

[Kirkland, Caroline.] "Illinois in Spring-time: With a Look at Chicago." *Atlantic Monthly* 2 (1858): 475–88.

Kitch, Edmund W., and Clara Ann Bowler. "The Facts of *Munn* v. *Illinois.*" In *1978: The Supreme Court Review,* edited by Philip B. Kurland and Gerhard Casper. Chicago: Univ. of Chicago Press, 1979.

Klein, Joseph J. "The Development of Mercantile Instruments of Credit in the United States." *Journal of Accountancy* 12 (1911): 321–45, 422–49, 526–37, 594–607; 13 (1912): 44–50, 122–32, 207–17.

Kleven, Bernhardt J. "The Mississippi River Logging Company." *Minn. Hist.* 27 (1946): 190–202.

Kline, Virginia M., and Grant Cottam. "Vegetation Response to Climate and Fire in the Driftless Area of Wisconsin." *Ecology* 60 (1979): 861–68.

Knapp, Joseph G. "A Review of Chicago Stock Yards History." *University [of Chicago] Journal of Business* 2 (1923–24): 331–46.

Knight, Oliver. "Toward an Understanding of the Western Town." *WHQ* 4 (1973): 27–42.

Kohlmeyer, Frederick W. "Northern Pine Lumbermen: A Study in Origins and Migrations." *JEH* 16 (1956): 529–38.

Krog, Carl. "Marinette Lumbermen." *Journal of Forest History* 21 (1977): 97–100.

Kuhlmann, Charles B. "The Influence of the Minneapolis Flour Mills upon the Economic Development of Minnesota and the Northwest." *Minn. Hist.* 6 (1925): 141–54.

Kujovich, Mary Yeager. "The Refrigerator Car and the Growth of the American Dressed Beef Industry." *Bus. Hist. Rev.* 44 (1970): 460–82.

Lampard, Eric E. "The History of Cities in the Economically Advanced Areas." *Economic Development and Cultural Change* 3 (1955): 81–136.

Langdale, John. "The Impact of the Telegraph on the Buffalo Agricultural Commodity Market: 1846–1848." *Professional Geographer* 31 (1979): 165–69.

Lanterman, Alice. "The Development of Kansas City as a Grain and Milling Center." *Mo. Hist. Rev.* 42 (1947): 20–33.

Larsen, Lawrence H. "Chicago's Midwest Rivals: Cincinnati, St. Louis, and Milwaukee." *Chicago History* 5 (1976): 141–51.

Larsen, Lawrence H., and Robert L. Branyon. "The Development of an Urban Civilization on the Frontier of the American West." *Societas* 1 (1971): 33–50.

Larson, Floyd. "The Role of the Bison in Maintaining the Short Grass Plains." *Ecology* 21 (1940): 113–21.

Lauer, Jeanette C., and Robert H. Lauer. "St. Louis and the 1880 Census: The Shock of Collective Failure." *Mo. Hist. Rev.* 76 (1982): 151–63.

Laurent, Jerome K. "Trade, Transport and Technology: The American Great Lakes, 1866–1910." *Journal of Transport History,* 3d ser., 4 (1983): 1–24.

Lawrence, Lee E. "The Wisconsin Ice Trade." *Wis. Mag. Hist.* 48 (1965): 257–67.

Leavitt, Charles T. "Some Economic Aspects of the Western Meat-Packing Industry, 1830–1860." *Journal of Business* 4 (1931): 68–90.

Lee, Guy A. "The Historical Significance of the Chicago Grain Elevator System." *Ag. Hist.* 11 (1937): 16–32.

Lefferts, Marshall. "The Electric Telegraph: Its Influence and Geographical Distribution." *Bulletin of the American Geographical and Statistical Society* 2 (1857): 242–64.

Lewis, Russell. "Everything under One Roof: World's Fairs and Department Stores in Paris and Chicago." *Chicago History* 12, no. 3 (Fall 1983): 28–47.

Lightner, David L. "Railroads and the American Economy: The Fogel Thesis in Retrospect." *Journal of Transport History,* 3d ser., 4, no. 2 (Sept. 1983): 20–34.

Lindstrom, Diane, and John Sharpless. "Urban Growth and Economic Structure in Antebellum America." *Research in Economic History* 3 (1978): 161–216.

Lippincott, Isaac. "A History of River Improvement." *J. Pol. Econ.* 22 (1914): 630–60.

———. "Internal Trade of the United States, 1700–1860." *Washington University Studies* 4 (1916): 63–150.

Lösch, August. "The Nature of Economic Regions." *Southern Economic Journal* 5 (1938): 71–78.

Luckingham, Bradford. "The City in the Westward Movement: A Bibliographical Note." *WHQ* 5 (1974): 295–306.

Lukermann, Fred. "Empirical Expressions of Nodality and Hierarchy in a Circulation Manifold." *East Lakes Geographer* 2 (Aug. 1966): 17–44.

Lyon, Bessie L. "The Menace of the Blue-stem." *Palimpsest* 21 (1940): 247–58.

Macbride, Thomas H. "Landscapes of Early Iowa." 1895. Reprint. *Palimpsest* 7 (1926): 283–93.

MacVeagh, Franklin. "Chicago's Part in the World's Fair." *Scribner's Magazine* 12 (1892): 551–57.

Madden, Carl H. "On Some Indications of Stability in the Growth of Cities in the United States." *Economic Development and Cultural Change* 4 (1956): 236–52.

Mahoney, Timothy R. "Urban History in a Regional Context: River Towns on the Upper Mississippi, 1840–1860." *JAH* 72 (1985): 318–39.

Marx, Leo. "Pastoral Ideas and City Troubles." *Journal of General Education* 20 (Jan. 1969): 251–71.

Mavor, James. "The Economic Results of the Specialist Production and Marketing of Wheat." *Political Science Quarterly* 26 (1911): 659–75.

Maybee, Rolland H. "Michigan's White Pine Era, 1840–1900." *Mich. Hist.* 43 (1959): 385–432.

Mayer, Harold M. "The Launching of Chicago: The Situation and the Site." *Chicago History* 9, no. 2 (Summer 1980): 68–79.

McAfee, R. Preston. "American Economic Growth and the Voyage of Columbus." *American Economic Review* 73 (1983): 735–40.

McCarty, H. H., and C. W. Thompson. *Meatpacking in Iowa.* Iowa Studies in Business, vol. 12 (Iowa City, 1933).

McFadden, Joseph M. "Monopoly in Barbed Wire: The Formation of the American Steel and Wire Company." *Bus. Hist. Rev.* 52 (1978): 465–89.

McLear, Patrick E. "John Stephen Wright and Urban and Regional Promotion in the Nineteenth Century." *J. Ill. State Hist. Soc.* 68 (1975): 407–20.

———. "Logan U. Reavis: Nineteenth Century Urban Promoter." *Mo. Hist. Rev.* 66 (1972): 567–88.

———. "Rivalry between Chicago and Wisconsin Lake Ports for Control of the Grain Trade." *Inland Seas* 24 (1968): 225–33.

———. "Speculation, Promotion, and the Panic of 1837 in Chicago." *J. Ill. State Hist. Soc.* 42 (1969): 135–46.

Mears, Carrie E. "Charles Mears, Lumberman." *Mich. Hist.* 30 (1946): 535–45.

Metcalf, P. Richard. "Who Should Rule at Home? Native American Politics and Indian-White Relations." *JAH* 61 (1974): 651–65.

"The Metropolis of the Prairies." *Harper's New Monthly Magazine* 61 (1880): 711–31.

Meyer, David R. "A Dynamic Model of the Integration of Frontier Urban Places into the United States System of Cities." *Economic Geography* 56 (1980): 120–40.

———. "Emergence of the American Manufacturing Belt: An Interpretation." *Journal of Historical Geography* 2 (1983): 145–74.

———. "Midwestern Industrialization and the American Manufacturing Belt in the Nineteenth Century." *JEH* 49 (1989): 921–37.

Meyerowitz, Joanne. "Women and Migration: Autonomous Female Migrants to Chicago, 1880–1930." *J. Urban Hist.* 13 (1987): 147–68.

Miller, George H. "Origins of the Iowa Granger Law." *MVHR* 40 (1954): 657–80.

Morton, W. L. "The Significance of Site in the Settlement of the American and Canadian Wests." *Ag. Hist.* 25 (1951): 97–104.

Mosher, A. A. "The Wisconsin Lakes." *Outing* 16 (1890): 170–78.

Muller, Edward K. "Regional Urbanization and the Selective Growth of Towns in North American Regions." *Journal of Historical Geography* 3 (1977): 21–39.

———. "Selective Urban Growth in the Middle Ohio Valley, 1800–1860." *Geographical Review* 66 (1976): 178–99.

Nagel, Paul C. "Twice to the Fair." *Chicago History* 14, no. 1 (Spring 1985): 4–19.

Newcomb, H. T. "The Decline in Railway Rates; Some of Its Causes and Results." *J. Pol. Econ.* 6 (1897–98): 457–75.

"The New Time Standards." *Railway Age* 8, no. 46 (Nov. 15, 1883): 722.

Nichols, Roger L. "The Black Hawk War in Retrospect." *Wis. Mag. Hist.* 65 (1982): 238–46.

Nickerson, J. F. "The Development of Refrigeration in the United States." *Ice and Refrigeration* 49, no. 4 (Oct. 1, 1915): 170–77.

Nord, David Paul. "The Public Community: The Urbanization of Journalism in Chicago." *J. Urban Hist.* 11 (1985): 411–41.

Norris, James D., and James Livingston. "Joy Morton and the Conduct of Modern Business Enterprise." *Chicago History* 10, no. 1 (Spring 1981): 13–25.

North, Douglass C. "Agriculture in Regional Economic Growth." *Journal of Farm Economics* 41 (1959): 943–51.

Odle, Thomas D. "The American Grain Trade of the Great Lakes, 1825–1873." *Inland Seas* 7 (1951): 237–45; 8 (1952): 23–28, 99–104, 177–78, 187–92, 248–54; 9 (1953): 52–58, 105–9, 162–68, 256–62.

———. "Entrepreneurial Cooperation on the Great Lakes: The Origin of the Methods of American Grain Marketing." *Bus. Hist. Rev.* 38 (1964): 439–55.

Olmstead, Alan L. "The Mechanization of Reaping and Mowing in American Agriculture, 1833–1870." *JEH* 35 (1975): 327–52.

Ortner, Sherry. "Is Female to Male as Nature Is to Culture?" In *Women, Culture, and Society,* edited by Michelle Zimbalist Rosaldo and Louise Lamphere. Stanford: Stanford Univ. Press, 1974.

Parker, William N., and Judith L. V. Klein. "Productivity Growth in Grain Production in the United States, 1840–60 and 1900–10." In *Output, Employment, and Productivity in the United States after 1800,* Conference on Research in Income and Wealth, Studies in Income and Wealth, vol. 30. New York: National Bureau of Economic Research, 1966.

[Parton, James.] "Chicago," *Atlantic Monthly* 19 (1867): 325–45.

Pauly, John J. "The Great Chicago Fire as a National Event." *American Quarterly* 36 (1984): 668–83.

Paxson, Frederic L. "The Railroads of the 'Old Northwest' before the Civil War." *Transactions of the Wisconsin Academy of Sciences, Arts, and Letters* 17 (1914): 243–74.

Peet, J. Richard. "The Spatial Expansion of Commercial Agriculture in the Nineteenth Century: A Von Thünen Interpretation." *Economic Geography* 45 (1969): 283–301.

———. "Von Thünen Theory and the Dynamics of Agricultural Expansion." *Explorations in Economic History* 8 (1970–71): 181–201.

Perren, Richard. "The North American Beef and Cattle Trade with Great Britain, 1870–1914." *Economic History Review,* 2d ser., 24 (1971): 430–44.

Peterson, Jacqueline. "Goodbye, Madore Beaubien: The Americanization of Early Chicago Society." *Chicago History* 9, no. 2 (Summer 1980): 98–111.

———. " 'Wild' Chicago: The Formation and Destruction of a Multiracial Community on the Midwestern Frontier, 1816–1837." In *The Ethnic Frontier: Essays in the History of Group Survival in Chicago and the Midwest,* edited by Melvin G. Holli and Peter d'A. Jones. Grand Rapids: William B. Eerdmans, 1977.

Pierson, George Wilson. "American Historians and the Frontier Hypothesis in 1941." *Wis. Mag. Hist.* 26 (1942): 36–60, 170–85.

Pilcher, John E. "Charles Brewster of Fort Madison: A Profile in Enterprise, 1845–1875." *Annals of Iowa,* 3d ser., 44, (Spring 1979): 602–26.

Pisani, Donald J. "Forests and Conservation, 1865–1890." *JAH* 72 (1985): 340–59.

———. "Promotion and Regulation: Constitutionalism and the American Economy." *JAH* 74 (1987): 740–68.

Pomeroy, Earl. "The Urban Frontier of the Far West." In *The Frontier Challenge: Responses to the Trans-Mississippi West,* edited by John G. Clark. Lawrence: Univ. Press of Kansas, 1971.

Popplewell, Frank S. "St. Joseph, Missouri, as a Center of the Cattle Trade." *Mo. Hist. Rev.* 32 (1938): 443–57.

Preston, Richard E. "The Structure of Central Place Systems." *Economic Geography* 47 (1971): 136–55.

Putnam, Jackson K. "The Turner Thesis and the Westward Movement: A Reappraisal." *WHQ* 7 (1976): 377–404.

Quaife, Milo Milton. "The Chicago Treaty of 1833." *Wis. Mag. Hist.* 1 (1918): 287–303.

Raney, William F. "Pine Lumbering in Wisconsin." *Wis. Mag. Hist.* 19 (1935): 71–90.

Rector, William G. "From Woods to Sawmill: Transportation Problems in Logging." *Ag. Hist.* 23 (1949): 239–44.

Renner, G. K. "The Kansas City Meat Packing Industry before 1900." *Mo. Hist. Rev.* 55 (1961): 18–29.

Richardson, Harry W. "Theory of the Distribution of City Sizes: Review and Prospects." *Regional Studies* 7 (1973): 239–51.

Robinson, Chas. D. "The Lumber Trade of Green Bay," *Transactions of the Wisconsin State Agricultural Society* 5 (1858–59): 401–3.

Rodgers, Cassandra S., and Roger C. Anderson. "Presettlement Vegetation of Two Prairie Peninsula Counties." *Botanical Gazette* 140 (1979): 232–40.

Rogers, George D. "History of Flour Manufacture in Minnesota." *Minnesota Historical Society Collections* 10, pt. 1 (1900–04): 35–55.

Rohe, Randall E. "The Evolution of the Great Lakes Logging Camp, 1830–1930." *Journal of Forest History* 30 (1986): 17–28.

———. "Place-names: Relics of the Great Lakes Lumber Era." *Journal of Forest History* 28 (1984): 126–35.

Rosen, Christine Meisner. "Infrastructural Improvement in Nineteenth-Century Cities: A Conceptual Framework and Cases." *J. Urban Hist.* 12 (1986): 211–56.

Rothstein, Morton. "America in the International Rivalry for the British Wheat Market, 1860–1914." *MVHR* 47 (1960): 401–18.

———. "Antebellum Wheat and Cotton Exports: A Contrast in Marketing Organization and Economic Development." *Ag. Hist.* 40 (1966): 91–100.

———. "Frank Norris and Popular Perceptions of the Market." *Ag. Hist.* 56 (1982): 50–66.

———. "The International Market for Agricultural Commodities, 1850–1873." In *Economic Change in the Civil War Era,* edited by David T. Gilchrist and W. David Lewis. Greenville, Del.: Eleutherian Mills–Hagley Foundation, 1965.

Rusk, J. M. "American Farming a Hundred Years Hence." *No. Am. Rev.* 436 (March 1893): 257–64.

Saloutos, Theodore. "The Spring-Wheat Farmer in a Maturing Economy, 1870–1920." *JEH* 6 (1946): 173–90.

Sawislak, Karen. "Smoldering City." *Chicago History* 17, nos. 3–4 (Fall–Winter 1988–89): 70–101.

Sawyer, Alvah L. "The Forests of the Upper Peninsula and Their Place in History." *Mich. Hist.* 3 (1919): 367–83.

Scheiber, Harry N. "The Road to *Munn:* Eminent Domain and the Concept of Public Purpose in the State Courts." *Perspectives in American History* 7 (1971): 327–402.

———. "Turner's Legacy and the Search for a Reorientation of Western History: A Review Essay." *New Mexico Historical Review* 44 (1969): 231–48.

———. "Urban Rivalry and Internal Improvements in the Old Northwest, 1820–1860." *Ohio History* 71 (1962): 227–39, 289–92.

Schlebecker, John T. "The World Metropolis and the History of American Agriculture." *JEH* 20 (1960): 187–208.

Schlesinger, Arthur M. "The City in American History." *MVHR* 27 (1940–41): 43–66.

Schmidt, Louis B. "Internal Commerce and the Development of National Economy before 1860." *J. Pol. Econ.* 47 (1939): 798–822.

Schnell, J. Christopher. "Chicago versus St. Louis: A Reassessment of the Great Rivalry." *Mo. Hist. Rev.* 71 (1977): 245–65.

Schnell, J. Christopher, and Katherine B. Clinton. "The New West: Themes in Nineteenth Century Urban Promotion, 1815–1880." *Bull. Mo. Hist. Soc.* 30 (1974): 75–88.

Schnell, J. Christopher, and Patrick E. McLear. "Why the Cities Grew: A Historiographical Essay on Western Urban Growth, 1850–1880." *Bull. Mo. Hist. Soc.* 28 (1972): 162–77

[Scott, Jesup W.] "Commercial Cities and Towns of the United States." *Hunt's Merch. Mag.* 19 (1848): 383–86.

———. "Internal Trade of the United States," *Hunt's Merch. Mag.* 8 (1843): 321–30, 447–58; 9 (1843): 31–47.

———. "Our American Lake Cities," *Hunt's Merch. Mag.* 31 (1854): 403–13.

———. "The Progress of the West." *Hunt's Merch. Mag.* 14 (1846): 163–65.

———. "Westward the Star of Empire." *De Bow's Review* 27 (1859): 125–36.

Scriabine, Christine. "Upton Sinclair and the Writing of *The Jungle.*" *Chicago History* 10, no. 1 (Spring 1981): 26–37.

Sheldon, J. P. "Report on the American and Canadian Meat Trade." *Journal of the Royal Agricultural Society of England,* 2d ser., 13 (1877): 295–355.

Sieber, George W. "Railroads and Lumber Marketing, 1858–78: The Relationship between an Iowa Sawmill Firm and the Chicago and Northwestern Railroad." *Annals of Iowa,* 3d ser. 39 (1967): 33–46.

Smith, Charles Clinton. "The Effect of Overgrazing and Erosion upon the Biota of the Mixed-Grass Prairie of Oklahoma." *Ecology* 21 (1940): 381–97.

Smolensky, Eugene, and Donald Ratajczak. "The Conception of Cities." *Explorations in Entrepreneurial History* 2 (1964): 90–131.

Spears, Timothy B. "A Grip on the Land." *Chicago History* 17, nos. 3–4 (Fall–Winter 1988–89): 4–25.

Stafford, H. A., Jr. "The Functional Bases of Small Towns." *Economic Geography* 39 (1963): 165–75.

"Standard Time—The Change Successfully Adopted," *Railway Age* 8, no. 47 (Nov. 22, 1883): 743.

Stead, William T. "My First Visit to America: An Open Letter to My Readers." *Review of Reviews* (London ed.), 9 (1894): 410–17.

Steffen, Jerome O. "Some Observations on the Turner Thesis: A Polemic." *Papers in Anthropology* 14 (1973): 16–30.

Stern, Steve J. "Feudalism, Capitalism, and the World-System in the Perspective of Latin America and the Caribbean." *AHR* 93 (1988): 829–72.

Stevens, Albert Clark. " 'Futures' in the Wheat Market." *Quarterly Journal of Economics* 2 (1888): 37–63.

———. "The Utility of Speculation in Modern Commerce." *Political Science Quarterly* 7 (1892): 419–30.

"St. Louis." *Harper's New Monthly Magazine* 68 (March 1884): 497–517.

Stone, Melville E. "Chicago before the Fire, after the Fire, and To-day." *Scribner's Magazine* 17 (1895): 663–79.

Taaffe, Edward J., Richard L. Morrill, and Peter R. Gould. "Transport Expansion in Underdeveloped Countries: A Comparative Analysis." *Geographical Review* 53 (1963): 503–29.

Taylor, Alonzo E. "Speculation, Short Selling, and the Price of Wheat." *Wheat Studies* 7 (1931): 231–66.

"The Metropolis of the Prairies." *Harper's New Monthly Magazine* 61 (1880): 711–31.

"The New Time Standards," *Railway Age* 8, no. 46 (Nov. 15, 1883): 722.

"The Union Stockyards December 25, 1865." *Chicago History* 7 (1965–66): 289–96.

Thomas, Edwin N., Richard A. Mitchell, and Donald A. Blome. "The Spatial Behavior of a Dispersed Non-farm Population." *Papers and Proceedings of the Regional Science Association* 9 (1962): 107–33.

Thompson, C. W. "The Movement of Wheat-Growing: A Study of a Leading State." *Quarterly Journal of Economics* 18 (1903–04): 570–84.

Thompson, John Giffin. "The Rise and Decline of the Wheat Growing Industry in Wisconsin." *Bulletin of the University of Wisconsin,* no. 292, *Economic and Political Science Series* 5, no. 3 (1909): 295–544.

Thrower, Norman J. W. "The County Atlas of the United States." *Surveying and Mapping* 21 (1961): 365–73.

Transeau, Edgar Nelson. "The Prairie Peninsula." *Ecology* 16 (1935): 423–37.

Treleven, Dale E. "Railroads, Elevators, and Grain Dealers: The Genesis of Antimonopolism in Milwaukee." *Wis. Mag. Hist.* 51 (1969): 205–22.

Trimble, William. "Historical Aspects of the Surplus Food Production of the United States, 1862–1902." *American Historical Association Annual Report for 1918.* (Washington, D.C.: GPO, 1921), 223–39.

Tunell, George G. "The Diversion of the Flour and Grain Traffic from the Great Lakes to the Railroads." *J. Pol. Econ.* 5 (1897): 340–75, 413–20.

Twining, Charles. "The Apostle Islands and the Lumbering Frontier." *Wis. Mag. Hist.* 66 (1983): 205–20.

———. "Plunder and Progress: The Lumbering Industry in Perspective." *Wis. Mag. Hist.* 47 (1963): 116–24.

Twyman, Robert W. "Potter Palmer: Merchandising Innovator of the West." *Explorations in Entrepreneurial History* 4 (1951–52): 58–72.

Ullman, Edward. "A Theory of Location for Cities." *American Journal of Sociology* 46 (1940–41): 853–64.

"The Union Stockyards December 25, 1865." *Chicago History* 7 (1965–66): 289–96.

Van Zanten, Ann Lorenz. "The Marshall Field Annex and the New Urban Order of Daniel Burnham's Chicago." *Chicago History* 11, no. 3 (Fall–Winter 1982): 130–41.

Veblen, Thorstein B. "The Price of Wheat since 1867." *J. Pol. Econ.* 1 (1892–93): 68–103.

"A Visit to the States: The Metropolis of the Lakes." (London) *Times*, Oct. 21, 24, 1887.

Wade, Richard C. "Urban Life in Western America, 1790–1830." *AHR* 44 (1958): 14–30.

Wallace, Anthony F. C. "Prelude to Disaster: The Course of Indian-White Relations Which Led to the Black Hawk War of 1832." *Collections of the Illinois State Historical Library* 35 (1970): 1–51.

Walsh, Margaret. "From Pork Merchant to Meat Packer: The Midwestern Meat Industry in the Mid Nineteenth Century." *Ag. Hist.* 56 (1982): 127–37, 167–71.

———. "Pork Packing as a Leading Edge of Midwestern Industry, 1835–1875." *Ag. Hist.* 51 (1977): 702–17.

———. "The Spatial Evolution of the Mid-western Pork Industry, 1835–75." *Journal of Historical Geography* 4 (1978): 1–22.

Ward, Richard T. "Vegetational Change in a Southern Wisconsin Township." *Proceedings of the Iowa Academy of Science* 63 (1956): 321–26.

Warren, Arthur. "Philip D. Armour: His Manner of Life, His Immense Enterprises in Trade and Philanthropy." *McClure's Magazine* 2 (1893–94): 260–80.

Wasson, D. A. "The Modern Type of Oppression." *No. Am. Rev.* 245 (Oct. 1874): 253–85.

Watkins, Melville H. "A Staple Theory of Economic Growth." *Canadian Journal of Economics and Political Science* 29 (1963): 141–58.

Watson, Russell. "Forest Devastation in Michigan: A Study of Some of Its Deleterious Economic Effects." *Journal of Forestry* 21 (1923): 425–51.

Weaver, J. E. "Some Ecological Aspects of Agriculture in the Prairie." *Ecology* 8 (1927): 1–17.

Weaver, J. E., and T. J. Fitzpatrick. "The Prairie." *Ecological Monographs* 4 (1934): 109–295.

Webb, Thompson III. "The Past 11,000 Years of Vegetational Change in Eastern North America." *Bioscience* 31 (1981): 501–6.

Westfall, Carroll William. "Home at the Top: Domesticating Chicago's Tall Apartment Buildings." *Chicago History* 14, no. 1 (Spring 1985): 20–39.

Whelpley, J. D. "American Control of England's Food Supply." *No. Am. Rev.* 174 (1902): 796–806.

"Where the Beef Comes From." *Lippincott's Magazine* 24 (1879): 573–79.

White, Richard. "The Winning of the West: The Expansion of the Western Sioux in the Eighteenth and Nineteenth Centuries." *JAH* 55 (1978): 319–43.

White, Wilford L. "The Refrigerator Car and the Effect upon the Public of Packer Control of Refrigerator Lines." *Southwestern Political and Social Science Quarterly* 10 (1930): 388–400.

White, William Allen. "The Business of a Wheat Farm." *Scribner's Magazine* 22 (1897): 530–48.

Whitney, Ellen M., ed. *The Black Hawk War, 1831–1832.* 4 vols. *Collections of the Illinois State Historical Library* 35 (1970).

Williams, Egerton R. "Thirty Years in the Grain Trade." *No. Am. Rev.* 161 (1895): 25–33.

Williams, Jeffrey C. "The Origin of Futures Markets." *Ag. Hist.* 56 (1982): 306–16.

Williamson, Jeffrey G. "Greasing the Wheels of Sputtering Export Engines: Midwestern Grains and American Growth." *Explorations in Economic History* 17 (1980): 189–217.

———. "The Railroads and Midwestern Development, 1870–1890: A General Equilibrium History." In *Essays in Nineteenth Century Economic History: The Old Northwest,* edited by David C. Klingaman and Richard K. Vedder. Athens: Ohio Univ. Press, 1975.

Williamson, Samuel H. "The Growth of the Great Lakes as a Major Transportation Resource, 1870–1911." *Research in Economic History* 2 (1977): 173–248.

Wohl, R. Richard. "The 'Country Boy' Myth and Its Place in American Urban Culture: The Nineteenth-Century Contribution." *Perspectives in American History* 3 (1969): 75–156.

Wohl, R. Richard, and A. Theodore Brown. "The Usable Past: A Study of Historical Traditions in Kansas City." *Huntington Library Quarterly* 23 (1960): 237–59.

Woodman, Harold D. "Chicago Businessmen and the 'Granger Laws.' " *Ag. Hist.* 36 (1962): 16–24.

Working, Holbrook. "Financial Results of Speculative Holding of Wheat." *Wheat Studies* 7 (1931): 405–37.

———. "Hedging Reconsidered." *Journal of Farm Economics* 35 (1953): 544–61.

———. "Wheat Acreage and Production in the United States since 1866: A Revision of Official Estimates." *Wheat Studies* 2 (1926): 237–64.

Wright, H. E., Jr. "Late Quaternary Vegetational History of North America." In *Late Cenozoic Glacial Ages,* edited by Karl K. Turekian. New Haven: Yale Univ. Press, 1971.

Wright, John A. "Effects of Internal Improvements on Commercial Cities: With Reference to the Pennsylvania Central Railroad." *Hunt's Merch. Mag.* 16 (1847): 263–72.

Zimmerman, Wm. David. "Live Cattle Export Trade between United States and Great Britain, 1868–1885." *Ag. Hist.* 36 (1962): 46–52.

UNPUBLISHED THESES AND DISSERTATIONS

Benson, Barbara Ellen. "Logs and Lumber: The Development of the Lumber Industry in Michigan's Lower Peninsula, 1837–1870." Ph.D. thesis, Indiana Univ., 1976.

Branch, Maurice Lloyd. "The Paper Industry in the Lake States Region, 1834–1947." Ph.D. thesis, Univ. of Wisconsin, 1954.

Canuteson, Richard L. "The Railway Development of Northern Wisconsin." M.A. thesis, Univ. of Wisconsin, 1930.

Conzen, Michael Peter. "Metropolitan Dominance in the American Midwest during the Later Nineteenth Century." Ph.D. thesis, Univ. of Wisconsin, 1972.

Dailey, Don Marcus. "The Development of Banking in Chicago before 1890." Ph.D. thesis, Northwestern Univ., 1934.

Dobyns, Lloyd Francis. "The History of Lumbering in Marinette County, Wisconsin." M.A. thesis, Univ. of Iowa, 1942.

Engberg, George B. "Labor in the Lake States Lumber Industry, 1830–1930." Ph.D. thesis, Univ. of Minnesota, 1949.

Engle, Robert H. "The Trends of Agriculture in the Chicago Region." Ph.D. thesis, Univ. of Chicago, 1941.

Finley, Robert W. "The Original Vegetation Cover of Wisconsin." Ph.D. thesis, Univ. of Wisconsin, 1951.

Flippo, Forrest Dean. "The McCormick Reaper and the Development of United States Wheat Production in the Ante-bellum Years." M.S. thesis, Univ. of Wisconsin, 1964.

Gitlin, Jay. "The Bourgeois Frontier: French Creole Communities in the American Midwest, 1770–1840." Ph.D. thesis, Yale Univ., forthcoming.

Glasgow, James. "Muskegon, Michigan: The Evolution of a Lake Port." Ph.D. thesis, Univ. of Chicago, 1939.

Jacklin, Kathleen B. "Local Aid to Railroads in Illinois, 1848–1870." M.A. thesis, Cornell Univ., 1958.

Kann, Kenneth Lyle. "Working Class Culture and the Labor Movement in Nineteenth Century Chicago." Ph.D. thesis, Univ. of California, Berkeley, 1977.

Kleven, Bernhardt J. "Wisconsin Lumber Industry." Ph.D. thesis, Univ. of Minnesota, 1941.

Krog, Carl Edward. "Marinette: Biography of a Nineteenth Century Lumbering Town." Ph.D. thesis, Univ. of Wisconsin, Madison, 1971.

Leavitt, Charles Townsend. "The Meat and Dairy Livestock Industry." Ph.D. thesis, Univ. of Chicago, 1931.

Lee, Guy A. "History of the Chicago Grain Elevator Industry, 1840–1890." Ph.D. thesis, Harvard Univ., 1938.

Marquardt, Mary Oona. "Sources of Capital of Early Illinois Manufacturers, 1840–1880." Ph.D. thesis, Univ. of Illinois, 1960.

Marshall, Ralph William. "The Early History of the Galena and Chicago Union Railroad." M.A. thesis, Univ. of Chicago, 1937.

Morgan, James Edward. "Sources of Capital for Railroads in the Old Northwest before the Civil War." Ph.D. thesis, Univ. of Wisconsin, 1964.

O'Connell, James C. "Technology and Pollution: Chicago's Water Policy, 1833–1930." Ph.D. thesis, Univ. of Chicago, 1980.

Philip, William Booth. "Chicago and the Down State: A Study of Their Conflicts, 1870–1934." Ph.D. thesis, Univ. of Chicago, 1940.

Posadas, Barbara Mercedes. "Community Structures of Chicago's Northwest Side: The Transition from Rural to Urban, 1830–1889." Ph.D. thesis, Northwestern Univ., 1976.

Rips, Rae Elizabeth. "An Introductory Study of the Role of the Mail Order Business in American History, 1872–1914." M.A. thesis, Univ. of Chicago, 1938.

Sawislak, Karen. "Smoldering City: Class, Ethnicity, and Politics in Chicago, 1867–1877." Ph.D. thesis, Yale Univ., 1990.

Schilling, Philip Alan. "Farmers and Railroads: A Case Study of Farmer Attitudes in the Promotion of the Milwaukee and Mississippi Railroad Company." M.S. Thesis, Univ. of Wisconsin, 1964.

Sereiko, George Eugene. "Chicago and Its Book Trade, 1871–1893." Ph.D. thesis, Case Western Reserve Univ., 1973.

Sieber, George W. "Sawmilling on the Mississippi: The W. J. Young Lumber Company, 1858–1900." Ph.D. thesis, Univ. of Iowa, 1960.

Smith, James B. "Lumbertowns in the Cutover: A Comparative Study of the Stage Hypothesis of Urban Growth." Ph.D. thesis, Univ. of Wisconsin, Madison, 1973.

Sturm, James Lester. "Railroads and Market Growth: The Case of Peoria and Chicago, 1850–1900." M.A. thesis, Univ. of Wisconsin, 1965.

Sutton, Robert Mise. "The Illinois Central Railroad in Peace and War, 1858–1868." Ph.D. thesis, Univ. of Illinois, 1948.

Treleven, Dale Emory. "Commissions, Corners and Conveyance: The Origins of Anti-Monopolism in Milwaukee." M.A. thesis, Univ. of Wisconsin, 1968.

Unfer, Louis. "Swift and Company: The Development of the Packing Industry, 1875 to 1912." Ph.D. thesis, Univ. of Illinois, 1951.

White, William Alan. "Chicago and Toronto: A Comparative Study in Early Growth." Ph.D. thesis, Northwestern Univ., 1974.

Yetter, Ruby. "Some Aspects of the Commercial Growth of Chicago, 1835–1850." M.A. thesis, Univ. of Chicago, 1937.

Index

Page numbers beginning with 392 refer to notes.